Contemporary
Clinical Psychology

Contemporary
Clinical Psychology

Thomas G. Plante
Santa Clara University and
Stanford University

John Wiley & Sons, Inc.
New York   Chichester   Weinheim   Brisbane   Singapore   Toronto

Dedication

For Lori and Zachary,
who make everything worthwhile

Acquisitions Editor Ellen Schatz
Marketing Manager Bonnie Cabot
Production Director Pamela Kennedy
Production Editor Barbara Russiello
Art Direction Dawn L. Stanley
Cover Designer David Levy
Cover Painting "Fall Hikers" by Connie Hayes
Photo Editor Lisa Gee
Illustration Editor Edward Starr
Illustration Precision Graphics

This book was set in 10/12 Times Ten by The PRD Group, Inc., and printed and bound by Hamilton Printing Co. The cover was printed by The Lehigh Press, Inc.

Recognizing the importance of preserving what has been written, it is a policy of John Wiley & Sons, Inc. to have books of enduring value published in the United States printed on acid-free paper, and we exert our best efforts to that end.

The paper on this book was manufactured by a mill whose forest management programs include sustained yield harvesting of its timberlands. Sustained yield harvesting principles ensure that the number of trees cut each year does not exceed the amount of new growth.

Library of Congress Catagloging-in-Publication Data:
Plante, Thomas G.
    Contemporary clinical psychology / Thomas G. Plante.
      p.   cm.
    Includes bibliographical references and index.
    ISBN 0-471-31626-1 (cloth : alk. paper)
    1. Clinical psychology. 2. Psychotherapy.   I. Title.
    [DNLM: 1. Psychology, Clinical. 2. Mental Disorders—
    therapy. 3. Psychotherapy.   WM 105 P713c 1999]
    RC467.P56 1999
    616.89—dc21
DNLM/DLC
for Library of Congress   98-20474
                                      CIP

Printed in the United States of America

10 9 8 7 6 5 4 3 2

ABOUT THE AUTHOR

Thomas G. Plante is an associate professor of psychology at Santa Clara University, a clinical assistant professor of psychiatry and behavioral sciences at Stanford University School of Medicine, and a consulting associate professor in the school of education at Stanford. He teaches undergraduate courses in Introduction to Psychology, Abnormal Psychology, Clinical Psychology, Health Psychology, Psychosomatic Medicine, and Ethics at Santa Clara and Professional Issues and Ethics for clinical psychology interns, postdoctoral fellows, and psychiatric residents as well as a clinical case conference seminar to doctoral students in counseling psychology at Stanford.

He is a licensed psychologist in California and a Diplomate of the American Board of Professional Psychology in Clinical Psychology maintaining a private practice in Menlo Park, California. He is a fellow in the Academy of Clinical Psychology. He acts as a licensing examiner for the State of California as well as a diplomate examiner for the American Board of Professional Psychology. He is the former chief psychologist and mental health director of the Children's Health Council, a private, non-profit agency serving children and families with behavioral, educational, and emotional problems affiliated with Stanford University as well as a former staff psychologist and medical staff member at Stanford Hospital.

He has published over 60 professional journal articles on topics such as clinical psychology training and professional issues, psychological benefits of exercise, personality and stress, and psychological issues among Catholic clergy. He recently co-authored a statistics textbook and is completing an edited book on sex-offending clergy to be published by Praeger/Greenwood.

Dr. Plante lives in the San Francisco Bay area with his wife, Lori, and son, Zachary.

PREFACE

The goals, activities, and contributions of contemporary clinical psychology are very appealing to many who are fascinated by human behavior and relationships. The enormous popularity of psychology as an undergraduate major, of clinical psychology as a career option, and of popular press psychology books are a testament to the inherent interest of clinical psychology. The goal of clinical psychology is noble: to use the principles of psychology and our understanding of human behavior to promote health, happiness, and quality of life.

Contemporary clinical psychology is changing and growing at a rapid pace. The advent of managed health care, the changing needs of a multicultural society, changes in training models, the shift from primarily a male to a female profession, technological and other scientific advances, complex problems in today's culture, all have greatly impacted both the science and practice of contemporary clinical psychology. Some of these changes are very positive; some are negative. Despite the challenges confronting clinical psychology, the field remains a fascinating and exciting endeavor with tremendous potential to help individuals, groups, and society.

As more research evidence emerges concerning the interplay of biological, psychological, and social influences on behavior, contemporary clinical psychologists must incorporate new knowledge to develop better applications in their efforts to understand and help others. Biopsychosocial integration in many ways best reflects contemporary clinical psychology, expanding the range and usefulness of its efforts.

This book seeks to provide students with an overview of contemporary clinical psychology from an integrative biopsychosocial perspective. The book highlights the various activities, roles, and responsibilities of the contemporary clinical psychologist as well as provides a foundation of the discipline through a detailed review of its history, scientific underpinnings, and theoretical orientations. The book also provides an overview of contemporary issues in clinical psychology as well as a road map for those interested in pursuing clinical psychology as a career option.

Each chapter includes a highlight of a contemporary clinical psychologist who provides the reader with a frank reflection on the pros and cons of contemporary clinical psychology as well as their view of the future of the field. A typical schedule is also provided so that the reader can get a sense of what a day in the life of a contemporary clinical psychologist might be like. Whereas some of the schedules were provided verbatim from the psychologist highlighted, a few of them were constructed from either telephone, electronic mail, or other methods provided by each psychologist. It is important to mention that the psychologists were chosen to reflect the broad range of people who are clinical psychologists. Whereas some of the psychologists are well known, others are not. Several work in colleges and universities conducting research and teaching. Several work in solo or group private practice. Some work in hospitals, government agencies, or university counseling clinics. One works in the United States Senate. Some combine work in several diverse settings. Some work part-time while raising a family. Psychologists from all over the United States, from diverse training programs, from both genders, a variety of ethnic groups, and with disabilities are represented. The range of activities, roles, and responsibilities of these psychologists reflects the diversity of careers open to the contemporary clinical psychologist.

Each chapter includes a detailed list of key points and terms to help enhance understanding. Each chapter also includes a section entitled The Big Picture, which provides a "bottom line" or "take home message" summary of the chapter as well as a look towards the future of the topic covered in that particular chapter.

A great deal of clinical case material is presented throughout the book as well. Several cases such as Mary, a 50-year-old woman with a long history of panic attacks, are discussed in several chapters for the reader to trace the theoretical conceptualization, assessment, and treatment of one case in some detail. All of the patients presented are based on actual clinical cases. All of the examples from testing, therapy, consultation, and ethics are also based on actual cases. However, some of the details have been altered to protect patient and psychologist confidentiality.

This book is different from others in several important ways. First, it uses an integrative biopsychosocial approach throughout. This approach best reflects the perspective of most contemporary clinical psychologists. Less emphasis is placed on traditional theoretical models such as behavioral, psychodynamic, and humanistic approaches since most contemporary clinical psychologists integrate these and other approaches and orientations rather than using only one. Second, although scholarly and research based, an emphasis is placed on the real world of clinical psychology to provide the reader with a window into how the science and practice of clinical psychology is actually conducted. While I, like all authors of clinical psychology textbooks, work as a professor of psychology at a university, I maintain a small private practice and have worked for many years as a mental health director for a child and family agency, a staff psychologist and medical staff member at a university hospital, and a consultant to businesses, religious orders, schools, and law firms. Thus, I have attempted to provide the reader with a realistic, practical, and current portrayal of the contemporary clinical psychology field in many different settings. Finally, unlike other texts available, this book provides a separate chapter on ethics and a separate chapter on the consultation, administration, and teaching responsibilities of clinical psychologists. Ethical issues and these additional roles for clinical psychologists have received more attention in recent years and are thus reflected in this book. The book also provides a chapter on ten common questions asked about psychotherapy. Finally, emphasis is placed on contemporary issues in clinical psychology such as diversity, managed health care, and other hot topics.

The instructor's guide that accompanies this book provides faculty with a detailed book outline, multiple choice and essay examination questions, transparencies for class use, a list of references, web sites, popular and educational films, class activities, and a sample course syllabus. The instructor's guide is available on computer disc as well so faculty can alter these materials to best suit their needs.

The book assumes that students have already completed undergraduate courses in introductory and abnormal psychology. The book is appropriate for upper division college students who are likely to be psychology majors or first-year graduate students in clinical psychology. The book might also be a helpful reference for those who provide career guidance for students potentially interested in a career in psychology or related fields.

I welcome comments about the book from both students and faculty. These comments will be used to create improved future editions. Thank you for reading this book and welcome to the exciting, fascinating, and ever-changing world of contemporary clinical psychology.

ACKNOWLEDGMENTS

Numerous people other than the author assist in the development and completion of a book. Some provide help in a direct and concrete manner while others provide help in less direct and more supportive ways. I would like to acknowledge the assistance of the many people who have helped in both ways and have contributed to the development of the book and of me.

First, I would like to thank the many wonderful people at John Wiley & Sons who have enthusiastically worked to publish this book. I'd like to thank editor Ellen Schatz and executive editor Chris Rogers for their strong interest in the project as well as their high level of professionalism and vision. Their kindness and sense of humor are especially appreciated. I would also like to thank the production staff including Bonnie Cabot, Tammy McGinnis, Alison Kam, Barbara Russiello, Lisa Gee, Dawn Stanley, and Christine Marra.

Second, I would like to thank my textbook writing mentor, Wayne Weiten, who has generously offered his advice and counsel concerning the challenges of both writing a textbook and working with publishers. It would have been very difficult for the project to be completed without his wisdom, experience, and efforts on my behalf.

Third, I would like to thank Lori Goldfarb Plante for helpful editing, feedback, and suggestions as well as providing some clinical case material. Her writing skills and clinical savvy are evident throughout the book and the project would have been much more difficult to complete without her gracious efforts.

Fourth, I would like to acknowledge the anonymous patients referred to in this book; allowing their life experiences and concerns to be an instrument of learning for others.

Fifth, I would like to thank the many reviewers from across the United States and Canada for offering their helpful suggestions and perspectives on earlier drafts of the book. These include:

Allen Sherman
University of Arkansas

Rick Ingram
San Diego State University

Jefferson Singer
Connecticut College

Julie Sincoff Jampel
Tufts University

Elizabeth Dykens
University of California, Los Angeles

Scott Vrana
Purdue University

Wayne Weiten
Santa Clara University

Frank Collins
Oklahoma State University

David Harder
Tufts University

William Iacono
University of Minnesota

Heidi Inderbitzen-Nolan
University of Nebraska-Lincoln

Marvin Kumler
Bowling Green State University

Liliana Lengua
University of Washington

Scott Monroe
University of Oregon

Beverly Palmer
California State University-Dominguez Hills

Chris Peterson
University of Michigan

C. Rick Snyder
University of Kansas

Brian Stagner
Texas A & M University

Charlotte VanOyen Witvliet
Hope College

Nancy Vogeltanz
University of North Dakota

Douglas Whitman
Wayne State University

Michael York
University of New Haven

Sixth, I would like to thank my many students for helping me better understand what is useful, interesting, and helpful for them to learn and for providing me with inspiration. I'd like to especially thank students who have reviewed parts of the book and offered feedback. These include Connie Hoffman, Dusty Pardini, Lisa Telford, Marcus Boccincini, Heather McLain, Amy Lantis, and Jennifer Booth.

Finally, I would like to thank friends, colleagues, mentors, and family who have been supportive and instructive in a variety of diverse ways over the years. These include Eli and Marilyn Goldfarb, Jackie Dormitzer, Sonny Manuel, Peter Merenda, John Sousa, Richard Walker, Anthony Davids, Gary Schwartz, Judith Rodin, Chris Hayward, Marcia Plante, Mary Beauchemin, Lee Sperduti, Henry and Anna McCormick, and Margaret Condon. Most especially, I would like to thank my wife, Lori, and son, Zachary, for their love, support, and for making everything worthwhile.

BRIEF CONTENTS

TABLE OF CONTENTS

Contemporary Clinical Psychology

PART 1

Foundations and Fundamentals

CHAPTER 1

What Is Contemporary Clinical Psychology?

Chapter Outline

Highlight of a Contemporary Clinical Psychologist:
    Patrick H. DeLeon, Ph.D., ABPP
Clinical Psychology: Definition and Inherent Intrigue
Clinical Psychology: Perspective and Philosophy
Clinical Psychology Education and Training
Clinical Psychology Activities
Clinical Psychology Subspecialties
Clinical Psychology Organizations
**How Does Clinical Psychology Differ From Related
    Fields?**

HIGHLIGHT OF A CONTEMPORARY CLINICAL PSYCHOLOGIST:

Patrick H. DeLeon, Ph.D., ABPP

Dr. Leon uses his training and skills as a clinical psychologist by working on Capital Hill. He helps shape policy and legislation that best reflects both the science and application of clinical psychology.

Birth Date: January 6, 1943

College: Amherst College (B.A. Liberal Arts), 1964

Graduate Program: Purdue University (M.S. Psychology), 1966; Purdue University (Ph.D. Clinical Psychology), 1969; University of Hawaii (M.P.H., Health Services Administration), 1973; Catholic University, Columbus School of Law (J.D.), 1980

Clinical Internship: Fort Logan Mental Health Center, Denver, Colorado

Current Job: Administrative Assistant (Chief of Staff), U.S. Senator D.K. Inouye, United States Senate

Pros and cons of being a clinical psychologist:

Pros: "Substantive knowledge about people, systems, health care, etc."

Cons: "Most psychologists or psychology colleagues do not appreciate how little they know about public policy and national trends."

Future of clinical psychology: "The knowledge base will continue to expand; whether services are provided by psychologists or other professionals is an open question. Psychology controls its own destiny—to not seek new agendas and to not save society means to be replaced by nursing and social work."

Typical schedule:

9:00   Meet with Legislative Assistants and committee staff members concerning upcoming legislation.

10:00   Attend senate hearing on issues related to managed health care (Labor, House of Human Services Appropriations Subcommittee).

11:00   Senate hearings continue.

12:00   Lunch

1:00   Attend briefing on health care issues for the elderly.

2:00   Meet with constituents and advocacy groups (e.g., members of APA regarding upcoming vote on legislation relevant to psychology; mental health professionals from Hawaii).

3:00   Respond to e-mail and phone calls.

4:00   Meet with Senator Inouye for briefing and review of activities of the day.

5:00   Stand-by in office until Senate adjourns to provide information to Senator Inouye for a pending vote.

Case Study: Carlos

Carlos is a biracial (part Latino and part Caucasian) 14-year-old boy who feels isolated, depressed, and hopeless. He has few friends, his school work is poor, and he feels uncomfortable in his predominately Caucasian high school. He is new at school, recently moving to a new town from out of state. He complains that he doesn't fit in and misses his old middle school, which had predominately Latino and African-American students. He was evaluated by a psychologist at school when he was 9-years-old and was found to experience an attentional problem as well as a learning disability that makes reading difficult. He has taken medication in the past for his attentional problem and he also takes insulin for his diabetes.

Carlos' mother is Latina and works as a social worker at a local hospital. She was recently diagnosed with breast cancer. His father is Caucasian from German descent and works as a clerk at a large computer company. His mother is Roman Catholic and very active in her church whereas his father was raised as a Lutheran but describes himself as an atheist. His father has had an alcohol problem for many years and has suffered from depression as well. He has been fired from several jobs due to his alcohol troubles and temper. He also had attentional and learning difficulties in school but coped fairly well with these problems and graduated from community college with good grades.

Carlos' parents have had a great deal of marital conflict and have separated on several occasions. Their differences in faith, ethnic background, financial concerns, and

his father's alcohol abuse, depression, and temper have taken a toll on the family. Carlos' younger sister is a "star" student, has lots of friends, and seems to cope very well with stress in the family. Carlos feels that his sister makes him "look bad."

Carlos' mother felt that Carlos should see a clinical psychologist about his depressive mood. Her managed care health insurance will allow Carlos and his family up to six sessions with a local clinical psychologist who is on the company's list of preferred providers. Carlos is willing to get help but feels that there is little anyone can do for him. He also worries about confidentiality because he does not want his parents to know that he has been sexually active and has used alcohol and drugs on occasion. He would like to see a Latino psychologist but the managed care company does not have one on their local panel of providers.

If you were the clinical psychologist Carlos and his family came to, how would you help them during the allotted six sessions? How would you further evaluate Carlos and his family? What would you suggest they do to help themselves and each other? How would you manage confidentiality arrangements? What research is available to guide you in your work? How much can you accomplish in six sessions? What do you do if after six sessions Carlos and his family still need your help? How do you evaluate if your work has been helpful? What do you do if Carlos becomes in danger of hurting himself?

As you can tell from this example, clinical psychology is a complex field that parallels the complexity of human behavior and emotion. Just as we are defined by more than blood and tissue, emotions and ideas, or our relationships to others, the field of clinical psychology is, by necessity, an integrative effort to understand the interaction of biological, psychological, and social factors in making each of us "tick." Furthermore, modern clinical psychology must respond to contemporary issues that impact all of our lives. For example, the importance of ethnicity, culture and gender in today's society informs and enriches the field of contemporary clinical psychology as do current issues related to economics, technology, ethics, and popular culture.

Like medicine and other fields, the roots of clinical psychology are now viewed as simplistic and narrowly conceived. However, with scientific advancements and collaboration between various

fields and schools of thought, contemporary clinical psychology champions a sophisticated integration that pulls together the best of these models for optimal treatment, assessment, consultation, and research.

Before describing the historical evolution of clinical psychology into it's contemporary form, this chapter will define clinical psychology and the varied roles and activities of today's clinical psychologist. In addition, the integrative nature of contemporary clinical psychology will be highlighted. The purpose of this chapter is to examine exactly what clinical psychology is all about. I will define clinical psychology as well as outline the educational process for clinical psychologists, detail their typical roles and professional activities, list the usual employment settings, the various subspecialties within clinical psychology, the professional organizations of clinical psychology, and the similarities and differences between clinical psychology and related fields. Subsequent chapters will highlight these issues (and others) in much more detail. In doing so, a comprehensive and realistic view of the field of clinical psychology will be presented.

Throughout the course of this book I will discuss the field of clinical psychology as understood and practiced in the United States. However, clinical psychology is recognized and practiced in many other countries around the world. The American Psychological Association and the Canadian Psychological Association, for example, have more similarities than differences and often host joint meetings and other professional activities. Unfortunately, it is beyond the scope of this book to detail the training, history, and activities of clinical psychologists from around the world. However, much of the information presented is relevant to clinical psychologists in other countries.

Clinical Psychology: Definition and Inherent Intrigue

What could be more intriguing than human behavior and interpersonal relationships in all their complexity? A visit to any major bookstore reveals that topics such as clinical psychology, self-help, and the general use of psychological principles in understanding our lives are enormously popular and pervasive. Hundreds of books are published each year, which focus on ways to better understand human behavior, replete with methods to improve psychological functioning as it interacts with physical well being, emotions, and interpersonal relationships.

Although the discipline of psychology is only about 100 years old, psychology is one of the most popular current undergraduate majors in most colleges and universities. Furthermore, clinical psychology is the most popular speciality area within psychology (American Psychological Association, 1995b; Mayne, Norcross, & Sayette, 1994a). Doctorates in psychology are more common than any other doctoral degree awarded in the United States with the majority of psychology doctorates being awarded in clinical psychology (American Psychological Association, 1995a, 1997b). The majority of members of the American Psychological Associa-

tion (APA) list clinical psychology as their area of specialization (American Psychological Association, 1993a, 1995a, 1997a, 1997b; Howard, Pion, Gottfredson, Flattau, Oskamp, Pfafflin, & Bray, 1986).

How is clinical psychology defined? Clinical psychology focuses on the **assessment, treatment,** and understanding of psychological and behavioral problems and disorders. In fact, clinical psychology focuses its efforts on the ways in which the human psyche interacts with physical, emotional, and social aspects of health and dysfunction. According to the American Psychological Association, **clinical psychology** attempts to use the principles of psychology to better understand, predict, and alleviate "intellectual, emotional, psychological, and behavioral disability and discomfort" (American Psychological Association, 1981, p. 642). Clinical psychology is "the aspect of psychological science and practice concerned with the analysis, treatment, and prevention of human psychological disabilities and with the enhancing of personal adjustment and effectiveness" (Rodnick, 1985, p. 1929). Thus, clinical psychology uses what is known about the principles of human behavior to help people with the numerous troubles and concerns they experience during the course of life in their relationships, emotions, and physical selves. For example, a clinical psychologist might evaluate a child using intellectual and educational tests to determine if the child has a learning disability or an attentional problem that might contribute to poor school performance. Another example includes a psychologist who treats an adult experiencing severe depression following a recent divorce. People experiencing alcohol addiction, hallucinations, compulsive eating, sexual dysfunction, physical abuse, suicidal impulses, and head injuries are a few of the many problem areas that are of interest to clinical psychologists.

Who is a clinical psychologist? Many people with different types of training and experience are involved with helping understand, assess, and treat people with problems in living. Counselors, nurses, psychiatrists, peer-helpers, and others are involved with the areas of concern already listed. Clinical psychologists "have a doctoral degree from a regionally accredited university or professional school providing an organized, sequential clinical psychology program in a department of psychology" (American Psychological Association, 1981, p. 641).

Although many universities offer master's degree training programs in clinical psychology, the doctorate is considered to be the minimal level of training to be considered a clinical psychologist. Clinical psychology is not so much a specialty separate from psychology, but is more a unique application of psychology to the realm of emotional and behavioral problems (Matarazzo, 1987).

Clinical Psychology: Perspective and Philosophy

Clinical psychology uses the scientific method to approach and understand human problems in behavior, emotions, thinking, relationships, and health. Rigorous scientific inquiry is used to select and evaluate assessment and treatment approaches and activities. Treatment outcome research helps to determine which treatments might be most effective for people seeking help with particular clinical problems. However, clinical psychology is both a science and an art. Findings from scientific investigations must be applied to the unique and special needs of an individual, group, or organization. What might be helpful to one person may not be to another even if they both experience the same diagnosis or problems. The science of clinical psychology informs the art while the art also informs the science. For example, research findings from experiments on psychotherapy outcome are used to determine which type of psychotherapy is most useful with people experiencing depression whereas clinical experience working with people struggling with depression is used to better design and implement psychotherapy outcome research.

Contemporary clinical psychology utilizes integrative approaches to understanding and addressing problems in human behavior. While a wealth of individual perspectives contribute important pieces of understanding to the puzzle of human behavior, these pieces must often be joined in novel ways to provide the most complete and holistic perspective. For example, advances in biology have provided important knowledge about the role of neurotransmitters in depression. Similarly, personal variables such as history of loss and trauma, as well as sociocultural factors such as poverty, discrimination and community support in depression, are well appreciated. Ultimately, an intelligent melding of these biological, psychological, and social factors leads to intervention strategies that best address the complex needs of depressed individuals. Therefore, this book will emphasize integrative efforts to address human behavior, referring to biopsychosocial factors throughout.

Although individual clinical psychologists may be closely aligned with particular theoretical perspectives on human behavior, most contemporary clinical psychologists also appreciate the integral roles of biopsychological factors in health and illness. The biopsychosocial perspective, an example of an integrative approach, will be more fully described in Chapter 5. For the time being, however, in order to understand psychology's roots and gradual development into its present form as an integrative endeavor, it is important to keep in mind the impact of biopsychosocial issues simply as the interplay of relevant biological, psychological, and social factors in human behavior.

Research and practice in clinical psychology has found that certain approaches to understanding and treating problems may be especially useful for certain people and problems while different approaches might be most helpful for others. For example, some people who experience depression respond well to medication while others respond to cognitive-behavioral psychotherapy. Others respond well to supportive therapies such as the humanistic approach. Still others respond to a combination of these and other approaches. Although medication might be useful to treat someone with depression, family therapy, vocational counseling, and group social skills training may enhance treatment success.

Many people who seek the services of a clinical psychologist often have several problems or diagnoses occurring at the same time. For example, the person who experiences depression may also suffer from a chronic illness, a personality disorder, a learning disability, and marital discord. Furthermore, stressful life events, intellectual functioning, ethnic background, religious orientation, and other factors contribute to the manifestation of the depressive disorder and other problems. One theoretical orientation may not address the complexity of the person seeking help. Although various clinical psychologists may be closely aligned with one particular theoretical or philosophical orientation, most contemporary clinical psychologists believe that problems in human behavior are multidimensional. They use an integrative approach that suggests that interacting causal factors generally contribute to human problems and that a multidimensional approach is usually needed to tackle these issues. Thus, many factors may contribute to human problems and a selection of factors must be utilized to help alleviate these concerns. Today, many clinical psychologists use an integrative perspective that maintains a biopsychosocial orientation.

The **biopsychosocial perspective** emphasizes the interaction of biological, psychological, and social influences on behavior and psychological functioning. Each must be carefully considered and the individual viewed in their broader biopsychosocial context in order to best understand the complexities of human behavior and the most effective means of intervention (Engel, 1977, 1980; Schwartz, 1982, 1984). Although clinical psychologists may not be able to intervene at the biological, psychological, and social level, they must take into consideration these influencing factors in understanding and treating people who seek their services. For example, psychologists cannot prescribe medication, conduct physical examinations, or offer surgery to their patients. They cannot alter ethnic, religious, socioeconomic, and cultural backgrounds. However, clinical psychologists can work to understand these influences on behavior and clinical problems and can consult with others who can provide additional services such as medication management and surgery.

The biopsychosocial approach is a systemic perspective (Schwartz, 1982, 1984) in that changes in one area of functioning will likely impact functioning in other areas. The fluid and systemic nature of the biopsychosocial approach highlights the mutual interdependence of each system on each of the other systems. For example, feelings of depression may be associated with brain neurochemicals, interpersonal conflicts, disappointments in life, stresses at home and at work, unrealistic expectations, cultural context, and many other interacting factors. Someone might be genetically or biologically vulnerable to depression due to brain chemistry. Stressful life events such as a divorce, illness, or job loss may trigger a depressive episode. Feelings of depression may result in poor work performance, social isolation, feelings of hopelessness, and lower self-esteem

that may deepen the depression as well as trigger brain chemistry that, in turn, further worsens the depression. Educational, cultural, socioeconomic, and other factors might influence whatever treatment, if any, is pursued by the depressed person. Treatment success may be influenced by both patient and therapist motivation, expectations, and comfort with the treatment plan.

Details on theoretical orientations and the biopsychosocial perspective will be discussed more fully in Chapters 4 and 5.

Clinical Psychology Education and Training

Few people are aware of the long and intensive training process that is involved in becoming a clinical psychologist. Most do not realize that the training process includes experimental research as well as clinical training in psychological testing and psychotherapy. Many do not know that although master's degrees are awarded in clinical psychology as well as other areas of applied psychology (e.g., school psychology), the doctorate is considered the minimal educational requirement to become a clinical psychologist (American Psychological Association, 1987b). Finally, many do not realize that mandatory training continues even beyond the doctorate. The road to becoming a clinical psychologist is a long one divided by a number of distinct stages and phases that include college, graduate school, clinical internship, postdoctoral fellowship, licensure, and finally employment, continuing education, and advanced certification. Although a brief overview of the training process is presented here, details of the training of clinical psychologists are outlined in Chapter 15.

Overall, students interested in becoming clinical psychologists and gaining admission into quality graduate programs must take their college experience very seriously. Completing courses in psychology, research design, and statistics as well as having excellent grades, Graduate Record Examination (GRE) scores, and high quality research and clinical experience during the college years are important to acquire.

Graduate training in clinical psychology involves course work as well as clinical and research experiences and training. Graduate school in clinical psychology takes at least five years to complete, including a one-year clinical internship. However, many students find that they need more than five years to complete their graduate education. Dissertation projects and other factors often extend the training process to an average of six to eight years. A student interested in obtaining a doctorate in clinical psychology can choose between two types of degrees: the traditional **Ph.D. (Doctor of Philosophy)** or the **Psy.D. (Doctor of Psychology).** Although the American Psychological Association recommends a core curriculum of courses and activities (American Psychological Association, 1987b), each program maintains its own unique orientation based on the faculty and traditions of the program. In researching graduate programs, one will find that each program has its own unique balance on emphasizing the roles of biological, psychological, and social factors in human behavior.

Almost all graduate training programs in clinical psychology require that students complete a one-year, full-time (or two-year, part-time) clinical internship prior to being awarded the doctorate. The internship is the most focused clinical training experience generally available during graduate training. The training usually occurs in hospitals, clinics, or various clinical settings throughout the United States and Canada. The activities during the clinical internship focus specifically on clinical training, such as the practice of psychotherapy, psychological testing, and consultation activities with a variety of patient or client populations.

Almost all states now require one to two years of postdoctoral training and supervision before one is eligible to take the national and state licensing examinations. Postdoctoral training occurs in a wide variety of settings including hospitals, clinics, counseling centers, universities, and even private practices. Postdoctoral training can include clinical work as well as research, teaching, and other professional activities.

Each state offers appropriately trained psychologists an opportunity to acquire a license to practice psychology and offer professional services to the public. Licensing attempts to protect the public from untrained or unethical practitioners and helps to protect the integrity of the profession by offering minimum standards of care. All states use the same national written examination for licensing (i.e., the

Examination for Professional Practice in Psychology, EPPP). After successful completion of the written examination, many states then require an oral (or sometimes an essay) examination before obtaining the license. Following licensure, most states require continuing education in order to renew the psychology license.

After being awarded the doctorate, a clinical psychologist is eligible to become a diplomate, an advanced level of certification. This diploma is an optional post-licensing certification that reflects advanced competency in a subspecialty area of professional practice. The American Board of Professional Psychology (ABPP) acts as the credentialing agency for psychology diplomates in a variety of speciality areas (e.g., clinical psychology, counseling psychology, neuropsychology, school psychology, health psychology).

Clinical Psychology Activities

Clinical psychologists certainly do more than talk to people who are distressed about personal matters. Clinical psychologists often do vastly different types of activities from teaching to psychotherapy to laboratory research. Clinical psychologists also may be involved in a wide range of professional activities including teaching at the college or university level, conducting independent and/or collaborative research, providing consultation to a variety of professionals and organizations, conducting psychotherapy, and providing psychological assessment and diagnostic services. Clinical psychologists work in a plethora of environments such as universities, hospitals, clinics, schools, businesses, military institutions, and private or group practices. These varied roles and settings often assist the clinical psychologist in appreciating multidimensional factors and integrating key approaches into his or her work.

Research

Research is at the foundation of all clinical psychology activities. Research conducted by psychologists or others in the behavioral sciences provides the basis and direction for all professional activities. Clinical psychologists often conduct and publish a wide variety of research studies. **Research programs** might help to determine which assessment or treatment approach might be most effective for a particular clinical problem such as depression, anxiety, eating disorders, or substance abuse problems. Projects may help identify those at risk for the development of certain psychological problems. Other projects might evaluate methods to better determine clinical diagnoses. The types of research activities conducted by clinical psychologists are extremely diverse.

Most psychologists who are actively engaged in research are faculty members at colleges, universities, or medical schools. They, like faculty in other academic disciplines, may conduct research on a wide range of subject areas, publish their findings in professional journals, and present their research at national and regional professional conferences. Psychologists who are not academic faculty members at colleges or universities might also conduct research at their hospitals, clinics, government agencies (e.g., National Institute of Mental Health), industry (e.g., pharmaceutical companies, psychological testing companies, managed care insurance companies), or private practices. Research in clinical psychology encompasses biological, psychological, and social aspects of human behavior, from research exploring neuroimaging techniques, to ethnic factors in hypertension, to spiritual aspects of love and intimacy.

Although not all clinical psychologists conduct and publish their own research, all are expected to be constant consumers of research in order to inform their professional activities. Clinical psychologists must understand the research findings of others in order to improve their own clinical practice activities. Many regularly read professional journals that cover topics of special interest.

Assessment

Many clinical psychologists use psychological tests and procedures in order to assess or diagnose various psychiatric (e.g., depression, psychosis, personality disorders, dementia) as well as nonpsychiatric issues (e.g., relationship conflicts, learning differences, educational potential, career interests and skills). Generally, psychologists are the only mental health professional that administers psychological tests. In fact, clinical psychologists not only conduct psychological evaluations with individuals to assess intellectual, educational, personality, and neuropsy-

chological functioning, but also assess groups of people (e.g., families) and even organizations.

There are numerous components to psychological **assessment,** including cognitive, personality, behavioral, neuropsychological, and observational measures. For example, a neuropsychologist may be called upon to evaluate an urban Latino adolescent boy for temporal lobe epilepsy, which often involves impulsive behavior and aggression. Neuroimaging techniques conducted by a physician will augment the findings, as well as a developmental history, to rule out personality or environmental factors such as trauma as causal in the behavioral manifestations of the disorder. Thus, while focusing on neuropsychological measures, the psychologist needs to be keenly aware of medical, psychological, and social factors that may contribute to or otherwise explain "seizurelike" symptomology.

Integration in assessment will be more fully explored in conjunction with its component elements in Chapters 7 and 8. An extremely challenging and exciting area of clinical psychology, assessment requires the psychologist to be something of a psychological sleuth, utilizing an arsenal of tools in determining subtle and often hidden problems and syndromes in the context of biological, psychological, and sociocultural factors.

Treatment

Contemporary psychological interventions address a tremendous range of human problems through a diversity of approaches. Psychotherapy may involve individuals, couples, families, and groups, and address an endless array of target problems. Anxiety, phobias, depression, shyness, physical illness, loss, trauma, drug addiction, eating difficulties, sexuality concerns, hallucinations, relationship problems, and work difficulties may all prompt individuals to seek psychological **treatment.** Furthermore, it has become increasingly incumbent upon psychologists to become educated and sensitized to cultural factors in treating clients, as well as the entire spectrum of individual differences (e.g., sexual preference, religious faith, disabilities, economic status) that comprise today's mosaic society.

Various treatment approaches and theoretical models are utilized to treat psychological and behavioral problems. Most psychologists use an eclectic strategy, defined as integrating a variety of perspectives and clinical approaches in their treatment (Norcross, Karg, & Prochaska, 1997a). Others tend to specialize in one of a number of treatment approaches, such as psychoanalysis, family therapy, or hypnosis. The major theoretical schools of thought in psychology are psychodynamic, cognitive behavioral, humanistic/existential, and family systems. Each of these theoretical orientations or perspectives will be discussed in detail in Chapter 4, leading to our current understanding of integrative models.

Recent efforts to develop *empirically validated* or *evidence based* treatments to assist clinicians and researchers in providing structured treatments and the use of treatment manuals that are based on treatment outcome research findings has received a great deal of attention and support from the American Psychological Association and others (American Psychological Association, 1995g; Crits-Christoph, Chambless, Frank, Brody, et al., 1995; Sanderson, 1994; Sanderson & Woody, 1995). Empirically validated treatments hinge on the notion that psychological treatment approaches should always be based on solid research data and supported by professional organizations such as the American Psychological Association. Empirically validated treatment approaches have been developed for a variety of clinical problems such as depression (Cornes & Frank, 1994; Hollon & Beck, 1994), anxiety (Newman & Borkovec, 1995), and conduct disordered children (Feldman & Kazdin, 1995). For example, cognitive and interpersonal psychotherapy have been determined to be empirically validated treatments for both depression and bulimia while exposure and response prevention have been found to be an empirically validated treatment for obsessive-compulsive disorder (Crits-Christoph et al., 1995). While many treatment approaches are based on research support, the concept of empirically validated treatments is the most recent effort to systematize service delivery to carefully studied populations and problems. Controversy exists over the development of "approved" treatment approaches for various clinical problems. These issues will be further discussed in detail in Chapter 14.

Teaching

Many clinical psychologists teach in a variety of settings. Some are full-time professors in colleges and universities across the United States and else-

where. These professionals teach undergraduates, graduate students, and/or postgraduate students. Other psychologists might teach on a very part-time basis at local colleges and universities as adjunct professors or lecturers. Still others might teach by providing one-on-one clinical supervision of graduate students, interns, or postdoctoral fellows. During supervision, psychologists discuss the trainees' clinical cases in depth while providing therapeutic guidance as they learn psychotherapy or psychological testing skills. **Teaching** may also occur in hospitals, clinics, or business environments. For example, a clinical psychologist might offer a stress management course for stressed attorneys, business executives, nurses, clergy, police officers, or others. A psychologist might also teach a workshop on intimate relationships to young couples about to be married. A psychologist might teach other professionals such as doctors or clergy how to better maintain professional boundaries or understand psychopathology among the persons they counsel. As in psychological treatment facilities, there are numerous examples and opportunities for psychologists to teach in a wide variety of professional settings.

Consultation

Many clinical psychologists provide **consultation** to health care professionals, business persons, schools, organizations, and even to other mental health professionals. Consultation might involve an informal discussion, a brief report, or a more ongoing and formal consultation arrangement. For example, companies might consult with a psychologist to help reduce co-worker conflicts or provide stress management strategies for high stress employees such as business executives, fire fighters, police officers, or prison guards. Consultation might involve helping a physician to better manage patient noncompliance with unpleasant medical procedures. Consultation could include working with a religious superior in helping to better select applicants who wish to enter a religious order. Many clinical psychologists provide professional consultation in a wide variety of settings using a range of techniques. Consultation might also include assessment, teaching, research, and brief psychotherapy activities.

Administration

Many clinical psychologists find themselves (intentionally or unintentionally) in administrative positions. Administrative duties might include serving as chairperson of a psychology department, or dean, provost, or even president of a college or university. Other psychologists might hold administrative positions in hospitals, mental health clinics, or other agencies. They may act as a unit chief directing a psychiatric hospital unit or ward, or direct mental health services for a community mental health clinic. They may act as directors of training in numerous clinical settings. In **administration,** these psychologists generally manage a budget, lead a multidisciplinary professional and support staff, make hiring and firing decisions, and develop policies and procedures for clinical or research operations.

Clinical Psychology Employment Settings

Clinical psychologists work in many different employment settings including hospitals, medical schools, outpatient clinics, colleges and universities, businesses and industry, and private or group practices. Many clinical psychologists work in some type of part-time or full-time private practice as well. Following private practice, teaching in colleges and universities is the second most common employment choice for clinical psychologists (Norcross, Karg, & Prochaska, 1997a; Norcross, Prochaska, & Gallagher, 1989). Many psychologists work in more than one setting, combining various positions and activities. For example, it is common for a clinical psychologist to work at a hospital or clinic several days per week, teach a course or two at a local college or university, and conduct a private practice one or more days each week. A clinical psychologist may be a full-time professor teaching and conducting research while also operating a small private practice and offering consultation services to various clinics, hospitals, or businesses. The diversity of experiences available to psychologists is quite appealing and offers tremendous flexibility and options.

Private or Group Practices

About 35 percent of clinical psychologists primarily work in solo or group private practices (American Psychological Association, 1993a, 1995a; Norcross,

Karg, & Prochaska, 1997a; Norcross, Prochaska, & Gallagher, 1989). Professionals in private practice may provide clinical services in their own solo practice or in conjunction with other mental health or health care practitioners in a multidisciplinary setting. Many psychologists are drawn to independently providing direct clinical, consultation, and other professional services to their own patients and clients and enjoy being their own boss and setting their own hours and policies. In fact, private practitioners report more job satisfaction (Norcross & Prochaska, 1983; Norcross, Karg, & Prochaska, 1997a) and less job stress than psychologists employed in other settings such as academia (e.g., Boice & Myers, 1987). However, recent significant changes in managed health care and insurance reimbursement for psychological services are likely to alter this rosy view of private practice for many professionals in the future. Many private practice psychologists, along with other mental and health care professionals operating practices, have experienced reductions in profits and freedoms as a result of the changing health care industry. In fact, some authors have suggested that solo private practice (as commonly provided by clinicians in the 1980s and 1990s) will no longer exist within the next several years (Cummings, 1995). Cummings predicted that these clinicians will be employed primarily in multidisciplinary health settings such as health maintenance organizations (HMOs) or very large and comprehensive medical group practices.

Colleges and Universities

About 20 percent of clinical psychologists are employed in academic environments (American Psychological Association, 1993a, 1995a; Norcross, Karg, & Prochaska, 1997; Norcross, Prochaska, & Gallagher, 1989). Most of these psychologists work as professors at colleges and universities across the United States and Canada. They generally teach psychology courses, supervise the clinical and/or research work of psychology students, and conduct both independent and collaborative research. They also typically serve on various college or university committees, providing leadership and assistance with the academic community. Some clinical psychologists work in academic clinical settings, such as student counseling centers, providing direct clinical services to students.

Hospitals

Many clinical psychologists work in hospital settings. They may conduct psychological testing, provide individual, family, or group psychotherapy, act as a consultant to other mental health or medical professionals on psychiatric or general medical hospital units, and may serve in administrative roles such as unit chief on a psychiatric ward. Many states now allow psychologists to become full members of the medical staff of hospitals. The *CAPP* v *Rank* decision in California, for example, allowed psychologists to have full admitting, discharge, and treatment privileges at appropriate California hospitals. Full medical staff privileges allow psychologists to treat their patients when they are hospitalized and allows psychologists to participate in hospital committees, including holding elected positions. The majority of psychologists working in hospital settings are affiliated with Veteran Administration (VA) hospitals. In fact, the majority of internship training sites are located in VA hospitals (Association of Psychology Postdoctoral and Internship Centers, 1996).

Medical Schools

Some hospitals and medical centers are affiliated with medical schools. In addition to the professional hospital activities mentioned previously, clinical psychologists serve on the faculties of many medical schools. They typically act as "clinical faculty," which generally involves several hours (i.e., two to four) per week of pro bono time contributed to the training of medical center trainees. These trainees might include psychiatry residents, other medical residents (e.g., pediatric residents), medical students, nursing students, or nonmedical hospital trainees such as psychology interns or postdoctoral fellows, social work interns, nursing students, or chaplaincy interns. These psychologists might teach a seminar or provide individual case supervision and consultation. Psychologists may also serve as academic or research faculty at medical schools. In fact, approximately 3000 psychologists are employed as faculty in medical schools (Sweet, Rozensky, & Tovian, 1991). These psychologists tend to primarily conduct research and are often funded by national grants (e.g., National Institute of Mental Health, National Science Foundation, American

Heart Association) to pay their salaries, thus allowing them to conduct their research. Finally, many psychologists employed in medical school settings evaluate, treat, and consult on patient care.

Outpatient Clinics

Many clinical psychologists work in various outpatient clinics such as community mental health centers. These psychologists often provide a range of clinical services to other professionals and organizations. For example, these psychologists might provide psychotherapy for children who have been abused or group therapy for adult substance abusers. They might also provide parent education classes. While psychologists in these settings may conduct research, direct clinical service is often the primary activity and priority of these settings.

Business and Industry

Many clinical psychologists working in business and industry settings offer consultation services to management, assessment and brief psychotherapy to employees, and conduct research on various psychosocial issues important to company functioning and performance. For example, these psychologists might consult with the human resource department, provide stress management workshops, or conduct interpersonal skills building workshops. Psychologists might help managers learn to improve their ability to motivate and supervise their employees. They may also assist in developing strategies for interviewing and hiring job applicants.

Military

Many clinical psychologists are employed by one of the branches of the American military such as the Navy, Air Force, or Army. They often provide direct clinical services. Some conduct research while others act as administrators in military hospitals and clinics. Typically, psychologists working in the military hold an officer rank such as captain. Other psychologists are civilians working in military hospitals such as Veteran Administration (VA) hospitals. In fact, since World War II, VA hospitals have been one the largest employers of clinical psychologists.

Other Locations

Clinical psychologists are also employed in a variety of other settings such as police departments, prisons, juvenile hall and detention centers, rehabilitation centers for disabled children and/or adults, substance abuse and/or mental illness halfway houses, battered women's shelters, schools and many other work environments. These psychologists provide a wide range of professional services such as psychological assessment, consultation, and counseling.

Clinical Psychology Subspecialties

Most clinical psychologists are trained in the research, assessment, and treatment of a variety of clinical issues pertaining to a diverse set of client populations. The core curriculum for all clinical psychologists include course work on the biological, social, cognitive, and individual influences on behavior as well as classes on research, statistics, ethics, assessment, and treatment. The core curriculum can then be applied, with additional specialty training, to various populations such as children and adults. Further training may be offered in many different subspecialty areas. Although a core set of competencies are expected from all clinical psychologists, not all clinical psychologists are trained exactly alike. Many clinical psychologists ultimately specialize in one or more areas of research or practice. Just as medicine offers doctors various specialties such as pediatrics, oncology, psychiatry, internal medicine, and cardiology, there are many clinical psychology subspecialties. Some of the most common specialities include child clinical psychology, clinical health psychology, clinical neuropsychology, forensic psychology, and geropsychology. Furthermore, each specialty includes a variety of subspecialties. For example, child clinical psychologists might specialize in working with very young children or adolescents. Clinical health psychologists might choose to specialize in eating disorders, anxiety disorders, or pain disorders, for example.

Child Clinical Psychology

Child clinical psychologists specialize in working with both children and families. A recent survey by the American Psychological Association revealed that about 1000 APA members (about 1%) identify themselves as specializing in **child clinical psychology** (American Psychological Association, 1995b). A child and family focus in clinical training has become enormously popular within graduate training programs (Sayette & Mayne, 1990). In addition to standard training in general clinical psychology, these psychologists obtain in-depth training in developmental psychology and child assessment (e.g., behavioral disorders, learning disabilities, and motor developmental delays) and treatment (e.g., play therapy, group therapy, parent consultation). **They commonly work in community mental health clinics, child guidance clinics, schools, children's hospitals, and in private practices. Child clinical psychologists may work with children who have experienced physical and/or sexual abuse or who experience attention deficit hyperactivity disorder, conduct disorders, autism, enuresis (bed wetting), learning disabilities, serious illness, school phobia, post traumatic stress disorder, or a host of other emotional, behavioral, or medical problems. These psychologists may provide consultation to teachers, school counselors, pediatricians, day care workers, parents, and others. They may assist teachers in classroom behavior management or parents in developing better parenting skills.**

Pediatric psychologists are child clinical psychologists who generally work with children and families in hospital settings where the child has a significant medical disorder. These medical problems might include, for example, cancer, epilepsy, diabetes, cystic fibrosis, and neurological disorders and disabilities. The pediatric psychologist might offer pain management strategies to a child while helping the family cope more effectively with and locate community resources. They may act as a consultant to various medical units and departments to help physicians, nurses, and others deal with the emotional and behavioral consequences of severe medical illnesses in children. For example, a pediatric psychologist might consult with a physician about an adolescent with diabetes who refuses to monitor his or her blood sugar level due to concerns about being different relative to peers. A pediatric psychologist might consult with nurses about a child who is hospitalized with cystic fibrosis and struggling with significant depression and social isolation.

Clinical Health Psychology

The field of clinical **health psychology** formally began around 1980 (Matarazzo, 1980) and has been defined as:

> . . . the aggregate of the specific educational, scientific, and professional contributions of the discipline of psychology to the promotion and maintenance of health, the prevention and treatment of illness, the identification of etiologic and diagnostic correlates of health, illness, and related dysfunction, and to the analysis and improvement of the health care system and health policy formation. (Matarazzo, 1982, p. 4)

Since its inception during the early 1980s, health psychology has become one of the fastest growing areas of clinical psychology and the most popular area of research in graduate training programs (Sayette & Mayne, 1990). This subspecialty serves as an excellent example of integrative trends in the field.

It has been estimated that 50 percent of all deaths are caused by lifestyle factors such as smoking cigarettes, drinking too much alcohol, eating high fat food, not exercising, and refusing to wear seat belts (Centers for Disease Control, 1980; National Center for Health Statistics, 1992, 1993; Taylor, 1995). Furthermore, over 15 percent of the gross national product is devoted to health care (Carmody & Matarazzo, 1991; Taylor, 1995). Health psychologists work to help healthy people stay healthy and assist people with various illnesses or risk factors to cope more effectively with their symptoms. Health psychologists work toward helping others develop health enhancing lifestyles, which can be a surprisingly difficult task. For example, about 95 percent of those who lose weight tend to regain all their lost weight within five years (Brownell, 1993; Wadden, Sternberg, Letizia, Stunkard, & Foster, 1989). Over 50 percent of those who start an exercise program drop it within six months, while 75 percent drop it within nine months (Dishman, 1982). Health psychologists work with individuals and groups in order to maximize health enhancing behaviors (e.g., exercise, low fat food consumption, smoking cessation) and minimize health damaging behaviors (e.g., smoking, stress, drinking alcohol). They also help in the treatment of chronic pain, panic disorders, and migraine headaches, and other physical conditions with prominent biopsychosocial features.

Health psychologists are often trained in clinical psychology, counseling psychology, social psychology, or child clinical psychology but specialize in health-related problems and interventions. Health psychologists typically work in hospital settings, however, many also work in academic, business, and outpatient clinic settings. Health psychologists often utilize specialized techniques such as biofeedback, hypnosis, relaxation training, and self-management strategies in addition to general psychotherapy in the course of the overall treatment process.

Clinical Neuropsychology

Neuropsychology focuses on brain–behavior relationships. These are defined as how brain functioning impacts behavior and behavior problems. Neuropsychologists assess brain and behavior functioning and offer strategies for patients suffering from brain impairment due to a large range of problems such as dementia, head injuries, tumors, stroke, AIDS, Alzheimer's Disease, epilepsy, and other problems that result in cognitive and neurological dysfunction. Neuropsychologists are well trained in assessing a range of cognitive abilities including executive or higher order cognitive functioning (i.e., planning, judgement, problem solving), sensory and motor functioning, memory skills and abstract reasoning, and use a variety of specialized tests to assess these brain–behavior relationships. Many psychologists who specialize in neuropsychology are often trained as clinical or counseling psychologists or they may be trained in cognitive science or neuroscience. Most neuropsychologists work in hospital, rehabilitation, or clinic settings. Some specialize in working with children. Many also work in private or group practice environments.

Forensic Psychology

Forensic psychology is usually defined as the "application of psychology to legal issues" (Cooke, 1984, p. 29). Forensic psychologists specialize in using principles of human behavior in the judicial and legal systems. They are often trained as clinical or counseling psychologists with a specialty in forensic work. Forensic psychologists may conduct psychological evaluations with defendants and present their findings as an expert witness in court. They may also provide evaluations for child custody arrangements, or be asked to predict dangerousness or competency to stand trial. They may be asked to participate in worker's compensation claims, or serve as a consultant to attorneys who are selecting a jury.

Geropsychology

Psychologists who specialize in **geropsychology** provide a range of psychological services to elderly members of society. The elderly are the largest growing segment of today's society and are often in need of professional psychological services. In fact, the number of elderly Americans has increased from 3.1 million to over 30 million during the twentieth century and will constitute an estimated 22 percent of the population by the year 2030 (American Association of Retired Persons, 1989). Geropsychologists might consult with senior centers, convalescent or nursing homes, and hospital medical units that serve elderly patients. These psychologists might provide psychological or neuropsychological testing, provide brief individual or family psychotherapy, and consult on strategies to maximize independence and self-care. These psychologists might develop activities to enhance self-esteem, control, and alleviate depression among elderly patients.

Clinical Psychology Organizations

As in most professions, clinical psychology boasts a variety of professional organizations. These organizations provide an opportunity for their members to meet and collaborate, attend yearly conventions and learn about new advances in the field, and participate in a number of activities that help psychologists as well as the public. These organizations are international, national, regional, and local.

American Psychological Association (APA)

Clinical psychologists are usually members of several professional organizations. Most are members of the **American Psychological Association** (APA). The APA was founded in 1892 and is the largest organization of psychologists anywhere in the world. There are 83,000 members of the organization (American Psychological Association, 1997a) representing all specialities within psychology (e.g., clinical psychology, social psychology, school psychology, experimental psychology). Students of psychology and associates of psychology (e.g., high school psychology teachers) are also included in the APA. In a recent survey, approximately 35,000 APA members (about 42%) identified themselves within clinical psychology (American Psychological Association, 1995b). About 62,000 psychologists have a license to practice in one or more states (American Psychological Association, 1988). The APA was incorporated in 1925 and is located in Washington, DC. Since the first meeting in Philadelphia in 1892, the APA holds a yearly national convention each August in a large American or Canadian city. The APA is divided into four directorates focusing on professional practice, education, public policy, and science.

The APA is also home to 51 topic interest divisions (e.g., Division 2 is Teaching of Psychology, Division 12 is Clinical Psychology, Division 36 is Psychologists interested in Religious Issues, Division 38 is Health Psychology). Numbering 93,640 currently, APA members and affiliates belong to an APA division (Fowler, 1995). About 7000 psychologists (about 8%) are members of the APA's Division 12 (Clinical Psychology). The APA publishes numerous professional journals (e.g., *American Psychologist, Professional Psychology: Research and Practice, Journal of Consulting and Clinical Psychology, Journal of Abnormal Psychology*) as well as many books. The APA acts a lobbying force in Washington DC, promoting legislation that will be favorable to psychology as a profession and to consumers of psychological services. The APA also provides standards for the education, certification, and ethical conduct of psychologists.

American Psychological Society (APS)

In 1988, the **American Psychological Society** (APS) was founded. Many of the psychologists in the APA who regarded themselves as academically and scientifically focused felt that the APA no longer adequately represented their interests. Founding members of the APS felt that the APA had become too focused on professional practice and was becoming neglectful of the science of psychology. A proposal was considered to either reorganize the APA to reflect these concerns or start a new organization dedicated to the science of psychology only. Clinical psychologists who were especially interested in the science of psychology joined APS. Many psychologists belong to both organizations while others resigned from the APA to join the APS.

State and County Psychological Associations

Each state and most counties maintain psychological associations. Many practicing clinical psychologists join their state psychological associations and may also join their county psychology associations. Approximately 33,000 members or about 40 percent (both clinical and other psychologists) of the American Psychological Association are also members of their state psychological association (American Psychological Association, 1995b). These organizations provide networking opportunities for psychologists as well as assistance in lobbying state legislatures regarding issues important to psychologists and the public's psychological welfare. Most state and county psychological associations provide workshops and conferences for its members that address various clinical and research topics. The state psychological associations frequently work closely with the state boards of psychology to assist in the policing of unethical and illegal conduct of psychologists as well as in developing licensing laws and criteria for acceptable professional practice.

American Board of Professional Psychology (ABPP)

The **American Board of Professional Psychology** (ABPP) was founded in 1947 as an agency that would certify psychologists in several specialty areas. The ABPP diploma is considered an advanced level of accomplishment beyond a state license to practice as a psychologist. The ABPP is an independent organization closely associated with the American Psychological Association. The ABPP diploma is offered in a number of specialty areas: the majority of diplomas are in clinical psychology. Approximately 2000 psychologists hold the ABPP diploma in clinical psychology (American Psychological Association, 1995b, 1997a).

Other Organizations

There are a number of other national and regional organizations that many clinical psychologists may join depending on their specialty interests. For example, many clinical psychologists are members of the Society of Behavioral Medicine (SBM), the Society of Pediatric Psychology, the International Neuropsychology Society (INS), the Association for Advancement of Behavior Therapy (AABT), the Association of Behavior Analysis (ABA) or many other organizations. Most of these organizations sponsor a yearly national conference, publish one or more professional journals, are involved in lobbying efforts of interest to their membership, and provide members with a range of services.

Many other countries also maintain psychological associations. The Canadian Psychological Association (CPA), for example, has a long and distinguished history providing yearly conventions, maintaining an ethics code, and accrediting programs throughout Canada, among other activities.

How Does Clinical Psychology Differ from Related Fields?

Many people are unaware of the similarities and differences between clinical psychology and related fields. For example, a popular question is, "what is the difference between a psychologist and a psychiatrist?" It can be confusing to the public (and even to professionals in the field) to understand the similarities and differences between mental health disciplines. Since almost all of the mental health disciplines share certain activities such as conducting psychotherapy, understanding differences between these fields can be very challenging.

Many professionals and members of the public wonder how clinical psychology differs from related mental health fields such as counseling psychology, school psychology, psychiatry, nursing, social work, and counseling. A brief overview of these disciplines will be provided and can be reviewed in Table 1.1.

Counseling Psychologists (Ph.D.)

Of all the different mental health professionals, **counseling psychologists** are perhaps the most simi-

Table 1.1 Mental Health Professionals

Degree	Program	Years of Training Prior to Degree[a]	Years of Postdegree Training	License
Ph.D.	Clinical Psych	4–5	1–2	Psychologist
	Counseling Psych	4–5	1–2	Psychologist
Ph.D.	School Psych	4	1–2	School Psychologist
Psy.D.	Clinical Psych	4–5	1–2	Psychologist
M.A./M.S.	Clinical Psych	2	1–2	MFCC
M.A./M.S.	Counseling Psych	2	1–2	MFCC
M.A./M.S.	School Psych	2	1	School Psychologist
M.S.W.	Social Work	2	1–2	Social Worker
M.D.	Medicine	4	3–4	Physician (e.g., Psychiatrist)

[a] While graduate school can take 4 to 5 years to complete, this is highly variable. Research projects such as dissertations as well as practicum experiences often result in a longer period of time to complete training.

lar to clinical psychologists in actual practice. While there are generally differences in philosophy, training emphases, and curriculum between clinical and counseling graduate programs, differences between clinical and counseling psychologists are subtle. Like clinical psychologists, counseling psychologists generally major in psychology as undergraduates, attend a four-year graduate training program (however, in counseling psychology rather than clinical psychology), complete a one-year clinical internship and complete postdoctoral training prior to obtaining their license as a psychologist. The differences between clinical and counseling psychology were more dramatic several decades ago in comparison to current times. Historically, counseling psychologists worked in outpatient, college, and vocational settings with people who did not experience major psychiatric difficulties. They often provided educational and occupational counseling to students and employees. Testing conducted by counseling psychologists generally involved career and vocational interests and skills. Today, counseling psychologists can be found in hospital, clinic, industry, and private practice settings. In fact, in most states, counseling psychologists practice under the same license as clinical psychologists. Some authors have argued that distinctions between clinical and counseling psychology, along with separate training programs, may no longer be warranted (e.g., Beutler & Fisher, 1994). There are about three times more clinical psychologists than counseling psychologists in the United States. For example, while 1372 Ph.D.s were awarded in clinical psychology in 1993, 488 were awarded in counseling psychology (American Psychological Association, 1995b). According to a recent survey conducted by the American Psychological Association (1995b), there are about 8000 APA members (about 10%) who identify themselves as counseling psychologists.

School Psychologists (M.A. or Ph.D.)

While doctorates in school psychology are available (e.g., 94 were awarded in 1993; American Psychological Association, 1995a), a master's degree is generally the degree of choice for school psychologists. A recent survey by the American Psychological Association (1995b) revealed that about 3000 members (about 4%) identify themselves as working in the field of school psychology. **School psychologists** typically work in elementary, secondary, or special education schools providing cognitive testing, brief counseling, and consultation to school teachers, administrators, parents, and students. Some school psychologists also provide tutoring help and some maintain private practices. School psychologists often work with children receiving special education services for problems such as attention deficit hyperactivity disorder, learning disabilities, or mental retardation. These professionals often provide guidance to both children and their families concerning educational and psychological concerns. School psychologists interested in careers in research, academics, or administration usually choose Ph.D. programs while those most interested in practice with children and families generally choose M.A. programs.

Psychiatry (M.D.)

Psychiatrists are physicians who earn a medical degree (M.D.) and complete residency training in **psychiatry.** The American Psychiatric Association reports that there are approximately 40,000 psychiatrists who are members of the association (American Psychiatric Association, 1995). Approximately 40 percent of psychiatrists work in solo private practices; 20 percent work in a state or federal hospital; 11 percent work in private psychiatric hospitals; and 5 percent work as academics in medical schools. About 67 percent of psychiatrists work in direct patient care; 12 percent work as administrators; 6 percent primarily work as teachers; 5 percent work in consultation; and 4 percent work in research (Dorwart, Chartock, Dial, Fenton, Knesper, Koran, Leaf, Pinus, Smith, Weissman, & Winkelmeyer, 1992).

Typically, psychiatrists receive their bachelor's degrees in pre-medical related fields (e.g., biology, chemistry), and then complete four years of medical school to obtain an M.D. degree. Subsequently, a one-year medical clinical internship is completed, prior to a residency (usually three years) in psychiatry. Unlike the internship completed in clinical psychology, the medical internship focuses on general medical (not psychiatric) training. While the residency training years may include some training activities similar to that obtained by clinical psychology interns (e.g., psychotherapy), most programs focus on medication management and other medical approaches to psychiatric disorders. The residency is usually completed in a hospital or medical center environment. However, residency training can also occur in outpatient settings such as community mental health clinics. These physicians obtain their medical license following medical school and often take their boards to become board certified in a speciality area (e.g., child psychiatry) when they complete their residency program.

Because psychiatrists are physicians, they use their medical training to diagnose and treat a wide spectrum of mental illnesses. Psychiatrists, as M.D.s, can prescribe medication, treat physical illnesses, and may utilize other biological interventions (e.g., electro-convulsive therapy). Although there are exceptions, psychiatry training generally focuses on clinical diagnoses and treatment of major psychopathology (i.e., affective or mood disorders, such as bipolar disorder, and psychotic disorders, such as schizophrenia). Training in general human behavior and research is usually minimal.

Relative to other mental health disciplines, there are a variety of pros and cons to being a psychiatrist. Advantages include several factors. First, as physicians, psychiatrists have extensive training in the biological basis of behavior and behavior problems. They are able to use this expertise to understand and treat a wide range of medical and psychiatric problems. Psychiatrists have superior knowledge of medical aspects of certain disorders, and have been trained to take a leadership role vis-à-vis these patients. Thus, they can prescribe medication and other biological treatments for their patients, whereas other clinicians must refer patients to an M.D. if medication or other biological interventions are indicated. However, efforts endorsed by the American Psychological Association are under way to enable psychologists with specialized training to prescribe medication (Smyer, Balster, Egli, Johnson, Kilbey, Leith, & Puente, 1993). Second, psychiatrists have a much higher earning potential than any other mental health professional. Starting salaries typically are around $80,000 with average salaries about $100,000 depending on the work setting (Dorwart et al., 1992). Third, as physicians, psychiatrists generally hold greater status and positions of greater authority, especially in hospital or other medical settings. Higher salaries and prestige are due to the costs and competitiveness of medical education as well as society's admiration of physicians in general.

There are several important disadvantages to becoming a psychiatrist. First, the costs of medical training are extremely high compared to the training costs of other mental health professionals. Second, psychiatrists tend to have much less training in general human behavior and psychotherapy than many other mental health professionals. For example, while most psychologists spend four undergraduate, five graduate, and one to two postdoctoral years focusing specifically on psychology and psychotherapy, psychiatrists only spend the three residency years focused on psychiatry. Thus, many first year psychiatry residents are far "greener," for example, than most advanced psychology graduate students or predoctoral psychology interns. Third, psychiatrists also are not trained in psychological testing and assessment, and must defer to clinical psychologists in order to acquire this often critical information. Fourth, psychiatrists are rarely trained as extensively as clinical psychologists in rigorous research methodology. Finally, fewer and fewer medical students choose psychiatry as a specialty. Psychiatry salaries, although high in comparison to nonM.D. mental health professionals, are very low compared to other physicians. Traditional psychodynamic and interpersonal relational approaches to psychiatry have given way to more biological approaches, partially due to new discoveries in the neurosciences, psychopharmacology, genetics, and other areas of medicine (Fleck, 1995; Michels, 1995), as well as the demand by managed care insurance companies and patients for quicker acting treatment approaches (Cummings, 1995).

Social Work (M.S.W.)

There are approximately 150,000 members of the National Association of Social Workers (NASW, 1995). Social workers have typically obtained a bachelor's degree in a social science such as psychology or sociology and subsequently enter a two-year graduate program to attain their master's degree in social work (M.S.W.). Next, they must complete up to two years of supervised clinical experience (depending upon the state) to become licensed as a Licensed Clinical Social Worker, or L.C.S.W. Similar to the clinical psychology internship, many social workers receive training in psychotherapy and psychiatric diagnoses during their year or years of supervised clinical experience. Unlike psychology they generally do not obtain extensive training in conducting research or using psychological testing instruments. However, those who earn a doctorate degree in **social work** (D.S.W.) often are interested in research and academic careers.

Historically, social workers focused on patient case management (i.e., helping the patient get the most out of his or her inpatient or outpatient treatment and helping patients transition to work or further treatment following discharge), patient advocacy, and a liason to optimal social service agencies and benefits. Whereas psychiatrists have

historically focused on biological theories and interventions and psychologists have focused on psychological theories and intervention, social workers have focused on social theories and interventions. Today, social workers can conduct psychotherapy with individuals, families or groups, or undertake administrative roles within agencies, hospitals, or social service settings. Providing direct clinical services to clients and patients is the most frequently reported activity of social workers (National Association of Social Workers, 1995). Social workers can be employed in numerous settings including schools, hospitals, clinics, and private practice. Employment in social service agencies and both inpatient and outpatient health facilities are the most common setting for social workers while about 12 percent are engaged in private practice (National Association of Social Workers, 1995). Social workers also may act as patient case managers and advocates, securing necessary follow-up care and social services following hospital discharge, for example.

Advantages to becoming a social worker include a shorter (and, thus, less expensive) length of graduate training (i.e., two years as opposed to the minimum five years necessary for a Ph.D. degree in clinical psychology). Second, training in social work tends to highlight social factors such as poverty, crime, racism, and oppression that influence individual, group, and organizational behavior as well as emphasizing advocacy for the rights of others. Third, no dissertation or large research study master's thesis is required for those who are not interested in conducting these types of large scale research projects. Disadvantages include less training and emphasis on the biological influences on behavior and less attention on research. Additional disadvantages include lower earning ability than psychologists and psychiatrists. Starting salaries tend to be about $30,000 depending on the position and location. Of course, social workers, like any clinician, can specialize and become expert in any nonprescribing or nonpsychological assessment enterprise.

Psychiatric Nursing (R.N.)

There are over 11,000 **psychiatric nurses** who have specialty training in psychiatric illnesses and treatment (Dial, Tebbutt, Pion, Kohout, VandenBos, Johnson, Schervish, Whiting, Fox, & Merwin, 1990).

They usually obtain both an undergraduate and master's degree in nursing. They are licensed as registered nurses (R.N.) following the completion of their undergraduate degree. During their training, they, like other mental health professionals, learn about psychiatric diagnosis and treatment. However, they also learn about psychopharmacology and are often involved in the dispensing of psychotropic medications to patients. Psychiatric nurses provide psychotherapy to individuals, families, and groups as well as assisting in medical management of psychotropic medications. Many psychiatric nurses are employed in hospitals and clinics, however, many maintain private practices as well.

Marriage, Family, and Child Counselors (MFCC)

The mental health discipline of **Marriage, Family, and Child Counseling** is unique to California and some other states, and comprises the most loosely defined and regulated licensed mental health specialty. There are approximately 22,000 MFCCs in California alone and about 46,000 nationally. The Association of Marriage and Family Therapists have about 22,000 members nationally. MFCCs typically complete a bachelor's degree in any field (typically a social science discipline such as psychology, sociology, political science), and later pursue a master's degree in a terminal master's counseling or psychology program. Following up to two years of supervised experience, MFCCs can be licensed to practice independently in several states. Despite the title, MFCCs are not necessarily experts solely in marriage, family, or child counseling. Often, they treat adults in individual therapy, as well. Advantages to becoming an MFCC include the ease of acceptance into programs and the one to two years necessary to obtain a master's degree. Disadvantages include the general mixed quality and training of professionals in this field.

Several states, such as Massachusetts, offer licensure as a Licensed Mental Health Counselor (LMHC) designed for master's-level practitioners. The training and experience for this profession tends to be similar to those outlined for MFCCs.

Other Counselors

Many hospitals and clinics employ a variety of counselors such as occupational therapists, activity thera-

pists, alcohol counselors, art therapists, psychiatric technicians, and others. These professionals provide a wide variety of services to patients including individual, family, and group counseling, and therapeutic activities such as art, dance, and music groups. Some of these professionals obtain a license or certification to practice (e.g., occupational therapists) while others do not (e.g., psychiatric technicians). Legislation in many states, such as Missouri, have been proposed or passed allowing occupational therapists, for example, to be licensed as "mental health professionals."

Other Psychologists

There are many different types of psychologists besides clinical, counseling, and school psychologists previously described. Cognitive, developmental, experimental, social, personality, industrial–organizational, physiological and other types of psychologists are represented in the field. They complete a doctoral degree in psychology with specialization in one or more of the areas already listed. Unlike clinical psychologists, they are not mandated to complete an internship or postdoctoral fellowship. These psychologists work in educational settings such as colleges and universities as well as in business, government, and the military. They conduct research, consult with individuals and groups, and develop policies. They have different areas of expertise and skill but generally do not assess or treat patients experiencing emotional, behavioral, interpersonal or other clinical problems. They are not considered mental health professionals and may not even be interested in human behavior. For example, an experimental psychologist might conduct research on the memory functioning of rats or the visual functioning of cats. A social psychologist might be interested in the social functioning of groups of primates. A physiological psychologist might be interested in how organisms such as snails learn new behaviors. These psychologists might be interested in human behavior but not in abnormal or clinical problems. For example, an industrial–organizational psychologist might help an executive interact with employees to improve morale. A cognitive psychologist might study how medications impact attentional processes and sleeping behavior. A developmental psychologist might be interested in how children who are in full-time day care that starts during the first weeks of life bond with their mothers. With the exception of industrial–organizational psychologists, these psy-

chologists do not obtain a license to practice psychology and therefore do not treat clinical problems.

The Big Picture

The goals, activities, and contributions of clinical psychologists are very appealing to many who are fascinated by human behavior and relationships. Contemporary clinical psychology can be defined as the assessment, treatment, and study of human behavior in the context of biological, psychological, and social factors. There, integration as well as awareness of such individual differences such as culture, ethnicity, and gender are part and parcel of the state of this current art and science. The enormous popularity of psychology as an undergraduate major, of clinical psychology as a career option, and of popular press psychology books are a testament to the inherent interest of clinical psychology. Most psychologists report a high degree of satisfaction with their career choice, and enjoy

the tremendous flexibility and diversity of potential employment settings, the opportunity to work with people from diverse backgrounds, and participation in the rapid scientific advances impacting the field. However, changes in health care delivery and reimbursement, the large number of degrees being awarded in clinical psychology and other mental health disciplines, and the moderate salaries of most psychologists must be viewed realistically along with the many advantages of clinical psychology as a career option. The goals and activities of clinical psychology are noble: to use the principles of psychology and our understanding of human behavior to promote health, happiness, and quality of life.

Key Points

1. Clinical psychology focuses on the diagnosis, treatment, and study of psychological and behavioral problems and disorders. Clinical psychology attempts to use the principles of psychology to better understand, predict, and alleviate "intellectual, emotional, psychological, and behavioral disability and discomfort" (American Psychological Association, 1981, p. 642).

2. The road to becoming a clinical psychologist is a long one divided by a number of distinct stages and phases, which include college, graduate school, clinical internship, postdoctoral fellowship, licensure, and finally employment. However, academic positions are usually available following receipt of a doctorate degree and prior to licensure.

3. One of the great advantages of being a clinical psychologist is that there are a wide variety of activities and employment settings in which to work. Becoming a clinical psychologist allows one to teach at the university level, conduct research, provide consultation to a wide variety of professionals and organizations, and conduct psychotherapy and psychological testing with a wide range of populations.

4. Clinical psychologists work in many different employment settings including hospitals, medical schools, outpa-

tient clinics, colleges and universities, business and industry settings, and private or group practices. The majority of clinical psychologists work in some type of part-time or full-time private practice. Following private practice, educational settings, such as academic careers in colleges and universities, are the second most common employment setting for clinical psychologists.

5. Many clinical psychologists ultimately specialize in one or more areas of research or practice. While there are many types of clinical psychology subspecialties, the most common include child clinical psychology, health psychology, neuropsychology, and forensic psychology.

6. Clinical psychologist are organized into a wide variety of professional organizations. Most psychologists are members of the American Psychological Association (APA). The APA is also divided into 51 topic interest divisions. About 7000 psychologists are members of the APA Division 12 (Clinical Psychology).

7. In 1988, the American Psychological Society (APS) was founded by many of the academic or science-minded psychologists in the APA who felt that the APA no longer adequately represented their interests. Founding members of the APS felt that the APA had become too focused on professional practice and was becoming less and less attuned to the science of psychology.

8. Each state and most counties maintain psychological associations. Most clinical psychologists join their state psychological associations and may also join their county psychology associations.

9. The American Board of Professional Psychology (ABPP) was founded in 1947 as an agency that would certify psychologists in several speciality areas. The ABPP diploma is considered an advanced level of recognition and is certification beyond a state license to practice as a psychologist.

10. Clinical psychology maintains both similarities and differences with other mental health related fields such as counseling psychology, school psychology, psychiatry, social work, nursing, and marriage, family, and child counseling.

11. Changes in health care delivery and reimbursement, the large number of degrees being awarded in clinical psychology and other mental health disciplines, and the moderate salaries of most psychologists can be viewed as some disadvantages of clinical psychology as a career option.

12. The field of clinical psychology is dedicated to humanitarian concerns. Clinical psychology seeks to use the principles of human behavior to minimize or eliminate human suffering and enhance and improve human quality of life. Clinical psychology attempts to help individuals, couples, families, groups, organizations, and society achieve healthier, happier, and more effective functioning.

Key Terms

Administration

American Board of Professional
  Psychology

American Psychological
  Association

American Psychological Society

Assessment

Biopsychosocial Perspective

Child Clinical Psychology

Clinical Psychology

Consultation

Counseling Psychologists

Doctor of Philosophy (Ph.D.)

Doctor of Psychology (Psy.D.)

Forensic Psychology

Geropsychology

Health Psychology

Marriage, Family, and Child
  Counseling

Neuropsychology

Psychiatric Nurses

Psychiatry

Research program

School Psychologists

Social Work

Teaching

Treatment

For Reflection

1. Define clinical psychology.

2. Why do you think clinical psychology is so popular?

3. Outline the major stages of clinical psychology training.

4. Outline the six major activities of clinical psychology.

5. Where do most clinical psychologists work?

6. Discuss the major subspecialties in clinical psychology.

7. Outline the major professional organizations associated with clinical psychology.

8. How do clinical psychologists differ from other psychologists?

9. How do clinical psychologists differ from other mental health professionals?

CHAPTER 2

Foundations and Early History of Clinical Psychology

Chapter Outline

Highlight of a Contemporary Clinical Psychologist: Gerdenio "Sonny" Manuel, Ph.D., S.J.

Setting the Stage: Early Conceptions of Mental Illness: Mind and Body Paradigms

The Founding of Clinical Psychology: Lightmer Witmer and the University of Pennsylvania

The Influence of Binet's Intelligence Test

The Influence of the Mental Health and Child Guidance Movement

The Influence of Sigmund Freud in America

The American Psychological Association and Early Clinical Psychology

The Influence of World War I

Clinical Psychology Between World Wars I and II

HIGHLIGHT OF A CONTEMPORARY CLINICAL PSYCHOLOGIST:

Gerdenio "Sonny" Manuel, Ph.D., S.J.

Dr. Manuel is both a clinical psychologist and a Roman Catholic priest in the Jesuit religious order. He oversees the formation, or training, of Jesuits in one of the ten Jesuit Provinces in the United States in addition to his academic position. He is of Filipino descent.

Birth Date: June 8, 1952

College: University of San Francisco (B.A. in Political Science), 1971

Graduate Program: Duke University (M.A. and Ph.D. in Clinical Psychology), 1985

Clinical Internship: Cambridge Hospital/ Harvard University School of Medicine (1984–1985)

Postdoctoral Fellowship: Cambridge Hospital/ Harvard University School of Medicine (1985–1986)

Current Job: Associate Professor of Psychology, Santa Clara University
Director of Formation, California Province of Society of Jesus

Pros and cons of being a clinical psychologist:

Pros: "Insight into life and life's meaning, an appreciation of the lights, shadows, and dreams of human life."

Cons: "Allowing oneself spontaneity in nonclinical situations; it's hard to give up the therapist role in off hours."

Future of clinical psychology: "The importance and contribution of clinical psychology will be enhanced as a counterbalance to technology or to humanize technology's impact on our lives."

Typical Schedule:

8:00	Office hours at university; meet with students regarding practicum placements.
9:00	Staff meeting with Provincial office
10:00	Meet with applicant to religious order.
11:00	Meet with priest concerning stress at a local Catholic high school.
12:00	Mass
1:00	Lunch meeting with several clergy about new policies for training of priests
2:00	Teach seminar in advanced topics in clinical and abnormal psychology.
3:30	Psychotherapy patient: 42-year-old Caucasian woman depressed regarding recent divorce
4:30	Psychotherapy patient: 28-year-old Latino male anxious about his performance in law school
5:30	Community dinner
6:30	Community meeting with fellow priests

Today, clinical psychology is a complex and diverse field encompassing numerous subspecialties and a continuum of scientific and practitioner focused enterprises. In seeking to alleviate human suffering in emotional, behavioral, and physical realms, clinical psychology has borrowed from philosophical, medical, and scientific advances throughout the centuries. Chapters 2 and 3 will highlight the seminal historical influences and fundamental contributors to the ever-evolving science and practice of today's clinical psychology. First, the evolution of Western medicine from a nonscientific endeavor to today's high-tech standard of practice will be traced. Central to this evolution has been the titanic human struggle to understand abnormal behavior in the context of the mind and the body. As you will see, an integration between the forces of mind and body has been long in coming, developing in fits and starts throughout the ages into today's biopsychosocial appreciation for the dynamic forces that join to create behavior. And just as this mind–body integration has developed, the practice and training of clinical psychologists has mirrored landmark scientific changes in this evolving field of study.

This chapter will highlight the early influences and foundations that led to the development of clinical psychology as an independent science and profession. It will trace the history and development of issues relevant to contemporary clinical psychology, from ancient times until World War I. Ideas, events, institutions, and people associated with this history will be highlighted. Also, Table 2.1 provides an outline of significant events in the field prior to World War II. The influence of biological, psychological, and social factors and the roots of integration of perspectives will be noted. Of course, it is unlikely that the people associated with these ideas and events could have predicted how they might influ-

ence further generations to derive at the perspectives of today. The next chapter will examine the more recent developments in the field, from World War II until the present. A full understanding of contemporary clinical psychology hinges upon a sound appreciation and understanding of its foundation and history.

Setting the Stage: Early Conceptions of Mental Illness: Mind and Body Paradigms

The Greeks

Several Greek thinkers were pivotal in the early development of integrative approaches to illness, and, thus, were precursors to a biopsychosocial perspective. Although the ancient Greeks felt that the gods ultimately controlled both health and illness, they looked beyond supernatural influences and explored biological, psychological, and social influences on illness (Maher & Maher, 1985a). The Greeks believed that the mind and body were closely interconnected. Somewhat similar to today's health resorts, ill Greeks often would spend a few days at a temple where they would engage in treatments that might include prayer, special foods, bathing, dream analysis, and animal sacrifice. The doctor-priest who conducted these treatments believed that healing could occur through activation of a life force stimulated by the treatment protocols (Mora, 1985).

The famous Greek physician, Hippocrates (460–377 B.C.), who led the writing of the *Hippocratic Corpus,* felt that disease was primarily the result of an imbalance in four bodily fluids or *humors,* rather than to spiritual factors (Maher & Maher, 1985a). These fluids were black bile, yellow bile, phlegm, and blood. Furthermore, Hippocrates felt that the relationship between these bodily fluids also determined temperament and personality. For example, too much yellow bile resulted in a *choleric* (angry, irritable) temperament, whereas too much black bile resulted in a *melancholic* (sadness, hopelessness) personality. Hippocrates felt that these imbalances might originate in the patient's environment. For example, it was believed that water quality, altitude, wind, and time of year were important considerations in the etiology of illness. Hip-

Table 2.1 Significant Events in Clinical Psychology Prior to World War II

Before Psychology was founded as a field

2500–500 B.C.	Supernatural, magic, herbs, and reason was the approach to mental and physical illness
470–322 B.C.	Greeks use holistic approach to illness, which is attentive to biological, psychological, and social influences
130–200 A.D.	Galen develops foundation of Western medicine based on the influence of the Greeks, which lasts 1000 years
500–1450	Middle Ages believe supernatural forces influence health and illness
1225–1274	Saint Thomas Aquinas uses scientific thinking to help explain health and illness
1490–1541	Paracelsus suggests that the movements of the stars, moon, sun, and planets influence behavior
1500–1700	Renaissance witnesses numerous scientific discoveries suggesting that biological factors influence health and illness
1596–1650	René Descarte develops mind/body dualism
1745–1826	Pinel, in France, develops humane moral therapy to treat mentally ill
1802–1887	Dorothea Dix advocates for humane treatment of mentally ill in America
1848	New Jersey becomes first state to build a hospital for mentally ill patients

After Psychology was founded as a field and until World War II

1879	Wilhelm Wundt develops first laboratory in psychology
1879	William James develops first American psychology laboratory at Harvard
1883	G. Stanley Hall develops second psychology laboratory at Johns Hopkins
1888	James McKean Cattell develops third American psychology laboratory
1890	James publishes *Principles of Psychology*
1890	Cattell defines *mental test*
1892	American Psychological Association founded
1896	Lightner Witmer establishes first psychology clinic at the University of Pennsylvania
1900	Freud publishes *The Interpretation of Dreams*
1904	Alfred Binet begins developing an intelligence test
1905	Binet and Theodore Simon offer Binet-Simon scale of intelligence
1905	Carl Jung creates a word association test
1907	*Psychological Clinic,* first clinical journal, is published
1908	Clifford Beers begins mental hygiene movement
1909	Clinical psychology section formed at APA
1909	Freud's only visit to America at Clark University
1909	William Healy develops child guidance clinic in Chicago
1916	Lewis Terman develops Stanford-Binet Intelligence Test
1917	Clinicians of APA leave to form American Association of Clinical Psychologists (AACP)
1917	Robert Yerkes and committee develop Army Alpha test
1919	AACP rejoins APA
1921	Cattell develops Psychological Corporation
1921	Hermann Rorschach presents his inkblot test
1924	Mary Cover Jones uses learning principles to treat children's fears
1935	APA Committee on Standards and Training define clinical psychology
1936	Louttit publishes first clinical psychology textbook
1937	Clinicians leave APA again to form American Association of Applied Psychology (AAAP)
1937	*Journal of Consulting Psychology* begins
1939	The Wechsler-Bellevue Intelligence Scale is published
1945	AAAP rejoins APA

pocrates encouraged fellow doctors to be gentle and patient with their patients because various stressors were viewed as capable of preventing healing. Hippocrates maintained a holistic approach to health and illness reflected in his statement: "In order to cure the human body, it is necessary to have a knowledge of the whole of things." He also felt that head trauma and heredity could also account for abnormal behavior and illness. He was sensitive to interpersonal, psychological, and stress factors that contribute to problem behavior. The thinking and writing of Hippocrates helped to move from a spiritualistic toward a more naturalistic view or model of health and illness. Hippocrates suggested that biological, psychological, and social factors all contribute to both physical and emotional illness. This early biopsychosocial perspective was further championed by Plato, Aristotle, and Galen until its temporary demise in the Middle Ages.

Plato (427–347 B.C.) saw the spirit or soul as being in charge of the body and that problems residing in the soul could result in physical illness (Mora, 1985). Plato quoted Socrates (470–399 B.C.) as stating: "As it is not proper to cure the eyes without the head, nor the head without the body, so neither is it proper to cure the body without the soul." Plato felt that mental illness resulted from sickness in the *logistikon* or the part of the soul that operates in the head, controlling reason. He felt that personality, a lack of harmony, and ignorance about the self were responsible for mental illness symptoms. Aristotle (384–322 B.C.) maintained a scientific emphasis and felt that certain distinct emotional states including joy, anger, fear, and courage impacted the functioning of the human body. Aristotle felt that treatment for mental problems should include talking and the use of logic to influence the soul and psyche (Maher & Maher, 1985a). The use of logic and reason to influence emotional and behavioral problems is one of the major principles behind today's cognitive therapy. These Greek philosophers and physicians viewed health, illness, personality, and behavior as being intimately interconnected.

Galen (130–200 A.D.) was a Greek physician who integrated the work and perspectives outlined by Hippocrates, Plato, Aristotle, and others and developed a holistic program of medical practice that became the foundation of medicine in Europe for 1000 years (Maher & Maher, 1985a; Mora, 1985). Like his Greek colleagues, Galen also used the hu-

moral theory of balance between the four bodily fluids discussed previously as a foundation for treatments. Induced vomiting to treat depression as well as induced bleeding or *bloodletting* to treat a variety of ailments were common treatments used for centuries (Burton, 1621/1977; Kemp, 1990). Galen also felt that the brain was the rational soul and the center of sensation and reason. Additionally, he thought that humans experienced one of two irrational subsouls, one for males and one for females. The male subsoul was thought to be located in the heart, whereas the female subsoul was thought to be located in the liver. Unlike Plato, Galen felt that the soul was the slave and not the master of the body, and that wishes of the souls in the body resulted in health and illness.

Together, the Greeks developed a remarkably holistic perspective in which we can see many of the roots of our current beliefs on mind and body interactions in mental and physical illness. However, the ensuing Middle Ages would temporarily derail from this line of reasoning, instead embracing largely supernatural views of illness.

The Middle Ages

During the Middle Ages (500–1450 A.D.), earlier notions regarding the relationship among health, illness, mind, and body reemerged (Kemp, 1990). Perhaps as a response to the highly turbulent, frightening, and stressful times during the black plague, numerous wars, and the split within the Roman Catholic Church resulting in two Catholic centers and popes, the focus on supernatural influences to explain events became commonplace. Disease and "insanity," many believed, were caused by spiritual matters such as the influence of demons, witches, and sin. Therefore, healing and treatment became, once more, a spiritual rather than a medical issue using integrative biopsychosocial strategies. Those who were ill would consult with priests or other clergy, and atonement for sins would likely be prescribed as the road to recovery. People who were "insane" would often be treated by exorcism. Some were chained to church walls in order to benefit from prayers; some were tortured and killed. In fact, in 1484, Pope Innocent VIII issued a papal statement approving of the persecution of "witches." Although the mentally ill were certainly not the only people targeted, it has been estimated that 150,000 people were executed in the name of religion during this time period (Kemp, 1990).

Although most modern people would agree that the supernatural emphasis and inhumane treatments during the Middle Ages were unhelpful, some of the same type of thinking and blaming of the victim is common during more current times. For example, many of the problems of the Germans during the 1930s and early 1940s were blamed on the Jews. During the 1980s many (including several United States senators) suggested that AIDS was a plague from God for "immoral" homosexual behavior. Today, many blame illegal immigration as a critical factor in many societal ills, including problems such as economic woes, violence, and youth crime.

Not everyone during the Middle Ages believed that good and evil, spirits and demons, sorcery and witchcraft contributed to mental illness (Kemp, 1990; Maher & Maher, 1985a). Some, such as Saint Thomas Aquinas (1225–1274), felt that there was both theological truth and scientific truth. For example, Aquinas reasoned that the soul was unable to become "sick" and, therefore, **mental illness** must have a physical cause or be due to problems in reason or passion (Aglioni, 1982). The late fourteenth-century French bishop Nicholas Oresme felt that abnormal behavior and mental illness were due to diseases such as melancholy (today's depression). Furthermore, the insane were sometimes humanely and compassionately cared for by people living in rural villages.

Another model to explain abnormal behavior, which became especially popular during the sixteenth century, was the influence of the moon, stars, and alignment of the planets. A Swiss physician, Paracelsus (1490–1541), popularized the notion that various movements of the stars, moon, and planets influenced mood and behavior. Paracelsus also focused on the biological foundations of mental illness and developed humane treatments. Juan Luis Vives (1492–1540) and Johann Weyer (1515–1588) helped to shift theories of mental illness from a focus on the soul to an emphasis on behavior and promoted humane treatments of the mentally ill. Therefore, the biological, psychological, social, astrological, and supernatural influences on behavior were believed to be responsible for mental illness and abnormal behavior during the Middle Ages. Different institutions, groups, and individuals main-

tained different opinions concerning which of these factors could explain behavior the best. Sadly, some of these beliefs resulted in poor or no treatment as well as inhumane behavior towards others.

The Renaissance

During the Renaissance, renewed interest in the physical and medical worlds emerged, overshadowing previously supernatural and religious viewpoints. Interest in the mind and soul were considered unscientific and thus relegated to the philosophers and clergy. New discoveries in chemistry, physics, biology, and mathematics unfolded rapidly and were met with great enthusiasm (Mora, 1985). Morgagni (1682–1771), for example, discovered through autopsy that a diseased organ in the body could cause illness and death. Andreas Vesalius, a Dutch physician, published an anatomy textbook in 1543 delineating dissection of the human body. The emphasis on scientific observation and experimentation rather than reason, mythology, religious beliefs, and dogma provided a model for future research and teaching. When William Harvey, an English physician, used the scientific method in 1628 to determine that blood circulated through the body because of the function of the heart, the Greek notion of imbalance of bodily fluids vanished from medical thinking.

New medical discoveries during the Renaissance resulted in biomedical reductionism in that disease, including mental illness, could be understood by scientific observation and experimentation rather than beliefs about mind and soul. The biological side of the integrative biopsychosocial perspective was emphasized. René Descartes (1596–1650), a French philosopher, argued that the mind and body were separate. This dualism of mind and body then became the basis for Western medicine until recently. The mind and body were viewed historically as split, in that diseases of the body were studied by the medical sciences while problems with the mind or emotional life were delegated to the philosophers and clergy. However, mental illness was often considered a disease of the brain, and thus the insane were treated using the medical orientation of the time.

Treatment of mental illness, however, lagged behind these medical developments. During this period, physicians treated people who were considered deviant or abnormal by confining them to hospitals and asylums. Little treatment, other than custodial care, was provided to these patients and thus these asylums were renowned for their prison-like environments. The term *bedlam* (a variant of *Bethlehem*), connoting chaos and hellish circumstances, originated when St. Mary's of Bethlehem was opened in London during 1547. Active treatments, besides custodial care, included restrictive cribs, hunger cures, bloodletting, cold water dunking or *hydrotherapy,* and other painful treatments (Kemp, 1990; Mora, 1985).

The Nineteenth Century

The nineteenth century experienced numerous advances in understanding mental and physical illness and allowed for a more sophisticated understanding of the relationship between body and mind in both health and illness. A breakthrough of the nineteenth century involved the discovery by Rudolf Virchow (1821–1902), Louis Pasteur (1822–1895), and others that disease and illness could be attributed to dysfunction at the cellular level (Maher & Maher, 1985a). For example, the discovery that syphilis was caused by microorganisms entering the brain following sexual activity helped to support the biological model of mental illness. The laboratory thus earned center stage as the arena for the investigation of disease. The nineteenth-century discovery that *germs* or microorganisms can cause disease, along with the twentieth-century advances in medical, genetic, and technological discoveries have continued to support the "Cartesian dualism" perspective of René Descartes and the seventeenth century.

However, **dualism** was tempered in the last part of the eighteenth century and during the nineteenth century due to the work and influence of a variety of physicians who believed that the mind and body were connected, not separate. Benjamin Rush (1745–1813) authored the first American text in psychiatry, positing that the mind could cause a variety of diseases. Franz Mesmer (1733–1815), an Austrian physician, and others noticed that many people experiencing paralysis, deafness, and blindness had no biomedical pathology, leaving psychological causes suspect. Claude Bernard (1813–1878) was a prominent physician who argued for recognition of the role of psychological factors in physical illness. Jean Martin Charcot (1825–1893), a French

physician, used hypnosis to treat a wide variety of conversion disorders (i.e., physical symptoms such as paralysis, blindness, deafness without apparent physical cause). Thus, many nineteenth-century physicians laid the groundwork for today's current theories and practices integrating the influences of physical, psychological, and social factors on health and well-being.

These advances lead to greater sensitivity and sophistication regarding the treatment of individuals with mental illness. A psychosocial approach to mental illness called **moral therapy,** emerged during this time. Moral therapy sought to treat patients as humanely as possible and encouraged the nurturance of interpersonal relationships. Its founder, French physician, Philippe Pinel (1745–1826), did much to improve the living conditions and treatment approaches used by mental hospitals during the nineteenth century. He became director of several mental hospitals in France (first at La Bicetre and then at La Salpetriere) and altered the treatment facilities in order to maximize patient welfare and humane forms of treatment. Using the same principles in the United States, Eli Todd developed a retreatlike program for the treatment of the mentally ill in Hartford, Connecticut. This program is still in operation today and is called the Institute of Living. William Tuke (1732–1822) also developed more humane treatment approaches in English mental hospitals. Dorothea Dix (1802–1887), a Massachusetts school teacher, worked heroically for 40 years to improve treatment conditions for the mentally ill in the United States. During the Civil War, she acted as the head nurse for the Union military. Due to her efforts, New Jersey became the first state to build a hospital for the mentally ill in 1848. Many states quickly followed suit.

Significant improvements in the diagnosis of mental illness emerged during this time as well. Efforts to apply scientific methodology in order to better classify and diagnose abnormal behavior were implemented. For example, influential German physician Emil Kraeplin (1856–1926) defined the term *dementia praecox* to describe the constellation of behaviors we generally now consider *schizophrenia* [coined by Eugen Bleuler (1857–1930)]. Kraeplin also asserted that mental disorders were brain disorders, and mental illness could be classified as rising from either exogenous or endogenous influences. The thinking and work of Kraeplin,

Bleuler, and others during this period not only helped to better understand mental disorders as medical problems but also assisted in developing a classification system for understanding and categorizing many mental disorders.

Franz Alexander (1891–1964) also studied the association between psychological factors and both physical and mental illnesses (Mora, 1985). He proposed that as a specific stressor occurred, a genetically predetermined organ system of the body responded. By repressing conflict, for example, Alexander felt that psychic energy could be channeled into the sympathetic division of the autonomic nervous system, thus overstimulating this system and producing disease. Therefore, while one person might repress conflict and eventually develop an ulcer (due to gastric acid secretion), another person might develop colitis, headache, or asthma. Alexander argued that specific personality styles, as opposed to unconscious conflicts, resulted in specific disease. For example, he felt that dependence would typically result in the development of ulcers while repressed rage would result in hypertension. Research continues to reveal biological, psychological, and social influences in the development of ulcers, hypertension, and other diseases.

A confluence of factors thus led to the birth of psychology as an independent discipline and science separate from, but related to, philosophy, medicine, and theology. In this history, we see the roots of today's mind–body integrative and biopsychosocial perspective. The evolution of the Western view of medicine and of abnormal behavior; the use of the scientific method to make new discoveries in biology, chemistry, physics, and math; the emergence of psychoanalytic thinking; and the interest in individual differences in behavior together combined to set the stage for the subsequent emergence of the science and practice of psychology.

The Birth of Psychology

In 1860, Theodor Fechner (1801–1887) published *The Elements of Psychophysics* while Wilhelm Wundt (1832–1920) published the *Principles of Physiological Psychology* in 1874. These publications were the first to indicate clearly that techniques of physiology and physics could be used to answer psychological questions. The first laboratory of psychology was subsequently developed by Wundt at the University of Leipzig, Germany in 1879 and with it, psychology was born. Wundt was especially interested in individual and group differences in sensation and perception, studying human reaction times in various laboratory experiments. He was also interested in using both the scientific method and introspection to better understand the structure and components of the mind. William James also established a psychology laboratory at Harvard University at about the same time that Wundt was developing his laboratory. Whereas Yale University offered the first formal Ph.D. in "Philosophy and Psychology" in 1861, Harvard University offered the first American Ph.D. in psychology in 1878. G. Stanley Hall established the second American psychology laboratory at Johns Hopkins University in 1883 while James McKeen Cattell established the third American laboratory in 1888. Hall also established the first independent psychology department at Clark University in 1887.

In 1890, James published *Principles of Psychology,* which became the first classic psychology text. In 1891, James Baldwin established the first psychology laboratory in Canada at the University of Toronto. In 1892, the **American Psychological Association** was founded, and G. Stanley Hall elected as its first president. During the beginning months and years of this new field, American psychology nurtured its roots in experimental psychology and was less interested in clinical or applied psychology. The early members of the American Psychological Association tended to be academics in universities conducting empirical research.

In addition to sensation, perception, and understanding the dimensions of the mind through experimentation, the early psychologists were interested in the development and use of mental tests. Although not a psychologist, Francis Galton, a relative of Charles Darwin, was interested in statistical analysis of differences among people in reaction time, sensory experiences, and motor behavior. He developed a laboratory in England to study these issues in 1882. In the United States, James McKeen Cattell (1860–1944) also studied reaction time and other differences in human behavior. Cattell coined the term mental test in 1890 to refer to measures that he developed in the hopes of tapping intellectual abilities. At the University of Freiburg, Germany, Hugo Münsterberg also developed a series of tests to investigate the mental abilities of children in

1891. This emerging interest in testing will later grow into one of the fundamental cornerstones and contributions of the discipline of clinical psychology.

Thus, psychology was founded, and its early years were launched by academic psychologists interested in empirically measuring various aspects of human behavior in order to better understand the components of the mind. They had very little interest in applying their findings in order to assist people with emotional, behavioral, or intellectual problems or disorders. The desire to apply these newly developed methods and principles of psychology to people in need was soon to result in the birth of clinical psychology (Maher & Maher, 1985b).

The Founding of Clinical Psychology: Lightner Witmer and the University of Pennsylvania

While psychology was born as a distinct discipline with the founding of the American Psychological Association in 1892, the birth of clinical psychology as a speciality area occurred four years later in 1896 with the opening of the first psychological clinic at the University of Pennsylvania by Lightner Witmer (1867–1956). Witmer completed his undergraduate studies at the University of Pennsylvania in 1888 and earned his Ph.D. in psychology at the University of Leipzig under Wilhelm Wundt in 1892. Following his doctoral studies, Witmer returned to the University of Pennsylvania to become director of their psychology laboratory.

Witmer became the first psychologist to use his understanding of the principles of human behavior to help an individual with a particular problem. He was asked by a teacher to help one of her students who was not performing well in school. After assessing the child's problem, Witmer developed a specific treatment program. He had found that the child had difficulty in spelling, reading, and memory, and recommended tutoring, which later proved to be a successful intervention (McReynolds, 1987).

In 1896, Witmer described his methods of diagnosis and treatment to members of the newly formed American Psychological Association. He proposed that a psychological clinic could be devoted to diagnosis and evaluation, individual treatment, public service, research, and the training of students. Apparently, his thoughts were not well received by his professional colleagues at the time (Brotemarkle, 1947; Reisman, 1976). His colleagues disliked the notion that psychology as a science should be applied to actual clinical problems. It is important to note that during this time, psychology was considered a science and its purpose was to better understand general (not abnormal or dysfunctional) human behavior. Despite the lukewarm reception, Witmer independently developed his psychological clinic at the University of Pennsylvania and developed programs to assist children with primarily school related difficulties and challenges.

A celebration of 100 years of clinical psychology recently occurred at the University of Pennsylvania in 1996 with events examining the influence of Witmer's work on contemporary clinical psychology. Many of the principles that Witmer developed in his psychological clinic are still used today. For example, he favored a diagnostic evaluation prior to offering treatment procedures and services. Second, he favored a multidisciplinary team approach as opposed to individual consultation. Third, he used interventions and diagnostic strategies based on research evidence. Finally, he was interested in preventing problems before they emerged.

By 1904, the University of Pennsylvania began offering formal courses in clinical psychology. In 1906, Morton Price published the first edition of the *Journal of Abnormal Psychology*. By 1907, Witmer began the first professional journal dedicated to the field of clinical psychology entitled *The Psychological Clinic*. Through these activities and landmark events clinical psychology was born. However, while Witmer helped launch the clinical psychology spe-

Figure 2.1 Lightner Witmer

cialty, a variety of other people and events further molded clinical psychology into its current form.

The Influence of Binet's Intelligence Test

In 1885, Alfred Binet, a French scientist and attorney, founded (along with Henri Beaunis) the first psychology laboratory in France. Binet and his colleagues were especially interested in developing tests to investigate mental abilities in children. In 1904, a French commission invited Binet and his colleague, Theodore Simon, to develop a method to assist in providing mentally disabled children with appropriate educational services. Binet and Simon developed an intelligence test that could be used with children in order to assist teachers and schools in identifying children whose mental abilities prevented them from benefitting from regular classroom instruction. The Binet-Simon scale was then developed in 1908 specifically for school use. Binet felt that the test did not provide a comprehensive and objective index of intellectual functioning and highlighted the limitations of his testing methods for use beyond the classroom.

Henry Goddard, who had developed a clinic for children at the Vineland Training School in New Jersey, learned about the Binet-Simon scale while in Europe during 1908. He was impressed with the scale and brought it back to the United States for translation and use. In 1916, Stanford University psychologist Lewis Terman revised the scale and renamed it the Stanford-Binet. The Binet approach to testing became remarkably popular in the United States, as various institutions throughout the country adopted the Binet-Simon and later the Stanford-Binet tests to assess children. By 1914, over 20 university psychology clinics were utilizing the Binet approach. Therefore, measuring the intellectual abilities of children quickly became a major activity of clinical psychologists during the early days of the field.

The Influence of the Mental Health and Child Guidance Movements

The momentum achieved through the emergence of psychological clinics and psychological testing

soon progressed into the realm of mental illness and problematic behavior. A former mental patient, Clifford Beers, who may be credited with the expansion, founded the National Committee for Mental Hygiene, which later became known as the National Association for Mental Health. Beers was hospitalized with severe depression that also included episodes of mania. Today, he would have likely been diagnosed with bipolar disorder (manic depression). His treatment, from a contemporary viewpoint, would be considered inhumane although it was common at the time. Once he was released from the hospital, he wrote a book entitled *A Mind That Found Itself,* published in 1908. The book focused on the inhumane treatment he experienced while hospitalized. The mission of his post-hospitalization life and his newly founded association was to improve the prevention and treatment of those suffering from mental illness.

Beers and his organization were successful due in part to the support of prominent psychologist and Harvard professor William James and prominent psychiatrist Adolf Meyer. This success led to the opening of William Healy's Juvenile Psychopathic Institute in 1909 and to the subsequent establishment of child guidance clinics throughout the country. Unlike Witmer's focus on learning differences and educational challenges, the child guidance clinics, such as the one developed by Healy, focused on disruptive behaviors of children interacting with schools, police, and the courts. The philosophy of these clinics was based on the view that disruptive behavior in children was due to mental illness and that intervention should occur early before significant problems such as stealing, fire-setting, and robbery began. In 1917, Healy founded the influential Judge Baker Foundation in Boston, Massachusetts. The child guidance movement applied the new principles of psychology to the treatment of children and their families encountering mental illness and problem behaviors. Thus, the child guidance perspective helped to emphasize the psychological and social influences of behavior and mental illness.

The Influence of Sigmund Freud in America

The work and writings of Sigmund Freud (1856–1939) and his colleagues was highly influential in further understanding the connection between the mind and body. Freud proposed that unconscious conflicts and emotional influences could bring about mental and physical illness. Freud reawakened earlier Greek notions that a more holistic view of health and illness including the study of emotional experience was necessary for a fuller understanding of health, illness, and abnormal behavior. Freud's 1900 publication of *The Interpretation of Dreams* resulted in mainstream acceptance of the psychoanalytic perspective.

Freud had little influence on the development of clinical psychology in the United States until September, 1909. At the time, Freud made his landmark and only trip to the United States in response to an invitation by G. Stanley Hall (the American Psychological Association's first president and president of Clark University in Worcester, Massachusetts). Clark University was celebrating its 20th anniversary as an institution and Hall invited a large number of prominent psychologists, psychiatrists, and academics for a series of lectures. In addition to Freud, Carl Jung, Otto Rank, Sandor Ferenczi, James McKeen Cattell, E. B. Titchener, and William James were also in attendance—a veritable "who's who" of influential names at the time (see photo below). This conference stimulated the widespread acceptance of Freud's psychoanalytic theories in the United States. The psychological and child guidance clinics, quickly growing in the United

Figure 2.2 1909 Psychology Conference at Clark University, Worcester, MA: (Front row, left to right) Franz Boas, E. B. Titchener, William James, William Stern, Leo Burgerstein, G. S. Hall, Sigmund Freud, C. G. Jung, Adolf Meyer, and H. S. Jennings. James McKeen Cattell is behind and to the right of William James. Sandor Ferenczi is in the third row between Hall and Freud.

States at the time, tended to adopt Freud's orientation to mental illness and treatment after the 1909 lectures. Thus, the psychoanalytic perspective to behavioral and mental problems was highlighted in these clinics. Furthermore, the enthusiasm afforded psychological testing in the wake of the Binet-Simon scale grew dramatically during this period as well.

The American Psychological Association and Early Clinical Psychology

The first two decades of the twentieth century witnessed tremendous growth in the field of clinical psychology. What were the activities and preoccupations of the American Psychological Association during this time? The answer might be surprising. The American Psychological Association was interested primarily in scientific research in academic settings and was largely disinterested in clinical applications in the field. Therefore, these rapid developments in the provision of psychological services in psychological clinics and child guidance clinics were generally ignored by the association. The growth of clinical psychology therefore occurred not because of the American Psychological Association but in spite of it. Clinicians frustrated with the lack of interest and support by the APA decided to leave the organization and form the American Association of Clinical Psychologists (AACP) in 1917. This separation did not last and in 1919, the AACP and APA agreed to a reconciliation of sorts and the AACP rejoined the APA as a clinical section.

The Influence of World War I

When the United States entered World War I in 1917, a large number of potential soldiers needed to be classified based on their intellectual and psychological functioning. The United States Army Medical Department contacted the current president of the American Psychological Association (Robert Yerkes) to assist in developing an appropriate test for the military recruits. A committee was formed that included Henry Goddard, Lewis Terman, and Guy Whipple (who had published a book entitled *Manual of Mental and Physical Tests* in 1910). The committee developed what became known as the Army Alpha and Army Beta intelligence tests. The Army Alpha was a verbal test while the Army Beta was a nonverbal test. Unlike intelligence tests such as the Stanford-Binet that could only be administered to one subject at a time, the Army Alpha and Army Beta tests could be group administered to very large numbers of people. Furthermore, the tests could be used for both literate and nonliterate adults. In order to assess psychological functioning, the committee suggested that the Psychoneurotic Inventory (developed by Robert Woodworth in 1917) also be used. Approximately 2 million people were evaluated using these tests by 1918. This opportunity for psychology to contribute to the war effort through the application of psychological tests increased the status and visibility of psychologists and of psychological testing.

Clinical Psychology Between World Wars I and II

Psychological Testing

Following World War I, psychologists became well known for their testing skills (Kiesler & Zaro, 1981; Maher & Maher, 1985b). A testing development explosion occurred, such that by 1940 over 500 psychological tests had been produced. These tests included both verbal and nonverbal intelligence tests, personality and psychological functioning tests, and career interest and vocational skill tests. Tests were available for children of all ages and abilities as well as for adults. The more popular and well-known tests included the Rorschach Inkblot Test (1921), the Miller Analogies Test (1927), the Word Association Test developed by Carl Jung (1919), the Goodenough Draw-A-Man Test (1926), the Thematic Apperception Test (1935), and the Wechsler-Bellevue Intelligence Scale (1939). In fact, testing boomed to such an extent that in 1921 James McKeen Cattell founded the Psychological Corporation to sell psychological tests to various organizations and professionals.

Projective testing became very popular with the 1921 publication of Hermann Rorschach's *Psycho-*

diagnostik, the famous "inkblot" test. Rorschach was a Swiss psychiatrist who died shortly after the publication of his famous test. In 1937, S. J. Beck and Bruno Klopfer both published comprehensivescoring procedures for the Rorschach Inkblot Test that facilitated much more research to be conducted using the instrument. In 1939, David Wechsler developed the first comprehensive and individually administered intelligence test for adults. The Wechsler-Bellevue (and subsequent revisions) quickly became the standard measure with which to assess adult intellectual abilities.

By the 1930s, 50 psychological clinics and about 12 child guidance clinics were operating in the United States. By the end of the 1930s, some clinical psychologists began to offer their professional services to clients and patients in private practice.

Psychotherapy

The early work of clinical psychologists involved primarily psychological and intellectual testing. Psychotherapy and other treatment services for those suffering from mental illness were conducted primarily by psychiatrists. Most psychotherapy during this time utilized Freud's psychoanalytic principles and techniques. Although Freud disagreed (Freud, 1959), psychiatrists in the United States believed that only physicians could adequately provide psychotherapy, thus preventing clinical psychologists and other nonphysicians from conducting psychotherapy services. In fact, it wasn't until a major lawsuit in the late 1980s that psychologists won the right to be admitted as full members of American psychoanalytic institutes, resulting in their current ability to conduct psychoanalysis with patients (DeAngelis, 1989). Prior to the lawsuit, most psychoanalytic institutes admitting psychologists required that they use their training for research rather than clinical purposes.

Despite this initial prohibition, clinical psychologists gradually began providing consultation as an outgrowth of their assessment work with children. Consultation as well as treatment evolved naturally from the testing process. Consultation with teachers, children, and parents eventually lead to the provision of a full range of psychotherapy and other intervention services. Unlike the psychoanalytic treatment provided by psychiatrists at the time, psy-

chological treatment was more behavioral in orientation, reflecting the research developments in academic laboratories. For example, in 1920, John Watson detailed the well-known case of little Albert who was conditioned to be fearful to white furry objects (Watson & Rayner, 1920), while Mary Cover Jones (1924) demonstrated how these types of fears could be removed using conditioning techniques.

Training

By the early 1940s, there were no official training programs or policies regulating the field of clinical psychology. Though the majority of clinical psychologists had earned B.A. degrees, very few had earned Ph.D. or even M.A. degrees. In order to be employed as a clinical psychologist, one merely needed to have a few courses in psychological testing, child development, and abnormal psychology. The APA was of little help because of their discomfort with "applied" psychology. The vast majority of the APA membership still consisted of academics primarily interested in research rather than practice applications. However, in 1935 the APA Committee on Standards of Training in Clinical Psychology recommended that a Ph.D. and one year of supervised clinical experience be required to become a clinical psychologist. The recommendation was largely ignored because the APA did nothing to enforce their recommendation at that time (Sharow, 1947).

Organizational Split and New Publications

As in 1917, a large group of clinicians again left the APA in frustration during 1937 to form a new organization, the American Association of Applied Psychology (AAAP). History repeated itself when this new organization rejoined the APA, this time eight years later in 1945. The split between basic experimentalists and those interested in applied areas of psychology have ebbed and flowed throughout psychology's history. Nonetheless, clinical psychology continued to develop and define itself. The first clinical psychology textbook was published in 1936 by Chauncey Louttit while the *Journal of Consulting Psychology* (now called the *Journal of Consulting and Clinical Psychology*) was first published in 1937.

The Big Picture

Although clinical psychology did not become a specialty within psychology until 1896, the many different perspectives in understanding, assessing, and treating emotional and behavioral problems during the preceeding centuries set the stage for its development. Understanding the influences of biological, psychological, and social factors in the development and maintainence of problem behavior and emotional distress evolved over many years. Each generation grappled with trying to best understand the influences of various factors on behavior. As more and more scientfic discoveries were revealed, theories about the relative importance of biological, psychological, and social factors on behavior and emotions were altered to accomodate the most up-to-date discoveries and thinking. However, historical events, influencial people, and social perspectives influenced past and current thinking about topics of interest to clinical psychology.

Prior to World War II, clinical psychology was essentially defining itself, struggling with its relationship with the American Psychological Association, and making scientific and clinical inroads (Kiesler & Zaro, 1981; Maher & Maher, 1985a). However, World War II and especially the aftermath of the war changed clinical psychology significantly. Chapter three will chronical the history and development of clinical psychology in modern times, beginning with World War II.

Humankind has struggled inexorably to make sense of human behavior in the context of changing social, theological, and political times. Changing notions of how the mind, body, and environment interact to create mental health and illness has developed through fits and starts into the roots of our current integrative appreciation for the dynamic interplay of biological, psychological, and social factors. Psychology as a science and clinical psychology as a discipline have emerged in these early eras through experimentation, testing, and, eventually, consultation and treatment. Yet to come, however, is the modern era of clinical psychology, and the exciting explosion of ideas, methods and practices applied to human problems in our contemporary world.

Key Points

1. Before Lightner Witmer opened the first psychological clinic at the University of Pennsylvania and coined the term *clinical psychology* in 1896, a number of events during the course of history set the stage for the development of clinical psychology as a profession.

2. The ancient Greeks felt that the gods were the cause of both health and illness and that the mind and body were closely interconnected. The famous Greek physician, Hippocrates (460–370 B.C.) believed that disease was primarily the result of an imbalance of four bodily fluids or *humors* rather than through spiritual factors.

3. During the Middle Ages (500–1450 A.D.) the early notions of the relationship between health, illness, mind, and body returned. Disease and insanity, it was believed, were caused by spiritual matters such as the influence of demons, witches, and the results of sin.

4. During the Renaissance, renewed interest in the physical and medical world emerged once again with diminishing influences of the supernatural or religious viewpoints. New medical discoveries during the Renaissance resulted in biomedical reductionism in that disease, including mental illness, could be understood by scientific observation and experimentation rather than beliefs about mind and soul.

5. It wasn't until the work of Sigmund Freud (1856–1939) and colleagues, that the connection between mind and body reemerged. Freud demonstrated that unconscious conflicts and emotional influences could bring about diseases. As the ancient Greeks believed, Freud reawakened the notion that a more holistic view of health, which included the role of emotional life, was necessary to a fuller understanding of health, illness, and abnormal behavior.

6. Psychology was born when the first laboratory of psychology was developed by Wilhelm Wundt at the University of Leipzig, Germany in 1879. In 1890, William James published *Principles of Psychology,* which became the first classic psychology text, and in 1892, the American Psychological Association was founded and elected G. Stanley Hall as its president.

7. The birth of clinical psychology occurred in 1896 with the opening of the first psychological clinic at the University of Pennsylvania by Lightner Witmer (1867–1956). Witmer became the first psychologist to use his understanding of the principles of human behavior to help an individual with a particular problem: He was asked by a teacher to help one of her students who was not performing well in school.

8. Alfred Binet and Theodore Simon developed an intelligence test that could be used with children in order to assist teachers and schools identify children whose mental abilities prevented them benefitting from regular classroom instruction. The Binet-Simon scale was developed in 1908 specifically for school use. In 1916, Stanford University psychologist Lewis Terman revised the scale and renamed it the Stanford-Binet. The Binet approach to testing became remarkably popular in the United States. Various institutions throughout the country adopted the Binet-Simon and later Stanford-Binet approach to assess children.

9. Former mental patient Clifford Beers founded the National Committee for Mental Hygiene, which was concerned about the inhumane treatment mental patients experience while hospitalized. The mission of Beers' post-hospitalization life and his newly found association was to improve treatment for those suffering from mental illness as well as assist in the prevention of mental disorders. Beers and his association founded the child guidance movement, which used the new principles of psychology to help children and their families deal with mental illness and problem behaviors.

10. During World War I, millions of men needed to be evaluated for psychological and intellectual functioning. The military turned to psychology for tests with which to evaluate the troops.

Key Terms

American Psychological Association

Dementia Praecox

Dualism

Mental Illness

Moral Therapy

For Reflection

1. What influence did the Greeks have on clinical psychology?

2. Explain how the Greeks combined several perspectives on health and illness.

3. Why did the Middle Ages represent a step backwards in mind and body understanding?

4. What factors contributed to the rise of supernatural beliefs regarding mental illness during the Middle Ages?

5. What was the seventeenth century's influence on medicine and ultimately, clinical psychology?

6. Why did clinical psychology and the American Psychological Association often have significant differences of opinion?

7. How did the first World War influence the formation of clinical psychology?

8. What happened at Clark University in 1909 that shaped clinical psychology?

9. What causal themes continue to exist in our understanding of the factors that contribute to health and illness?

CHAPTER 3

Recent History of Clinical Psychology

Chapter Outline

Highlight of a Contemporary Clinical Psychologist: Amy Bassell Crowe, Ph.D.

The Influence of World War II

Clinical Psychology Immediately after World War II

The Rise of Alternatives to the Psychodynamic Approach

A New Training Model Emerges: The Vail Model and Professional Schools of Psychology

HIGHLIGHT OF A CONTEMPORARY CLINICAL PSYCHOLOGIST:

Amy Bassell Crowe, Ph.D.

Dr. Bassell Crowe combines a part-time private practice with being the mom of three girls.

Birth Date: December 27, 1956

College: Wellesley College (B.A. in Psychology), 1978

Graduate Program: Masters of Public Health (M.P.H.), University of California, Berkeley, 1982
Ph.D., California School of Professional Psychology (Alameda Campus), 1990

Clinical Internship: San Mateo County Mental Health Department (1989–1990)

Postdoctoral Fellowship: The Children's Health Council/Stanford University School of Medicine (1990–1991)

Current Job: Psychologist, Private Practice (San Jose and Menlo Park, CA)

Pros and cons of being a clinical psychologist:

Pros: "*Versatility.* A clinical psychologist is in the unique position of choosing various positions and functions. The opportunity to do research, teach, and/or clinical treatment and evaluation is unparalleled in other professions. My work is never dull as no two days are ever the same. In addition, as a mother of three, I have found that being a clinical psychologist offers me the ability to determine my hours and caseload in a manner commensurate with my desire to be an involved parent as well as a committed professional. While it is always a challenge to be successful in each domain, clinical psychology allows me the flexibility which few, if any, other careers can offer."

Cons: "One of the most frustrating aspects to being a clinical psychologist in the 1990s is working with third-party payers. There is increasingly more paperwork required to justify treatment, and treatment is less determined by the treating professional, but more by the requirements of an insurance policy's mental health benefits. In addition, many insurance policies offer preferred providers who are the only professionals covered by that plan. It is very difficult to become a member of these plans, thus leaving many qualified professionals financially inaccessible to many people."

Future of clinical psychology: "It is difficult to know what course the profession will take, but it appears that specialization is on the horizon. This will clearly have a dramatic impact on training as well as how the general public can utilize the clinical psychologist. In addition, as a clinical psychologist working with children, I believe it is increasingly important for us to work in a multidisciplinary manner. Many of the youngsters I see for evaluation and treatment present with increasingly complex histories. Thus, it becomes even more important for the psychologist to feel comfortable and competent working with school personnel, learning disability specialists, pediatricians, social service staff, and other health professionals to accurately diagnose and treat youngsters. The clinical psychologist plays a vital role in these coordinated efforts, but I believe it behooves us to think in broader terms about the people who are asking for our assistance."

Typical Schedule:

8:30 Psychological evaluation of a mixed race eight-year-old male (half Caucasian, half African-American) for possible learning disability and/or attention deficit disorder

10:30 Individual psychotherapy with 45-year-old Caucasian female with post traumatic stress disorder and major depression subsequent to abuse and divorce

11:30 Consultation with parents and teacher of local elementary school to design an appropriate educational program for five-year-old Caucasian child born with early brain injury

1:00 Individual psychotherapy with 51-year-old Latino male for treatment of generalized anxiety disorder

2:00 Individual psychotherapy with adopted 10-year-old Korean-American male for treatment of depression

3:15 Leave work and pick up children in carpool.

3:30 Attend daughter's basketball game.

4:30 Bring other daughter to piano lesson.

5:50 Home for dinner and family time

The past fifty years have shaped clinical psychology every bit as significantly as the previous 2000 years. Since World War II, clinical psychology has defined, refined, and expanded itself in concert with contemporary issues and demands. New theories, medications, and integrative views have led to today's field of clinical psychology. Similarly, current compelling issues related to gender, culture, ethnicity, other individual differences and the changing economic climate of healthcare, have demanded an up-to-date awareness and sensitivity for today's psychologists. This chapter will detail the major developments in clinical psychology from World War II to the present and provide an outline of these events in Table 3.1. The conclusion contains a description of contemporary factors in training, sensitivity to individual differences, and healthcare.

The Influence of World War II

With the United States' involvement in World War II, the need to assess military recruits again became pressing. As during World War I, a committee of psychologists was formed to develop an assessment procedure to efficiently evaluate intellectual and psychological functioning as well as other skills of potential soldiers (Maher & Maher, 1985b). Reflecting the rapid development in psychological testing since World War I, the testing conducted during World War II was much more extensive and sophisticated than the Army Alpha and Army Beta used

earlier. The committee developed a group administered intelligence test called the Army General Classification Test. The committee also recommended several other tests, such as the Personal Inventory, which assessed psychiatric problems, and brief versions of the Rorschach Inkblot Test and the Thematic Apperception Test to assess personality. Additionally, various ability tests were used to assess military officers and certain specialty military groups. These tests were given to over 20 million people during World War II (Reisman, 1976). Due to the military's desperate need for psychological services beyond testing, psychologists were called upon to provide other clinical services such as psychotherapy and consultation (Maher & Maher, 1985b; Miller, 1946).

In addition to the enormous needs of the military during the war effort, additional advances and developments were associated with the growth of clinical psychology. For example, new tests were developed such as the Minnesota Multiphasic Personality Inventory (MMPI) (Hathaway, 1943). The MMPI was developed as an objective personality inventory geared toward assessing psychiatric problems. The MMPI and current revisions (MMPI-2, MMPI-A) are amongst the most widely utilized psychological tests administered today. In 1949, David Wechsler published an intelligence test for children called the Wechsler Intelligence Scale for Children (WISC), which became the first significant alternative to the well-known and most often used Stanford-Binet. The current version of the WISC

Table 3.1 Significant Events in Clinical Psychology Since World War II

1940s
1945	AAAP rejoins APA.
1945	Connecticut passes first certification law for psychology.
1946	VA and NIMH fund clinical psychology training.
1947	ABEPP is founded to certify clinicians.
1949	Halstead presents neuropsychological testing battery.
1949	Boulder Conference defines scientist-practitioner model of training.

1950s
1950	Dollard and Miller publish *Personality and psychotherapy: An analysis in terms of learning, thinking, and culture.*
1951	Rogers publishes *Client-Centered Therapy.*
1952	Eysenck publishes *The effects of psychotherapy: An evaluation.*
1952	American Psychiatric Association publishes diagnostic categories in *Diagnostic and Statistical Manual* (DSM-I).
1953	APA publishes *Ethical Standards.*
1953	Skinner presents operant principles.
1955	Joint Commission on Mental Health and Illness founded.
1956	Stanford University training conference
1958	Wolpe publishes *Psychotherapy by reciprocal inhibition.*
1958	Miami training conference
1959	Mental Research Institute (MRI) founded.

1960s
1960	Eysenck publishes *Handbook of abnormal psychology: An experimental approach.*
1963	Congress passes legislation creating community mental health centers.
1965	Chicago training conference
1965	Conference at Swamscott, MA starts community psychology movement.
1967	Association for Advancement in Behavior therapy founded.
1968	First Psy.D. program founded at the University of Illinois.
1969	First free standing professional school of psychology founded at California School of Professional Psychology.

1970s
1970	DSM II published.
1973	Vail training conference
1976	National Council of Schools of Professional Psychology (NCSPP) founded.
1977	George Engel publishes paper in *Science* defining biopsychosocial model.
1977	Wachtel publishes *Psychoanalysis and behavior therapy: Toward an integration.*

1980s
1980	DSM III published.
1981	APA ethical standards revised.
1982	Health psychology defined.
1986	NCSPP Mission Bay training conference
1987	Salt Lake City training conference
1987	DSM III-R published.
1988	American Psychological Society founded.
1989	NCSPP San Juan training conference

1990s
1990	NCSPP Gainesville training conference
1991	NCSPP San Antonio training conference
1992	Michigan Conference on postdoctoral training
1994	DMS IV published.
1995	APA publishes a list of empirically validated treatments.

(the WISC-III) is the most commonly used intelligence test for children aged 6 to 16 given today.

In 1945, Connecticut became the first of many states to pass a certification law for psychologists, thereby launching the regulation of the practice of clinical psychology among qualified professionals. Thus, the practice of psychology became regulated by the state such that only those deemed qualified by training and experience could call themselves "psychologists" and offer services to the public for a fee. In 1946, the first edition of the *American Psychologist* was published, and the American Board of Examiners in Professional Psychology (ABEPP) was created to certify psychologists. The ABEPP developed a national examination for all clinical psychologists seeking licensure. This frequently revised examination is now used in every state.

Clinical Psychology Immediately After World War II

The Veterans Administration (VA)

Following the war, over 40,000 veterans were hospitalized in **Veterans Administration** Hospitals for psychiatric reasons, representing about 60 percent of the total VA hospital patient population (Miller, 1946). Psychiatrists and other physicians were unable to meet the treatment demands of these enormous numbers of veterans. Therefore, the overwhelming need for clinical services resulted in a huge increase in the number of clinical psychologists who could provide a full range of comprehensive psychological services, including psychological testing, psychotherapy, consultation, and research. In 1946, the VA requested 4700 clinical psychologists be employed in the VA system. In fact, the chief medical director of the VA system met with officials from a group of major universities to request that formal training programs in clinical psychology be developed. By later that year, 200 graduate students in clinical psychology were being trained at 22 VA institutions (Peck & Ash, 1964). VA hospitals offered clinical psychologists secure job positions, attractive salaries, and the freedom to provide a full range of professional services. By the early 1950s, the VA Hospitals became the largest single employer of clinical psychologists in the United States (Maher & Maher, 1985b; Peck & Ash, 1964).

Academic psychologists had mixed feelings about the tremendous boom in clinical psychology due to the needs of the VA Hospitals. Many thought that this was an opportunity to increase the activities, prestige, and influence of clinical psychology. Many others were disinterested in the applied aspects of psychology, preferring to focus solely on the science of psychology in academic environments. This division between science and practice has remained an area of contention within psychology from the very earliest days of the discipline until the present.

Training

The need for qualified mental health professionals after World War II resulted in the National Institute of Mental Health (NIMH) developing grant programs to help train clinical psychologists (as well as psychiatrists, nurses, and social workers). The grant program started with $212,000 in 1948 and rose to $10 million in 1980 (Kiesler & Zaro, 1981). These monies attracted more and more students to the mental health fields making both new training programs and new guidelines quickly needed.

The APA Committee on Training in Clinical Psychology under the leadership of David Shakow sought, in 1947, to develop training standards and guidelines for graduate and internship training in clinical psychology (Shakow, 1947). Ultimately, the committee's guidelines not only became the "gold standard" for clinical training but were used to determine if federal monies would be used to support these graduate training programs. The guidelines included the central admonishment that clinical psychologists be trained rigorously in a four-year doctoral program along with a one-year clinical internship. The guidelines also created the standard that training include several different content areas such the biological, cognitive, individual difference, and social aspects of behavior (Shakow, 1947, 1976, 1978). In addition, psychologists were to be trained as both scientists and clinicians. The committee recommended that training be comprehensive in research, treatment, and assessment. In 1948, the American Psychological Association began to carefully evaluate, critique, and accredit doctoral training programs. These guidelines led to the most influential training conference that has occurred in the history of clinical psychology: The 1949 Boulder Conference.

The Boulder Conference

Two years after the training report was released, a committee met in Boulder, Colorado and formally adopted the advised model of clinical training. The conference was financially supported by the Veterans Administration as well as the United States Public Health Service via the National Institute of Mental Health. The financial support provided by these government agencies reflected the enormous interest and stake the United States government had in the field of clinical psychology. Clinical psychology had come a long way since its humble beginnings in Witmer's clinic in 1886. The **Boulder model** also became known as the **scientist-practitioner model**, and emphasized that clinical psychologists should be competent in both conducting research as well as in providing professional psychological services such as psychotherapy and assessment. This training model stated that a Ph.D. degree in psychology from a university-based training program plus a one-year clinical internship were necessary for adequate preparation. This model has been, in effect, the predominant training approach for the past 50 years (Norcross, Karg & Prochaska, 1997a; Shakow, 1978). By 1948, there were 22 APA-accredited clinical psychology training programs in universities and by 1949, 42 schools offered accredited doctoral training in clinical psychology, almost doubling the number in just one year.

Post-Boulder Conference Events

Not everyone was pleased with the results and recommendations of the Boulder conference (Frank, 1984; Korman, 1976; Strother, 1956). Additional conferences convened following the 1949 Boulder conference to discuss the pros and cons of the clinical psychology training model. Conferences occurred at Stanford University in 1955 (Strother, 1956), Miami Beach in 1958 (Roe, Gustad, Moore, Ross, & Skodak, 1959), Chicago in 1965 (Zimet & Throne, 1965), Vail in 1973 (Korman, 1976), and Salt Lake City in 1987 (Bickman, 1987). The Chicago conference was the first to question seriously the wisdom of the Boulder model. Some conference participants felt that because only about 10 percent of psychologists actually publish research, too much emphasis and energy were being spent teaching graduate students how to conduct psychological research (Brems, Johnson, & Gallucci, 1996; Levy, 1962; Frank, 1984). Although this concern has continued to be expressed over the years, no resolution regarding this conflict has occurred in university-based training programs. The advent of the Psy.D. degree and freestanding professional schools of psychology have attempted to deal with this issue by offering more practiced based (and less research based) training.

By the early 1950s, over 1000 members of the APA were members of the Clinical Division. The growth of clinical psychology during the 1950s was enormous. APA membership more than doubled during the 1950s and federal research grants supporting psychology training and research tripled during the same time period.

In 1953, the first attempt to outline ethical principles for psychologists was published. The ethical principles have been revised eight times since then and as recently as 1992. The Ethics Code outlines expected behavior among all psychologists including those involved with clinical, research, teaching, forensic, and administrative activities and will be discussed in detail in Chapter 13.

The Rise of Alternatives to the Psychodynamic Approach

During the first half of the twentieth century, the psychoanalytic approach founded by Freud and, to a much lesser extent, the behavioral conditioning approach founded by John Watson served as the eminent theoretical and treatment approach to mental illness. During the 1950s, 1960s, and 1970s, many new approaches were developed as alternatives to the traditional psychodynamic approach. Psychologists were becoming well established in psychotherapy, augmenting their already acknowledged testing services. The humanistic, behavioral, cognitive-behavioral, and family systems approaches to treatment emerged as compelling and popular alternatives to the more traditional theories and interventions. Furthermore, the rise of the community mental health movement in the 1960s as well as the introduction of psychotropic medication in treating mental illness had powerful influences on clinical psychology. During the turbulent yet optimistic 1960s and early 1970s, clinical psychology continued to expand with increasing knowledge, tools, and professional resources. Finally, integrative approaches, such as the biopsychosocial perspective emerged, adding to the sophistication of thought and practice in the field. In this chapter, I will examine these alternatives to the psychodynamic viewpoint from a historical perspective. I will introduce the persons responsible for these theories and how they emerged over time. In the next two chapters I will highlight these perspectives in more detail focusing on how the theories and principles are applied to issues of concern in clinical psychology.

The Behavioral Approach

The behavioral approach applies theories of learning and conditioning to the understanding of human behavior and the treatment of behavioral and psychological problems. Rooted in the conditioning research of Ivan Pavlov (1849–1936) in Russia as well as the American research on behaviorism and learning theory conducted by John Watson, Edward Thorndike, Clark Hull, John Dollard, Neal Miller, and B.F. Skinner, **behavioral** principles in psychological treatment became an attractive alternative to medical and psychodynamic strategies during the 1950s and 1960s. Many psychologists were unimpressed with both the methods and outcomes of the medical or psychodynamic approaches practiced by psychiatrists and other professionals. For example, the review article by Eysenck (1952) examining psychotherapy treatment results was not favorable to psychoanalytic techniques. The behavioral platform was especially attractive to research oriented clinicians who felt that behavior therapy approaches proved more effective in empirical research trials relative to traditional theories and methods such as psychoanalysis. Therefore, the behavioral approach to understanding human behavior, diagnosis, and treatment of mental illness was viewed by many as more scientifically based, and thus justified, than the psychodynamic approach. Furthermore, behavior therapy approaches were advanced by researchers because, more than other treatment modalities, behavioral techniques were more readily operation-

alized to allow for research. For example, it was easier to measure the number of times a child had a temper tantrum or a person had a panic attack than measuring constructs such as the id, transference, or unconscious conflicts. Behavioral approaches allowed for greater ease of measuring outcome data, defining concepts, and statistical analysis.

Behavior therapy approaches to treatment were being developed in both South Africa by Joseph Wolpe and colleagues as well as in England by Hans Eysenck, M.B. Shapiro, Stanley Rachman, among others. Wolpe (1958) had developed systematic desensitization to treat a variety of anxiety-based disorders such as phobias. Eysenck and colleagues at the University of London Institute of Psychiatry and the Maudsley Hospital used research supported techniques guided by learning theory to treat a number of psychiatric complaints (Eysenck, 1960). These later researchers were applying the principles of conditioning and learning theory to treat a variety of clinical problems including phobia, obsessive-compulsive behavior, anxiety, and disruptive behavior in children. The publication of several books by these professionals set the stage for behavior therapy to be widely accepted and practiced in the United States (e.g., Eysenck, 1960; Krasner & Ulmann, 1965; Skinner, 1953; Wolpe, 1958; Wolpe & Lazarus, 1966).

Behavior therapy was also well suited to the Boulder training model because clinical psychology training was designed to emphasize both the science and practice of psychology. The behavioral approach also was well suited to the social and political influences of the time which included the optimistic notion that we could create a more perfect society using social engineering and conditioning techniques (Skinner, 1948).

Although there are various types of behavior therapy such as applied behavioral analysis (Wilson & Frank, 1982), social learning theory-based treatment (Bandura, 1969, 1982), and cognitive-behavioral therapy (Kendall & Bemis, 1983), there are also several commonalities to the behavior therapies in terms of their understanding of human behavior and approach to assisting those who experience emotional and behavioral problems. These include the notion that most problematic behavior is learned and can be altered through the use of learning principles. Furthermore, treatment methods are based on scientifically derived procedures and can be objectively used and evaluated. Finally, behavior therapy is not imposed on others but is agreed to by clients through a collaborative and contractual relationship (O'Leary & Wilson, 1987). In 1967, the Association for Advancement of Behavior Therapy (AABT) was founded and remains as one of the major professional organizations for clinical psychologists who not only conduct behavior therapy but who are broadly interested in the applied application of scientifically derived data.

The Cognitive-Behavioral Approach

Although the cognitive approach became popular during the 1970s after the rise of several other methods that will be discussed later in this chapter, since it is closely related, the cognitive approach is presented here following the behavioral discussion. During the 1970s, many researchers and clinicians adhering to the behavioral approach to research and treatment acknowledged a number of significant limitations in their model. Primarily, a strict focus on overt behavior neglected the contributions of thinking and attitudes in human behavior. The work of Albert Ellis (Ellis, 1962; Ellis & Grieger, 1977) using Rational-Emotive Therapy (RET; now called Rational-Emotive Behavior Therapy, REBT); Aaron Beck (1976) using cognitive treatments for depression; the cognitive restructuring work of Mahoney (1974); the stress inoculation work of Meichenbaum (1977); and the self-efficacy work of Bandura (1969, 1982) led the charge in integrating cognitive approaches with behavioral approaches. Treatment focusing on changing thinking, feeling, and expectations became as important as the goal of changing overt behavior.

For example, Ellis' Rational-Emotive Behavior Therapy attempts to alter the patient's irrational beliefs concerning the "shoulds" and "oughts" about themselves and others. Beck's cognitive approach focuses on the notion that depressed people tend to view themselves, others, and the world as more negative than nondepressed persons. Altering maladaptive thought patterns and developing more adaptive ways of thinking are central to Beck's approach. Meichenbaum's self-instructional approach uses *self-talk* to guide and alter problematic thinking and behavior. While there are a number of different cognitive therapies, commonalities include the no-

tion that learning and behavior are cognitively mediated by attitudes and attributions and that the role of the therapist is to serve as a coach, educator, or consultant in assisting the alteration of maladaptive cognitive processes and behavior (Ingram & Scott, 1990; Kendall & Bemis, 1983). The cognitive approach has become so popular that by 1990 the majority of AABT members (69%) identified themselves as being **cognitive-behavioral** while only 27 percent reported being strictly behavioral in orientation (Craighead, 1990).

The Humanistic Approach

The **humanistic** approach employed philosophy, existentialism, and theories of human growth and potential to understand human behavior and offer strategies for psychological treatment. The humanistic approach focused on the patient's experience or phenomenology of their concerns and offered warmth, empathy, and unconditional positive regard in psychotherapeutic interactions. During the 1950s and 1960s (during an age of anxiety following World War II and during the cold war), the humanistic approach to psychological treatment gained widespread acceptance. Frustrated with the limitations of the psychodynamic and behavioral approaches regarding treatment process, outcome, and both client and therapist satisfaction, as well as the perceived negative psychodynamic and behavioral views of human nature (e.g., the psychodynamic emphasis on neuroses as well as infantile and primitive needs; the behavioral focus on governing behavior through external reinforcement), many mental health professionals began to incorporate the more optimistic and embracing views purported by the humanistic school of thought. The humanistic approach became known as the *third force* in psychology following the psychodynamic and behavioral approaches.

The humanistic approach was strongly influenced by philosophy as well as the existential approach to psychotherapy. The existential approach became especially popular after the atrocities of World War I and most especially in response to Nazi Germany during World War II (Frankl, 1963, 1965). The existential approach had its roots in European philosophy in the works of Kierkegaard, Nietzsche, Sartre, Buber, and Heidegger among others. This approach focused, for example, on the human need to seek and define meaning in life. American writers such as psychologist Rollo May (May, 1977; May, Angel, & Ellenberger, 1958) and psychiatrist Irvin Yalom (1981) helped to delineate and popularize the existential approach to humanistic therapy in the United States. Psychoanalytic writers such as Hans Kohut, Otto Kernberg, and Merton Gil have integrated some of the humanistic perspective into their writing as well.

Leading humanistic psychotherapists and theorists such as Carl Rogers, Abraham Maslow, Frederick Perls, Victor Frankl, and others all uniquely contributed to the development of the humanistic approaches to professional psychotherapy. Whereas each offered a somewhat different approach, their commonalities are notable and together comprise the humanistic school. These commonalities include the commitment to the phenomenological model that emphasizes that humans are able to be consciously reflective and have the ability to experience self-determination and freedom. Thus, therapists must be able to fully understand a person's perception of internal and external reality in order to not only better understand their feelings and behavior but also offer assistance. Another commonality included the notion that humans strive towards growth and are not, for example, trying to maintain homeostasis by satisfying various primitive needs and conflicts. The humanistic approach also championed a belief in free will and regarded human behavior as not just a by-product of early childhood experiences or merely conditioned responses to the external environment. Finally, the humanistic approach is person-centered with maximum respect for the individual and their experiences (Tageson, 1982).

The client-centered and phenomenological approach of Carl Rogers became the most influential humanistic therapy. While Rogers was trained in the more traditional psychodynamic approach, he rejected it to provide a compelling alternative with the client-centered approach. The approach emphasizes therapist empathy, unconditional positive regard, congruence, intensive active listening, and support to help individuals and groups reach their full human potential (Rogers, 1951, 1954, 1961). Rogers felt that humans naturally strive towards their potential and that psychotherapy was a catalyst that could assist them in this endeavor.

The Family Systems Approaches

Unlike the psychodynamic, behavioral, and humanistic approaches already outlined, the **family systems** approaches tend to utilize the entire family in understanding and treating problematic feelings and behavior. Rather than working with an individual patient who reports problematic symptoms, the family approaches generally work with the entire (or a subset of the) family. Prior to the 1950s, most psychological treatment focused on the *identified patient* defined as the person regarded within the family as manifesting problematic symptoms, behaviors, or attitudes. The family members of the identified patient were generally left out of the treatment and not viewed as potentially active agents of dysfunction and potential recovery. During the 1950s, 1960s, and especially during the 1970s, the family systems approach to treatment became popular among clinical psychologists and other mental health professionals (Haley, 1976; Minuchin, 1974). The systems approach took exception to the notion that only the identified patient was in need of intervention services. In fact, the systems approach asserted that the dysfunction resided in the family as an interrelated system and not only in one family member. For example, therapists observed that patient functioning often deteriorated when they interacted with their family members. Therefore, all family members were treated together—a radical departure from traditional treatment modalities. Family therapy became a very common intervention strategy for numerous problems.

The family systems approach emerged from the Bateson Project during the 1950s in California. Gregory Bateson, an anthropologist, was especially interested in communication styles, collaborating with Jay Haley (an expert in communications), John Weakland (an engineer), and Don Jackson (a psychiatrist) to examine communication styles such as *double-bind communication* and *metamessages* in psychiatric patients (especially schizophrenic patients) at the Palo Alto Veterans Hospital (Bateson, Jackson, Haley, & Weakland, 1956). Double-bind messages include impossible-to-satisfy requests (e.g., someone ordering another person to be spontaneous) while metamessages involve what someone really means rather than what they actually say (e.g., someone may report deeply loving someone but never show any actions or sincere statements that support the claim). Jackson later founded the Mental Research Institute (MRI) in Palo Alto, CA in 1959 in conjunction with another well-known family therapist, Virginia Satir.

Jay Haley later left the Bateson Project and joined forces with Salvador Minuchin to develop the structural family therapy model at the Philadelphia Child Guidance Clinic. Haley later moved to Washington, DC in the 1970s and founded the Washington Family Institute where his wife, Cloe Madanes, developed the strategic therapy model (Haley, 1976). Strategic therapy uses paradoxical intention, or *reverse psychology,* and techniques to effect behavior change. This model of family therapy prescribes the symptom in order to cope with resistance in treatment. Further details regarding this and other family therapy approaches will be provided in the next chapter.

During the 1960s and 1970s a variety of models of family therapy emerged in various parts of the United States and Europe. For example, Maria Selvini-Palazoli and colleagues founded the Milan Associates in the late 1960s to treat families confronted with anorexia nervosa in a family member. The Milan group sought to use family systems theory to better understand family rules and to avoid getting trapped into family alliances and coalitions. Being trapped or manipulated into family alliances (e.g., joining or agreeing with the parents that all of the problems in the family are due to the child's aggressive behavior or the spouse's infidelity) may prevent effective therapy for the whole family. Watzlawick, Weakland, and Fisch (1974) developed the Brief Therapy Project at the Mental Research Institute. The program focused on repetitive cycles of interpersonal behavior that often tend to reinforce problems rather than solve them. Some family theorists (such as John Bell, Ivan Nagy, James Framo, Lyman Wynne, and Murray Bowen) used psychoanalytic theory in their application of family therapy (Bell, 1961; Bowen, 1978). Others, such as Carl Whitaker and Virginia Satir, focused on experiential models with an emphasis on intuition and feelings (Whitaker & Keith, 1981; Satir, 1967, 1972). Still others, such as Nathan Ackerman and Salvador Minuchin, developed structural family therapy and focused on family boundaries and generational hierarchies, especially among child-focused families.

While a wide variety of family therapy approaches and strategies emerged following the Bateson Project throughout the later part of the 20th century (especially during the 1960s and 1970s), commonalities primarily included a focus on the role of the entire family system in producing and maintaining problematic behavior, communication patterns associated with family problems, and ongoing maladaptive relationship patterns among family members. Intervention at the family level rather than at the individual level became the goal of each of these treatment strategies.

Psychotropic Medication

Although biological treatments and medications such as opium, insulin, bromides, and electric convulsive therapy (ECT) were used to treat mental illnesses during the early and mid part of the twentieth century, it was not until the 1950s that effective medications were developed to treat severe disorders such as schizophrenia and bipolar illness. Typical of many discoveries, it was by accident that these **psychotropic medications** were found to be effective in the treatment of mental illness.

Australian psychiatrist, John Cade, noticed that guinea pigs became calm when they were given lithium chloride, a natural salt. Dr. Cade then gave lithium to psychotic patients and found that it had the same calming effect as discovered in the guinea pigs. French physician, Henri Laborit, used the medication in an attempt to lower blood pressure prior to surgery and found that it lowered patient anxiety. In 1952, two French psychiatrists (Pierre Deniker and Jean Delay) gave the medication (chlorpromazine or Thorazine) to psychiatric patients. They found that patients were less anxious and that schizophrenic patients experienced fewer hallucinations and delusions. Thus, the discovery of rauwolfia serpentona (or reserpine) and the neuroleptics (such as Thorazine and Haldol) proved helpful in reducing the hallucinations, delusions, and agitation of psychotic patients. Furthermore, benzodiazepines (such as Valium) were found in the early 1960s to be effective in reducing profound symptoms of anxiety.

The initial response to the discovery of these medications was marked by tremendous enthusiasm in the professional and lay communities. Later, however, problematic side effects and treatment limitations tempered the initial enthusiasm. Nonetheless, the effectiveness of these treatments ultimately enabled patients to leave mental hospitals in droves. For example, in 1950 there were approximately 500,000 patients hospitalized in state and county mental hospitals in the United States. This number dropped to only 100,000 by 1988 (Mechanic & Rochefort, 1992). These medications also provided a new role for psychiatrists who were generally providing only psychoanalytic, limited biological (e.g., electro convulsive therapy), and custodial treatments for their patients. The effectiveness of medication further solidified the notion that many mental illnesses were brain diseases and thus did not emerge from unconscious conflicts alone. The rising use of medication to treat psychiatric problems also promulgated the frequent leadership role physicians currently take in treating mental illness. Today, about 20 percent of all medications prescribed are intended to impact emotional or behavioral factors such as depression, anxiety, and impulsive behavior (Baldessarini, 1990).

Community Mental Health Movement

During the 1950s, psychotropic medication allowed many psychiatric patients to leave the institutional setting of mental hospitals and reenter society. Furthermore, reflecting the sociopolitical climate of the time, the "warehousing" of patients in mental hospitals was replaced by more humane community based treatments. During this period of deinstitutionalization, psychiatric patients needed outpatient services to readjust to society, obtain gainful employment, and cope with the stresses of life and increased social demands and opportunities. Furthermore, interest in the prevention of mental illness as well as the social factors that contribute to mental illness—such as poverty, homelessness, racism, unemployment, and divorce—developed a more prominent role in the theories and interventions associated with mental illness. This resulted in the rise of the **community mental health movement.** Congress passed legislation in 1955 to create the Joint Commission on Mental Health and Illness, which sought to develop community mental health services outside of the inpatient mental hospital setting. In 1963, legislation was passed to use federal monies to create community mental health centers throughout the United States. In 1965 a group of

psychologists met in Swampscott, Massachusetts to plan for the unique role psychology would play in this movement. The mission of the community mental health movement and of community psychology was to provide affordable mental health services to all aspects of society on an outpatient basis, as well as to prevent mental illness from developing via early intervention and detection programs. The community mental health clinics that opened throughout the United States were typically funded by state and federal grant monies. The movement resulted in opportunities for psychologists to provide a wide range of professional services including psychological testing, consultation, treatment, crisis intervention, and services focused on the prevention of mental illness (e.g., education). However, within 20 years of passing the legislation that created the community mental health movement, the federal and state governments significantly reduced funding and most of the programs closed, reduced services, or were incorporated into private clinics.

The Integrative Approaches

After the explosion of new theories and approaches during the 1950s, 1960s, and 1970s, many researchers and clinicians felt dissatisfied with strict adherence to one particular theory or theoretical orientation. Each school of thought (behavioral, cognitive-behavioral, humanistic, family systems, psychodynamic) developed their own philosophy or world view of human behavior and translated these views into strategies for effecting positive change in feelings, behavior, and relationships. During the late 1970s and early 1980s, many professionals sought to integrate the best that the various schools of thought had to offer on a case-by-case basis. Rather than focusing on the differences in these approaches, an emphasis was placed on common factors. The fact that research was unable to demonstrate that any one treatment approach or theoretical orientation was superior relative to the others (Smith, Glass, & Miller, 1980) and the finding that the majority of practicing clinicians identified themselves as being eclectic (Garfield & Kurtz, 1976; Norcross & Prochaska, 1983) further motivated the professional community to consider **integrative** approaches to theory, research, and practice.

In the 1950s, Dollard and Miller (1950) attempted to understand psychodynamic concepts through behavioral or learning theory language. Other authors, especially during the 1970s, took an interest in integrating psychodynamic and behavioral concepts and techniques (Feather & Rhoads, 1972; Wachtel, 1975, 1977). The most notable work in this area was the work of Paul Wachtel (1975, 1977, 1984). Wachtel sought to take the strengths of each approach by incorporating elements of both in a logical and consistent manner. He focused on the importance of unconscious influences, meaning, and fantasies as well as the importance of empirical evidence, the patient's goals of treatment, and respect for the environmental influences and context of behavior.

Jerome Frank (1961, 1982) examined the commonalities of various treatment methods (as well as placebo effects and faith healing) and found that they all include instilling hope and emotional arousal in the patient, encouraging improved morale and understanding of self and others, a healing setting (e.g., psychotherapy office), and supporting change outside of the treatment environment. Other authors focused on the nature of the professional relationship as being a common curative factor in all types of therapies (Rogers, 1954; Schofield, 1964; Truax & Mitchell, 1971).

Other, more recent, authors have focused on eclecticism and the integrative use of techniques from various theoretical orientations without specific allegiance to the theoretical underpinnings of these techniques (Beutler, 1986; Lazarus, 1981, 1986). These approaches focus on a more functional and pragmatic approach to incorporating various treatment strategies to fit the needs of the individual patient.

The Biopsychosocial Approach

Ever since the seventeenth century and the influence of Descartes and Newton, theories of health and illness have tended to separate the mind from the body. Thus, Western medicine often tends to view illness, including mental illness, as either being influenced by biology, such as genetics and neurochemical imbalances, or by the mind, such as personality and interpersonal conflicts. Advances in medicine, science, psychology, sociology, ethnic and minority studies, and other fields during the last half of the twentieth century have provided evidence for interactive multidimensional influences on health and illness, including mental illness. New discoveries in genetics and neurochemistry, along with new techniques to investigate the brain such as neuroimaging, have solidified the contribution of biology to emotion and behavior. The effectiveness of psychotropic medications further provided clues as to the profound biological influences impacting behavior. The new theories and supporting research proposed by the behavioral, cognitive-behavioral, humanistic, and family systems perspectives provided further evidence and credence to psychological and social factors influencing health, illness, emotions, and behavior. Finally, the community mental health movement beginning in the 1960s demonstrated the influence of social, cultural, and economic factors in mental illness. The confluence of these new discoveries and perspectives allowed a **biopsychosocial** orientation to emerge during the late 1970s.

In 1977, George Engel published a paper in the journal *Science* that proposed the biopsychosocial approach as the optimal model of understanding and treating illness. The approach, with its roots in the ancient Greek notions of Hippocrates discussed earlier, suggests that physical and psychological problems are likely to have a biological, psychological, and social element that should be understood in order to provide effective intervention strategies. Thus, rather than a unidimensional causal approach to problems, the biopsychosocial perspective utilizes a multidimensional and interactive approach. The biopsychosocial framework suggests that the biological, psychological, and social aspects of health and illness intimately influence each other.

The biopsychosocial perspective is not new. As was discussed in the previous chapter, the appreciation for biological, psychological, and social influences on behavior, emotions, and health was recognized centuries ago. However, over the years, emphasis has been placed on different elements of the perspective, which has sometimes excluded other elements. Furthermore, scientific discoveries, influencial people, and social thinking of the time has tended to highlight either biological, psychological, or social influences.

The biopsychosocial approach has been accepted in both medicine and psychology with research support to demonstrate its usefulness (McDaniel, 1995). For example, research has indicated that many diverse problems such as obesity, alcoholism, learning disabilities, anxiety, and depressive disorders all involve a complex interaction between biological, psychological, and social influences. An understanding of and appreciation for these interactions should be taken into consideration when designing treatment and prevention interventions. The biopsychosocial approach became the foundation for the field of health psychology in the early 1980s (Schwartz, 1982). It has become an influential perspective in clinical psychology as well. Therefore, psychologists must be aware of multidimensional biopsychosocial influences in order to understand and treat others.

A New Training Model Emerges: The Vail Model and Professional Schools of Psychology

The Vail Conference

A turning point in the philosophy of clinical psychology training occurred during the 1973 Vail conference held in Vail, Colorado (Korman, 1976). The conference was held to discuss how training could be altered to accomodate the changing needs of both clinical psychology students and society. The National Conference on Levels and Patterns of Professional Training in Psychology received financial support from the National Institute of Mental Health (NIMH). The most significant outcome of the conference was the acceptance of a new training model for clinical psychology. In addition to the Boulder or scientist-practitioner model, the Vail or **scholar-practitioner model** was endorsed as an appropriate alternative. This model suggested that clinical training could emphasize the delivery of professional psychological services while minimizing research training. Furthermore, the conference endorsed the notion that graduate training need not occur only in university psychology departments but could also occur in free standing professional schools of psychology. Free standing schools were developed independent of university affiliation.

One of the first and largest schools is the California School of Professional Psychology with four campuses and over 5000 students enrolled. Shortly following the conference in 1973, the National Council of Schools of Professional Psychology was formed to address issues unique to these new schools and programs. Finally, the conference endorsed the Psy.D. (or doctor of psychology) degree as an alternative to the Ph.D. degree. The Psy.D. degree would be given to clinicians trained in the **Vail model** who were more practitioner-oriented than those trained in the traditional Boulder model, which emphasized both research and clinical training. This new model allowed students to choose the type of emphasis they wanted in their graduate education. These choices are still available for current students seeking graduate training. The first Psy.D. program was developed in 1968 at the University of Illinois (Peterson, 1968). However, that program is no longer in existence.

For the first time ever, the Vail conference also endorsed the notion that recipients of a terminal master's degree be considered professional psychologists rather than only prospective the recipients of a doctoral degree. However, in 1977, the APA stated that a doctorate was needed for the title *psychologist,* thereby diminishing the role of the terminal master's degree supported by the Vail conference. Although numerous graduate programs across the United States and Canada offer terminal master's degree programs in clinical psychology and many states license master's level professionals as counselors, the APA has chosen not to support terminal master's degree education as adequate for the independent practice of psychology. In practice, professionals with master's degrees often provide independent professional services under the title *counselor* but not *psychologist.*

Salt Lake City Conference

During 1987, the National Conference held yet another meeting to examine how training models best fit the needs of students, society, and the profession. The conference endorsed the notion that all graduate training in clinical psychology, regardless of the degree (Ph.D. or Psy.D.) or setting (university or free standing professional school), should include a core curriculum containing courses such as research methods, statistics, professional ethics, history and systems, psychological assessment, and on the biological, social, cognitive, and individual difference bases of behavior. However, the Salt Lake City conference tempered the Vail conference's enthusiasm for free standing professional school training of clinical psychologists. Most notably, the conference stated that by 1995, all APA accredited programs should at least be affiliated with a regionally accredited university. This measure was passed in order to maintain better control over the training conducted at the rapidly proliferating free standing professional schools (Bickman, 1987). However, this recommendation has largely been ignored to the extent that, by 1995, the majority of free standing professional schools of psychology are still not associated with any universities. In fact, 50 percent of all doctorates in psychology are now awarded from these free standing professional schools not associated with universities, with the vast majority being located in California.

Additional Conferences

The National Council of Schools in Professional Psychology held several national meetings in Mission Bay in 1986, San Juan in 1989, Gainesville in 1990, and San Antonio in 1991. These meetings led to a refinement of the mission of Professional Schools of Psychology. New goals included an emphasis on adequate training in service to ethnic minorities and underserved groups as well as a recommitment to integrating science and practice into clinical training.

Michigan Conference on Postdoctoral Training

In October of 1992, the National Conference on Postdoctoral Training in Professional Psychology was held at the University of Michigan to specifically address postdoctoral training issues in psychology (Larsen, Belar, Bieliauskas, Klepac, Stigall, & Zimet, 1993). While the APA accredits and provides detailed guidelines for graduate and internship training, no comprehensive APA guidelines have historically been provided for postdoctoral training. Since most all states require postdoctoral training prior to licensure, almost all clinical psychologists

had been participating in postdoctoral training programs without APA guidance. Many professionals have called for national standards for postdoctoral training (Belar, Bieliauskas, Larsen, Mensh, Poey, & Roehike, 1989; Plante, 1988). The Michigan conference developed guidelines and plans for further control and regulation of postdoctoral training in clinical psychology. For example, recommendations included the completion of APA-accredited doctoral and internship training programs prior to admission to accredited postdoctoral training programs; at least two hours per week of face-to-face supervision by a licensed psychologist; and a systematic evaluation mechanism for examining the trainees and program among others.

Present History

Contemporary clinical psychology, ever evolving, is currently adapting to numerous changes and challenges. While a detailed discussion will address these current issues in Chapter 14, brief mention is warranted at this point regarding clinical psychology's response to increasing imperatives regarding diversity and cultural sensitivity, changing trends in professional training, and ongoing economic factors affecting the study and practice of clinical psychology.

The United States is both blessed and challenged with tremendous diversity. Diversity in gender, culture, ethnicity, language, religious faith, sexual orientation, physical ability and disability, and the entire spectrum of individual differences has necessarily informed and enriched the practice and study of psychology. No longer can researchers, educators or clinicians assume a white, male, English speaking, heterosexual population. Increasingly, it has become incumbent upon clinical psychologists to acquire the education and insight necessary to develop important sensitivities in their work with diverse individuals and populations. The contribution of diversity to the field is more fully explored in Chapter 14, but can be seen throughout this book given its contemporary emphasis. Training itself is undergoing significant changes. First, more than half of all clinical psychologists now train in free standing professional schools of psychology rather than in traditional university programs. This has resulted in many more psychologists seeking employment, as well as many more being trained within the Vail (i.e., scholar-practitioner), rather than the Boulder (i.e., scientist-practitioner), model. Second, after being predominantly a male profession, the gender distribution of students and new graduates in clinical psychology has changed from being mostly men to being mostly women. While about 60 percent of the APA members are men (representing all areas of psychology), the majority of new doctorates in clinical psychology are now awarded to women (American Psychological Association, 1995). For example, between 1973 and 1991, the number of men who entered the field of psychology rose by 130 percent while the number of women choosing psychology as a career increased by 530 percent (American Psychological Association, 1995d). The feminization of psychology in general and clinical psychology in particular has significantly altered the face of the field.

Economic factors in health care are also significantly altering the landscape for psychologists. Significant reductions in federal grant funding have resulted in far less federal dollars available for clinical psychology research and training. This has resulted in more competition for limited research funding. While the number of clinical psychologists choosing full-time private practice as their career choice has grown steadily over the past several decades, the trend may be starting to reverse itself due to significant and sweeping changes in health care. Thus, solo independent practice may become less attractive as a career option for psychologists. Clinical psychology has expanded beyond the mental health field into the general health care and preventative health care fields. Therefore, clinical psychology has found its way into general health care with applications to numerous medical problems and issues. Clinical psychology has also secured more independence, for example, gaining hospital admitting privileges in many states, as well as the ability to prescribe medication in certain settings, such as in the military. This has expanded the types of professional activities and roles available to clinical psychologists. Finally, changes in the health care delivery and reimbursement systems in the United States have posed one of the biggest challenges to clinical psychology and other health related fields. Limited services and monies are available from insurance companies to treat mental and physical problems. Each of these current issues will be discussed in more detail in Chapter 14.

The Big Picture

Clinical psychology has come a long way since Witmer founded the specialty by opening the first psychological clinic in 1886. It is hard to imagine that about 50 years ago there were no psychology licensing laws in any state and no comprehensive clinical psychology training guidelines, accreditation standards, or models of training. Furthermore, it is astonishing that 50 years ago, clinical psychologists were often not allowed to conduct psychotherapy since it was the exclusive domain of psychiatrists. Today, clinical psychology is a thriving field, utilizing the integrated resources of numerous perspectives and interventions. Clinical psychology is now practiced in a wide variety of hospitals, clinics, businesses, and educational settings, among other locations.

Curiously, while clinical psychology has come such a long way, its progress has sometimes occurred, not because of but, in spite of the American Psychological Association. Several times the clinical psychologists resigned from the APA to form their own independent group. Each time they later decided to rejoin the APA. The differences of opinion between the applied clinical professionals and the majority academic and scientific members of APA have been a fact of life since the APA was founded. The tension between the science and practice of psychology has existed for 100 years and will likely continue.

Today, contemporary clinical psychology seeks to address and incorporate the important issues of diversity, scientific advances, and changes in professional training and economic factors affecting healthcare in this country. Ultimately, the science and practice of clinical psychology has contributed broadly to our understanding and treatment of human difficulties. The science and application of clinical psychology has proved effective in enhancing the quality of life for numerous people throughout the world. It certainly is an exciting time in the clinical psychology field. This excitement is likely to continue for future clinical psychologists.

Key Points

1. During World War I and World War II, millions of men needed to be evaluated for psychological and intellectual functioning. The military turned to psychology to provide them with testing in order to evaluate the troops.

2. Following World War II, over 40,000 veterans were hospitalized in Veterans Administration Hospitals for psychiatric reasons. The overwhelming need for clinical services for these men resulted in a huge increase in clinical psychologists providing a full range of comprehensive psychological services, including psychological testing, psychotherapy, consultation, and research. In 1946, the VA requested about 4700 clinical psychologists to be employed in the VA system.

3. The APA Committee on Training in Clinical Psychology met in 1947 and sought to develop training standards and guidelines for graduate and internship training in clinical psychology. Ultimately, the committee's guidelines became the "gold standard" for clinical training. The report included the notion that clinical psychologists should be trained rigorously in a four-year doctoral program as well as with a one-year clinical internship and be trained as both scientists and clinicians. The committee recommended that training be comprehensive in research, treatment, and assessment. In 1949 a committee met in Boulder, Colorado and developed the *Boulder model* (also know as the scientist-practitioner model) of clinical training.

4. During the 1950s, 1960s, and 1970s, many new treatment and intervention approaches and perspectives were offered as an alternative to the traditional psychodynamic approach. Psychologists were becoming well established in their psychotherapy skills in addition to their testing services. The family systems, behavioral, cognitive-behavioral, and humanistic approaches to intervention emerged as compelling and popular alternatives to the more traditional theories and interventions. Furthermore, the rise of the community mental health movement in the 1960s as well as the advent of psychotropic medication to treat mental illness exerted powerful influences on clinical psychology.

5. A turning point in the philosophy of clinical psychology training occurred during the 1973 Vail conference held in Vail, Colorado. The most significant outcome of the conference was the acceptance of a new training model for clinical psychology. In addition to the Boulder, or scientist-practitioner model, the Vail, or the scholar-practitioner model, was endorsed. This model suggested that clinical training could emphasize the delivery of professional psychological services while minimizing research training. Furthermore, the conference endorsed the notion that graduate training did not need to occur only in academic psychology departments at major universities but could also occur in free standing professionals schools of psychology. Finally, the conference endorsed the Psy.D. degree as an alternative to the Ph.D. degree.

6. In 1977, George Engel offered the biopsychosocial approach as the best possible model of understanding and treating physical and mental illness. The approach suggests that all physical and psychological illnesses and problems are likely to have a biological, psychological, and social element, which should be understood in order to provide the most effective intervention strategies. The biopsychosocial model has been widely accepted in both medicine and psychology with strong research support to demonstrate its effectiveness. The biopsychosocial perspective has quickly become an influential model in clinical psychology.

Key Terms

Behavioral	Family Systems	Scholar-Practitioner Model
Biopsychosocial	Humanistic	Scientist-Practitioner Model
Boulder Model	Integrative	Vail Model
Cognitive-Behavioral	Psychotropic Medication	Veterans Administration
Community Mental Health Movement		

For Reflection

1. How did the two World Wars influence the formation of clinical psychology?

2. Why was the VA Hospital so supportive of clinical psychology?

3. Why did the government feel compelled to financially support the training of clinical psychologists?

4. What was the major outcome of the Boulder training conference?

5. What was the major outcome of the Vail training conference?

6. What do the changes in health care have to do with clinical psychology?

7. What theoretical orientations became popular between 1950 and 1980?

8. Compare and contrast the behavioral, cognitive-behavioral, humanistic, and family systems approaches.

9. How did psychotropic medication revolutionize the field of clinical psychology during the 1950s?

10. What does the biopsychosocial approach have to do with clinical psychology?

CHAPTER 4

The Major Theoretical Models: Paving the Way Towards Integration

Chapter Outline

Highlight of a Contemporary Clinical Psychologist: Marcia Johnston Wood, Ph.D.

The Four Major Theoretical Models in Clinical Psychology

Understanding Mary from Different Theoretical Orientations

HIGHLIGHT OF A CONTEMPORARY CLINICAL PSYCHOLOGIST:

Marcia Johnston Wood, Ph.D.

Dr. Johnston Wood works in a part-time private practice, teaches several college courses, and is the mom for two young children.

Birth Date: December 21, 1956

College: Williams College, 1979 (English)

Graduate Program: Long Island University, Clinical Psychology, 1987

Clinical Internship: Yale University School of Medicine

Postdoctoral Fellowship: New York Hospital–Cornell Medical Center

Current Job: Private Practice, Portland, OR; Adjunct teaching at Portland State University

Pros and cons of being a clinical psychologist:

Pros: 1. emotional and intellectual stimulation. 2. satisfaction and interest in helping people understand and change their lives. 3. flexible schedule.

Cons: 1. can be emotionally draining and anxiety provoking (e.g., suicidal clients). 2. always (unless on vacation) "on call." 3. people's resistance to change.

Future of clinical psychology: "The need for psychotherapeutic help is not going to disappear and I hope that we will soon see the decline of some kinds of managed care and capitation contracts that may not be truly in a client's best interest. As consumers realize that cost containment is important but not always effective in anything more than the very short-term and also as more outcome and therapy research is done, therapies are becoming more tailored to effectively address particular diagnostic groups and problems so they can be targeted more specifically to match a client's needs."

Nature of practice: "I see adolescents, adults, and couples in psychotherapy. Occasionally family members may join a session or part of it if it would be helpful to the client. I see many clients who are depressed, suicidal, have relationship problems or other life problems/issues to solve, as well as clients with personality disorders. Sometimes my clients (most often for depression or anxiety) are also on psychiatric medication so I coordinate treatment with a psychiatrist. Occasionally, I have to help arrange hospitalization for a severely depressed or suicidal client."

Typical Schedule:

9:30   Psychotherapy patient: 16-year-old Caucasian girl experiencing depression with suicidal thinking.

10:30	Psychotherapy patient: 33-year-old Latino woman experiencing relationship and work conflicts associated with a personality disorder.
11:30	Psychotherapy patient: 29-year-old Caucasian

	man experiencing anxiety, depression and spiritual issues.
1:00	Teach Theory and Practice of Counseling Psychology class at Portland State University.
3:00	Pick up children from school and do "mom time."

The field of clinical psychology in the contemporary era has been founded on four predominant theoretical models or orientations to the understanding and treatment of human difficulties. Theoretical models can be understood as world views or philosophies about human behavior that provide a conceptual framework for research, assessment, and treatment of psychological problems. These four psychological orientations include the psychodynamic, cognitive-behavioral, humanistic, and family systems models and each have received substantial research and clinical support. Whereas the previous chapter introduced these theories and persons responsible for their development from a historical perspective, these fundamental psychological perspectives will be reviewed in greater depth in this chapter in terms of how they are applied to actual clinical issues. Although each approach can be used to understand behavior in a wide range of settings, the use of each method in treatment of psychological and behavioral problems will be highlighted here. Discussing how each approach is used in the treatment of behavioral problems is helpful to illustrate the differences between them and how they can be applied to actual clinical problem areas. Keep in mind, however, that in contemporary science and practice, it has become increasingly difficult to adhere to one single **theoretical orientation** in considering all

problems and questions regarding human behavior. Although some professionals still closely align themselves with one of these orientations, most psychologists today utilize a combination of these perspectives in order to most fully understand and assist others. Nonetheless, a sound knowledge of each of the four major theoretical models is essential to a thorough grounding in the building blocks of contemporary clinical psychology.

The theorectical models will be used throughout the chapter to understand the panic and other problematic symptoms experienced by Mary, a middle-aged Caucasian woman presented in the case study.

The Four Major Theoretical Models in Clinical Psychology

The Psychodynamic Approach

The **psychodynamic** approach began with the work of Sigmund Freud. Often people assume that those who utilize the psychodynamic approach are Freudian and that they will most likely look and act like Freud. People frequently imagine a psychodynamic psychologist as being a middle-aged or elderly man with a beard, sporting a tweed jacket replete with a

Case Study: Mary

Brief Identifying Information: Mary is a 50-year-old Irish Catholic Caucasian woman who lives with her husband. She is the mother of three adult children, and has never worked outside of the home. She is presently significantly overweight. Following the death of her father from a cardiac arrest when she was 5 she was raised by a single mother who also suffered from panic attacks and was the eldest of two children, having a brother two years her junior.

Presenting Problem: Mary experiences frequent and severe panic attacks involving symptoms of rapid breathing, trembling, faintness, and intense fear. During these episodes, which only occur outside her home, she fears that she will die of a heart attack. Her symptoms have confined her to her home and several other "safe" locations such as her church and her daughter's house. She is also expressing some marital conflict centering around her perceived inability to work despite a recent financial setback in the home.

pipe. They often envision someone who will analyze everything and require that their patients lay on a couch, talk about their relationship with their mother, and disclose all of their sexual fantasies. Of course, various films and other media influences have perpetuated this stereotype of the psychodynamic therapist. This narrow stereotype of psychodynamically-oriented professionals is obviously outdated and inaccurate. Psychologists of all ages, ethnicities, and both genders identify themselves as being psychodynamically oriented. While Freud is usually credited with being the founding father of the psychodynamic perspective, many neo-Freudians and other revisionists have greatly adapted, broadened, and challenged Freud's basic approach over the past 100 years. Freud, if alive today, might even be surprised (or appalled) to behold the array of current theories and intervention strategies utilized by modern psychodynamic psychologists.

The psychodynamic perspective maintains certain assumptions about human behavior and psychological problems (Table 4.1). First, the psychodynamic perspective holds that human behavior is influenced by *intrapsychic* (within the mind) drives, motives, conflicts, and impulses, which are primarily unconscious. Second, various adaptive and maladaptive ego defense mechanisms are used to deal with unresolved conflicts, needs, wishes, and fantasies that contribute to both normal and abnormal

behavior. Third, early experiences and relationships, such as the relationship between children and their parents, play a critical and enduring role in psychological development and adult behavior. Fourth, insight into these mostly unconscious influences combined with working through them (discussing and integrating them into everyday life) help to improve psychological functioning and behavior. Finally, the analysis of the transferential relationship that develops between the patient and therapist also helps to resolve conflicts and improve psychological functioning and behavior. **Transference** involves the projection of early relationship dynamics onto the therapist who represents an authority figure similar to the patient's parents, for example. **Countertransference** involves projection by the therapist onto the patient in response to the patient's transference behavior.

The psychodynamic approach can be generally classified into several categories, including the traditional Freudian perspective, the revisionist perspective, and the modern object relations perspective. While there are numerous further divisions of psychodynamic theory, these three major views will be presented here.

Freud's Psychoanalytic Perspective Freud's psychoanalytic perspective is often called classical analysis or classical freudian analysis. Freud developed an understanding of human behavior based on three

Table 4.1 Examples of Psychodynamic Techniques and Concepts

Free Association	Stating whatever is on the patient's mind without filtering. For example, Mary is encouraged to say whatever is on her mind no matter how silly or embarrassing it may be to her.
Transference	Projecting the issues and dynamics between the patient and significant figures in their lives (e.g., mother, father) onto the therapist. For example, Mary's feelings of love and longing for her father are projected onto her male therapist.
Insight	Better understanding unconscious influences and impulses. Making the unconscious conscious. For example, Mary learns that she really hates her mother and her panic is partially a guilt reaction to her wish that her mother died when she experienced episodes of panic.
Working Through	Assimilating and incorporating new insights into daily life. For example, Mary learns to accept and cope with her new insight concerning the hate she experienced regarding her mother.
Dream Analysis	Understanding the unconscious influence of dreams in everyday life. For example, Mary reports that she had a dream that she came to a therapy session and her therapist was not there to see her. In discussing her dream, she reports fears of being abandoned by her therapist as well as other important figures in her life.
Countertransference	Therapist responding to the transference of the patient through projecting their needs, wishes, and dynamics onto the patient. For example, Mary's therapist experiences Mary as being similar to his mother and behaves towards her as he would behave towards his mother.

mental structures that are usually in conflict. The **id,** developed at birth, operates on the pleasure principle and represents all of our primitive wishes, needs, and desires. The **ego,** developed at about age one, operates on the reality principle and represents the rational and reasonable aspects of our personality helping us to adapt to a challenging world. Finally, the **superego,** developed at about age 5 following the successful resolution of the Oedipal complex, represents the internalization of familial, cultural, and societal norms and mores. The superego includes the *ego ideal* (the perfect image or representation of who we are and who we can become) and our *conscience* (the rules of good and bad feelings, thinking, and behavior). The conscience involves what we perceive to be "right" and "wrong."

Inevitable conflict between the id, ego, and superego lead to anxiety and discomfort and the need to utilize ego defense mechanisms. **Defense mechanisms** are strategies developed by the ego to protect the person from these internal and mostly unconscious conflicts Table 4.2). Thus, they help us cope, either adaptively or maladaptively, with the inevitable anxiety and discomfort associated with being human. There are a variety of ego defense mechanisms individuals can draw upon. Examples include **repression** (keeping unpleasant thoughts, feelings, wishes, and conflicts out of consciousness), **denial** (denying that problematic feelings, thoughts, or behaviors exist), *reaction formation* (consciously thinking or feeling the opposite of the unconscious

impulse), *projection* (one's own unconscious conflicts, feelings, and drives are perceived in someone else), *sublimation* (channeling unacceptable impulses and desires into socially acceptable activities) and *displacement* (channeling unacceptable impulses toward less threatening sources). The maladaptive use of these defense mechanisms to cope with anxiety and conflict often lead to psychopathology.

Freud also outlined several **psychosexual stages** of development that he regarded as universal. These include the *oral, anal, phallic, latency,* and *genital* phases. *Libidinal,* or life energies, are channeled towards different areas of the body that demand gratification during each of these phases. Potential conflicts and problems can develop as a by-product of fixations at any one of these stages. For example, one might become fixated at one stage of development (e.g., oral) due to too much or too little stimulation during that stage. This fixation may then result in problems in adulthood such as smoking, eating, or drinking too much. Freud especially focused on the **Oedipal complex** (named after a character in the Greek tragedy, Oedipus Rex) that occurs during the phallic stage of development. Although one of Freud's most well-known theories, this complex notion was not a central feature of many of his writings. During the Oedipal phase, a boy develops incestuous and murderous desires, wishing to be unified with his mother while necessarily eliminating his father. The resulting fears of retaliation and castration result in repression of these

Table 4.2 Examples of Ego Defense Mechanisms Using the Case Study of Mary

Repression	Mary's hate of her mother is so anxiety and guilt provoking she does not allow these feelings to become conscious—keeping them repressed into her unconscious.
Denial	Mary denies having hateful feelings towards her mother.
Reaction Formation	Mary's hateful feelings towards her mother are so powerful and frightening that she feels and behaves in a very loving manner towards her mother. She expresses a great deal of affection for her and has difficulty not being in close contact with her.
Projection	Mary's dislike of her mother is projected onto her female therapist who she feels is cold, aloof, and uncaring.
Sublimation	Mary's hate of her mother has led her to channel these feelings into nonprofit organizations that work to prevent child abuse. She has become an active volunteer in efforts to help children who are abused by their parents.
Displacement	Mary's hate towards her mother can not be channelled towards her for fear of retaliation along with the experience of extreme anxiety and guilt. However, Mary becomes very irritable and critical of her husband for no apparent reason.

impulses and the use of reaction formation to iden- tify with the father instead. Freud felt that a similar situation occurs for girls involving the desire for unification with the father and elimination of the mother. This female variation of the Oedipal com- plex is referred to as the *Electra complex* although Freud himself did not like or use this term.

The goal of Freud's approach was **insight** (un- derstanding the unconscious factors that lead to problematic feelings, thinking, and behavior) and **working through** of the insights to improve daily functioning. The working-through process involves a careful and in-depth examination of the role of unconscious wishes, drives, impulses, and conflicts in everyday life. Techniques such as **free association** (saying whatever is on one's mind without censor- ing), *dream analysis* and *interpretation,* and the *anal- ysis of transference* as well as everyday thoughts, feelings, and behavior were used to help understand and treat various problems. Furthermore, under- standing and analyzing inevitable defensiveness and resistance to treatment is also a goal of psychody- namic therapy.

The Revisionist or Neo-Freudian Perspective The psychodynamic perspective proposed by Freud has been expanded and adapted in various ways by nu- merous theorists since the days of Freud. These revisions actually began during Freud's lifetime. Carl Jung (1875–1965) was one of the first members of Freud's inner circle to disagree with fundamental aspects of Freud's theory and develop a revision of the psychodynamic perspective. In fact, Freud had hoped that Jung would be his protégé and heir, carrying on his work after his death. Freud's disap- pointment with Jung's iconoclasm led to a great deal of bitterness and many angry letters between the two men.

Most adaptations of Freud's original theories focus on the role of development beyond childhood, the role of societal and cultural influences, and the role of interpersonal relationships, and involve a de-emphasis on unconscious and id-driven impulses and behaviors such as sexuality. Erik Erikson (1909–1993), for example, developed a lifespan per- spective stating that psychosocial development con- tinues far beyond the five psychosexual stages of childhood outlined by Freud. Alfred Adler (1870– 1937) felt that Freud's emphasis on the id and sexu- ality as well as his underemphasis of the ego were

critical flaws in his approach. Furthermore, unlike Freud, Adler felt that compensation for feelings of inferiority were very important in the formation of personality and psychological functioning. Carl Jung also rejected Freud's emphasis on sexuality. Furthermore, Jung emphasized spiritual influences as well as the role of the collective unconscious (symbols and innate ideas that are shared with our ancestors). Harry Stack Sullivan (1892–1949) fo- cused on the role of interpersonal relationships in personality and psychological development. Karen Horney (1885–1952) took issue with Freud's theo- ries of penis envy and the role of women.

The contributions of these neo-Freudians, or **revisionists,** significantly diverged from Freud's original theories. Fundamentally, Freud's emphasis on the id was de-emphasized among the revisionists who developed theories that focused more on the functioning of the ego. Thus, the theories of many of the revisionists have become known as forming the basis of *ego psychology.* Furthermore, most of the revisionists agreed that the role of interpersonal relationships was fundamental in the development of personality and psychological functioning. Fi- nally, the revisionists generally agreed that psycho- logical development continues beyond the early years addressed by Freud. These aspects of the revi- sionists' theories set the stage for current object relations theory.

The Object Relations Perspective Even though Freud's psychoanalytic theory focused heavily on early childhood experiences, he never once treated a child in psychoanalysis. Freud made inferences about childhood development and experiences through his analysis of adult patients who reflected on their childhoods. Critics of Freud often state that because his theories were based on his experience of treating a small number of upper-class and primarily adult female patients in Vienna during the Victorian period rather than on more broad and scientifically based research and experience, his theories are sus- pect. One of the first psychoanalytic writers who focused on the direct treatment of children was Melanie Klein (1952). Klein felt that the internal emotional world of children focuses on interper- sonal relationships rather than on the control of impulses and drives. Klein and several colleagues including W. R. D. Fairbairn (1954) and Margaret Mahler (1952) became known as the British School of object relations theory, whereas the American contributions of Otto Kernberg (1975, 1976, 1984), James Masterson (1981), and Heinz Kohut (1971, 1977, 1984) further developed **object relations** theory in the United States. Object relations theorists have been especially influential in further developing and fine-tuning current psychodynamic theory, research, and practice.

The object relations theorists view infants as being relationship or *object* seeking rather than pleasure seeking. The early relationship with the mother provides the framework for the development of the sense of self. Thus, attachment to the mother provides the structure and approach for the development of psychological functioning and future relationships. Through interactions with the mother during breast feeding and other activities, the child internalizes, or *introjects,* various qualities of the person or object with whom they are interacting. The child then separates, or *splits,* these internalized aspects of the mother into various positive (the good rewarding mother, or the "good breast") and negative (the bad or punishing mother, or the "bad breast") aspects. Attachment to the mother may be either secure or insecure. These divisions provide a template for future interactions with the world in general. Therefore, if the mother–child relationship is primarily negative and filled with unsatisfying and frustrating experiences, the child is likely to have a difficult time developing an adequate and positive sense of self or achieving satisfying and trusting intimate adult relationships. Therefore, object relations theorists tend to view behavior as a manifestation of early childhood experiences with the mother and other important figures in the child's life. Object relation theorists, however, generally neglected the influence of the father–child relationship. The early relationship foundation develops the sense of self as well as a framework for negotiating all future interpersonal relationships.

Psychodynamic professionals today are likely to focus on early childhood experiences and relationships, the enduring personality structure of a person, and the influences of unconscious fantasies, wishes, and impulses. The analysis of dreams, transference, and resistance with the goal of increased insight into the unconscious are still important goals of current psychodynamic approaches. Psychodynamic psychotherapy historically would take

years to conduct and involve four or five sessions each week. Recent psychodynamic theorists have now developed short-term treatments (Goldfried, Greenberg, & Marmar, 1990; Strupp & Binder, 1984; Horowitz, Marmar, Krupnick, Wilner, Kaltreider, & Wallerstein, 1984), which focus on the application of psychodynamic principles in treatment over the course of several weeks or a few months. Research has found that these brief psychodynamic treatments are effective (Anderson & Lambert, 1995). In fact brief psychodynamic psychotherapy is considered to be an empirically validated treatment supported by the American Psychological Association when applied to opiate dependence and depression (Chambless et al., 1996).

The Behavioral and Cognitive-Behavioral Approaches

Unlike the image of the pipe smoking, middle-aged gentleman wearing a tweed jacket while silently listening to his patient free associate on a couch, the typical image of a psychologist from the behavioral or cognitive-behavioral perspective is quite different. Often people assume that someone who maintains a behavioral orientation might wear a white lab coat and dark horn-rim glasses. The behavioral psychologist is often thought to control and manipulate behavior by giving reinforcements (such as M&M candies) to people when they behave in a desired manner and punishments (such as electric shocks) when they behave in an undesirable manner. Sometimes people assume that psychologists who are behavioral in orientation are not warm and caring and that they have little interest or tolerance for nonobservable behavior such as feelings and fantasies. Popular films also help to perpetuate the image of a cold, aloof, mechanistic behaviorist concerned with specific behaviors rather than individuals. Similar to the stereotype of the psychodynamic professional, the stereotype of the behaviorist is also outdated and inaccurate.

Both behavioral and cognitive (thoughts and beliefs) focuses make up the broad behavioral/cognitive-behavioral perspective. Although some would argue that the behavioral and cognitive-behavioral viewpoints are separate, in this review, I will combine these perspectives because they are generally more similar than divergent in their assumptions about human nature and behavior change. Furthermore, the cognitive-behavioral approach generally draws on behaviorism rather than cognitive neuroscience or cognitive psychology. However, many contemporary cognitive theorists use cognitive science and information processing methods to enhance their theories and applications. I will refer to the cognitive-behavioral perspective as including both the strictly traditional behavioral perspective (the theories of B. F. Skinner) as well as the newer cognitive perspective. Like the psychodynamic approach, the cognitive-behavior approach subsumes a wealth of subperspectives associated with specific leading authors who develop and advocate certain theories and techniques. These leaders in cognitive-behavioral psychology include Albert Ellis, Aaron Beck, Arnold Lazarus, Leonard Krasner, Joseph Wolpe, B. F. Skinner, Donald Meichenbaum, Marsha Linehan, among others.

The **cognitive-behavioral** approach is historically based on the principles of learning and has its roots in the academic experimental psychology and conditioning research conducted by B. F. Skinner,

John Watson, Clarke Hull, Edward William James, Ivan Pavlov, and cognitive-behavioral approach focuses on overt (i.e., observable behavior) and covert (nonobservable behavior such as thinking) behaviors acquired through learning and conditioning in the social environment (Table 4.3). Basic assumptions that provide the foundation of the cognitive-behavioral approach include a focus on current rather than past experiences, the emphasis on measurable and observable behavior, the importance of environmental influences on the development of both normal and problematic behavior, and an emphasis on empirical research methods to develop assessment and treatment strategies and interventions.

Cognitive-behavioral perspectives include principles of operant conditioning, classical conditioning, social learning, and attribution theories to help assess and treat a wide variety of difficulties (Table 4.3). For example, operant conditioning may be used to help a child improve his or her behavior and performance in a classroom setting. A child might obtain reinforcements such as stickers or so-

Table 4.3 Examples of Cognitive–Behavioral Techniques and Concepts

Contingency management	Changing behavior by altering the consequences that follow behavior. For example, Mary takes the bus after the friendly bus driver and her children offer social praise.
Counterconditioning	Developing a more adaptive response to environmental stimuli. For example, Mary does aerobic exercise when feeling anxious rather than taking antianxiety medication.
Exposure	Gradual or all at once approach to the feared situation or stimuli. For example, Mary is encouraged to gradually take longer and longer bus rides.
Behavioral contract	An agreement between therapist and patient that outlines specific consequences of behavior. For example, Mary agrees to decrease coffee consumption by two cups per week until she no longer drinks caffeinated coffee.
Participant modeling	Demonstrating the desired behavior for the patient. For example, Mary watches others confidently learn to drive a car without fear before she tries to do the same.
Behavioral rehearsal	Practicing how one might handle a given problem situation. For example, Mary frequently practices diaphragmatic breathing techniques so that they become automatic.
Thought Stopping	Stopping irrational or defeating thoughts by interrupting the negative or problematic pattern of thinking (e.g., yelling "stop" to oneself, snapping an elastic band around the wrist) and inserting more positive and adaptive thoughts (e.g., "I can handle it, I'm as worthy of love as anyone else"). For example, Mary stops her thoughts that she cannot handle walking into the bank by yelling "stop" to herself when she finds herself engaged in maladaptive and negative thinking, and inserts more positive thoughts in their place such as "I enjoy my new found independence by going to the bank anxiety free."

cial praise from the teacher for improved classroom behavior that is defined, for example, as being more attentive, talking less with peers during classroom instruction, and improving test scores. **Contingency management** (changing behavior by altering the consequences that follow behavior) and **behavioral rehearsal** (practicing appropriate behavior) may also be used. Classical conditioning techniques might be used to help someone overcome various fears and anxieties. Someone who is fearful of dogs, for example, might learn to overcome this fear through the use of systematic desensitization (a technique developed by Wolpe, 1958), **counter conditioning** (developing a more adaptive response to dogs), or by **exposure** such as a gradual approach to being with dogs. Social learning might be used to help a child undergoing a painful medical procedure (such as a bone marrow transplant) to cope with the anxiety and pain associated with the procedure. For example, the child might watch an educational video of other children who cope well with the medical procedure. Furthermore, long-standing and maladaptive beliefs may contribute to many psychological problems such as depression and anxiety. Maladaptive irrational and automatic thoughts such as, "I'm a failure," "No one will love me," and "I can't do anything right," might be examined, challenged, and altered using cognitive-behavioral techniques such as **thought stopping** and rehearsal of positive self statements. There are numerous cognitive-behavioral techniques that may be employed to help assess and alter behavior. Each of these general frameworks (classical, operant, social learning, and cognitive) will be reviewed next.

The Classical Conditioning Perspective The **classical conditioning** perspective originated with the work of Ivan Pavlov as well as the work of Joseph Wolpe and Hans Eysenck. This viewpoint maintains learning occurs and subsequently, behavior, through the association of conditioned and unconditioned stimuli. Thus, two or more random events (stimuli) that are paired together become associated over time. For example, a psychologist using the classical conditioning perspective with Mary might examine the pairing of Mary's panic and fear with going to church, the grocery store, and the bank. When Mary had her first panic attack at church, she associated the church with the uncomfortable and frightening feelings that accompany panic, thereby

causing her to avoid the church in the future. Panic attacks in other places such as the grocery store, on the bus, and in the bank all become associated through classical conditioning, resulting in more and more avoidance of various places. Furthermore, generalization occurs, for example, although Mary may have had a panic attack at one specific branch office of a bank, she feels fearful of entering any bank. A therapist using a classical conditioning approach may choose to treat Mary's anxiety with *systematic desensitization* (SD; Wolpe, 1958). The therapist would ask Mary to create a hierarchy of anxiety-provoking situations from less anxiety-provoking situations such as walking on the sidewalk outside of her home to extremely anxiety-provoking situations such as flying in an airplane. The therapist would train Mary in a relaxation procedure and then pair relaxation with each of the anxiety-provoking situations that she would imagine. Thus, each step of the hierarchy would be paired with relaxation using classical conditioning strategies.

The Operant Perspective The **operant perspective** of the behavioral approach originated with the work of B. F. Skinner. This viewpoint maintains that all behavior can be understood through a functional analysis of *antecedents* (the conditions present just before a target behavior occurs) and *consequences* (what occurs following the target behavior) of behavior. This is often referred to as Functional Behavioral Analysis or the A-B-Cs of behaviorism: *Antecedents, Behavior, Consequences.* Thus, behavior is learned and developed through interaction with the environment. If behavior is reinforced in some way, it will continue, while behavior that is punished or not reinforced will be diminished. The gradual shaping of desired behavior is achieved by reinforcing small increments towards the target behavior. Problematic behavior, such as aggressiveness in children, fears and phobias, and overeating can be altered by changing the reinforcements associated with the target behavior (Plaud & Gaither, 1996). For example, a psychologist using the operant perspective might be concerned that Mary, the patient with panic disorder, might receive reinforcement for her panic behavior (e.g., not having to work, attention from her husband and other family members). Intervention might include an analysis of the antecedents (the conditions present just before her panic symptoms) and consequences of her panic behavior followed by reinforcement of desired behavior (e.g., praise when Mary has no panic symptoms while taking a bus). The reinforcement would likely include shaping the successive approximations of targeted behavior towards the goal of engaging in specific activities outside of the home such as food shopping and other errands.

The Social Learning Perspective   The social learning perspective originated with the work of Albert Bandura. This viewpoint maintains that learning occurs through observational or vicarious methods. Thus, behaviors can be learned and developed by watching others perform various behaviors rather than by practicing a behavior or being personally reinforced for a given behavior. For example, someone might learn to avoid walking through a surprisingly deep puddle by watching someone else get uncomfortably wet when they walk through it. The psychologist working with Mary might use the **social learning** perspective in understanding how Mary learned panic behaviors from her mother who also had panic attacks. Mary's mother might have been reinforced for her panic behavior through attention, distracting family members from other problems or conflicts, and avoiding work or household chores. Thus, by observing her mother Mary may have learned that panic behaviors result in a variety of secondary gains such as avoiding things you do not want to do.

The social learning perspective also incorporates the role of expectations in behavior development. For example, Julian Rotter (1954) proposed that behavior develops as a by-product of what someone expects to happen after they make a given response. The importance of the desired outcome also impacts the likelihood of that behavior. For example, someone will pay a large sum of money and dedicate several years of their life in order to obtain a college degree because they expect that a college degree will result in a satisfying career and life. Thus, Mary avoids the grocery store, the bank, and her church because she expects that she will experience a panic attack at these locations. The fear of having a panic attack is so great that she makes a great effort to avoid these places.

An important variation concerning the role that expectations play in behavior involves the concept of **self-efficacy** (Bandura, 1986). Self-efficacy refers to the belief that one can successfully perform a particular behavior. For example, someone is more likely to kick a field goal in football or make a free throw in basketball if he or she believe that they can accomplish these athletic tasks. Thus, confidence in one's ability to successfully accomplish a task results in greater likelihood of success in the given task. Mary is more likely to take the bus to the grocery store if she believes that she will be able to adequately cope with her anxiety by practicing positive self statements such as "I can handle this," employing breathing techniques, and feeling confident that she can shop with minimal stress.

The Cognitive Perspective: Beliefs, Appraisals, and Attributions   The cognitive perspective originated with the work and writings of several professionals notably including Aaron Beck and Albert Ellis. The cognitive perspective suggests that our beliefs, appraisals, and attributions play a significant role in behavior and behavior problems. *Appraisals* include the manner in which we examine or evaluate our behavior. For example, if a soccer player thinks her athletic abilities are mediocre, she will evaluate all of her successes and failures in this light. If the soccer player has an exceptionally great game, she may attribute her good fortune to luck or poor performance on the part of the opposing team. If Mary feels that her attempts to develop more independence are hampered by marginal skills and motivation, she will more likely fail.

Attributions refer to theories regarding the causes of behavior. We generally make attributions about behavior based on several factors. These factors include the concepts of the internal versus external locus of control as well as situational versus dispositional characteristics. *Internal locus of control* refers to feeling that we have control and influence over much of our life experiences while *external locus of control* refers to feeling that we have very little control or influence over what happens to us. For example, success in life due to hard work and being smart reflects an internal locus of control while luck or fate reflects an external locus of control.

Situational factors refer to external influences impacting behavior, and *dispositional factors* refer to enduring characteristics of the person impacting behavior. For example, driving through a red light without stopping due to distraction from a heated conversation with a passenger would reflect a situational attribution while driving through the red light because the person is a careless and reckless driver would reflect a dispositional attribution. Thus, a professional football player might attribute missing an easy field goal to distraction from a loud audience or from the sun in his eyes (external locus of control), low self-esteem or anxiety during the game (internal locus of control), having a bad day (situational), or being a bad player in general (dispositional). Depression and learned helplessness can develop, for example, in people who make frequent dispositional and internal locus of control attributions about their perceived problematic feelings and behavior (Rosenhan & Seligman, 1989; Seligman, Peterson, Kaslow, Tanenbaum, Alloy, & Abramson, 1984). For example, Mary feels depressed and hopeless believing that she will never get over her panic attacks because she experiences her fears as being due to her long-term "character flaws" and "weaknesses."

Albert Ellis (1962, 1977, 1980) and other professionals have focused on irrational beliefs and self-talk that lead to problematic feelings and behavior. For example, common beliefs such as "everyone should agree with me," "everyone should appreciate me and my talents," " no one could love someone as unattractive as me," and "I should always be patient with my children and spouse" result in inevitable failure and disappointment. Ellis and others use techniques such as *Rational-Emotive Therapy* (RET) to help individuals think and process beliefs in a more rational manner. These techniques involve using logic and reason to challenge irrational and maladaptive thoughts and beliefs (e.g., "So do you really think that everyone you meet must like you in order to be a worthy human being?"). This approach relies on persuasion and reason to alter beliefs about self and others. For example, Ellis's focus on irrational beliefs is related to Mary's beliefs about her panic. Mary feels that if she feels even a little anxiety while taking a bus or sitting in church, she is a failure and a weak person. The therapist helps Mary to see that her beliefs are irrational and unrealistic and encourages her to develop more adaptive self-talk regarding her anxiety (e.g., "Even if I'm anxious, I can still overcome my fear and take the bus. I don't need to have my anxiety control me; I can control it").

Aaron Beck (1963, 1976) developed *cognitive therapy* (CT) to treat depression and other disorders. Beck posits that as people develop, they formulate rules about how the world works that tend to be simplistic, rigid, and often based on erroneous assumptions. A schema or template develops to the extent that all new incoming data is filtered through these rules and distortions. Thus overgeneralization (e.g., "everyone at work hates me"), all-or-none thinking (e.g., "If I don't get this job my career will be ruined"), or exaggeration or downplaying the meaning or significance of events (e.g., "my divorce was no big deal and didn't affect me or my children at all") are typical ways of interpreting our world and experiences. Problematic behavior and attitudes are associated with these unrealistic and erroneous rules and interpretation of events. Like Ellis, Beck evaluates and challenges these beliefs and assumptions and trains people to monitor and alter their automatic thoughts. However, Beck focuses on the treatment of beliefs as hypotheses that must be tested and evaluated to best determine whether the beliefs are useful and realistic.

A variety of variations on cognitive-behavioral psychotherapy has emerged over the years. For example, Marsha Linehan developed Dialectical Behavior Therapy (DBT) to treat people experiencing borderline personality disorders (Linehan, 1993). DBT uses cognitive-behavioral strategies along with psychodynamic, client-centered, family systems, and crisis intervention perspectives. DBT focuses on acceptance of self and experiences along with efforts towards behavior change. These changes are sought through a three stage process that includes a pretreatment commitment phase, an exposure and emotional processing phase of past events, and a synthesis phase integrating progress from the first two stages to achieve treatment goals. Another example includes David Barlow's Panic Control Treatments (PCT) developed to help those experiencing panic attacks (Barlow & Craske, 1994). In PCT, patients are exposed to the sensations that remind them of their panic attacks. For example, patients would participate in exercise to elevate their heart rates or shake their heads to create dizziness. Attitudes and fears about these induced panic-like symptoms are explored and demonstrated as harmless to the patient's health. Furthermore, patients are taught breathing and relaxation exercises to help reduce anxiety.

The Humanistic Approach

The stereotype of the **humanistic** practitioner typically conjures a warm and supportive individual who does not provide any direct advice or suggestions to their patients. The humanistic therapist is often thought to be more casually dressed in perhaps a turtleneck or Hawaiian shirt wearing some kind of beads around the neck and sandals. The stereotype of the humanistic psychologist involves an individual who, although friendly, says little more than, "uhmm" and benign comments such as "I hear you" or "I feel your pain." Images of encounter groups or T-groups from the 1960s might emerge. Again, like the behavioral and psychodynamic orientations, stereotypes about the humanistic approach are also outdated and inaccurate.

The humanistic approach has its roots in European philosophy as well as in the psychotherapeutic work of Victor Frankl, Carl Rogers, Abraham Maslow, Rollo May, Fritz Perls, and other mental health professionals. In rejecting the basic assumptions of the psychodynamic and behavioral theories, the humanistic theorists assume a *phenomenological* approach that emphasizes each individual's perception and experience of his or her world (Table 4.4). The humanistic perspective tends to view people as being active, thinking, creative, and growth-oriented. Helping others is partially accomplished through understanding concerns, feelings, and behavior through the eyes of the patient. Humanistic professionals tend to assume that people are basically well-intentioned and that they naturally strive towards growth, love, creativity, and self-actualization. Self-actualization helps to produce the forward movement in life towards greater growth, peace, and acceptance of self and others. Rather than focusing on the influences of the past, humanistic theorists focus on the "here and now" or present. The client-

centered approach of Carl Rogers, the humanistic approach of Abraham Maslow, and the Gestalt approach of Fritz Perls will be briefly reviewed next. Of course, there are many additional perspectives and variations of these approaches. However, the contributions of Rogers, Maslow, and Perls have been the most influential within the humanistic perspective.

The Client-Centered Perspective The **client-centered** perspective of Carl Rogers stands out as the most classic example of the humanistic approach. Rogers used non-directive techniques such as **active listening, empathy,** congruence, and unconditional positive regard to understand and help others. Rogers felt that sincere empathy was needed in order for people to feel accepted and understood, and ultimately to enable growth to occur. **Unconditional positive regard** refers to the belief that no one should be negatively judged or evaluated in the therapy experience or elsewhere. Rather, respect and acceptance should prevail. Unconditional positive regard can be a challenge for professionals working with individuals who have attitudes or behaviors that one finds offensive (e.g., sexual abuse of children, stealing, racist comments). Unconditional positive regard does not mean that these behaviors or attitudes are accepted as being okay. Rather, it is the person who is fully accepted. Therefore, respect and a nonjudgmental attitude are advocated. **Congruence,** or genuineness, refers to harmony between ones feelings and actions. Thus, the professional should strive towards emotional honesty in his or her relationship with others. Genuineness also implies that the professional will not try to hide his or her feelings from others, yet still present a professional attitude and demeanor. Rogers was also instrumental in developing ways to assess treatment

Table 4.4   Examples of Humanistic Concepts and Techniques

Active Listening	Intense listening to the patient using paraphrasing, summaries, reflection, and other techniques.
Empathy	Conveying a sense of being heard and understood.
Unconditional Positive Regard	Fully accepting the feelings and thoughts of the patient.
Congruence	Being genuine in behavior.
Self-Actualization	Innate movement towards growth and fulfilling one's potential.
Peak Experiences	Moments when self-actualization is reached.

process and outcome. This included an individualized assessment technique such as the Q-sort (sorting a variety of cards with descriptive feelings in several categories) to assess functioning and outcome.

The client-centered approach maintains that people have an innate drive towards growth. Because the development of the self and attempts at growth are often met with various social consequences (such as praise or punishment), individuals may develop patterns of behavior that are inconsistent with growth. For example, a parent may wish that their child will eventually take over the family accounting business. However, the child may be very creative and prefer to pursue interests in music and dance. The parents may exert pressure on the child through conditioned love to pursue education and skills in accounting and business rather than the creative arts. The child, wishing to please his parents may do so, but at a high price in terms of incongruence with their self-actualizing motive and potential. Mary, for example, may feel "boxed in" to her role as housewife and mother. She actually had harbored a strong interest in joining religious life as a nun. However, her parents more highly valued family life and encouraged her to get married and have children, thus discouraging her call to religious life. This conflict with her family resulted in incongruence, causing her to feel trapped, out of control in her life, and possibly, more prone to anxiety.

Maslow's Humanistic Perspective   Abraham Maslow (Maslow, 1954, 1971) originated a further variation of the humanistic approach. He emphasized the importance of **self-actualization** which refers to the impulse and desire to develop fully one's potential. His focus on self-actualization highlighted the role of unmet needs. He felt that humans have a hierarchy of needs beginning with basic biological requirements for food, water, and warmth. Once these needs are met, one is free to focus on higher level needs such as safety and security. Again, as these higher level needs are met, one can then focus on needs for love, belonging, and acceptance. Finally, at the top of the hierarchy is self-actualization. Maslow believed that people who experienced self-actualization were characterized by an acceptance of themselves and others, efficient perceptions of reality, social interests, creativeness, mystical or

LITZLER

"WELL I'VE HAD MY COFFEE SO I GUESS IT'S ON TO THE REST OF MASLOW'S LIST."

"peak" experiences, as well as other qualities (Maslow, 1971). Although Maslow believed that everyone has the potential to achieve self-actualization, few were thought to succeed because of unmet needs at lower levels. Maslow felt that less than 1 percent of the population ever reach self-actualization. Therefore, problems in feelings, thoughts, behavior, and relationships emerge because many people are *deficiency-motivated* in that they are trying to fulfill unmet needs. Maslow referred to those moments when self-actualization is actually reached as peak experiences. Although Maslow's theories have received a great deal of attention and acceptance, he offered little in terms of specific techniques to use in psychological assessment or treatment.

The Gestalt Perspective   The **gestalt** perspective within the humanistic approach originated with the work of Fritz Perls (Perls, 1947, 1969). Assumptions of the gestalt approach include the notion that problems occur due to our inability to be truly aware of our current feelings, thoughts, and behavior and to our inordinate focus on the past and future rather than the present. The gestalt approach focuses on being keenly aware of one's *here and now* or present experience. The gestalt approach seeks to help people live in the immediate moment by frequently requesting that people work towards an awareness of current thoughts and feelings. Taking personal responsibility for one's feelings, thoughts, behavior, and choices is also of paramount importance for those using the gestalt perspective. Techniques include making believe that an important someone such as a spouse, boss, or mother is in the room with you sitting in an empty chair. Talking to the person as if they were there helps someone become better in touch with feelings and behavior. For example, Mary might be asked to pretend that her mother is in the room with her. The gestalt therapist might encourage Mary to talk with her mother as if she was sitting in an empty chair in the office. Mary would be asked about her immediate feelings and thoughts as she spoke with her mother in the room.

The Family Systems Approach

The **family systems** approach emerged to overcome the limitations of other perspectives seeking to work only with the identified individual patient. The family systems approach emerged from research and treatments geared to address problems associated with interpersonal communication among schizophrenic patients and between family members. As mentioned in Chapter 3, the family systems approach began with the Bateson group in Palo Alto, California during the 1950s.

The goals of the family systems approach commonly include improved communication among family members and a de-emphasis on the problems of any one member in favor of attention to the family system as a whole. Family systems professionals meet with all family members rather than with just the person who has the identified problem(s). Family systems professionals might also involve extended members of the family or other significant figures in the life of the family such as neighbors, friends, and teachers in their therapeutic work. Family systems perspectives maintain a systemic view of problems and relationships. That is, they suggest that any change in the behavior or

functioning of any one member of the family system is likely to influence other members of the system. Therefore, even if improved psychological functioning and behavior is achieved in individual members, others must adjust to and contribute to these new changes in family functioning. Paradoxically, improvements among some family members may lead to problems among other family members. For example, if Mary becomes less fearful and more independent, she may no longer need her husband to drive her around town for errands. Her husband would then lose an important and powerful role in his relationship with his wife, perhaps feeling somewhat uncomfortable and even threatened by her new found independence. This change might result in marital discord that may encourage Mary to relapse into her panic behaviors.

Like the previously reviewed approaches, there are many variations of the family systems approach identified with individual professionals (Table 4.5, p. 66). These include, for example, the communication approach of Virginia Satir, the structural approach of Salvador Minuchin, the strategic perspectives of Jay Haley and Milton Erickson, and the narrative approach of Michael White. While there are many other perspectives within family systems, five main orientations will be briefly presented.

The Communication Approach   The communication approach was developed by Virginia Satir (1967) and colleagues at the Mental Research Institute (MRI) in Palo Alto, California. The approach suggests that problems in effective communication contribute to family problems and dysfunction. Unspoken and unreasonable expectations, rules, and assumptions about how family members should relate to one another and live their lives result in conflict and problems in family functioning. Satir outlined several communication styles in families, which include placating, blaming, superreasonable, irrelevant, and congruent. In problem families the father may be *superreasonable,* maintaining a rational style and keeping his feelings to himself. The mother may placate the father by agreeing with him and not expressing her feelings. One of the children may use a *blaming* style attributing all of his or her problems in school and at home on someone else. *Irrelevant communication* might involve annoying habits on the part of a sibling. Satir encourages

Table 4.5   Examples of Family Systems Concepts and Techniques

Reframing	Altering the way one understands and interprets a given behavior. For example, Mary's panic might be reframed as an attempt to engage her husband into her life and assist him in feeling more manly.
Paradoxical Intention	Prescribing the problematic symptom in order to combat resistance to treatment. For example, ask Mary to schedule a number of panic attacks each day.
Joining	Therapist attempts to connect with the family and become part of the family unit rather than act in an detached observer manner in the sessions.
Enmeshment	Over and maladaptive involvement in the lives of family members. For example, Mary's overinvolvement in her son's life results in her being highly critical of all work and relationship decisions that he makes that are not consistent with her interests.
Disengagement	Over detachment of one family member from others. For example, Mary's daughter has little interest in activities and functioning of the family and prefers to stay out of any emotional involvement with the family.

family members to embrace *congruent communication,* which focuses on expressing genuine feelings.

A communications approach may encourage Mary to express her true feelings more directly about needing to be taken care of by her husband. Her panic behavior might be viewed as a way to communicate a need for attention and care by her husband and others. Her husband may be encouraged to express his feelings about his need to feel important and useful in the relationship. Taking care of Mary during panic episodes may be a way to feel powerful and important in the relationship.

The Structural Approach   The structural approach was developed by Salvador Minuchin (1974) and focuses on altering and restructuring the pattern of relationships between family members. The structural perspective focuses on appropriate and adaptive levels of **differentiation, enmeshment,** and **disengagement** among family members (Minuchin, 1974; Minuchin & Fishman, 1981). For example, a mother and daughter may be overly enmeshed with each other resulting in distance and disengagement in the father. Furthermore, the daughter's overinvolvement in her mother's life and troubles may make it difficult for her to develop satisfying peer relationships and levels of independence. The mother's overinvolvement with her daughter may result in less interest and energy for her relationship with her husband. Due to dysfunctional family patterns, conflicts and problems emerge within the family unit as a whole. The **structural** perspective emphasizes more functional, balanced, and hierarchical family

relationships. The therapist may actually rearrange seating in the therapy session in order to join the family and to alter the structure of family dyads and interactions. For example, Mary may be overly involved with her son, resulting in resentment from her daughter and husband. Furthermore, her son may feel that her overinvolvement makes it difficult for him to develop more independence and greater connection with his father. The therapist might try to assist Mary in disengaging from her son (starting by having her sit away from her son during the session) and engaging more with her daughter and husband.

The Milan Approach   In the **Milan approach,** the professional is viewed as an integral part of the family system or unit (Boscolo, Cecchin, Hoffman, & Penn, 1987). The Milan approach highly values neutrality as well as acceptance and respect for the family system. The Milan approach uses hypothesizing as well as positive, logical connotation (Selvini Palazzoli, Boscolo, Cecchin, & Prata, 1980) to assist in better understanding family dynamics. Hypothesizing helps to better understand the function and dynamics of the family, whereas positive, logical connotation reframes the behavior of the family in more positive and accepting terms.

The Milan school also encourages the use of a team approach. For example, family systems professionals using the Milan approach might request that Mary bring her entire family to the treatment sessions. While a therapist meets with Mary's family, several colleagues observe the session using a one-way mirror. Efforts at hypothesizing and positive, logical connotation would be aimed at a better understanding of family interactions and a more acceptable, positive reframing of family issues. The treatment team discusses the session as it occurs and offers suggestions to the therapist working with the family via a telephone in the treatment room. Following the session, the family might be invited to observe the treatment team as they discuss the session with the treating therapist. The Milan school also utilizes "rituals," asking the family to behave in certain prescribed ways between sessions.

The Strategic Approach The **strategic approach** was developed by Jay Haley (1973, 1987) and others such as Milton Erikson (1980) to help professionals deal more effectively with resistance in their work. The approach utilizes very active and direct involvement by the clinician. The strategic perspective maintains that any attempt to change a member or set of members within a family system will be met with resistance and sabotage (conscious or unconscious). Therefore, the professional must find ways to combat this resistance by directing and altering the behavior of the family. One of the most common and well-known examples of a strategic intervention involves the use of "paradoxical" techniques. Paradoxical approaches are often referred to by the general public as "reverse psychology." **Paradoxical techniques** involve prescribing the symptom of concern in an exaggerated form and so it appears on the surface to contradict the goals of intervention. For example, a child who terrorizes the family with frequent and intense temper tantrums might be encouraged by the professional to yell and scream louder: "Yell louder—I don't think you are trying hard enough and I'm sure people in the next room cannot hear you." Strategic theorists believe that since people will resist direct interventions to change the family system, the clinician can assist others in reaching intervention goals by asking them to do the opposite of those goals. For example, a strategic therapist might encourage Mary to schedule her panic attacks throughout the day and to never leave her house. Since resistance can be expected, Mary would likely have difficulty scheduling frequent panic attacks and have trouble staying in her home. Therefore, the ultimate goals of therapy (decreased panic and increased independence) are

likely to be met. Using these paradoxical techniques are both controversial and risky (e.g., asking an anorexia nervosa patient to further decrease food consumption could be ill-advised and tantamount to malpractice).

Strategic techniques not only assume that people will be resistant to the suggestions, but they also assist the client in being more aware of the undesirability of the problematic behaviors as well as provide the client with a greater sense of control. For example, Mary may find it dull to stay home all day beyond her usual at-home schedule and she may wish to do something other than have a panic attack at the therapist's prescribed time of day.

Another technique utilized by strategic clinicians is reframing. **Reframing** involves reinterpretation of a behavior or issue in a new and different light. Therefore, behaviors considered negative by the family may be reinterpreted as being positive. For example, a child who steals might be viewed as trying to alert the family to their emotional deprivation and neediness. Mary's panic behavior might be reframed as being an attempt to stay close to her husband and to help him feel more powerful and masculine. An adolescent who has run away from home and made poor choices could be viewed as "doing the wrong things for the right reasons" (i.e., increased independence).

The Narrative Approach The **narrative** approach originates from the work of Michael White (White, 1986; White & Epston, 1990). The narrative approach holds that family members conceptualize their problems and concerns through a series of stories about their lives and various members of the family system. Using techniques such as externalizing and relative influence questioning, professionals assist family members in relating their stories in a more objective manner, allowing them to take a less negative and blaming approach to family problems. The narrative approach highlights the restraining influence that certain ideas and stories place on people. For example, an abusive male may feel that women are property and that they should have less power and influence than men. He may feel that he protects his weak, unstable, and inferior wife and that she would be in a great deal of trouble trying to survive without him. He may describe their relationship as one where he constantly protects her while she resists his efforts. These myths and world views influence his behavior towards women. Mary and her family might be asked, for example, to relate their story of Mary's mother's panic attacks and the role Mary's mother had on the development of family relationships and activities. They may be asked to discuss family stories about Mary's mother and examine what beliefs and myths play a role in current family functioning.

Understanding Mary from Different Theoretical Orientations

Each of the major theoretical models frequently are applied to clinical cases encountered by practicing psychologists. Mary's case study will be presented and separate psychodynamic, cognitive-behavioral, humanistic and family systems formulations applied in order to illustrate the use of these models in actual practice. It is important to note the unidimensional nature of the formulations presented, as they further illustrate the usefulness of integration and multidimensional intervention subsequently emphasized in Chapter 5.

Psychodynamic Formulation and Plan

Mary's panic attacks and agoraphobia (fear of leaving home and other safe places) hearken back to the intense anxiety and guilt associated with the loss of her father during the heightened attachment of the Oedipal period of development. Mary has not worked through this loss, so this interrupted attachment has led to tentative object relations, a view of the world as unpredictable and dangerous, and intense insecurity and lack of ego strength, which manifests in overt panic away from home, church, and other secure attachments. Mary's own mother's depression and anxiety after her husband's death may have rendered her emotionally unavailable to Mary, thus heightening Mary's oral dependency needs and weight problem. Psychoanalytically-oriented treatment would focus on a working through of the loss of her mother. Transference themes involving ambivalent attachment to the therapist (i.e., conflicting feelings of neediness and fear of loss), anger at anticipated loss and rejection, and the desire to be emotionally nurtured likely will be areas of focus leading ultimately to greater trust in relationships, a strengthened ego, and the ultimate resolution of her symptoms.

Cognitive-Behavioral Formulation and Plan

Mary's panic and agoraphobia are the result of learned behavior modeled by her own mother's struggle with these behaviors. Mary learned a set of beliefs through her mother's example that the world was not safe, sudden death was imminent, and she had little resources with which to cope independent of the help of others. Mary and her mother also attained significant reinforcement for their symptoms, as their confinement to home, inability to work, and dependent behaviors successfully solicited assistance, nurturance, and protection from others. Treatment would best incorporate cognitive-behavioral techniques involving exposure, response prevention, shaping, and reinforcement. Thus, Mary would be encouraged to recreate her symptoms of panic in the therapist's office, and develop strategies to interrupt and overcome these symptoms. She would be encouraged to gradually expose herself to feared situations, such as taking a bus or going alone to the store, and learning that each situation does not result in panic. Her therapist will teach her relaxation techniques such as diaphragmatic breathing to afford her tools for alleviating her own symptoms if and when they occur. Reinforcers, such as her family's admiration and praise and greater freedom to leave home will encourage healthy behavior. A behavioral program could also be implemented to assist Mary with weight loss. Thus, a set of cognitive-behavioral interventions will be useful in reducing Mary's symptoms of panic, agoraphobia, and inability to work and lose weight.

Humanistic Formulation and Plan

Mary's panic mirrors her existential anxiety and phenomenological experience of the world as lonely and risky. Mary has been deprived of support, empathy, and validation for her internal experience, and by feeling disempowered, has not assumed responsibility for herself and her life. Humanistic therapy would involve a highly supportive and empathetic approach wherein the therapist listens with respect and positive regard for Mary without judgement or pathologizing of Mary's experience. The therapist would encourage Mary to express all of her feelings, fears, and beliefs while supportively affirming her experience and gently helping her move toward assuming greater levels of acceptance and responsibility for herself.

Family Systems Formulation and Plan

Mary, the identified patient, is manifesting symptoms of a larger dysfunctional system. Mary's family of origin encouraged dependent behavior in the service of keeping family members closely tied to one another. In Mary's present family, Mary's dependent role is supported by her husband and children in several ways. First, generational boundaries have been altered such that Mary's children assumed a parentified role in taking care of her, affording them a closer alliance with their father and a relief from their mother's threatened anxiety attacks. Mary's husband had been empowered in his role as Mary's driver escort, and sole breadwinner, until recent financial circumstances have threatened the family system. Treatment would involve family sessions with the entire family initially and later with Mary and her husband. A strategic intervention might involve having Mary's family members insist on escorting her everywhere and helping her with everything, exaggerating her symptoms to the point where these interactions become unbearably smothering, resulting in her insistence on independence.

Her symptoms could be reframed as forms of communication. Instead of expressing panic, Mary could be encouraged by family members to explicitly state the intended communication, for example, "I need to know that I am cared about." Generational boundaries would be restructured such that Mary and her husband unite in the parental role and enable the children to assume less responsibility for Mary's needs in the future.

Conclusion

The case example of Mary explicates how each of the four major theoretical models might be applied toward understanding and treating problematic behavior. Each school of thought has strengths and weaknesses and makes some contribution to both understanding Mary's concerns and offering intervention strategies. However, the reality of contemporary psychology involves integrative ideas and efforts. For example, it may be useful to provide cognitive-behavioral interventions to Mary in the context of a supportive therapeutic relationship that assists her in resolving the death of her father and developing a heightened sense of self-efficacy. Involving her husband in the treatment may also have numerous benefits, which collaboration with medical professionals, her priest and church community, and other resources may provide a comprehensive and perhaps optimal treatment approach. Chapter 5 fully expands this theme of integration in contemporary clinical psychology and explores the advances and applications of integrative perspectives to emotional and behavioral problems.

The Big Picture

Theoretical approaches provide a comprehensive framework for understanding behavior and planning intervention. Whether a psychologist is conducting research, teaching, or providing clinical services, using a theoretical approach helps to provide competent and theory-driven strategies. Without perspectives, a professional would "wing it" each time he or she engaged in professional activities, deprived of useful guidelines for direction in his or her work. Some professionals mistakenly maintain

rigid adherence to a particular approach hoping that it can be universally applied to each and every situation and person. Strict adherence to a theoretical approach or to a proponent of an approach can result in limited, rigid views of human behavior and behavior change and cult-like zealousness. Whereas each approach has its advantages for understanding behavior and offering ideas for intervention, this limited view might lead a psychologist to overlook important alternatives to understand, explain, and treat patients and thus fail to provide effective assessment and treatment.

Some perspectives lend themselves to research better than other approaches. For example, research has been extensively conducted on assessment and treatment using the behavioral approach while much less research has been conducted using the humanistic/existential approach. The vast majority of empirically validated treatments favor the behavioral approach. However, it would be incorrect to suggest that the behavioral approach is the superior approach. Each of the four major psychological perspectives offer a helpful way to view human behavior and offer useful strategies for assessment and intervention. Furthermore, all four approaches have been enormously influential in contemporary clinical psychology and have been integrated into current theory and practice.

The evolution of clinical psychology has witnessed increasing integration of various theoretical perspectives. While some argue that integrating approaches is a mistake and akin to mixing apples and oranges, more and more psychologists are integrating various theoretical perspectives and techniques with success. Biological, psychological, and social factors clearly influence emotional, behavioral, and interpersonal functioning. Furthermore, as more research and clinical experience help to uncover the mysteries of human behavior, approaches need to be adapted and shaped in order to best accommodate these new discoveries and knowledge. The future will likely further expand the biopsychosocial perspective by better understanding the interplay between biological, psychological, and social influences on behavior and targeting interventions that better suit these influences.

Key Points

1. Theoretical approaches are world views or philosophies about human behavior. They provide a psychologist with a conceptual understanding of why humans behave as they do, and provide a coherent structure for conducting research, assessment, treatment, and consultation concerning emotional, behavioral, or interpersonal problems. As clinical psychology has evolved over the past several decades, more integrative perspectives have emerged.

2. The psychodynamic perspective suggests that human behavior is influenced by intrapsychic drives, motives, conflicts, impulses and other largely unconscious forces. Various adaptive and maladaptive defense mechanisms are used by the ego to deal with conflicts, needs, wishes, and anxieties. Early experiences and relationships are viewed as playing a critical and enduring role in development and adult behavior. Insight into these mostly unconscious influences, as well as the working-through process, help to improve psychological functioning and behavior. The psychodynamic method subsumes Freud's psychoanalytic approach, the revisionist approaches, and object relations theories.

3. Basic assumptions that comprise the foundation of the cognitive-behavioral approach include: emphasis on current rather than past experiences, and measurable and observable behavior, the importance of environmental influences on the development of both normal and problematic behavior, and empirical research methods to validate assessment and treatment strategies. Operant conditioning, classical conditioning, social-learning, and cognitive perspectives represent variations within the cognitive-behavioral perspective.

4. The humanistic perspective assumes a phenomenological approach that emphasizes the person's perception and experience of their world. The humanistic perspective tends to view people as being active, thinking, creative, and growth-oriented. Helping others is partially accomplished through understanding concerns, feelings, and behavior through the eyes of the patient. Humanistic therapists tend to assume that people are basically well intentioned and that they naturally strive towards growth, love, creativity, and self-actualization. The humanistic perspective includes the client-centered approach, Maslow's hierarchy of needs, and the gestalt approach.

5. The family systems approach focuses on improved communication among family members and a de-emphasis on the problems of any one member of the family. The family systems approach emphasizes systems theory, that is, any change or problem in one aspect of the system impacts and alters other aspects of the family system. Structural, strategic, Milan, and narrative methods represent some of the variations within family systems theory and practice.

Key Terms

Active Listening	Exposure	Psychosexual Stages
Behavioral Rehearsal	Family Systems	Reframing
Classical Conditioning	Free Association	Repression
Client-centered	Gestalt	Revisionists
Cognitive-behavioral	Humanistic	Self-actualization
Congruence	Id	Self Efficacy
Contingency Management	Insight	Social Learning
Counterconditioning	Joining	Strategic
Countertransference	Milan Approach	Structural Approach
Defense Mechanisms	Narrative	Superego
Denial	Object Relations	Theoretical Orientation
Differentiation	Oedipal Complex	Thought Stopping
Disengagement	Operant	Transference
Ego	Paradoxical Technique	Unconditional Positive Regard
Empathy	Peak Experience	Working Through
Enmeshment	Psychodynamic	

For Reflection

1. What are theoretical approaches in clinical psychology and how are they used?

2. What are the advantages and disadvantages of using theoretical approaches?

3. What are the advantages and disadvantages of integrating theoretical approaches?

4. Compare and contrast the psychodynamic, cognitive-behavioral, humanistic, and family systems approaches. What are the strengths and weaknesses of each approach?

5. How does the Freudian approach differ from the revisionists and object relations approaches?

6. How does the operant approach differ from the classical conditioning and social learning approach?

7. How does the cognitive approach differ from the strict behavioral approach?

8. How does the client-centered approach differ from the gestalt approach?

9. How does the structural approach differ from the strategic approach?

10. Who are the founding fathers (or mothers) of the psychodynamic, cognitive-behavioral, humanistic, and family systems approaches?

11. What unique contribution is provided in understanding behavior and offering assessment and intervention strategies for each of the major theoretical approaches?

CHAPTER 5

Integrative and Biopsychosocial Approaches in Contemporary Clinical Psychology

Chapter Outline

Highlight of a Contemporary Clinical Psychologist: Paul L. Wachtel, Ph.D.
The Call to Integration
Biopsychosocial Integration
Synthesizing Biological, Psychological, and Social Factors in Contemporary Integration
Application of the Biopsychosocial Perspective to Contemporary Clinical Psychology Problems

HIGHLIGHT OF A CONTEMPORARY CLINICAL PSYCHOLOGIST:

Paul L. Wachtel, Ph.D.

Dr. Wachtel combines a full-time academic career with a small private practice.

Birth Date: July 28, 1940

College: Columbia University, 1961 (A. B., Psychology)

Graduate Program: Yale University, 1965 (Ph.D., Clinical Psychology)

Clinical Internship: Yale Psychiatric Institute

Postdoctoral Fellowship: New York University (Psychoanalysis and Psychotherapy)

Current Job: Distinguished Professor of Psychology, City University of New York

Pros and cons of being a clinical psychologist:

Pros: "For me, what is most exciting about the field is that one can bring into play one's heart and one's mind, and that they are not in opposition but work in tandem. The fact that ours is a field with strong contending points of view presents a stimulating intellectual challenge to integrate and reconcile these opposing positions."

Cons: "I don't know if this is a con, but clinical psychology is not a field for anyone who does not have considerable tolerance for ambiguity. Those who need to impose a false or premature clarity oversimplify and do a disservice to the field and to themselves."

Future of clinical psychology: "Much depends on how long the public tolerates the privations managed care will force upon them. When the bottom line takes precedence over human needs, we are manifesting a false understanding of economy or efficiency. If there is public outcry over lack of choice and decreased access to treatment, the future of the field is bright. If the public passively accepts a decline in our quality of life, not only clinical psychology will suffer."

Typical Schedule:

8:00   See patient in psychotherapy session.
9:00   Travel to university and work on research.
10:00 Research session continues.
11:00 Research session continues.
12:00 Meet with students.
1:00   Meet with students.
2:00   Teach class.
3:00   Teach class.
4:00   Meet with students and travel back to private office.
5:00   See patient in psychotherapy.

Having now reviewed the four major theoretical models in psychology, this chapter will seek to illustrate how integration is achieved in the actual science and practice of clinical psychology. In addition to psychological perspectives per se, a full integration of human functioning demands a synthesis of psychological factors with both biological and social elements. This combination of biological, psychological, and social factors comprises an example of contemporary integration in the form of the biopsychosocial perspective. This chapter will therefore describe the evolution of individual psychological perspectives into a more comprehensive biopsychosocial synthesis perhaps first touched upon 2500 years ago by the Greeks.

The Call to Integration

While there are over 400 different types of approaches to psychotherapy and other professional services offered by clinical psychologists (Karasu, 1986), the major schools of thought reviewed and illustrated in the previous chapter have emerged during the 20th century as the primary perspectives in clinical psychology. As mentioned, these include the psychodynamic, cognitive-behavioral, humanistic, and family systems approaches. Prior to the 1980s, most psychologists tended to adhere to one of these theoretical approaches in their research, psychotherapy, assessment, and consultation. In fact, numerous institutes, centers, and professional journals were (and still are) devoted to the advancement, research, and practice of individual perspectives (e.g., *Behavior Therapy* and *International Journal of Psychoanalysis*). Professionals typically affiliate themselves with one perspective as well as the professional journals and organizations represented by that perspective (e.g., Association for the Advancement of Behavior Therapy), and have little interaction or experience with the other perspectives or organizations. Opinions are often dogmatic and other perspectives and organizations viewed with skepticism or even disdain. Surprisingly, psychologists with research and science training sometimes choose not to use their objective and critical thinking skills when discussing the merits and limitations of theoretical frameworks different from their own. Choice of theoretical orientation is typically a by-product of graduate and postgraduate training,

the personality of the professional, and the general world view held of human nature. Even geographical regions of the country have been historically associated with theoretical orientations among psychologists and other mental health professionals. For example, the psychoanalytic approach has been especially popular in the northeasten part of the United States, and the behavioral approach has been especially popular in the midwestern and southern parts of the United States.

However, unidimensional approaches have been found to be lacking and of limited use in their approach to the full spectrum of psychological problems. Research has generally failed to demonstrate that one treatment perspective is more effective than another (Beckham, 1990; Lambert, Shapiro, & Bergin, 1986; Smith, Glass, & Miller, 1980). About 45 percent of the improvements in psychotherapy, for example, may be attributable to common factors found in all major theories and approaches (Lambert, 1986). Furthermore, some research has suggested that less than 15 percent of treatment outcome variance can be accounted for by specific techniques (Beutler, Mohr, Grawe, Engle, & MacDonald, 1991; Lambert, 1986). Studies have suggested that a combination of perspectives and techniques may even have powerful synergistic effects (Lazarus, 1989; Norcross & Goldfried, 1992). Therefore, both research and practice suggest that religious adherence to only one perspective may be counterproductive and naive.

In reviewing the major theoretical approaches in clinical psychology, it may seem clear that each

"Sir, the following paradigm shifts occurred while you were out."

perspective offers unique contributions towards better understanding human behavior and assisting those who seek professional psychological services. Adherence to only one school of thought, however, can be rigid and ultimately limiting. In the words of Arnold Lazarus, "Given the complexity of the subject matter, it seems unlikely that any single approach can possess all the answers. So why wear blinders? Why not borrow, purchase, pilfer, import, and otherwise draw upon conceptions and methods from diverse systems so as to harness their combined powers" (Lazarus, 1995, p. 399). While no one theory has a lock on the truth nor the keys to behavior change, perhaps each has something very important to offer in the greater puzzle of "truth." Furthermore, debate about which school of thought reigns supreme seems to become moot in the ensuing context of integration (Arnkoff & Glass, 1992). In the words of Sol Garfield and Allen Bergin, "a decisive shift in opinion has quietly occurred . . . the new view is that the long-term dominance of the major theories is over and that an eclectic position has taken precedence" (Garfield & Bergin, 1986, p. 7).

Commonalities Among Approaches

With so much emphasis on differences, it is often overlooked that there is some degree of overlap among many of these perspectives. For example, some of the major concepts articulated in one perspective are also expressed in other perspectives, using different terms and language. *Free association* in the psychodynamic framework and *automatic thoughts* (or self-talk) in the cognitive-behavioral orientation provide a helpful example. Thus, those immediate and unfiltered thoughts and feelings that come to mind are referred to as free associations for those from a psychodynamic perspective and automatic thoughts in the cognitive-behavioral lexicon. Both approaches highly value and integrate free association/self-talk into their understanding and treatment of human behavior. Attempts to translate the language of one perspective into another have occurred since 1950, beginning with the work of Dollard and Miller.

Since research tends to support the notion that one theoretical framework is not superior to another in treating all types of problems, the examination of common denominators among the different

theoretical perspectives has attempted to isolate common factors (Goldfried, 1991). This research has suggested that providing the patient with new experiences within and outside of the therapy session is common in all types of psychotherapies (Brady, et al., 1980). Goldfried (1991) stated that all psychotherapies encourage the patient to engage in corrective experiences and that they all provide some form of feedback to the patient. Additional similarities discussed by Frank (1973, 1982) and others include a professional office associated with healing and being helped; a trained mental health professional who is supportive, thoughtful, professional, and perceived as an expert in human behavior; enhanced hope that thoughts, feelings, and behaviors can change for the better; fees associated with service; and the avoidance of dual relationships (e.g., avoidance of sexual relationships or friendships with patients).

James Prochaska (1984) discussed commonalities among theoretical orientations by examining the process of change across different types of problems and different methods of treatment. In his analysis of different orientations to behavior change, he isolated a variety of universal stages, levels, and processes of change. His theory includes five stages of change (i.e., precontemplation, contemplation, preparation, action, and maintenance), five levels of change (i.e., symptoms, maladaptive cognition, current interpersonal conflicts, family/systems conflicts, past interpersonal conflicts), and ten change processes (i.e., consciousness raising, catharsis/dramatic relief, self-evaluation, environmental reevaluation, self-liberation, social liberation, counterconditioning, stimulus control, contingency management, and helping relationship). While it is beyond the scope of this chapter to outline the specifics of Prochaska's model, the interested reader may wish to read a more detailed account (see Prochaska, 1984, 1995; Prochaska & Norcross, 1994). Although Prochaska's perspective has a cognitive-behavioral flavor to it, his theory of change is atheoretical in that it is not based on any one theoretical perspective and can be applied to all perspectives.

Efforts Toward Integration

The integration of theoretical and treatment perspectives is challenging and complex. Each perspective has its own language, leaders, and practices. Furthermore, research is challenging to conduct because what happens in a laboratory or research clinic may be very different from what happens in a clinician's office. For example, a treatment manual that clearly specifies a behavioral intervention for panic disorder used in research is likely not used in clinical practice. Efforts at **integration** tend to occur in one of three ways: (1) integrating the theories associated with each perspective, (2) developing an understanding of the common factors associated with each perspective, and (3) using eclectism in a practical way to provide a range of available intervention strategies (Arkowitz, 1989, 1992). Most attempts to integrate perspectives have involved the integration of psychodynamic and behavioral approaches. Perhaps this is due to the fact that during most of the twentieth century, the majority of clinical psychologists have identified themselves (with the exception of eclectism) as being either psychodynamically or cognitive-behaviorally oriented.

Paul Wachtel (1977, 1982, 1987) has been a significant contributor to the evolving framework of integration between the psychodynamic and behavioral points of view. Wachtel was one of the first professionals to integrate psychodynamic and behavioral approaches. For example, Wachtel uses the psychodynamic perspective in focusing on early childhood experiences as well as the notion that unconscious conflicts result in problematic feelings and behaviors. He uses the behavioral principal of reinforcement in the present environment to understand various ongoing emotional, psychological, and behavioral problems. Wachtel further notes that behavioral interventions can improve insight while insight can lead to behavioral change (Wachtel, 1982).

Gill (1984) reports that psychodynamic and cognitive-behavioral theories have clearly been integrated with much success. Psychodynamic therapies have increasingly incorporated cognitive-behavioral theories and practices into their perspectives. For example, many psychodynamic thinkers have become interested in the cognitive influences of maladaptive beliefs about self and others in interpersonal relationships (Horowitz, 1988; Strupp & Binder, 1984). Furthermore, interest in providing briefer treatments has resulted in the incorporation of cognitive-behavioral problem-solving strategies in dynamic therapy (Strupp & Binder, 1984). Some psychodynamic approaches have also endorsed the

behavioral and humanistic principles of focusing on the present or *here and now* (Weiner, 1975). Contemporary cognitive-behavioral orientations have incorporated the psychodynamic view that attention must be paid to the nature of the therapeutic relationship between the therapist and patient as well as the need for insight to secure behavior change (Dobson & Block, 1988; Mahoney, 1988).

Other efforts toward theoretical integration have occurred using family systems theory (Kirschner & Kirschner, 1986; Lebow, 1984), humanistic approaches (Wandersman, Poppen, & Ricks, 1976), and interpersonal theory (Andrews, 1991). For example, the humanistic orientations have endorsed the scientific approach of the cognitive-behavioral orientation (Bugental, 1987) as well as the role of cognition in promoting growth (Bohart, 1982; Ellis, 1980). The behavioral approaches have incorporated family systems theory into their efforts at developing behavioral family therapy (Jacobson & Margolin, 1979; Jacobson, 1985). Using a broader framework, some authors have looked towards an integration of biological, cognitive, affective, behavioral, and interpersonal elements of human behavior (Andrews, 1991; Beckham, 1990; Schwartz, 1984, 1991). Rather than looking at the major theoretical perspectives as being mutually exclusive, these authors experience them as all having some corner of the truth, which needs to be examined and pieced together in order to understand behavior and offer useful intervention strategies.

Eclecticism

Professionals maintaining an eclectic or integrative approach to their work tend to use whatever theories and techniques appear to work best for a given patient or problem. Thus, once the psychologist has an adequate understanding of the patient's problems or symptoms, he or she uses strategies from various perspectives in order to design a treatment plan best suited to the unique needs of each patient. Lazarus (1971) argued that professionals can use techniques from various theoretical orientations without necessarily accepting the theory behind them. For example, a psychodynamically-oriented psychologist might help a patient learn relaxation techniques such as diaphragmatic breathing or muscle relaxation in order to help control feelings of anxiety and panic. The therapy would continue to pursue the underlying basis for these symptoms while affording the patient some immediate relief. A cognitive-behaviorally oriented psychologist might ask a patient who is troubled by insomnia associated with frequent nightmares to describe his or her disturbing dreams and inquire about the patient's insights into these dreams. A humanistic psychologist might invite a patient to examine irrational beliefs. Irving Weiner stated that, "effective psychotherapy is defined not by its brand name, but by how well it meets the needs of the patient" (Weiner, 1975, p.44). This has become the "battle cry" of many clinical psychologists today. In many ways, someone seeking the professional services of a clinical psychologist is much more interested in obtaining help for his or her particular problem(s) than embracing the particular theoretical orientation of the psychologist. Also, they generally want immediate help with what ails them, not an intellectual discussion or understanding about the philosophy of human behavior. Also, they usually want an approach that is consistent with their personality and own perspective to problems. However, Eysenck (1970) and others have warned that eclecticism can be a "mish-mash of theories, a hugger-mugger of procedures, a gallimaufry of therapies" (p. 145). Concerns about eclecticism suggest that it can result in a passing familiarity with many approaches but competence in none, as well as muddled and unfocused thinking. Nonetheless, numerous surveys have revealed that eclectic approaches have become more and more common and popular among clinical psychologists (e.g., Norcross & Prochaska, 1988; Norcross, Prochaska, & Gallagher, 1989).

An excellent and influential example of an eclectic approach is the *multimodal* approach of Arnold Lazarus (Lazarus, 1971, 1985, 1986, 1996). In the multimodal approach, treatment reflects the patient's needs based on seven aspects of behavior. These include behavior, affect, sensation, imagery, cognition, interpersonal relationships, and drugs (referred to as BASIC ID). Interventions include cognitive-behavioral techniques such as imagery, biological interventions such as medication, and humanistic strategies such as empty chair exercises and reflection. Although the work of Lazarus has a cognitive-behavioral slant, many noncognitive-behavioral techniques and approaches are utilized in the multimodal approach.

Beyond Psychological Models

As clinical psychology has evolved, more complex theories of human behavior and behavior change have developed utilizing and integrating the major theoretical psychological perspectives in conjunction with biological and social factors. Furthermore, multidimensional and integrative approaches to intervention that reflect a biopsychosocial synthesis have become the trend in contemporary clinical psychology (Lam, 1991). In fact, formal education in the biological, psychological, and social influences of behavior have become a requirement for licensure in most states. No longer can a psychologist master only one theoretical perspective while remaining oblivious to other perspectives and hope to obtain a license to practice in his or her state. For example, if a patient requests treatment by a clinical psychologist for tension headaches associated with stress, the psychologist must be able to appreciate the biological, psychological, and social influences on the patient's symptoms. While not all psychologists can treat all problems, it is incumbent on practitioners to at least know when to make appropriate referrals. For example, the headaches might be associated with stress but they could also be associated with medical problems such as a migraine, brain tumor, or other serious neurological condition. The competent psychologist would request that the patient be evaluated by a physician in order to rule out these other important medical possibilities prior to treating the headaches with biofeedback, relaxation training, psychotherapy, or other psychosocial interventions and strategies in conjunction with any appropriate medical treatment. If a member of a particular religious or ethnic group seeks treatment for an emotional problem, it is important to have adequate awareness and understanding regarding the influences of culture on the behavior or problem in question (Sue, 1983, 1988). Ignorance regarding the role of ethnicity, culture, and gender in behavior is no longer tolerated in most professional circles. Examining the biological, psychological, and social influences on behavior has become fundamental in clinical psychology and defines the biopsychosocial framework.

For example, a disabled Latino child, recently immigrating from El Salvador, experiences depression and posttraumatic stress disorder following an experience of sexual abuse perpetrated by a family member. The school teacher notices an increase in sexualized and inattentive behavior and refers the child to a psychologist who consults with the school. The child tells the psychologist about the sexual abuse and the psychologist, as required by law, must break confidentiality and report the abuse to the state child protection agency. The bilingual psychologist might treat the child and members of the family with a variety of intervention strategies. The range of interventions might include (1) psychodynamic approaches to increase insight and access unconscious anger and resentment, (2) cognitive-behavioral strategies to manage anxiety symptoms and inattentive behavior at school, (3) referral to a psychiatrist for evaluation of the possible use of medication to address the depression, (4) referral to a pediatrician to evaluate potential medical problems associated with the abuse, (5) social and community support and interventions to address cultural issues associated with being an El Salvadoran immigrant as well as legal issues associated with the victimization, (6) family systems approaches to help the entire family cope with the current crisis and avoid future abuse, and (7) humanistic approaches to help support and accept the feelings and behavior of the child and family. This example demonstrates the need to intervene broadly with a wide arsenal of tools given the complexity of issues within the individual and larger family and social systems.

Biopsychosocial Integration

Whereas psychologists have increasingly utilized combined and multimodal psychological models and interventions, contemporary psychology has looked beyond even its own field into biological and sociological realms to enhance its scope and usefulness. The combined integration of biological, psychological and social factors on behavior have led to the term *biopsychosocial,* and represents an increasingly appreciated comprehensive approach in clinical psychology. It is important to note that while biological, psychological, and social factors are all viewed as relevant in this perspective, they may not each be equal in their contribution to every problem or disorder. Thus, in the case of a primarily biological disorder such as childhood leukemia, for

example, psychological and social factors provide important contributions to the course and treatment of the disease but are not given equal etiological or treatment consideration. Similarly, while a grief reaction following the loss of a loved one may at first glance appear purely psychological, social factors such as family and community support as well as biological factors such as sleeping and eating patterns can complicate or alleviate the severity of symptoms. Thus, an intelligent blending and weighing of these three factors comprise the challenge of biopsychosocial integration. Having described the major psychological approaches in detail in Chapter 4, the nature of biological and social factors on behavior will be described in this section, leading to clinical examples of biopsychosocial integration in contemporary practice.

Biological Factors

Since Hippocrates, the close association between biology and behavior has been acknowledged, but not always fully integrated into treatment. Recent advances in medicine and the biological sciences have furthered our awareness of the intimate connection between our physical and psychological selves. A full understanding of any emotional or behavioral problem must therefore take into consideration potential biological factors.

Some authors have attempted to explain human behavior in terms of biological, genetic, and evolutionary influences. For example, it is well known that there is a strong genetic influence on physical characteristics such as height, weight, hair color, and eye color. Furthermore, it is well known that a variety of physical illnesses such as Huntington's chorea, phenylketonuria (PKU), Tay-Sachs, Down Syndrome, heart disease, cancer, mental retardation, and psychiatric illnesses such as schizophrenia, bipolar disorder, and alcoholism have strong biological or genetic influences (e.g., Dykens & Hodapp, 1997; Gottesman, 1991). This does not mean that a psychiatric condition such as schizophrenia is completely attributable to genetic influences. In fact, an identical twin has about a 50 percent chance of *not* developing schizophrenia if his or her twin has the disorder (Gottesman, 1991). The point is that biological and genetic influences have a significant but incomplete contribution to the development and course of many illnesses.

Genetically-based chromosomal dysfunction can lead to a number of conditions that involve behavior and learning problems of interest to clinical psychologists. For example, Fragile X, Williams, and Prader-Willi syndromes all involve deletion or dysfunction of chromosomes due to genetic influences resulting in a variety of cognitive, intellectual, learning, and behavioral problems (Dykens & Hodapp, 1997). Behavioral and learning problems associated with these disorders have intervention implications that involve both biological and psychosocial strategies.

Even personality traits such as shyness have been shown to have a genetic component (e.g., Kagan, Reznick, & Snidman, 1988; Plomin, 1990). Research studying identical twins reared apart from birth have revealed many striking research findings that support the notion of a strong biological influence associated with human health, illness, and behavior. Of course genetic and **biological vulnerabilities** and predispositions do not necessarily result in the expression of a particular illness or trait. For example, while someone may inherit the vulnerability to develop PKU, environmental factors such as diet determine if the trait is expressed. Therefore, biological predispositions must be examined in the context of the environment.

Furthermore, additional biological influences on behavior, such as the role of brain chemicals called neurotransmitters, have demonstrated that brain functioning plays a significant role in human behavior. For example, serotonin (5-hydroxytryptamine or 5-HT) is a neurotransmitter associated with a variety of instinctual behaviors such as eating, sexuality, and moodiness. Low levels of serotonin at the synapse have been associated with impulsive behavior and depression (Spoont, 1992). Another neurotransmitter, dopamine, has been linked to schizophrenia but also corresponding medications to treat its troubling symptoms. Therefore, many psychologists and others maintain that biological influences such as inherited characteristics and brain neurochemistry (such as the role of neurotransmitters) greatly influence both normal and abnormal behavior. The goal of the biological approach is to understand these biological and chemical influences and use interventions such as medication to help those with certain emotional, behavioral, and/or interpersonal problems.

Professionals with strong biological training, such as many psychiatrists, generally favor biological interventions in treating patients. Various types of psychotropic medications such as antipsychotic, antianxiety, and antidepressant medications are frequently used to treat a wide variety of emotional, psychological, and behavioral problems. For example, lithium is typically used to treat bipolar disorder (commonly referred to by the general population as manic-depression), while neuroleptics such as Haldol, Thorazine, and Risperdal are often used to treat psychotic disorders such as schizophrenia. The benzodiazepines such as Valium and Xanax are frequently used to treat anxiety-based disorders such as panic and phobia. Finally, tricyclics such as Elavil, the monoamine oxidase (MAO) inhibitors, and a new class of medications called the selective serotonin reuptake inhibitors (SSRIs), which include the popular Prozac, are used to treat depressive disorders. Tricyclics such as imipramine are also used to treat panic and phobic disorders. Electroconvulsive therapy (ECT) is frequently used to treat severe and resistant depression. The technique involves applying a small amount of electrical current (usually 20–30 milliamps) to the patient's temples for about one minute while patients are sedated. The treatment results in a seizure or convulsion, which is subsequently associated with a reduction in symptoms.

These biological interventions are not without important side effects. For example, the benzodiazepines can cause drowsiness, tolerance, and both physical and psychological dependence or addiction (Baldessarini & Cole, 1988; Hayward, Wardle, & Higgitt, 1989). Antidepressants such as Prozac can cause insomnia, nervousness, and inhibited orgasms (Kaplan & Sadock, 1993). Antipsychotic medication can produce muscle rigidity, weight gain, dry mouth, constipation, a shuffling walk, and an irreversible condition called *tardive dyskinesia* characterized by involuntary facial and limb movements (Breggin, 1991). Tardive dyskinesia can render patients socially impaired if the symptoms cannot be managed by other medications. Although research has failed to find that ECT causes structural damage to the brain (Devanand, Dwork, Hutchinson, Blowig, & Sackheim, 1994; Devanand & Sackeim, 1995; Scott, 1995), memory deficits, usually associated with events occurring around the time of ECT administration, are a common side effect. Biological interventions may be used effectively with certain patients but also have important side effects. Therefore, a perfect pill or "magic bullet" that completely fixes a problem without any side effects or negative factors does not exist.

While medication can greatly help to minimize or eliminate problematic symptoms, additional problems associated with a mental illness may continue to exist. For example, antipsychotic medication or neuroleptics such as Thorazine, Mellaril, or Risperdal may reduce or eliminate the hallucinations and delusional thinking associated with schizophrenia. Therefore, the patient is bothered no longer by hearing voices or beliefs that have no basis in reality. However, problems with social skills, self-esteem, fears, and comfort with others may not be altered by the use of these powerful medications and must be dealt with using other means (e.g., social skills training, psychotherapy, job skill training).

In addition to medications and other biological treatments such as ECT, technological advances such as the development of computer neuroimaging techniques (CAT and PET Scans, and functional MRIs) have improved our understanding of brain-behavior relationships (Mazziotta, 1996). CAT scans (Computerized Axial Tomography) were developed in the early 1970s to better view the structures of the brain. CAT scans provide computer enhanced multiple X-ray like pictures of the brain from multiple angles. CAT scan research has, for example, discovered that schizophrenics have enlarged ventricles or spaces in the brain and experience cortical atrophy over time. PET (Positron Emission Tomography) scans use radioactive isotopes injected into the bloodstream of a patient to create gamma rays in the body. PET scans provide not only a view of brain structure but also provide information on brain function (Fischbach, 1992). Research using PET scan technology has revealed changes in brain blood flow during different intellectual tasks and during different emotional states such as anxiety (Fischbach, 1992). PET scan research has determined that panic is associated with brain cells located in the locus ceruleus in the brainstem which are also sensitive to the benzodiazepines (Barlow, 1988; Reiman, Fusselman, Fox, & Raichle, 1989). Finally, MRI (Magnetic Resonance Imaging) was developed in the early 1980s and provides a detailed visual reconstruction of the brain's anatomy (Andreasen & Black, 1995). The MRI analyzes the nuclear magnetic movements of hydrogen in the water and fat of the body. MRI research has helped to uncover the role of possible frontal lobe damage among schizophrenic patients (Andreasen, 1989) as well as potential tissue loss in bipolar patients (Andreasen & Black, 1995).

Clinical psychologists, at this time, are unable to prescribe ECT, medication, or any other biological interventions (e.g., CAT or PET scans, MRI). Therefore, psychologists interested in the use of these interventions must work collaboratively with physicians (such as psychiatrists). However, efforts are underway by the United States military, the American Psychological Association, and other organizations to work towards allowing psychologists, with the appropriate training, supervision, and experience, to legally prescribe medications in the future. This would allow psychologists to more fully integrate biological interventions with the psychosocial interventions they already provide. Prescribing medications by psychologists will be discussed in more detail in Chapter 14.

Some authors also view evolutionary influences as powerful contributors to human behavior (Wilson, 1991, 1983, 1978). Although speculative and not based on controlled scientific experimentation, evolutionary explanations for a variety of behaviors and behavior problems have become popular in recent years. For example, some researchers report that many experiences and difficulties with intimate relationships can be traced to evolutionary influences (Buss, 1994; Fisher, 1992). For example, Fisher (1992) explained that divorces occur often and usually fairly early in a relationship (after about four years) for evolutionary reasons, because about four years were needed to conceive and raise a child to a minimal level of independence. Once a child is about three years old, members of a clan could adequately continue with child rearing. Fisher and others explain infidelity as evolutionarily helpful because by distributing our genes by mating with a number of partners we will most likely keep our genes from dying out. Because life was tenuous for our ancestors—death was a realistic daily possibility—having some reproductive options with several people increased the possibility of mating as well as having help taking care of young infants. Maximizing reproductive success and perpetuating the species is enhanced if people mate often and with a variety of partners. Whereas these researchers provide compelling explanations for human intimate relationships from studying the behavior of animals as well as the behavior of our ancient ancestors, people are often very quick to proclaim that human behavior is driven by strong biological forces and therefore, we cannot help being who we are and behaving as we do. Thus, someone engaged in an extramarital affair who blames their behavior on his or her genetic makeup is likely (and rightfully) to be viewed with skepticism.

Biologically-oriented factors emphasize the influence of the brain, neurochemistry, and genetic influences on behavior. They typically lead to biologically-oriented approaches to study, assess, and treat a wide range of emotional, psychological, medical, and behavioral problems. Evolutionarily-oriented professionals focus on understanding human behavior in the context of our sociobiological roots. The biological and evolutionary perspectives on behavior have become increasingly influential. New discoveries in genetics such as genetic markers for depression, panic, anxiety, obesity, and schizophrenia as well as new discoveries in brain structure and function associated with schizophrenia, homosexuality, and violence have contributed to the ascendancy of the biological perspective. Finally, psychiatry's emphasis on biological theories of mental illness and medication interventions have also fueled the current focus on biological factors in understanding, diagnosing, and treating mental illness (Fleck, 1995; Kramer, 1993; Michels, 1995).

Social Factors

Many clinical psychologists have begun to focus more on both cultural and social influences on be-havior. Sociologists, anthropologists and social workers have been investigating these influences for many years. While most practicing clinical psychologists today still primarily work with individuals, couples, and families rather than with large organizations or groups, issues such as culture, socioeconomic factors, ethnicity, sexual orientation, religious background, social support, and community resources have received a great deal of attention concerning their important influences on human behavior (American Psychological Association, 1993b; Brown, 1990; Greene, 1993; Jones, 1994; Lopez, Grover, Holland, Johnson, Kain, Kanel, Mellins, & Rhyne, 1989; National Mental Health Association, 1986; Sue, 1983, 1988; Tharp, 1991; U.S. Department of Health and Human Services, 1990).

Professionals maintain that individual behavior is often influenced by the cultural environment as well as by larger social and even political factors. Homelessness, poverty, racism, ethnicity, underemployment, abuse, and even the weather can influence behavior (American Psychological Association, 1993b; Lewis, 1969; Lex, 1985; Tharp, 1991). Thus, individual human behavior cannot be viewed apart from the larger social context. For example, compelling research has demonstrated that developing schizophrenia is 38 percent more likely for those living in urban environments relative to rural environments (Lewis, David, Andreasson, & Allsbeck, 1992). While no one would suggest that city living alone would cause someone to become schizophrenic, perhaps vulnerable persons who are at risk for the development of schizophrenia are more likely to develop symptoms in an urban rather than a suburban or rural environment. Depression

---

Case Study of Mary: Integrating Biological Factors

Given the significant research into biological aspects of panic disorder, several key insights are germane to Mary's case. First, panic and other anxiety disorders have a strong familial contribution, in that individuals whose family members have these disorders are at increased risk of also developing the disorders. Second, neurotransmitters associated with the GABA-benzodiazepine and serotonergic systems have been implicated in the development of panic disorder (Deakin & Graeff, 1991; Gray, 1982, 1991). Therefore, medications prescribed by a physician such as benzodiazepines (e.g., Valium and Xanax) and antidepressants (e.g., Tofranil) may be helpful in altering the biological neurochemistry associated with Mary's panic symptoms (e.g., Klosko, Barlow, Tassinari, & Cerny, 1990). However, potential side effects would need to be fully discussed and Mary clearly informed as to her biological and other treatment options.

and drug abuse are also more prevalent in urban environments while alcoholism is more common in rural places (Eaton, et al., 1984; Regier, et al., 1984). Although disorders such as schizophrenia, depression, and substance abuse can be found in all cultures and countries, social factors such as culture, social expectations, racism, and economic factors often determine how symptoms are presented. For example, while auditory hallucinations are most common in developed countries such as the United States, visual hallucinations are most common in less developed countries such as those in many parts of Africa and Central America (Ndetei & Singh, 1983).

Social relationships appear influential in protecting individuals from a variety of physical and psychological problems including depression, hypertension, and alcoholism (House, Landis, & Umberson, 1988). In fact, many research studies in several countries have found that a large network of social contacts increase the chance of living a long life (Berkman & Syme, 1979; House, Robbins, & Metzner, 1982). The relationship between social support and longevity exists even after accounting for other important risk factors such as hypertension, smoking, and alcoholism. Social support also helps people cope more effectively and recover more quickly from both physical and psychological problems (McLeod, Kessler, & Landis, 1992).

Social factors can also be damaging as well. Social influences can be so powerful that they can even lead to death. For example, disease and death frequently closely follows separation from a spouse through death or divorce. This relationship is especially common among elderly men (Arling, 1976).

Professionals with a great deal of training and experience in the social influences on behavior, such as social workers, generally favor social interventions in helping patients. Interventions such as improved housing and employment opportunities, community interventions such as Project Head-Start providing low cost and high quality preschool experiences for low income and high risk families, and legal strategies such as laws to protect battered women and abused children are often the focus of many of these professionals.

The powerful influences of cultural and ethnic background as well as social issues such as poverty, homelessness, racism, violence, and crime have been associated with psychological functioning and human behavior, lending support to the importance of more global social and systems thinking (American Psychological Association, 1993b; Lopez et al., 1989; Schwartz, 1982, 1984, 1991; Tharp, 1991). No contemporary clinical psychologist can overlook social context when seeking to understand and treat psychological problems. In fact, the American Psychological Association provides guidelines to psychologists that include that they "recognize ethnicity and culture as significant parameters in understanding psychological processes" (American Psychological Association, 1993b, p. 46). These issues are further discussed in Chapter 14.

Synthesizing Biological, Psychological, and Social Factors in Contemporary Integration

Several theories have influenced the development of this integrative and contemporary biopsychosocial perspective and a brief review of them is warranted. This group includes the diathesis-

---

Case Study of Mary: Integrating Social Factors

A number of social factors further contribute to an understanding of Mary. First, Mary's Irish Catholic upbringing was marked by repression of feelings and a tendency to experience intense guilt. Her current social environment is exceedingly narrow, limited by her agoraphobia and avoidance of new situations. It may therefore be useful to first engage her priest and church community in both working through deeply-held religious beliefs that con-tribute to her sense of guilt and emotional restriction and toward broadening her contact with others. Connection to social support through her church community could lead to some volunteer responsibilities and eventually, greater contact and involvement in the larger community. Thus, sociocultural and religious factors contribute largely to Mary's experience and can be utilized in a positive manner to assist her.

stress perspective, the reciprocal-gene-environment perspective, and the psychosocial influence on biology perspective.

The Diathesis-Stress Perspective

The **diathesis-stress** perspective is a causal perspective for illness or problems. It suggests that a biological or other type of vulnerability in combination with psychosocial or environmental stress (e.g., divorce, financial troubles, unemployment) creates the necessary conditions for illness to occur (Eisenberg, 1968; Meehl, 1962; Segal & Ingram, 1994; Zubin & Spring, 1977). The diathesis-stress perspective states that people have a biological, genetic, cognitive or other tendency towards certain behaviors and problems. A susceptibility emerges such that certain individuals are more prone to developing potential traits, tendencies, or problems. For example, if someone has one biological parent with hypertension (i.e., high blood pressure), they have a 45 percent chance of developing high blood pressure themselves even if they maintain normal weight, minimize their fat and salt intake, and obtain adequate physical exercise. If both biological parents have hypertension, the odds soar to 90 percent (Taylor, 1995). Another example includes schizophrenia, since in fact, much of the research supporting the diathesis-stress perspective focuses on this serious mental illness (Eisenberg, 1968). Schizophrenia occurs in about 1 percent of the population. However, if a person has an identical twin with schizophrenia, there is a 48 percent chance of developing the disorder. If a person has a fraternal twin with schizophrenia, there is a 17 percent chance of developing the problem (Gottesman, 1991). Therefore, diathesis means that someone is susceptible to developing a particular problem due to some inherent vulnerability. When certain stressors emerge or the conditions are right, the problem then becomes manifest.

A disorder will occur when the biological or other vulnerability and environmental stressors interact in a sufficient manner to unleash the problem (Fig. 5.1). For example, people with significant family histories of schizophrenia may experience their first psychotic episode during the stress of moving to a new city or starting college. Or individuals with a family history of alcoholism might develop the problem during college when many opportunities to drink are available and reinforced by peers. For example, Mary (the patient example from the previous chapter) may have a biological predisposition to panic and anxiety disorders due to her genetic and biological make-up. The stress of her father's death and her failure to develop necessary levels of self-confidence may have resulted in this predisposition becoming expressed in the form of a panic disorder.

The Reciprocal-Gene-Environment Perspective

Some argue that genetic influences might actually increase the likelihood that an individual will experience certain life events (Rende & Plomin, 1992). Thus, certain individuals may have the genetic tendency to experience or seek out certain stressful situations. For example, someone with a genetic tendency towards alcoholism may develop a drinking problem that results in work, relationship, and financial strains. These stressors may result in further drinking, thus worsening both the alcohol problem and life stressors. Someone with a genetic predisposition towards attention deficit hyperactivity disorder (ADHD) is likely to be impulsive. This impulsivity might result in making poor decisions concerning potential marital partners leading to divorce and other relationship problems. Stressful relationships and divorce may then exacerbate their attention problems. The reciprocal-gene-environment perspective suggests that there is a close relationship between biological or genetic vulnerability and life events such that each continuously influences the other. Some research suggests that the reciprocal gene-environment perspective may also help to explain depression (McGuffin, Katz, & Bebbington, 1988) and even divorce (McGue & Lykken, 1992).

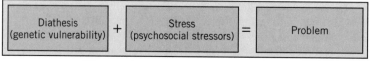

Figure 5.1 The diathesis-stress model.

Psychosocial Influences on Biology

In addition to the notion that biology influences psychosocial issues, an alternate theory suggests that psychosocial factors actually alter biology. For example, research has found that monkeys reared with a high degree of control over their choice of food and activities were not anxious but were aggressive when injected with an anxiety-inducing medication (i.e., a benzodiazepine inverse agonist) that generally causes anxiety compared with a group of monkeys raised with no control over their food and activity choices (Insel, Champoux, Scanlan, & Soumi, 1986). Thus, early rearing experiences greatly influenced how monkeys responded to the effects of medication influencing neurotransmitter activity. Other research has demonstrated that psychosocial influences can alter neurotransmitter circuits (Anisman, 1984). Animals raised with a great deal of exercise and stimulation have been found to have more neural connections in various parts of the brain than animals without an active background (Greenough, Withers, & Wallace, 1990). Other psychosocial factors appear to impact biological functioning as well. For example, social isolation, interpersonal and environmental stress, pessimism, depression, and anger have all been found to be closely associated with the development of various illnesses and even death. These illnesses include cardiovascular disease such as hypertension and heart attacks as well as cancer (see Goleman, 1995 and Shorter, 1994 for reviews). Hostility, for example, has been found to be an independent risk factor for coronary heart disease. It is believed that the heightened physiological arousal associated with chronic feelings of anger may promote problematic atherogenic changes in the cardiovascular system (Miller, Smith, Turner, Guijarro, & Hallet, 1996).

Development of the Biopsychosocial Perspective

In 1977, George Engel published a paper in the journal *Science* championing the **biopsychosocial** perspective in understanding and treating physical and mental illness. This perspective suggests that all physical and psychological illnesses and problems have biological, psychological, and social elements that require attention in any effective intervention. The biopsychosocial perspective further suggests

that the biological, psychological, and social aspects of health and illness influence each other. The biopsychosocial perspective has been accepted in both medicine and psychology with research support demonstrating its validity (Carmody & Matarazzo, 1991; Miller, 1987). The biopsychosocial perspective became the foundation for the field of health psychology in the early 1980s (Schwartz, 1982), and has quickly become an influential perspective in clinical psychology (Lam, 1991; Levy, 1984; McDaniel, 1995; Sweet, Rozensky, & Tovian, 1991). It is important to mention that the biopsychosocial approach is not another term for the medical model. Nor is it another term for a biological approach to psychology and clinical problems.

The biopsychosocial approach is contextual and states that the interaction of biological, psychological, and social influences on behavior should be addressed in order to improve the complex lives and functioning of people who seek professional health and mental health services (Engel, 1977, 1980; Lam, 1991; McDaniel, 1995; Schwartz, 1982, 1984). The biopsychosocial framework applies a systems theory perspective to emotional, psychological, physical, and behavioral functioning (Levy, 1984; Lam, 1991; McDaniel, 1995; Schwartz, 1982, 1984). The "approach assumes that all human problems are biopsychosocial systems problems; each biological problem has psychosocial consequences, and each psychosocial problem has biological correlates" (McDaniel, 1995, p. 117). Miller (1978), for example, discussed seven levels of systems, each interdependent on the other. These include functioning at the cellular, organ, organism, group, organization, society, and supernatural levels. Furthermore, Miller outlined 19 additional sublevels present at each of the major 7 levels of functioning. Dysfunction at any level of functioning leads to dysregulation, which in turn results in dysfunction at other levels. Thus, changes in one area of functioning (such as the biological area) will likely impact functioning in other areas (e.g., psychological area). For example, chemical imbalances might occur at the cellular level in the brain, which leads to mood dysfunction in the form of depression. The depressive feelings may then lead to interpersonal difficulties that further impact job performance and self-esteem. Stress associated with these problems at work and home may then lead to further brain chemical imbalances and further depression. Similarly, in an adolescent, Japanese-American female with anorexia nervosa, the intimate interaction between (a) psychological needs for control and mastery, (b) cultural expectations of thinness in women and achievement in Japanese-American culture, combined with (c) pubertal hormonal changes, all conspire to create a dysregulated system with biological, psychological, and social factors compounding and contributing to the dysfunction of each other. Thus, the systems perspective of the biopsychosocial perspective highlights the mutual interdependence of all systems. The biopsychosocial perspective is holistic in that it considers the whole person and specifically, the holistic interaction of biological, psychological, and social influences.

Application of the Biopsychosocial Perspective to Contemporary Clinical Psychology Problems

The biopsychosocial perspective is generally viewed as a useful contemporary approach to clinical psychology problems (Fig. 5.2, Lam, 1991; McDaniel, 1995). It will be helpful now to illustrate how this multidimensional, systemic, and holistic approach is employed with the complex problems faced by clinical psychology and related disciplines.

Biopsychosocial Model

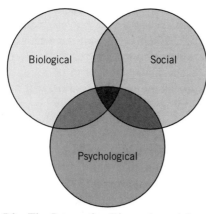

Figure 5.2 The Integrative Biopsychosocial Perspective

Obsessive-Compulsive Disorder

Obsessive-Compulsive Disorder (OCD) is an anxiety disorder involving obsessions (recurrent and persistent thoughts, images, impulses) and compulsions (repetitive behaviors such as hand washing, checking, ordering, or acts) (American Psychiatric Association, 1994). Frequent obsessions might include wishing to hurt oneself or others, or fear of contamination through contact with germs or others. Compulsions might include repeatedly checking to ensure that the stove is turned off or that the door is locked, constantly washing hands to avoid germs and contamination, or performing bizarre rituals. OCD occurs among approximately 3 percent of the population (American Psychiatric Association, 1994). However, milder forms of obsessions and compulsions that are not severe enough to be considered a disorder commonly occur among many people. OCD tends to be more common among males than females and symptoms generally first appear during adolescence or early adulthood (American Psychiatric Association, 1994).

Brain imaging techniques have failed to find structural differences between those with and without OCD. However, research has found that OCD patients have hyperactivity in the orbital surface of the frontal lobe, the cingulate gyrus, and the caudate nucleus (Breiter, Rauch, Kwong, & Baker, 1996; Insel, 1992). Furthermore, the neurotransmitter, serotonin, appears to be particularly active in these areas of the brain. OCD patients are believed to have less serotonin available than nonOCD controls. It is, however, unclear what causes these brain differences. Does the biology impact the behavior or does the behavior impact the biology? In other words, does the activity of neurotransmitters in certain sections of the brain cause people to develop OCD symptoms or do the symptoms themselves alter brain chemistry? Research evidence suggests that there may be an interaction (Baxter, et al., 1992; Insel, 1992). For example, evidence has shown that a person can develop OCD following surgery to remove a brain tumor in the orbital frontal area of the brain (Insel, 1992). Thus, a specific trauma to the brain can result in OCD in individuals never troubled by obsessions or compulsions. Evidence has also shown that psychological interventions such as the cognitive-behavioral techniques of exposure and response prevention can alter brain circuitry

(Baxter et al., 1992). Thus, an interaction between biological and psychological influences is likely to create or reduce OCD behavior. Additionally, social influences such as culture, religious faith, and social support influence the nature, course, and prognosis of OCD (Greist, 1990; Insel, 1984, 1992; Riggs & Foa, 1993). Current treatments may involve a biopsychosocial approach that includes a drug such as Prozac that inhibits the reuptake of serotonin; neurosurgery (in extreme cases); cognitive-behavioral psychotherapy using exposure and response prevention techniques; social support and education through psychoeducational groups; and psychotherapy, which may include marital and/or

---

Biopsychosocial Case Study: Obsessive-Compulsive Disorder in Hector

Brief identifying information: Hector is an eighteen-year-old first generation Mexican–American living with his immigrant parents, two sisters, and maternal grandmother. Hector has recently completed high school, and has deferred his acceptance to a university due to the severity of his current symptoms. Hector's first language is Spanish, and he is also fluent in English.

Presenting Problem: Hector suffers from an obsessive-compulsive disorder that first emerged at age fourteen. His symptoms involve fears of contamination through contact with germs, blood, or other people. His fears compel him to wash his hands excessively throughout the day, disinfect his room at home, repeatedly cleanse any foods he consumes, wear gloves in public, and refuse to use public restrooms or restaurants. Hector's symptoms have greatly interfered with his social life, and he is largely isolated from peers or others outside of his immediate family. He is underweight due to his fear of many food items' safety and because of the extensive rituals he performs to cleanse anything he consumes. He also expresses some depressive symptoms in light of his feeling a prisoner to his obsessions and compulsions and due to their negative impact on his social and career goals.

Biological Factors: Hector's family history is positive for several paternal relatives having symptoms suggestive of obsessive-compulsive disorder, and research strongly supports a prominent biological/genetic role in the etiology of this disorder. Therefore, abnormalities in neurochemistry may be contributing greatly to his debilitating obsessions and compulsions.

Psychological Factors: Hector has always had a cautious personality, marked by a desire for order and predictability and a perfectionistic style. His ability to achieve success through highly ordered, careful, and perfectionistic behavior has ultimately served to reduce anxiety and enhance his self-esteem and family's pride in him. His high need for control extends into his grooming, exercising, eating, socializing, and academics.

Social Factors: Hector's family-centered upbringing has nurtured his increasing desire to stay within his home, to perform well, to aspire toward educational achievement and career success, and to feel a deep attachment to his family and Mexican heritage. Due to his parents' experience as primarily Spanish speaking immigrants, he shares their suspicion of mental health professionals and other services that are perceived as having "official" or government ties.

Biopsychosocial Formulation and Plan: Hector's significant family history of obsessive-compulsive behavior speaks to a strong biological/genetic vulnerability to obsessive-compulsive disorder. While viewed by many as primarily a biological disorder, both psychological and social factors and interventions are essential to any successful treatment with Hector. Both his personality style and stressful school environment and social context that encourages achievement, home life, and suspicion of mental health professionals may subtly impact the course and treatment of Hector's obsessive-compulsive symptoms.

Treatment should involve a comprehensive approach sensitive to the experience of Mexican–Americans and immigrants, and should involve a bilingual clinician to assist communication with Hector's parents and extended family members. Treatment might incorporate medication to decrease obsessive-compulsive impulses and behavior as well as cognitive-behavioral techniques such as exposure, response prevention, thought stopping, relaxation, and problem-solving to manage symptoms and to learn new adaptive skills. Psychoeducational group therapy may be used to help Hector learn more about the disorder as well as obtain group support from others experiencing similar problems. Psychotherapy might assist Hector to better understand and cope with his struggles, discuss feelings of anxiety, depression, and alienation, and obtain additional support. Family consultation might also assist in providing an optimal treatment approach by helping family members better understand Hector's condition.

family counseling as well as supportive and insight-oriented approaches (Koran, Thienemann, & Davenport, 1996). A biopsychosocial perspective of OCD has been developed and illustrated by Barlow (1988) and is found in Figure 5-3.

Panic Disorder and Anxiety

Anxiety related panic disorder provides another useful application of the biopsychosocial perspective. While everyone has experienced anxiety at various times in their lives, some experience full-blown panic attacks. Panic attacks are characterized by an intense fear that arises quickly and contributes to a variety of symptoms including heart palpitations, sweating, chest pain, shortness of breath, dizziness, and depersonalization (American Psychiatric Association, 1994). While intense fear can be an adaptive mobilizing response in the face of real danger (e.g., preventing a car accident or running away from an assailant), people with panic attacks have a maladaptive response to an imagined threat that often prevents them from engaging in a variety of activities most people take for granted, such as grocery shopping, traveling over bridges, or leaving

their home to run errands in a car. About 4 percent of the population experience panic disorder with onset typically occurring during adolescence or early adulthood (American Psychiatric Association, 1994). Although panic disorder is found throughout the world, symptoms manifest differently depending on the cultural context.

Biopsychosocial factors influence the development, maintenance, and prognosis of panic behavior (Roth, 1996). First, evidence suggests that a combination of genetic factors make some people vulnerable to experiencing anxiety or panic attacks (Barlow, 1988). Furthermore, neurotransmitter activity, specifically the influence of gamma amino butyric acid (GABA), serotonin, and norepinephrine, have been associated with people who experience panic (Deakin & Graeff, 1991; Gray, 1991). Neurotransmitter activity in the brain stem and midbrain have been implicated (Gray, 1991). Second, psychological contributions to the development of panic involve learning through modeling (Bandura, 1986) as well as emotionally feeling out of control of many important aspects of one's life (Barlow, 1988). Cognitive explanations and situational cues also appear to contribute to panic (Clark, 1988; Roth, 1996). For example, heart rate increases due to exercise or excitement may result in fear that panic is imminent. Panic sufferers are thus more vigilant regarding their bodily sensations. This awareness fuels further panic, resulting in a cycle of anxiety. Panic thus becomes a learned alarm (Barlow, 1988). Finally, social factors such as family and work experiences, relationship conflicts, and cultural expectations may all contribute to the development and resolution of panic. Thus, biological vulnerability coupled with psychological and social factors create the conditions for fear and panic to occur. A biopsychosocial perspective of panic has been developed by Barlow (1988) and is illustrated in Figure 5-4.

Treatment for panic also reflects the biopsychosocial nature of the disorder. Medications that impact the serotonin and norepinephrine neurotransmitter systems such as tricyclic antidepressants (e.g., imipramine) as well as benzodiazepines (e.g., Xanax) are often used (Klosko, Barlow, Tassinari, & Cerny, 1990; Roth, 1996) in conjunction with psychological treatments that involve gradual exposure to the feared situations, relaxation train-

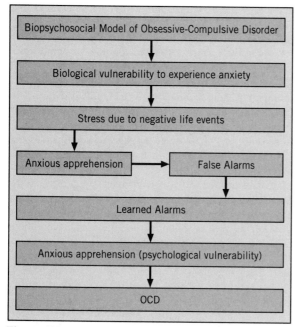

Figure 5.3 Biopsychosocial perspective of obsessive-compulsive disorder according to Barlow (1988)

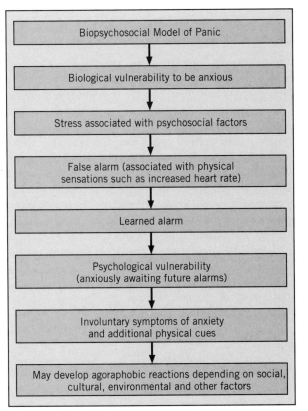

Figure 5.4 Biopsychosocial perspective of panic according to Barlow (1988)

ing, breathing exercises, cognitive therapy, and both insight-oriented and supportive psychotherapy (Barlow, 1988; Barlow & Craske, 1989; Craske, Brown, & Barlow, 1991; Klosko et al., 1990). Group treatment, contact with social support systems and access to community resources also may provide a social component in treatment.

In addition to panic disorder, less severe forms of anxiety that are experienced by many can also be viewed from a biopsychosocial perspective. School phobia, separation anxiety, posttraumatic stress disorder and other anxiety-based problems pose frequent clinical challenges. For example, many students experience test anxiety. Test anxiety not only results in feelings of intense discomfort prior to completing examinations but can also significantly impact performance. Some students are so anxious prior to an examination that they have difficulty sleeping and eating prior to the test. Some even routinely vomit. Biological vulnerability to anxiety

as previously discussed is also a factor for many who experience test anxiety. They often tend to be more anxious in general and have family members who are anxious. This anxiety creates problems with bodily functioning such as eating and sleeping, which contributes to further anxiety about an exam in that they may feel more vulnerable to failure because they have been unable to sleep and eat. Psychological factors such as fear of failure, low self-esteem, depression also contribute to test anxiety. Social factors such as expectations from parents, cultural norms, minority or language differences, and comparison to peers, siblings, and others may further increase anxiety.

Cardiovascular Disease

In addition to common mental health problems such as obsessive-compulsive disorder, anxiety and depressive disorders, and schizophrenia, the use of the biopsychosocial perspective in clinical psychology has been effectively extended to understand and treat major medical diseases. Thus, clinical psychologists are now involved in disorders that fall directly under the purview of medicine. Cardiovascular disease provides an excellent example of the biopsychosocial perspective's utility for clinical psychology in better understanding, preventing, and treating this problem. Cardiovascular disease (CVD) is the nation's number one killer, having been the leading cause of premature death in the United States since the 1930s (Jenkins, 1988). As mentioned earlier, it has been estimated that 50 percent of the top ten causes of all deaths are due to lifestyle factors such as smoking, drinking alcohol, high fat diets, and sedentary lifestyles (U.S. Department of Health and Human Services, 1985a; Taylor, 1995). These lifestyle factors are especially closely associated with the development of CVD (Krantz, Contrada, Hill, & Friedler, 1988). In addition to lifestyle factors, personality, anger, anxiety, family medical history, and gender also contribute to CVD (Barlow, 1988; Contrada & Krantz, 1988; Jorgensen, Johnson, Kolodziej, & Schreer, 1996; Thoresen & Powell, 1992). Even how one responds to stressful life events may contribute to CVD, as high stress responsivity has been reported to be an independent risk factor for the development of hyperten-

Biopsychosocial Case Study: School Phobia in Nicole

Brief Identifying Information: Nicole is a nine-year-old Caucasian female who lives with her mother. Nicole's father has never lived with the family and has not been in contact for many years. Nicole is a fourth grade student at an urban elementary school and her mother works as an assistant at a veterinary hospital. Nicole and her mother moved to the city within the past year.

Presenting Problem: For the past several weeks, Nicole has increasingly refused to attend school. Initially, Nicole claimed illness in order to stay home, but lately has been tearfully refusing to go to school because she "wants to stay home" and is "scared to go back" to her classroom. Her mother has been forced to take time off from work, and occasionally enlists neighbors to stay with Nicole when she has to work. School officials are insisting that Nicole return to school immediately or begin a program of home tutoring.

Biological Factors: Nicole has always been an anxious child who had difficulty with separation and new experiences. While her mother is unaware of any family history of anxiety disorders, she claims that Nicole has seemed "edgy" and "fearful" from "day one". Nicole's diet is significant for her lack of appetite—excessive consumption of caffeine-rich cola beverages (approximately 6 cans per day)—and she also complains of sleep difficulties.

Psychological Factors: Nicole is deeply attached to her mother who works full time. Her mother finds it challenging to parent such a needy child. Nicole is beset by ongoing anxiety, particularly in response to separation experiences such as going to school and sleep overs at friends' homes. She has numerous strengths, such as her high intellect, loving nature, and artistic skill. She has poor self-esteem, and is riddled with feelings of inadequacy.

Social Factors: Nicole lives and attends school in an urban environment. Having moved to the city only recently, Nicole and her mother feel relatively isolated and feel tentative in a big city with significant crime and hustle bustle. Nicole's relatives all live in distant cities, and her mother's work demands have limited their ability to make social or community connections.

Biopsychosocial Formulation and Plan: Nicole, who may or may not have a biological tendency toward anxiety, is certainly not benefitting from the high levels of caffeine she is consuming. Caffeine may be contibuting to some degree to her sleeplessness, low appetite, and possibly even her anxiety. Most prominent, however, appears to be Nicole's sense of isolation in a new and intimidating environment and her necessary dependence on her single, full-time working mother. By staying home from school, Nicole (perhaps unconsciously) succeeds in securing her mother's presence, or at least the attention of a neighbor. Nicole's school refusal may be inadvertently reinforced by the companionship and attention of her mother and neighbors, as well as by relief from the more challenging aspects of getting to school on public transportation and contending with school demands. The lack of a secure social support network appears to be enhancing her dependency on her mother and generating fearfulness and school refusal.

Treatment should progress in a number of ways. First, a behavioral program should be instituted whereby shaping is utilized to gradually reinforce Nicole's reentry to school. For example, Nicole's mother could spend the first hour of her school day during her first week back at school, then only the first thirty minutes, then only accompany her to school, etcetera. Nicole's successes could be reinforced by special time with her mother, enjoyable experiences with friends, or other desirable incentives. This behavioral plan should be augmented by some supportive psychotherapy to help Nicole express her fears and dependency needs, both verbally and through nonverbal means such as play and drawing. Efforts should also be encouraged for the family to extend their social network, and consultation could be provided to determine available resources and strategies. Nicole's participation in activities (such as group art projects), which can enhance her sense of esteem and competence, would also be beneficial. Finally, all caffeine should be eliminated from Nicole's diet.

---

sion (Jorgensen et al., 1996; Matthews, Woodall, & Allen, 1993). Thus, *how* one responds to stress even when family history, gender, lifestyle, and personality factors are statistically accounted for and controlled is associated with the development of CVD. Furthermore, cultural, occupational, and socioeco-

nomic factors also contribute to CVD. For example, Type A personalities in so-called white collar positions are more likely to develop CVD than Type A personalities in blue collar positions (Eaker, Pinsky, & Castelli, 1992; Haynes, Feinleib, & Kannel, 1980). Women with low levels of education are at

Biopsychosocial Case Study: Cardiovascular Disease in Taylor

Brief Identifying Information: Taylor is a 60-year-old bi-racial male of African-American and Korean heritage who works as a trial lawyer. Taylor has been divorced from his wife for the past three years following a highly contentious settlement and has one adult son who is married with two children.

Presenting Problem: Taylor recently experienced a cardiac arrest after a longstanding history of hypertension. He smokes a pack of cigarettes a day, exercises rarely, and works long hours in a high stress job. His father died of a heart attack in his fifties, and cardiovascular disease is rampant throughout his paternal family history. Taylor's cardiologist has recommended that he make significant lifestyle and behavioral changes in order to maximize his opportunities for medical rehabilitation.

Biological Factors: Taylor's extensive family history of cardiovascular disease and his African-American ethnicity clearly place him at increased risk for hypertension and heart attack. However, Taylor's cigarette smoking, lack of exercise, and stressful work likely exacerbate his medical condition.

Psychological Factors: Taylor manifests the classic Type A personality as a hard-driving, competitive, high achieving, aggressive, time urgent individual. The Type A personality is associated with cardiovascular disease, as are high stress jobs and lifestyles. Thus, Taylor's personality, stressful work, and personal life may be contributing to his health problems. Finally, his smoking and lack of exercise further reflect his tension and poor health.

Social Factors: Taylor's recent divorce and lack of social life outside his work contribute to his high stress level and lack of support. Taylor's biracial ethnicity has prompted him to feel the need to perform exceptionally well in order to succeed as an ethnic minority in the field of law. Finally, Taylor has identified more strongly with his mother's Korean ancestry and traditions, which were actively integrated into the home, and yet has ultimately felt conflicted and alienated from both heritages given his dominantly African-American appearance and love for his father as well.

Biopsychosocial Formulation and Plan: In addition to the regimen of medication and follow-up prescribed by his physician, Taylor would benefit from a number of other interventions as well. While his physician has told him to "stop smoking and start exercising," behavior and life-style are exceedingly difficult to change, and Taylor may well benefit from psychological consultation to develop a smoking cessation and exercise program. Cognitive-behavioral, group and medical (e.g., nicotine patch, nicotine gum) interventions may be combined to assist with smoking cessation, while a behavioral program may be developed in conjunction with an exercise physiologist to develop a gradual build up in exercise.

Psychological intervention would also be useful in contending with Taylor's Type A personality and response to the considerable work and personal stressors in his life, such as cognitive-behavioral, psychoeducational and supportive techniques. Finally, Taylor may benefit from increased social support. Consultation regarding his family relationships, ethnic attitudes and identities, and leisure needs could be beneficial.

---

higher risk for developing CVD than women from higher educational levels (Eaker et al., 1992). African-Americans are twice as likely to develop hypertension than other Americans (Anderson & Jackson, 1987).

Research suggests that those who have an immediate parental history of CVD are more likely to develop CVD as compared to those lacking this family history even when diet, weight, exercise, life stress, and other commonly known correlates of hypertension are statistically controlled (Fredrickson & Matthews, 1990; Jorgensen *et al.*, 1996). For example, it has been estimated that 95 percent of those offspring whose biological parents both experience hypertension will develop hypertension, while 45 percent of offspring with one biological parent demonstrating hypertension will develop the condition (Smith, Turner, Ford, Hunt, Barlow, Stults, & Williams, 1987).

Clearly, biopsychosocial factors play a significant role in the development of CVD. Furthermore, evidence suggests that these factors interact with and influence each other (Barlow, 1988; Carmody & Matarazzo, 1991; Haynes et al., 1980; Sweet et al., 1991). Treatment for CVD's symptons including hypertension, cardiac arrhythmias, postmyocardial infarction, and other cardiac-related diseases reflect the biopsychosocial emphasis. These treatments may include an individualized approach involving surgery, medication, education, lifestyle management, relaxation treatment, biofeedback, psychotherapy, and social support depending upon the diagnosis and progression of the disease as well as the individual needs of the patient and the patient's family (Carmody & Matarazzo, 1991).

Cancer

Cancer is another serious medical problem that is of interest to contemporary clinical psychologists. Principles of the biopsychosocial perspective offer assistance in understanding the disease as well as in developing intervention strategies for prevention and rehabilitation (Andersen, 1996). Cancer is the second leading cause of death in the United States, affecting approximately 25 percent of the population and killing about 600,000 people per year (American Cancer Society, 1989, 1996; Taylor, 1995). Deaths associated with cancer have increased steadily during the past several decades with large increases in lung cancer (especially among women) and both breast and prostate cancer (American Cancer Society, 1996). Cancer is a general term that subsumes more than 100 types of illnesses that have several similarities (Taylor, 1995). These primarily include problems associated with maladaptive cell growth and reproduction programmed by DNA at the cellular level. Some forms of cancer have a well-known etiology such as exposure to cancer-causing toxins associated with poisons and pollutants. The poison DDT, the building material asbestos, as well as cigarette smoke and sun exposure are good examples. However, many forms of cancer develop without known causative factors. Some forms of cancer are easier to diagnose and treat than others and cell growth associated with cancer can be rapid and life threatening or slow and easy to abate. Many forms of cancer are curable when caught and treated early in the development of the disease (McCaul, Branstetter, Schroeder, & Glasgow, 1996).

Biopsychosocial factors interact and contribute to the development of many forms of cancer. First, genetic factors influence the development of many types of cancer. For example, colon and breast can-

cer have been found to be highly associated with genetic factors and tend to run in families. Specific inherited genes have been found to place some people at much higher risk for developing cancer than others. Second, some cancers are related to lifestyle and ethnic factors (American Cancer Society, 1989, 1996; Andersen, 1996). For example, Caucasian men are more likely to develop skin and bladder cancer than nonCaucasians. Women from northern European backgrounds are at much higher risk for developing breast cancer than Asian women. African-American men are at higher risk for prostate cancer, whereas Japanese-Americans are at higher risk for stomach cancer. Third, cancer is related to lifestyle factors such as high fat diets, sunbathing, smoking, alcohol consumption, and sedentary lifestyles (American Cancer Society, 1989, 1996; Fitzgibbon, Stolley, Avellone, Sugerman, & Chavez, 1996; Levy, 1983). Finally, psychosocial factors such as social support, stress, mood (e.g., depression and hopelessness), and even personality (e.g., repressiveness) have been associated with cancer in some studies (Classen, Koopman, Angell, & Spiegel, 1996; Fox, 1988; Kaplan & Reynolds, 1988; Scherg, 1987; Sklar & Anisman, 1981). Although the relationships between all of these biopsychosocial factors and the development of cancer are unclear and even controversial, it appears that biological or genetic vulnerability interacts with life events and environmental factors (e.g., exposure to toxins, stress) to set the stage for the emergence and course of many forms of cancer.

Once cancer develops, the interaction of biopsychosocial factors contribute to the course of the illness. For example, negative emotions have been found to be associated with poorer prognosis among skin and breast cancer patients (Classen et al., 1996; Temoshok, 1987). Depression among smokers leads to poorer outcome than among either nondepressed smokers or nonsmokers (Linkins & Comstock, 1988). Stress has been hypothesized to interfere with DNA repair also resulting in poorer cancer prognosis (Levy, 1983). Furthermore, health promoting behaviors such as healthy diets, exercise, stress reduction; compliance with medical evaluations and treatments; and the minimization of health damaging behaviors such as alcohol and drug consumption, smoking, sunbathing, and exposure to

Biopsychosocial Case Study: Cancer in Marilyn

Brief Identifying Information: Marilyn is a 68-year-old Jewish female who lives with her husband. She has three adult children and four grandchildren. She has been retired from a long career as a high level school administrator.

Presenting Problem: Marilyn has recently been diagnosed with invasive lobular breast carcinoma, a serious form of breast cancer discovered in a very early stage during a routine mammogram. Marilyn's mother died from bilateral lobular breast cancer diagnosed at age 69. Marilyn must decide on a course of treatment: mastectomy without radiation or lumpectomy with radiation and chemotherapy.

Biological Factors: Breast cancer is a disease that tends to run in families. Marilyn's mother's history of the disease places her at increased risk, however unknown environmental and biological factors may also contribute to the development of breast cancer. Genetic concerns will cause her additional worry over her own daughter and three granddaughters.

Psychological Factors: In combatting this fundamentally biological disease, emotional factors weigh heavily in treatment choice, outcome, and even ultimate mortality. First, Marilyn's surgical options are highly personal, and involve feelings related to her sexuality, appearance, and feelings about both surgery and radiation. Second, adjust-ing to the longterm fears and vulnerabilities associated with being a cancer victim poses a significant challenge. Psychoeducational needs also vary among individuals. In Marilyn's case, her desire to be well informed must be integrated into any treatment plan.

Social Factors: Social support has been shown to be a significant factor in outcome and longevity in breast cancer survivors. Both family and group support will be essential to Marilyn's decision making, adjustment and long-term quality of life. Her husband's support will also be critical in Marilyn's adjustment, to the bodily changes associated with surgery, as will the support of her many friendships developed over years of involvement in her temple and Hadassah.

Biopsychosocial Formulation and Plan: Marilyn's treatment would best integrate psychoeducational and social supportive interventions into her medical regimen of surgery, radiation and chemotherapy. A "no-nonsense" type of person, Marilyn would likely benefit from informational access to physicians, libraries, and other breast cancer survivors in both group and individual contexts. Sensitive consultation on the part of medical and mental health professionals could assist Marilyn in making highly personal medical decisions and obtaining needed emotional support from community and family resources.

---

environmental and occupational toxins are often necessary to improve recovery (Andersen, 1996; Fitzgibbon et al., 1996; Levy, 1983; McCaul et al., 1996; Taylor, 1995).

Treatment for cancer also reflects the biopsychosocial perspective. In addition to medical treatments such as chemotherapy, radiation, and surgery, social support and psychotherapy have been found to enhance rehabilitation and even longevity (Classen et al., 1996; Spiegal, Bloom, Kraemer, & Gottheil, 1989). Medical treatment for cancer often has problematic side effects such as nausea and vomiting associated with chemotherapy and a host of problems following surgery such as the loss of bodily function, pain, and fatigue. Cancer patients are understandably often depressed and anxious.

They must learn to cope with both the physical and emotional ramifications of a truly frightening disease. Marital and family relationships and work-related problems also are common among cancer patients. Psychosocial treatments including hypnosis, visual imaging, relaxation training, psychotherapy, group therapy, and peer support have all been used with cancer patients (Andersen, 1992, 1996; Burish & Trope, 1992; Turk & Fernandez, 1990).

Many additional medical problems such as AIDS, arthritis, pain, headaches, and irritable bowel syndrome all involve biological, psychological, and social components in their development, maintenance, and outcome (Gatchel & Blanchard, 1993). These and other medical problems often involve biological vulnerability, environmental stress, personality, culture, and their ultimate interaction. Contemporary clinical psychology, along with traditional medical intervention, is useful in developing comprehensive prevention and intervention approaches for many of these problems.

Conclusion

The biopsychosocial perspective provides invaluable and comprehensive means of understanding and treating a wide variety of physical and emotional problems. Research evidence and clinical practice both tend to support the use of this perspective in treating many types of problems that are of interest to clinical psychologists and other professionals. Human difficulties are certainly complex with unidimensional theories proving less and less fruitful as more information becomes available concerning how people develop problems in their lives. The biopsychosocial perspective serves as an example of a current integrated orientation aimed at managing this complexity by approaching problems in a holistic, systemic, and multidimensional manner.

Case Study of Mary: Biopsychosocial Synthesis

Let us now reexamine the case of Mary from an integrative biopsychosocial perspective.

Biological Factors: Mary may have a biological/genetic predisposition to panic disorder, agoraphobia, and anxiety-related conditions in light of her mother's history of these symptoms and research highlighting this association. She may be prone to experiencing anxiety through intense physiological reactions, especially under certain psychological and environmental conditions.

Psychological Factors: Mary presents a personality profile that places her at risk for anxiety. The sudden death of her father and subsequent loss of her mother due to her grief and anxiety resulted in tremendous emotional vulnerability to loss and separation. This underlying insecurity is further compounded in Mary by her failure to develop an internal sense of competence and developmentally appropriate independence to assist her in traversing life's challenges. Together, Mary experiences both her internal and external worlds as fragile, and is vulnerable to genuine panic away from known safety zones.

Social Factors: Mary's Irish Catholic cultural and religious upbringing has provided both resources and liabilities. First, the traditions, rituals, and strong religious faith of her family and church community have contributed a sense of belonging, meaning, and safety in these contexts. However, her family's emphasis on the common good as opposed to individual development thwarted her separation from home; her cultural context that favored repression over expression of feelings and needs has stifled her expression and development; and her perceived view of the church's teachings as encouraging self-sacrifice and denial of personal needs has perhaps contributed to Mary's inability to develop autonomous coping skills and values. Finally, Mary's role model of womanhood in our society, her mother, perhaps taught her the dependency and fearfulness she herself experiences.

Biopsychosocial Formulation and Plan: Mary's biological vulnerability to anxiety has been spurred into a full blown panic disorder in the context of her personality and cultural development. A multidimensional treatment approach is clearly indicated, and should include the following integrated components:

1. Individual psychotherapy that combines a supportive therapeutic relationship wherein Mary can safely explore her difficulties, work through her losses, and develop enhanced tools for autonomous and competent functioning.

2. Cognitive-behavioral strategies will be essential in assisting Mary with her immediate symptoms of panic, including the techniques of relaxation, exposure, and response prevention.

3. Adjunctive couple's work may be useful in enlisting Mary's husband's support and encouragement for Mary to take on a more healthy and autonomous role without feeling her attachment to her husband (and others) threatened.

4. Utilization of church resources to assist Mary in greater mobility and in addressing some of her religious concerns.

5. Consultation with a psychiatrist may be useful in exploring the possible benefits and side-effects associated with the use of psychoactive medication in treating Mary's symptoms of panic.

The Big Picture

It has become important for contemporary clinical psychologists to heed the call to integration in an increasingly complex field and society. The intelligent and sensitive synthesis of psychological approaches with relevant biological and social factors has led to an increasingly integrative field. While biological, psychological, and social factors may not always share equal weight in either cause or treatment, on a case-by-case basis attention to the delicate interaction between these factors richly informs any study or intervention regarding clinical issues. Biopsychosocial integration in many ways is intimate with contemporary clinical psychology, expanding the range and usefulness of its efforts. As more research evidence emerges concerning the interplay of biological, psychological, and social influences on behavior, contemporary clinical psychologists will incorporate new knowledge to develop better applications in their efforts to help others.

Key Points

1. Today, the vast majority of clinical psychologists identify themselves as being integrative in orientation rather than adhering to one singular theoretical point of view. Clinical psychology has evolved in such a way that one theoretical approach no longer appears to adequately provide a satisfactory theory of human behavior and behavior change for most professionals. Integration of theoretical approachs and available techniques has become the norm rather than the exception.

2. The integration of approaches is a complex and challenging endeavor. Each approach has its own language, leaders, and practices. However, attempts at the integration of these major theoretical approachs tend to occur in one of three ways, which include (1) integrating the theory associated with each approach, (2) developing an understanding of the common factors associated with each approach, and (3) using eclectism in a practical way to provide a range of available techniques to assist others.

3. The biopsychosocial approach is contextual and suggests that the interaction of biological, psychological, and social influences on behavior must be carefully addressed in order to understand the complexities of human behav-

ior and help improve the lives of people who seek professional health and mental health services. The biopsychosocial approach applies a systems theory perspective to emotional, psychological, physical, and behavioral functioning in that each of these areas are intimately related and interdependent.

4. Professionals with a biological viewpoint generally favor biological interventions. Of course, they tend to treat problems suited to this approach. For example, electroconvulsive therapy (ECT) and medications are frequently used to treat depressions, mania associated with bipolar disorder, and schizophrenia.

5. Many clinical psychologists have begun to increasingly focus on the cultural and social influences on behavior that sociologists and anthropologists have been investigating for many years. While most practicing clinical psychologists still primarily work with individuals, couples, and families, rather than large organizations or groups, the influence of issues such as culture, socioeconomic factors, ethnicity, and community have received a great deal of attention concerning their relative contributions to human functioning and variation.

Key Terms

Biological Vulnerability
Biopsychosocial

Diathesis-stress
Integration

For Reflection

1. Why is it harder to conduct research on some of the approachs than others?

2. Which approach has the most research support and why?

3. What are the disadvantages to adherence to one approach?

4. What theoretical approaches have generally been integrated?

5. What are some of the advantages of approach integration?

6. What is the biopsychosocial approach and how does it apply to clinical psychology?

7. What are the advantages and disadvantages of the biopsychosocial approach?

8. Use the biopsychosocial approach to discuss schizophrenia, depression, and cancer.

PART 2

Research, Practice, and Varied Roles and Responsibilities

CHAPTER 6

Research in Contemporary Clinical Psychology: Design and Outcome

Chapter Outline

Highlight of a Contemporary Clinical Psychologist: Alan E. Kazdin, Ph.D., ABPD

Research Methods and Designs

Treatment Outcome Research

Questions and Challenges in Conducting Treatment Outcome Research

Contemporary Issues in Clinical Psychology Treatment Outcome Research

How and Where Is Research Conducted in Clinical Psychology and How Is It Funded?

HIGHLIGHT OF A CONTEMPORARY CLINICAL PSYCHOLOGIST:

Alan E. Kazdin, Ph.D., ABPP

Dr. Kazdin maintains a full-time academic career focusing on research methodology and conduct disorders.

Birth date: January 24, 1945

College: San Jose State University, B.A. 1967 (Psychology/Philosophy)

Graduate Program: Northwestern University, (M.A. and Ph.D. in Clinical Psychology) 1970

Clinical Internship: North Shore Association, Evanston, IL

ABPP: Behavioral Psychology

Current Job: Professor of Psychology and Professor of Child Study (child psychiatry), Yale University, Director, Yale Child Conduct Clinic

Pros and cons of being a clinical psychologist:

Pros: "A career in clinical psychology has an extraordinary number of options. My own area of interest, developmental psychopathology, focuses on understanding adjustment, adaptation, and clinical dysfunction among children and adolescents, and is particularly rich in career opportunities. Among the many highlights are opportunities to work and to collaborate with colleagues from related disciplines (e.g., epidemiology, genetics, psychiatry, sociology) that are critical to understanding psychological processes and their emergence and course. There are many urgent questions for research that have broad implications for individuals and for society at large. My own energies permit consideration of only a few of the exciting topics including aggressive and antisocial behavior, childhood depression and suicidality, and child and adolescent therapy."

Future of clinical psychology: "I hesitate to predict the future of clinical psychology; postdiction is clearly the wiser strategy. Currently, there continues to be significant growth within core areas of psychology including the vast domains of neuroscience, cognition, and memory, to mention a few. Within clinical psychology, improvements in methodology, research quality, and increased accountability in relation to clinical work are additional influences that will direct advances and directions in research."

Typical schedule: "On a typical day, I teach undergraduate or graduate classes, work with graduate and undergraduate students on their projects, work on clinical-research at a clinic I direct, and supervise treatment of children and families. The goals of the Yale Conduct Clinic, the primary site of my research, are to develop effective treatments for aggressive and antisocial (conduct disorder) children and their families, to understand child, parent, and family factors that contribute to treatment outcome, and to trace development of dysfunction over time."

9:00   Teach research methods class for graduate students.

10:00   Class continues.

11:00   Supervise several graduate students working in clinic. Discuss several cases of adolescents with conduct disorders.

12:00   Attend clinical lunch meeting with faculty and graduate students.

1:00   Teach abnormal psychology class for undergraduates.

2:00   Class continues.

3:00   Work on grant concerning conduct disorders.

4:00   Work on grant continues.

5:00   Work on research paper.

6:00   Work on paper continues.

Most people think of psychologists as practitioners who conduct psychotherapy rather than investigators who conduct research. Yet research forms the very foundation of clinical psychology. Basic and applied research provides many of the clues to important questions about diagnosis, treatment, and general human behavior, thus allowing practitioners to implement their techniques and theories with confidence. In fact, psychology is the only mental health discipline that has its roots in academic research rather than in practice. Psychiatry, social work, and marriage and family counseling, for example, all have their roots in practice rather than in research. Even the academic degree awarded in psychology reflects its unique role and foundation in research: the Ph.D. (Doctor of Philosophy) is historically a research degree awarded from an academic department at a university. In contrast, the M.D. (Doctor of Medicine), J.D. (Doctor of Law), and M.S.W. (Master of Social Work) degrees are generally awarded from professional schools at universities and emphasize practice rather than research. Both the scientist-practitioner, or Boulder, model and the scholar-practitioner, or Vail, model of training in clinical psychology emphasize the value placed on conducting research and remaining an informed consumer of research. In many ways the Vail model in psychology, usually associated with the Psy.D. degree, is similar to the professional school degrees awarded in medicine, law, and social work in that emphasis is generally placed on practice and consuming research rather than conducting research. However, research is fundamental to both the science and the practice of clinical psychology regardless of the training model used in graduate school.

Clinical psychologists conduct research in hospitals and clinics, in schools and universities, in the military, and in business settings. Some researchers use questionnaires, whereas others perform laboratory experiments with people or animals. The research may be archival, using data from existing charts or records, or it may involve the study of a single subject over time. Research skills and knowledge are important even for clinical psychologists who do not actively conduct research studies. Those who maintain professional independent practices, for example, must be able to ascertain what new findings and discoveries are worthy of incorporation into their clinical work.

Research is needed not only to better understand human behavior but also to develop psychological assessment techniques and treatment strategies that are reliable, valid, and effective. Nevertheless, as discussed in Chapter 3, tensions have existed between the research and applied interests of psychology since clinical psychology began in 1896. For example, clinicians often feel that researchers conduct studies that are too obscure or irrelevant to be of help with actual patients, while researchers often feel that clinicians provide services that feel right rather than selecting those that are supported by empirical research. Furthermore, researchers often do not provide clinical services in a practice setting, and clinicians often do not conduct empirical research. This situation tends to enlarge the chasm between science and practice.

This chapter will examine the research foundation of clinical psychology and discuss the manner in which research is designed and conducted in clinical psychology. Several important research challenges in clinical psychology will also be highlighted.

Research Methods and Designs

The general goal of research in clinical psychology is to acquire knowledge about human behavior and use this knowledge to help improve the lives of individuals, families, and groups. Clinical psychologists use the scientific method in conducting research activities. The scientific method is a set of rules and procedures that describe, explain, and predict a particular phenomenon. This method includes the observation of a phenomenon, the development of hypotheses about the phenomenon, the empirical testing of the hypotheses, and the alteration of hypotheses to accommodate the new data collected and interpreted.

During the first stage of inquiry, the clinical psychologist must objectively describe a given phenomenon. One important research tool for this purpose is the Diagnostic and Statistical Manual, Fourth Edition (DSM IV), published by the American Psychiatric Association (APA). The manual describes numerous clinical syndromes and lists highly specific diagnostic criteria for each psychiatric problem thus enabling researchers to better ensure that the same criteria are used to describe each popula-

tion studied. The diagnostic criteria describe the thinking, feeling, and behavior associated with a particular clinical syndrome. For example, Table 6.1 outlines the DSM IV diagnostic criteria for a panic attack. The DSM will be discussed in more detail later. While other diagnostic manuals are used such as the International Classification of Impairments, Activities and Participation (ICIDH) and others, the DSM system is most commonly used in the United States and Canada (Mjoseth, 1998).

Once a careful description is constructed, a hypothesis must be developed and tested to adequately explain the behavior of interest. For example, researchers may be interested in learning more about the sexual response changes experienced by patients utilizing Prozac versus Elavil, two very different antidepressants. They may hypothesize that unlike the inhibited orgasms experienced by women taking Elavil, Prozac users do not experience this particular side effect to any noticeable degree. Researchers may be interested in examining the influence of poverty on urban elderly residents' cognitive functioning by measuring their memory and motor performances in comparison to those members of other elderly groups. Once a hypothesis is devel-

Table 6.1   DSM IV Criteria for Panic Attack

A discrete period of intense fear or discomfort, in which four (or more) of the following symptoms developed abruptly and reached a peak within 10 minutes:

1. palpitations, pounding heart, or accelerated heart rate
2. sweating
3. trembling or shaking
4. sensations of shortness of breath or smothering
5. feelings of choking
6. chest pain or discomfort
7. nausea or abdominal distress
8. feeling dizzy, unsteady, lightheaded, or faint
9. derealization (feeling of unreality) or depersonalization (being detached from oneself)
10. fear of losing control or going crazy
11. fear of dying
12. paresthesia (numbness or tingling sensations)
13. chills or hot flushes

Source: American Psychiatric Association (1994). *Diagnostic and Statistical Manual-IV* (DSM-IV). Washington, DC: Author. Reprinted with permission from the American Psychiatric Association.

oped, it must be tested to determine its accuracy and usefulness, and adapted to accommodate consistent and inconsistent research findings. A valid hypothesis can then be used both to explain and to predict behavior. Accurately predicting behavior based on hypotheses becomes an index demonstrating that those hypotheses are indeed valid. Many different types of research experiments and investigations are used to test hypotheses.

Experiments

Conducting an experiment is the fundamental way to utilize the scientific method in answering research questions. For example, suppose we were interested in designing a procedure for reducing student test-taking anxiety. We wish to find out if relaxation or aerobic exercise might be useful in helping to reduce test anxiety prior to a stressful exam. First, a hypothesis is needed. In this case, we may believe that while both aerobic exercise and relaxation might help to lower test-taking anxiety relative to a control (comparison or baseline) condition, the relaxation technique might prove the superior method. Relaxation has been shown to be helpful with other types of fears and anxieties, and it helps to reduce the physiological arousal (e.g., elevated heart rate and blood pressure) associated with anxiety.

Identifying Independent and Dependent Variables
After a hypothesis is proposed, an experiment must be designed to evaluate the hypothesis. The researcher must select both independent and dependent variables. The *independent* variable is manipulated by the researcher and provides the structure for the study. Therefore treatment condition (i.e., relaxation, aerobic exercise, or a control condition) would be the independent variable in the test-anxiety study. The *dependent* variable is the variable that is expected to change as a result of the influence of the independent variable. In other words, the dependent variable is what is measured by the researcher to determine whether the hypothesis can be supported or not. In this case, scores on a test-anxiety scale following treatment might be the dependent variable. Research studies evaluate the influence of the independent variable(s) on the dependent measure(s). The study must be constructed such that all other factors that might influence the dependent variable are controlled, with the excep-

tion of the influence of the independent variable. Thus the experiment must minimize systematic and random error. Error occurs from unforeseen or uncontrolled influences on the dependent measure.

Minimizing Experimental Error   A critical goal of all experiments is to minimize experimental error. *Experimental error* occurs when changes in the dependent variable are due to factors other than the influence of the independent variable. For example, if the experimenter is aware of the hypothesis that relaxation is superior to aerobic exercise in reducing test-taking anxiety, yet conducts both laboratory sessions with the research subjects, his or her biases may influence the results. The experimenter might behave differently toward the subjects in the relaxation condition, perhaps being more friendly to them than to subjects in the exercise or control conditions. This scenario is termed *experimenter expectancy effects.*

The experimenter must minimize potential error or bias by controlling potentially influencing variables (other than the independent variable manipulated by the experimenter). For example, the experimenter might avoid bias in conducting the laboratory sessions by using a research assistant who was unaware of (and uninvested in) the hypotheses of the study. The research assistant might also be instructed to read from a prepared script and wear the same lab coat so that all interactions with each subject are consistent.

Furthermore, the experimenter would minimize potential error or bias caused by unknown or uncontrollable influences by using a randomization procedure. The experimenter randomly varies a variable across experimental and control conditions such that the influence of the variable does not differentially affect one or more of the experimental or control conditions. For example, test-anxious students may differ in the intensity or degree of their anxiety, in their belief that test-anxiety intervention techniques might prove useful to them, in academic performance, and in a host of other variables. Because all of these potentially confounding (influencing) variables cannot be controlled or accounted for in the experiment, the researcher would randomly assign the pool of research subjects to experimental and control conditions. Therefore the potential influence of these variables would be (theoretically) evenly distributed across experimental and control conditions.

Experimenters must use both reliable and valid measures of assessment in research studies as well. *Reliability* refers to the stability or consistency of a measurement procedure. For example, a method for assessing test anxiety should result in similar scores whether the test is administered early in the day, late in the day, or by different research assistants. *Validity* refers to the notion that an instrument should measure what it was designed to measure. An instrument measuring test anxiety should indeed measure the construct we call "test anxiety" rather than other constructs such as depression, general anxiety, or low self-esteem. Any measures used in a research study must demonstrate that they have adequate reliability and validity.

Furthermore, experimenters can make errors in their choice of instruments and in data collection, scoring, and analysis. Objective and precise scoring methods that are both reliable and valid must be designed and implemented to minimize error. Checking and rechecking of coded data, data entry, and data analysis are necessary in order to spot mistakes and ensure that the data are completely free of error.

Maximizing Internal and External Validity Research experiments must be designed not only to minimize experimental error and bias but also to maximize both internal and external validity. *Internal validity* refers to the condition in which only the influence of the independent variable in an experiment accounts for results obtained on the dependent variable. Any potential extraneous influences on the dependent variable (other than the influence of the independent variable) becomes a **threat to** the experiment's **internal validity.** Thus, the experimenter designs a well-constructed and methodologically sound research study to ensure internal validity.

Extraneous variables that may threaten the internal validity of any research study include the effects of history, maturation, testing, instrumentation, statistical regression, selection bias, and experimental mortality (Campbell & Stanley, 1963). **History** refers to events outside the experimental situation (e.g., earthquakes, death of a loved one, marriage) that could have a significant impact on the results of the study. **Maturation** refers to changes

within subjects over the passage of time (e.g., aging; becoming fatigued, bored, or stronger) that may influence the experimental results. For example, students who report that they are test anxious at the beginning of an academic year may feel less anxious as the term proceeds owing to positive experiences with in-class exams. Others may feel more anxious because of negative experiences with in-class exams and stress associated with approaching finals. Someone participating in a lengthy study may become tired and bored and therefore answer research questions differently at the end of the study than at the beginning. **Testing** concerns the influence of the testing or evaluation process itself on research results such as in the use of repeated measures obtained on the same subjects over time. For example, one might answer a series of questions following treatment for test anxiety in a similar manner as prior to treatment due to practice or familiarity effects. **Instrumentation** refers to the influences of the tests and measurement devices used to measure constructs in the study. For example, the test anxiety scale may not be validated for use with the intended population or it may not reliably assess test anxiety. Furthermore, subjects may respond differently on a scale at different periods of the experiment.

Statistical regression concerns the tendency of extreme scores on a measure to move toward the mean over time. For example, subjects who score very high in test-taking anxiety only to score lower at a later date may reflect regression toward the mean rather than a reduction in anxiety associated with treatment. **Selection bias** refers to a differential and problematic selection procedure for choosing research subjects. For example, bias would occur when students selected to participate in the experimental treatment groups on test-taking anxiety are selected from a campus student health clinic while control subjects are selected from an introductory psychology class. Bias occurs since the treatment and control subjects were selected from different populations of students. As discussed earlier, random assignment into experimental and control conditions is usually performed in order to minimize the chance of any selection bias. Finally, **experimental mortality** refers to attrition or subject drop out in an experiment. For example, experimental mortality would be a problem if 50 percent of the subjects in the control condition dropped out of the experiment on test-taking anxiety while only 10 percent of the subjects in the experimental condition did so. Experimenters must evaluate their research designs in order to minimize the influence of these seven threats to internal validity prior to conducting an experiment. If any threat is operating in a research study, results are likely to be uninterpretable and the experimenters will be unable to reach meaningful conclusions based on their data.

External validity refers to the generalizability of the research results. The more similar the research experiment is to a "real world" situation, the more generalizable the findings. However, the more careful an experimenter is about maximizing internal validity, the more likely he or she will minimize external validity. A high degree of control and precision is necessary to minimize experimental and random error and thus maximize internal validity. Therefore, carefully constructed laboratory-based research maximizing internal validity may jeopardize the generalizability (external validity) of the results. For example, in the experiment on test-taking anxiety, all subjects completed the same stressful "IQ" test administered in a laboratory rather than a "real" test such as a final examination in one of their college courses. Allowing subjects in this study to take a real examination would increase the generalizability of the results but compromise the internal validity of the study because course exams cannot be uniform. Some exams are in chemistry, physics, psychology, or business. Exams can be multiple choice, essay, or oral. Furthermore, some exams are scheduled on a Monday, some on a Friday, some in the morning, and some in the afternoon. All these conditions might influence the results if they are not uniform or constant for all experimental and control subjects.

Researchers must carefully examine **threats to external validity** prior to conducting their experiments. These threats include testing, reactivity, multiple-treatment interference, and the interaction of selection biases (Campbell & Stanley, 1963). **Testing** refers to the use of a questionnaire or other assessment device that may sensitize and alter the subject's response and therefore influence the dependent measure. For example, completing questionnaires on anxiety may increase the research subject's experience of anxiety. **Reactivity** concerns the subject's potential response to participating in an experiment. The subject may behave

differently in an experiment than in the natural environment. For example, a subject who knows that he or she is being observed during an experiment may behave in a more socially desirable manner. **Multiple-treatment interference** refers to exposing a subject to several treatment conditions or factors such that the experimenter cannot isolate any specific condition or factors. For example, a subject in the relaxation condition may receive a videotape that presents relaxing music, nature scenes, and instructions in guided imagery and progressive muscle relaxation. So many different treatment influences (e.g., gentle music, pretty images, progressive muscle relaxation instruction, distraction) could be in operation that the isolation of only one influencing factor becomes impossible. Finally, the **interaction of selection biases** concerns the notion that subjects in one group may have been differentially responsive to the experimental condition in some unique manner. For instance, subjects assigned to a relaxation group for test-taking anxiety may enjoy or respond differently than subjects assigned to another treatment condition (e.g., exercise). Responses may be a by-product of their enjoyment of the activity and not due to assumed therapeutic value of the activity itself. Thus, experimenters must carefully evaluate these threats to external validity as well as balance the dual goals of maximizing both internal and external validity prior to conducting an experiment and drawing conclusions based on obtained research data.

Another important threat to external validity includes the specific population sampled and how similar or different the group is relative to the overall population of interest to the researchers. For example, if all of the students in the test-taking anxiety example were middle-class Caucasian college students then the results could not be generalized to include nonmiddle-class Caucasian students or to students in elementary or high school settings. Therefore, researchers must pay careful attention to the population sampled to ensure that the group adequately represents the larger population of interest.

Experimental Designs

There are many different means of carrying out a research experiment. Each approach offers unique advantages and disadvantages. No single approach is superior to another for answering every research question, and all can be rendered useless if not carefully designed and applied. The trick is to use the right **experimental design** with the right research question and to construct each experiment to maximize both internal and external validity.

True Experimental Designs To demonstrate cause-and-effect relationships (e.g., specific treatment may cause improvement in functioning), **true experiments** that use randomization procedures with experimental and control conditions must be conducted, and all efforts made to minimize and control potential error and bias as well as to maximize both internal and external validity. *Randomization* is a procedure where research subjects are selected in such a way that they all have an equal chance of being placed in the different experimental and control groups. No bias can occur in deciding which conditions subjects are placed into during the experiment. In conducting experiments using randomization procedures, the experimenter is best able to determine that outcome measures obtained on the dependent variable must be due to the influence of the experimenter-manipulated independent variable and unlikely due to error or other factors.

However, several unique challenges are associated with such studies in clinical psychology. First, it is often impossible or unethical to randomly assign human beings to certain experimental or control conditions. For example, an experimenter interested in the effects of sexual abuse and maternal deprivation on depression could not randomly assign children to an experimental group in which the children would be either sexually abused or deprived of contact with their mothers. Second, it is often impossible or unethical to assign patients to a control condition in which they do not receive treatment. For example, it would be unethical to assign suicidal patients to a control condition for several months without any form of treatment. Furthermore, many patients would refuse to wait for treatment or knowingly accept a placebo treatment. Third, certain disorders are fairly rare, making it difficult to obtain enough subjects for various experimental and control conditions. For example, an experimenter interested in different treatment approaches for children with trichotillomania (i.e., a disorder that involves compulsively pulling out one's hair) may be unable to find enough subjects

for group-designed research conditions in a timely manner. Fourth, because many patients experiencing psychological distress have several diagnoses, comorbidity (two or more diagnoses) is likely to be the rule rather than the exception. Thus it is often difficult to find people who experience only the specific disorder under investigation. For example, many children with attention deficit disorders also experience depression, oppositional defiant disorder, learning disabilities, low self-esteem, and other problems. An experimenter might think that he or she is treating the attention deficit disorder, whereas the personal contact between child and therapist might actually be treating the depression.

In addition to true experimental designs that include randomization, there are quasi-experimental designs; between, within, and mixed group designs; analogue designs; case studies; correlational methods; epidemiological methods; and longitudinal and cross-sectional designs. Many of these designs are not mutually exclusive. For example, correlational designs can be either longitudinal or cross-sectional, or both. A study can include both between and within group designs. The experimental and quasi-experimental approaches can also use between, within, and mixed group designs. A brief review of each of these alternative designs follows.

Quasi-Experimental Designs When random assignment to experimental and control conditions is not possible because of ethical or other limitations, an experimenter may choose to use a **quasi-experimental** design. For example, a treatment-outcome study conducted at a child guidance clinic must use patients already being treated at the clinic (Plante, Couchman, & Diaz, 1995). Client satisfaction as well as assessment of problematic symptoms are conducted at the beginning, during, and at the end of treatment. Control subjects may include persons not being treated at the clinic or those on a wait-list for treatment. Because the experimenters cannot always decide who can receive treatment and who must remain wait-listed, randomization is impossible. Therefore many important differences between treated children and children not being treated at the clinic may exist and cannot be adequately controlled. Such practical limitations require much more caution in the interpretation of research findings than is the case with true experimental techniques, and direct cause-and-effect relationships cannot be inferred.

Between Group Designs   **Between group** designs use two or more separate groups of subjects, each of which receives a different type of intervention or, in the case of a control condition, no intervention. Therefore the independent variable is manipulated by the experimenter so that different groups of subjects receive different types of experiences. In the test-taking anxiety example, one group of subjects received relaxation, a second group received aerobic exercise, while a third group received a control condition (i.e., magazine reading). Ideally, subjects are randomly assigned to treatment and control conditions in a between group design. The experimenter then assumes that all other factors that could potentially influence the study results (e.g., age, motivation, intelligence, severity of anxiety) will be evenly distributed between the groups. To ensure that potential factors that might influence the results do not differentially affect the experimental and control groups, the experimenter may wish to use a matching procedure. For example, to ensure that gender and age are similar in each experimental and control condition, the experimenter would match subjects such that males and females as well as different ages are evenly distributed across the groups. Or in the test-taking anxiety example, to ensure that the severity of test-taking anxiety is evenly distributed among the groups, the experimenter would match subjects in each group on the basis of the severity of anxiety.

There are several different types of between group research designs. The *pretest-posttest control group design* includes two or more subject groups. While one group receives treatment, the other does not. Subjects are evaluated both before and after treatment on the dimension of interest. For example, a test-anxiety questionnaire might be used both before the treatment begins and after the completion of treatment. Control subjects (i.e., those not receiving treatment) would complete the test-anxiety questionnaire at the same time the experimental group completes the materials. One disadvantage of the pretest-posttest design is that the administration of a pretest might sensitize subjects or influence their response to treatment. A posttest-only control group could be added to control for pretest sensitivity.

Another between group design, the *factorial design,* provides an opportunity to study two or more factors in a given study. Therefore two independent variables of interest (e.g., gender and ethnic background of therapist) can be examined at the same time. For example, treatment might be conducted with four groups: male African-American therapist, female African-American therapist, male Caucasian therapist, female Caucasian therapist. This would be considered a 2 × 2 factorial design. Adding two additional ethnic groups to the design (e.g., Asian-American, Hispanic-American) would create a 2 (gender) × 4 (ethnicity) factorial design. An advantage of conducting factorial designed studies is that the experimenter can examine the role of interactions between factors.

Within Group Designs   **Within group** designs are used to examine the influence of the independent variable (such as treatment) on the same subjects over time. Subjects are not assigned to different experimental and control groups as they are in a between group design but are all assigned to experience the same research procedure, treatment, or protocol. The same patient is examined at different points of time, such as during a baseline or pretreatment period, a treatment intervention period, and a follow-up or posttreatment period. Thus each subject serves as his or her own control. For example, subjects at risk for the development of hypertension were asked to participate in a study to examine their blood pressure and heart rates while they performed different intellectual and cognitive tasks (Plante, Lantis, & Checa, 1997). All subjects had their heart rates and blood pressures taken before, during, and after a series of laboratory experiences. Changes within the same subjects over time allowed the experimenters to study the association between stress and physiological reactivity among hypertensive high risk persons.

There are several within group designs to choose from in conducting clinical psychology research. Since experimenters using within group designs must be especially careful with ordering or sequencing effects, most variations on the design methods attempt to control for these influences. *Ordering effects* refers to the influence of the order in which treatment or experimental conditions are presented to the subjects. The experimental or treatment condition in the *crossover design* switches or "crosses over" during the course of the experiment. Generally two or more groups receive the same treatments; only the order of presentation is altered for each group. The crossover design counterbalances the treatments so that order of presentation is controlled. For example, the hypertension study just discussed (Plante, Lantis, & Checa, 1997) counterbalanced two laboratory stressors (i.e., a stressful IQ test and the Stroop Color Naming test) such that for half the subjects one stressor was presented before the second, while for the other half the second stressor was presented before the first.

Three or more treatments make crossover designs very complicated. These designs are called *multiple-treatment counterbalanced designs.* For example, if three treatments or experimental conditions are used, six counterbalanced presentations are needed. Suppose three different treatment strategies were being used to treat cannabis abuse. These could include behavioral contracting, group therapy, and interpersonal psychotherapy. All subjects would receive the same three treatments, but the order of presentation would be altered so that various subgroups of subjects would receive the treatments in different order. Controlling the order of presentation is necessary because treatment effects could be influenced by which treatment was experienced first, second, or third. If group therapy were provided to all subjects first, it would be difficult to determine if subjects benefited from the behavioral contracting or interpersonal psychotherapy procedures because of carryover or residual effects of the group treatment experience. Table 6.2 outlines the different counterbalanced presentations needed in a three-treatment study.

Table 6.2 Order of Presentation
in a Three-treatment Counterbalanced Design

First	Second	Third
Treatment 1	Treatment 2	Treatment 3
Treatment 2	Treatment 3	Treatment 1
Treatment 3	Treatment 1	Treatment 2
Treatment 1	Treatment 3	Treatment 2
Treatment 2	Treatment 1	Treatment 3
Treatment 3	Treatment 2	Treatment 1
Example:	Treatment 1 (relaxation training)	
	Treatment 2 (aerobic exercise)	
	Treatment 3 (thought stopping)	

Mixed Group Designs **Mixed group** designs include elements of both between and within group designs. In mixed group designs, experiments are constructed in such a way that different groups of subjects receive different treatment or experimental experiences (between group) while subject responses are assessed over time at different phases of the experiment (within group). For example, in the hypertension study mentioned earlier, control groups of subjects who were not at risk for the development of hypertension were also used. Thus, the presence or absence of hypertension risk acted as a between group variable, while the experimental tasks were within group variables. Mixed group designs, which are more complex than between or within group designs alone, are very commonly used in clinical psychology.

Analogue Designs **Analogue** designed studies use procedures, subjects, and measures that approximate a "real life" clinical situation and are usually conducted in a laboratory where experimental conditions can be controlled better than in the natural environment. For example, subjects may or may not be suffering from disorders that are of interest to the experimenter. Procedures may or may not be identical to those used in the natural or clinical environment. Therapists may or may not be licensed mental health providers. The test-anxiety experiment previously mentioned was conducted in a laboratory using a testing condition that was somewhat removed from testing conditions experienced by test anxious students (e.g., final examinations). The subjects were students who identified themselves as being test anxious and who scored high on a questionnaire measuring test anxiety rather than students who sought treatment for the condition at a campus counseling center. Furthermore, the treatment conditions of relaxation training and aerobic exercise were conducted in the laboratory rather than in a more natural setting (e.g., a dorm room or campus apartment, a health club, a clinic). Analogue studies may use trained research assistants to conduct "treatment conditions" and may involve subjects who do not meet specific diagnostic criteria for a particular disorder. The advantages of analogue designs are that they maximize internal validity more effectively than studies conducted in a more natural environment. However, disadvantages include threats to external validity, since generalizability of research findings may be compromised. For example, subjects may respond less genuinely and honestly in a laboratory environment than in a clinical environment, or, treatment provided by research assistants may differ in important ways from treatment provided by licensed clinicians in practice.

Case Studies

A **case study** is an in-depth investigation, observation, and description of a single person or situation. The case study method was the primary technique used by Sigmund Freud and his colleagues to describe cases of hysteria and other problems. For example, Breuer & Freud (1895/1957) described the hysterical symptoms of Anna O. using the case study approach. Case studies are not experiments, because they lack dependent variables, experimenter manipulation of independent variables, and randomized assignment of subjects into treatment and control conditions. Rather, case studies provide an intensive observation of a person and phenomenon that allows for the development of hypotheses and theories. Case studies can be especially helpful for examining a new, rare, or unusual phenomenon or during the early descriptive stages of a research program. Theories developed through case study methods can be tested later with more intensive research designs.

One of the most famous case studies in psychology is the case of Anna O. described by Joseph Breuer and Sigmund Freud (Breuer & Freud, 1895/1957). Anna O. experienced *hysteria,* or what the DSM IV would term a *conversion disorder* today. She was healthy and relatively problem free until she was 21 years old, and caring for her failing father. After several months of care giving, Anna O. developed unusual vision difficulties as well as motor problems with her right arm and legs that could not be explained medically. She also had trouble speaking and developed other symptoms (e.g., headaches, recurrent cough, fear of drinking). She sought treatment from Joseph Breuer, who conducted hypnosis and treated one symptom at a time. Breuer noticed that symptoms disappeared following the hypnosis. The development of both hypnosis as well as psychoanalytic theory (e.g., theories of repression) occurred partly through the case study of Anna O. Specific single-case research designs have been developed to further objectify the case

study method. Empirical experimental procedures applied to single case studies will be briefly reviewed here.

Single Subject Designs Single case designs blend case study and experimental techniques. While these designs offer the scientific rigor of experimental methods, they also allow for practical clinical relevance because they are used with only one patient or case. Therefore clinicians can use these methods to both study and treat individual patients in their practice. Another advantage of the single subject design is its robustness in that it avoids the problems associated with variability among a large number of subjects. Single subject designs use time-series methodologies (Barlow, Hayes, & Nelson, 1984), which require a series of measures conducted on the same person over a period of time (i.e., a pretreatment phase, a treatment phase, and a post-treatment phase). Rather than using a separate control group or control subject, the individual patient acts as his or her own control during the baseline phase when data are collected on a phenomenon of interest without any active treatment or intervention. For example, binge-eating behavior might be assessed in a bulimic patient by using a questionnaire both before, during, and after treatment and during follow-up. Changes in self-reported binge-eating behavior can then be compared to baseline measures in order to document change. Various baseline and intervention phases or conditions can be implemented to examine the short-term and long-term effectiveness of the intervention.

One of the most commonly used single subject designs is the *ABAB design.* The ABAB refers to alternating between baseline (or no treatment) and treatment phases during a single subject intervention for a particular clinical problem. The ABAB is both a single subject design and a within subjects design. It is also referred to as an intrasubject-replication design. Thus an initial baseline period (A) occurs when the problem behavior is assessed without any intervention, followed by a treatment intervention (B), followed by a return to no treatment (A), followed by a second treatment intervention (B). Treatment–no treatment phases can alternate numerous times depending on the needs of the research and/or treatment. For example, a child who has an attention deficit hyperactivity disorder might frequently and impulsively leave his or her seat in a classroom setting. This behavior might be highly disruptive to other students and the teacher and prevent the child from completing classroom assignments. The teacher might use social reinforcement such as praise when the child is behaving appropriately while sitting in his or her chair. The teacher might record the number of times the child leaves the chair without any reinforcement (i.e., A), and then the number of times the problematic behavior occurs while offering the social praise reinforcement (i.e., B). The teacher then withholds reinforcement, continuing to count the frequency of the problem behavior (i.e., A), and then reinstates the social praise reinforcement condition (i.e., B). Collected data (e.g., number of times child left classroom seat without permission) can be tabulated for each baseline and intervention period for analysis of the success of the intervention.

One cautionary note expressed about ABAB designs concerns the ethics associated with withdrawing helpful treatment during the A phases of the design. For example, some children engage in problematic head-banging or other self destructive and aggressive activities that could be highly dangerous if allowed to be untreated during baseline assessment and treatment withdrawal phases.

A second concern regarding ABAB designs is the limitation of focusing on only one problematic behavior. Rarely do patients present with only one specific target behavior. For example, the child mentioned earlier may not only leave the classroom seat but also impulsively and poorly complete assignments, interrupt and disturb other children, and have temper tantrums. An adult who is depressed may also have obsessive-compulsive traits, an eating or sleeping disturbance, suicidal thoughts, relationship conflicts, and alcohol abuse problems. Multiple baseline designs are used when more than one target behavior is evaluated and treated.

An additional problem with the ABAB design is that it is often impossible to withdraw treatment because a new skill has been learned in the "A" condition. Therefore, once a new skill has been learned it may be impossible to "unlearn" it during the "B" condition.

Multiple Baseline Designs With a multiple baseline design, baseline data are collected for all the behaviors of interest. Then treatment is provided for one target behavior while baseline data are still collected on the other behaviors. Treatment intervention might then target a second behavior while continuing or removing treatment for the first behavior. For example, the child with attention deficit disorder mentioned earlier might not complete homework assignments and might also get into frequent fights with other children during recess periods at school. Baseline data such as the daily frequency of these problematic behaviors are tabulated. Reinforcements such as earning points toward a special gift or privilege might be used to target improvement in getting homework assignments completed. Following several weeks of treatment, reinforcement for the homework assignments is supplemented with social praise for playing cooperatively with other children. Social praise is used to improve the child's social behavior for several weeks. Data concerning the frequency of the problematic behaviors are collected continuously throughout the various baseline and intervention periods. If target behaviors do not improve during the intervention periods, new intervention strategies can be developed and implemented later on. Figure 6.1 provides an example of a multiple baseline design used for several children with autism to improve both social interaction and reading skills through tutoring.

Although all single subject designs can provide a great deal of information about treatment for one individual, generalizing and applying the findings to others is of serious concern. Treatment interventions, for example, may work well for one person but not for another. Replication of the interventions aimed at target behaviors would need to be conducted with many others to determine whether generalizability exists. While most single subject study designs such as ABAB are used by professionals with behavioral or cognitive-behavioral orientations, the principles can be extended to assess any range of interventions as well as integrated into biopsychosocial or multimodal approaches.

Multiple baseline designs can be used to investigate two or more behaviors, settings, or individuals. Multiple baseline designs are often used when a return to baseline without reinforcement might prove to be problematic or dangerous. For example, if a child with attentional and impulsivity problems engages in dangerous behaviors such as running into a busy street, it would likely be too dangerous to withdraw reinforcement and risk that the child

Figure 6.1 Multiple baseline results for cooperative behavior among children in several preschool classes

could get injured or killed. A multiple baseline design might be used to first collect baseline data at school and home and then provide reinforcement (e.g., social praise, rewards) at the school setting first, followed by reinforcement at the home setting. Once the reinforcement begins, it is not withdrawn. If reinforcement works, it would be expected that improvements in behavior would be noted in the school environment first, followed by the home environment.

Multiple baseline designs can mix individuals, settings, and behaviors and may withdraw interventions at some levels but not others. For instance, Bay-Hinitz, Peterson, and Quilitch (1994) conducted a study that used a multiple baseline design to investigate the influence of competitive and cooperative games on aggression and cooperative behavior among preschool children. Children from

four different preschool classes were used in the study. Results demonstrate that while cooperative games increased cooperative behavior and decreased aggressive behavior, competitive games increased aggressive behavior and decreased cooperative behavior. Figure 6.2 provides data from this study.

Correlational Methods

The *sin qua non* of experimental research, random-assignment experimental and control conditions, is often impossible to implement in clinical psychology research. Single case study designs are also not feasible in many clinical or research settings. Ethical, legal, and other limitations on experimentation with human beings must be taken into consideration before a research design can be selected. Many of the limitations that prevent experimental methods from being used can be alternatively addressed through the application of correlational methods. **Correlational** designs examine the degree of association between two or more variables. While correlational designs do not allow cause-and-effect conclusions (e.g., treatment cured a problem), they do provide researchers and clinicians useful information concerning the degree of association between constructs of interest. Thus, correlational methods inform the experimenter how closely two or more variables tend to correspond to each other.

Correlations can be either positive or negative. A *positive correlation* refers to two or more variables that move in the same direction. As one variable increases, so does the other. For example, the more depressed someone feels, the more hopeless he or she may feel. Thus depression and hopelessness tend to correlate and in the same direction (i.e., high degrees of depression are associated with high degrees of hopelessness, whereas low degrees of depression are associated with low degrees of hopelessness). The more marital arguments a couple experiences, the more dissatisfied they are with their marriage. The more alcohol one consumes, the more work or school days he or she is likely to miss.

A *negative correlation* refers to two or more variables that move in opposite directions. As one variable increases, the other decreases. For example, the more television a student watches, the less time he or she devotes to studying. Thus television

Figure 6.2 Example of multiple baseline approach for several children with autism

viewing and studying tend to go together in different directions (i.e., a lot of time watching television is associated with little time studying, whereas little time watching television is associated with a lot of time studying). The more depressed someone feels, the less time he or she spends with friends. Therefore negative correlations imply that two or more variables tend to go together in opposite directions.

None of these correlations or associations between variables is perfect. In other words, some variation is expected in all the examples presented. For instance, some couples who tend to have frequent arguments may report high marital satisfaction, while some students who watch a great deal of television may still be able to spend many hours studying. The degree of association between variables is expressed by a correlation coefficient. A *correlation coefficient* is a score ranging from -1.00 to $+1.00$. Scores close to -1.00 reflect a nearly perfect negative correlation, that is, while one variable is high, the other is low. For example, if hours of television watching and studying were assessed in a large class and it was determined that all the students who watched a lot of television studied infrequently while all of the students who did not watch television studied frequently, a perfect -1.00 correlation coefficient would likely surface from the statistical equation that calculates the coefficient. Scores close to $+1.00$ reflect a nearly perfect positive correlation; as scores on one variable increases, so do the scores on the other. Furthermore, a positive correlation also occurs when scores on both variables of interest are low. For example, if scores on depression and scores on hopelessness are assessed in a large group of people, they are likely to be positively correlated. Thus, those who tend to score high on depression are also likely to score high on hopelessness, while those who score low on depression are also likely to score low on hopelessness. When there is no correlation between two variables (e.g., shoe size and intelligence), the correlation is close to .00.

It is important to emphasize that the association between two or more variables does not mean that one necessarily caused the other. Correlation does not imply causality. Thus, television viewing does not necessarily cause inadequate studying, and depression does not necessarily cause hopelessness. Additional variables not assessed in a given experiment or study may operate to influence the correlation coefficient. For example, perhaps unmotivated students watch a great deal of television and spend very little time studying. Perhaps these students would spend very little time studying no matter how much television they watched. Other factors (e.g., interest in the subject matter) may also play a role.

Epidemiological Methods

Clinical psychologists are often interested in the use and results of epidemiological research methods. *Epidemiology* refers to the examination of the incidence or distribution of a particular clinical problem or variable of interest. **Epidemiological** research describes the prevalence and incidence of a particular issue of concern, seeking to answer questions such as "How many people have alcohol problems? How many college students are clinically depressed? How many people have schizophrenia? How many new cases of attention deficit hyperactivity disorder were diagnosed last year? How many adolescent girls have unwanted pregnancies?" Epidemiological data may be collected from a variety of sources including government census, survey approaches, and hospital records. For example, epidemiological research has indicated that approximately 750,000 people die of heart disease each year (American Heart Association, 1993), and that about 10.5 million people in the United States are alcoholics (U.S. Department of Health and Human Services, 1990b). Epidemiological research has shown that approximately 1 percent of the United States population experiences schizophrenia, and between 0.5 percent and 1 percent of female adolescents or young adults experience anorexia nervosa (American Psychiatric Association, 1994). Not only does epidemiological research attempt to accurately estimate the number of people who experience certain problems, but it also tries to provide detailed information concerning other demographic characteristics of interest (e.g., ethnic, economic, age, or gender differences in those who have heart attacks before age 55). Data from epidemiological research is usually collected from government documents and records, hospital and clinic records, national polls, generalized from large scale multisite research projects and other sources of information usually outside of the controlled laboratory experiments.

Cross-Sectional and Longitudinal Designs

Experimental, correlational, epidemiological, and even single case designs can be constructed to be cross-sectional or longitudinal. Many studies can incorporate both cross-sectional and longitudinal methods into the same investigation and are called cross-sequential designs. **Cross-sectional** designs provide a "snapshot" view of behavior at a given moment in time. Most of the research in clinical psychology as well as most other areas of psychology applies cross-sectional methods because they are generally easier and less expensive to complete. The study on test-taking anxiety mentioned earlier is an example of a cross-sectional research design. Test-anxious subjects were provided laboratory "treatment" and then participated in a simulated "IQ test" during one brief laboratory session. The study provided a snapshot view of test-anxious students to determine whether a brief treatment might be useful in reducing anxiety during one isolated laboratory session. **Longitudinal** designs generally collect research data over a long period of time. Examining test-anxious subjects throughout the course of their high school and college education would be an example of a longitudinal design method. In this example, levels of test-taking anxiety would be assessed periodically during high school and college and thus would take approximately eight years to collect.

Suppose a clinical psychologist were interested in determining whether the development of hypertension (high blood pressure) was associated with a person's reaction to stress over time. Using a cross-sectional approach, the psychologist might take self-report and physiological (e.g., blood pressure) measures during a stressful laboratory procedure. He or she might be interested in determining whether hypertensive patients experience greater reactivity to the laboratory procedure than do nonhypertensive control subjects. On the other hand, a researcher who decided to use a longitudinal approach might assess a random group of people on their self-reported and physiological responses to laboratory stress periodically for many years. Then the researcher would determine which subjects developed hypertension and which subjects did not. The researcher would then determine whether earlier measurements could have predicted the later development of hypertension. While longitudinal designs can be extremely useful, their cost and other limitations often make this type of research difficult to conduct.

Treatment Outcome Research

Clinical psychologists conduct research to answer questions on the development of reliable and valid assessment instruments, on strategies to better understand and diagnose clinical syndromes, and on predicting problematic behavior such as aggression and suicide. But perhaps the most frequently asked and compelling research questions concern treatment outcome: Does psychotherapy work? Which type of therapy works best for which type of condition? Is longer-term treatment better than shorter-term treatment? Which therapist characteristics are associated with treatment success? Which patient characteristics are associated with treatment success? A great deal of research in clinical psychology attempts to answer one or more of these questions. Treatment outcome research has become critical in recent years. Although treatment outcome research has been conducted for many years, the changes in the health care delivery and reimbursement systems have demanded that treatment outcome research demonstrate that psychological and other forms of

treatment do indeed work and therefore justify the expenditure of funds.

To conduct research on treatment outcome, different strategies are employed depending on the specific question of interest. Kazdin (1991) outlined seven **treatment outcome research strategies** for effectively evaluating treatment outcome research. These include treatment "package" strategy, dismantling treatment strategy, constructive treatment strategy, parametric treatment strategy, comparative treatment strategy, client and therapist variation strategy, and process research strategy (Table 6.3). Each method will be briefly described in the following section.

Treatment Package Strategy

The **treatment** package strategy approach attempts to answer the basic question, "Does treatment work?" This approach seeks to determine whether a specific treatment is effective for a specific clinical problem or disorder. In this approach, a treatment package is usually employed, while a control condition such as a no-treatment control or a wait-list control group is used for comparison. *Package* refers to the fact that most treatment approaches include a variety of potentially helpful components. For example, relaxation training might include the learning of specific breathing techniques, muscle relaxation techniques, and visual imagery techniques, as well as problem-solving strategies to use

Table 6.3 Treatment Outcome Research

Treatment Outcome Research Strategy Approaches	Questions Attempted to Answer
Treatment	"Does treatment work?"
Dismantling	"What aspect of treatment works?"
Constructive	"What might be added to an effective treatment to make it even more effective?"
Parametric	"What aspect of treatment can be altered to make treatment work better?"
Comparative	"Which treatment approach works better?"
Client and therapist variation	"Which type of therapist or which type of patient is treatment most likely to be effective?"
Process	"How does the actual process of therapy impact treatment outcome?"

Source: Kazdin, A. E. (1991). Treatment research: The investigation and evaluation of psychotherapy. In M. Hersen, A. E. Kazdin, & A. S. Bellack (Eds.), *The clinical psychology handbook, second edition.* New York: Pergamon.

the techniques on a daily basis. A package approach does not isolate one or several highly specific components that are believed responsible for the positive therapeutic effects. Because many nonspecific factors (e.g., attendance at sessions, belief that therapist is helpful and knowledgeable) could also be involved in patient improvement, researchers usually include a control condition that involves some form of *pseudotreatment.* A pseudotreatment might involve many aspects of real treatment (e.g., meeting with a mental health professional in a professional setting, discussion of problems, regular sessions) but would not involve what the researchers believe are the active ingredients of treatment (e.g., specific techniques or strategies). For example, suppose researchers conducting the test-anxiety study mentioned earlier wanted to know if relaxation training actually helped test-anxious students reduce anxiety. One group might receive relaxation therapy including instructions on specific techniques presented on videotape. Another group might watch a videotape that had pleasant pictures and music but no specific instructions on how to use relaxation techniques. A third group might receive nothing. Additional groups could be used to determine if other strategies helped to reduce anxiety.

Dismantling Treatment Strategies

Dismantling treatment strategies attempt to answer the question, "Which aspect of treatment works?" The focus of dismantling treatment strategies is to identify the active ingredient of a particular treatment strategy after the treatment has been determined effective. To conduct a dismantling research study, different patients or groups of patients receive different aspects of a given treatment. Some may receive the entire treatment, while others receive the treatment without an important component. For example, interpersonal psychotherapy has been found to be helpful in treating patients with binge-eating disorder (Agras, Telch, Arnow, Eldredge, Detzer, Henderson, & Marnell, 1995; Wilfley, Agras, Telch, Rossiter, Schneider, Cole, Sifford, & Raeburn, 1993). A dismantling strategy might include one group that receives standard interpersonal psychotherapy conducted by a licensed psychologist in a clinic setting. Another group might

receive the same treatment, conducted by a fellow group member in a self-help format. A third group might receive the same treatment but use a workbook rather than an actual treatment provider. Therefore the therapist role is examined using a dismantling strategy to determine if experience, training, and face-to-face contact are necessary for interpersonal psychotherapy to work in the case of binge eating. The dismantling strategy thus seeks to determine the basis for change during treatment.

Constructive Treatment Strategies

Constructive treatment strategies attempt to answer the question, "What might be added to an effective treatment to make it even more effective?" The constructive treatment approach adds various components to the treatment to determine whether the additions will improve treatment outcome. For example, interpersonal treatment for binge eating might be enhanced if the treatment also included additional sessions with family members or a reading list for patient use. Furthermore, adding cognitive-behavioral treatment to the interpersonal therapy may be helpful (Agras et al., 1995). One group of patients might receive the standard treatment, while others receive the standard treatment with different additional components. The constructive treatment approach allows the researcher to empirically construct a treatment package by adding new components piece by piece.

Parametric Treatment Strategy

The **parametric** treatment strategy seeks to answer the question, "What aspect of treatment can be altered to make treatment work better?" This approach changes a specific aspect of the treatment to determine whether the change can enhance treatment effectiveness. Often the parametric approach involves altering the treatment time or intensity. For example, interpersonal therapy for binge eating might be enhanced (i.e., fewer symptoms following treatment and client reported satisfaction with treatment) if the standard treatment were conducted for a longer period (e.g., 90 minute sessions instead of 60 minutes, 20 weeks of treatment instead of 12 weeks) or with scheduled follow-up sessions.

Thus, a parametric treatment strategy might include a group of patients receiving standard treatment while another group receives longer and more intense treatment.

Comparative Treatment Strategy

The **comparative** treatment strategy attempts to answer the question, "Which treatment approach works better?" This approach generally compares different strategies for producing change in a clinical problem. For example, a comparative treatment approach to binge-eating might include a group receiving cognitive-behavioral psychotherapy, a second group receiving interpersonal psychotherapy, and a third group receiving a combination of both cognitive-behavioral and interpersonal psychotherapy. Each group of patients would be evaluated to determine if symptoms were reduced more in one group relative to the others.

Client-Therapist Variation Strategy

The **client-therapist** variation strategy seeks to answer the question, "With which type of therapist or for which type of patient is treatment most likely to be effective?" Thus, the client-therapist variation strategy alters the types of therapists or patients to determine which combinations optimize treatment outcome. For example, would treatment work better if the therapist were of the same gender, sex, or ethnicity as the patient? Might treatment outcome improve if the therapist has also experienced the disorder first-hand (e.g., sponsors in Alcoholic Anonymous)? Might treatment be more effective if the patient is highly motivated rather than only moderately motivated?

Process Research Strategy

Finally, the **process** research strategy attempts to answer the question, "How does the actual process of therapy impact treatment outcome?" This research approach seeks to determine which aspects of the psychotherapeutic process are associated with positive treatment outcome. The process approach might attempt to answer specific process questions such as, "What makes a satisfying and productive session between a therapist and patient?" For exam-

ple, patient hostility, therapist friendliness, and level of patient disclosure might affect treatment process and outcome.

Questions and Challenges in Conducting Treatment Outcome Research

Conducting treatment outcome research is extremely challenging. Problems associated with the design, implementation, and interpretation of research results are common to this realm of research. Several common questions regarding treatment outcome research will be briefly reviewed here.

Is a Research Program's Treatment Similar to the Treatment in Actual Practice?

To conduct an effective research study, a great deal of control and precision are needed to determine whether changes in the dependent variable are due to the manipulation of the independent variable. Therefore, research strategies must be employed very carefully in any study. However, treatment designed for a research study may or may not be typical of the treatment provided in the professional community. For example, suppose a researcher wished to compare cognitive-behavioral therapy with psychodynamic therapy for a particular clinical population such as obsessive-compulsive disorder. To ensure that patients receive the same type of therapy, the researcher might use treatment manuals and instruct the therapists participating in the study never to deviate from the manual as they work with obsessive-compulsive research subjects and patients. To ensure that the therapists do not deviate from the treatment manuals, sessions might be videotaped and evaluated by trained experts. To control the duration of treatment for the two groups, each therapist might be required to see the patients for 12 consecutive weeks (1 session per week) and terminate treatment on the 12th session. These strict limitations generally do not occur in actual clinical practice. Patients may often be seen for longer or shorter lengths of time; integrative treatment approaches using, for example, both psychodynamic and cognitive-behavioral techniques are common in actual practice; videotaping of sessions rarely occurs in most practices; and participation in a research study in and of itself might alter the patient's perception of the treatment. Therefore results from the study may not be generalizable. Researchers must design studies that approximate the real world of practice as much as possible in order to maximize the external validity of their study, while monitoring experimental control to maximize its internal validity.

Are the Patients and Therapists Used in a Research Study Typical of Those in Actual Practice?

A patient who is willing to receive treatment provided in a research study may or may not be typical of someone who seeks treatment privately through the services of a mental health professional in the community. Often patients who agree to participate in a research study are able to get professional services at no cost or may even be paid to participate. These financial incentives may or may not result in securing a pool of research patients that are typical of the patient population at large. Furthermore, research studies often need to be very specific about the criteria used to select patients for the study. For example, if a researcher is interested in studying obsessive-compulsive disorder, he or she may wish to secure a patient subject pool that meets the DSM IV diagnostic criteria for obsessive-compulsive disorder without also having other coexisting psychiatric problems (e.g., depression, personality disorder, eating disorder). While selectivity in deciding who should participate in the research project enhances the internal validity of the study, the resulting subjects may or may not be representative of patients with obsessive-compulsive disorder in the general population.

Similar concerns exist regarding the selection of therapists. Therapists participating in the study may or may not be representative of therapists in the community providing treatment. For example, research experiments may use licensed mental health professionals working in a hospital, clinic, or university setting or research assistants with no professional license to practice. Research studies often use clinicians who are primarily researchers rather than clinicians. Researchers may use thera-

pists with highly specialized treatment approaches (e.g., hypnosis for pain control) that may not reflect the type of approaches the average clinician in the community might choose to use. Again, efforts to enhance internal validity may compromise external validity. Therapist characteristics such as age, gender, ethnicity, experience, warmth, orientation, and other factors must be taken into consideration as well.

How and When Is Treatment Outcome Measured?

The assessment of treatment outcome is much more complicated than, at the end of treatment, merely asking patients if they feel better or are no longer troubled by specific problems. Bias and demand characteristics may operate in effecting how a patient or therapist perceives the success of treatment. For example, both a therapist and a patient would likely be highly motivated to believe that treatment was useful after investing a significant amount of time and energy into the process. To overcome potential bias, outcome measures must be obtained in a variety of ways (e.g., direct observation, self-report, other-report). Outcome measurements might include the viewpoint of the patient, of the therapist, and of significant others (e.g., spouse, boss, coworkers, parents), as well as that of impartial outside observers. Furthermore, reliable and valid instruments must be used in any attempt to measure outcome. Many instruments and programs have been developed to specifically measure treatment effectiveness as well as client satisfaction with treatment (e.g., Ellsworth, 1981; Nguyen, Attkisson, & Stegner, 1983; Overall & Pfefferbaum, 1962; Plante, Couchman, & Diaz, 1995; Plante, Couchman, & Hoffman, 1998; Speer & Newman, 1996). The timing of the assessment is critical as well. Assessment of treatment effectiveness or outcome is needed not only at the termination of treatment but also during periodic follow-up sessions one to several years after treatment is completed (Craighead, Stunkard, & O'Brien, 1981; Jacobson, 1984; Speer & Newman, 1996). Treatment outcome measurements conducted at the end of treatment may reveal different results than measurements conducted several weeks or months later.

Statistical Versus Clinical Significance

To determine whether research hypotheses are supported, probability and statistical significance have been traditionally used in psychology as well as in most other scientific fields. *Statistical significance* refers to the very small probability of obtaining a particular finding by error or chance. The convention is that if there is less than a 5 in 100 times chance that the means of two groups come from the same population, then the null hypothesis (i.e., no difference) is rejected and the hypothesis of the study is supported. This is referred to as $p < .05$; that is, the probability of error is less than 5 percent. A number of statistical techniques or tests can be used to derive this probability statement for a given study (e.g., *t*-test, analysis of variance, multiple analysis of variance). Statistical tests have also been developed to measure the size of a given effect beyond merely determining statistical significance. These tests measure what is referred to as *effect size*. Effect size reflects the strength or degree of impact a given result or effect has on the results of the study. The design and purpose of the study determine which statistical test is used.

Many researchers feel that demonstrating statistical significance in treatment outcome and other clinical psychology research is insufficient. They argue that researchers must be able to demonstrate clinical or practical significance in addition to statistical significance for a research finding to have meaning (Jacobson & Revenstorf, 1988; Kazdin, 1991; Kendall & Norton-Ford, 1982). For example, a study was conducted to examine personality differences among 80 hospitalized clergy who sexually abused minors and 80 hospitalized clergy who did not sexually abuse minors (Plante, Manual, & Bryant, 1996). All the clergy were hospitalized in a psychiatric facility that specialized in the treatment of clergy. A number of psychological tests were administered to the patients, including both personality and cognitive tests. One of the findings of the study included a significant difference between the two clergy groups on a measure of overcontrolled hostility from the Minnesota Multiphasic Personality Inventory-2 (MMPI-2). Overcontrolled hostility refers to the tendency to try to suppress aggressive and hostile impulses. Using analysis of variance (ANOVA), the researchers found that the overcontrolled hostility measure was significantly higher in

the sexually abusive group ($p < .05$). Therefore hospitalized clergy who sexually abused minors tended to experience more overcontrolled hostility than those who did not sexually abuse minors. However, the actual mean scores on overcontrolled hostility for the sexual abusive group was 56 while for the nonabusing clergy it was 53. Although the difference between the two scores might be statistically significant if the study had used a large number of subjects, little practical or clinical significance can be obtained from these results. It would therefore be inappropriate for a clinician to use the overcontrolled hostility measure as a screening instrument for sexual abuse based on this study. Another example might include measuring change in depression following a given treatment. Patients may have lower scores on measures of depression following treatment but still may feel depressed. While they may be less depressed than they were when they entered treatment and score significantly lower on a standard measure of depression (e.g., Beck Depression Inventory), they may still feel unhappy when they terminate treatment.

It has been suggested that treatment outcome research use other criteria more relevant than statistical significance to determine treatment effectiveness. These criteria might include a return to premorbid or baseline level of functioning, change that results in improvement in social or occupational functioning, or the elimination of the presenting symptoms (Jacobson & Revenstorf, 1988; Kendall & Norton-Ford, 1982). Many investigators have called for treatment outcome and other clinical psychology research to move away from the use of statistical significance as the only measure of success and to use more useful and practical measures such as evidence that the patient has moved from a dysfunctional to a more functional state (Kazdin, 1991; Speer & Newman, 1996).

How Can Treatment Outcome Decisions Be Made when Studies Come to Different Conclusions?

Research investigations attempting to answer similar research questions often do not agree. Threats to both internal and external validity may play a role in what appear to be contradictory conclusions. Furthermore, research must be replicated in order to develop confidence in the conclusions obtained. One popular yet controversial method to examine all the research conducted on a given topic or question is the use of meta-analysis (Smith, Glass, & Miller, 1980). **Meta-analysis** is a statistical method for examining the results of a large number of research studies. Effect size, or result, is estimated by, for example, subtracting the average outcome score of a control group from the average outcome score of the treatment or experimental group and then dividing the difference by the standard deviation of the control group. The larger the effect size, the larger the treatment effect. For example, in a frequently quoted study of the use of meta-analysis for psychotherapy treatment outcome, Smith and Glass (1977) reported that the effect size for the studies they reviewed was 0.68 and concluded that the average patient would have a better outcome with psychotherapy than without psychotherapy about 75 percent of the time.

Many authorities have criticized the Smith and Glass (1977, 1980) studies for a wide range of procedural and statistical reasons (e.g., Landman & Dawes, 1982; Wilson & Rachman, 1983). Critics argue that only high quality research studies should be used when conducting meta-analysis, and that using results from mediocre or flawed studies will result in erroneous conclusions. In other words, "garbage in, garbage out." In addition to statistical techniques such as meta-analysis, the development of a program of research examining research findings and designing additional studies to continue fine-tuning hypotheses is also used by researchers. A program of research allows one study to inform the development of a second study, which then informs the design and implementation of further studies in a step-by-step and organized manner.

What Is a Program of Research and How Is It Conducted?

Often people assume that one research study can confidently answer an important research question. Newspapers frequently report the results of a recently published study and make sweeping generalizations based on those results. For example, a study may report that oat bran lowers cholesterol or that drinking moderate amounts of red wine reduces the risk of heart attack. A single research study,

however, rarely provides a full understanding of a particular phenomenon. Even the best designed and completed studies have limitations. Furthermore, replication is needed to ensure that the results are consistent and stable and not due to chance or unknown factors. Therefore the understanding of various phenomenon develops through a series of related research studies or programs of research rather than from a single study.

Agras and Berkowitz (1980) outlined a research program method to assist in gaining a better understanding of the treatment outcome of new intervention techniques. First, a new technique or procedure can be used in several case studies to determine whether it appears to be a reasonable intervention. Then short-term outcome studies can be designed to compare the new procedure to no treatment. If the short-term effectiveness of the procedure is supported, then studies can be designed to examine the most effective and efficient manner to utilize the procedure as well as to understand the basic ingredient that results in positive treatment outcome. The next step is to conduct field effectiveness research to determine whether the procedures developed and studied in a laboratory setting can be applied to various clinical settings (e.g., private practice, clinics). All the research designs and approaches discussed in this chapter (e.g., single case study designs, correlational designs, experimental designs) could be utilized in various stages to determine the usefulness of a new therapeutic technique or procedure. Usually these **research programs** start with uncontrolled case studies and then lead from single case study designs to between group designs with a small number of patients over a short period of time, followed by between group designs with a large number of patients over a long period of time. Wilson (1981) also proposes a model of research that starts in the laboratory and ends in the consultation room of a clinician (Table 6-4).

Contemporary Issues in Clinical Psychology Treatment Outcome Research

Research conducted in clinical psychology has evolved to a high level of sophistication and complexity. Contemporary clinical psychology treat-

Table 6.4   Different Levels of Research from Basic Research to Clinical Practice

Level 1	Basic laboratory research on factors associated with behavior change
Level 2	Analogue treatment research to identify effective ingredients of therapeutic procedures under controlled laboratory conditions
Level 3	Controlled clinical research with patient populations
Level 4	Clinical practice. Therapists may measure outcome in case studies or clinical series

Source: Wilson, G. T. (1981). Some comments on clinical research. *Behavioral Assessment, 3,* 217–226. Reprinted by permission, Association for Advancement of Behavior Therapy.

ment outcome research involves much more than determining if a particular treatment approach works relative to a control group conducted by a few therapists in one clinic location. While there are many fascinating current issues and trends in contemporary clinical psychology treatment outcome research, several selected compelling ones will be highlighted in this section. These include research regarding biopsychosocial approaches to psychopathology research, meta-analysis, empirically validated treatments, large comprehensive and collaborative multisite research projects, and large scale community wide interventions.

Biopsychosocial Approaches to Psychopathology Research

Research on psychopathology historically focused on specific and unidimensional influences on the development, maintenance, and treatment of psychopathology. Some researchers would focus on the biological influences while others would investigate psychological or social influences. Whereas many researchers continued their focus on the influence of a very specific variable on human behavior and psychopathology, researchers now recognize the complex influence of numerous interacting factors. As more and more research has been conducted, complex and interactive biopsychosocial influences on psychopathology have been described, and research designs adapted to better study these complex interactions.

Alcohol abuse is an excellent example of a complex biopsychosocial problem. Biological factors including genetic predisposition, physical dependency, and tolerance conspire with psychological vulnerabilities (e.g., depression, denial, stress) and social factors (e.g., friends gather at local pub, raised

in family where drinking was excessive, media depictions of drinking as macho) to create the pervasive physical, interpersonal, intrapsychic and work-related difficulties associated with alcoholism. Treatments are therefore largely multidimensional. In order to evaluate the efficacy of a treatment program that utilizes inpatient detoxification, group therapy, and antabuse follow-up (i.e., a medication which causes violent illness when combined with alcohol), a constructive treatment strategy research design may be applied. Thus, outcome measures would be taken at baseline, after the completion of inpatient treatment, then after the addition of group therapy, and finally, again after the addition of antabuse. Thus, the relative contributions of each component and their synergistic effects can be statistically analyzed and scientifically tested.

Depending upon the specific research questions of interest to an experimenter, research investigating treatment outcome must take these biopsychosocial influences into consideration. For example, programs of research in these and other areas may use a variety of research design strategies to answer important questions. Although all of the designs discussed earlier may be used in a particular study, the comparative and constructive treatment strategies as well as longitudinal designs are often especially useful. These designs better reflect the types of complex questions asked of researchers in contemporary clinical psychology regarding the multiple influences on clinical problems.

Comprehensive biopsychosocial treatments often must intervene at multiple levels and examine or account for multiple influencing factors. For example, treatment outcome research for schizophrenia must reflect realistic clinical practice and examine the role of medication, social support, individual, family, and group psychotherapy, vocational counseling, housing assistance, and other possible intervention strategies. Contemporary treatments rarely use one narrowly defined intervention strategy but rather attempt intervention at multiple biological, psychological, and social levels. Therefore, researchers now must follow suit and design research programs that take this compexity into account.

Meta-analysis

As mentioned earlier, meta-analysis is a statistical technique that allows researchers to examine the results from numerous research studies. Ever since Smith and Glass (1977; Smith, Glass, and Miller, 1980) conducted their landmark studies on the effectiveness of psychotherapy, meta-analytic approaches have been widely used in treatment outcome research. Because hundreds and perhaps thousands of research studies examining treatment outcome and other topics have been conducted over the years, this technique is especially useful in consolidating overall results across studies. Criteria are developed to determine which studies to include and which must be excluded. The measurement of effect size or the strength of a treatment effect relative to control conditions is determined for each study and evaluated with other studies. The use of well designed and controlled research studies is fundamental to the meta-analysis technique (Wilson & Rachman, 1983). More and more research conducted in contemporary clinical psychology utilizes meta-analysis techniques.

Empirically Validated Treatments

Research is needed to determine if treatments used in clinical psychology are effective. The Task Force on Promotion and Dissemination of Psychological Procedures (1995) of the APA Division of Clinical Psychology (Division 12) has developed guidelines for psychotherapy treatments based on solid research findings (Chambless, et al., 1996). **Empirically validated treatments** are well established treatment approaches that have received significant research support demonstrating their efficacy (Rehm, 1997; Sanderson, 1994; Sanderson & Woody, 1995). Criteria for acceptance as empirically validated treatments include the demonstration of efficacy using well designed between group and/or a large series of single case design experiments. Results from these experiments must have demonstrated treatment superiority to placebo or other treatments as well as having used enough subjects to have adequate statistical power. Furthermore, the experiments must be conducted using treatment manuals and the characteristics of the clients must be very clearly specified. Finally the effects must be found by at least two independent researchers or research teams. These standards have been applied to the numerous treatment approaches that have been used to treat a large range of problems.

Empirically validated treatments have been developed for the treatment of chemical abuse and dependency, anxiety, depressive, sexual, eating, and health problems. Examples of empirically validated treatments include exposure treatment for phobias and posttraumatic stress disorder, cognitive-behavior therapy for headache, panic, irritable bowel syndrome, and bulimia, and insight-oriented dynamic therapy for depression and marital discord. Many contemporary clinical psychologists argue that only empirically validated treatments should be used in clinical practice (Chambless, 1996; Crits-Christoph, 1996; Meehl, 1997; Rehm, 1997). Others are more skeptical of empirically validated approaches citing limitations to these approaches (Garfield, 1996; Havik & VandenBos, 1996). Skeptics often cite problems such as the difficulty making the generalization from research findings to actual clinical practice and the complexity of each unique individual as reasons for being less enthusiastic about the development of these treatment approaches. Nonetheless, contemporary clinical psychology research focuses on developing empirically validated treatments and using them in many research and clinical investigations.

Although developing empirically validated treatments have been of interest to clinical psychologists for several decades, recent changes in health care reimbursement systems and the advent of managed health care has resulted in a great deal of recent financial impetus to research and develop validated treatments. Funding sources are in increasingly shorter supply, and require increasing assurance of cost effectiveness prior to committing resources. While managed health care will be discussed in detail in Chapter 14, the increased demand for accountability in both cost effective and validated treatments has been of interest to contemporary mental health professionals, managed care companies, and the public.

Comprehensive and Collaborative Multisite Clinical Trial Research Projects

Whereas clinical psychology treatment outcome research was conducted historically in isolated clinic, hospital, or practice settings by one primary investigator, contemporary research approaches use comprehensive and collaborative multiple sites in large scale studies. Conducting collaborative research in many different sites across the country and using many different therapists enhances the external validity of treatment studies by representing more of a cross section of treatment situations. One of the best known and often cited comprehensive and **collaborative multisite research projects** in treatment outcome is the National Institute of Mental Health (NIMH) depression study (Elkin, 1994; Elkin, Parloff, Hadley, & Autry, 1985; Elkin, et al., 1989). The NIMH study will be briefly discussed as an example of these research methods.

The goal of the NIMH depression study was to utilize a large scale collaborative clinical trial study to evaluate the effectiveness of several brief treatments for depression. Large scale collaborative clinical trials have been used frequently in medicine to investigate the effectiveness of medication and other medical interventions but had not been used in clinical psychology until this study. A collaborative clinical trial is a well-controlled treatment outcome study in a wide variety of settings that provides support for the reliability, validity, and generalizability of results. The NIMH depression study compared cognitive-behavioral psychotherapy, interpersonal psychotherapy, and medication with case management for treating depression at three research sites (University of Pittsburgh, George Washington University, and University of Oklahoma) as well as at three training sites (Yale University, Clark University, and Rush Presbyterian-St. Luke's Medical Center). A medication with case management placebo control condition was also in-

cluded. Two-hundred-fifty patients were randomly assigned to the four treatment conditions at the three research sites. Experienced clinicians were used as therapists in the study and were audiotaped to ensure that they followed treatment protocols. Results included assessment before, during, and after treatment. These results revealed that all treatments proved useful relative to the control condition. Medication resulted in a quicker treatment response but psychotherapy proved equally as effective as medication over time. Collaborative multisite treatment outcome studies have been conducted investigating other disorders such as panic and attention- deficit disorders (Sholomskas, Barlow, Cohen, Gorman, Moras, Papp, Shear, & Wood, 1990).

Community-wide Interventions

Contemporary clinical psychology research seeks to study and influence entire communities in addition to involving individuals (Cohen, Stunkard, & Feliz, 1986). While there are many examples of research and intervention projects being conducted on a large scale community level, the Stanford Heart Disease Prevention Program (Meyer, Maccoby, & Farquhar, 1980; Meyer, Nash, McAlister, Maccoby, & Farquhar, 1980) serves as an excellent example of this type of clinical research project. The purpose of the Stanford program was to alter health damaging behavior in several California communities. Two towns were provided with an intense mass media campaign to encourage residents to stop smoking and improve their diet and exercise in an effort to lower their risks of developing cardiovascular disease. Television, radio, mailings, and telephone contacts were all employed to attempt to help residents live a more healthy lifestyle. A third town served as a control condition and thus was evaluated without any intervention. In addition to mass media appeals, specific behavioral instructions were provided to at-risk subjects. Results indicated that lower blood pressure and reductions in smoking occurred as a result of the community-wide intervention project (Meyer et al., 1980). Other **community-wide intervention** projects such as the Multiple Risk Factor Intervention Trial (MRFIT) and the North Karelia project in Finland have been used to alter high risk behavior. Studies designed to minimize teen pregnancy, sexually transmitted diseases, and violence have been developed as well. In this way, clinical psychology has expanded its techniques to influence the behavior and health of entire communities.

How and Where Is Research Conducted in Clinical Psychology and How Is It Funded?

Research in clinical psychology is conducted in numerous settings including colleges and universities, hospitals, outpatient clinics, independent research institutes, and even private practices. However, most clinical psychology research is conducted in academic settings such as colleges, universities, and university-affiliated medical settings or in institutions (e.g., clinics, hospitals).

Research is funded by various sources. Grants from government agencies such as the National Institute of Mental Health (NIMH), the National Institutes of Health (NIH), the Veterans Administration (VA), and the National Science Foundation (NSF) fund research in clinical psychology. Private foundations such as the American Heart Association, the March of Dimes, the American Cancer Foundation, the John D. and Catherine T. McArthur Foundation, and the James T. Irvine Foundation also fund clinical psychology research projects. Many colleges, universities, hospitals, and corporations budget some money to provide small grants to researchers affiliated with their institutions. A researcher completes an application form and research proposal, hoping that his or her project will be selected for funding. Most national granting programs are highly competitive. For example, only approximately 18 percent of NIMH grant applications are funded.

Often research can be conducted without grant money or other financial support. Many agencies allow some release time from clinical, teaching, or other professional responsibilities to allow time for research projects; they may also provide support such as secretarial time as well as photocopying, computer, and telephone services to assist in the completion of research projects. Finally, volunteers such as college and graduate students are often instrumental in helping to complete research projects.

How Are Research Results Communicated and Incorporated into Practice?

Completed research is usually communicated to the professional community through publication in scholarly professional journals and through presentation at national and regional conferences. When a project is submitted to a professional journal, it is generally mailed to several experts in the field for peer review. Usually 2 to 4 professionals as well as the editor or associate editor of the professional journal carefully review the research paper to determine whether it is worthy of publication. To minimize potential bias, the reviews are sometimes conducted anonymously. Thus the authors' names and affiliations are removed from the research paper while under review, and the names of the reviewers are withheld from the authors of the paper. The review process often takes three to eight months to complete before feedback is provided to the authors. The reviewers may accept the paper as written, or with revisions requested, or they may reject the paper. If a paper is rejected, the authors usually incorporate the feedback of the reviewers to enhance the quality of the paper or subsequent investigation. Once a paper is accepted and the requested revisions are made, it can take several months to a year or more before the paper is published. Therefore, several years can elapse between the time a research project is submitted to when it is actually published. Authors are allowed to submit their research to only one professional journal at a time and therefore cannot submit their paper to several journals in the hope that one of many will accept their work. Nor do they get paid for their article when it is accepted and published in a professional journal.

While this peer review process has a number of disadvantages (e.g., the length of time for publication), advantages include careful review by experts in the field to maximize the chances that only high quality and significant research is published. Although researchers are interested in learning more about their field of inquiry and sharing their findings with the professional community, regular publishing is generally expected and required for job retention (e.g., tenure) and promotion in academic, medical, and other settings. The well-known phrase "publish or perish" captures these publishing requirements and pressures. Of the numerous professional journals in clinical psychology, some are highly competitive, accepting few papers submitted to them by researchers; others are moderately competitive; and still others are fairly uncompetitive.

The peer review process is also used for submissions to professional conferences. Most professional organizations at both the national and regional levels (e.g., American Psychological Association, American Psychological Society, Western Psychological Association, New England Psychological Association, Society of Behavioral Medicine) hold a yearly conference for their members and others interested in the field. Papers, posters, and symposiums are presented over several days in various cities across the country (for national organizations) or across the region (for smaller regional conferences). Research papers are submitted about six months prior to the conference and are reviewed by experts in the field.

Many have expressed concern that research findings tend to be communicated more to the research community than to the clinical community (e.g., Beutler, Williams, Wakefield, & Entwistle, 1995; Fensterheim & Raw, 1996; Nezu, 1996). For example, practitioners often do not read many of the professional scientific journals nor do they regularly attend national or regional conferences. Rather, they learn of new techniques and strategies by attending continuing education workshops or hospital grand rounds presentations. Some argue that because research precision is so highly valued and many projects focus on such specialized areas of study that they are not useful to the average clinician practicing in the field. The dilemma is exacerbated by the fact that many researchers know few clinicians and many clinicians know few researchers. Hence academic and clinical circles do not always overlap. This separation between research and practice has been an important issue in psychology since the field began in 1896 and continues to be a hotly debated topic (Clement, 1996; Fensterheim & Raw, 1996; Hayes, 1996; Nezu, 1996; Rice, 1997).

Researchers often argue that some clinicians are misguided and uninformed in their efforts to help their patients and that quality research is needed to correct this problem (Davison & Lazarus, 1994; Garfield, 1994). Clinicians often feel that many research studies are oversimplified and that researchers are not in touch with the complicated challenges that clinicians face in trying to help their patients (Clement, 1996; Edelson, 1994; Havens, 1994). However, recent studies suggest that clinicians value research more than researchers generally believe they do, and that clinicians try to incorporate research findings into their practices whereas researchers tend less often to incorporate the concerns of clinicians into their research (Beutler et al., 1995).

Several professional journals have been developed to specifically bridge the gap between research and practice (e.g., *Clinical Psychology: Science and Practice; In Session: Psychotherapy in Practice*). Talley, Strupp, and Butler (1994) propose that research be made more relevant to clinicians by providing a therapeutic context for research results and interpretation, and that research funding be made more sensitive to the needs of clinicians. Stricker and Trierweiler (1995) and Clement (1996) suggested that clinicians bring the same rigorous scientific thinking and attitude to their practice as researchers bring to their experiments. Fensterheim and Raw (1996) suggested that clinical research and practice are such distinct areas that they should "deintegrate clinical research from clinical practice so that workers from each area can meet as peers, each accepting that the other has different modes of thinking, of researching, and respecting that difference" (p. 170).

The Big Picture

Research is fundamental to the goals and activities of clinical psychology. Research provides helpful answers to important questions about human nature and ways to improve the quality of life for many. For instance, quality research can be used to design studies investigating improved ways to assess and treat numerous clinical problems. Research can also help validate and fine-tune biopsychosocial models of psychopathology and treatment. Furthermore, research training helps to develop critical thinking skills that can be employed in both research and nonresearch activities and settings. Psychologists have developed a wide variety of sophisticated research design methods to use with various research and clinical questions. All of the different designs and research methods seek to study a particular issue of importance to clinical psychology while minimizing or eliminating potential research error and bias but maximizing internal and external validity. The scientific method is used in all areas of clinical psychology research and can be successfully employed in clinical practice as well as in research laboratories. Conducting high quality, ethical, and useful research programs and incorporating these findings into the actual practice of psychologists is a challenging goal for contemporary psychology. Clinical psychologists who do not actually conduct research must be informed consumers of research in order to evaluate findings and incorporate the information into their clinical or other professional work. Future clinical psychologists will likely use more sophisticated research methods to answer more complex questions about the workings of the mind and behavior. These strategies will likely integrate methods and knowledge from other disciplines such as medicine, sociology, and epidemiology.

Key Points

1. Research is at the very foundation of clinical psychology. Basic and applied research provides many of the answers to important questions about diagnosis, treatment, and general human behavior, thus allowing both researchers and practitioners to use their techniques and theories with confidence. Research is fundamental to both the science and practice of clinical psychology.

2. The general goal of research in clinical psychology is to acquire knowledge about human behavior and use this knowledge to help improve the lives of others. Clinical psychologists use the scientific method in conducting their research activities. The scientific method is a set of rules and procedures that describe, explain, and predict a particular phenomenon.

3. Conducting an experiment is the typical and basic way to utilize the scientific method in answering research questions. Experiments must identify the independent and dependent variables, minimize experimenter error and bias, and maximize internal and external validity.

4. There are several types of extraneous variables that threaten internal and external validity, which must be considered and addressed in any research study. Threats to internal validity include the effects of history, maturation, testing, instrumentation, statistical regression, selection bias, and experimental mortality. Threats to external validity include testing, reactivity, multiple-treatment interference, and the interaction of selection biases.

5. There are many different approaches to constructing and carrying out a research experiment. Many of the different experimental designs offer unique advantages and disadvantages. These include experimental designs, quasi-experimental designs, between group designs, within group designs, mixed group designs, analogue designs, case studies, correlational designs, epidemiological designs, cross-sectional designs, and longitudinal designs.

6. The cornerstone of true experiments that allow cause-and-effect statements is randomization. Randomization of subjects into experimental and control conditions is the hallmark of true experiments. However, randomization is often impossible in many clinical psychology research studies due to legal, ethical, and practical limitations.

7. Between group designs use two or more separate groups of subjects, each of which receive a different type of intervention or no intervention in the case of a control condition. Therefore, the independent variable is manipulated by the experimenter in such a way that different groups of subjects receive different types of experiences that are being investigated.

8. Within group designs examine the influence of the independent variable (such as treatment) with the same subjects over time. Therefore, subjects are not assigned to different experimental and control groups as they are in a between group design but are all likely to experience the same research protocol. In within group designs comparisons are made with the same patient at different points of time, such as during a baseline or pre-treatment period, during a treatment intervention period, and during a follow-up or posttreatment period.

9. Case studies provide an intensive observation of a person and phenomenon, which allows for hypotheses and theories to be developed. Case studies can be especially helpful when researchers and clinicians are interested in examining a new, rare, or unusual phenomenon, or during the early descriptive stages of a research program.

10. Analogue designs use procedures, subjects, and measures that approximate a "real life" clinical situation and are usually conducted in a laboratory where experimental conditions can be controlled better than in the natural environment.

11. Correlational designs examine the degree of association between two or more variables. While correlational designs do not allow cause-and-effect conclusions from being made (e.g., treatment cured a problem), they do provide researchers and clinicians alike useful information concerning the degree of association between constructs of interest.

12. Cross-sectional studies provide a "snap shot" view of behavior at a given moment of time while longitudinal designs generally collect research data over a long period of time.

13. While clinical psychology research is conducted to investigate numerous research questions, the evaluation of treatment outcome is one of the most common areas of study. There are many different ways to conduct research on treatment outcome. Different strategies are employed depending upon the specific research questions of interest. Kazdin (1991) has outlined seven specific research strategies for effectively evaluating treatment outcome research. These include the treatment strategy approach, the dismantling treatment strategy approach, the constructive treatment strategy approach, the parametric treatment strategy approach, the comparative treatment

strategy approach, the client and therapist variation strategy approach, and the process research strategy approach.

14. Research in clinical psychology is conducted in numerous settings including colleges and universities, hospitals, outpatient clinics, independent research institutes, and even private practices. However, most research in clinical psychology is conducted in academic settings such as colleges, universities, and university-affiliated medical settings or in institutions (e.g., clinics or hospitals) that are affiliated with academic facilities.

15. One research study rarely results in a full understanding of a particular phenomenon being studied. Even the best designed and completed studies have limitations. Furthermore, replication is needed to ensure that the results of a particular study are consistent and stable and not due to chance or some unknown factor or factors. Therefore, understanding various phenomena occurs through a series of related research studies or a program of research rather than from a single study.

16. Contemporary clinical psychology treatment outcome research involves much more than determining if a particular treatment approach works relative to a control group conducted by a few therapists in one clinic location. Current issues include biopsychosocial approaches to psychopathology research, meta-analysis, empirically validated treatments, large comprehensive and collaborative multisite research projects, and large scale community-wide interventions.

Key Terms

Collaborative multisite research projects
Community-wide intervention
Empirically validated treatments
Experimental Designs
   Analogue
   Between Group
   Case Study
   Correlational
   Cross-sectional
   Epidemiological
   Longitudinal
   Mixed Group
   Quasi-Experimental

   True Experimential
   Within Group
Meta-analysis
Research Program
Threats to External Validity
   Interaction of Selection Biases
   Multiple-Treatment Interference
   Reactivity
   Testing
Threats to Internal Validity
   Experimental Mortality
   History
   Instrumentation

   Maturation
   Selection Bias
   Statistical Regression
   Testing
Treatment Outcome Research Strategy
   Client and Therapist Variation
   Comparative
   Constructive
   Dismantling
   Parametric
   Process
   Treatment

For Reflection

1. Why is research needed in clinical psychology?
2. What are the considerations that are needed in order to design a quality research experiment?
3. What are the different design methods used in clinical psychology and what are the advantages and disadvantages to each?
4. What are the different methods to conduct treatment outcome research and what are some of the advantages and disadvantages of each?
5. How are research ideas communicated?
6. How do research findings get incorporated into practical clinical activities such as professional practice?
7. How is research funded?
8. What are some advantages and disadvantages of the peer-review process for publishing research findings?
9. How can the needs to maximize internal validity and external validity be balanced?
10. How is error and bias minimized in research studies?
11. Design a research study to investigate three treatments for depression.
12. Why is a program of research important and beneficial when compared to the results of one research study?
13. Why is meta-analysis used in research?
14. Why are biopsychosocial approaches needed in treatment outcome research?
15. What are empirically validated treatments?
16. What are some advantages of large scale collaborative multisite research projects?

CHAPTER 7

Contemporary Psychological Assessment I: Interviewing and Observing Behavior

Chapter Outline

Highlight of a Contemporary Clinical Psychologist: Stanley Sue, Ph.D.

Goals, Purposes, and Types of Assessment

Reliability and Validity

Interviewing

Types of Interviews

Potential Threats to Effective Interviewing

Behavioral Observations

Checklists and Inventories

Physiological Testing

HIGHLIGHT OF A CONTEMPORARY CLINICAL PSYCHOLOGIST:

Stanley Sue, Ph.D.

Dr. Sue maintains a full-time academic and administrative career focusing on Asian-American issues.

Birth Date: February 13, 1944

College: University of Oregon (B.A. in Psychology), 1966

Graduate Program: University of California at Los Angeles (Ph.D. in Clinical Psychology), 1971

Clinical Internship: Student Health Psychiatric Clinic, University of California at Los Angeles

Current Job: Professor of Psychology and Director of Asian American Studies, University of California at Davis

Pros and cons of being a clinical psychologist:

Pros: Interesting and important work with people. Variety of possible roles in teaching, research, clinical practice, consulting, and administration.

Cons: Can experience burnout in clinical practice.

Future of clinical psychology: "The future looks bright. Employment possibilities are strong despite managed care. In the future, better integration of research funds with clinical practice."

Typical Schedule:

8:00	Communicate on e-mail
9:00	Administrative work on research center. Organize seminar on mental health issues of Asian Americans.
10:00	Administrative and organizational work continues.
11:00	Meet with students concerning research about the importance of culture in mental health assessment issues.
12:00	Communicate on e-mail
1:00	Research and writing. Working on paper for publication and grant application concerning training culturally competent mental health professionals.
2:00	Research and writing continues.
3:00	Teach Abnormal Psychology class.
4:00	Office hours

Assessing an individual's psychological makeup in the course of a few meetings is a formidable undertaking. This ability to access, identify, describe, and meaningfully integrate the quintessential workings of an individual's mind and emotional soul challenges both the human and intellectual resources of the psychologist.

Since the earliest days of professional psychology, assessment and testing have been important clinical activities. *Psychological assessment* is the process psychologists use to collect and evaluate information in order to make diagnoses, plan treatment, and predict behavior. Assessment may include interviewing the patient, reviewing past records (such as medical or school records), observing behavior, and administering psychological tests to measure various cognitive, behavioral, personality, family, and even biological factors. *Psychological testing* involves specific assessment techniques utilizing reliable and valid testing instruments that enable the psychologist to compare individual scores with the scores obtained from normative samples.

Assessment was the primary applied activity of clinical psychologists from the emergence of clinical psychology in 1896 to the end of World War II. As discussed in Chapter 3, the need to evaluate not only children who were struggling in school but also military recruits in the two world wars quickly propelled clinical psychology into the assessment and testing enterprise. Today many clinical psychologists specialize in general psychological testing or the testing of specific populations (e.g., neuropsychological testing of elderly stroke patients, cognitive testing of preschoolers, personality testing of disturbed adolescents). In fact, psychological assessment and testing, with its numerous procedures and products, has become a multimillion dollar industry.

In this chapter, psychological assessment through interviewing and behavioral observation will be reviewed. In Chapter 8, the major undertakings of cognitive and neuropsychological assessment as well as personality assessment will be discussed. Throughout, case examples will be utilized to illustrate the actual use and application of assessment tools and measures.

Goals, Purposes, and Types of Assessment

People requesting the services of a clinical psychologist are typically motivated to seek help because of certain thoughts, feelings, or behaviors that cause them or others discomfort and concern. The symptoms they present may include anxiety, depression, anger, poor grades, interpersonal conflict, overeating, sleeplessness, loneliness or irritability. They find such symptoms distressing and wish to obtain professional help in eliminating them. Routinely, important questions emerge during the sessions. The psychologist's job is to help answer fundamental questions such as the following:

Why is my son not behaving well in school?

Why can't I get over the breakup with my girlfriend six months ago?

How can I overcome my intense fear and panic whenever I drive over a bridge?

What can I do to help my adult son cope with his bipolar illness?

How can my husband and I get along better?

Is my child mentally retarded?

Are my headaches caused by stress or by some serious medical problem like a brain tumor?

Why do I feel so depressed when things in life appear to be going fine?

How can I overcome the low self-esteem that prevents me from doing better at work?

Before the psychologist can help the patient, an initial assessment is necessary. The goal of assessment is usually to size up the situation by developing a fuller understanding of the factors that contribute to the presenting problem(s). Then the psychologist can make a diagnosis and outline a subsequent treatment or intervention plan. For example, someone may come to a psychologist for help in coping with frequent hallucinations and delusions. Various biological, psychological, and/or social factors might contribute to these symptoms. The person may have a medical problem, such as a tumor, or the hallucinations and delusions may be associated with amphetamine abuse or seizures. The symptoms may also be associated with post-traumatic stress disorder or schizophrenia. The symptoms might also be associated with important social factors, for example, they may have worsened in the face of a financial crisis or violent trauma. Thus, the hallucinations and delusions could be associated with a variety of biological, psychological, and social factors, and ultimately, a number of different diagnoses. An assessment of the influence of these factors is critical in developing a satisfactory diagnostic and treatment plan. For example, treatment would be vastly different if the hallucinations and delusions are associated with amphetamine abuse, schizophrenia, bipolar illness, post-truamatic stress disorder or organic brain disease.

Sometimes the presenting problem or symptom is not the real problem. For instance, someone may seek help specifically for the treatment of tension headaches. Perhaps the patient is interested in using biofeedback or developing relaxation strategies to reduce the frequency, duration, and intensity of the headaches. However, after a session or two the patient reports that her marriage is falling apart and she is fearful that her spouse is having an affair. The headaches may be associated with the stress of marital discord, but focusing on the headaches during the first few sessions might have felt less threatening than launching into the more compelling and painful topic of marital discord and infidelity. Thus the headaches were a "ticket" into psychotherapy with marital issues comprising the core area of concern.

Depression is another example of a symptom that can be due to many different causes. Again, an assessment of the biological, psychological, and social influences on each case of depression is necessary in order to develop an adequate disgnostic understanding and intervention strategy. For example, depression often runs in families and research suggests that there is frequently a genetic or biological vulnerability to depression among family members. Thus, if several biological relatives such as a parent, sibling, and/or grandparent have a history of a depressive disorder, the odds are higher that other family members will also develop depressive symptoms. Furthermore, depressive symptoms may be a side effect of various medications or may be associated with a number of physical ailments and conditions (e.g., heart disease, diabetes, cancer, chronic fatigue syndrome, irritable bowel syndrome, chronic illness, sleep apnea). Psychological factors associated with depression may include stress at home or work, significant losses (e.g., death or separation from loved ones), relationship conflicts, personality disorders such as borderline or antisocial personality, as well as numerous other psychological factors. Social factors including homelessness, cultural conflicts, racism, sexual harassment, financial problems, and other issues could also play a significant role in the manifestation of depressive symptoms. For many people, a constellation of biological, psychological, and social factors leads to depressive symptoms. Finally, other potential psychiatric

problems are also associated with depression such as attention deficit hyperactivity disorder, post-traumatic stress disorder, oppositional defiant disorder, eating disorders (e.g., obesity, anorexia nervosa, bulimia), and thought disorders (e.g., schizophrenia) among others. Therefore, comorbidity defined as the coexistence of two or more clinical problems, needs to be adequately addressed in order to more fully understand the factors contributing to the depressive symptoms and the development of an appropriate diagnostic and treatment plan.

Assessment is fundamental to any professional psychological service and may take many different forms. For example, it could include clinical interviews with a patient or significant other (family member, friend, colleague); behavioral observations (classroom observation, role plays); the use of checklists, inventories, and psychological tests (IQ and personality tests); the review of previous records (medical charts, school records); and discussions with other professionals familiar with the person or situation in question (physician, school teacher, school counselor, clergy, probation officer, attorney). The choice of assessment tools depends on the nature of the presenting problem(s), the skills and perspective of the psychologist, the objectives and willingness of the patient, and practical matters such as cost and time.

Reliability and Validity

Regardless of the assessment approach used, the method must be both reliable and valid in order to be useful. *Reliability* is a term used to refer to the consistency of results. In order to develop conclusions and general principles from collected data, the data must be deemed reliable or consistent. Reliability might concern the ability of an examiner to obtain similar test scores on the same person on two different occasions. For example, scores obtained on an IQ test given to a child on Monday should not significantly differ if the test was administered by the same person to the same child on Wednesday. Reliability also may involve the ability to obtain the same scores on a test regardless of the identity of the examiner. For example, the child in the above example should obtain the same IQ score whether Dr. A, B, or C is the test administrator. Reliability might also involve having several people or raters observe the same behavior of interest and provide independent ratings or scores for comparison. This refers to *interrater* or *interobserver* reliability. For example, while Dr. A is conducting an IQ test with a child, Dr. B and Dr. C observe the testing administration and score the test as well. There should be a high degree of agreement between the raters for the test to be reliable.

There are many different types of reliability that evaluate the consistency of an assessment procedure. These include test-retest reliability, alternate-form reliability, split-half reliability, Kuder-Richardson reliability and Cronbach's coefficient alpha, and scorer or interrater reliability (Anastasi, 1988). *Test-retest* reliability refers to obtaining the same results when the test is given on two separate occasions. *Alternate-form* reliability refers to getting the same results even when two different but equal versions of the test are administered. *Split-half* reliability concerns getting the same results even when the test is evaluated in separate but equal parts (e.g., comparing scores from the odd numbered items with the even numbered items). *Kuder-Richardson* and *Cronbach's coefficient alpha* reliability refer to statistical procedures that measure the internal consistency of an assessment procedure. Finally, *scorer* reliability concerns how well two or more examiners conduct the evaluation and are consistent in their testing administration and scoring. All of these types of reliability measure a different type of consistency. Reliability is rarely perfect and a small amount of error or imperfection can be expected from all tests. For example, a child may not obtain the exact same scores on two equivalent forms of an IQ test or two raters may not agree on every aspect of their evaluation of the same person. However, for a test to be reliable the conclusions drawn from these scores must be the same.

In addition to reliability, assessment procedures must be valid. *Validity* refers to how well the assessment approach measures what it purports to measure. Does an IQ test really measure intelligence? Does a personality test really measure "personality"? Does the SAT really measure college aptitude? Like reliability, there are many different types of validity: results from research must be deemed valid in order to draw conclusions and generalize findings. These include content, criterion (predictive and concurrent), construct validity, and discriminant (Anastasi, 1988). *Content validity* refers to

whether the assessment procedure covers a representative sample of the behaviors it is designed to measure. For example, an IQ test that only includes vocabulary items would not adequately represent all aspects of intelligence (e.g., problem-solving, abstract reasoning, visual-motor skills). *Criterion validity* refers to how well an assessment instrument predicts performance on another test or in a specific activity. For example, performance on an SAT should highly correlate with college performance. This is *predictive* criterion validity since SAT scores taken during high school are used to predict performance in college at a future date. *Concurrent validity* occurs when the two measures of interest are available at the same time. For example, SAT scores may be used to assess concurrent validity with the ACT examination, an alternative high school test used in place of the SAT in many high schools. Since the SAT and ACT can both be administered at about the same time, concurrent validity is assessed. *Construct validity* refers to how well the assessment device measures the theoretical construct it purports to measure. For example, does a test of anxiety truly measure the construct of anxiety? *Discriminant validity* refers to two or more measures that are appropriately unrelated. For example, SAT scores should be unrelated to shoe size, height, and social skills. Like reliability, the assessment of validity is rarely perfect. Some degree of error in measurement can be expected. For example, SAT scores do not perfectly predict college performance. Acceptable levels of validity may differ depending upon the criteria of an investigator or the purpose of the validity assessment.

The assessment approaches discussed in this chapter and the next are used to diagnose, describe, explain, and predict behavior in a reliable and valid manner. Typically, assessment then leads to recommendations regarding treatment, selection (e.g., job or school program selection), or other intervention strategies. Since assessment is used to make important decisions effecting the lives of many, it is critical that reliable and valid procedures are used and used cautiously. Therefore, these measures must have appropriate clinical utility. *Clinical utility* refers to the notion that assessment devices must maximize the number of true positives and true negatives while minimizing false positives and false negatives. For example, if testing is used to determine who might be admitted to a psychiatric inpatient unit against their will (i.e., involuntary commitment), it is imperative the testing maximizes the odds of making a correct decision and minimizes any possibility that someone would be admitted against their will based on faulty, unreliable, and invalid test findings.

Interviewing

Most helping professionals use interviewing as a standard approach to assessing problems and formulating hypotheses and conclusions. Talking with appropriate, interested, and knowledgable parties (the patient, family members, school teachers, physicians) is usually an important early step in conducting an assessment. Interviewing in clinical psychology entails much more than posing a series of questions to collect data about a case. Asking critical questions, carefully listening to answers, attending to missing or inconsistent information, observing nonverbal behavior, developing hypotheses, and ruling out alternative hypotheses are all part of the interviewing process.

The interview is a thoughtful, well-planned, and deliberate conversation designed to acquire important information (facts, attitudes, beliefs) that enables the psychologist to develop a working hypothesis of the problem(s) and its best solution. Whereas some interviews are highly structured with very specific questions and directions [such as those provided by the Diagnostic Interview Schedule (DIS) and the Structured Clinical Interview for DSM IV (SCID)], others are unstructured and evolve as the conversation develops. While structured interviews are often used in research settings, unstructured interviews are generally used in practice settings. Structured interviews provide more precision but do not allow the flexibility to tailor the experience to the individual needs of the person being interviewed. The use of structured or unstructured interviews is based on the goals of the interview. Effective interviewing is both an art and a science. Although a great deal of research has been conducted on interviewing skills, the psychologist does not read a manual on how to conduct an interview and then become an expert. Effective interviewing is developed over time with practice, supervision, experience, and natural skill.

While the actual information obtained might vary greatly depending on the specific purpose of the interview, generally a list of standard data is collected and discussed (Table 7.1). This includes demographic information such as name, address, telephone number, age, gender, or grade in school, occupation, ethnicity, marital status, and living arrangements. Information about current and past medical and psychiatric problems and treatments are also usually requested. The chief complaint or a list of symptoms experienced by the patient is discussed as well as the patient's hypotheses regarding the contributing factors associated with the development and maintenance of the problem(s). The interviewer often wants to know how the person has tried to cope with the problem(s) and why he or she wishes to obtain professional services now.

Interviewing is used for a wide variety of purposes. For example, an interview is typically conducted whenever a psychologist begins psychotherapy with a new patient. Interviews are also conducted to determine whether someone is in a crisis and might be at risk for self-injury or injury to others. An interview might be conducted to determine the current mental status (e.g., is alert and oriented toward time, place, and person) of a patient at a given moment. An interview is generally conducted as part of any psychological evaluation. Al-

Table 7.1 Typical List of Information Requested During a Standard Clinical Interview

Identifying Information (e.g., name, age, gender, address, date, marital status, education level)
Referral Source (who referred the person and why)
Chief Complaint or Presenting Problems (list of symptoms)
Family Background
Health Background
Educational Background
Employment Background
Developmental History (birth and early child development history)
Sexual History (sexual experiences, orientation, concerns)
Previous Medical Treatment
Previous Psychiatric Treatment
History of Traumas (e.g., physical or sexual abuse, major losses, major accidents)
Current Treatment Goals

though numerous different interviewing situations exist, certain techniques and skills are necessary for nearly all types of interviews. These include developing rapport, effective listening skills, effective communication, observation of behavior, and asking the right questions.

Rapport

When patients talk with a psychologist about problems they are experiencing, they are often uncomfortable sharing their intimate concerns with a complete stranger. They may have never discussed these concerns with anyone before, including their best friends, parents, or spouse. They may worry that the psychologist might make negative judgements about their problems. They may feel embarrassed, silly, worried, angry, or uncomfortable in a vareity of ways. An individual from an ethnic, racial, or sexual minority may fear being misunderstood or maltreated. To develop a helpful, productive, and effective interview, the psychologist must develop rapport with the person he or she is interviewing. **Rapport** is a term used to describe the comfortable working relationship that develops between the professional and the interviewee. The psychologist seeks to develop an atmosphere and relationship that is positive, trusting, accepting, respectful, and helpful.

Although there is no specific formula for developing rapport, several principles are generally followed. First, the professional must be attentive. He or she must focus complete attention on the patient without interruption from distractions such as telephone calls or personal concerns. Second, the professional must maintain a rapport-building posture—for example, by maintaining eye contact and facing the patient with an open posture without a physical barrier such as a large desk impeding communication. Third, the psychologist actively and carefully listens to the patient, allowing him or her to answer questions without constant interruption. Fourth, the psychologist is nonjudgmental and noncritical when interacting with the patient, especially in regard to personal disclosures. The professional also strives toward genuine respect, empathy, sincerity, and acceptance, without acting as a friend or a know-it-all. He or she tries to create a supportive, professional, and respectful environment that will help the patient feel as comfortable and as well understood as possible during the interview.

Effective Listening Skills

In addition to the development of rapport, an effective interviewer must be a good listener. While this may appear obvious, good listening skills are important to develop and generally do not come naturally for most people. People often find it challenging to fully listen to another without being distracted by their thoughts and concerns. Many are too focused on what they are thinking or want to say rather than on listening to someone else. Furthermore, careful listening must occur at many different levels. This includes the *content* of what is being said as well as the *feelings* behind what is being said. Listening also involves paying attention to not only what is being said but how it is presented. For example, someone may deny that he or she is angry yet have their arms crossed and teeth clenched, thus suggesting otherwise. Listening also includes paying attention to what is not being said. Thus listening involves a great deal of attention and skill including the ability to "read between the lines."

Effective interviewers must learn to use and develop **active listening** skills, which include paraphrasing, reflection, summarization, and clarification techniques (Cormier & Cormier, 1979). **Paraphrasing** involves rephrasing the content of what is being said. It means careful listening to another's story and then attempting to put the content of the story into a brief summary. The purpose of paraphrasing is to help the person focus and attend to the content of his or her message. In contrast, **reflection** involves rephrasing the feelings of what is being said in order to encourage the person to express and understand his or her feelings better. **Summarization** involves both paraphrasing and reflection in attempting to pull together several points into a coherent brief review of the message. Summarization is used to highlight a common overall theme of the message. Finally, **clarification** includes asking questions to ensure that the message is being fully understood. Clarification is needed to ensure that the interviewer understands the message as well as helping the person elaborate on their message.

Examples of these techniques are provided in the following example of a couple trying to decide if they should get married. Eduardo is a 36-year-old Latino man who has been dating Janice, a 33-year-old Caucasian woman, for several years. He feels that he cannot commit to marriage because he feels unsure if Janice is the "right one" for him.

Janice wants to marry Eduardo and reports feeling frustrated that he has so many doubts. Eduardo further reports that he is unsure if he could stay faithful to one person for the rest of his life.

Eduardo: "I'm not much of a believer in the institution of marriage. It seems to me that it made sense when the average life span was only 30 years or so. How can someone make a decision like this during their 20s or 30s and have it be a good decision for 50 years or more? My parents are still married after 50 years but they hate each other. I don't know why they stay together. Janice is really nice and I like being with her but who knows what the future will hold for us. She has a lot of great qualities but some characteristics drive me nuts. For example, I really don't like some of her friends. They are boring. She's really a practical person, which I like, but sometimes there isn't a lot of excitement in our relationship."

Examples of active listening techniques offered by the therapist follow:

Paraphrase: "So you seem to be unsure if marriage to Janice or anyone for that matter is right for you."

Reflection: "To some degree you feel bored in your relationship."

Summarization: "You are unsure if marriage is right for you and you are concerned that Janice may not be the right person for you regardless of your views on marriage."

Clarification: "When you say that your relationship lacks excitment are you also referring to your sexual relationship?"

Effective Communication

To conduct a successful interview, effective communication is a requirement. The professional must use language appropriate to the patient, whether a young child, an adolescent, or a highly educated adult. The interviewer generally avoids the use of professional jargon, or psychobabble, and speaks in terms that are easily understood. The interviewer tries to fully understand what the patient is trying to communicate and asks for clarification when he or she is unsure.

Observation of Behavior

The interviewer pays attention not only to what is being said during a clinical interview, but also to how it is being said. Observation of nonverbal communication (e.g., body posture or body language, eye contact, voice tone, attire) provides potentially useful information. For example, a patient may describe severe depressive symptoms and suicidal thoughts, yet smile a great deal and appear energized and in good spirits during the interview. Another patient might state that he or she feels completely comfortable, yet sits with arms and legs tightly crossed while avoiding eye contact. Inappropriate dress (e.g., T-shirt and shorts on a very cold winter day or for a job interview) or a disheveled apperance may provide further insight into the nature of the patient's difficulties.

Asking the Right Questions

A good interviewer must ask the right questions. All too often, inexperienced interviewers forget to ask a critical question only to remember it after the patient has left. Experience with interviewing and a solid understanding of psychopathology and human behavior are needed in order to ask the right questions. Typical questions deal with issues such as the frequency, duration, severity, and patient's perception of the etiology of the presenting problem. A careful understanding of the symptoms as well as the patient's efforts to cope with the problem is usually important. A comprehensive examination of biological, psychological, and social factors associated with the problem is useful, as are questions pertaining to suicide risk and other dangerous behaviors where indicated.

In the following case study, the interviewer's questions lead to a better understanding of the factors that may be associated with Joe's depression. Joe's long work hours as well as his conflictual relationships with both his boss and his father appear to play important roles in his self-esteem and depression. On the basis of the information given, the depression does not appear severe enough to require hospitalization or other dramatic interventions (e.g., electro-convulsive therapy, medication). Continued individual therapy appears warranted, however.

Case Study: Joe

Brief Identifying Information: Joe is a 35-year-old Caucasian middle manager of a large construction company. He has been married for five years and has no children.

Presenting Problem: Joe is concerned about his feelings of depression. He experiences sadness, hopelessness, feelings of worthlessness, and general lassitude. He reports that these feelings occur about 10 or so days each month and are usually associated with a conflict or problem at work. The following is a transcript from a segment of the initial interview conducted by a clinical psychologist.

Interviewer: How long have you had these feelings of depression? (duration of problem).

Patient: Oh, probably about 20 years.

Interviewer: Do you remember what happened 20 years ago that started these feelings? (etiology of problem)

Patient: No.

Interviewer: Have you ever sought professional help for these problems during the past 20 years? (previous history of treatment)

Patient: No. I have never seen a psychologist or anyone else about them before. In fact, other than my wife, I don't think anyone knows about them.

Interviewer: What made you decide to do something about them now? (antecedents for current help seeking)

Patient: Well, my wife encouraged me to see someone—I think because she recently saw a psychologist for feelings of panic and anxiety whenever she drives over a major bridge. Since she found it helpful, she thought I might talk this over with someone. Also, my new insurance plan at work allows me up to 12 free sessions, and so I thought I might as well take advantage of it.

Interviewer: Do you feel comfortable doing this? (assess feelings associated with help-seeking)

Patient: Yes. I feel good about finally doing something about my depression.

Interviewer: What exactly happens when you feel depressed? (assess patient symptoms)

Patient: Well, I just feel worthless, like my self-esteem takes a hit.

Interviewer: So you generally feel bad about yourself?

Patient: Yes, definitely.

Interviewer: Any troubles or changes with sleeping or eating? (assess vegetative signs)

Patient: Not really. I sleep okay and eat fine. In fact, I probably could lose a few pounds. I have a weak spot for chocolate, especially See's dark chocolate cremes.

Interviewer: How do you try to cope with these feelings when they occur?

Patient: I generally talk it over with my wife, who is very supportive. I also usually try to do some exercise like taking a hard run or bike ride. I think the distraction of exercise helps me a great deal. Sometimes, when I feel especially bad, I cry a little and the release makes me feel better.

Interviewer: So you either distract yourself with physical activity or cry when things are really bad.

Patient: Right.

Interviewer: Do other members of your family have trouble with depression or other mood problems?

Patient: Not really. My mother had bouts of depression now and then but nothing serious. My brothers and sisters, my father, my grandparents all seem to have no significant trouble with depression or mood problems.

Interviewer: Do you (or any family members) ever experience the opposite of depression? Do you or do they ever feel very euphoric, maybe get little sleep, spend a lot of money, feel on top of the world?

Patient: No, if you mean do I ever feel manic, I don't. No one in my family does either, that I know of.

Interviewer: Do you ever feel so low that you think of hurting yourself?

Patient: Not really, I might have a fleeting thought that I wish I were dead, but I never feel what I would call suicidal and I would never hurt myself.

Interviewer: Have you ever tried to hurt yourself?

Patient: No, never.

Interviewer: What do you think contributes to your feelings of depression?

Patient: Well, I work really hard. Usually I start work at 7 A.M. and finish at 7- to-8 P.M. Sometimes my boss drives me crazy. He is so controlling. You always feel like he stands over your shoulder and tells you how you could be doing your job better. Generally, I like my job. It pays very well and I like the type of work I do, but I don't like the hours or my boss.

Interviewer: So the job has some major pros, like money, yet major cons like long hours and a challenging boss.

Patient: Right.

Interviewer: Does your boss remind you of anyone else in your life?

Patient: Well, to tell you the truth, he does remind me of my dad a bit. My dad, bless his heart, is a loving guy, and I have a good relationship with him, but his one major flaw is that he is controlling and always has an opinion on how you could do something better. He means well, but he sure can be annoying.

Interviewer: Do you think the similarity between your boss and your father might have anything to do with your depressive feelings?

Patient: I'm not sure. I never really thought about it or made a connection between the two.

Types of Interviews

There are many different types of interviews conducted by psychologists. Some interviews are conducted prior to admission to a clinic or hospital, some are conducted to determine if a patient is in danger of injuring themself or someone else, some are conducted to determine a diagnosis. Whereas some interviews are highly structured with specific questions asked of all patients, others are unstructured and spontaneous. While not an exhaustive list, this section will briefly review examples of the major types of interviews conducted by clinical psychologists.

Initial Intake or Admissions Interview

The purpose of the initial intake, or admissions, interview is to develop a better understanding of the patient's symptoms or concerns in order to recommend the most appropriate treatment or intervention plan. Whether the interview is conducted for admission to a hospital, an outpatient clinic, a private practice, or some other setting, the initial interview attempts to evaluate the patient's situation as efficiently as possible (Fig. 7.1). In addition to learning more about the patient's problems and needs, the psychologist also seeks to determine whether the services provided by the hospital, the clinic, or the practitioner can adequately meet the patient's needs. For example, someone might request services for treating depression, yet during the course of the initial interview, the patient reveals that he has a significant alcohol and cocaine problem. If the psychologist feels that substance abuse treatment is warranted, he or she might refer the patient to a colleague or clinic that specializes in substance abuse problems rather than undertaking treatment of a problem outside his or her area of expertise. Another goal of the initial interview is to orient the patient to the hospital, clinic, or practice. For example, the psychologist typically discusses treatment and payment options, informs the patient about the policies and procedures of the treatment facility or practice, and answers the patient's questions about the services offered. Finally, the initial interview often attempts to instill trust, rapport, and hope that the treatment professional(s) and/or facility will professionally and competently deal with the patient's concerns.

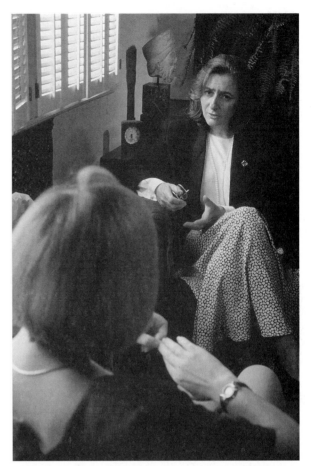

Figure 7.1 A psychologist conducts a clinical interview.

Mental Status Interview

Often a **mental status interview** is conducted to screen the patient's level of psychological functioning and the presence or absence of abnormal mental phenomena such as delusions, delirium, or dementia. Mental status exams include a brief evaluation and observation of the patient's appearance and manner, speech characteristics, mood, thought processes, insight, judgement, attention, concentration, memory, and orientation. Results from the mental status examination provides preliminary information about the likely psychiatric diagnoses experienced by the patient as well as offering some direction for further assessment and intervention (e.g., referral to a specialist, admission to psychiatric unit, evaluation for medical problems that impact psychological functioning). For instance, mental status interviews typically include questions and tasks to determine orientation to time (e.g., "What day is it? What month is it? What year is it?"), place ("What city are you in? Where are you now? Which hospital are you in?"), and person ("Who am I? Who are you? Who is the president of the United States?"). Also, the mental status interview assesses short term memory (e.g., "I am going to name three objects I'd like you to try and remember: dog, pencil, and vase") and attention-concentration (e.g., "Count down by 7s starting at 100. For example, 100, 93, and so forth").

While there are some mental status examinations that are structured resulting in scores that can be compared to national norms, most are unstructured and do not offer a scoring or norming option. During the examination the interviewer notes any unusual behavior or answers to questions that might be indicative of psychiatric disturbance. For example, being unaware of the month, year, or the name of the current President of the United States usually indicates mental problems. This can result in bias based on the interviewer's clinical judgement during an evaluation (Herbert, Nelson, & Herbert, 1988).

Crisis Interview

A crisis interview occurs when a patient is in the middle of a significant and often traumatic or life-threatening crisis. The psychologist or other mental health professional or paraprofessional (e.g., a trained volunteer) might encounter such a situation while working at a suicide or poison control hotline, an emergency room, a community mental health clinic, a student health service on campus, or in many other settings. Although many of the interviewing principles discussed earlier still apply (e.g., asking the right questions, attentive listening), the nature of the emergency dictates a rapid, "get to the point" style of interview as well as quick decision making in the context of a calming style. For example, it may be critical to determine whether the person is at significant risk of hurting him- or herself or others. Or it may be important to determine whether the alcohol, drugs, and/or medication the person ingested is a lethal dose. The interviewer must maintain a calm and clear-headed manner while asking critical questions in order to deal with the situation effectively. The interviewer may need to be more directive (e.g., encouraging the person to phone the police, unload a gun, provide instruc-

tions to induce vomiting, or step away from a tall building or bridge); break confidentiality if the person (or someone else, such as a child) is in serious and immediate danger; or enlist the help of others (e.g., police department, ambulance).

Diagnostic Interview

The purpose of a diagnostic interview is to obtain a clear understanding of the patient's particular diagnosis. Thus patient-reported symptoms and problems are examined in order to classify the concerns into a diagnosis. Typically, the Diagnostic and Statistical Manual IV (DSM IV; American Psychiatric Association, 1994) is used to develop a diagnosis based on five categories, or axes. The DSM IV is the psychiatric "bible" in that it is used by hospitals, clinics, insurance companies, and the vast majority of mental health professionals to classify and diagnose psychiatric problems. While the DSM system is the most widely used diagnostic classification of psychiatric disorders in the United States, other classification systems exist and have both advantages and disadvantages relative to DSM (Mjoseth, 1998). The five axes for each diagnosis provide information concerning the clinical syndromes, influence of potential personality disorders, medical problems, psychosocial stressors, and level of functioning. Specifically, Axis I includes the presence of clinical syndromes (e.g., depression, panic disorder, schizophrenia). Axis II includes potential personality disorders (e.g., paranoid, antisocial, borderline). Axis III includes physical and medical problems (e.g., heart disease, diabetes, cancer). Axis IV includes psychosocial stressors currently experienced by the patient (e.g., fired from job, marital discord, financial hardship). Axis V (Global Assessment of Functioning or GAF) includes a clinician rating of how well the patient is coping with his or her problems (1 = poor coping, 100 = excellent coping). The interview is conducted to rule out inapplicable diagnoses and rule in applicable ones. Thus, the goal of the interview is to determine whether the patient meets the diagnostic criteria of a particular disorder. The diagnostic categories outlined in the DSM IV are presented in Table 7.2.

Diagnostic interviewing can be challenging. It is frequently difficult to ascertain the precise diagnosis through interview alone. Also, comorbidity may

Table 7.2   Diagnostic Categories in the DSM IV and Examples

Disorders Usually First Diagnosed in Infancy, Childhood, or Adolescence (e.g., Mild Mental
  Retardation, Autistic Disorder, Attention Deficit Hyperactivity Disorder, Conduct Disorder)
Delirium, Dementia, and Amnesia and Other Cognitive Disorders (e.g., Dementia of
  the Alzheimer's Type, Vascular Dementia, Dementia Due to Parkinson's Disease)
Mental Disorders Due to a General Medical Condition (e.g., Personality Change Due to Head Injury)
Substance-Related Disorders (e.g., Alcohol Abuse, Caffeine Intoxication,
  Cannabis-Induced Anxiety Disorder, Inhalant Abuse)
Schizophrenia and Other Psychotic Disorders (e.g., Schizophrenia, Paranoid Type,
  Schizoaffective Disorder, Shared Psychotic Disorder)
Mood Disorders (e.g., Major Depressive Disorder, Bipolar I Disorder, Dysthymic Disorder, Cyclothymic Disorder)
Anxiety Disorders (e.g., Panic Disorder with Agoraphobia, Social Phobia,
  Post-traumatic Stress Disorder, Obsessive-Compulsive Disorder)
Somatoform Disorders (e.g., Hypochondriasis, Conversion Disorder, Body Dysmorphic Disorder)
Factitious Disorders (e.g., Factitious Disorder with Predominantly Physical Signs and Symptoms)
Dissociative Disorders (e.g., Dissociative Amnesia, Depersonalization Disorder)
Sexual and Gender Identity Disorders (e.g., Sexual Aversion Disorder,
  Male Erectile Disorder, Exhibitionism, Pedophilia)
Eating Disorders (e.g., Anorexia Nervosa, Bulimia Nervosa)
Sleep Disorders (e.g., Primary Insomnia, Sleepwalking Disorder, Nightmare Disorder)
Impulse-Control Disorders Not Elsewhere Classified (e.g., Kleptomania, Pathological Gambling, Trichotillomania)
Adjustment Disorders (e.g., Adjustment Disorder with Depressed Mood,
  Adjustment Disorder with Disturbance of Conduct)
Personality Disorders (e.g., Paranoid Personality Disorder, Borderline
  Personality Disorder, Histrionic Personality Disorder)
Other Conditions That May Be a Focus of Clinical Attention (e.g., Psychological Factors Affecting
  Physical Condition, Relational Problems, Malingering, Religious or Spiritual Problem)

complicate the clinical picture. For instance, a patient who has been losing a lot of weight might be interviewed to determine whether he or she has anorexia nervosa, a disorder that results in self-starvation. Most people who have anorexia nervosa are adolescent girls. Significant weight loss may also be associated with a number of medical problems (e.g., brain tumor) or other psychiatric problems (e.g., depression). To determine whether the weight loss symptoms might be associated with anorexia nervosa, the clinician may wish to conduct a diagnostic interview to see if the patient meets the DSM IV diagnostic criteria for anorexia nervosa. Furthermore, additional possible diagnoses may need to be considered as well (e.g., depression, phobia, borderline personality). While some clinicians might choose to use a structured clinical interview such as the DIS or SCID approach (see next section for description of structured interview approaches), most would conduct their own clinical interview.

Table 7.3 lists the DSM IV diagnostic criteria for anorexia nervosa that would be used during the interview process. Table 7.4 provides several examples of diagnoses among chidlren.

Structured Interviews

In an effort to increase the reliability and validity of clinical interviews, a number of **structured interviews** have been developed [e.g., The Anxiety Disorders Interview Schedule for Children, Silverman & Nelles, 1988; Diagnostic Interview Schedule (DIS), Robins, Helzer, Croughan, & Ratcliff, 1994; Structured Clinical Interview for DSM-IV (SCID-I and SCID-II), First, Spitzer, Gibbon, & Williams, 1997; Structured Interview for the Five-Factor Model of Personality (SIFFM), Trull & Widiger, 1997]. Although the SCID interview is the most common one used, each has both advantages and disadvantages depending on the goals of the

Table 7.3 Example of the Diagnostic Criteria of a Psychiatric Problem

---

DSM IV Criteria for Anorexia Nervosa

A. Refused to maintain body weight at or above a minimally normal weight for age and height (e.g., weight loss leading to maintenance of body weight less than 85% of that expected; or failure to make expected weight gain during period of growth, leading to body weight less than 85% of that expected).

B. Intense fear of gaining weight or becoming fat, even though underweight.

C. Disturbance in the way in which one's body weight or shape is experienced, undue influence of body weight or shape on self-evaluation, or denial of the seriousness of the current low body weight.

D. In postmenarcheal females, amenorrhea, i.e., the absence of at least three consecutive menstrual cycles. (A woman is considered to have amenorrhea if her periods occur only following hormone, e.g., estrogen, administration.)

Specify types:

Restricting Types: during the current episode of Anorexia Nervosa, the person has not regularly engaged in binge eating or purging behavior (i.e., self-induced vomiting or the misuse of laxatives, diuretics, or enemas).

Binge-Eating/Purging Type: During the current episode of Anorexia Nervosa, the person has regularly engaged in binge-eating or purging behavior (i.e., self-induced vomiting or the misuse of laxatives, diuretics, or enemas).

Source: American Psychiatric Association (1994). *Diagnostic and Statistical Manual-IV* (DMS-IV). Washington, D.C.: Author. Reprinted with permission from the American Psychiatric Association.

Table 7.4 Examples of DSM IV Diagnoses for Three Children

Jim:

Axis I: Separation Anxiety Disorder (309.21)
           Learning Disorder NOS (315.90)
Axis II: No Diagnosis on Axis II (V71.09)
Axis III: Type I Diabetes
Axis IV: Psychosocial Stressors: is picked on in school, mother has cancer
Axis V: GAF: Current (61), Past Year (65)

Peter:

Axis I: Attention Deficit/Hyperactivity Disorder, Predominantly Inattentive Type (314.01), Mild
           Disruptive Behavior Disorder, Not Otherwise Specified (312.9), Mild
           Depressive Disorder, Not Otherwise Specified (311.00)
Axis II: No Diagnosis on Axis II (V71.09)
Axis III: None reported
Axis IV: Psychosocial and Environmental Problems: father lost job,
              shares room with two other siblings in very small apartment
Axis V: GAF: Current (55), Past Year (65)

Beth:

Axis I: Oppositional Defiant Disorder (313.81)
           Academic Problem (V62.30)
Axis II: Mild Mental Retardation (317.00)
Axis III: Allergies
Axis IV: Psychosocial Stressors: parents divorce, moved to new school
Axis V: GAF: Current (55), Past Year (65)

interview and the patient involved (First et al., 1997). Structured interviews include very specific questions (e.g., "Have you ever had a spell or attack when all of a sudden you felt frightened, anxious, or very uneasy in situations when most people would not be afraid?" Robins et al., 1994) asked in a detailed flowchart format. The goal is to obtain necessary information to make an appropriate diagnosis, to determine whether a patient is appropriate for a specific treatment or research program, and to secure critical data that are needed for patient care. The questions are generally organized and developed in a decision tree format. If a patient answers yes to a particular question (such as in the example about panic), a list of additional questions might be asked to obtain details and clarification (e.g., "During this spell did your heart pound? Did you have tightness or pain in your chest? Did you sweat? Did you tremble or shake?" Robins et al., 1994). If the patient answers no to a particular question, the follow-up questions are skipped. Clinical judgment and spontaneity are minimized or eliminated in structured interviews. The interview proceeds in the same precise manner no matter who conducts it. Thus the interview resembles an oral questionnaire more than a conversation. Structured interviews have become a popular means of objectifying the interviewing process (Edelbrock & Costello, 1984; First et al., 1997; First, Gibbon, Spitzer, Williams, & Benjamin, 1997; Robins et al., 1994; Silverman & Nelles, 1988; Trull & Widiger, 1997; Wiens, 1989). Semistructured interviews offer some degree of flexibility in the questions asked by the interviewer. Structured and semistructured interviews tend to be used in research environments more than in clinical environments such as private practice or clinics. Paraprofessionals, nonprofessionals, and clinical or research assistants are often trained to conduct structured interviews to reduce the costs and enhance the uniformity associated with the interview process. An example of part of a structured interview is provided in Table 7.5. The interview is designed for diagnosing and better understanding social phobia among adolescents. A second example of part of a structured interview examining phobia is provided in Table 7.6.

Computer-Assisted Interviews

A next step in the evolution of structured interviews involves computer interviewing. As computers be-

come more sophisticated and less expensive, programs can be developed to administer highly complex, efficient, and effective interviews. Computers can be used to ask patients questions and record their responses in a very objective manner. Numerous decision trees can be employed for appropriate follow-up questions to patient's answers. Furthermore, some patients feel more comfortable answering sensitive and potentially embarrassing questions via computer rather than talking face-to-face with a human interviewer (Farrell, Complair, & McCullough, 1987). However, some people are uncomfortable with using computers in this way and prefer to talk with a professional person about problems.

Computer-assisted interviews have been used in clinic settings where patients can answer a variety of questions about their concerns while waiting in a waiting area prior to their face-to-face meeting with a counselor. Results from the computer interview can be provided to the counselor to help in the treatment process. Confidentiality concerns must be addressed when sensitive material is being requested in a public area (e.g., waiting room) and when access to computer files is not closely controlled.

Exit or Termination Interview

After treatment is completed, an exit, or termination, interview may be used to help evaluate the effectiveness of treatment or to smooth the patient's transition to the next psychotherapeutic step (e.g., discharge from a hospital to a group home or to an outpatient facility). The interview might focus on how the patient experienced the treatment, what the patient found useful or not useful, and how he or she might best deal with problems in the future. Another goal of the exit interview may be to determine what residual problems still need to be addressed or to give the patient a sense of closure regarding the therapeutic experience. The interview may or may not be conducted by the treating professional. Especially in large treatment facilities such as hospitals and clinics, someone other than the treating professional might conduct a termination interview in order to minimize bias. For example, it may be difficult for a patient to tell his or her therapist directly that the treatment was unhelpful or to criticize the clinician's techniques. However,

Table 7.5 Example of a Structured Interview

SOCIAL PHOBIA (SOCIAL ANXIETY DISORDER)

I. INITIAL INQUIRY

Many times kids (teenagers) feel scared or uncomfortable in situations or places with other people. They get nervous about what other people might think, or that they might make mistakes and look silly or foolish and then get embarrassed. But some kids (teenagers) feel <u>really</u> scared and uncomfortable in situations with other people—so scared and uncomfortable that they might want to <u>stay away</u> from these places. Some kids (teenagers) might also cry, or even have a temper tantrum, or get angry when they have to be in situations with other people. What happens is that they might be told to go to these places, but they would rather not. They are much more afraid of these situations than other kids their age are. I want to know if this sounds at all like you.

_____ Yes _____ No _____ Other

If "Yes" or "Other", **Can you tell me about that?** _____

_____

Make sure that the child is responding to anxiety and fear in social situations. If Unclear, ask: **Okay, but tell me, is there any time that you feel nervous or scared when you're in school, or with friends, or when you have to do things in front of people, like give an oral report, or just talking to another person?**

_____ Yes _____ No _____ Other

When is that? Can you tell me more about that? _____

_____

_____

* *

If the child has a social-related situation, or if unsure, continue.
Otherwise, skip to **SPECIFIC PHOBIA** (p. 20).

* *

1a. **When you are in certain places with other people like school, restaurants, or parties, do you feel that these people might think that something you do is stupid or dumb?**

_____ Yes _____ No _____ Other

1b. **When you are in certain places with other people, like school, restaurants, or parties, do you think these people might laugh at you?**

_____ Yes _____ No _____ Other

1c. **When you are in these situations with other people, do you worry that you might do something that will make you feel ashamed or embarrassed?**

_____ Yes _____ No _____ Other

For any question(s) 1a-c that the child endorsed, the interviewer might wish to obtain further elaborations to determine if those areas are clinically significant.

_____

_____

_____

_____

FEAR (Yes/No)

2a. **Now I am going to give you a list of some situations and ask you if you think you get more nervous or scared in these situations than other kids your age do. Answer "Yes" if you think you get more nervous than others. Also, answer "Yes" only if these situations almost always make you scared or nervous, not if it's just happened once or twice. First just tell me "Yes" or "No".**

NOTE: The interviewer may use discretion inquiring about age-relevant situations. Those situations more common to older children and adolescents are grouped at the end of the list.

138

Table 7.5 (*continued*)

FEAR RATING (0-4)

2b. For each situation to which the child responded "Yes," obtain fear ratings using the Feelings Thermometer. Ask, **When you say that you're afraid or nervous** (e.g., giving an oral report), **how afraid do you feel when you're** (e.g., giving an oral report)? **Use the thermometer to show me how afraid or nervous you get.**

AVOIDANCE (Yes/No)

2c. For each situation to which the child responded with a 2 or greater for fear, inquire for avoidance behavior. Ask, **When you say that you're scared or nervous** (e.g., working in a group), **do you ever try to avoid or stay away from** (e.g., working in groups)?

	Yes	No	Fear (0-4)	Avoidance (Yes/No)
Answering questions in class	—	—	—	———
Giving a report or reading aloud in front of the class	—	—	—	———
	Yes	No	Fear	Avoidance
Asking the teacher a question or for help	—	—	—	———
Taking tests	—	—	—	———
Writing on the blackboard	—	—	—	———
Working or playing with a group of kids	—	—	—	———
Gym class	—	—	—	———
Walking in the hallways/hanging out by your locker	—	—	—	———
Starting or joining in on a conversation	—	—	—	———
Using school or public bathrooms	—	—	—	———
Eating in front of others (e.g., home, school cafeteria, restaurants)	—	—	—	———
Meetings such as girl/boy scouts or team meetings	—	—	—	———
Answering or talking on the telephone	—	—	—	———
Musical or athletic performances	—	—	—	———
Inviting a friend to get together	—	—	—	———
Speaking to adults (e.g., store clerk, waiters, principal)	—	—	—	———
Talking to persons you don't know well (e.g., strangers, new or unfamiliar people)	—	—	—	———
Attending parties, dances or school activity nights	—	—	—	———
Having your picture taken (e.g., for the yearbook)	—	—	—	———
Dating	—	—	—	———
Being asked to do something that you really don't want to do, but you can't say no. For example, if someone wants to borrow your homework or favorite toy, is it hard to say no?	—	—	—	———
Having someone do something to you that you don't like, but you can't tell them to stop. For example, if someone is teasing you, is it really hard for you to tell them to leave you alone?	—	—	—	———

Are there any other times that being around people makes you nervous or scared?

———— Yes ———— No

If "Yes", **Could you tell me about that?** _____

_____

_____

* *

If the child responded "No" to any of Questions 1a-c, and reports no fear or avoidance in any situation in Question 2, skip to **SPECIFIC PHOBIA** (p. 20).

* *

Table 7.5   (*continued*)

To meet Diagnostic Criteria for Social Phobia, the child must respond "Yes" to at least 1 question from 1a-1c of any situation listed in Question 2 and either avoid or endure social situation with intense anxiety or distress. In addition, there must be evidence of significant interference in the child's normal routine in Section II.

Now I want to find out more details about some of those things that bother you. When you tell me that (insert specifics of the child's fear, for example, "you don't like to start a conversation"):

3. **Does it make a difference if the people are friends or strangers?**

_____ Yes _____ No _____ Other

If "Yes", **Which is easier?** _____

4. **Does it make a difference if the group is boys, girls, or boys and girls?**

_____ Yes _____ No _____ Other

If "Yes", **Which is easier?**   _____ Boys _____ Girls _____ Boys & Girls Together

5. **Does the age of the people matter?**   _____ Yes _____ No _____ Other

If "Yes", **Which is easier: older than you, younger than you, or the same age as you?**

_____ Older than you _____ Younger than you _____ Your age

6. **Does the size of the group make a difference?**   _____ Yes _____ No _____ Other

If "Yes", **Which is easier: big groups, small groups, or medium size groups?**

_____ Big _____ Small _____ Medium

7. **What do you think will happen when you are in (give specifics of feared social situation?**

_____
_____
_____

II. INTERFERENCE

Okay, I want to know how much this problem has messed things up in your life. That is, how much has it messed things up for you with friends, in school, or at home? How much does it stop you from doing things you would like to do? Tell me how much by using the thermometer we discussed earlier, okay? If necessary, the interviewer should review the scale with the child. Show the child the Feeling Thermometer and obtain an overall rating of interference.

Child's Rating _____

OPTIONAL INTERFERENCE INQUIRY

To obtain a breakdown of specific areas of interference, the interviewer may ask the following questions.

Does this problem mess things up for you at school? Think about whether it stops you from doing things at school and makes it hard for you to have fun at school.

_____ Yes _____ No _____ Other

Does this problem mess things up with friends? Think about whether it keeps you from making friends or doing things with friends.

_____ Yes _____ No _____ Other

Does this problem mess things up for you with your family? Think about whether it keeps you and your family from doing things you would all like to do.

_____ Yes _____ No _____ Other

Does this problem mess things up for you, such as sleeping, eating, or concentrating on things like homework? Does it cause you to cry or to get upset easily?

_____ Yes _____ No _____ Other

Source: Adapted from *The Anxiety Disorders Interview Schedule for Children* (Silverman & Nelles, 1988).

Table 7.6 Example of Part of a Structured Interview from the SCID-I

SPECIFIC PHOBIA	SPECIFIC PHOBIA CRITERIA	SCREEN Q #7		
		YES	**NO**	
IF SCREENING QUESTION #7 ANSWERED "NO," SKIP TO OBSESSIVE-COMPULSIVE DISORDER			IF NO: GO TO OBSESSIVE-COMPULSIVE DISORDER	
IF QUESTION #7 ANSWERED "YES": You've said that there are other things that you've been especially afraid of, like flying, seeing blood, getting a shot, heights, closed places, or certain kinds of animals or insects. . .				
IF SCREENER NOT USED: Are there any other things that you have been especially afraid of, like flying, seeing blood, getting a shot, heights, closed places, or certain kinds of animals of insects? Tell me about that. What were you afraid would happen when (CONFRONTED WITH PHOBIC STIMULUS)?	A. Marked and persistent fear that is excessive or unreasonable, cued by the presence of anticipation of a specific object or situation (e.g., flying, heights, animals, receiving an injection, seeing blood).	? 1 2 3 ↓ GO TO OBSESSIVE-COMPULSIVE DISORDER		F67
Did you always feel frightened when you (CONFRONTED PHOBIC STIMULUS)?	B. Exposure to the phobic stimulus almost invariably provokes an immediate anxiety response, which may take the form of a situationally bound or situationally predisposed panic attack. Note: in children, the anxiety may be expressed by crying, tantrums, freezing, or clinging.	? 1 2 3 ↓ GO TO OBSESSIVE-COMPULSIVE DISORDER		F68
Did you think that you were more afraid of (PHOBIC STIMULUS) than you should have been (or than made sense)?	C. The person recognizes that the fear is excessive or unreasonable. Note: in children, this feature may be absent	? 1 2 3 ↓ GO TO OBSESSIVE-COMPULSIVE DISORDER		F69

? = inadequate information 1 = absent or false 2 = subthreshold 3 = threshold or true

Source: Specific Phobia section of the Structured Clinical Interview for DSM-IV Axis I Disorders, or SCID-I. From *Structured Clinical Interview for DSM-IV Axis I Disorder,* by M. B. First, R. L. Spitzer, and J. B. W. Williams, pp F16-F19. Copyright © 1996 Biometrics Research. Reprinted by permission.

in smaller treatment facilities, such as a solo independent practice, the treating professional usually conducts the termination interview.

Potential Threats to Effective Interviewing

Bias

Interviewers may be biased. Their personality, theoretical orientation, interests, values, previous experiences, cultural background, and other factors may influence how they conduct an interview, what they attend to, and what they conclude. Interviewers may consciously or unconsciously distort information collected during an interview based on their own slant on the patient or the patient's problems. For example, a psychologist is an expert on child sexual abuse. She treats patients who have been sexually abused as children and publishes professional articles and books on the topic. She is often asked to give lectures around the country on the subject. When a patient describes symptoms often associated with child sexual abuse such as depression, anxiety, low self-esteem, relationship conflicts, and sexuality concerns, the psychologist assumes that the symptoms are associated with sexual abuse. When a patient denies any experience of sexual abuse, the psychologist assumes that the patient has repressed or forgotten the traumatic memory. She then works to help the patient uncover the repressed memory in order to realize that they have been abused. Clearly, this example illustrates how **bias** can lead to distorted or even destructive approaches.

Reliability and Validity

Reliability and validity may also be threatened. For example, if two or more interviewers conduct independent interviews with a patient, they may or may not end up with the same diagnosis, hypotheses, conclusions, or treatment plans. Furthermore, patients may not report the same information when questioned by several different interviewers (Hubert, Wachs, Peters-Martin, & Gandour, 1982). Interviewer gender, race, age, and skill level are some of the factors that may affect patient response during an interview (Grantham, 1973). Emotional

level may also have an impact on reporting of information (Kolko, Kazdin, & Meyer, 1985). For example, personal questions regarding sexual behavior, alcohol use, child abuse, or other sensitive issues may elicit varying responses from patients under different circumstances. Reliability and validity may be enhanced by using structured interviews, asking similar questions in different ways, using multiple interviewers, and supplementing interview information from other sources (e.g., medical records, observers, questionnaires).

Behavioral Observations

Seeing is believing. Behavioral observations are an attempt by the psychologist or other trained observer to watch the problems and behaviors in question unfold naturally in the real world. While a clinical interview can provide a psychologist with a great deal of helpful information, this approach to assessment has a number of limitations. Perhaps most importantly, the clinical interview relies on self-report information that may or may not be accurate. Interview information is filtered through the perception, experience, and impression management orientation of the person being interviewed. Therefore, information obtained through an interview may be biased. For example, patients may minimize the degree of distress they experience. People with an alcohol problem may underreport the daily amount of alcohol they consume because of embarrassment and/or denial that they have a problem. Children who are reportedly disruptive and inattentive in class may appear attentive and well-behaved during an interview session when talking one-on-one with a psychologist. Information provided in an interview session may be intentionally or unintentionally distorted. Behavioral observations, whether naturalistic, self-monitoring, or controlled, provide an opportunity for the psychologist to see for himself or herself the concerns in question.

An important concept in behavioral observations include functional analysis (Skinner, 1953). **Functional analysis** refers to a behavioral analysis of the antecedents, or what led up to the behavior in question, as well as the consequences of the behavior. For example, if a child is disruptive in class, the behavior in question might involve speaking to his peers, leaving his seat, and refusing to complete assignments. A functional analysis of the behavior may reveal that being ignored by a teacher may precede the display of the problematic disruptive behavior and the consequences might include a great deal of attention (although negative attention) from the teacher and perhaps other school personnel (e.g., teacher's aide, principle) following the behavior. Functional analysis assumes that behaviors are learned and that antecedents result in the opportunity for the behavior to manifest itself while consequences maintain or reinforce the behavior.

Another important concept regarding behavioral observations includes selection of target behaviors. *Target behaviors* are specific behaviors that are examined, evaluated, and hopefully altered by interventions (Hawkins, 1987). It is often very difficult to isolate target behaviors. Many people seeking the consultation of a psychologist have vague complaints that may be difficult to observe and understand. For example, the teacher in the example might complain that a child is "unmotivated" in school and not "working to potential." The couple mentioned earlier who are unsure if they should marry might complain of a lack of passion in the relationship and feelings of boredom. Behavioral observations must identify clear target behaviors to observe. Developing operational definitions (i.e., specifically defined behaviors or concepts using reliable and valid measures for assessment) to clearly define target behaviors is needed for effective behavioral observations. For example, the term *unmotivated* might involve target behaviors such as not attending class, sloppy and incomplete homework, and looking out the window during classroom instruction. Lack of passion might be defined as infrequent sexual contact and/or highly unsatisfying sexual experiences.

Naturalistic Observation

Observing patients in their natural environments often helps psychologists develop a more comprehensive and realistic understanding of the problems that need to be addressed. For example, a child may be highly disruptive in class, get into frequent fights on the playground, and have numerous conflicts at home over homework or household chores. Teachers or parents may suspect an attention deficit disorder and refer the child to a psychologist for an evaluation. In addition to conducting an interview

with the child, family, and teachers, the psychologist might wish to observe the child at home and/or at school. In doing so, the psychologist can obtain firsthand information about the child's problematic behavior as well as examining the environmental and social influences (e.g., teacher, peer, and/or parental response to disruptive behavior, classroom seating arrangements) that may reinforce or encourage the child's disruptive behavior. Therefore **naturalistic observation** involves entering into the world of the patient in order to observe the person interacting with the environment in which problems occur.

Although there are many obvious advantages to observation in a natural environment, several important disadvantages should be addressed. First, naturalistic observations can be time consuming and expensive. The psychologist must travel to the home, school, or work environment as well as conduct the observation and then travel back to the office. The psychologist can therefore spend many hours out of a day involved with just one case. Second, confidentiality can be compromised when teachers, co-workers, peers, and others know that a psychologist is coming to observe so-and-so. Third, most people behave differently when they know they are being watched. This is refered to as *reactivity,* reflecting the notion that people often behave differently in private than in public while being watched by certain others (e.g., researchers or parents). For example, a disruptive child may be on his or her best behavior knowing that a psychologist is observing in the classroom or on the playground. Fourth, the problematic behavior may or may not occur when the psychologist is conducting his or her observation. The observation is a small snapshot of behavior that may not represent typical behavior. Finally, the observation may be biased. The psychologist may expect to see certain behavior (e.g., inattentiveness, impulsivity, and disruptive behavior) based on the information collected during the interview session. Furthermore, interested parties may try to influence the psychologist's judgment because they have a hidden agenda in the outcome of the evaluation. For example, a teacher may wish to have a perceived problem student taken out of the class. Thus the psychologist may focus on expected behaviors and ignore unexpected behaviors. These disadvantages often prohibit most psychologists from conducting on-site observations. Those who do conduct naturalistic observations often work on-site where direct observation is convenient and inexpensive. For example, school psychologists who work in an elementary or secondary school can easily observe a classroom or playground that may be located on the same premises as their office.

Many efforts have been made to increase the convenience, reliability, and validity of naturalistic observations. For example, Patterson (1977) developed the Behavioral Coding System (BCS), which provides a structured and research-based observational coding system for trained observers to record and classify disruptive behavior at home. Others have developed structured observational coding methods for specific populations (e.g., children, mentally challenged adults, hospitalized psychiatric patients) and problems (e.g., depression, anxiety, work behaviors, Jones, Ulicny, Czyzewski, & Plante, 1987; Lewinsohn & Shaffer, 1971; Mariotto & Paul, 1974; O'Leary & Becker, 1967). Many of these scales can be used by trained paraprofessionals to reduce the costs associated with conducting naturalistic observations. However, most of these techniques and scales are still employed primarily for research purposes and only infrequently for clinical purposes.

Self-Monitoring

Whereas naturalistic observations are conducted by a trained clinician, researcher, paraprofessional, or appropriate person other than the patient, **self-monitoring** is conducted by the identified patient. The patient is instructed in how to observe and record his or her own behavior in an objective manner. Self-monitoring has become a very commonly used tool not only for assessing problems but also as an intervention.

Patients are instructed to maintain a diary or log where they can record the problematic behaviors as well as other important information such as feelings and thoughts associated with each behavioral occurrence. For example, someone who is trying to lose weight might be asked to write down everything he or she eats for several weeks. The food item, quantity, and time might be recorded for each eating episode. The person might be asked to also record feelings and thoughts at the time as well as what happened before and after each eating episode. In this way, both patient and psychologist develop a better understanding of the target behavior, or

problem, as well as the factors that may encourage or reinforce it. These self-monitoring diaries can then be analyzed in various ways. For instance, total calorie consumption, percentage of fat in the diet, and stress-related eating episodes can be more closely assessed using this method than with a traditional interview. Although many people might find self-monitoring boring and a chore, computer technology (e.g., self-monitoring computer software and small datebook-size hand-held computers) as well as other methods have made self-monitoring easier and more pleasant (e.g., Taylor, Agras, Losch, Plante, & Burnett, 1991). Self-monitoring has been successfully employed with a large number of problem behaviors other than eating problems, including smoking (Pomerleau & Pomerleau, 1977), sleeping problems (Miller & DiPilato, 1983), anxiety symptoms (Cooper & Clum, 1989), and criminal behavior (Shapiro, 1984).

There are also several important disadvantages to self-monitoring. First, patients often have some reaction to the process of recording their behavior, which changes the very behavior that is being assessed. Paradoxically, this disadvantage in getting an accurate assessment can become a treatment advantage. For example, if patients know that they must write down everything they eat, they may think twice before impulsively eating a high-fat, high-calorie treat such as candy or cookies (Fig. 7.2). Thus self-monitoring is often used as both an intervention and an assessment technique. A second disadvantage is that few people are willing to self-monitor for a long period of time. Thus compliance to the self-monitoring task can be a challenge for many. Finally, embarrassment and denial may prevent people from honestly completing the self-monitoring assignment. For example, someone who has to report in to a professional might shy away from recording a binge-eating episode for fear of reproach.

Controlled Observations

In a **controlled observation,** the psychologist attempts to observe behavior in a prescribed manner. Rather than waiting (and hoping) for target behaviors to unfold in the natural environment or for the patient to report on the behavior using a self-monitoring technique, controlled observations force the behavior of interest to occur in a simulated

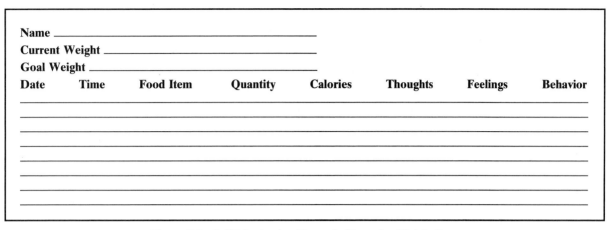

Name _____

Current Weight _____

Goal Weight _____

Date	Time	Food Item	Quantity	Calories	Thoughts	Feelings	Behavior

Figure 7.2   Self-Monitoring Example Form for Weight Loss

manner. For example, a person who is interested in reducing public-speaking anxiety may be asked to present a speech in front of the psychologist and other patients who also have public-speaking anxiety. In this way the psychologist can observe at first hand the patient's behavior in a controlled, confidential, and unthreatening environment. Stress interviews are another kind of controlled observation. To determine how someone copes with stress, the person may be asked to participate in a stressful interview situation or be required to complete a stressful task while being observed. These techniques were especially popular in the military following World War II (OSS Assessment Staff, 1948; Vernon, 1950). One example employed by a graduate school admissions committee involved asking a candidate to open a window in a room with several members of the committee present. The window, unbeknownst to the applicant, had been nailed shut. The committee observed how the applicant handled the impossible task of trying to open the window. Another technique entails the use of leaderless groups (Ansbacher, 1951). Small groups of people without a designated leader are required to solve a problem or participate in a discussion, with observers watching behind a one-way mirror. The observers see who develops as a leader in the group and who takes a passive role.

Perhaps the most commonly used type of controlled observation is the role play. Role plays require people to act as if they were in a particular situation that causes them concern. For example, patients who have trouble making new friends might

be asked to role play with the psychologist (or a research or clinical assistant) how they might try to meet a new neighbor. People who have trouble being assertive with family members might be asked to role play telling their mothers they are not coming home for Thanksgiving dinner. Thus, in conducting a role play, the patient and other participants are requested to act as if they were in a brief play. They are asked to stay in role as if they were indeed in the prescribed situation. Role plays might be videotaped to review later for teaching purposes. Role plays can be used both for the assessment of a particular problem and for treatment interventions. For example, they are frequently used to help people become more assertive or socially skilled (Plante, Pinder, & Howe, 1988).

Checklists and Inventories

Interviews and behavioral observations can provide a great deal of helpful information in a psychological assessment. However, a major disadvantage of both methods is that they generally take a lot of time to complete and therefore tend to be expensive. It is not uncommon for several hundred and even thousands of dollars to be billed for interview and observational assessments. Additionally, if many assessments are needed (e.g., screening military recruits, factory workers, hospital employees), it is often impractical to conduct intensive interviews and behavioral observations for each person. Concerns regarding reliability and validity also emerge when using these techniques. As mentioned earlier, the expectations, interests, perspectives, and prejudices of the interviewer and observer may uniquely influence each assessment.

To avoid these disadvantages, many psychologists utilize checklists and inventories to assess behavior. These are brief pencil-and-paper questionnaires that assess one or more traits or problem areas. They can be administered to a large number of people at one time, are inexpensive, and can be quickly scored and analysized. Clinical information obtained from checklists and inventories tends to be more reliable and valid than information collected through most interview and observational methods. This is because extensive research is conducted on most of these measures before they become available for purchase and use. Numerous checklists and inventories have been developed to assess and diagnose a wide variety of problems such as anxiety, depression, eating disorders, and attention deficit disorders. These instruments generally are very brief, easy to complete, and need little instruction or supervision from a professional. They may focus on feelings, thoughts, and/or behavior and are typically either hand or computer scored. While seemingly straightforward, checklists and inventories also need to be sensitively interpreted in the context of other measures as well as biological, psychological, and social factors. This section highlights three of the most commonly used instruments in clinical psychology: the Beck Inventories, the Child Behavior Checklist, and the Symptom Checklist 90-Revised.

Beck Inventories

Aaron Beck, a founding father of cognitive-behavioral psychotherapy, has developed a series of inventories to assess depression, anxiety, hopelessness, and suicidal ideation (thoughts of hurting oneself). All the **Beck Scales** are brief (all include 21 items, except the 20-item hopelessness inventory) and are used with persons who range in age from 17 to 80 years. Each scale takes only 5 to 10 minutes to complete and employs a simple scoring system so that hand scoring is both easy and quick. The Beck Depression Inventory (BDI; Beck 1987, 1993; Beck, Steer, & Brown, 1996) has become the most widely-used checklist instrument to assess the severity of depressive symptoms. The BDI has been revised and updated several times with the most

recent version (BDI-II) published in 1996. The Beck Anxiety Scale (BAS; Beck 1990, 1993) is a popular instrument for assessing the intensity of anxiety symptoms. The Beck Hopelessness Scale (BHS; Beck 1988, 1993) assesses hopelessness about the future and examines feelings regarding the loss of motivation and expectations. Finally, the Beck Scale for Suicide Ideation (BSS; Beck 1991) assesses suicidal thinking. Research demonstrates that the Beck Scales are both reliable and valid. These inventories often are used during an initial assessment evaluation as well as during the course of psychotherapy to assess progress and treatment outcome.

Child Behavior Checklist (CBCL)

The **Child Behavior Checklist** (CBCL; Achenbach, 1991) is a checklist of over 100 problem behaviors or symptoms (e.g., disobedient at school, cries a lot) experienced by children aged 4 through 18. Parents are asked to evaluate their child using a 3-point scale on each of the symptoms. The CBCL also includes a series of questions concerning the child's activities, chores, friends, and grades. A teacher's version of the checklist is available [i.e., Teacher's Report Form (TRF)] as well as a self-report form for children aged 11 to 18 to complete [i.e., Youth Self-Report (YSR)]. Furthermore, a semistructured clinical interview [i.e., the Semistructured Clinical Interview for Children and Adolescents (SCICA)] and a direct observation form (i.e., DOF) are also available.

Each of the measures is hand or computer scored and compared with national norms. Separate scores are obtained on a number of both internalizing symptoms (e.g., anxious/depressed, social problems, attention problems) and externalizing symptoms (e.g., delinquent behavior, aggressive behavior). The CBCL and related instruments have satisfactory psychometric properties in terms of reliability and validity. Like the Beck scales, the CBCL is frequently incorporated into an initial evaluation and periodically both during and following treatment to evaluate progress and outcome.

The Symptom Checklist 90-Revised (SCL-90-R)

The **SCL-90-R** (Deregotis, 1983) is a brief and multidimensional self-report measure to screen persons for major psychiatric symptoms. The SCL-90-R consists of 90 items, scored on a 5-point scale, that reflect nine validated symptom dimensions (e.g., anxiety, depression, interpersonal sensitivity, obsessions, psychoticism). The checklist can be administered to people aged 13 through adulthood and generally takes 10 to 15 minutes to complete. A brief form of the SCL-90-R [i.e., the Brief Symptom Inventory (BSI); Derogatis, 1982] that includes only 53 items is also available. In addition to scores on each of the nine dimensions, a Global Severity Index is calculated to assess the depth of the disorder, and a Positive Symptom Distress Index is designed to assess the intensity of the symptoms. Reliability and validity research indicates that the SCL-90-R has satisfactory psychometric properties. It is also used throughout evaluation, treatment, and follow-up periods to evaluate progress and outcome.

Other Checklists and Inventories

In addition to the checklists and inventories already outlined, many other instruments have been developed for specific populations or clinical problems. These include, among others, the Conner's Rating Scales (Conners, 1989), which focus on the assessment of hyperactivity and other child behavioral problems; the Children's Depression Inventory (CDI; Kovacs, 1985); and the Goldfarb Fear of Fat Scale (GAFFS; Goldfarb, Dykens, & Gerrard, 1985) used with eating-disordered patients. Table

---

Case Study: Jose and the BDI, CBCL, and SCL-90-R

Brief Identifying Information: Jose is a 17-year-old Hispanic high school junior. He lives with his parents and three siblings. Jose identifies himself as homosexual.

Referral Question: Jose's parents have noticed an abrupt shift from Jose's typically cheerful and energetic demeanor to a pattern of tearfulness, lethargy, anxiety, irritability, and inability to eat or sleep adequately. Jose has told his parents that he has been feeling depressed and anxious about his college applications, stating "I don't know what I want to do with my life." He was referred by his parents for a psychological evaluation to determine the nature of his current symptoms and obtain appropriate recommendations. There is significant family history of depression and anxiety.

Tests Administered: Interview, BDI, CBCL, and SCL-90-R

Brief Summary and Interpretation of Results: Jose's score on the Beck Depression Inventory (23) places him in the "severely depressed" range of this measure. On the Child Behavior Checklist (Parent Report Form), significant elevations were obtained on the Anxious/Depressed, Attention Problems, Somatic Complaints, and Withdrawn scales. On the SCL-90-R, significant elevations were revealed on the Interpersonal Sensitivity, Depression, Anxiety, Paranoia, and Positive Symptom Distress Index scales. Taken together, these checklist measures clearly corroborate significant levels of depression and anxiety in Jose's profile. However, the cause, nature, and content of these symptoms still remain unanswered by these measures alone.

Results from the clinical interview revealed that Jose had become deeply depressed following the discovery that his former boyfriend tested positive for HIV, the virus associated with Acquired Immune Deficiency Syndrome (AIDS). This revelation has plummeted Jose into a state of fear, guilt, hopelessness and ultimately, major depression. While he has shared his sexual orientation with his parents, he has been afraid of telling them about his former boyfriend's HIV, and even more frightened to obtain an HIV test himself. His family history of depression and anxiety may make him biologically vulnerable to depression in the context of significant psychosocial stress.

The clinical psychologist assessing Jose made the following recommendations. First, Jose requires ongoing therapy with a supportive clinician who can assist him in traversing this difficult crisis. A clinician especially sensitive to homosexuality, terminal illness, and Hispanic culture would be indicated. Second, adjunctive work with Jose's parents, given his consent, will be useful in assisting them in supporting their beloved son. Third, a psychiatric consultation may be useful to determine whether antidepressant medications are indicated to assist in treating Jose's depression. Fourth, assisting Jose in developing contacts with community resources, such as a group for young gay men and AIDS information hotline, would be beneficial. Fifth and finally, processing with Jose the emotional and medical implications of obtaining an HIV test while remaining alert to his fears will be necessary to assist him in making a responsible choice with adequate preparation.

7.7 provides a list of checklists and inventories used in clinical practice and research.

Like all assessment procedures, checklists and inventories have some disadvantages as well as advantages. Because these instruments rely on self-report information, people may distort their answers or try to present themselves in a favorable or unfavorable light. Furthermore, checklists and inventories do not provide the depth and complexity of information obtainable through interview, observation, and other assessment measures. Thus, they are typically used as a screening tool rather than for an in-depth analysis of a particular person or problem. Screening is a useful means of determining the need for further assessment in specific areas. Cognitive and personality testing seeks to obtain more detailed, complex, and comprehensive data than available from checklists and inventories.

Physiological Testing

Physiological tests have increasingly been integrated into contemporary clinical psychology. Psy-

Table 7.7   Examples of Checklists and Inventories

Alcohol Beliefs Scale
Assertion Inventory
Brief Depression Rating Scale
Compulsiveness Inventory
Dieting Beliefs Scale
Fear of AIDS Scale
Fear of Intimacy Scale
Goldfarb Fear of Fat Scale
Hopelessness Scale for Children
Hospital Fears Rating Scale
Illness Behavior Inventory
Interpersonal Dependency Inventory
McGill Pain Questionnaire
Panic Attack Symptoms Questionnaire
Physical Self-Efficacy Scale
Rational Behavior Inventory
Santa Clara Strength of Religious Faith Questionnaire
Self-Control Schedule
Self-Esteem Rating Scale
Sexual Behavior Inventory
Social Fear Scale
Social Support Appraisals Scale
Stress-Arousal Checklist
West Haven-Yale Multidimensional Pain Inventory

Source: Fischer, J., & Corcoran, K. (1994). *Measures for clinical practice: A sourcebook* (Vol. 2, Adults). New York: Free Press.

chological states such as anxiety and stress can be assessed through noninvasive techniques that measure physiological activity (e.g., blood pressure, heart rate, and sweating, respiration, and muscle tension; Blascovich & Katkin, 1993; Gatchel & Blanchard, 1993). Physicians may order and interpret **neuroimaging** techniques such as Magnetic Resonance Imaging (MRI), Computerized Axial Tomography (CAT), and Position Emission Tomography (PET) scans to examine physiological activities associated with mood and other psychological states. Some clinical psychologists use polygraph or biofeedback equipment to assess physiological activities such as blood pressure, heart rate, respiration, and muscle tension, which indicate levels of arousal, stress, and anxiety. **Polygraphs,** or lie detector tests, measure physiological reactions but have been highly criticized for being unreliable and invalid (Lykken, 1991). Whereas polygraphs measure physiological activity in a reliable and valid way, most professionals feel that to attribute certain physiological states to the act of lying is a stretch that is not supported by research data (Lykken, 1991).

Biofeedback equipment is similar to polygraphs in that it measures physiological activity. Unlike polygraphs, biofeedback provides information to patients or subjects about their level of physiological arousal through visual or auditory feedback (e.g., high-pitched tone sounds when heart rate is fast and low-pitched tone sounds when heart rate is slow). Technological advances have resulted in the development of small and inexpensive devices that measure these physiological states. Thus, the devices can be used in professional offices or at home by patients. They are also used to assess and treat people with disorders associated with overactivity of the sympathetic nervous system (e.g., Raynaud's disease, irritable bowel syndrome, Type A behavior pattern, headaches, and anxiety disorders). Biofeedback provides this information to patients who then try to lower their physiological arousal through the use of relaxation or other techniques. For example, thermal biofeedback, which provides patients with information regarding their hand temperature, is the treatment of choice for Raynaud's disease, a condition of restricted blood flow that causes cold and often pain in the hands and feet (Freedman, 1993). The use of these technological advancements

Figure 7.3 (*left*) A medical technician operates a Magnetic Resonance Imaging (MRI) installation with brain image on screen and patient module in background; (*right*) A patient receives biofeedback treatment.

is likely to be helpful in the assessment of a wide variety of mental and physical health problems of interest to clinical psychologists and others in the future.

The Big Picture

Clinical psychologists provide a unique and extremely challenging and useful skill in the form of psychological testing. Interviews, behavioral observations, checklists and inventories, and physiological measures provide important information that can be used in conjunction with other tests to make diagnostic conclusions and intervention decisions. Always, these tests need to be contextualized given the unique constellation of biopsychosocial factors affecting individual's and their test results. Future clinical psychologists will likely fine-tune these instruments making them more reliable, valid, and useful among diverse populations. In Chapter 8, the assessment of cognitive functioning and personality will be described, as these tools assist the clinical psychologist in delving deeper and deeper into the intellectual, emotional, and interpersonal worlds of patients.

Key Points

1. Since the earliest days of clinical psychology, assessment and testing have been important professional activities. Psychological assessment and testing are the major professional activities of many clinical psychologists.

2. Psychological assessment is the process psychologists use to collect and evaluate information in order to make diagnoses, plan treatment, and predict behavior. Assessment may include interviewing the patient, reviewing past records (such as medical or school records), observing behavior, and administering psychological tests to measure various cognitive, behavioral, personality, family, and even biological variables. Psychological testing is a specific assessment technique utilizing reliable and valid testing instruments. Tests usually compare individual scores with the scores obtained from normative samples.

3. The goal of assessment is usually to size up the situation by developing a fuller understanding of the factors that contribute to the presenting problem(s). An assessment is necessary in order to make a diagnosis and outline a subsequent treatment or intervention plan.

4. The clinical interview is a thoughtful and deliberate conversation designed to acquire important information (facts, attitudes, beliefs) that allows the psychologist to develop a working hypothesis of what the problem(s) is/ are about. Although there are numerous examples of interviewing situations (initial intake or admissions interview, mental status interview, crisis interview, structured interview, computer-assisted interview, exit, or termination interview), several techniques and skills are necessary for all types of interviews. These include developing rapport, active listening, effective communication, observation of behavior, and asking the right questions.

5. Potential threats to effective interviewing include bias as well as inadequate reliability and validity. The patient's background and other factors may bias or influence the manner in which an interview is conducted as well as what might be attended to and concluded. Interviewers may consciously or unconsciously distort information collected during an interview based on their own slant on the patient or the patient's problems. Reliability and validity may also be threatened. For example, two or more professionals interviewing the same person may come to very different conclusions.

6. Behavioral observations are an attempt by the psychologist or other trained observers to watch the problems and behaviors in question unfold naturally in the real world. There are several different types of behavioral observations including naturalistic, self-monitoring, and controlled. Naturalistic observations involve entering into the world of the patient in order to observe the person

interacting with the environment in which problems occur. Self-monitoring is conducted by the identified patient who is instructed in how to observe and record his or her own behavior in an objective manner. Controlled observations force the behavior of interest to occur in a simulated manner, such as during a role play.

7. Checklists and inventories are brief pencil-and-paper questionnaires that assess one or more trait or problem areas. They provide a quick, inexpensive, reliable, and valid way to obtain useful clinical information. Examples include the Beck Scales, the Child Behavior Checklist, and the Symptom Checklist 90-Revised.

8. Psychological states such as anxiety and stress can be assessed through noninvasive techniques that measure physiological activity (e.g., blood pressure, heart rate, and sweating, respiration, and muscle tension). Clinical psychologists often use polygraph or biofeedback equipment to assess physiological activity such as blood pressure and heart rate, which indicate levels of arousal, stress, and anxiety.

Key Terms

Active Listening	Mental Status Interview	Rapport
Beck Scales	Naturalistic Observation	Reflection
Bias	Neuroimaging	Symptom Checklist 90-Revised (SCL-90-R)
Biofeedback	Objective Testing	
Child Behavior Checklist (CBCL)	Paraphrasing	Self-Monitoring
Clarification	Polygraph	Structured Interview
Controlled Observation	Projective Testing	Summarization
Functional Analysis		

For Reflection

1. Why is assessment needed in clinical psychology?

2. How is psychological assessment and psychological testing the same or different?

3. What are the factors that contribute to effective interviewing?

4. What are the different types of clinical interviews?

5. What are major threats to effective interviewing?

6. What are the major methods to directly observe behavior in an assessment?

7. What are some of the advantages of checklists and inventories?

8. What types of constructs are checklists and inventories likely to assess?

9. What are examples of assessment procedures that measure physiological activity?

10. Why might a psychologist be interested in assessing physiological activity?

CHAPTER 8

Contemporary Psychological Assessment II: Cognitive and Personality Assessment

Chapter Outline

Highlight of a Contemporary Clinical Psychologist: Lori Goldfarb Plante, Ph.D.

Congnitive Testing

Intellectual Assessment Case Study: WAIS-III with Gabriel

Intellectual Assessment Case Study: WISC-III with Lillian

Personality Testing

Clinical Inference and Judgment

Communicating Assessment Results

HIGHLIGHT OF A CONTEMPORARY CLINICAL PSYCHOLOGIST:

Lori Goldfarb Plante, Ph.D.

Dr. Goldfarb Plante maintains a part-time private practice and teaches a seminar for clinical psychology interns while being a mom to a young son.

Birth Date: January 22, 1959

College: Pitzer College (B.A. in Psychology), 1982

Graduate Program: University of Kansas (M.A. and Ph.D. in Clinical Psychology),1987

Clinical Internship: Yale University School of Medicine (1986–1987)

Postdoctoral Fellowship: Cornell University Medical College, New York Hospital (1987–1988)

Current Job: Clinical Assistant Professor, Stanford University School of Medicine; Private Practice

Pros and cons of being a clinical psychologist:

Pros: 1. tremendous gratification in helping others
2. fascinating problems and people
3. autonomy and freedom

Cons: 1. low salaries
2. a great deal of responsibility

Future of clinical psychology:
1. Increased need for specialization
2. Increasingly complex presenting problems of patients and less insurance coverage for adequate treatment
3. Decreased opportunities for private practice

Typical schedule:

9:00   Psychotherapy session with young, single mother having relationship difficulties with baby's father and also a history of bipolar illness.

10:00 Psychotherapy session with priest experiencing conflict with colleagues, stress, and health concerns

11:00 Teach seminar to Postdoctoral Fellows and Psychology Interns: Advanced Psychological Assessment of Children and Adolescents

1:00   Supervision of Postdoctoral Fellow: Assessment case

2:00   Paper work and phone calls

3:00   Psychotherapy session with adolescent male experiencing school expulsion and acting out difficulties

4:00   Two hour psychological assessment of teenage female to evaluate for depression and possible thought disorder following recent suicide attempt and violent threat towards her mother

151

This chapter expands the discussion of assessment in clinical psychology. Cognitive assessment measures a host of intellectual capacities and encompasses the subspecialty of neuropsychological assessment, which examines brain-behavior relationships. Personality testing accesses both underlying intrapsychic issues as well as overt behavioral manifestations of each individual's unique psyche. Once all the assessment data are collected and examined by the psychologist, decisions can be made regarding diagnosis, treatment plans, and predictions about future behavior. How does the psychologist integrate and draw conclusions from all the data? How does he or she communicate results to the patient and other interested parties (e.g., family members, school teachers, physicians, attorneys)? This fascinating and unique clinical psychology endeavor will be explored in depth.

Cognitive Testing

Cognitive testing is a general term referring to the assessment of a wide range of information-processing or thinking skills and behaviors. These comprise general neuropsychological functions involving brain-behavior relationships, general intellectual functions (such as reasoning and problem solving) as well as more specific cognitive skills (such as visual and auditory memory), language skills, pattern recognition, finger dexterity, visual-perceptual skills, academic skills, and motor functions. Cognitive testing may include aptitude testing, which assesses cognitive potential such as general intelligence, and achievement testing, which assesses proficiency in specific skills such as reading or mathematics. Cognitive testing utilizes well-known tests such as the Scholastic Aptitude Test (SAT) and all kinds of IQ tests. Thus, cognitive testing is an umbrella term that refers to many different types of tests measuring many different types of thinking and learning skills. While it is beyond the scope of this book to consider all the specific tests available, intelligence testing will be discussed in detail.

Intelligence Testing

Measuring intellectual ability has long been a major activity and interest of clinical psychologists. As noted in Chapter 3, the goals of **intellectual testing** during the earliest years of the field were to evaluate children in order to help them maximize their educational experience and to assist teachers in developing curricula for children with special needs. Intelligence testing was also used to screen military recruits. Today it is still used for these purposes. However, it is also employed for vocational planning, assessing learning disabilities, determining eligibility for gifted and special education programs, and examining brain-behavior relationships following head injuries, strokes, or other medical conditions. Intellectual testing is used to not only obtain an IQ score, but to learn more about an individual's overall cognitive strengths and weaknesses. Thus, it is used not only to measure intelligence but to assess cognitive functioning in general.

Many myths and misconceptions about intelligence testing persist. Alfred Binet (1857–1911), creator of the first IQ test, expressed concern about the misinterpretation, overgeneralization, and misuse of his test almost immediately after it was developed. Unfortunately, IQ testing has been frequently misused by some professionals as well as the public. Often people erroneously assume that IQ tests are perfect measures of an innate and stable ability we call "intelligence" and that these scores perfectly predict success in life and self-worth. Controversy continues over the reliability, validity, meaning, and usefulness of IQ scores and testing. Questions concerning IQ testing and racial bias, for example, have been the topic of best-selling books, feature articles in national magazines, and even legislative initiatives (Herrnstein & Murray, 1994). Some people have used the IQ as a way to perpetuate racist beliefs that certain ethnic groups are innately less intelligent than other groups. Before discussing the major intelligence tests, a brief discussion of the definition of intelligence is warranted.

What Is Intelligence? Unfortunately there is no definition or theory of intelligence that all experts agree upon. Controversy exists among the numerous professionals who specialize in intelligence research and testing concerning how best to define and understand intelligence (Sternberg, 1997). In fact, there are so many definitions that Sternberg and Kay (1982) suggested that there were more definitions than experts! Even as early as 1923, Boring (1923) cynically defined intelligence as what intelligence tests measure. The most influential and often-cited definitions and theories of intelligence include those offered by Spearman (1927), Thurstone (1931, 1938), Cattell (1963, 1971, 1979), Guilford (1967, 1979, 1985), Piaget (1952, 1970, 1972), and, more recently, Sternberg (1996, 1997), Gardner (1983, 1986, 1994), and Goleman (1995). While it is beyond the scope of this book to present detailed descriptions of all these definitions and theories, a brief overview will help put in context the types of tests currently available to measure intellectual, or cognitive, functioning.

Spearman (1927), well known and respected for his development of statistical techniques, offered a two-factor theory of intelligence that suggested that any intellectual task or challenge required the input of two factors: *general* abilities of intelligence (which Spearman referred to as *g*) and *specific* abilities of intelligence (referred to as *s*). Overall, Spearman emphasized through factor analysis research that intelligence was primarily a broad-based and general ability. Factor analysis is a complex statistical technique that helps to identify specific factors from sets of variables. Spearman's notion of intelligence as a comprehensive overall general ability has greatly influenced not only the conception of intelligence but also the development of intelligence tests for many years.

Also using factor analysis, Thurstone (1931, 1938) disagreed with Spearman and suggested that intelligence included nine separate group factors or *primary mental abilities.* Thurstone reasoned that intelligence did not comprise two but nine unique and independent skills or abilities. He termed these nine abilities verbal relations, words, perceptual ability, spatial ability, induction, deduction, numerical ability, arithmetic reasoning, and memory. Thurstone thus focused on distinct and separate abilities that together comprise intelligence.

Cattell (1963, 1971, 1979) expanded Spearman's two-factor theory regarding the notion of a broad-based general intelligence (*g*) factor and suggested that (*g*) consisted of two components, which included both fluid and crystallized abilities. Cattell defined *fluid abilities* as the person's genetic or inborn intellectual abilities, whereas *crystallized abilities* are what a person learns through experience, culture, and various opportunities arising from interaction with the world. Fluid abilities resemble

Spearman's *g* and refer to general problem-solving abilities, abstract reasoning, and ability to integrate and synthesize information quickly and efficiently. Crystallized abilities resemble Spearman's *s* and refer to specific skills developed and nurtured through training and experience. Cattell and colleagues also included the role of motivation, personality, and culture in their investigation and understanding of intelligence.

Guilford (1967, 1979, 1985) provided a comprehensive classification system of 150 specific intellectual abilities in his attempt to define intelligence. In contrast to the statistical and factor analytic approach and theories of Spearman, Thurstone, and Cattell, Guilford reasoned that intelligence consisted of three categories: operations (i.e., mental activity needed to solve a particular intellectual problem), contents (i.e., the specific issue or problem needing to be addressed), and products (i.e., the end result, or bottom line, of the mental activity). Guilford outlined five types of operations, i.e., memory, cognition, evaluation, divergent production, convergent production; five categories of content, i.e., visual, auditory, semantic, symbolic, and behavioral; and six products, i.e., class, relation, system, unit, transformation, implication. Each intellectual task required, according to Guilford, at least one element from each of the three categories for a possible combination of 150 factors of intelligence.

Unlike the theories of intelligence mentioned, Piaget (1952, 1970, 1972) added a developmental perspective to intellectual theory. Piaget sought to develop a theory of how humans understand their world through actively adapting and interpreting their life experiences. He suggested that humans have four major stages of cognitive development (i.e., sensorimotor, preoperational, concrete operational, and formal operations), each having a variety of substages. Piaget used the terms *assimilation* to refer to gathering information and *accommodation* to refer to changing existing cognitive structures (or schemes) to allow for the newly incorporated and assimilated information. Rather than using laboratory or statistical analyses, Piaget conducted cognitive tasks and experiments with his own children to develop his theories of intellectual and cognitive development.

These traditional theories of intelligence tend to focus on the discovery and understanding of the structure or components of intelligence. Tests were used and developed based on these theories in an attempt to measure a variety of skills such as reasoning, analytical thinking, and language skills. These theories and tests were designed to measure what we know or what we are able to accomplish with a new problem. More recent theories of intelligence use an information-processing model to better understand the process or manner in which we attempt to solve problems. The speed, level, and type of processing someone experiences when trying to solve problems are of interest to many experts in the field of intelligence research and testing today. Furthermore, contemporary views of intelligence include practical, creative, and emotional aspects in addition to more traditional abstract reasoning and academic abilities (Gardner, 1994; Goleman, 1995; Sternberg, 1996). Particularly influential recent developments in theories of intelligence include the work of Robert Sternberg (1996, 1997) and Howard Gardner (1983, 1986, 1994), and reflect a more biopsychosocial perspective in the description of intelligence.

Sternberg offered a triarchic theory of intelligence that identifies three categories of intelligence: componential, experiential, and contextual. This theory is consistent with the holistic biopsychosocial perspective. The *componential* aspect of intelligence includes analytical thinking, and the *experiential* factor includes creative abilities. The *contextual* factor refers to good "street smarts" and the ability to adapt to and manipulate the environment. Thus, Sternberg views intelligence as involving practical and creative elements, with biological, psychological, and social underpinings, traditionally ignored in both research and assessment of intellectual functioning.

Gardner (1983, 1986, 1994) developed a theory of multiple intelligences comprising six different types of intelligence: linguistic, logical-mathematical, musical, bodily-kinesthetic, spatial, and personal. Gardner's view thus includes music and body awareness, which have been ignored in earlier views of intelligence. Both Sternberg and Gardner have attempted to develop theories of intelligence that emphasize the practical aspects of human existence, accounting for a wider variety of skills and tasks and cultural contexts utilized to survive and thrive in the world. Recent emphasis on emotional intelligence (Goleman, 1995) further highlights the more holistic approach to understanding intellectual functioning and suggests that social skills and emotional functioning play an important role in "intelligence" as well as the ability to achieve goals and be successful. Knowing and managing one's emotions and recognizing emotions in others are part of emotional intelligence (Goleman, 1995), and have tremendous biopsychosocial implications. For example, social experiences may enhance or squelch the appreciation of and opportunities for the development of social skills and managing emotions to maximize social relationships. Psychological stress and trauma may also contribute to the inability to manage emotions and understand the emotions of others. At this time, however, these new views of intelligence offered by Sternberg, Gardner, and others have not resulted in the development of new tests that are commonly used in clinical psychology. Therefore, the traditional IQ tests will be presented here, and their interpretation highlighted with a more biopsychosocially informed appreciation.

How Do Clinical Psychologists Measure Intelligence? There are hundreds of tests that propose to measure intelligence or cognitive ability. Different tests have been developed for use with various populations such as children, adults, ethnic minority group members, the gifted, and the disabled (e.g., visually, hearing, or motorically impaired individuals). Some tests are administered individually, while others are administered in groups. Some tests have used extensive research to examine reliability and validity, whereas others have very little research support. Some are easy to administer and score, while others are very difficult to use. Although there are many intelligence tests to choose from, only a small handful of tests tend to be used consistently and widely by most psychologists. Clearly, the most popular and frequently administered tests include the **Wechsler Scales** [i.e., the Wechsler Adult Intelligence Scale-Third Edition (WAIS-III), the WAIS-R as a Neuropsychological Instrument (WAIS-R NI), the Wechsler Intelligence Scale of Children-Third Edition (WISC-III), the Wechsler Primary and Preschool Scale-Revised (WPPSI-R)]. The second most frequently used intelligence test is the Stanford-Binet (Fourth Edition). Other popular choices include the Kaufman Assessment Battery for Children (K-ABC) and the Woodcock-Johnson Psychoeducational Battery.

Wechsler Scales

Wechsler Scales for Adults. The Wechsler-Bellevue Intelligence Scale was developed and published by David Wechsler (1896–1981) in 1939. The test was revised in 1955 and renamed the Wechsler Adult Intelligence Scale (WAIS) and revised again in 1981 as the Wechsler Adult Intelligence Scale-Revised (WAIS-R; Wechsler, 1981). The most recent edition of the scale is the third edition published in 1997 (WAIS-III; Wechsler, 1997a) and thus the WAIS-III is the current version of the test in use today (Table 8.1). The WAIS-III consists of seven individual Verbal subtests (Information, Similarities, Arithmetic, Vocabulary, Comprehension, Digit Span, and Letter-Numbering Sequencing) and seven Performance (or nonverbal) subtests (Picture Completion, Picture Arrangement, Block Design, Object Assembly, Matrix Reasoning, Digit Symbol, and Symbol Search). Each subtest includes a variety of items that assess a particular intellectual skill of interest (e.g., the Vocabulary subtest includes a list of words that the respondent must define). The WAIS-III generally takes about one to one-and-a-half hours to individually administer to someone between the ages of 16 and 74. Three IQ scores are determined using the WAIS-III: a Verbal IQ, a Performance IQ, and a Full Scale (combining both Verbal and Performance) IQ score. The mean IQ score for each of these three categories is 100 with a standard deviation of 15. Scores between 90 and

Table 8.1 Descriptions of the WAIS-III Subtests

Subtest	Description
Picture Completion	A set of color pictures of common objects and settings, each of which is missing an important part that the examinee must identify
Vocabulary	A series of orally and visually presented words that the examinee orally defines
Digit Symbol—Coding	A series of numbers, each of which is paired with its own corresponding hieroglyphic-like symbol. Using a key, the examinee writes the symbol corresponding to its number
Similarities	A series of orally presented pairs of words for which the examinee explains the similarity of the common objects or concepts they represent
Block Design	A set of modeled or printed two-dimensional geometric patterns that the examinee replicates using two-color cubes
Arithmetic	A series of arithmetic problems that the examinee solves mentally and responds to orally
Matrix Reasoning	A series of incomplete gridded patterns that the examinee completes by pointing to or saying the number of the correct response from five possible choices.
Digit Span	A series of orally presented number sequences that the examinee repeats verbatim for Digits Forward and in reverse for Digits Backward
Information	A series of orally presented questions that tap the examinee's knowledge of common events, objects, places, and people
Picture Arrangement	A set of pictures presented in a mixed-up order that the examinee rearranges into a logical story sequence
Comprehension	A series of orally presented questions that require the examinee to understand and articulate social rule and concepts or solutions to everyday problems
Symbol Search	A series of paired groups, each pair consisting of a target group and a search group. The examinees indicates, by marking the appropriate box, whether either target symbol appears in the search group
Letter–Number Sequencing	A series of orally presented sequences of letters and numbers that the examinee simultaneously tracks and orally repeats, with the number in ascending order and the letters in alphabetical order
Object Assembly	A seat of puzzles of common objects, each presented in a standardized configuration, that the examinee assembles to form a meaningful whole

Source: From Wechsler (1997).

110 are considered within the average range of intellectual functioning. Scores below 70 are considered to be in the mentally deficient range, while scores above 130 are considered to be in the very superior range. The individual subtests (e.g., Vocabulary, Block Design) have a mean of 10 and a standard deviation of 3. These subtests form the basis for subtle observations about the relative strengths and weaknesses possessed by each individual.

The Wechsler scales has been shown to have acceptable reliability, validity, and stability (Anastasi, 1988; Parker, Hanson, & Hunsley, 1988; Wechsler, 1981, 1997). Factor analytic research has suggested that the Wechsler scales consists of two factors: a Verbal/Comprehension factor (primarily assessed using the Information, Comprehension, Similarities, and Vocabulary subtests) and a Perceptual/Organizational factor (primarily assessed using the Block Design and Object Assembly subtests; Gutkin, Reynolds, & Galvin, 1984). However, Parker (1983) suggests a third factor in addition to the two outlined by Gutkin et al. (1984). The third factor is a Freedom from Distractibility factor (primarily assessed using the Digit Symbol, Arithmetic, and Digit Span subtest).

Edith Kaplan and associates have developed an expanded version of the WAIS-R called the WAIS-R as a Neuropsychological Instrument (WAIS-R NI; Kaplan, Fein, Morris, Delis, 1991). The WAIS-R NI contains additional subtests (e.g., Sentence Arrangement, Spatial Span, Symbol Copy) as well as modifications for administration and scoring (e.g., using pencil and paper for the Arithmetic subtest and multiple choice for the Vocabulary, Information, and Similarities subtests) in order to be more useful for individuals who may have brain dysfunction. This is just one of an arsenal of neuropsychological tests utilized in psychology, an area of testing covered more fully later in this chapter.

In addition to overall IQ scores, most psychologists make inferences about cognitive strengths and weaknesses by examining the pattern of scores obtained on each WAIS-III subtest. For example, high scores on the vocabulary subtest relative to very low scores on the block design subject might suggest that the person has good use of language in solving problems and a poorer ability to solve problems using certain perceptual and motor integration skills. Additionally, the Wechsler scales can be helpful in learning about neuropsychological problems

such as brain damage (Kaplan et al., 1991), as well as psychological and personality functioning (Allison, Blatt, & Zimet, 1968). For example, low scores on performance subtests of the WAIS-III, such as picture completion, picture arrangement, and block design relative to high scores on the verbal subtests, such as information, vocabulary, and comprehension, has been associated with certain brain impairment associated with alcoholism and dementia (Kaplan et al., 1991).

Finally, IQ tests should always be interpreted in the context of other assessment measures. As subsequent examples will illustrate, even a seemingly straightforward IQ test needs to be integrated with other test results as well as the panoply of biopsychosocial factors impacting the individual and his or her performance. Otherwise, the scores in isolation can be rendered meaningless or even misleading.

The Wechsler Scales for Children. The Wechsler Intelligence Scale for Children (WISC) was first published in 1949 and was revised in 1974 (and renamed the Wechsler Intelligence Scale for Children-Revised; WISC-R) and revised again in 1991 (renamed the Wechsler Intelligence Scale for Children-Third Edition; WISC-III). The WISC-III is the current version of the test used today. The WISC-III has both Verbal and Performance scales similar to those used on the WAIS-R. However, WISC-III questions are generally simpler because they were developed for children aged 6 to 16. The Verbal scales consist of the following six subscales: Information, Similarities, Arithmetic, Vocabulary, Comprehension, and Digit Span. The Digit Span subtest, however, is not calculated in the overall Verbal IQ score, and is included as an optional scale. The Performance scale consists of the following five subtests: Picture Completion, Picture Arrangement, Block Design, Object Assembly, and Coding. Additional and optional subtests include Mazes and Symbol Search, which are not calculated as part of the overal Performance IQ score. Optional subtests are used to assess aspects of cognitive functioning which are not considered part of the IQ such as processing speed (Symbol Search) and immediate memory (Digit Span). Like the WAIS-III, the WISC-III provides three IQ Scores: Verbal, Performance, and Full Scale with mean IQs set at 100 with a standard deviation of 15. The

Intellectual Assessment Case Study: WAIS-III with Gabriel

Brief Identifying Information: Gabriel is a 64-year-old unmarried Caucasian male who lives alone and is presently unemployed. He has periodically worked as a cook. He was adopted at birth and little is known about his biological parents.

Referral Question: Gabriel was referred for cognitive and personality testing by his physician due to concerns related to depression, relationship difficulties and conflicts with coworkers, and inability to hold a job. He is repeatedly fired from his jobs for inadequate performance. Intellectual testing was conducted as part of a complete psychological battery to determine his cognitive functioning as it may relate to his present work-related difficulties. His WAIS-III subtest scaled scores were as follows:

Verbal Subtests	Scaled Scores	Performance Subtests	Scaled Scores
Information	14	Picture Completion	7
Similarities	14	Picture Arrangement	12
Arithmetic	12	Block Design	8
Vocabulary	19	Object Assembly	10
Comprehension	19	Digit Symbol	8
Digit Span	12	Matrix Reasoning	10
Letter–Number Sequencing	15	Symbol Search	9

Scaled scores between 7 and 13 are within normal limits

Verbal Score	= 133	(99th percentile)
Performance Score	= 104	(61st percentile)
Full Scale Score	= 123	(87th percentile)

Brief Summary of IQ Results: Gabriel is a very intelligent man currently functioning in the superior range of overall (full scale) intelligence. However, there is a significant discrepancy between his very superior Verbal IQ and average Performance IQ, pointing to relative difficulties in his perceptual-motor abilities. Depression may also contribute to these score differences. While Gabriel demonstrates exceptional strengths in verbal abilities, such as knowledge of vocabulary and social norms, his relative verbal weaknesses in the areas of arithmetic and remembering number series (i.e., digit span) further points to underlying perceptual and numerical limitations. His nonverbal performance skills, while average, represent a significant relative weakness.

Brief Interpretation of IQ Results: While IQ results must be interpreted in the context of other test results, several important findings emerge. First, Gabriel's perceptual-motor relative weakness may impact the physical aspects of his work as a cook, such as skills requiring manual dexterity, quickness, and strength in lifting heavy pots, etc. Second, visual perceptual skills are essential to interpersonal skills in that attention to nonverbal cues informs us in our social relationships. Finally, depression may contribute to lower perceptual-motor scores and should be further evaluated. Gabriel may therefore have subtle cognitive-relative weaknesses that contribute to his difficulties with coworkers and general social isolation. Further, personality, mood, and perceptual motor testing is necessary to fully address the biological, psychological, and social aspects of Gabriel's difficulties.

WISC-III also calculates four index scores: Verbal-Comprehension, Perceptual-Organization, Freedom from Distractibility, and Processing Speed. These index scores were developed using factor analytic techniques in understanding how several subtests assess different aspects of the same overall skill. For example, the vocabulary, information, comprehension, and similarities subtests combine to assess overall verbal-comprehension skills. As with the WAIS-III, each subtest score has a mean of 10 and a standard deviation of 3. The WISC-III has been shown to have satisfactory reliability, validity, and stability (Wechsler, 1991).

The *Wechsler Preschool and Primary Scale of Intelligence* (WPPSI) was developed and published in 1967 for use with children aged 4 to 6. The test was revised in 1989 and became known as the Wechsler Preschool and Primary Scale of Intelligence-Revised (WPPSI-R). The WPPSI-R is the current version of the test being used today. The WPPSI-R is used for children ranging in age from 3 to 7. Like the other Wechsler scales (WAIS-III, WAIS-III NI, WISC III), the WPPSI-R has both Verbal and Performance scales resulting in three IQ scores: Verbal IQ, Performance IQ, and Full Scale IQ. Similar to the other Wechsler scales, IQ scores have a

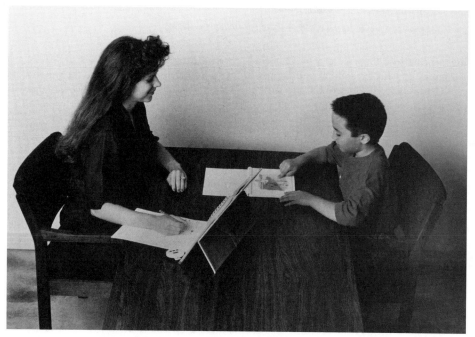

Figure 8.1 A child taking the WISC-III

mean of 100 and a standard deviation of 15, while the subtest scores have a mean of 10 and a standard deviation of 3. The Verbal subtests include Information, Vocabulary, Similarities, Arithmetic, Comprehension and an optional subtest entitled Sentences. The Performance subtests include Picture Completion, Block Design, Object Assembly, Mazes, and two optional subtests called Animal Pegs and Geometric Design. The WPPSI-R has been shown to have satisfactory reliability, validity, and stability (Wechsler, 1989).

Stanford-Binet Scales   The Stanford-Binet is a revised version of the first standardized intelligence test, developed by Alfred Binet in 1905. The test has been revised many times—in 1916, 1937, 1960, and most recently, in 1986. The current version of the test is called the Stanford-Binet—Fourth Edition (Thorndike, Hagen, & Sattler, 1986). The Stanford-Binet can be used with individuals from 2 years of age through adulthood, but standardization research was conducted with individuals from age 2 to 23. Therefore the test must be used cautiously with persons above age 23. The **Stanford-Binet Scales** consists of 15 subtests that result in separate scores in four intellectual areas of functioning. The Verbal Reasoning subtests include Vocabulary,

Comprehension, Absurdities, and Verbal Relations. The Abstract/Visual Reasoning subtests consist of Pattern Analysis, Copying, Matrices, and Paper Folding and Cutting. The Quantitative Reasoning subtests include Quantitative, Number Series, and Equation Building. Finally, the Short-Term memory subtests consist of Bead Memory, Memory for Sentences, Memory for Digits, and Memory for Objects. Unlike the Wechsler scales, only certain Stanford-Binet subtests are used with certain subjects. The age of the subject determines which subtests are used in any given evaluation. Scores from all subtest categories are used to derive an overall standard age score, or SAS, based on a mean of 100 and a standard deviation of 16. Research suggests that the Stanford-Binet has satisfactory reliability, validity, and stability (Anastasi, 1988; Thorndike et al., 1986). One important concern regarding the standardization sample is that children with parents from high socioeconomic levels were overrepresented in the development of the instrument (Kaufman & Harrison, 1991). Table 8.2 provides a list of the Stanford-Binet subtests and the types of items used.

Other Tests of Intellectual Ability   Numerous tests other than the Wechsler and Stanford-Binet are

Intellectual Assessment Case Study: WISC-III with Lillian

Brief Identifying Information: Lillian is a 12-year-old African-American girl currently in the seventh grade in a large public junior high. Lillian lives with her mother who is divorced from her father. She is closely involved with her father who has shared custody, resulting in Lillian spending one week with her mother, followed by one week at her father's home.

Referral Question: Lillian's teachers have recommended psychological evaluation in light of Lillian's poor attention in class, generally disruptive nature, and seeming disorganization around homework and studying. She appears bright, yet is performing poorly in most academic subjects. What is the basis for Lillian's behavior and low achievement? Her WISC-III subtest scaled scores follow:

Verbal Subtests	Scaled Scores	Performance Subtests	Scaled Scores
Information	12	Picture Completion	12
Similarities	15	Picture Arrangement	18
Arithmetic	7	Block Design	14
Vocabulary	12	Object Assembly	17
Comprehension	16	Coding	14
Digit Span	11		

Scaled scores between 7 and 13 are within normal limits

Verbal Score	=	114	(82nd percentile)
Performance Score	=	133	(99th percentile)
Full Scale Score	=	126	(96th percentile)
Verbal/ Comprehension Factor	=	122	(93rd percentile)
Perceptual/ Organizational Factor	=	132	(98th percentile)
Freedom from Distractibility Factor	=	96	(39th percentile)

Brief Summary of IQ Results: Lillian is indeed an extremely intelligent, energetic, and vivacious child who demonstrates superior overall intelligence in the context of above average verbal and very superior nonverbal (performance) skills. Her index scores are further revealing in that Freedom from Distractibility (comprised of the arithmetic and digit span scores) appears significantly impaired relative to her other index scores. Thus, Lillian, who was distractible and inattentive during the evaluation, appears to have some difficulties with these cognitive functions. Her high picture arrangement (tapping social planning skills) and verbal social comprehension scores point to her special talent with social relationships.

Brief Interpretation of IQ Results: Lillian is an extremely bright child who has the intellectual capacity to perform at a much higher academic level. However, her difficulties with attention and concentration may be impeding her ability to learn and perform both in the classroom and at home. She may therefore expend her energy on social relationships given her strong interpersonal interest and easy distraction from academics. Furthermore, the disruptions engendered by her moving between her parents' homes may be adding to her difficulties with organization, studying, and homework completion. Finally, as an African-American student in a predominantly Caucasian classroom, Lillian may feel uncomfortable and poorly integrated into the class milieu. Further assessment is necessary to determine whether Lillian may have an Attention Deficit Disorder and in order to assess biological, psychological, and social factors that may be contributing to her disruptive and inattentive behavior.

available for use with specific populations. For example, alternative tests may be used with special populations such as gifted children, nonverbal or hearing impaired individuals, or with minority group members. They may also be used as a second opinion following a Wechsler test or Stanford-Binet or to obtain additional cognitive information not available through the administration of the Wechsler or Stanford-Binet scales (e.g., reading achievement). While it is beyond the scope of this book to discuss all the available tests in detail, some of the more popular ones follow, and the reader may wish to consult other resources for more information concerning these tests (e.g., Anastasi, 1988). Examples of these alternative tests include the Kaufman Tests (Kaufman Assessment Battery for Children (K-ABC; Kaufman & Kaufman, 1983), which offer, for example, African- American norms, the Kaufman Brief Intelligence Test (K-BIT; Kaufman & Kaufman, 1990), the Kaufman Adolescent

Table 8.2   Subtests and Types of Test Items from the Stanford-Binet (Fourth Edition)

Subtests	Test Type Items
Verbal Reasoning	
Vocabulary	Define bus, mistake
Comprehension	Why should people exercise?
Absurdities	Identify the error in a series of pictures
Verbal Relations	How are three words alike yet different from a fourth word
	(e.g., How are mouse, bird, and ape alike yet different from a man)
Abstract/Visual Reasoning	
Pattern Analysis	
Copying	Arrange blocks to look like a design
Matrices	
Paper Folding and	
Cutting	
Quantitative Reasoning	
Quantitative	
Number Series	Which number comes next after a series of numbers: e.g., 5, 10, 15, ____, ____
Equation Building	
Short Term Memory	
Bead Memory	Arrange colored beads to look like pictures of beads organized in various ways
Memory for Sentences	
Memory for Digits	
Memory for Objects	Select the correct order of pictures that were presented earlier

and Adult Intelligence Test (KAIT; Kaufman & Kaufman, 1993), the Peabody Picture Vocabulary Test-Revised (PPVT-R; Dunn & Dunn, 1981), the Woodcock-Johnson Psychoeducational Battery, Raven's Progressive Matrices (Raven, 1993), the General Ability Measure for Adults (GAMA; Neglieri & Bardos, 1997), and the System of Multicultural Pluralistic Assessment (SOMPA; Lewis & Mercer, 1978; Mercer & Lewis, 1979). The K-ABC and SOMPA will be briefly outlined next.

The K-ABC is administered to children between the ages of 2.5 and 12.5 and has four global scales including Sequential Processing, Simultaneous Processing, Mental Processing Composite (combining both the Sequential and Simultaneous Processing measures), and Achievement. The development of the K-ABC reflects a different theoretical approach to intellectual assessment relative to the Wechsler scales. Sequential processing refers to problem-solving skills that use a step-by-step approach while simultaneous processing uses information from several sources to arrive at an answer all at once. Means are set at 100 with standard deviations of 15. The K-ABC was developed from research and theory in neuropsychology and, unlike both the Wechsler and Stanford-Binet scales, has achievement scores to measure skills such as reading ability. Many clinicians feel that the K-ABC is more enjoyable and engaging for children than the Wechsler scales and Stanford-Binet, as well as a less verbally dependent test. Furthermore, the K-ABC generally takes less time to administer than the Wechsler and Stanford-Binet.

The SOMPA is a comprehensive assessment of intellectual functioning for children aged 5 to 11 and is especially designed for children from minority groups such as African-American and Latino populations. SOMPA provides nine different measurements of cognitive functioning and includes a structured parent interview as part of the evaluation process. Many professionals feel that the SOMPA is much more useful with minority groups than the

Wechsler and Stanford-Binet measures. Issues regarding testing bias among minority group will be addressed later in this chapter.

Other Tests of Cognitive Ability   Some tests are not intelligence tests per se, but also measure cognitive abilities. For example, the Bayley Scales of Infant Development, Second Edition (BSID-II; Bayley, 1993), measures mental, motor, and developmental abilities among very young children aged 1 month to 42 months. The Vineland Adaptive Behavior Scales (Sparrow, Balla, & Cicchetti, 1986) and the Adaptive Behavior Scales, Second Edition (Lambert, Eland, & Nihira, 1992), examine adaptive behavior (e.g., dressing and eating independently) among children by focusing on socialization and the development of social competence. These scales are critical, for example, in documenting mental retardation in conjunction with IQ scores. Thus, IQ scores below 70 (reflecting 2 standard deviations below the mean) in conjunction with adaptive behaviors significantly below expectation for a given age are used to diagnose mental retardation. The Wide Range Achievement Test-3 (Jastak & Wilkinson, 1993) measures reading, writing, and mathematical skills for individuals aged 5 to 75. The Woodcock-Johnson test includes an achievement as well as aptitude component, measuring skills such as reading, writing, and mathematics.

Neuropsychological Testing   Other tests focus on brain-behavior relationships and thus measure neuropsychological functioning. Brain impairment due to head injury, substance abuse, stroke, or other illnesses and injuries often impact the cognitive ability to use language, think and make appropriate judgements, adequately perceive and respond to stimuli, and remember old or new information. **Neuropsychological testing** assesses brain-behavior skills such as intellectual, abstract reasoning, memory, visual-perceptual, attention, concentration, gross and fine motor, and language functioning. Since neuropsychological topics are highlighted in Chapter 11 it will be only briefly addressed here.

Neuropsychological tests include test batteries as well as individual tests. The Halstead-Reitan Battery (Boll, 1981; Halstead, 1947; Reitan & Davison, 1974) and the Luria-Nebraska Battery (Golden, Hammeke, & Purisch, 1980) are the most commonly used test batteries. The Halstead-Reitan Battery can be administered to persons aged 15 through adulthood and consists of 12 separate tests along with the administration of the MMPI-2 and the WAIS-III. The battery takes approximately 6–8 hours to administer and provides an overall impairment index as well as separate scores on each subtest assessing skills such as memory, sensory-perceptual skills, and the ability to solve new learning problems (Table 8.3). Other versions of the test are available

Table 8.3   Halstead-Reitan Neuropsychological Test Battery

Category Test	Current learning, abstract concept formation
Tactual Performance Test	Motor speed, psychomotor coordination
Rhythm Test	Attention, concentration, auditory perception
Speech Sounds Perception Test	Attention, concentration, coordination of language processing
Finger Oscillation Test	Finger tapping skill
Trail Making Test	Psychomotor speed, sequencing, maintain & shift sets
Strength of Grip Test	Gross motor strength
Sensory-Perceptual Examination	Ability to perceive stimuli to both body sides
Tactile Perception	Tactile finger localization
Modified Halstead-Wepman Aphasia Screening Test	Screening of language skill
Wechsler Adult Intelligence Scale-III (WAIS-III)	Intellectual functioning
Minnesota Multiphasic Personality Inventory-2 (MMPI-2)	Personality and psychological functioning

for children between ages 5 and 14. The Luria-Nebraska Battery consists of 11 subtests for a total of 269 separate testing tasks. The subtests assess reading, writing, receptive and expressive speech, memory, arithmetic, and other skills. The Luria-Nebraska battery takes about 2.5 hours to administer.

Another neuropsychological testing approach is represented by the **Boston Process Approach** (Goodglass, 1986; Milberg, Hebben, & Kaplan, 1986). The Boston process approach uses a variety of different tests depending upon the nature of the referral question (Table 8.4). Rather than using a

standard test battery, the Boston Process Approach uses a subset of a wide variety of tests in order to answer specific neuropsychological questions. Performance on one test determines which tests or subtests, if any, will be used next. The testing process could be short or long involving few or many tests and subtests depending upon what is needed to adequately evaluate strengths and weaknesses in functioning. For example, if a neuropsychological evaluation of a head injured patient was to focus on memory skills following a car accident, several tests would be considered for use. These might include the Benton Visual Retention Test, the Wechsler Memory Scale-III, and the Wisconsin Card Sorting Test. Each of these tests measure a different facet of memory functioning. Results provide a clearer picture of short- and long-term memory as well as visual, auditory, and sensory memory. If, during testing, language problems were detected, the receptive and expressive language sections of the Luria-Nebraska might be added to the battery to assess language skills. The language assessment might help to better understand the relationship between memory and language skills in this patient.

Some of the commonly used individual neuropsychological tests include the Wechsler Memory Scale-III (Wechsler, 1997b), the Benton Visual Retention Test (Benton, 1991), the WAIS-R as a Neuropsychological Instrument (Kaplan, Fein, Morris, & Delis, 1991), the Kaufman Short Neuropsychological Assessment Procedure (K-SNAP; Kaufman & Kaufman, 1994), the California Verbal Learning Test (Delis, Kramer, Kaplan, & Ober, 1987) and the California Verbal Learning Test-Children's Version (Delis, Kramer, Kaplan, & Ober, 1994), and the Wisconsin Card Sorting Test (Grant & Berg, 1993). These tests measure various aspects of cognitive functioning that reflect strengths and weaknesses associated with brain-behavior relationships. Results from these tests are compared with national norms to develop a clearer understanding of the interaction between brain functioning and behavior, emotions, and thoughts as well as to help locate the site of brain impairment.

Some authors have suggested that physiological tests such as evoked potentials, electroencephalography (EEG), and reaction time measures may be useful in the assessment of intelligence and cognitive abilities (Matarazzo, 1992; Reed & Jensen, 1991). Evoked potentials assess the brain's ability

Table 8.4 Sample of Tests Used in the Boston Process Approach to Neuropsychological Assessment

Intellectual and Conceptual Skills
Wechsler Adult Intelligence Scale-III (WAIS-III)
Standard Progressive Matrices
Shipley Institute of Living Scale
Wisconsin Card Sorting Test
Proverbs Test

Memory Skills
Wechsler Memory Scale-Revised
Rey Auditory Verbal Learning Test
Rey-Osterrieth Complex Figure
Benton Visual Recognition Test
Consonant Trigrams Test
Cowboy Story Reading Memory Test
Corsi Blocks

Language Skills
Narrative Writing Sample
Tests of Verbal Fluency (Word List Generation)

Visual-Perceptual Skills
Cow and Circle Experimental Test
Automobile Puzzle
Parietal Lobe Battery
Hooper Visual Organization Test

Academic Skills
Wide Range Achievement Test

Motor and Impulse Control Skills
Porteus Maze Test
Stroop Color-Word Interference Test
Luria Three-Step Motor Program
Finger Tapping

to process the perception of a stimulus, and EEG measures electrical activity of the brain. Although psychologists are currently not licensed to administer or interpret neuroimaging techniques such as computerized axial tomography (CAT), magnetic resonance imaging (MRI), and positron emission tomography (PET), these techniques allow examination of brain structure and function, which is useful in assessing brain-behavior relationships such as cognitive abilities. For example, cortical atrophy, shrinkage, or actual loss of brain tissue has been associated with schizophrenia, Alzheimer's disease, anorexia nervosa, alcoholism, and mood disorders (e.g., Andreasen, 1989, Andreasen & Black, 1995; Fischbach, 1992).

Contemporary neuropsychological testing integrates specialized tests along with additional sources of information. The tests are often used in conjunction with data obtained from clinical interviews, behavioral observations, and other cognitive, personality, and physiological assessment tools. Thus, neuropsychological testing is not isolated from other evaluation techniques used by contemporary clinical psychologists. While neuropsychological assessment is a subspecialty of clinical psychology, it overlaps with many of the skills and techniques of general clinical psychologists. In addition to specialized testing, neuropsychologists must have a high level of understanding of brain structure and functioning.

Questions and Controversies Concerning IQ and Cognitive Testing

Are We Born With a Certain IQ?   Often people assume that we are born with an innately determined level of intellectual ability that is not influenced by social, emotional, and environmental factors (Herrnstein & Murray, 1994). Some suggest that **IQ, Intellectual Quotient,** differences found among different racial groups might be due to inborn differences in intelligence. A great deal of controversy has raged in this debate for many years. The publication of the book *The Bell Curve* (Herrnstein & Murray, 1994) reignited this controversy by suggesting that African-Americans were innately less intelligent than Caucasians while Caucasians were less intelligent than Asians. Research examining genetic influences on intelligence generally studies the heritability (i.e., the estimate of genetic contribution to a given trait) of IQ using twin studies. Identical (monozygotic) and fraternal (dizygotic) twins reared together and reared apart present a unique research opportunity for examining the influence of both genetic and environmental contributions to a wide variety of traits. It has been estimated that the heritability of intelligence is be-

---

Neuropsychological Case Study: Robert

Brief Identifying Information: Robert is a 17-year-old Caucasian male who is a senior in high school. He lives with his father and younger sister. Robert was shot in the head when he was 11 years old during a robbery at a neighborhood store. His mother was also shot and tragically killed during the robbery. Robert has received surgery to obtain a cranial plate and glass eye. He experiences seizures and is being administered 100 milligrams of Dilantin per day.

Referral Question: Robert has been evidencing antisocial behavior over the past three years, including lying, stealing, truancy, and angry and aggressive outbursts. Neuropsychological testing was requested in order to determine the basis for his behavior in light of his brain damage.

Tests Administered: The Halstead-Reitan Neuropsychological Battery

Brief Summary and Interpretation of Test Results: Robert achieved an average Full Scale IQ, above average Verbal IQ, and average Performance IQ. Test results indicated some difficulties in sensory-perceptual functioning such that he experiences mild to moderate right upper extremity sensory-perceptual dysfunction consistent with left posterior frontal (i.e., sensory strip) and parietal compromise. Thus, he has difficulty moving and feeling with his right arm and shoulder. The nature of Robert's mild neuropsychological compromise is chronic, nonprogressive, and residual from his head trauma. Therefore, only a portion of his current behavioral problems can be attributed to neuropsychological compromise. Personality testing is recommended to evaluate the psychosocial basis for his antisocial behavior in the context of his traumatic brain injury.

tween .40 and .80. Thus between 16 percent and 64 percent of the variance in intellectual ability is due to genetic influence (Hale, 1991; Sattler, 1988, 1992). Research generally supports the notion of at least some significant genetic influence in intellectual ability (Neisser, et al., 1996). However, biological (e.g., prenatal care, genetics, nutrition), psychological (e.g., anxiety, motivation, self-esteem), and social (e.g., culture, socioeconomic status) influences all appear to be associated with intelligence or at least with IQ scores on standardized tests (Hale, 1991; Neisser et al., 1996; Sternberg, 1997).

Are IQ Scores Stable Over Time? Measures of attention, memory, and other cognitive abilities assessed during the first year of life generally are moderately associated (i.e., $r = .36$) with intelligence test scores assessed later in childhood (McCall & Garriger, 1993). Often people assume that an IQ score obtained in childhood is stable over time. Thus, many people erroneously believe that someone who obtained an IQ of 120 in the first grade will also have an IQ of 120 in adulthood. Intelligence tests, however, provide an index of current functioning, and scores may change significantly over time. Many factors influence the stability of IQ scores. First, scores obtained when a child is very young (e.g., age 3) are likely to be less stable than scores obtained when a child is older (e.g., age 16). This is partially because early childhood tests focus on perceptual and motor skills, whereas tests for older children and adults focus more on verbal skills (Anastasi, 1988; Brody, 1997; Hale, 1991; Sattler, 1988, 1992). Second, the longer the time between testing administrations, the more unstable the IQ score will appear. Thus, the difference between scores obtained at ages 3 and 30 is likely to be greater than the difference between scores obtained at ages 16 and 19. Furthermore, environmental factors such as stress, nutrition, educational opportunities, exposure to toxins such as lead, and illness, among other influences, all play a role in the determination of IQ scores (Anastasi, 1988; Hale, 1991; Sattler, 1988, 1992).

Are IQ Scores Biased? Many people are concerned about potential bias in intelligence testing (Cole, 1981; Greenfield, 1997; Helms, 1992; Neisser et al., 1996; Sandoval, 1989; Schiele, 1991). For example, many feel that IQ testing may be biased in

that children from high socioeconomic-level homes tend to perform better on standardized tests than those from lower socioeconomic-level homes. Furthermore, some argue that currently available intelligence tests may not be appropriate for use with individuals from many ethnic minority groups (Sandoval, 1989; Sattler, 1988, 1992; Schiele, 1991; Suzuki & Valencia, 1997). In fact, California passed legislation that prohibited intelligence testing from being used for school placement of African-American children (*Larry P.* v. *Wilson Riles*). The ruling suggested that intelligence testing was biased against African Americans and that they were disproportionately represented in educable mental retardation (EMR) classrooms. Bias is determined by examining the test's validity across different groups. A test is biased if the validity of the test varies from group to group. Research suggests that most standardized IQ tests such as the Wechsler and Stanford-Binet scales are not biased (Hale, 1991; Reynolds, 1982). However, tests can be misused by both unqualified and well-meaning people (Suzuki & Valencia, 1997).

Should the Terms Intelligence Quotient *or* IQ *Continue to be Used?* A number of misconceptions and myths about IQ exist. These include the notion that the IQ measures an innate or genetically-determined intelligence level, that IQ scores are fixed and never change, and that IQ scores generated from different tests mean the same thing (Hale, 1991; Sattler, 1988, 1992). These concerns have led some experts to suggest that general IQ scores be eliminated (Turnbull, 1979) in favor of standard scores that more accurately describe specific skills. In fact, many recent tests of intellectual and cognitive ability have not used the terms *intelligence quotient* or *IQ* at all. These include the Woodcock-Johnson Psychoeducational Battery, the Kaufman Assessment Battery for Children, and the newest version of the Stanford-Binet.

Conclusion Tests of cognitive ability are used to answer a wide variety of important clinical questions. In addition to identifying overall intellectual skills and cognitive strengths and weaknesses, these tests are frequently employed to assess the presence of learning disabilities, predict academic success in school, examine brain dysfunction, and assess personality. Any competent psychologist must be cautious in the use of intellectual, neuropsychological, achievement, and all other forms of cognitive testing. Professionals must be aware of the limitations of the testing situation and the limitations of the particular test they have chosen. They must be careful to use tests for the purpose for which the test was developed and researched, and in conjuction with other appropriate tests. They must also be able to understand the results in terms of the context of the individual's testing response style and the biopsychosocial influences that might affect particular scores. For instance, scores may not accurately reflect potential if a child is distracted due to severe stress or family conflict, chronic illness; compromised by poor nutrition; or disadvantaged due to poverty or frequent school disruption. In fact, some research has indicated that stress level and coping abilities are significantly associated with performance on intelligence and other tests of cognitive abilities (Plante, Goldfarb, & Wadley, 1993; Plante & Sykora, 1994).

Personality Testing

Personality testing in a sense accesses the heart and soul of an individual's psyche. **Personality testing** strives to observe and describe the structure and content of personality, which can be defined as the characteristic ways in which an individual thinks, feels, and behaves. Personality testing is particularly useful in clarifying diagnosis, problematic patterns and symptoms, intrapsychic and interpersonal dynamics, and treatment implications. Personality testing involves a wide variety of both objective and projective measures, both of which will be discussed in detail after the following explanations of the concepts *personality* and *psychological functioning.*

What Are Personality and Psychological Functioning?

Each human being has a unique manner of interacting with the world. Some people tend to be shy and withdrawn, while others are generally outgoing and gregarious. Some tend to be anxious worriers, while others are generally calm and relaxed. Some are highly organized and pay attention to detail, while others are disorganized and impressionistic. *Personality* refers to the enduring styles of think-

ing and behaving when interacting with the world (MacKinnon, 1944; Hogan, Hogan, & Roberts, 1996). Thus, it includes characteristic patterns that make each person unique. These characteristics can be assessed and compared with those of others. Personality is influenced by biological, psychological, and social factors. For example, research has shown that between 20 percent and 60 percent of the variance in personality traits (e.g., extroversion, sociability) are influenced by genetic factors (Loehlin, 1992; Plomin, 1990), with the remainder influenced by psychosocial factors (e.g., relationships that develop with parents, siblings, and friends, as well as life events; Bouchard & McGue, 1990). While the nature versus nurture debate rages on well beyond statistical models, personality development clearly reflects biological, psychological, and social factors.

Personality theories provide a way to understand how people develop, change, and experience generally stable and enduring behavior and thinking patterns. These theories also help us to understand the differences among people that make each person unique. Ultimately, personality theory is used to understand and predict behavior. This understanding is then used to develop intervention strategies to help people change problematic patterns.

Psychological functioning is a more general term referring to the individual's cognitive, personality, and emotional worlds. Thus, psychological functioning includes personality as well as other aspects of emotional, behavioral, cognitive, and interpersonal functioning. In this section, psychological functioning will refer to particularly noncognitive areas of functioning such as mood and interpersonal relationships. For example, while anxiety, depression, and anger may all be enduring personality traits, they can also be temporary mood states. Someone facing stressful life events, such as the death of a loved one or criminal victimization, may experience severe anxiety, depression, or anger. However, these mood states may not be associated with enduring personality characteristics. Thus, the individual may feel and behave in an anxious or depressed manner as a reaction to the stressful event(s) but does not tend to be anxious or depressed most of the time. Therefore, psychological functioning can be viewed as encompassing the gamut of component psychological processes as they impact one's ability to cope with life's pleasures and demands and uniquely combine to define personality.

Is Personality Really Enduring?

While a tremendous amount of research has been conducted on personality, controversy still exists concerning its definition and characteristics (Kenrick & Funder, 1988; West & Graziano, 1989). Some people question the very notion of personality, suggesting that enduring behavioral characteristics do not exist. While many believe that behavior is consistent across situations (e.g., a shy person is likely to behave in a shy manner wherever he or she goes), many argue that behavior is generally situation specific. Thus, someone may behave in a shy manner in a social situation with people he or she does not know very well while he or she might behave in a very outgoing manner at work or with close friends. Most professionals in the area of personality theory, research, and practice support an interactional approach (Kenrick & Funder, 1988). This approach suggests that behavior is predictable but is not rigidly consistent in an absolute sense. Therefore, people have personality styles that are generally consistent but interact with situational factors; personality and behavior differs somewhat from situation to situation.

How Do Clinical Psychologists Measure Personality and Psychological Functioning?

In addition to using interviews, observations, checklists, inventories, and even biological assessments (e.g., neuroimaging techniques such as PET scans), clinical psychologists generally use a range of tests to assess personality and psychological functioning. Most of these tests can be classified as either objective or projective. **Objective testing** presents very specific questions (e.g., Do you feel sad more days than not?) or statements (e.g., I feel rested) to which the person responds by using specific answers (e.g., yes/no, true/false, multiple choice) or a rating scale (e.g., 1 = strongly disagree, 10 = strongly agree). Scores are tabulated and then compared with those of reference groups, using national norms. Thus, scores that reflect specific constructs (e.g., anxiety, depression, psychotic thinking, stress) may be compared to determine exactly how anxious, depressed,

psychotic, or stressed someone might be relative to the norm. The checklists described in the previous chapter are examples of objective tests. **Projective testing** uses ambiguous or unstructured testing stimuli such as inkblots, incomplete sentences, or pictures of people engaged in various activities. Rather than answering specific questions using specific structured responses (e.g., yes/no, true/false, agree/disagree) subjects are asked to respond freely to the testing stimuli. For example, they are asked to tell stories about pictures, or describe what they see in an inkblot, or say the first thing that comes to their mind when hearing a word or sentence fragment. The theory behind projective testing is that unconscious or conscious needs, interests, dynamics, and motivations are projected onto the ambiguous testing stimuli, thereby revealing the internal dynamics or personality. Projective responses are generally much more challenging to score and interpret than objective responses.

Objective Testing   There are hundreds of objective tests of personality and psychological functioning. The reader may wish to consult other resources for detailed information about these instruments (e.g., Anastasi, 1988). Clinical psychologists usually employ a small set of objective tests to evaluate personality and psychological functioning. By far the most commonly used test is the Minnesota Multiphasic Personality Inventory (MMPI), now in its second edition (MMPI-2). The MMPI also includes an adolescent version called the Minnesota Multiphasic Personality Inventory-Adolescents (MMPI-A). Other objective tests such as the Millon Clinical Multiaxial Inventory-III (MCMI-III), the 16 Personality Factors Questionnaire, Fifth Edition (16PF), and the NEO-Personality Inventory-Revised (NEO-PI-R) will also be briefly discussed below.

The Minnesota Multiphasic Personality Inventory (MMPI, MMPI-2, MMPI-A).   The original MMPI was developed during the late 1930s and published in 1943 by psychologist Starke Hathaway and psychiatrist J.C. McKinley. The MMPI was revised and became available as the MMPI-2 in 1989. The original MMPI consisted of 550 true/false items. The items were selected from a series of other personality tests and from the developers' clinical experience in an effort to provide psychiatric diagnoses for mental patients. The original pool of about 1000 test items were considered and about 500 items were administered to psychiatric patients and visitors at the University of Minnesota hospitals. The **MMPI** was designed to be used with individuals aged 16 through adulthood. However, the test has been frequently used with adolescents younger than 16. The MMPI takes about one to one-and-a-half hours to complete.

Scoring the MMPI results in four validity measures and ten clinical measures. The validity measures include the ? (Cannot Say), L (Lie), F (Validity), and K (Correction) scales. Admitting to many problems or "faking bad" is reflected in an inverted V configuration with low scores on the L and K scales and a high score on the F scale. Presenting oneself in a favorable light or "faking good" is reflected in a V configuration with high scores on the L and K scales and a low score on the F scale. The clinical scales include Hypochondriasis (Hs), Depression (D), Conversion Hysteria (Hy), Psychopathic deviate (Pd), Masculinity-femininity (Mf), Paranoia (Pa), Psychasthenia (Pt), Schizophrenia (Sc), Hypomania (Ma), and Social Introversion (Si). Scores are normed using standardized T-scores, meaning that each scale has a mean of 50 and a standard deviation of 10. Scores above 65 (representing one-and-one-half standard deviations above

the mean) are considered elevated, and in the clinical range. While 65 is the cut off score on the MMPI-2 and MMPI-A, 70 is used with the original MMPI. Table 8.5 provides a description of each of the MMPI scales.

Since the MMPI was originally published, a number of additional subscales have been developed, including measures such as Repression, Anxiety, Ego Strength, Overcontrolled Hostility, and Dominance. It has been estimated that there are over 400 subtests of the MMPI (Dahlstrom, Welsh, & Dahlstrom, 1975). The MMPI has been used in well over 10,000 studies that examine a wide range of clinical issues and problems (Graham, 1990). Although the original MMPI was the most widely used psychological test, a revision was needed. For example, the MMPI did not use a representative sample when it was constructed. The original sample included Caucasians living in the Minneapolis, Minnesota, area who were either patients or visitors at the University of Minnesota hospitals. Also, many of the more sophisticated methods of test construction and analysis used today were not available in the late 1930s when the test was developed. Therefore, during the late 1980s, the test was restandardized and many of the test items were rewritten. Furthermore, many new test items were added, and outdated items were eliminated. The

Table 8.5   MMPI-2 Scales and Personality Dimension Measured

Scale Name	Personality Dimension Measured
Validity Scales	
? (Cannot Say)	Number of items unanswered
L (Lie)	Overly positive self report
F (Validity)	Admitting to many problems
K (Correction)	Defensiveness
Clinical Scales	
1 Hypochondriasis (Hs)	Concern regarding bodily functioning
2 Depression (D)	Hopelessness, pessimism
3 Conversion Hysteria (Hy)	Psychological conflict and distress manifested as somatic problems
4 Psychopathic Deviate (Pd)	Oppositional, disregard for social convention
5 Masculinity-Feminity (Mf)	Traditional masculine or feminine interests
6 Paranoia (Pa)	Mistrust, suspiciousness
7 Psychasthenia (Pt)	Fears, guilt, anxiety
8 Schizophrenia (Sc)	Idiosyncratic thinking, unusual thoughts & behavior
9 Hypomania (Ma)	Overactivity, emotional excitement
0 Social Introversion (Si)	Shy, insecurity

resulting MMPI-2 (Butcher, Dahlstrom, Graham, Tellegen, & Kaemmer, 1989) consists of 567 items and can be used with individuals aged 18 through adulthood. The MMPI-2 uses the same validity and clinical scale names as the MMPI. Importantly, many have noted that the names reflecting each of the MMPI (or MMPI-2) scales are misleading. For example, a high score on the Schizophrenia (Sc) scale does not necessarily mean that the person who completed the test is schizophrenic. Therefore, many clinicians and researchers prefer to ignore the scale names and use numbers to reflect each scale instead. For example, the Schizophrenia (Sc) scale is referred to as Scale 8 (see Table 8.5). Like the original MMPI, the MMPI-2 has numerous sub-scales, including measures such as Type A behavior, post-traumatic stress, obsessions, and fears.

The Minnesota Multiphasic Personality Inventory-Adolescent (MMPI-A) (Butcher, et al., 1992) was developed for use with teens between the ages of 14 and 18. The MMPI-A has 478 true/false items and includes a number of validity measures in addition to those available in the MMPI and MMPI-2. The MMPI, MMPI-2, and MMPI-A can be scored by hand using templates for each scale or they can be computer scored. Most commercially available computer scoring programs offer in-depth interpretive reports that fully describe the testing results and offer suggestions for treatment or other interventions. Scores are typically interpreted by reviewing the entire resulting profile rather than individual scale scores. Profile analysis is highlighted by examining pairs of high scores combinations. For example, high scores on the first three scales of the MMPI are referred to as the *neurotic triad* reflecting anxiety, depression, and somatic complaints. Research indicates that the MMPI, MMPI-2, and MMPI-A have acceptable reliability, stability, and validity (Butcher et al., 1989; Butcher et al., 1992; Graham, 1990; Parker, Hanson, & Hunsley, 1988). However, controversy exits concerning many aspects of the test. For example, the MacAndrew Scale was designed as a supplementary scale to classify those people with alcohol-related problems. The validity of the scale has been criticized and some authors have suggested that the scale no longer be used to examine alcohol problems (Gottesman & Prescott, 1989). Figure 8.2 provides an example of an MMPI-2 profile of a 60-year-old male high school teacher convicted of sexually abusing adolescent boys. The evaluation, which included a comprehensive psychological battery, revealed him to be actively alcoholic, depressed, and suffering from a personality disorder.

The Millon Clinical Multiaxial Inventories (MCMI). The **Millon Clinical Multiaxial Inventories (MCMI)** include several tests that assess personality functioning using the DSM IV classification system and the Theodore Millon theory of personality (Millon, 1981). Unlike the MMPI-2, the Millon was specifically designed to assess personality disorders outlined in the DSM such as histrionic, borderline, paranoid, and obsessive compulsive personalities. The first Millon test was published in 1982; additional tests and revisions quickly developed during the 1980s and 1990s. The current tests include the Millon Clinical Multiaxial Inventory-III (MCMI-III; Millon, Millon, & Davis, 1994), the Millon Adolescent Clinical Inventory (MACI; Millon, Millon, & Davis, 1994), the Millon Behavioral Health Inventory (MBHI; Millon, Green, & Meagher, 1982), the Millon Clinical Multiaxial Inventory-II (MCMI-II; Millon, 1987), and the Millon Adolescent Personality Inventory (MAPI; Millon, Millon, & Davis, 1982). The MBHI, however, is a health behavior inventory and not a measure of personality or psychological functioning per se. The MCMI-III will be highlighted here. The MCMI-III is a 175 true/false item questionnaire designed for persons aged 18 through adulthood and takes approximately 30 minutes to complete. It was designed to assess personality disorders and syndromes based on the DSM IV system of classification. The MCMI-III includes 24 scales, including 14 personality pattern scales and 10 clinical syndrome scales. Furthermore, the MCMI-III also includes several validity measures. Table 8.6 provides a list of the measured characteristics.

The Sixteen Personality Factors (16PF). The **16PF** was developed by Raymond Cattell and colleagues and is currently in its fifth edition (Cattell, Cattell, & Cattell, 1993). It is a 185-item multiple-choice questionnaire that takes approximately 45 minutes to

---

Figure 8.2 Minnesota Multiphasic Personality Inventory-2, profile of EL, a 60-year-old high school teacher convicted of sexual abuse of minors (on facing page)

MMPI-2 Minnesota Multiphasic Personality Inventory-2™

Profile for Basic Scales

Name EL

Address

Occupation

Education SJ   Age 60   Marital Status S

Referred By SJ   Date Tested 9/18/93

MMPI-2 Code

Scorer's Initials TGP

LEGEND
L   Lie
F   Infrequency
K   Correction
Hs Hypochondriasis
D   Depression
Hy Conversion Hysteria
Pd Psychopathic Deviate
Mf Masculinity-Femininity
Pa Paranoia
Pt Psychasthenia
Sc Schizophrenia
Ma Hypomania
Si Social Introversion

MALE

	L	F	K	Hs+.5K 1	D 2	Hy 3	Pd+.4K 4	Mf 5	Pa 6	Pt+1K 7	Sc+1K 8	Ma+.2K 9	Si 0
Raw Score	9	13	13	13	25	30	25	31	17	26	24	26	30
K to be Added				7			5			13	13	3	
Raw Score with K			20	30			30			39	37	29	

? Raw Score

Raw Score 1

CD987843

Product Number 24001

169

Table 8.6   MCMI-III Scales

Clinical Personality Patterns Scales

Scale 1	Schizoid
Scale 2A	Avoidant
Scale 2B	Depressive
Scale 3	Dependent
Scale 4	Histrionic
Scale 5	Narcissistic
Scale 6A	Antisocial
Scale 6B	Aggressive (Sadistic)
Scale 7	Compulsive
Scale 8A	Passive-Aggressive (Negativistic)
Scale 8B	Self-Defeating

Clinical Syndrome Scales

Scale A	Anxiety
Scale H	Somatoform
Scale N	Bipolar: Manic
Scale D	Dysthymia
Scale B	Alcohol Dependence
Scale T	Drug Dependence
Scale R	Post-traumatic Stress Disorder

Severe Syndrome Scales

Scale SS	Thought Disorder
Scale CC	Major Depression
Scale PP	Delusional Disorder

Severe Personality Pathology Scales

Scale S	Schizotypal
Scale C	Borderline
Scale P	Paranoid

Modifying Indices (Correction Scales)

Scale X	Disclosure
Scale Y	Desirability
Scale Z	Debasement

complete. The 16PF is administered to individuals aged 16 years through adulthood. Scoring the 16PF results in 16 primary personality traits (e.g., guilt prone) and five global factors that assess second-order personality characteristics (e.g., anxiety). Standardized scores from 1 to 10 or sten scores are used with means set at 5 and a standard deviation of 3. Table 8.7 lists the 16PF scales. The 16PF has been found to have acceptable stability, reliability, and validity (Anastasi, 1988; Cattell *et al.,* 1993).

The NEO-Personality Inventory-Revised (NEO-PI-R). The NEO-PI-R (Costa & McCrae, 1985, 1989, 1992) is a 240-item questionnaire that uses a 5-point rating system. A brief 60-item version of the NEO-PI-R called the NEO-Five Factor Inventory (NEO-FF)

is also available as well as a observer rating version (Form R). The NEO-PI-R measures the big five personality dimensions: neuroticism, extroversion, openness, agreeableness, and conscientiousness. The *big five* or the five-factor model has been found to be consistent personality dimensions from factor analytic research conducted for over 40 years (Digman, 1990). The NEO-PI traits are referred to as the big five because in many research studies they have been found to account for a great deal of variability in personality test scores (Wiggins & Pincus, 1989). The NEO-PI-R has been found to be both reliable and valid (Costa & McGrae, 1992). Unlike the other objective tests mentioned, the NEO-PI-R does not include validity scales to assess subject response set.

Other Objective Tests.   Additional objective personality tests include the Edwards Personal Preference Schedule (EPPS: Edwards, 1959), a 225-item paired-comparison test assessing 15 personality variables, and the Eysenck Personality Questionnaire (Eysenck & Eysenck, 1975), measuring three basic personality characteristics: psychoti-

Table 8.7   16PF (Fifth Edition) Measures

Global Factors Scales

EX	Extroversion
AX	Anxiety
TM	Tough-Mindedness
IN	Independence
SC	Self-Control

16 Primary Personality Traits

A	Warmth
B	Reasoning
C	Emotional Stability
E	Dominance
F	Liveliness
G	Rule Consciousness
H	Social Boldness
I	Sensitivity
L	Vigilance
M	Abstractedness
N	Privateness
O	Apprehension
Q1	Openness to change
Q2	Self Reliance
Q3	Perfectionism
Q4	Tension

cism, introversion-extroversion, and emotionality-stability. Many other tests are available as well, however, they generally are not as commonly used as those previously discussed.

Projective Testing   Just as there are numerous objective personality and psychological functioning instruments, there are many projective instruments. Most psychologists use a small number of preferred projective tests—typically the Rorschach, the Thematic Apperception Test (TAT), Projective Drawings, and Incomplete Sentences.

The Rorschach.   The **Rorschach** is the famous ink-blot test (Rorschach, 1921/1942, 1951). Many people are fascinated by the idea of using inkblots to investigate personality and psychological functioning. Of course, many people (including psychologists) are skeptical of projective techniques such as the Rorschach, questioning its validity as a measure of psychological functioning (Dawes, 1994). The Ror-

Figure 8.3   An example of a Rorschach ink blot.

schach is often mentioned in television shows or in films depicting psychological evaluations. Curiously, the idea of seeing objects in inkblots came from a common game in the 1800s called Blotto. Someone would put a drop of ink on a blank piece of paper and fold the paper in half, creating a unique inkblot. Others would then take turns identifying objects in the inkblots. Alfred Binet used this technique to examine imagination among children. Swiss psychiatrist Hermann Rorschach noticed that mental patients tended to respond very differently to this game relative to others. Thus, Blotto became the basis for the Rorschach test (Exner, 1976).

Rorschach Case Study: Martha

Martha is a 24-year-old biracial (Caucasian and Iranian) woman who was referred for psychological testing by her psychiatrist. She had several hospital admissions due to depression and suicide attempts. Martha was diagnosed with both major depression and a borderline personality disorder. She was resistant to testing and complied only because "my shrink and father are making me do this." The following represents the free-association portion of the first five cards of the Rorschach administration.

Card I

Psychologist: What might this be?
Martha: (long pause) You mean besides just a blot of ink?
Psychologist: Yes.
Martha: Well, some kind of big black animal looking into the water. An ugly animal.
Psychologist: Most people see more than one thing.
Martha: Well I don't. That's it.

Card II

Psychologist: What might this be?
Martha: This looks like a head and hands touching and feet here (points). That's the only thing I see. They all look like mirror reflections so far. There's blood there (points).

Card III

Psychologist: What might this be?
Martha: Two people spinning. I don't know what these red things are. Could be they got shot. Would you like me to move the cards around?
Psychologist: It's up to you.

Martha: That little figure looks like a person leaning back with their legs in front of them and that looks sort of like a fish. Looks like a human fish.

Card IV

Psychologist: What might this be?
Martha: This seems stupid. I don't see how this will help me. I don't know, it looks like some sort of charred monster. I suppose you want to know how it looks like a monster.
Psychologist: Sure.
Martha: This is the head and claws, big feet here, and a tail coming through the bottom (points).

Card V

Psychologist: What might this be?
Martha: Looks like a moth or a bat or something. That looks like an alligator or crocodile head, at least part of it does.

Although a complex scoring system would be used to analyze Martha's response, her angry, oppositional, and depressive feeling and impulses are evident in the responses to these few inkblots. For example, the image of the "big, black . . . ugly animal" on Card I and the "charred monster" on Card IV likely reflect her depressive emotions and may speak to the manner in which she views herself. Her oppositional behavior and anger is well reflected in her response to Card I when she stated, "You mean besides just a blot of ink?" and on Card IV when she stated, "This seems stupid." Her response to Card III seeing a "human fish" is concerning and unusual. These incongruent combinations that do not exist in reality but are reported by adults may be an indication of thought disturbance.

The Rorschach consists of 10 inkblots that are symmetrical; that is, the left side of each card is essentially a mirror image of the right side. Figure 8.3 provides an example of the type of inkblot used in the test. The same 10 inkblots have been used (in the same order of presentation) since they were first developed by Herman Rorschach in 1921 (Rorschach, 1921/1942). Half of the cards are black, white, and gray, and half use color. While there are several different ways to administer the Rorschach and score, the vast majority of psychologists today use the method developed by John Exner (Exner, 1974, 1976, 1986; Exner & Weiner, 1995). Each card is handed to the patient with the question, "What might this be?" The psychologist writes down everything the patient says verbatim. During this free-association portion of the test, the psychologist does not question the patient. After all 10 cards are administered, the psychologist shows the patient each card a second time and asks questions that will help in scoring the test. For example, the psychologist might say, "Now I'd like to show you the cards once again and ask you several questions about each card so that I can be sure that I see it as you do." With each card, he or she asks a nonleading question such as, "What about the card made it look like a —— to you?" The psychologist looks for answers that will help him or her score the test in several

Rorschach Case Example: Xavier

Xavier is a 48-year-old Caucasian attorney hospitalized for mania associated with a bipolar disorder. He was spending a great deal of money, which he could not afford to do, and behaving in a hypersexual manner, not sleeping, and getting into fights. The following represents the free-association portion of the first five cards of the Rorschach administration. Compare Xavier's responses to those of Martha. Remember that they are both looking at the same five Rorschach cards and yet their responses differ greatly.

Card I

Psychologist: What might this be?
Xavier: It's a butterfly. It could be a Halloween mask too. Here, at the top it looks like dogs. It also looks like something sinister going on inside, a horror mask. It looks like a vagina in the middle. Little children are looking out from the womb of the mother.

Card II

Psychologist: What might this be?
Xavier: Two long-snouted animals kissing in the middle with their hearts in the middle. The top red part is a mask or something. Looks like little sheep, teddy bears, or dogs.

Card III

Psychologist: What might this be?
Xavier: Looks like Africans dancing around pots. This looks like a bow tie or a hip bone. This looks like an inverted fish that swims.

Card IV

Psychologist: What might this be?
Xavier: This looks sinister. Looks like I'm looking on top of this huge rug or rodent. Maybe a bat looking down from the top. This looks like antenna or antlers. Maybe an Indian rug.

Card V

Psychologist: What might this be?
Xavier: It looks like a bat or butterfly. It also could be a Rodin.

Xavier's responses include "sinister" images on Cards I and V which may reflect feelings of mistrust or suspiciousness. The sexual response in Card I is unusual and might be associated with a lack of impulse control as well as his hypersexual sensitivity common among those with manic symptoms. Scoring the entire record would be most helpful in understanding Xavier's psychological functioning.

---

categories such as location (i.e., the area of the blot being used), content (i.e., the nature of the object being described, such as a person, animal, or element of nature), determinants (i.e., the parts of the blot that the patient used in the response, such as form, color, shading, and movement), and populars (i.e., the responses typically seen by others). This portion of the test is referred to as the inquiry. Once the test is completed, scoring involves a highly complex system and analysis. Each response is carefully scored based on the content, location, determinants, and quality of the response. An actual scoring sheet, once completed, resembles a highly specialized and foreign language. Because the scoring process can be very complicated and may take a long time to complete, many experienced psychologists do not score the test in fine detail but rely on their clinical inference, experience, and judgment to answer clinical questions such as, Is the patient psychotic or not? Is the patient repressive or not? Is the patient depressed? The case studies of Martha and Xavier illustrate the use of the Rorschach.

Various aspects of the Rorschach responses are associated with psychological functioning. For example, the frequent use of shading is generally considered to be reflective of anxiety and depression. The use of human movement and adequate number of popular responses are usually associated with adaptive and well-integrated psychological functioning. Numerous responses that attend to minor details of the blots often reflect obsessive-compulsive traits. Frequent use of the white space around the blot is generally associated with oppositionality and/or avoidance.

Many have argued that the Rorschach is not a reliable and valid instrument. In fact Robyn Dawes calls the Rorschach a "shoddy (instrument that) . . . is not a valid test of anything" (Dawes, 1994, pp. 123 & 146). In fact many graduate training programs have stopped using it. Some attempts to improve the psychometric properties of the Rorschach, such as the development of the Holtzman Inkblot Technique (HIT; Holtzman, Thorpe, Swartz, & Herron, 1961; Holtzman, 1975), have not caught on with clinicians. However, the development of John Exner's Comprehensive System and his research on the Rorschach (Exner, 1974, 1976, 1986; Exner & Weiner, 1995; Weiner, 1996) have helped to improve the scientific basis of the test. Exner has developed a method with highly precise scoring criteria and has used this method to demonstrate reliability and validity of the approach. Many have criticized Exner's system for not publishing his findings in peer-reviewed journals. Others question some of his assumptions regarding reliability and validity (Dawes, 1994). Thus, many still remain skeptical of the Rorschach's use even with the available and much improved scoring and interpretation techniques. However, a review of Rorschach research revealed reliability coefficients to be in the .80s and the average validity coefficient to be about .42 (Ornberg & Zalewski, 1994; Parker, Hanson, & Hunsley, 1988; Weiner, 1996), suggesting that the Rorschach does maintain acceptable levels of reliability and validity (Weiner, 1996). Ultimately, it may be reasonable to refer to the Rorschach and other projective instruments as *tools* as opposed to tests *per se.*

The Thematic Apperception Test (TAT). The **TAT** (Murray & Bellack, 1942; Tomkins, 1947) was developed during the late 1930s by Henry Murray and Christiana Morgan at Harvard University. The TAT was originally designed to measure personality factors in research settings. Specifically, it was used to investigate goals, central conflicts, needs, press (i.e., factors that facilitate or impede progress towards reaching goals) and achievement strivings associated with Henry Murray's theory of *personology* (Murray, 1938). The TAT consists of 31 pictures (one of which is blank), most all of which depict people rather than objects. Some of the pictures are designed to be administered to males, some to females, and others to both genders (Fig. 8.4). Generally only a selected number of cards (e.g., 10) are administered to any one patient.

The psychologist introduces the test by telling the patient that he or she will be given a series of pictures and requested to tell a story about each. The patient is instructed to make up a story that reflects what the people in the picture are thinking, feeling, and doing and also to speculate on what led up to the events depicted in the picture and

what will happen in the future. After each card is presented to the patient, the psychologist writes down everything that is said verbatim. Although a variety of complex scoring approaches have been developed (Murray, 1943; Shneidman, 1951), most clinicians use their clinical experience and judgment to analyze the themes that emerge from the patient's stories. Since clinicians generally do not officially score the TAT, conducting reliability and validity research is challenging. Many feel that the TAT and other projective tests are more like a clinical interview than a test, and that the experience, training, and clinical judgment of the clinician determines the usefulness and accuracy of these instruments.

Other tests similar to the TAT have been developed for special populations, such as the Robert's Apperception Test for Children (RATC; McArthur & Roberts, 1982) for use with elementary school children. The 27 pictures depict children interacting with parents, teachers, and peers. The Children's Apperception Test (CAT; Bellak, 1986) was developed for very young children and depicts animals interacting in various ways.

Projective Drawings. Many clinicians ask both children and adults to draw pictures in order to assess their psychological functioning. Typically, people are asked to draw a house, a tree, a person, and their family doing something together. For the Draw-a-Person test (Machover, 1949), the House-Tree-Person Technique (Buck, 1948), and the Kinetic Family Drawing Technique, the patient is instructed to draw each picture in pencil on a separate blank piece of paper and to avoid the use of stick figures. Variations on the instructions have been used by many clinicians. For example, a popular variation on the Draw-a-Person test instructs the patient to draw persons of the same and opposite sex and a person in the rain. Attempts to develop scoring criteria as well as research on the reliability and validity of these drawing techniques have been only moderately successful. Some researchers have been involved with developing scientific scoring procedures that maximize both reliability and validity and can be used as screening measures for cognitive and emotional impairment (Sopchak, Sopchak, & Kohlbrenner, 1993; Trevisaw, 1996). Yet these attempts have not generally been embraced by practicing clinicians. Many clinicians feel that these techniques are quick and easy methods to establish rapport with children or with those who have great difficulty expressing their feelings verbally. Unfortunately, some clinicians overinterpret **projective drawings** without adequate research support to justify their interpretations. Figure 8.5 shows several drawings by Debbie, the 24-year-old female patient described in the TAT case study.

Sentence Completion Techniques. Another projective technique involves the use of **sentence completion.** There are many different versions of this technique (e.g., Forer, 1957; Goldberg, 1965; Lanyon & Lanyon, 1980; Rotter & Rafferty, 1950; Rotter, 1954). The patient is presented (either orally by the examiner or in writing through a questionnaire) a series of sentence fragments. These might include items such as, "When he answered the phone he ———— " or "Most mothers are ———— ". The patient is asked to give the first response that he or she thinks of and complete the sentence. Again, like projective drawings and the TAT, several scoring systems have been developed to assist in interpretation. However, these scoring approaches are generally used only in research settings; most clinicians prefer to use their own experience and

Figure 8.4 An example of a TAT card.

TAT Case Study: Debbie

Debbie is a 24-year-old physically disabled Caucasian female patient who has experienced alcoholism, depression, and intense feelings of death anxiety. She also reported feeling stressed from too many job and home responsibilities as well as alcoholism among several family members. She felt that she was the "glue that keeps the family together" and had been overly responsible for her family's functioning and happiness. The following is an example of Debbie's response to one of the TAT cards depicting three people (2 female and 1 male) in an outdoor farm scene.

Debbie: I've seen this one before, okay, she is her daughter and she just came home from school and is looking around at her father and her pregnant mother and wondering if school will get her out of this achorion (i.e., fungus-like) existence (laughs). She looks con-

cerned that she'll end up like her mother. She's going to be in the same trap and never be out of this crummy situation.

Psychologist: How does the father feel?

Debbie: He's pretty tired and has his back towards her. He knows she's there. It's late in the day and he's still plowing and she doesn't identify with that or doesn't want to.

Psychologist: What will happen in the future?

Debbie: She looks despondent and looks like she'll be in the same situation as her mother or father.

Debbie's response to the TAT card likely reflects her concerns about the marital problems among her parents and her worries about what her future relationships might be like. Her response suggests that she feels that following in her mother's footsteps might be inevitable.

Figure 8.5 Projective drawings from Debbie, a 24-year-old disabled woman with alcoholism, depression, and family conflicts

clinical judgment to interpret the themes that emerge from the completed sentences.

Questions and Controversies Concerning Personality and Psychological Testing

Are Personality Results Assessed Through Testing Stable? Traditionally, many psychologists have assumed that personality is a fairly stable phenomenon—that each individual's personality traits and style are consistent over time and in varying situations (e.g., home, work, school). Thus, someone who tends to be friendly is likely to be friendly most of the time and in most circumstances. Personality testing using the MMPI-2, MCMI-III, or 16PF, for example, might be considered useful in evaluating and measuring fairly stable personality characteris-

---

Sentence Completion Case Study: Xavier

Xavier is the attorney who was hospitalized during a manic episode of bipolar disorder. The following is a sample of his responses on a sentence completion test (Forer, 1957).

I used to feel I was being held back by *limited people.*

He often wished he could *fulfill his potential.*
Sometimes he wished he *could do it all.*
I was most annoyed when *big egos demand attention and don't work.*
I feel guilty about *overspending.*
More than anything else, he needed *love.*

Sentence Completion Case Study: Elias

Elias is a 37-year-old African-American computer programmer who is seeking psychotherapy for symptoms of anxiety and depression. He has recently had several poor job performance ratings and has been told that he is not a "team player." The following is a sample of his responses on a sentence completion test (Forer, 1957).

Most fathers *don't spend enough time with their sons.*
I used to feel *that I was being held back by my lack of people skills.*
My father always *doesn't understand me.*

I was most annoyed when *my Dad pooh-poohed my ideas.*
At times he worried about *getting bad reviews at work.*
I felt most dissatisfied when *I did not get the recognition I thought I should.*
Sometimes I feel *that my boss doesn't care about my career interests.*
He felt inferior *when he got bad reviews at work relating to his people skills.*

tics. However, several researchers have demonstrated that personality is not as stable as many people assume but instead partially depends on specific environmental and situational circumstances (Mischel, 1968, 1973). For example, rather than thinking of someone as an anxious person, it is more useful to evaluate and understand the circumstances in which he or she is likely to show anxiety (e.g., testing situations, speaking engagements, asking someone for a date). Mischel and others (Bem & Funder, 1978; Epstein, 1979; Magnusson, 1981) have advanced the person-situation interaction theory of personality. While recognizing that somewhat stable individual differences can exist in cognitive styles, the psychologist must consider behavior across similar situations, and self-reported personality traits, emphasizing situational factors and influences. Personality testing results must then be evaluated in light of these situation-specific factors, which should of course be part of any integrative biopsychosocial evaluation.

Are Projective Techniques Reliable and Valid?
Over the years numerous reviews have concluded that projective techniques have not demonstrated adequate reliability and validity to justify their use with patients (e.g., Cronbach, 1956; Dawes, 1994; Eysenck, 1958; Rotter, 1954; Suinn & Oskamp, 1969). Some proponents of projective testing have argued that it is inappropriate to use the same criteria for both objective tests and projective tests. They state that unlike objective tests, in which scores are determined and compared to national norms, pro-

jective tests are similar to structured interviews, whose purpose is to better know, understand, and describe a person (Blatt, 1975; Frank, 1948; Tomkins, 1947).

Most of the debate concerning the reliability and validity of projective testing has centered around the Rorschach. Many reviews of the literature on the Rorschach have found little support for the technique (Dawes, 1994; Schofield, 1952; Suinn & Oskamp, 1969; Windle, 1952; Ziskin & Faust, 1988; Zubin, 1954). However, more recent studies have been much more favorable in their analysis of the psychometric properties of the Rorschach (Exner, 1974, 1986; Exner & Weiner, 1995; Parker et al., 1988; Weiner, 1996). Weiner (1996) concluded his review of research on the validity of the Rorschach by stating that "properly used by informed clinicians . . . it functions with substantial validity and considerable utility in answering certain kinds of important questions related to personality processes" (p. 213).

Research on the psychometric properties of the TAT and projective drawing techniques have generally failed to provide research support for their reliability and validity (Harris, 1972; Swartz, 1978). Yet, these and other projective tests continue to be used by clinical psychologists (Lubin, Larsen, Matarazzo, & Seever, 1985; Piotrowski & Keller, 1989). Many clinicians report that these instruments provide useful information that helps them develop a better understanding of the patient, particularly when interpreted in concert with other measures.

Are Personality and Psychological Tests Appropriate for Use With Minority Group Members? The early developers of most personality and psychological tests such as the MMPI, Rorschach, and TAT did not consider ethnic and other diversity issues during the test construction and validation process. For example, using the original MMPI with members of ethnic minority groups is questionable since the test was validated using only Caucasians. Furthermore, many tests (e.g., Stanford-Binet) were first developed among people from the middle or upper-middle socioeconomic classes, thus using these tests for low socioeconomic groups may also compromise validity. Today, the professionals who update these tests and construct new ones are much more sensitive to issues of diversity. For example, the revisors of the MMPI (i.e., the MMPI-2) and the WISC (i.e., WISC-III) were careful to use a standardization sample that reflected geographic, socioeconomic, and ethnic diversity. Psychologists must be aware of the limitations of the tests that they use and be sensitive to diversity issues when making judgments based on psychological tests used with diverse populations (American Psychological Association, 1992a, 1993b).

Should Personality and Psychological Tests Be Used for Employment Decisions? Many employers use personality and psychological tests to screen job applicants for psychiatric disorders or personality problems that may interfere with work performance. Others are interested in screening for personalities that match the requirements for a particular position. As mentioned earlier, a shy and withdrawn person may not succeed as a salesperson; someone who is not detail-oriented may not succeed as an accountant. Some have argued that personality tests such as the MMPI, Rorschach, and WAIS-R were not specifically designed and validated for use in employment settings and therefore should not be used for employment decisions (Guion & Gottier, 1965). Others claim that personality measures can be successfully and appropriately used in employment settings (Bentz, 1985; Hogan, Hogan, & Roberts, 1996). Still others have designed specialized tests that have been validated for personnel selection in specific industries (Clarke, 1956; Gough, 1984).

Clinical Inference and Judgment

Psychological assessment and testing involve much more than administering tests and computing scores. Once a psychologist completes an interview, conducts a behavioral observation, and administers intellectual and personality testing, he or she must pull all the information together and make some important decisions regarding diagnosis and treatment recommendations. All of the information gathered may or may not agree with other data collected. Integrating convergent and divergent information from many different sources requires a great deal of skill, training, and experience. Although clinicians make many efforts to objectify **clinical judgments** by using structured interviews, computer interviewing, objective testing, and input from other highly skilled and experienced professionals, the clinician ultimately uses his or her own judgment, impressions, and experience along with objective data to make decisions. These judgements are not only needed to make sense of all of the data gathered to answer specific clinical questions about psychological functioning, diagnosis, prognosis, and treatment but are also used to decide which instruments and assessment approaches should be administered in the first place. There are hundreds and perhaps thousands of available tests and assessment approaches that can be enlisted to evaluate a person. Choosing the right techniques can often be a complex task.

The quality of clinical judgment can be enhanced by the use of multiple assessment sources (e.g., interview, case history, tests, observations). For instance, if a patient reports feeling depressed, if many of the stories that the patient tells in response to the TAT include depressive themes, and if the patient's scores on the MMPI-2, the Beck Depression Inventory (BDI), the Symptom Checklist 90-Revised (SCL-90-R), and depression index on the Rorschach are all elevated, it is likely that the clinician will accurately conclude that the patient is indeed depressed. Unfortunately, clinical decisions are not always so clear. For example, a patient may report feeling depressed, but scores on psychological tests measuring depression are not elevated. Alternatively, a patient may deny feeling depressed during the clinical interview, while testing scores indicate that he or she is depressed. Furthermore, depression may be associated with numerous diagnoses. Patients with a variety of medical conditions (e.g., irritable bowel syndrome, cardiac problems, diabetes, chronic pain) may feel depressed. People who experience personality disorders (e.g., antisocial, borderline) may also feel depressed. Depression is often associated with attention deficit disorders, learning disabilities, and other syndromes. Depression can be moderate in severity and chronic (i.e., dysthymia) or severe in intensity and of shorter duration (i.e., major depression). Someone may falsely report being depressed in order to get medical attention (e.g., Munchausen's syndrome) or to obtain some other type of secondary gain (e.g., obtain sympathy and attention from loved ones, staying home from work). Furthermore, many people who are depressed express their feelings through somatic complaints and do not consciously recognize their depression. Numerous factors in the environment may also lead to depression (e.g., loss of job or a loved one). How can the psychologist sort out all the available data and make judgments regarding diagnosis and treatment planning?

Psychologists must examine all the pieces of the puzzle and then make sense of them. Their theoretical framework, prior experience, clinical training, and intuitions all come into play. Clinicians do not put all of the data into a formula or computer program and get a fully objective answer to their questions. However, much research suggests that clinical judgments can be unreliable and invalid (Dawes, 1994; Faust, 1986; Meehl, 1954, 1965; Mischel, 1986)—not only in psychology but in medicine and other fields (Sanchez & Kahn, 1991). Others have criticized this research, stating that these studies are flawed and do not reflect the types of decisions typically made by practicing clinicians (Garb, 1988, 1989; Lambert & Wertheimer, 1988). Efforts are often made to increase the reliability and validity of clinical judgements. For example, many managed care insurance companies require clinicians to use highly specific assessment tools and to objectify target symptoms in psychological evaluations and treatment. Assessment is also encouraged on a regu-

lar basis rather than in a single snapshot of a person at the beginning of treatment. Initial formulations and impressions are constantly being challenged based on the discovery of further information. Given the complex nature of psychological assessment, psychologists make case formulations and an initial plan for treatment, for example, that is continually reassessed and revised as the need arises.

Some have suggested that psychologists should employ actuarial (i.e., statistical) approaches in their decision making rather than relying solely on clinical judgment. Thus, test scores, presenting symptoms, and other information can be quantified and entered into statistical equations to help determine a diagnosis and develop a treatment plan (Dawes, 1979, 1994; Gough, 1962). Others argue that the complexity of human nature cannot be quantified so easily and that professional clinical judgement is always needed (Blatt, 1975; Garb, 1988, 1989; MacDonald, 1996). Whereas many clinicians find it distasteful to rely on actuarial techniques, others feel it is critical to use any approach that has proved reliable, valid, and useful (Dawes, 1979, 1994). Most practicing clinicians rely more on clinical judgment than on actuarial approaches, whereas most researchers rely on actuarial approaches. The reality is that psychologists will likely always be required to make professional clinical judgements that are based on training, experience, and intuition. Efforts to increase their skills and achieve reliable, valid, and useful conclusions is certainly a worthy and welcomed endeavor (MacDonald, 1996).

Communicating Assessment Results

After testing is completed, analysized, and interpreted, the results are usually first communicated orally to patients and other interested parties. Of course, results are communicated to others only with the explicit permission of the person unless extraordinary conditions are involved (e.g., the patient is gravely disabled). After a psychological evaluation, the psychologist will often schedule a feedback session to show the patient the results, explain the findings in understandable language, and answer all questions. Often psychologists must also explain their assessment results to other interested parties such as parents, teachers, attorneys, and physicians.

In addition to oral feedback, the psychologist typically prepares a written report to communicate test findings. Table 8.8 provides an outline of a typical assessment report. Most testing reports include the reason for the referral and the identification of the referring party, the list of assessment instruments used, actual test scores (such as percentile ranks), the psychologist's interpretation of the scores and findings, a diagnostic impression, and recommendations. It is important to ascertain the audience for whom the report is being written. A report directed to another mental health professional may be very different from one to a school teacher or a parent. Most psychologists avoid professional jargon so that their reports will be understandable to nonpsychologists. Psychologists also must handle reports confidentially and send them only to appropriate persons.

Integrated Psychological Assessment Report

Having described various components of psychological assessment, the case study for Thomas will be used to demonstrate the actual integration of a complete psychological assessment battery. Note the diversity of measures, theoretical perspectives and biopsychsocial elements synthesized in the course of this evaluation.

This complex, integrative, and contemporary example of a psychological assessment case serves to illustrate several critical issues. First, a combination of psychological tests was utilized to most fully assess this child through observational, interviewing, intellectual, objective personality, and projective personality measures. Second, an integrated theoretical approach was utilized, taking into consideration intrapsychic psychodynamic issues (e.g., loneliness, low self-esteem), cognitive-behavioral factors (e.g., need for behavioral reinforcement program and social skills training), humanistic concerns (e.g., need for support and understanding in both Thomas and his parents) and family issues (e.g., adoption). Third, the intimate connection between biological (e.g., Asperger's is a neurological condition), psychological (e.g., social impairments, aggression) and social (e.g., interracial issues, classroom milieu) factors must be integrated into a meaningful formulation and set of recommendations. Finally, what on the surface may have appeared to be simply a boy having problems with aggression in the classroom was revealed through psychological assessment to be far more complex and elusive.

Table 8.8 Outline of Typical Psychological Report

---

1. Identifying information (name, sex, age, ethnicity, date of evaluation, referring clinician)
2. Referral question
3. Assessment procedures administered
4. Background (information clarifying referral question)
5. Summary of impressions and findings
   a. Cognitive (current cognitive functioning including intellectual, memory, perception, ideation as well as amount and likely cause of impairment relative to premorbid level of functioning)
   b. Affective and mood (current mood compared to premorbid level of functioning as well as degree, lability, and chronic versus nature of disturbance)
   c. Interpersonal-intrapersonal (interpersonal-intrapersonal conflicts, significance, coping, and defensive strategies, formulations of personality)
6. Diagnostic impressions
7. Recommendations (assessment of risk, need for confinement, medication, treatment recommendations)

Source: From "Integrating and Communicating Findings," by L. E. Beutler in Integrative Assessment of Adult Personality edited by L. E. Beutler and M. R. Berren, p. 36. Copyright © 1955 by Guilford Publications, Inc.

Psychological Assessment Report Example for Thomas

Patient: Thomas X
Date of Birth: May 12, 1991
Age: 6 years
Parents: Mr. and Mrs. X
Dates of Testing: June 23, 26, 1997
Clinician: Dr. Z

Brief Identifying and Referral Information: Thomas is a 6-year-old adopted Caucasian boy who has recently completed kindergarten. His adoptive mother is Japanese-American and his adoptive father is Caucasian. Little is known about Thomas's biological parents who apparently were teenagers who felt ill-prepared to care for a child. Thomas's parents chose to adopt due to infertility. Thomas was born at 27 weeks gestation, three months premature.

Thomas's parents are seeking an evaluation of Thomas in order to assist them with a number of school related decisions. First, it is unclear whether Thomas is ready for first grade, primarily in light of "explosive aggression" at school. His mother reports that while shy and introverted during preschool, Thomas has been highly aggressive in kindergarten, hitting, pushing, and punching other children. He is described as very active, bossy with other children, but bright and academically on track. Psychological testing was requested in order to shed light on Thomas's social difficulties and determine an optimal educational program.

Tests and Procedures Administered
Wechsler Intelligence Scale for Children-III (WISC-III)
Child Behavior Checklist (completed by his mother)
Sentence Completion Test (Haak version)
Child Depression Inventory
Robert's Apperception Test
Rorschach
Projective Drawings
Clinical Interview with Thomas' mother
Conversation with kindergarten teacher
Conversation with educational consultant

Interview Data: Thomas' development is significant for behavioral rigidity and fixated interests. Thomas' mother describes him as having tremendous difficulty adapting to changes in plans, frequently prompting tantrums. Similarly, Thomas is described as controlling and bossy with his peers, insisting that they play what and how he wants. Beginning at age two, Thomas has developed rigid food preferences and bedtime rituals, for example, Thomas must have his mother bring him a glass of water in bed. In terms of interests, he "becomes fixated for months at a time" on one particular preoccupation—currently sharks and previously dinosaurs.

He is an active child, but neither his teacher nor his mother feel that he is unusually overactive. He is also not described as unusually distractible or inattentive. He is, however, regarded by both his teacher and mother as impulsive, and easily frustrated. In the sensory realm, Thomas often licks objects and sniffs at foods before consuming them. In addition to the aggression with other children, he is unable to read social cues, appears to misperceive other children's communication, and is not attuned to others' emotions. He also compulsively labels other individual's according to their racial status, for example stating: "Joey is Mexican. His Mommy is Mexican, too."

There is no known history of significant trauma outside of Thomas's adoption experience. He is presently in excellent physical health.

Behavioral Observations: Because the evaluation was conducted during the summer, an in-class observation was not possible. In the office, Thomas engaged enthusiastically, cheerfully, and cooperatively in the testing. He demonstrated good attention and concentration despite being physically restless and squirmy during verbal portions of the assessment. He was easily redirected at each of these points. Thomas was tangential and perseverative in his speech, frequently telling long stories unrelated to the task. Many of his verbalizations were difficult to follow, and he spoke with a sing-song prosody in an overly loud voice.

Intellectual Functioning: Thomas is currently functioning within the Above Average Range of general mental abilities, achieving a Full Scale IQ score of 118. Thomas achieved a Superior Verbal IQ score of 121 and an Above Average Performance IQ score of 112. Thus, Thomas demonstrated above average to superior intellect, with no significant discrepancy between his verbal and nonverbal skills. There were no significant differences between index scores.

Verbal Scaled Score		Performance Scaled Score	
Information	13	Picture Completion	12
Similarities	15	Coding	16
Arithmetic	13	Picture Arrangement	11
Vocabulary	15	Block Design	12
Comprehension	11	Object Assembly	08
Digit Span	09		

Results of Personality and Psychological Functioning Tests: Emotionally, Thomas' test results revealed feelings of mild depression, anxiety, and aggressive content. On the Child Behavior Checklist (CBCL) completed by his mother, Thomas' profile shows significant levels of Anxiety/Depression, Aggression and Social Problems. On the Child Depression Inventory administered directly (and orally) to Thomas, he scored in the mildly depressed range (i.e., score of 11). These findings are consistent with a child who is aware to some degree of his present

Psychological Assessment Report Example for Thomas (*Continued*)

difficulties and is responding with understandable sadness and frustration.

On projective tests, Thomas first drew a series of person drawings significant for their tiny size, often associated with low self-esteem in children. These drawings are further suggestive of some tension due to the extremely heavy pencil pressure utilized and darkly shaded areas. Obsessive detail was also noted. His Sentence Completion Test responses were notable for the degree of difficulty meeting his social and emotional needs, for example stating: I feel sorry when I have . . . "no friends around to play with." Thomas' story responses to the Robert's cards were significant for aggression, sadness, tangentiality, and perseverativenes. Thomas' Rorschach responses focused on nonhuman, strange, or extraterrestrial figures, for example perceiving a "flying robot," "a really strange guy," and "a sea monster." Aggressive images were also pervasive. These responses may reflect Thomas's feelings of social alienation and the use of aggression to assert himself. On all of the projective measures, Thomas repeatedly referred to the racial status of himself and others, mentioning race no fewer than 22 recorded times during the evaluation, indicative of both his perserverative style and extreme focus on this issue.

Integration and Formulation: Thomas presents a complex profile of significant strengths and difficulties, and given his rapid development as a robust six year old, caution must be taken in applying diagnostic labels. Thomas' history and current test results are suggestive of a diagnosis of Asperger's Disorder, often viewed as "social dyslexia" or the highest functioning end of the Pervasive Developmental Disorders continuum. Consistent with this potential understanding is Thomas's pattern of behavioral rigidity, fixated interests, sensory abnormalities, social difficulties, and inability to perceive social cues, tangential speech and lack of relatedness in conversation, and associated feelings of frustration, anger, sadness, and anxiety.

Thomas' clinical picture is further complicated by his premature birth, adoptive status, and confusion regarding his racial identity in an interracial family. Thus, medical, cognitive, family, sociocultural, and emotional factors all deserve further attention in order to best assist Thomas in meeting the challenges ahead.

Recommendations

1. Social skills training (in a group context) is indicated to assist Thomas in acquiring improved tools for contending with peers and more effectively meeting his social needs and decreasing his aggressive behavior. The use of cognitive-behavioral techniques in a highly structured group format is indicated.

2. Parent consultation is recommended to support Thomas' parents, assist the family in processing adoption and racial issues, and in developing a behavioral program that breaks down social behavior into small steps and rewards desirable social behavior both at home and in school.

3. A speech and language evaluation is recommended in order to rule out a language learning disorder that may be contributing to Thomas' expressive and social difficulties.

4. Thomas is cognitively and academically prepared to move on to a first grade classroom that can collaborate with Thomas' parents and clinicians in assisting with and providing support for his social and behavioral difficulties.

The Big Picture

Psychological testing is truly a unique and invaluable skill offered by clinical psychologists. In addition to the interviewing and observational tools described in Chapter 7, the major areas of cognitive, neuropsychological, and personality assessment provide tremendous insights into the human mind and psyche. Formal psychological assessment, when carefully integrated with selected measures and biopsychosocial contexts, richly informs both diagnosis and treatment. Future clinical psychologists will improve these measures in order to make them more useful to diverse clinical populations. Information obtained from research and practice will be used to develop improved measures that increase reliability, validity, and utility. Future instruments will also likely attempt to assess psychological and other relevant constructs in a more efficient manner.

Key Points

1. Cognitive testing is a general term referring to the assessment of a wide range of information-processing or thinking skills and behaviors. These include general neuropsychological functioning involving brain-behavior relationships, general intellectual functioning (such as reasoning and problem-solving), as well as more specific cognitive skills such as visual and auditory memory, language skills, pattern recognition, finger dexterity, visual-perceptual skills, academic skills, and motor functioning.

2. Experts disagree on the definition of intelligence. Theories proposed by Spearman, Thurstone, Cattell, Guilford, Piaget, Sternberg, Gardner, and others have been considered. The Wechsler Scales are the most commonly used tests of intelligence assessing preschool children (WPPSI-R), elementary and secondary school children (WISC-III), and adults (WAIS-III and WAIS-R NI). The Stanford-Binet, Kaufman Scales, and other intelligence tests are also frequently used. In addition to overall intellectual skills and cognitive strengths and weaknesses, these tests are frequently used to assess the presence of learning disabilities, predict academic success in school, examine brain dysfunction, and assess personality.

3. Other cognitive tests include neuropsychological tests (e.g., the Halstead-Reitan, the Boston Process Approach, the Luria-Nebraska) and other nonintellectual tests of cognitive, social, and motor development.

4. Controversy exists concerning cognitive testing. Some have argued that many tests are biased and misused with minority group members. Others assume that cognitive skills such as intelligence is stable throughout the life span and are innately determined.

5. Many tests exist to measure personality and psychological functioning such as mood. Most of these tests can be classified as either objective or projective instruments.

6. Objective instruments present very specific questions or statements to which the person responds to using specific answers. Scores are tabulated and then compared with those of reference groups, using national norms. The most commonly used objective personality tests include the Minnesota Multiphasic Personality Inventory (MMPI, MMPI-2, MMPI-A), the Millon Clinical Inventories (MCMI-III, MCMI-II, MACI, MAPI, MBHI) and the 16 Personality Factors Questionnaire (16PF).

7. Projective tests use ambiguous or unstructured testing stimuli. Subjects are asked to respond freely to the testing stimuli such as telling stories about pictures, describing what they see in an inkblot, or saying the first thing that comes to their mind when hearing a word or sentence fragment. The most common projective tests used include the Rorschach, the TAT, Incomplete Sentences, and Drawings.

8. Traditionally, many psychologists have assumed that personality is a fairly stable phenomenon—that each person's personality traits and style are consistent over time and in varying situations (e.g., home, work, school). However, several of researchers have demonstrated that personality is not as stable as many people assume but instead partially depends on specific environmental and situational circumstances

9. Many authors have questioned the reliability and validity of projective tests. Over the years numerous reviews have concluded that projective techniques have not demonstrated adequate reliability and validity to justify their use with patients. Most of the debate concerning the reliability and validity of projective testing has centered around the Rorschach. Many conclude that research failing to support the reliability and validity of these tests does not deter them from using the instruments if they believe that helpful clinical information can be obtained.

10. The developers of most personality and psychological tests such as the MMPI, Rorschach, and TAT did not consider ethnic and other diversity issues during the test construction and validation process. The professionals who update these tests and construct new ones are much more sensitive to issues of diversity. Psychologists must be aware of the limitations of the tests that they use and be sensitive to diversity issues when making judgments based on tests administered with special populations.

11. Many employers use personality and psychological tests to screen job applicants for psychiatric disorders or personality problems that may interfere with work performance. Others are interested in screening for personalities that match the requirements for a particular position.

12. Psychologists must examine all of the available assessment data and make sense out of it. Their theoretical framework, prior experience, clinical training, and intuition play a role in decision making. However, research suggests that clinical judgments are sometimes unreliable. Some have suggested that psychologists employ actuarial approaches in their decision making rather than relying solely on clinical judgment. Most practicing clinicians rely more on clinical judgment than actuarial approaches while the most researchers rely on actuarial approaches.

13. Assessment results are often communicated verbally to interested parties. After a psychological evaluation a psychologist will often schedule a feedback session to show the person who was tested the results and explain the findings in language that is understandable to a non-psychologist. In addition to oral feedback, the psycholo-gist typically prepares a written report to communicate test findings. Most psychologists avoid professional jargon so that their reports will be understandable to nonpsy-chologists.

Key Terms

Boston Process Approach

Intellectual Testing

Intelligence Quotient (IQ)

Millon Clinical Multiaxial
Inventories (MCMI)

Minnesota Multiphasic Personality
Inventory (MMPI)

Neuropsychological Testing

Objective Testing

Personality Testing

Projective Drawings

Projective Testing

Rorschach

Sentence Completion

Sixteen Personality Factors
Questionnaire (16-PF)

Stanford-Binet Scales

Thematic Apperception Test
(TAT)

Wechsler Scales

For Reflection

1. What is cognitive testing?

2. What are the main approaches to assess intelligence?

3. What is neuropsychological assessment?

4. Will an IQ score obtained at age 5 be the same as an IQ score obtained at age 40 for the same person? Why or why not?

5. What are some of the different tests used to measure IQ and how are they similar and different?

6. What are the differences between objective and pro-jective psychological testing?

7. List the major objective and projective tests used in clinical psychology.

8. What are the main types of personality tests used?

9. Are projective tests valid?

10. Should psychological tests be used to hire employees? Why or why not?

11. Are psychological tests appropriate to use with peo-ple from ethnically diverse backgrounds?

12. How do psychologists make decisions based on test-ing data?

13. How are testing results communicated to others?

14. What are the advantages of and disadvantages of using an actuarial approach rather than a clinical ap-proach in making clinical judgements?

15. Why are multiple approaches to assessment often ad-vantageous?

CHAPTER 9

Psychotherapeutic Interventions in Contemporary Clinical Psychology

HIGHLIGHT OF A CONTEMPORARY CLINICAL PSYCHOLOGIST:

John C. Norcross, Ph.D.

Dr. Norcross maintains a full-time academic career with a part-time private practice.

Birth Date: August 13, 1957

College: Rutgers University (B.A., Psychology, 1980)

Graduate Program:
University of Rhode Island
(M.A., Ph.D., ClinicalPsychology, 1984)

Clinical Internship: Brown University School of Medicine

Current Job: Professor of Psychology, University of Scranton, Scranton, PA; Private Practice (part-time)

Pros and cons of being a clinical psychologist:

Pros: 1. Diversity of professional activities (e.g.,

teaching, psychotherapy, research, supervision)
2. Enhancing the life functioning and satisfaction of fellow humans (i.e., making a difference)
3. Combining the best of science and humanism in our pursuits (thinking with the mind of a scientist and feeling with the heart of the humanist, as I like to say.)

Cons: "Only serious con that comes to mind is that it can be quite exhausting at times."

Future of clinical psychology: "Innovation and expansion are the defining characteristics of clinical psychology in the past two decades. Innovation in designing and validating new treatments, for example; expansion into new areas and populations, such as health psychology, rehabilitation, prescription privileges (probably). Psychotherapy will come of age with new, prescriptive treatments that customize the technical methods and relationship stances to the unique needs of the individual client. Psychotherapy integration will become the predominant model."

Typical Schedule:

9:00	Office hour
10:00	Teach class—Clinical Psychology (lecture on psychotherapy).
11:00	Class continues.
12:00	Meet with undergraduate research assistants concerning work on a large scale survey of APA-approved doctoral programs
1:00	Clinical supervision
2:00	Play tennis or racquetball
3:00	Travel to my private practice; paperwork.
4:00	Conduct individual psychotherapy at private practice with 40-year-old depressed Caucasian man having marital dificulties.
5:00	Conduct individual psychotherapy at private practice with 32-year-old anxious Caucasian

| | woman with concerns about job performance. | | 7:00 | Conduct marital therapy session at private practice with Caucasian couple in their 50s regarding marital problems associated with an extra-marital affair. |
| 6:00 | Conduct individual psychotherapy at private practice with 38-year-old anxious Caucasian man with concerns about relationship conflicts with his spouse. | | 8:00 | Marital therapy session continues. |

Psychotherapy, to many, is the *sin qua non* of clinical psychology. The cumulative power of psychology's many efforts in research and assessment is perhaps best seen in the ultimate helpfulness it achieves in relieving suffering and effecting positive change. Psychotherapy is the general umbrella term for an enormous range of interventions, modalities, and integrative strategies employed in the service of improving quality of life and health. Contemporary psychotherapy combines the synergistic power of a wealth of biological, psychological, and social resources to create a multidimensional and integrative treatment. This tall order requires a great deal of creativity, competence, and collaboration on the part of the clinician. In this chapter, psychotherapy will be defined, its goals, common denominators, stages, and modes delineated, and finally, its contemporary incarnation in the form of integrative approaches as illustrated through case studies.

The word **psychotherapy** means caring for another person's soul or being, as derived from the Greek word *psyche* meaning "soul" or "being" and *therapeutikos* meaning "caring for another" (Kleinke, 1994). A useful definition, developed by Norcross (1990), follows: Psychotherapy is "the informed and intentional application of clinical methods and interpersonal stances derived from established psychological principles for the purpose of assisting people to modify their behaviors, cognitions, emotions, and/or other personal characteristics in directions that the participants deem desirable" (p. 218). While psychotherapy implies being treated by someone to cure or care for problems, the word *counseling* refers to providing advice and suggestions.

Psychotherapy is a unilateral professional relationship that is circumscribed by limits on time, frequency of contact, content of discussions, and level of intimacy in which a person may talk over problems with a specialist in human behavior. Confidentiality is assured in a professional relationship, so that a client or patient can express whatever is on his or her mind without concern that the informa-

tion will be disclosed to others. As will be discussed in Chapter 13, there are several selected ethical and legal limits to confidentiality, including serious and immediate danger to self and others. A professional relationship also must not be compromised by the development or maintenance of unethical dual relationships. A psychologist will not be effective if also trying to be a friend, a colleague, or a lover. One of the differences between talking to a friend and talking to a psychologist is that the professional relationship is a primarily unilateral, or "one-way," relationship in which the problems or concerns of the patient or client are discussed, not the needs or concerns of the psychologist. Thus, psychotherapy involves consulting with a mental health professional to obtain assistance in changing feelings, thoughts, or behaviors that one experiences as problematic and distressing. Psychotherapy utilizes theories of human behavior as well as a carefully integrative plan to improve the psychological and behavioral functioning of a person or group.

Those who choose to receive psychotherapy from a mental health professional tend to benefit from the experience. An extensive review of all the research studies concludes that psychotherapy does indeed work (Barlow, 1996; Hollon, 1996; VandenBos, 1996). Generally 70 percent to 80 percent of those treated in psychotherapy are improved (Smith, Glass, & Miller, 1980). Most people who participate in a psychotherapy experience are satisfied with their treatment (*Consumer Reports,* 1995; Seligman, 1995). However, some psychologists are critical of psychotherapy feeling that much more effort should be directed towards prevention rather than treatment of psychological problems (Albee & Gullotta, 1997; Albee & Perry, 1996).

Contemporary Integration in Psychotherapy

Contemporary approaches to treating emotional distress and other problems in psychotherapy are multidimensional, comprehensive and integrative. An integrative biopsychosocial perspective maintains that biological, psychological, and social influences on behavior interact and must be taken into consideration in both psychological and medical treatment. Although psychotherapy conducted by psychologists is primarily a psychological (rather than biological or social) intervention, the biological and social influences on behavior are assessed, discussed, and taken into consideration during psychotherapy. Often, social or medical interventions are sought through other professionals or resources. Leading experts expect that psychotherapy will become more integrative, psychoeducational, problem-focused, and briefer in the future (Norcross, Alford, & DeMichele, 1992).

For example, suppose a patient seeks psychotherapy for depression. The patient may have a *biological* or genetic predisposition to depression and other affective, or mood disorders. The patient's mother, father, siblings, grandparents, and/or other relatives may also have depressive disorders. Research has demonstrated that emotional problems such as depression tend to be two to three times more likely to occur if someone has a relative with depression (Gershon, 1990). Of course relatives usually share both genetic and environmental similarities. Twin studies have revealed further support for the genetic influence in the development of depression. For example, Bertelsen, Harvald, & Hauge (1977) and Nurnberger & Gershon (1992) report that an identical twin is about three times more likely to develop a mood disorder when their twin has a mood disorder compared with nonidentical (fraternal) twins. Depressed patients also appear to have lower levels of neurotransmitters such as serotonin, norepinephrine, and dopamine (Spoont, 1992). Furthermore, endocrine involvement is associated with depression in that depressed patients experience elevated levels of the stress hormone cortisol relative to nondepressed persons (Weller & Weller, 1988). Thus, people may be biologically vulnerable to developing certain types of psychological disorders such as depression, attention deficit hyperactivity disorder, schizophrenia, bipolar disorder, or panic disorder. The psychologist may discuss this biological aspect with the patient to help him or her better understand and cope with this aspect of the illness. The psychologist may, for instance, refer the patient to a psychiatrist for biological treat-

ments such as the use of antidepressant medication or electroconvulsive therapy (ECT).

The patient also inevitably experiences *psychological* concerns related to the depression. Low self-esteem, hopelessness, loss of pleasure in activities and relationships, and perceived inability to achieve's one's goals may all be distressing for the depressed patient. Attitudes and the interpretation of stressful life events may also contribute to feelings of depression. Beck and colleagues (Beck, 1976) have suggested that depressed persons maintain a "negative schema" which is a stable negative cognitive belief about their life. Thus, depressed people maintain automatic negative interpretations of life events. Seligman (1975) suggested that depressed persons develop a pessimistic style of understanding their world and maintain a "learned helplessness" feeling that they have no control over their life. Object relations theorists (e.g., Kernberg, 1976; Klein, 1952; Kohut, 1971) suggest that impaired early attachments make one vulnerable to depression. Psychological interventions such as psychotherapy generally focus on such concerns by examining the thoughts and feelings associated with depression.

Finally, *social* influences on depression might include the depressed patient's interaction with family members, work associates, friends and the larger cultural context. Stressful life events such as divorce is highly associated with the onset of depression, especially among men. While divorced women are three times more likely to develop severe depression relative to women who remain married, men are nine times more likely to develop depression following a divorce (Bruce & Kim, 1992). Cultural influences may also play an important role in depression. For instance, in various cultural groups, many members tend to express depressive symptoms through somatic complaints such as headaches and gastric discomfort (Shorter, 1994). How emotional distress is expressed is partially determined by the social and cultural context in which the distress is experienced. Some cultural groups are more apt than others to encourage the expression of feelings and support the concept of psychotherapy. Therefore, these influences must be examined in order to better understand and treat the patient. Involving family members in the psychotherapy or using culture-specific interventions or consultations may prove useful for the depressed patient.

In short, in even the seemingly straightforward "psychological" example of depression, biopsychosocial factors interact uniquely and importantly to inform and direct treatment. In the following discussion of psychotherapy, this complexity and richness will best be illustrated in the integrative case examples provided for each therapeutic modality described.

Goals of Psychotherapy

The list of possible goals of psychotherapy is endless. Goals may include behavioral change, enhanced interpersonal relationships, insight, support, or concrete outcomes such as finding a job or a partner, staying out of the hospital, or staying alive. The goals may also be different for the patient, for the significant others in the patient's life (e.g., spouse, parents, coworkers, teacher), and for the psychologist. Whereas the patient may have one goal (e.g., reduction of anxiety), the psychologist may have another (e.g., increased insight), and the patient's spouse may have yet a different goal (e.g., increased independence and responsibility for the patient).

Kleinke (1994) described six fundamental therapeutic goals common to almost all psychotherapies: (1) overcoming demoralization and gaining hope, (2) enhancing mastery and self-efficacy, (3) overcoming avoidance, (4) becoming aware of one's misconceptions, (5) accepting life's realities, and (6) achieving insight. Common concerns that bring many to psychotherapy (e.g., anxiety, depression, loneliness, low self-esteem, problematic symptoms and/or relationships) often lead to the patient's feeling hopeless and demoralized. Psychotherapy usually seeks to return or develop a sense of hope or optimism. Increasing one's sense of mastery, efficacy, and control can also heighten one's sense of hope. Avoidance of issues can lead to more serious problems. Denying, avoiding, and minimizing problems prevent a person from dealing directly with them. Psychotherapy often seeks ways to help patients confront problems and concerns in order to deal more effectively with them. Insight into the intrapsychic, interpersonal, biological, and social factors that lead to symptoms and problems are

likely to assist a person in coping more effectively with their concerns.

The goal of psychotherapy may include changing very specific problem behaviors. For example, the goal might be to reduce or minimize temper tantrums, fear while speaking in public, nail biting, binge eating, or smoking. Other goals might include improving certain target behaviors such as attention in class, performance on examinations, polite behavior, exercise, and healthy food consumption; enhancing awareness of and insight into anxieties, attitudes, beliefs, and feelings; or increasing self-efficacy and mastery over problems. Goals of treatment might also involve careful management of a crisis (e.g., trauma, suicidal or homicidal threats). The objectives of psychotherapy may change several times during the course of the therapy experience. Accordingly, psychotherapy hopes to address many different types of goals, depending on the specific needs, interests, and concerns of all interested parties. Sometimes the goals are difficult to define and articulate until the psychologist evaluates or gets to know the patient. Overall, the ultimate objective is to improve quality of life through self-understanding, behavioral and lifestyle change, improved coping and adaptation, and/or enhanced relationships. Psychotherapy attempts to utilize what is known about the biopsychosocial influences on human behavior and apply that knowledge to help individuals and groups contending with a wide range of difficulties.

Similarities or Common Denominators in Psychotherapy

Common denominators in all psychotherapy include a professional person or "expert" of varying degree, professional behavior or manner on the part of the psychologist, a professional setting where services meant to help the client are rendered, fees, and a schedule of sessions. All psychotherapy also includes (or should include) ethical conduct. Many professionals report that factors such as the development of a therapeutic relationship, a sense of mastery and control, and corrective emotional experiences are helpful to patients and can be found in all psychotherapies (Kleinke, 1994; Prochaska &

Norcross, 1994). Grencavage and Norcross (1990) report 89 commonalities in psychotherapy, which generally fall into one of two categories: positive expectations and a helpful therapeutic relationship. These common factors will be discussed in detail in the next chapter. Professional person, manner, setting, fees, and schedule issues are briefly discussed here.

Professional Person

Almost all psychotherapies involve working with a licensed mental health professional (e.g., psychologist, psychiatrist, social worker, psychiatric nurse, marriage and family counselor) or a formally supervised trainee in a mental health discipline. These professionals learn principles of human behavior and apply them to the individual needs and concerns expressed by those who seek their services. Most professional organizations suggest that the practice of psychotherapy is a challenging art and science. Most encourage or require their members to obtain many years of intensive training, experience, and supervision prior to licensing. Psychologists, psychiatrists, social workers, nurses, marriage and family counselors, and others have specific requirements for certification and continuing education. Curiously, the term *counselor* or *psychotherapist* is not regulated by the states. Therefore, anyone can be called a counselor or a psychotherapist without any specific training or certification. A wide variety of "psychotherapy" approaches and techniques are offered by untrained or marginally trained persons. Although some of these counselors can provide excellent services, many do not (Singer & Lalich, 1996). All the professional mental health disciplines demand that anyone who wishes to provide psychotherapeutic services be fully trained and supervised to protect both the public and the profession from potential harm.

Professional Manner

Almost all psychologists maintain a professional manner. This entails observing appropriate professional boundaries (e.g., not discussing one's own problems) as well as behaving in an attentive, caring, and helpful manner. Professional manner also re-

quires being physically and psychologically available to the patient during sessions. Psychologists should not, for example, take telephone calls, fall asleep, eat, be late for appointments, act impulsively, or allow themselves to be distracted from their patients during the session.

Professional Setting

Most psychotherapy occurs in the professional office of the service provider (Fig. 9.1). The office is usually equipped with comfortable seating and space and also allows for private conversation (e.g., so that others cannot see or hear the conversation). Although some professionals may meet with patients outside the office setting (e.g., at school), the

Figure 9.1 Psychologists may conduct psychotherapy sessions.

vast majority of psychotherapy takes place in the office of the mental health professional. Whenever psychotherapy is conducted outside the professional office setting, clinicians should have a compelling reason to do so. Therefore, home visits and meetings at school or in public places may be appropriate under certain circumstances. For example, a psychologist treating someone with an airplane phobia may appropriately conduct a session at an airport, and someone who is severely disabled and cannot leave home may be necessarily treated by the psychologist at home. However, psychotherapy sessions over lunch at a restaurant are considered unprofessional and inappropriate. Maintaining confidentiality and professional boundaries must be considered carefully when meeting outside the office setting.

Fees

Almost all psychotherapy involves fees. Patients and/or their insurance companies are required to pay for the psychotherapy sessions. Fees may range from about $30 per hour in low-fee training or community clinics to $150 or more per hour. Generally, mental health disciplines that require more years of training (e.g., psychiatry and psychology) charge more than disciplines requiring fewer years of training (e.g., social work, marriage and family counseling). Geographic location can also impact professional fees. Fees tend to be higher for professionals with more years of experience who live in expensive areas (e.g., New York City, San Francisco, Boston). Some professionals use a sliding fee schedule to accommodate those who cannot afford the expense or whose health insurance does not cover mental health services. Some psychologists offer services to a certain number of people for free, or *pro bono,* in order to help those who need services but cannot pay for them. However, psychologists must manage their fees in an appropriately professional manner that allows them to earn a living.

Duration of Sessions

Psychotherapy usually involves about an hour of service per session (e.g., 50 minutes). Longer sessions (e.g., 80 minutes) are often scheduled for fam-

ily or group psychotherapy. Although there is nothing magical about meeting for 50 minutes, most psychologists do not deviate significantly from the 50-minute-session format. Fifty minutes (rather than a full hour) is generally used to allow the psychologist to take notes following the session as well as make quick telephone calls and conduct other administrative tasks relevant to patients. Most psychologists have a clock that is easily seen by the therapist and the patient so that both can monitor their time and use it wisely.

Frequency of Sessions

Most outpatient psychotherapy is conducted on a once-per-week basis, whereas inpatient or hospital-based psychotherapy is usually conducted daily. However, there may be compelling reasons to alter the once-per-week format. For example, some outpatient psychotherapy is conducted twice, three times, or, in the case of psychoanalysis, four or five times per week. Frequency of sessions may change during the course of psychotherapy. Some people prefer once every other week, once per month, or on an as-needed basis, and each of these arrangements affords pros and cons. Insurance companies generally have guidelines concerning the frequency of sessions that they will reimburse. During a crisis, someone may schedule psychotherapy sessions several times per week and switch to a weekly, bi-monthly, or an as-needed basis following the resolution of the crisis. After most of the goals of psychotherapy are reached, periodic follow-up or "booster" sessions are often scheduled as needed or once every few months to monitor progress and deal with potential relapse.

Stages of Psychotherapy

Most psychotherapy is carried out in several stages: an initial consultation, assessment of the problem and situation, development of treatment goals, implementation of treatment, evaluation of treatment, termination of treatment, and perhaps follow-up.

Initial Consultation

An initial consultation generally involves a discussion of why the patient has decided to seek help and what the patient hopes to gain from the psychotherapy experience. The consultation provides an opportunity to determine whether there is a good fit between the needs, goals, and interests of the patient and the skills of the psychologist. Furthermore, the psychologist usually outlines the terms of professional services such as limits of confidentiality, fees, available appointment times, therapeutic approach, and so forth. The initial consultation helps both the patient and the psychologist answer the question, "Am I likely to be able to work with this person successfully?"

Following the initial consultation, several decisions are made regarding whether or not to schedule a second session. The patient may evaluate how adequately his or her needs can be met by working with the psychologist, and whether the practical terms of the therapy are acceptable (e.g., session availability, fees, office location, psychologist approach). The patient may also consider whether the psychologist has an appealing personality or professional manner. Additionally, given the information presented during the consultation session, the psychologist may determine whether he or she has the expertise to work effectively with the patient. Thus, both patient and psychologist mutually decide whether additional sessions are advisable.

The initial consultation may result in the decision not to continue services. The patient may decide that his or her goals and needs cannot be adequately met by the psychologist for a variety of reasons. For instance, the psychologist may seem too direct, quiet, aloof, old, young, expensive, or inexperienced. Or the patient's goals may no longer seem as reasonable as initially thought. For example, the patient may have requested global personality change during the course of limited sessions or may wish to reduce a long-standing problem that is not amenable to psychotherapy. Then, too, the patient may actually feel better and have some sense of direction after the initial consultation and thus feel less compelled to continue sessions. The psychologist may also refuse to provide continued services for several reasons. For example, the patient may reveal an alcohol problem, and the psychologist might wish to refer him or her to a specialist in the assessment and treatment of substance abuse problems. The psychologist may decide not to proceed if the goals outlined by the patient are unrealistic or inappropriate. Research discussed later in this chapter suggests that a sizable number of initial consultation sessions do not result in a second session.

Assessment

The psychologist must perform an assessment of the patient. This may or may not involve formal psychological testing or extended interviews. Essentially, the psychologist must size up the patient and situation to develop a reasonable level of understanding concerning the diagnosis and direction for designing a treatment program. The psychologist must gain some insight into the factors that led to the development of the problem(s), the maintenance of the problem(s), and appropriate strategies for helping the patient obtain relief from the problem(s).

Some psychologists perform formal assessments for each new patient in their practice. Many clinics, hospitals, prisons, and other facilities use a standard battery of tests for all persons undergoing psychotherapy. For example, each adult patient might be asked to complete the Minnesota Multiphasic Personality Inventory-2 (MMPI-2), Symptom Checklist-90-Revised (SCL-90), and Projective Drawings no matter what the presenting problem(s) might be. All parents might be asked to complete a Child Behavior Checklist (CBCL) or a Conner's Rating Scale prior to treatment services for their child. Other treatment facilities and individual practitioners may make assessment decisions on a case-by-case basis after the initial interview. Furthermore, many professionals weave assessment and treatment together, evaluating treatment goals, symptoms, and satisfaction with services on a regular basis throughout treatment as well as after its termination.

Development of Treatment Goals

Once a reasonable level of understanding about the nature of the problem(s) is established, treatment goals and objectives can be developed. Whereas some psychologists explicitly detail treatment goals with their patients and use formal instruments to complete this process, others are much more informal about the development of treatment goals. It is important, however, for both patient and psychologist to have some understanding of the goals that each has in mind so that both parties can work toward the same ends. Once treatment goals are developed, a treatment plan should be outlined to reach them.

Implementation of Treatment

The actual treatment is provided with the hope of reaching the treatment goals. The treatment plan may include individual, couple, family, or group psychotherapy in weekly, bi-weekly, or daily sessions. Inpatient, outpatient, and partial hospitalization all may be utilized in the implementation of treatment. Different theoretical approaches might be used as well, and biological, psychological, and social interventions carried out. The treatment might include "homework," self-help readings, or consultation with other professionals (e.g., physicians, clergy, vocational counselors, school teachers). The various combinations and permutations of the treatment plan are as unique as each person seeking psychotherapy.

Evaluation of Treatment

During the course of treatment, an evaluation of the treatment should be regularly conducted to determine whether the treatment plan is working effectively or needs to be altered to be more useful to the patient. Although some psychologists, treatment facilities, and even health insurance companies conduct periodic and formal treatment evaluations using questionnaires, checklists, and other instruments, most choose to discuss the progress of the treatment informally with their patients during periodic sessions. Treatment may be altered or even terminated based on the evaluation.

Termination

Once psychotherapy has successfully reached the treatment goals, psychotherapy is usually terminated. Sometimes treatment is terminated prematurely due to a variety of factors such as the patient's financial or time constraints or resistance to change;

a job change or move on the part of the patient or psychologist; changes in insurance coverage; and so forth. A discussion concerning relapse strategies and a review of psychotherapy progress usually occur during termination. Psychotherapy termination can be difficult for both patients and psychologists who have spent many months or even years working closely together.

Follow-up

Often, follow-up sessions are scheduled or at least offered to the patient to ensure that the changes achieved during the course of therapy are maintained after treatment is terminated. Periodical booster sessions might be scheduled to review progress and to work on problems that emerge later. Follow-up can provide a sense of continuity for patients, and alleviate the abruptness of termination after an intensive therapy.

Modes of Psychotherapy

Meeting individually with a psychologist is not the only way psychotherapy can occur. Psychotherapy can be provided in individual, couple, group, or family modes, and people may participate in several different modes at the same time. Each mode has advantages and disadvantages as well as different potential goals and objectives.

It is often difficult to understand what psychotherapy might be like without using actual case examples. Confidentiality concerns prevent most students and other interested parties from witnessing psychotherapy sessions in person or on videotape. Several brief examples of actual psychotherapy cases are provided in this chapter in a manner that protects patient confidentiality. Each of these cases provides a description of psychotherapy with either groups, couples, or individuals regarding specific difficulties.

Individual Psychotherapy

Individual psychotherapy is the most commonly practiced and researched mode of psychotherapy (Bergin & Garfield, 1994). Goals, techniques, and perspectives on how to conduct individual psychotherapy vary widely. Perhaps the only common denominator is that the patient meets alone with a psychologist. Individual psychotherapy involves conversations between a psychologist and patient who work as a team to help the patient overcome problems, improve insight and/or behavior, and enhance his or her quality of life. These conversations may focus on many different topics, depending on the problems and symptoms experienced by the patient as well as the skills and orientation of the psychologist. The discussion can focus on the development of techniques to cope with symptoms (e.g., thought stopping, relaxation), feelings associated with symptoms (e.g., alienation, fear) or on the actual relationship between the psychologist and patient (e.g., the transference and counter transference).

Case Study: Individual Child Therapy with Shawna

Brief Identifying Information: Shawna is an eleven-year-old Caucasian girl who lives with her parents, older sister (15), and two cats. She is presently in the sixth grade in a public school where she is performing very well academically. Shawna's family lives in a wealthy suburban area where achievement and success are strong community values. There are no significant current stressors in the home nor past traumas identified.

Presenting Problem: Shawna has been troubled by almost nightly enuresis, often referred to as "bedwetting", ever since she was "out of diapers". Both Shawna and her parents are deeply embarrassed by this problem, which has remained a deep family secret and prevented Shawna from the normal range of overnights and sleep away activities with her peers. Assessment of the enuresis does not reveal any consistent stressors or emotional antecedents to the almost nightly occurences. However, the consequences of the wetting involves Shawna's mother or older sister changing her bedclothes and informing her father: "Another wet night."

Key Biopsychosocial Factors:
   Biological: The clinician needs to rule out a medical basis for enuresis (e.g., bladder disease or abnormality). Some children sleep so deeply as to not heed the physiological sensation of a full bladder.
   Psychological: The clinician needs to rule out an emotional basis for enuresis (e.g., anxiety, trauma, stress). For example, shame and isolation as well as a lack of developmentally appropriate independence and autonomy may play a role.
   Social: Community values on success intimidate this family from sharing problems with friends and extended family and increase sense of shame and isolation.

Treatment Goals and Plans: Treatment will focus on resolving the enuresis, working through the shame and secrecy, and increasing Shawna's sense of competence and social access.

The treatment plan involves the following components.

1. A medical examination is required to rule out any physical basis for the enuresis.
2. In the absence of a medical problem, a behavioral program using a special device which buzzes at the first drop of moisture in bed will be employed. This techniques requires that Shawna take responsibility for attaching the device to her bed each night, and as soon as the alarm is activated, she is to get out of bed and go to the bathroom to urinate. (Eventually, children become conditioned to the association between a full bladder and the buzzer, and learn to awaken on their own.) Shawna is to record each morning whether the buzzer woke her, whether she woke herself, and other relevant details. She is also to handle her own linens, and her family members are only to be involved at her direct request.
3. Individual sessions will discuss the progress of this behavioral program while exploring her feelings of shame, success, isolation, etc. Fourth, intermittent family sessions will ensure that the family is allowing Shawna more autonomy and afford an opportunity to discuss embarrassment and the pressure to "always look good" in their community. As Shawna's enuresis resolves, her newfound pride and independence can be integrated through discussion and ventures into overnights, and therapy sessions eventually tapered.

This example illustrates the use of individual and family modalities in a combined behavioral and humanistic approach to understand, support, and increase self-efficacy around a specific problem. Medical consultation in addition to an understanding of the meaning of the problem in the larger sociocultural context further adds to the treatment efficacy.

Whereas individual psychotherapy for adults involves discussions with a psychologist, for young children it often incorporates play activities. Play therapy includes activities that are observed and interpreted by a psychologist. It is assumed that children work though emotional conflicts in their play, and that themes that develop and become reenacted during play sessions assist in the healing process. Play is also used with children to aid communication and as a distraction to assist children in feeling less self-conscious when talking about sensitive topics.

Case Study: Individual Psychotherapy with James

Brief Identifying Information: James is a 55-year-old biracial (Hawaiian and Caucasian) executive who lives alone following the death of his wife seven years ago. He has one daughter with a family of her own.

Presenting Problem: James presents in a manic stage of bipolar disorder, having had a number of previous episodes. James' maternal uncle and grandfather also had bipolar illness. This episode involved James discontinuing his lithium use, travelling to Los Angeles in the hopes of becoming an actor, spending thousands of dollars on extravagant merchandise, and finally, being arrested for drunk and disorderly conduct at a nightclub. James was hospitalized in an inpatient unit briefly, and is now seeking outpatient treatment.

Key Biopsychosocial Factors:
  Biological: There is a family (genetic) history of bipolar disorder as well as research supporting a biological basis of bipolar disorder. Medication is an essential treatment component.
  Psychological: James' lack of compliance with his lithium regimen, denial regarding chronicity of his bipolar disorder, enjoyment of the manic high, need for control and independence, emotional losses pertaining to wife's death and a severe chronic psychiatric condition all play a role in his illness.
  Social: Family and cultural traditions that (in James' family) distrust Western medicine and cultural and general social isolation also are likely to impact his illness.

Treatment Goals and Plan: James requires medication management in addition to individual therapy in order to achieve several immediate and longterm goals. After an initial consultation and assessment period with James, the following treatment goals were determined. First, James will seek to work through the various impediments to his reliable use of Lithium medication. These involve not only his need to be in control and not dependent on drugs (or others), but his family of origin's negative feelings about Western medicine. Second, James finds that when he becomes depressed, he longs for the "high" associated with mania. Therefore, the causes of his depression will be determined as well as improved coping skills. Third, James is lonely, misses his wife, and feels isolated from the Hawaiian heritage he cherishes. Thus, treatment will also address his interpersonal, social and cultural needs.

The treatment plan involves the following components:

1. Collaboration with James' physician regarding his lithium regimen.
2. Behavioral contracting, which involves James' commitment to maintain his lithium regimen for at least the first six weeks of psychotherapy.
3. Exploratory work to understand James' disdain for dependence and impediments to developing a more satisfying interpersonal life.
4. Psychoeducational materials regarding bipolar illness, lithium, and traditional Hawaiian healing techniques and rituals to aid James in understanding the similarities, differences, and potential virtues and liabilities of both traditions.
5. Problem solving regarding increasing social contacts and cultural identification.
6. Developing improved awareness and skills for combatting depression and curtailing future manic episodes.
7. Examination of the transference relationship between James and his psychologist to better understand James' interpersonal issues as well as his need for control and independence.

This case example serves to illustrate how personality and culture impact compliance with medical regimens such as medication, and the need to work through a variety of intrapsychic and social issues in managing a major psychiatric problem such as bipolar illness. The treatment by necessity is multidimensional and mindful of the biopsychosocial influences on human functioning.

Group Psychotherapy

Group psychotherapy comes in many shapes and sizes with various goals, techniques, and objectives. Some groups are conducted in hospital settings and meet daily or several times per week. Outpatient groups generally meet once per week or every other week. Some groups are homogeneous, specializing in the treatment of people who share a common clinical problem (e.g., bulimia, social phobia, alcoholism), whereas other groups are heterogeneous, with patients experiencing a wide range of concerns and diagnoses. All of the major theoretical orientations and their integration can be used to structure a psychotherapy group and formulate its goals.

Groups that are psychoeducational in orientation provide both useful information for patients experiencing similar problems and an opportunity for group support (e.g., sharing and expressing feelings and concerns and obtaining feedback from group members). Much like classroom instruction, information is provided, followed by group discussion and support (Fig. 9.2). Many psychoeducational groups also include guest speakers on relevant topics. Most hospitals offer psychoeducational support groups for patients with diabetes, cancer, multiple sclerosis, heart disease, bipolar disorder,

smoking, alcohol, obsessive-compulsive disorder, or other problems. Patients who share the same diagnosis meet together to learn how to manage their illness; they also share stories and give and receive support from each other. Group support not only is helpful for psychological health but has been associated with longevity among cancer patients and others (Spiegal, 1990, 1992).

Other forms of group psychotherapy may focus on interpersonal skill development rather than psychoeducation. These groups generally provide a forum for support and peer feedback as well as for the development of interpersonal skills. Patients can gain new insights and practice new ways of interacting with others during group sessions. Group cohesion and a sense of hope often emerges through these sessions. Patients frequently feel better knowing that they are not alone and that others, like them, struggle with similar issues and concerns. Advice, suggestions, and general feedback from peer group members can often be more powerful than those provided by the group leader(s). Table 9.1 provides a list of **curative factors** associated with group psychotherapy according to Irvin Yalom (1985).

Children's groups can be helpful for children having difficulty with socialization. Those who expe-

Figure 9.2   School-based discussion group among adolescents

Table 9.1   Curative Factors in Group Psychotherapy (Yalom, 1985)

Imparting information:	Advice and suggestions offered by group members and leaders
Instilling hope:	Others learning and dealing with concerns enhances hope
Universality:	Others share same problems and concerns
Altruism:	Helping others enhances self-esteem and confidence
Interpersonal learning:	Learning from others in open and honest manner
Corrective recapitulation of the primary family:	Group often takes on a family-like quality. New ways of interacting with others helps to improve ways of dealing with others
Catharsis:	Expressing emotions in a safe and trusting manner
Group cohension:	Feeling connected and close to the group
Development of socializing techniques:	Group provides chance to develop and improve social skills
Imitative behavior:	Group members learning by observing and modeling other group members as well as the group leader
Existential factors:	Group members learn about meaning in life, that life is not always as you plan, and that feelings of loneliness are common.

rience problems such as attention deficit hyperactivity disorder, pervasive developmental disorders, social phobia, and anxiety can often benefit from regular group psychotherapy. Children experiencing parental divorce, sexual abuse, or chronic illness also benefit from being with other children who share similar concerns and experiences. Groups for young children tend to have fewer verbal activities such as talking and usually include play, art, and other activities. Peer interactions, support, and feedback can be useful in all of these group activities

to improve self esteem, social skills, and general interpersonal functioning.

Couples Psychotherapy

Couples psychotherapy is often useful for those experiencing marital or couples discord. Rather than meeting with one person to discuss problems in the relationship, both parties meet with the psychologist to work on *in vivo* issues pertaining specifically to the relationship (e.g., communication problems,

Figure 9.3   A marriage therapy session

Case Study: Inpatient Group Psychotherapy

Patients hospitalized on an inpatient medical-psychiatric unit participate in daily group psychotherapy. The participants experience both medical and psychiatric problems such as eating disorders, chronic pain disorders, alcohol abuse and dependence, colitis, and Alzheimer's disease. Many of the patients have experienced depression, anxiety, and/or personality disorder as well. In addition to comprehensive individual medical and psychiatric treatment, patients attend psychoeducational groups (e.g., "How to Manage Your Illness"), as well as the psychotherapy group sessions conducted by a psychologist and a nurse. Patients are generally hospitalized for several days or weeks, and individuals are admitted to and discharged from the unit several times each day. Therefore, the composition of the psychotherapy group changes almost daily.

The purpose of the group is to encourage patients to discuss feelings and concerns in a safe and trusting environment. The group is highly structured, provides support, and emphasizes a "here and now" perspective. Structure, such as starting and ending the session on time, providing an introduction to the group so that all group members understand what can be expected from the group experience, introducing all members, and trying to elicit feelings and reflections from all members during the course of the session is provided in order to ensure that the group runs smoothly and that all patients have a positive group experience. Support is necessary to create a comfortable, accepting, and nonjudgmental environment. The "here and now" helps each group member stay focused on the present rather than revealing long stories about the past or worries about the future.

The following patients attended one of these actual inpatient group sessions.

Anna is a 58-year-old Latino woman who is hospitalized with obesity, sleep apnea, and depression. Her internal medicine physician is concerned that her obesity is making her sleep apnea (episodes of breathing cessation while asleep) much worse and that since she is depressed, she is unwilling to attempt to lose weight to minimize her health risks. In fact, Ann reports that she is very unhappy about family stress and conflicts and would prefer to die in her sleep. She hopes that her sleep apnea will kill her without pain.

Beth is a 19-year-old Caucasion college student with severe anorexia nervosa. She currently weighs 83 pounds and is 5′7″ tall. She is also obsessive-compulsive and depressed. She refuses to gain weight and had to withdraw from her classes due to her recent hospitalization.

Carl is a 34-year-old African-American man with severe colitis. He is highly anxious and experiences several phobias. He has recently had surgery for colon cancer as well. His doctors do not think that he will live for more than a few years.

Diane is a 43-year-old Caucasion woman who is dependent on alcohol, Valium, and several pain medications. She has been hospitalized many times during suicidal episodes as well as for detoxification. She is also diagnosed with borderline personality disorder and major depression. She was severely sexually abused as a child by her father and is currently married to a man who physically abuses her.

Esther is an 84-year-old African-American woman who is depressed, has Alzheimer's disease, and recently had a hip-replacement surgery. She is concerned that she must leave her own home and enter a nursing home when she is discharged from the hospital. She would like to stay hospitalized as long as possible to delay her inevitable move to the nursing home.

Fran is a 34-year-old Asian-American married woman who has a somatization disorder. While she has no known medical problems, she has numerous medical symptoms and complaints. She left her work on disability several years ago, and her husband and two children take turns caring for her. She complains that she can't walk well, move her arms, or see very well. She is also diagnosed with a histrionic personality disorder. She is especially angry because she feels that all the doctors and nurses think her problems are "all in her head." She has had over 20 hospitalizations for these symptoms. An excerpt from a group session follows:

Psychologist: Welcome to the group. We meet every day at 11:00 a.m. for one hour. The purpose of the group is to talk about feelings and issues in the moment. Anger, sadness, anxiety, interpersonal conflicts are, for example, typical topics that we discuss. We try to avoid talking about things in the past or future problems and concerns because we don't feel that we can be very helpful on these topics within our limited amount of time and given the number of people that participate in the group. Let's quickly go around the room and introduce ourselves and then let us go around a second time and state what topic or agenda you would like to talk about in our group today. My name is Dr. Gerard and I am a psychologist on the unit.

(Group members introduce themselves and then each states what his or her topic or agenda is for the day.)

Anna: I really have nothing to say today.

Psychologist: Anna, you seem angry when you said that. Are you feeling angry today?

Anna: Yes, I guess I am. I want to just go home. I'm sick of being locked up here. My doctor tells me that he thinks I should stay for at least another 4 days, but I don't think it is doing me any good.

Psychologist: Perhaps discussing your feelings of anger and frustration would be useful in the group today.

Case Study: Inpatient Group Psychotherapy (Continued)

Anna: Okay, I guess so. I suppose it can't hurt since I'm here anyway.

Psychologist: Okay, Anna, we'll get back to that issue. Beth, how about you.

Beth: I'm feeling very anxious and guilty today. I can't believe I had to drop out of school this term. I'll never graduate with my class and maybe never graduate at all. I feel like a total failure.

Psychologist: Thanks Beth, we'll come back to you. Carl?

Carl: I feel down too. I feel crummy. Angry too. I'm sick of being sick all the time. It stinks. I wish I didn't have to deal with this.

Diane: I'm okay today. I feel pretty good actually. I'm leaving the hospital later today and feel that I've made some good progress this time. I'll miss Beth, we've had some good talks since I've been here. I hope you'll stay in touch. I'm a bit anxious about how I'll do outside of the hospital, but I'm pretty excited about leaving. I've been here long enough.

Psychologist: We'll be sure to say our goodbyes and best wishes to you, Diane, before the group ends today.

Esther: I'm okay. I don't have anything to say.

Psychologist: How are you feeling right now, in the moment?

Esther: Okay, nothing really.

Psychologist: Okay, let us know, however, if something comes up for you and we'll check in with you as well.

Fran: I think this is all b.s. I'm sick of all this talk, talk, talk. I need answers to my medical problems and everyone around here wants me to talk about my feelings. I can't believe I even agreed to be admitted here. What a mistake. There is no way I'd do this again.

Psychologist: You sound pretty angry Fran. Perhaps we could talk about that in the group today.

Fran: See what I mean? Talk, talk, talk. I don't know. I'm angry for sure but I don't think talking will help much.

Psychologist: I hope that you'll try, Fran. While talking may not cure any of the medical problems that you experience, perhaps it will help you to feel better. Now that we've heard from everyone, let's try to work through the issues that were brought up in the group today. Anna and Fran are feeling pretty angry today, while Carl says that he's feeling down and Beth is feeling angry and guilty. Ester is doing okay and doesn't have an agenda in the moment. Let's do the best we can to talk about each agenda. Let's start with Anna and Fran's anger theme.

This brief excerpt from an inpatient group psychotherapy session illustrates several key themes. First, this particular psychotherapy is one part of a complex, multi-dimensional treatment program that utilizes biological, psychological and social interventions and various modalities during this inpatient phase of treatment. Second, it is clear from even these brief summaries of each patient's problems that clinical cases are usually highly complex and involved. Finally, the psychologist in this group provides structure, support and clarification in an effort to assist patient's in dealing with their immediate emotional states.

---

sexual concerns, commitment issues). Couples therapy includes unmarried as well as married partners; heterosexual as well as homosexual partners. There are as many approaches to couples psychotherapy as there are to individual psychotherapy; however, the focus is usually on improved communication and problem-solving strategies.

Family Therapy

Family psychotherapy involves the entire family—parents and children, and sometimes also grandparents, aunts and uncles, or various subsets of the family (e.g., mother and child dyad or pair). There are numerous approaches and perspectives to family psychotherapy. Like couples psychotherapy, the goals of family psychotherapy often include improving both communication between family members and problem-solving strategies. There is often an "identified patient" (e.g., an adolescent who is acting out), yet treatment focuses on how each family member is contributing to the maintenance of disharmony within the entire family system.

Nonpsychotherapy Approaches to Treatment: Biological and Social Interventions

Although clinical psychologists primarily rely on psychotherapy utilizing models explicated in Chapter 4 to treat difficulties, nonpsychotherapy interventions are also frequently used. Nonpsychotherapy interventions may include biological interventions such as the use of psychotropic medication, electroconvulsive therapy (ECT), and biofeedback or social interventions such as large-scale commu-

Case Study: Couples Therapy with Hans and Marta

Brief Identifying Information: Hans and Marta, a Caucasian couple of Austrian descent have been married for two years, and each have two children from their previous marriages currently living in the home. They also have an infant daughter of their own. Thus, this blended family combines five children and the challenges of relating to involved ex-spouses. Hans is employed as a contractor and Marta does not work outside of her considerable duties within the home.

Presenting Problem: Hans and Marta report frequent fighting and very low marital satisfaction. Hans is reportedly physically abusive of Marta, and a number of times has struck one of the children. Marta is therefore afraid to confront Hans about her unhappiness and has been withdrawn and disinterested in sex. Hans reports that Marta ignores him, is focused only on the children, and sometimes he just "loses it". Hans and Marta are asking for help with the fighting, the physical abuse, and the extremely low level of positive marital interaction.

Key Biopsychosocial Factors:

Biological: Hans' father was physically abusive, which may represent a biological or an environmental predisposition to violence. Marta gave birth only six months ago and is still resuming her normal hormonal and physical functioning. The extent of the physical abuse needs to be assessed in terms of the health of Marta and the children, and all family members protected from further violence.

Psychological: Marta is a battered woman and lives in constant fear for her own and her children's safety. She is attached to Hans and is unable to separate from him or assert her needs in the face of his violence. Hans is a classic batterer in the sense that he denies responsibility for the abuse, blames Marta for his behavior, and states that if she were only more loving and available he would not need to resort to such anger.

Social: The larger sociocultural context for violence is well established in that we live in a violent society that does not adequately protect victims or treat perpetrators. Hans' own abuse at the hands of his father may have imparted this tendency through social learning or identification with the aggressor.

Marta may feel dependent upon Hans and afraid to separate due to her fear that she may be unable to adequately house, clothe, and feed her children, and perhaps even lose custody.

Treatment Goals and Plan: The prevailing goal of treatment must be the physical safety of Marta and her children. Given that physical abuse of the children is being reported, the psychologist is legally and ethically mandated to make a report to Child Protective Services. If the couple are willing to remain in treatment in spite of this report, several goals will include (1) cessation of all physical violence within the home, (2) development of alternative means of expressing and working through anger and frustration, (3) insight into the origins and triggers of violence, (4) improved capacity for communication and intimacy.

The treatment plan will include:

1. Individual therapy for Hans to learn to control his temper and violence and for Marta to develop increased autonomy, assertiveness, and a plan of action in the face of future violence.
2. Develop alternative behavioral strategies for dealing with anger and create a contract between Hans and Marta for taking alternate steps to violence.
3. Family-of-origin work to understand the roots of violence for Hans and factors contributing to Marta's relationship to an abusive man.
4. Develop opportunities for the couple to engage in some mutually positive and pleasurable activities.
5. Locate social services and shelters for battered women.
6. A group therapy for Hans with other men who are abusive.
7. Collaboration with the individual psychologists, group therapist, family physician, child therapists and social services worker monitoring abuse within the home.

This couple's therapy case illustrates the high stakes and complex layers of relational problems. The outcome of this case, like most others, will depend largely on the cooperation and motivation of Hans and Marta to acknowledge their serious difficulties and take the necessary steps toward improvement. Various modalities, techniques, and social and medical elements also come into play in this complex yet all too common situation.

Case Study: Family Therapy with the Kaplans

Brief Identifying Information: The Kaplan family consists of Mr. Kaplan, his 16-year-old son David and 13-year-old daughter Barbara. Mrs. Kaplan tragically died one year ago after a long battle with lung cancer. The Kaplans live in an urban setting in a large city.

Presenting Problems: The Kaplans were referred for family therapy by David's individual psychologist who is treating David following a serious suicide attempt. This psychologist feels that family therapy is indicated in order to address issues of unresolved grief, anger, parenting, and communication.

As a family, the Kaplans report that since Mrs. Kaplan's death, the family has been in extreme turmoil. Mrs. Kaplan had always assumed the primary parenting and housekeeping duties, while Mr. Kaplan worked long hours as a city planner. David has been performing poorly in school, experimenting with drugs, and withdrawing from his home. Barbara has been depressed, anxious, and both clingy and demanding with her father. Mr. Kaplan is depressed, overwhelmed and frequently irritable with the children. All agreed that the family is in crisis, or as David put it: "Everything sucks."

Key Biopsychosocial Factors:
Biological: There is no known family history of psychiatric problems such as depression. Family members have not regulated well in the wake of their loss, and are eating and sleeping poorly.
Psychological: The Kaplans experience an ongoing grief reaction, depression in the wake of loss, associated anger and irritability, acting out of emotional distress, and reworking of attachments, roles, and structure within the family.

Social: The Kaplan children have experienced the loss of their mother as the keeper of family and religious traditions and rituals as well as changes in their social network, which was maintained by their mother.

Treatment Goals and Plan: The Kaplans agree to the following treatment goals in the context of family therapy: (1) Discuss each member's feelings regarding the loss of Mrs. Kaplan, (2) learn how these feelings impact current relationships within the family, and (3) figure out how to reorganize the household to reduce the present chaos and reclaim a sense of cohesion, stability and organization.

The treatment plan involves the following components:
1. During each session, each member will discuss their feelings of grief, sadness, anger, confusion, etcetera regarding the untimely loss of Mrs. Kaplan and refer to one interaction with another family member where these feelings interfered (e.g., lashed out at another due to anger at loss, was afraid to be alone because of fear of feeling overwhelmingly sad).
2. Problem solving will be utilized to develop plans for carrying out household tasks, resuming important rituals and traditions, redefining roles and in a sense, creating a new household structure.
3. Consultation with David's psychologist with David and his father's signed consent in order to keep abreast of important developments in both therapies.

This case illustrates the use of family therapy to alter systemic factors potentially responsible for generating symptoms and problems. Collaboration between the two treating psychologists will be important as will monitoring of family members' biological, psychological, and social functioning through the course of treatment.

---

nity education programs, structured residential communities (e.g., halfway houses), and various types of prevention programs. Nonpsychotherapy treatment and prevention interventions may be used in addition to psychotherapy or without psychotherapy. For example, a patient may routinely take an antidepressant medication such as Prozac or an antianxiety agent such as Xanax with or without participating in psychotherapy. The medications might be provided by a trained mental health professional such as a psychiatrist or by someone with minimal mental health training such as an internal medicine or family practice physician. A clinician might use biofeedback with or without psychother-

apy to treat a range of problems such as anxiety, phobia, headaches, or irritable bowel syndrome. Finally, a patient may enroll in a halfway house for substance abuse with or without individual, family, or group psychotherapy.

Biological Interventions

Currently psychologists are unable to provide invasive biological or medical interventions such as prescribing psychotropic medications or using ECT. However, efforts are under way to give psychologists limited prescription privileges, thereby allowing them to provide medications for their patients without physician supervision (American Psychological Association, 1992b; this controversial issue will be discussed in more detail in Chapter 14). Although psychologists at present cannot prescribe medication and must work with physician colleagues in treating patients using these medications, clinical psychologists need at least a basic understanding of commonly used psychotropic medications. They must be familiar with medications and their side effects and know when to refer a patient to a physician for a medication evaluation or treatment.

The most common classes of medications used in psychiatric treatment include antidepressant, antianxiety, and antipsychotic agents (Julien, 1995). However, psychostimulants and lithium are two other types of medication used for specific clinical problems. Antidepressant medication is usually classified in one of three categories. The first category includes the selective serotonin reuptake inhibitors (SSRIs) such as Prozac, Zoloft, and Paxil. The second class includes the tricyclics such as Elavil, Tofranil, and Anafranil. The third class includes the monoamine oxidase inhibitors (MAOIs) such as Parnate and Nardil. Antianxiety medications usually include the benzodiazepines such as Xanax, Valium, and Ativan. Antipsychotic medications (often called neuroleptics) include Haldol, Mellaril, Thorazine, and Risperdal. Psychostimulants such as Ritalin and Dexedrine are used to increase attention and concentration among children with attention-deficit and/or hyperactivity problems (Klein, 1995). Finally, lithium (lithium chloride) as well as anticonvulsant medications (e.g., Depakote, Tegretol) are used to treat bipolar disorder (commonly known as manic-depression; Julien, 1995).

Each medication has advantages and disadvantages (Julien, 1995; Klein, 1995; Kramer, 1993). Some medications work well for some people but not for others, even if they share the same diagnosis. Some people have negative reactions to some medications while others do not. Although helping to relieve symptoms such as anxiety, depression, and psychotic thinking, many medications have undesirable side effects (e.g., dry mouth, weight gain, constipation, diarrhea, physical and/or psychological

addiction). Some medications (e.g., MAO inhibitors) cannot be taken with certain foods (e.g., beer, wine, chocolate). Some are often extremely dangerous if used in suicide attempts (e.g., Valium). Research and development by pharmaceutical companies and other researchers work toward improved medications that are safe and effective and have minimal negative side effects. Much attention has been given to the selective serotonin reuptake inhibitors such as Prozac in recent years (Kramer, 1993). Many claim that Prozac is more effective than the other classes of antidepressant medications (i.e., tricyclics and MAO Inhibitors) without so many adverse side effects (Kramer, 1993). Importantly, medication is generally prescribed in the context of a therapeutic relationship, and research supports the combined efficacy.

It is important to mention that the positive effects of medication on disorders·such as depression, anxiety, and schizophrenia do not imply that these disorders are strictly a biological problem (Horgan, 1996). Again a biopsychosocial view is needed to understand and treat these and other disorders. Many people respond positively to medication due to a placebo effect, since many believe that the medication will help them and expectation therefore ensures that it does. Many people also do not respond well to psychotropic medications. In fact it has been estimated that about two-thirds of people using antidepressant medications experience no improvement or responded equally as well to a placebo drug (Fisher & Greenberg, 1989). Although medications such as Prozac are enormously popular with more than 20 million people taking the drug (Kramer, 1993; Horgan, 1996), research has not demonstrated that Prozac is more effective than psychotherapy in treating depression (Consumer Reports, 1995; Horgan, 1996; Seligman, 1995).

Biofeedback (Miller, 1969; Schwartz & Beatty, 1977) is another example of a nonpsychotherapy biological approach to treatment. As discussed in Chapter 8, biofeedback provides patients with information concerning their physiological arousal as measured by heart rate, blood pressure, muscle tension, respiration, sweating, and body temperature. Some or all of these physiological states are measured during office or home sessions. Patients are asked to lower their level of arousal through the use of relaxation, imagery, prayer, or any other technique that works for them. Feedback is provided by visual or auditory means such as tones or computer graphics. Unlike psychotropic medication, biofeedback is noninvasive, and psychologists can legally and ethically use it with their patients as long as they have adequate training and experience with the technique.

Social Interventions

Social and community interventions and programs often seek to improve psychological, interpersonal, social, and occupational functioning. Clinical psychologists frequently are involved with the design, implementation, and evaluation of these programs. They usually employ a psychoeducational approach, providing education, skill-building training, and support for those at risk for or already struggling with a significant psychiatric, medical, or other problem(s).

Community programs generally attempt to help at-risk persons to prevent the development of serious problems or to minimize the impact of an already present problem. The programs are usually categorized as primary, secondary, or tertiary. Primary prevention programs seek to prevent problems from developing through the use of education. For example, Head Start is a program developed to give young children from disadvantaged homes an opportunity to attend preschool without charge. The goal was to give these children a "head start" in school and allow their parents the opportunity to work or obtain further education to improve their socioeconomic status and quality of life. Primary prevention programs have been developed to help teen mothers learn child care and other skills (Abma & Mott, 1991). Other programs have been designed to teach school children how to minimize unsafe and high-risk sexual behavior (Howard & McCabe, 1990).

Secondary prevention programs attempt to intervene early during the course of problems to minimize the development of more serious problems. For example, people arrested for driving under the influence of alcohol (DUIs) are often offered the opportunity to attend a training program about substance abuse in order to avoid the loss of their driver's license. The goal of the program is to educate first-time offenders about the dangers of driving under the influence of drugs, thereby helping to prevent future incidents of drunk driving. Similar programs have been developed for adolescents arrested for various offenses and for people who seek the services of prostitutes. Secondary prevention might also involve outreach to homebound elderly individuals to mitigate loneliness and provide social and intellectual stimulation.

Tertiary prevention programs endeavor to minimize the impact of serious psychiatric or other problem(s). They are basically the same as other treatments but usually refer to community-based interventions. For example, halfway houses are designed to help patients recently released from hospitals, drug treatment programs, or prisons. They allow patients to live and work in the community and still receive professional supervision and skill-building training. They help transition patients from the highly structured hospital, drug treatment, or prison setting back to the community. Halfway houses typically specialize in certain populations such as adolescents or former convicts, or in certain problems such as alcohol and drug dependence, schizophrenia, or physical disabilities. Other tertiary prevention programs offer education and support for those with serious illnesses. For example, the American Cancer Society, along with other organizations, offers group support programs to help those coping with terminal or other forms of cancer. Alcoholics Anonymous (AA) is a well known example of a tertiary prevention program. AA started in 1935 and provides over 20,000 support groups around the globe (Nathan, 1993). AA uses a 12-step treatment approach that involves confidential group support for alcoholics. AA members report a very high degree of satisfaction with the program (*Consumer Reports,* 1995; Hogan, 1996).

Contemporary Case, Contemporary Treatment

Increasingly, psychologists are confronted with extremely "involved" cases, referring to the multidimensional complexities encountered in a typical caseload. Individuals are rarely "simple"; and neither can treatment be simple or unidimensional. The following case illustrates this complexity and the siren call to integration in contemporary clinical psychology.

Case Study: Mako
Contemporary Psychotherapy: Integration of Theories, Techniques, Modalities, and Biopsychosocial Factors in a Case of Anorexia Nervosa

Brief Identifying Information: Mako is a 14-year-old Japanese female who has lived in the United States since age 7. She lives with her parents and younger brother. Mako's father is a businessman who commutes between Japan and the United States, utilizing a work visa for he and his family. Mako is in the 8th grade in public junior high school, and attends a Japanese school 3 afternoons each week to maintain her Japanese language skills. Mako and her brother are fluently bilingual; her parents have some difficulty conversing in English.

Presenting Problem: Mako has been diagnosed with anorexia nervosa, a disorder that commonly afflicts adolescent females with a relentless drive toward thinness. Mako is severely emaciated due to self-starvation and excessive exercise, and also evidences amenorrhea (cessation of menstrual periods), intense fear of gaining weight, extreme fatigue, social withdrawal, and depression. She has received both a medical and a neurological evaluation to rule out a primary medical basis for her weight loss, and was determined to be suffering from anorexia nervosa.

Key Biopsychosocial Factors:

Biological: Mako experiences life-threatening malnutrition and emaciation, low heart rate and blood pressure, as well as hormonal and electrolyte imbalances. Mako's malnutrition also contributes to impaired reasoning and severe fatigue.

Psychological: Mako is presently genuinely terrified of losing control over her eating and becoming overweight. Her perfectionism and desire to achieve correspond to a strong need for control, yet also to an underlying fear of inadequacy in confronting the psychosocial and developmental challenges of adolescence. Depression, feelings of stigmatization, and loss of esteem are also relevant.

Social: Mako's family and cultural values emphasize cooperation, achievement, conformity and minimal expression of emotion and opinion. Mako is also experiencing cultural conflict in seeking to maintain her dual Japanese and American identities. The generally American premium on expressiveness and individuality is in direct conflict with her Japanese family's value on calm acceptance and conformity to parents and social norms. Finally, media and culture in both the United States and Japan glorify standards of thinness and beauty for females.

Treatment Goals: (1) Humanely assist Mako in resuming a healthy weight and healthy eating behavior, (2) address the underlying psychological, developmental, and familial basis for her anorexia nervosa, (3) assist the family in contending with this serious illness in the family, (4) assist Mako in resuming school and social activities.

Course of Treatment: Mako was initially hospitalized on an adolescent eating disorders unit in order to stabilize her medical condition and lay the foundation for outpatient treatment. During hospitalization, Mako was initially confined to bed during which time she was medically monitored, given intravenous fluids and electrolytes, and given the option of tubefeeding or eating substantially on her own. She opted to eat on her own (anorexics are typically ravenously hungry), and made good progress with gradual reintroduction of food.

Once stabilized, Mako was integrated into the ward milieu, participating in group psychotherapy where she learned that she was not alone with anorexia and was able to hear the experiences of others at varying stages of recovery. Mako began individual psychotherapy with a psychologist on the unit, and learned information about anorexia nervosa, the general course of treatment and for the first time entertained the idea that her dieting was not only about fearing fat but perhaps had other deeper causes as well. Family sessions were also begun while on the unit, and the stress of her illness, her father's frequent absences, and the challenges of straddling two cultures discussed. A behavioral contract guided her way toward some moderate weight gain, and contingencies were spelled out for continuing this progress outside the hospital lest she need to be rehospitalized. Her inpatient psychologist assisted Mako in discharge planning by locating a Japanese-American therapist with bilingual abilities, conferring with her physician, and arranging for her reintegration into both of her schools.

After discharge, Mako began individual therapy with occasional family sessions integrated into the treatment. While her physician monitored her weight and medical status and communicated this to her psychologist, Mako focused on the psychological, cultural, and family aspects of her life. The psychologist explored Mako's sense of anxiety and dependency regarding ensuing adolescence, and her trepidation regarding the pressure she felt from American peers to separate from family members and prematurely explore sexual behavior. Her desire to inte-

Case Study: Mako (Continued)

grate with her friends at school and adopt their more outgoing, expressive, even bold manner was in conflict with her family's style of quiet acceptance, good manners, and respect for authority. Mako discussed her perfectionism and obsessiveness regarding both schoolwork and eating behavior and developed cognitive-behavioral strategies with her psychologist to assist with decision-making, thought stopping, and reexamining her attitudes and expectations. Finally, when Mako's depression did not remit with adequate weight gain, she was referred to a psychiatrist for a medication consult and responded positively to Prozac.

Mako's family was integral to the treatment. In family sessions, her concerns were discussed and she found her parents remarkably respectful and attentive to her feelings. Her parents were encouraged to support her autonomous decisions when they did not contradict their values, and allow her to take steps toward independence while learning that her parents would neither condemn

nor abandon her. The family was able to openly discuss the challenges of dual American and Japanese identities as well as the stress of Mako's father's frequent absences.

Mako's treatment proceeded extremely smoothly relative to the often difficult courses in many cases of anorexia nervosa. Nevertheless, her individual therapy and medication treatment continued for three full years, as she gradually overcame her anorexia and developed significantly enhanced psychological, social, and family resources.

This case illustration exemplifies the necessity and utility of integrative strategies in treating complex problems. In a case such as anorexia nervosa where the biological, psychological, and social features are so compelling, neglect of any one factor can seriously limit or even compromise the treatment. This case demonstrates the trend in contemporary psychotherapy to integrate theories, techniques, modalities and biopsychosocial factors in order to best meet the comprehensive needs of the patient.

The Big Picture

Psychotherapy is one of the most common activities conducted by clinical psychologists and one that brings relief and tremendous assistance to many individuals and groups. Each patient, each psychologist, and each psychotherapy experience is unique. Psychotherapy has evolved over the years from several distinct theoretical perspectives to an integrative and biopsychosocial endeavor. No longer can a psychologist maintain an isolated practice

while conducting routine, rigid, and narrowly conceived treatment. Today, integration of theory, technique, modality, and biopsychosocial factors is the state-of-the-art standard to which psychologists aspire. The future of psychotherapy will attempt to use research and practice supported intervention strategies that can be administered in a brief, cost-effective manner to maximize treatment effectiveness while minimizing costs and time.

Key Points

1. Of all the professional activities conducted by clinical psychologists, psychotherapy is probably the most well known. Psychotherapy involves consulting with a mental health professional in order to obtain assistance in changing feelings, thoughts, or behaviors that the patient or client experiences as problematic and distressing. Psychotherapy includes theories of human behavior as well as specific treatment techniques to impact the psychological and behavioral functioning of a person or persons.

2. There are many different types of goals that psychotherapy hopes to reach depending upon the specific needs,

interest, and concerns of all of the interested parties. Overall, psychotherapy ultimately hopes to improve the quality of life through self-understanding, behavior and lifestyle change, coping with problems, and/or enhancing relationships. Psychotherapy attempts to utilize what is known about human behavior and apply that knowledge to help a particular person better deal with the issues that cause distress.

3. There are numerous types of psychotherapy. Psychotherapy may include individual, couple, family, group, or combinations of different types of treatment.

4. All psychotherapy tends to include several common denominators or certain similarities. They all include a professional person or "expert" of varying degree, professional behavior, or manner on the part of the psychologist, a professional setting where services are rendered, fees, and a schedule of sessions.

5. No matter what type or approach to psychotherapy a psychologist uses, most psychotherapy occurs in several stages. Generally, these include an initial consultation, assessment of the problem and situation, the development of treatment goals, the implementation of the treatment, an evaluation of the treatment, termination of treatment, and, perhaps, follow-up.

6. A biospsychosocial perspective suggests that psychotherapy consider biological, psychological, and social influences on behavior and behavior change. Although psychotherapy conducted by psychologists is usually a psychological (rather than biological or social) intervention, the biological and social influences on behavior are generally assessed and discussed during psychotherapy.

Key Terms

Curative Factors

Psychotherapy

For Reflection

1. How does psychotherapy differ from talking problems over with a friend or someone else you know?

2. What is psychotherapy?

3. What do most psychotherapies have in common?

4. Describe the stages of psychotherapy.

5. What are some of the biological approaches used to treat psychological disorders?

6. What are some of the social interventions used to treat psychological disorders?

7. How does psychotherapy differ from what is depicted in television and in films?

CHAPTER 10

Ten Essential Questions About Psychotherapy

Chapter Outline

Highlight of a Contemporary Clinical Psychologist: Allen Sherman, Ph.D.

Does Psychotherapy Work?

Is Long-Term Therapy Better Than Short-Term Treatment?

Who Stays In and Who Drops Out of Psychotherapy?

Is One Type of Therapy Better Than Another?

Do the Effects of Psychotherapy Last after Therapy Ends?

What Common Factors Are Associated With Positive Psychotherapy Outcome?

Why Is Change Difficult?

Must Someone Be a Professional To Be an Effective Therapist?

Does Psychotherapy Help Reduce Medical Costs?

Can Psychotherapy Be Harmful?

HIGHLIGHT OF A CONTEMPORARY CLINICAL PSYCHOLOGIST:

Allen Sherman, Ph.D.

Dr. Sherman uses his training and skills as a clinical psychologist working in a medical center with cancer patients.

Birth Date: August 4, 1960

College: Brown University, 1983 (A.B., Psychology)

Graduate Program:
University of Kansas, 1988 (Ph.D., Clinical Psychology)

Clinical Internship: Harvard Medical School, The Cambridge Hospital

Postdoctoral Fellowship: Harvard Medical School, The Cambridge Hospital

Current Job: Clinical Director, Behavioral Medicine Program, Arkansas Cancer Research Center, and Assistant Professor, Department of Otolaryngology and Head and Neck Cancer, University of Arkansas for Medical Sciences, Little Rock, Arkansas

Pros and cons of being a clinical psychologist:

Pros: "This is an intrinsically fascinating field if you're interested in psychological disorders, and more generally, in the way people behave, form relationships, and interact with the world around them. Clinical psychology is enormously diverse, with an opportunity to pursue many different roles in many different settings. This capacity to wear "different hats" (e.g., with respect to psychotherapy, consultation, supervision, teaching, research, administration, or public policy) is among the most appealing aspects of clinical psychology. In the last few years I've become especially interested in one area within clinical psychology—behavioral medicine, which concerns how mind and body interact to influence health and illness."

Cons: "Requires extensive training and graduate programs can be difficult to get into."

Future of clinical psychology: "The field of clinical psychology is evolving in response to a number of forces, some welcome and some stressful. Among these changes: (1) the advent of managed care in the public and private sectors means that, for clinicians, opportunities for private practice are becoming more limited, reimbursement for psychotherapy is becoming more restricted, and clinicians are faced with more paperwork and bureaucracy. (2) The decrease in federal funding means that, for researchers, competition for grant money is becoming tighter. (3) The field is becoming more specialized. Behavioral Medicine and Health Psychology are among the areas that are growing rapidly. Notwithstanding the changes that are moving through the field, clinical psychology offers an exciting career."

Typical Schedule:

9:00 Teach Behavioral Medicine Seminar (This weekly seminar is open to behavioral medicine staff, physicians and nurses in the medical school, and clinicians in the surrounding community. It focuses on topics in health psychology, mind-body interactions, and psychological services for patients with stress-related medical illnesses.)

10:00 Conduct Team Meeting (This weekly meeting is designed to provide an opportunity for the interdisciplinary treatment team to review all new cases admitted to the Clinic.)

11:00 Supervise psychology extern (Supervision usually revolves around assessment and treatment of patients with stress disorders or chronic medical conditions.)

12:00 Lunch

1:00 Supervise staff psychologists (Small group supervision with clinicians on staff involves discussion of cases being seen for consultation, individual, group, or family therapy. Many of these are cancer patients, struggling to cope with the stress of a life-threatening illness and demanding medical treatments.)

2:00 Psychotherapy (These cases often involve chronic pain, with patients seeking to learn self-regulation skills to manage pain and enhance quality of life.)

3:00 Group therapy or research meeting (Depending on the day of the week, this time might be filled by a short-term therapy group for cancer patients, or by research planning meetings. Some current research projects involve how women adapt and cope with breast cancer over the course of the first year following their diagnosis, and whether psychological adjustment and coping have any impact on long-term survival from the disease.)

4:00 Group therapy or research meeting

5:00 Paperwork and phone calls

While psychotherapy has been in existence for over 100 years and today enjoys tremendous popularity, this most common professional activity of clinical psychologists still remains shrouded in a certain degree of mystery. Many fundamental questions regarding psychotherapy are on the minds of its many consumers and students, and deserve direct attention. This chapter will respond to ten of the typical questions asked about psychotherapy, beginning with the very basic: "Does psychotherapy work?"

Does Psychotherapy Work?

Patients, insurance carriers, psychologists, and other interested parties (i.e., significant others of patients, school personnel, courts) frequently ask important questions about the usefulness of psychotherapy. For example: Are the time, expense, and effort of psychotherapy warranted by its results? Are people likely to be better off after psychotherapy than before? What are the expected benefits of psychotherapy? Unfortunately, such questions are difficult to answer and may vary from individual to individual and treatment to treatment. Psychotherapy is a highly personalized experience that is im-

pacted by the skills, interest, training, motivation, and personality of the psychotherapist and by the specific symptoms (e.g., etiology, duration, severity), motivation, personality, and resources of the patient. Furthermore, the unique therapist-patient interaction that emerges during psychotherapy as well as a wide range of nonspecific factors such as beliefs, attitudes, and expectations all play a significant role in treatment outcome. Positive treatment outcome may be associated not only with the psychotherapy experience but also with the passage of time (i.e., "time heals all wounds"), among many other factors. Thus, no two psychotherapy experiences can be exactly alike. Two patients with very similar symptoms seeing the same psychotherapist may experience two very different psychotherapies. Psychotherapy may be helpful to one but not to the other. Although many efforts have been made to make psychotherapy a precise scientific enterprise, psychotherapy involves a human relationship between therapist and patient: no human relationship can be reduced to a precise science.

How can we investigate whether psychotherapy works or not? Merely asking patients if they believe that the services were useful provides important but not sufficient data to answer this important ques-

"Well, I do have this recurring dream that one day I might see some results."

tion. Demand characteristics are likely to influence a patient's report that psychotherapy was or was not useful. The situation creates an environment where a certain response is expected. For example, it may be important for the patient to believe that psychotherapy was useful to justify spending a great deal of time, money, and effort in the psychotherapy process. Also, after spending so many sessions working with a psychotherapist, the patient may not want to tell him or her that the experience was not helpful. Therefore, determining whether psychotherapy is useful is a challenging research and clinical task.

Early psychotherapists used clinical case studies rather than controlled research investigations to evaluate treatment outcome. In fact, Freud felt that controlled research using statistical analysis was not a reasonable method for determining the effects of treatment (Freud, 1917/1963, 1933/1964). Freud and others felt that because psychotherapy was such a highly individualized experience, group findings based on averages and statistics were useless. Only since the 1950s have psychologists endorsed the notion that systematically studying psychotherapy outcome is a worthy endeavor. Once several controlled investigations of psychotherapy outcome were conducted, hundreds and perhaps thousands of studies have followed during the past 50 years. **Psychotherapy treatment outcome** has become one of the most

common topics of investigation in all psychology research.

In a classic and frequently cited research project, Hans Eysenck (1952) examined 24 research studies concerning both psychodynamic and eclectic techniques used for nonpsychotic patients. The results of his study failed to demonstrate that psychotherapy was effective. Furthermore, Eysenck suggested that spontaneous recovery (i.e., recovery from symptoms without any treatment intervention) from neurotic types of problems (e.g., anxiety and depression) could be expected about 72 percent of the time. Therefore he estimated that 72 percent of those experiencing psychological distress would improve without treatment. However, many critics of Eysenck's research methods have seriously questioned his conclusions (e.g., Bergin , 1971; Sanford, 1953; Strupp, 1963). For example, Bergin (1971) reexamined Eysenck's data and estimated that the rate of spontaneous recovery was about 30 percent rather than 72 percent and that the recovery rate from psychotherapy was much higher than that estimated by Eysenck.

In a much more rigorous and ambitious research project, Smith and Glass (1977) examined 375 research studies on psychotherapy treatment outcome by using meta-analysis and effect-size techniques. Results from the study revealed that patients receiving psychotherapy tended to be more improved than those who did not seek psychotherapy about 75 percent of the time. Furthermore, Smith and Glass examined the treatment outcomes of different types of psychotherapy (e.g., behavioral and psychodynamic) and failed to find superiority of one treatment approach over another. This comprehensive and extensive investigation contradicted the Eysenck study and provided compelling support for the effectiveness of psychotherapy. The Smith and Glass (1977) study, like the one by Eysenck (1952), became one of the most frequently cited research studies in clinical psychology.

The Smith and Glass (1977) study received a great deal of attention and a large response from the professional community. Many strongly criticized both the method and the conclusions of the investigation (Eysenck, 1978, 1983; Kazdin & Wilson, 1978; Rachman & Wilson, 1980: Searles, 1985). For example, some questioned the wisdom of using a wide variety of studies that focused on so many different types of treatments and patient problems. Others felt that the authors paid too little attention to the quality of the studies evaluated. Still others questioned the interpretation of the meta-analysis results. Smith, Glass, and Miller (1980) later extended the analysis to include 475 studies and improved upon several of the procedures from the earlier study. The 1980 study confirmed the earlier results and found that those receiving psychotherapy tended to be more improved than 80 percent of untreated persons and that behavioral therapies were more effective than verbal therapies. Perhaps one of the most positive outcomes of the Eysenck (1952) and Smith et al., (1977; 1980) investigations has been the subsequent stimulation of numerous research studies to assist in answering basic questions about the effectiveness of psychotherapy.

A large number of meta-analysis studies examining psychotherapy treatment outcome have been conducted since the Smith and Glass studies (Andrews & Harvey, 1981; Kazdin & Bass, 1989; Landman & Dawes, 1982; Lipsey & Wilson, 1993; Matt, 1989; Searles, 1985; Shapiro & Shapiro, 1982). The vast majority of these and other studies conclude that psychotherapy is generally effective. For example, Andrews and Harvey (1981) evaluated 475 controlled psychotherapy outcome studies and concluded that a patient receiving psychotherapy was better off than 77 percent of untreated control subjects and that relapse rates were very small.

Smith (1982) examined over 500 controlled psychotherapy outcome studies and concluded that psychotherapy was effective in improving psychological well-being and that duration, mode, and therapist training and experience were unrelated to outcome. Furthermore, Smith (1982) concluded that behavioral therapies were more effective than verbal therapies and that the use of medication without therapy was not more effective than psychotherapy alone. The positive effectiveness of psychotherapy has also been found among studies focusing on special populations such as children. Casey and Berman (1985), for example, found that treatment of children was equally effective whether the treatment was provided individually or in groups.

Consumer Reports (*Consumer Reports,* November, 1995; Seligman, 1995) conducted an extensive survey of psychotherapy outcome and found that people who participated in psychotherapy found the experience effective and that long-term treatment was superior to short-term treatment. Furthermore, the survey concluded that psychotherapy with medication was not superior to psychotherapy alone and that psychologists, psychiatrists, and social workers were equally effective and were, as a group, superior to marriage counselors. The survey also concluded that no particular psychotherapy orientation (e.g., psychodynamic, behavioral) was superior to other orientations regardless of the clinical problem of interest. People who used community interventions such as Alcoholics Anonymous (AA) were found to be especially satisfied with these experiences. The *Consumer Reports* survey concluded that while psychotherapy does appear to work and people are generally highly satisfied with their psychotherapy experience, low or no cost self-help community interventions are equally helpful.

An extensive review of all the research studies generally concludes that psychotherapy does indeed work (Barlow, 1996; Hollon, 1996; VandenBos, 1996). Numerous research and clinical examples provide convincing evidence that psychotherapy is effective. However, both researchers and clinicians have been trying to answer many additional follow-up questions that go well beyond whether psychotherapy works or not, such as: How does psychotherapy work and what types of treatment and therapists are effective for what types of problems and patients? Recent efforts by the American Psychological Association have attempted to identify specific treatment approaches for specific problem areas (Chambless, et al., 1996; Task Force on Promotion and Dissemination of Psychological Procedures, 1995). These empirically validated treatments have received a great deal of recent attention and support but remain controversial. While many feel that specific treatments can be targeted for specific problems, others feel that psychotherapy is too unique and complicated to routinely fit human beings into standardized treatment protocols (Garfield, 1996; Havik & VandenBos, 1996).

Seligman (1994) suggests that certain types of problems are more amenable to change than others. He states that the depth of a problem often predicts if the problem can be altered significantly through psychotherapy. For example, problems that are primarily biologically oriented and pervade all aspects of life are less appropriate for psychotherapy than problems that are learned and are less pervasive. Thus, he suggests that problems such as panic and phobia are much more responsive to therapy than obesity and alcoholism.

Is Long-Term Therapy Better Than Short-Term Treatment?

Psychotherapy can last for one session or for hundreds of sessions over the course of many years. The duration of psychotherapy depends on the symptoms, interest, motivation, and financial resources of the patient as well as on the orientation and skills of the therapist. Some types of psychotherapy tend to be very short while others tend to be remarkably long. For example, the average length of treatment using psychoanalysis is 835 sessions (Voth & Orth, 1973).

More and more emphasis is being placed on brief psychotherapy. Brief approaches to therapy are of interest to both patients and insurance companies. Patients who seek psychotherapy generally do so during an emotional crisis and wish to obtain relief as fast as possible. They generally expect to see quick results within just a few sessions, and complete recovery from presenting problems within 12 sessions (Garfield, 1986). Insurance companies and others are interested in briefer forms of treatment to reduce health care costs.

Most psychotherapy experiences do tend to be fairly brief. The majority of patients in psychotherapy terminate treatment before 10 sessions with the median number of sessions being about 6 (Blackwell, Gutmann, & Gutman, 1988; Garfield, 1986; Kleinke, 1994; Taube, Burns, & Kessler, 1984). In fact, about one-third of all persons who consult with a mental health professional for psychotherapy attend only one session (Bloom, 1981; Clarkin & Hull, 1991). Research has found that between 25 percent and 50 percent of people who consult with a mental health professional fail to attend a second session (Betz & Chullman, 1979; Phillips, & Fagan, 1982; Sue, McKinney, & Allen, 1976). Research on more than 2400 psychotherapy patients over 30 years of research suggests that 50 percent of psychotherapy patients were significantly improved by 8 sessions and 75 percent were improved by 26 sessions (Howard, Kopta, Krause, & Orlinsky, 1986). Surprisingly, research has found that even a single session of psychotherapy or consultation is associated with positive therapeutic outcomes such as a decrease in medical office visits (Goldberg, Krantz, & Locke, 1970) and in general medical utilization (Cummings, 1977). However, some meta-analysis research of treatment outcome has demonstrated that treatment duration is not necessarily associated with treatment outcome. For example, brief treatment results in about the same positive outcome as moderate or long-term treatment, according to Andrews and Harvey (1981). Yet the national survey conducted by *Consumer Reports* magazine as well as several other studies found that longer-term treatments tend to be more helpful than shorter-term treatments (Barlow, 1996; *Consumer Reports,* November 1995). Thus, while psychotherapy tends to be fairly brief in duration, it is difficult to make generalizations regarding the superiority of short versus long-term treatment.

Who Stays In and Who Drops Out of Psychotherapy?

If about a third of psychotherapy patients do not attend a second session, what factors might predict psychotherapy dropout? Several studies have found that socioeconomic status (Berrigan & Garfield,

1981; Dodd, 1970; Fiester & Rudestam, 1975; Kahn & Heiman, 1975; Pilkonis, Imber, Lewis, & Rubinsky, 1984) and educational level (Rabin, Kaslow, & Rehm, 1985) appear to be associated with psychotherapy dropout. Those from lower socioeconomic spheres and those who have less education tend to be more likely to quit psychotherapy. Research focusing on the influence of age, sex, race, psychological test results, and other patient variables of interest has proved inconclusive (Garfield, 1993). Thus, social and cultural factors deserve further investigations in order to understand their impact on therapy duration and outcome.

If the socioeconomic status and educational level of the patient predict psychotherapy dropout, what characteristics of the therapist might also predict it? The skill of the therapist is positively associated with continuation of psychotherapy (Baekeland & Lundwall, 1975; Dodd, 1970; McNeill, May, & Lee, 1987; Sloane, Staples, Cristol, Yorkston, & Whipple, 1975). However, a therapist's sex and professional affiliation (e.g., psychologist, psychiatrist, social worker) appear unrelated to psychotherapy continuation or dropout (Carpenter & Range, 1982; Mogul, 1982) although many additional factors may play a role. Patients may feel that the crisis that led them to psychotherapy has passed, and thus motivation for continuing has significantly decreased. Often patients feel better after just one session and do not wish or need to continue (Goldberg, Krantz, & Locke, 1970). The therapist and patient may not "click" during the first session as well. Patients who do not like their therapist or who feel that their needs are not being adequately met are less likely to schedule or attend additional sessions.

Is One Type of Therapy Better Than Another?

Is psychodynamic psychotherapy better than cognitive-behavioral psychotherapy? Is individual psychotherapy better than family-systems approaches to psychotherapy? Is any one type of psychotherapy superior to another? As discussed in earlier chapters, clinical psychology has had a long history of professionals claiming that their approach to psychotherapy is superior to other alternatives. However, as detailed in Chapter 4, more and more integrative approaches to psychotherapy have been developed and practiced during the past several decades as the field has grown and matured. Still, numerous research investigations have been and continue to be conducted to determine if one type of psychotherapy is superior to others. The vast majority of these studies compare verbal or insight-oriented psychotherapies (e.g., psychodynamic, humanistic) to action-oriented psychotherapies (e.g., behavioral, cognitive).

To ensure that these studies use pure forms of therapy and do not mix and match techniques and orientations, most of these research investigations incorporate treatment manuals and ask clinicians to follow these treatment manual protocols. These protocols provide specific guidelines in the administration of the treatment approach (e.g., Crits-Christoph & Mintz, 1991; Luborsky & DeRubeis, 1984; Rounsaville, O'Malley, Foley, & Weissman, 1988). Of course, clinicians tend not to use treatment manuals in actual practice and rarely focus their treatment with the use of techniques and approaches from only one theoretical perspective (Barlow, 1996; Goldfried & Wolfe, 1996; Seligman, 1996). Most of the research studies have ultimately failed to find that one type of psychotherapy is consistently superior to another. In fact, since the mid-1970s, Luborsky, Singer, and Luborsky (1975) and many others (e.g., Stiles, Shapiro, & Elliott, 1986) have referred to the equality of different types of psychotherapy as the "dodo bird verdict." This term comes from *Alice and Wonderland,* where the dodo bird states that "everyone has won and all must have prizes." However, a number of authors believe that the dodo bird verdict is a myth (London, 1988; Norcross, 1995). They suggest that different types of psychotherapy often result in different specific effects, and that these effects are not exclusive to only one type of therapy (Norcross, 1995). When these studies find differences between therapies, they generally support the notion that cognitive and behavioral treatments tend to result in more positive outcomes (usually measured by symptom reduction and behavior change) than psychodynamic or other more verbal treatment orientations (Andrews & Harvey, 1981; Searles, 1985; Shapiro & Shapiro, 1982; Svartberg & Stiles, 1991).

Studies have also attempted to determine whether psychotherapy is as effective as medication in treating anxiety, depression, and other symptoms (see Hollon, 1996 and Horgan, 1996 for review). A large-scale National Institute of Mental Health (NIMH) Collaborative Depression study compared cognitive-behavioral psychotherapy, interpersonal psychotherapy (i.e., a combination of psychodynamic and humanistic psychotherapy), medication (i.e., imipramine), and a drug placebo condition. The medication and drug placebo groups also received clinical case management. Two hundred fifty patients were treated in one of three major cities by either a psychiatrist or a psychologist. Results indicated that all the treatments, including the placebo condition, resulted in patient improvement and that differences in outcome between patients receiving the cognitive-behavioral and the interpersonal psychotherapy were minimal. Thus, medication has not proved superior to psychotherapies in treating many common psychological problems such as anxiety and depression. Although isolated studies do sometimes support one type of therapy over another, the overall picture is that most professionally administered and legitimate psychotherapy approaches are equally effective for most people (Horgan, 1996).

Although research does not support the notion that one type of legitimate psychotherapy is superior to another for treating all types of clinical problems, research that examines treatment approaches for very specific disorders does provide some support for the superiority of certain techniques. So, although no one type of therapy is superior to another for general issues of concern, several specific disorders tend to be treated more successfully using certain approaches. The Task Force on Promotion and Dissemination of Psychological Procedures (1995) of APA Division of Clinical Psychology (Division 12) has developed guidelines for psychotherapy treatments based on these solid research findings of specific disorders (Chambless et al., 1996). Empirically-validated treatments have been developed for the treatment of a variety of problem areas such as chemical abuse and dependence, and anxiety, depressive, sexual, eating, and health problems. Examples of empirically-validated treatments include exposure treatment for phobias and post-traumatic stress disorder, cognitive behavior therapy for headache, depression, irritable bowel syndrome, and bulimia, and insight-oriented dynamic therapy for depression and marital discord.

Do the Effects of Psychotherapy Last After Therapy Ends?

What happens when someone stops psychotherapy? Do people generally fall back into maladaptive patterns of thinking, feeling, and behaving? Do the gains obtained through psychotherapy last? It may be unrealistic to expect that psychotherapy will "cure" a problem or eliminate symptoms for life without any relapse. If someone is treated with psychotherapy for depression at age 20, one cannot expect that the person will never again feel depressed. Numerous studies have investigated the long-term effects of psychotherapy to determine whether symptoms reemerge following termination. Most of the data collected on psychotherapy follow-up range from several months to several years after treatment.

Research generally supports the contention that gains obtained in psychotherapy do last (Andrews & Harvey, 1981; Barlow, 1996; Jorm, 1989; Landman and Dawes, 1982; Nicholson & Berman, 1983; Nietzel, Russell, Hemmings, & Gretter, 1987). For example, Jorm (1989) examined the results of studies treating anxiety and found that anxiety reduction was maintained one year after treatment when compared to control subjects. Nietzel et al., (1987) investigated research that focused on the treatment of depression and found that treatment gains were maintained four months (on average) after termination of active treatment. Gallagher-Thompson, Hanley-Peterson, and Thompson (1990) also examined depression treatment outcome studies and found that therapy gains were generally maintained even two years after treatment. Similar findings have been reported when examining alcohol (Bellack & Hersen, 1990) and headache treatments (Blanchard, 1987). However, relapse is a common and worrisome problem for many. Researchers have developed programs and strategies to maximize maintenance of psychotherapy gains (e.g., Annis, 1990, Brownell & Jeffery,

1987; Cummings, Gordon, & Marlatt, 1980). Research tends to support the notion that the effects of psychotherapy last even after psychotherapy has terminated.

What Common Factors Are Associated with Positive Psychotherapy Outcome?

Overall, research suggests that psychotherapy is effective in treating numerous concerns compared with receiving no treatment, and that no one type of psychotherapy is superior to another (Lambert & Bergin, 1994). If most of the research on psychotherapy outcome supports the notion that different types of treatment are about equally effective, then specific theories and techniques associated with different types of psychotherapy (e.g., psychodynamic, behavioral, and family systems) do not significantly account for the curative effects of the therapy experience. The question then arises, if specific theories and techniques do not account for treatment outcome, then what does? One potential answer is that there are certain commonalities among all types of psychotherapies and that these commonalities are associated with treatment effectiveness. One might speculate that merely having someone with whom to talk over problems or having the attention of a caring and nurturing professional might be a powerful curative factor in all types of psychotherapy. The search for common denominators or **common factors** in psychotherapy is important to understanding how psychotherapy might work.

Goldfried and colleagues (Goldfried, Greenberg, & Marmar, 1990; Goldfried, 1991) proposed that all psychotherapies encourage the patient to engage in corrective emotional experiences and that they all provide some form of feedback to the patient. Karasu (1986) suggested that all useful psychotherapies include three common patient factors: affective experiencing, cognitive mastery, and behavioral regulation; and that all major schools of psychotherapy utilize these three ingredients to effect change. *Affect experiencing* refers to expressing feelings. *Cognitive mastery* refers to thinking about problems in a manner that enables the patient to experience control over attitudes, perceptions, and

beliefs about his or her problems. *Behavioral regulation* refers to developing strategies for controlling impulses and problematic behaviors. Additional commonalities outlined by Frank (1973, 1982) and others include a professional office associated with being helped; a trained mental health professional who is supportive; enhanced hope that thoughts, feelings, and behaviors can change for the better; fees associated with service; and the avoidance of dual relationships.

In reviewing the literature, Weinberger (1995) outlined five common factors associated with positive psychotherapy outcome. These include the therapeutic relationship, expectations of success, confronting a problem, providing the experience of mastery or control over the problem, and an attribution of success or failure. Each of these five common factors will be briefly reviewed. All major approaches to psychotherapy emphasize that the working relationship between the therapist and patient should be positive and that therapists should generally be empathic, genuine, warm, and professional (Lafferty, Beutler, & Crago, 1991; Lambert, 1986). This working alliance between therapist and patient is thought to be a critical ingredient for effective psychotherapy (Horvath & Symonds, 1991; Lambert, 1992; Lambert & Bergin, 1994; Norcross, 1995; Salvio, Beutler, Wood, & Engle, 1992; Strupp, 1995; Yalom, 1980). Strupp (1995), for example, states that "the quality of the interpersonal context is the *sine qua non* in all forms of psychotherapy" (p. 70) and that good therapists provide a patient with a corrective emotional experience and deal effectively with transference dynamics. Thus Strupp concluded that therapists must have "the ability to manage therapeutically a complex human relationship and . . . avoid enmeshments in the patient's unconscious self-defeating scenarios" (p. 71). Connecting to a therapist whom the patient perceives as helpful and accepting is a powerful common factor in almost all types of psychotherapy (Lambert, 1992; Norcross, 1995).

Expectancy is also a strong predictor of positive therapeutic outcome. Numerous studies have demonstrated and suggested that treatment is more effective when patients believe that the treatment is helpful (Bandura, 1989; Barker, Funk, & Houston, 1988; Frank, 1973, 1982; Hollon & Garber, 1990;

Kirsch, 1990; Rosenthal, 1987). Belief that psychotherapy can work is another important common factor in psychotherapy. In fact, because many improvements in psychotherapy may be attributed to placebos (Brody, 1983; Horvath, 1988), placebo control conditions must be utilized in treatment outcome research to ensure that outcome results are due to factors other than expectancy effects (Horvath, 1988; Kirsch, 1990; Weinberger, 1995).

Facing problems rather than avoiding, escaping, or denying them has been thought to be a critical variable in treatment outcome and is a common factor in all therapies (Kleinke, 1994; Orlinsky & Howard, 1986; Weinberger, 1995). All involve some degree of attention and plan of attack to confront problems and develop strategies to cope more effectively with various symptoms. Research has even supported the healing aspects of confronting problems outside a psychotherapeutic context. For example, Liberman (1978) and Pennebaker (1990) found that merely writing or talking about a problem in isolation without a therapist present results in improvement of symptoms. Therefore, working on problems and focusing on ways to overcome them are powerful common factors in all types of psychotherapy and are effective even outside the formal psychotherapy experience.

Mastery, or a sense of control, over a problem is a powerful predictor of therapy outcome and is hypothesized to be a very important common factor in all therapies (Kleinke, 1994; Liberman, 1978; Weinberger, 1995). Belief that one has a "leg up" on the problem or at least a reasonable plan to overcome it enhances one's sense of self-efficacy (Bandura, 1989).

Finally, patient attributions concerning the factors that they believe contribute to change appear to be a powerful predictor of therapy success or failure. Success in treatment is generally associated with internal attributions (e.g., the patient's own efforts, improved coping skills, positive personality changes; Bandura, 1989; Weinberger, 1995).

Murphy, Cramer, and Lillie (1984) asked patients to describe what they thought were the most important factors associated with positive psychotherapy outcome. The majority reported that getting advice and talking with someone who understands and is interested in their problems, and gives encouragement and hope, were *curative factors.* Lazarus (1971) found that the personal qualities of the therapist (e.g., gentle, honest) were more important to patients than the actual psychotherapy techniques used. Thus, the therapeutic relationship, beliefs about psychotherapy, working on problems, and developing control and mastery all seem to be common curative factors in psychotherapy.

Why Is Change Difficult?

Behavioral change, with or without the assistance of psychotherapy, is not easy to accomplish. Humans tend to be creatures of habit, and even behavior or thinking patterns that are destructive (e.g., temper tantrums, low self-esteem, smoking, eating high-fat foods) tend to be remarkably difficult to change. Furthermore, even positive change is not always welcomed. Often patients are ambivalent about change and may not be pleased with some of the consequences of change. For example, a patient who loses a lot of weight may find some of the attention he or she receives unpleasant. A patient who successfully overcomes panic attacks and other fears may be expected to develop more responsibility at home or at work. A child who no longer gets negative attention for temper tantrums in school may feel ignored. Resistance to change is very common among psychotherapy patients as well as, perhaps, the general public.

James Prochaska (1984) and colleagues have researched commonalities of behavioral change among theoretical orientations by examining the process of change across different types of problems and different methods of treatment. In his analysis of different orientations to behavior change, Prochaska isolated a variety of universal stages, levels, and processes of change. His theory includes five stages of change (i.e., precontemplation, contemplation, preparation, action, and maintenance), five levels of change (i.e., symptoms, maladaptive cognition, current interpersonal conflicts, family/systems conflicts, interpersonal conflicts), and ten change processes (i.e., consciousness raising, catharsis/dramatic relief, self-evaluation, environmental reevaluation, self-liberation, social liberation, counterconditioning, stimulus control, contingency management, and helping relationship). Although Prochaska's model has a cognitive-behavioral "flavor" to it, his theory of change is atheoretical since it is not based on any one model or perspective (Prochaska & Norcross, 1994). In view of the fact that up to 40 percent of change can be attributed to expectation or placebo (Lambert, 1992) and that consciousness raising is considered a critical ingredient in behavioral change for most psychotherapies (Prochaska & Norcross, 1994), the desire to change is likely to be a very important factor in explaining behavioral change.

Change is not easy to accomplish. Although patients generally enter a psychotherapy experience seeking to change their behavior (or the behavior of others), paradoxically many people are highly resistant to change. Resistance to change in psychotherapy has been recognized and highlighted by psychotherapists since the days of Freud. Kleinke (1994) outlined several important factors explaining why change is difficult to achieve and why resistance is so common in psychotherapy. First, change is threatening. Familiar ways of thinking, feeling, and behaving offer some degree of comfort even if they are maladaptive. For example, people who suffer from agoraphobia may be frustrated by their inability to feel comfortable traveling, going to the grocery store, or conducting other errands. They often feel most comfortable when they are close to home and can avoid the situations that provoke anxiety. Confronting these fears and working to increase independence is threatening and scary. Secondary gains (i.e., advantages to maintaining problems) associated with problematic symptoms may also be difficult to give up. For instance, the patient with agoraphobia may not work or be expected to run unappealing errands (e.g., picking up friends and family at the airport, grocery shopping). Family members and friends may be willing to do a lot for the agoraphobic person, affording the opportunity to avoid many unpleasant tasks. A third factor associated with resistance as outlined by Kleinke (1994) includes potential interference from others. Although a patient may wish to change behavior through psychotherapy, important others in the life of the patient may be motivated to maintain the status quo. For example, the spouse of the patient with agoraphobia may feel important and needed by the patient. Increased independence may be experienced by the spouse as a threat to his or her power and role in the relationship. If a patient is interested in minimizing alcohol consumption, family and friends who frequently drink with the person may feel displaced, guilty, and uncomfortable if he or she stops drinking and they no longer have this in common. A person trying to lose weight may find it difficult to maintain friendships with others who enjoy dining out together. Finally, many people resist change when they feel that their freedom is threatened (Brehm & Brehm, 1981). If a therapist is perceived as moving too quickly or having high expectations for change, the patient will likely repel and resist the change even if it is in the desirable direction.

Must Someone Be a Professional To Be an Effective Therapist?

Does someone really need to have a Ph.D. or other advanced degree (e.g., Psy.D., M.S.W., M.D.) to be an effective psychotherapist? Does someone really need four to seven years of postgraduate training to get a license to practice as a mental health professional? Aren't many caring and empathetic persons excellent "therapists" even if they have no formal training? Aren't a lot of friends, colleagues, and grandparents excellent "therapists"? If common factors such as warmth, empathy, honesty, and interest on the part of the psychotherapist are important and even vital to treatment outcome, couldn't any "nice" person with minimal training be an effective psychotherapist? If placebo conditions are associated with positive treatment outcome, might not good placebos administered by almost anyone be appropriate therapy? These challenging questions all center on the notion that someone might not need to be a professional to be a therapist. Compared to performing surgery, constructing an office building, or programming a computer, talking over problems with people is a natural human activity. Most people have had the experience of talking over problems and concerns with their friends, relatives, colleagues, or even strangers. Not every potential patient will feel that a particular psychotherapist is good. The fit between the therapist and patient is not only important but highly individual. Research tends to demonstrate that the therapist's psychological health and skill as well as a sincere interest in helping others are necessary qualities for being an effective psychotherapist (Kleinke, 1994).

Several studies have failed to find a difference in psychotherapy outcome between therapies provided by professionals versus paraprofessionals (Berman & Norton, 1985; Stein & Lambert, 1984). Surprisingly, some studies have found that the use of paraprofessionals results in superior outcomes relative to professionals (Hattie, Sharpley, & Rogers, 1984). The Hattie et al., (1984) study, however, has been severely criticized (e.g., Berman & Norton, 1985) for using poor quality research in their analysis and for considering social workers as paraprofessionals. However, other research has demonstrated that the experience and training of the therapist is important for positive therapeutic outcomes (Bergin & Lambert, 1978; *Consumer Reports,* 1995; Dush, Hirt, & Schroeder, 1989; Lyons & Woods, 1991; Seligman, 1995; Weisz, Weiss, Alicke, & Klotz, 1987). These studies have found that professionals with solid experience, training,

and credentials were more helpful to patients than were those with minimal experience, training, and credentials. For example, the aforementioned survey by *Consumer Reports* magazine (November, 1995; Seligman, 1995) found that patients were more satisfied and had better outcomes when treated by psychologists and psychiatrists than when treated by less-trained marriage counselors.

Although both well-trained and poorly trained therapists can both potentially provide poor professional service and in fact do harm, minimally trained therapists are more likely to provide a very narrow range of treatment options that often are not based on solid research support (Singer & Lalich, 1996). For example, many attend a weekend workshop in a particular technique such as hypnosis, biofeedback, or primal scream therapy and then attempt to apply these skills and techniques with all of their clients (Singer & Lalich, 1996). Highly trained professionals are more likely to have a wide range of treatment options available to them and use rigorous integrative thinking and judgment based on scientific support.

Overall, the professional literature has failed to demonstrate convincingly that trained professionals are superior to less-trained professionals in positive therapeutic outcome. Effective therapists may not necessarily be those with the most training, experience, and credentials. However, it is generally advisable to trust the professional judgments of highly trained professionals rather than minimally trained persons (Singer & Lalich, 1996).

Does Psychotherapy Help to Reduce Medical Costs?

Because a contemporary biopsychosocial perspective suggests that the mind, body, and social context are important in the development and maintenance of both physical and emotional health, one would expect that a more healthy emotional life may result in a healthier physical life as well. For example, an estimated 50 percent of all deaths are due to behavioral and lifestyle factors such as eating high-fat foods, being sedentary, and misusing alcohol (Taylor, 1995). Changing health care behavior and attitudes through psychotherapy may lead to healthier living and fewer illnesses. Additionally, an important question for government agencies, insurance companies, and health care facilities concerns the association between psychotherapy and health care costs. Is a person experiencing psychotherapy less likely to need or seek out medical attention? Research suggests that the answer is yes. Psychotherapy does appear to reduce medical costs.

It has been estimated that 50 percent to 70 percent of patients who seek medical treatment have no medical problems and that their symptoms are primarily due to psychological factors such as anxiety, stress, and depression (VandenBos & DeLeon, 1988). Emotional problems (most notably anxiety and depression) are associated with many medical problems such as heart disease, diabetes, and cancer as well as psychophysiological diseases such as dermatitis, irritable bowel syndrome, chronic headaches, Raynaud's disease, and asthma (Gatchel & Blanchard, 1993). Psychological interventions have also been found to be the treatment of choice for a number of "medical" problems such as tension headaches and irritable bowel syndrome (Chambless et al., 1996). Treatment of emotional and psychological factors through psychotherapy assists in the treatment of many of these medical problems and symptoms.

Those who experience a mental illness tend to use medical services a great deal. In fact it has been estimated that mental health patients use medical services more than twice as much as those who do not experience a mental health diagnosis (Brous & Olendzki, 1985). For example, about one third of depressed patients experience somatic complaints as a by-product of their depression (Shorter, 1994). Patients who receive psychotherapy tend to seek much less medical care than those who do not receive psychotherapy (Brous & Olendzki, 1985). Medical patients with chronic illnesses such as hypertension and diabetes lower medical costs by 18 percent to 31 percent when they receive psychological interventions (Lechnyr, 1992). Therefore, psychotherapy not only enhances psychological functioning and well-being but also improves medical symptoms that in turn reduce overall health care costs.

Can Psychotherapy Be Harmful?

Research has demonstrated that psychotherapy is generally helpful for the majority of people who participate in it. Even psychotherapy critics and skeptics often feel that the experience is benign and that people are usually not hurt as a result of it. How can talking over problems and concerns with a trained professional be harmful? Therapy, unlike a medical procedure such as surgery, does not seem to have life-and-death consequences if it goes poorly. The worst thing that could happen in psychotherapy is that someone might waste time and money and receive little if any benefit, right? Actually, psychotherapy may not be appropriate or useful for everyone who wants it. Some people may actually deteriorate in functioning during or after psychotherapy (Mays & Frank, 1980, 1985; Mohr, 1995; Singer & Lalich, 1996). In fact, Freud's most famous case example of Anna O. was a treatment failure: Anna O. had more severe symptoms after she began treatment with Freud. Research has often found that a sizable number of psychotherapy patients are worse off after psychotherapy than before (e.g., Colson, Lewis, & Horowitz, 1985; Shapiro & Shapiro, 1982; Stone, 1985). Some research has shown that patients in wait list or other control conditions may show less deterioration in functioning than some psychotherapy patients. For example, Shapiro and Shapiro (1982) found that about 11 percent of psychotherapies resulted in a negative outcome, and Colson et al., (1985) found that about 17 percent of patients were worse at psychotherapy termination than before psychotherapy began. Other studies generally report similar findings (e.g., Stone, 1985). Of course, a wide variety of factors associated with treatment failure may or may not be directly associated with the psychotherapy experience. These might, for example, include stressful life events that occur during the course of psychotherapy (e.g., divorce, loss of job, development of physical illness, death of a loved one). Furthermore, a number of both patient and therapist variables (e.g., patient diagnosis, therapist personality and technique) have been found to be associated with negative treatment outcome. Finally, minimally trained therapists have been found to be damaging when they offer inappropriate and even "crazy therapies" (Singer & Lalich, 1996).

How can psychotherapy result in deterioration in functioning, and what are the variables that predict negative outcome? Research has shown that a large number of variables are associated with poor treatment outcome such as characteristics of the patient and the therapist, and the interaction or fit between patient and therapist. For example, patient diagnosis, severity of symptoms, and psychotherapy that includes experiential, insight-oriented, or confrontational approaches are all associated with poor treatment outcome among certain patients. Patients who experience psychotic disorders such as schizophrenia (Feighner, Brown, & Oliver, 1973; Stone, 1985) or are diagnosed with borderline personality disorder (Horowitz, 1974; Kernberg, 1973; McGlashan, 1986; Mohr, 1995; Stone, 1985, 1990) often deteriorate in these types of expressive therapies. Furthermore, a number of researchers have also found a high incidence of deterioration among obsessive-compulsive patients as well (Foa & Steketee, 1977; Vaugh & Beech, 1985). Expressive psychotherapies, which may prove useful for many people under certain conditions, may not be the best choice for therapists working with patients who have many psychotic, borderline, or obsessive-compulsive disorders.

Patients who have little motivation for change, have low tolerance for anxiety, and have a history of inability to maintain satisfying interpersonal relationships also tend to do poorly in psychotherapy (Kernberg, 1973; Mohr, 1995; Strupp, 1980). Thus the old adage, "You can lead a horse to water but you cannot make him drink" may be an appropriate way to think about highly unmotivated patients or those who have tremendous difficulty maintaining a relationship and/or tolerating anxiety. Patients who are highly suspicious, mistrustful, and hostile also generally do poorly in psychotherapy (Mohr, et al., 1990; Strupp, 1980). Not all persons who present themselves to a therapist for psychotherapy are good candidates for it.

In addition to patient and patient-therapy fit variables, therapist characteristics have also been closely associated with poor treatment outcome. For example, therapists who lack empathy and are impatient and authoritarian tend to be associated with poor psychotherapy outcome (Lafferty, Beutler, & Crago, 1989; Yalom & Lieberman, 1971). Furthermore, therapists who fail to focus the therapy session, fail to deal with negative feelings of the patient toward the therapist or treatment, and inappropriately use various techniques are also associated with poor treatment outcomes (Sachs, 1983). Of course, unethical and incompetent therapists can certainly do a great deal of harm to their patients. For instance, sexual relationships between therapist and patient can be damaging (Apfel & Simon, 1985; Gabbard, 1994). Patients seeing poorly trained therapists or therapists who offer only one type of intervention applied to all types of problems are associated with poor outcomes (Singer & Lalich, 1996). Patient, therapist, and patient-therapist fit all must be taken into serious consideration prior to beginning psychotherapy in order to minimize potential harm to patients. Psychotherapy can be harmful if these factors are not examined and if both therapists and patients alike assume that a psychotherapy experience can do no harm.

The Big Picture

Psychotherapy is one of the most common activities conducted by clinical psychologists. Each patient, each psychologist, and each psychotherapy experience are unique. What works well with one person may not work well with another. Conducting useful research on psychotherapy is important yet challenging due to the uniqueness of each psychotherapeutic experience. Psychotherapy has evolved over the years from several distinct theoretical perspectives to an integrative and biopsychosocial contemporary practice. The good news is that research suggests that therapy does in fact work. Yet, the intricate process of change in therapy is dependent upon a range of specific and nonspecific factors, and the benefits, length, and patient-therapist variables involved in each treatment best assessed on a case-by-case basis.

Contemporary clinical psychologists must continue to work towards understanding what works well in psychotherapy and to provide this service in a cost-effective and efficient manner. The future of psychotherapy is likely to include efforts for more specific research supported guidelines to maximize treatment effectiveness. However, psychotherapy will always be a unique experience shared between a therapist and patient(s).

Key Points

1. An extensive review of all of the research studies conducted to determine if psychotherapy works generally concludes that psychotherapy does indeed work. Numerous research and clinical examples provide convincing evidence that psychotherapy is effective.

2. Research suggests that most psychotherapies tend to be very brief in duration with an average of 6 sessions per psychotherapy experiences. While most research suggests brief treatment is as effective as longer treatments, some data suggest that longer treatments are more beneficial.

3. Socioeconomic status and educational level appear to be associated with psychotherapy drop out. Those from lower socioeconomic classes and those who have less education are more likely to drop out of psychotherapy.

4. No one type of psychotherapy has been determined to be generally better or more effective than any other. Many authors suggest that different types of psychotherapy often result in different specific effects and yet, these effects are not exclusive to only one type of therapy.

5. Several common factors found in most psychotherapies have been associated with positive psychotherapy outcome. These include the therapeutic relationship, expectations of success, confronting a problem, providing the experience of mastery or control over the problem, and an attribution of success or failure. The therapeutic relationship, beliefs about psychotherapy, and working on problems developing control and mastery all seem to be common curative factors in psychotherapy.

6. Behavior change, with or without the assistance of psychotherapy, is generally not easy to accomplish. Humans tend to be creatures of habit and even behavior or thinking patterns that are destructive tend to be remarkably difficult to change.

7. The professional literature has failed to demonstrate convincingly that trained professionals are superior to less trained professionals in positive therapeutic outcome. Therefore, effective therapists may not necessarily be those with the most training, experience, and credentials. However, research and practice suggests that highly trained professionals are more likely to have a wide range of treatment options and skills available to them relative to minimally trained persons.

8. Those who experience a mental illness tend to use medical services a great deal. In fact it has been estimated that mental health patients use medical services more than twice of those who do not experience a mental health diagnosis. After patients receive psychotherapy, they tend to seek much less medical care than those who need but do not receive psychotherapy. Medical patients with chronic illnesses such as hypertension and diabetes lower their future medical costs by 18–31 percent when they receive psychological interventions. Thus, psychotherapy not only improves psychological functioning and well-being but also improves many medical symptoms and conditions as well as reducing overall health care costs.

9. Research has shown that there are a large number of variables associated with poor treatment outcome. These variables include characteristics of the patient, the therapist, and the interaction or fit between patient and therapist. Patients who have little motivation for change, have little tolerance for anxiety, and have a history of an inability to maintain satisfying interpersonal relationships also tend to do poorly in psychotherapy. Unethical and incompetent therapists can certainly do a great deal of harm.

Key Terms

Common Factors   Curative Factors   Psychotherapy Treatment Outcome

For Reflection

1. Does psychotherapy work?

2. How might psychotherapy work?

3. Is long-term psychotherapy superior to short-term psychotherapy?

4. Which type of psychotherapy seems to work best?

5. Name curative factors associated with psychotherapy.

6. Under what circumstances might psychotherapy be harmful?

7. Is a volunteer paraprofessional likely to be as good of a psychotherapist as a psychologist or psychiatrist? Why or why not?

CHAPTER 11

Areas of Specialization in Contemporary Clinical Psychology

Chapter Outline

Highlight of a Contemporary Clinical Psychologist: Micheline Beam, Ph.D.
Clinical Health Psychology
Child Clinical Psychology
Clinical Neuropsychology
Forensic Psychology
Other Subspecialties

HIGHLIGHT OF A CONTEMPORARY CLINICAL PSYCHOLOGIST:

Micheline Beam, Ph.D.

Dr. Beam is a young child specialist who combines consultation, clinical assessment, and teaching activities.

Birth Date: August 27, 1950
College: Mills College (B.A. in Psychology), 1972
Graduate Program: Michigan State University (M.A. and Ph.D. in Clinical Psychology), 1980
Clinical Internship: St. Vincent's Hospital, New York, NY
Current Job: Adjunct Faculty, California School of Professional Psychology (Alameda Campus)
  Private Practice

Pros and cons of being a clinical psychologist:

Pros: "Positive interactions with parents of young children and their willingness to be involved in altering behavioral problems. Joy of working with young children and the rapid changes that occur in treatment."

Cons: "Managed care has posed a serious threat to the therapeutic relationship and dictates treatment options. Psychologists must be vigilant to this danger and make every effort to maintain the integrity of the profession and our ability to determine within the therapeutic relationship what is best for our clients."

Future of clinical psychology: "Psychologists of the future will need to prepare for the changing demographics of America and the impact of managed care. We will need to be more versatile in our service delivery models, develop skill in providing short-term treatment and diversify our roles as care-givers to the community."

Typical Schedule:

9:00 Teach assessment seminar at California School of Professional Psychology for second-year graduate students in clinical psychology (lecture on testing young children).

10:00 Assessment seminar continues.

11:00 Assessment seminar continues.

12:00 Provide consultation to foster care/adoption agency. Consult with family who has adopted an 8-year-old African-American boy who has some trouble with attachment to his adopted family as well as depression and disruptive behaviors at school.

1:00 Consult with social workers at agency concerning ways to improve family involvement with a 12-year-old Caucasian boy with disruptive behaviors associated with attention deficit hyperactivity disorder.

2:00   Provide a training seminar for case workers on signs and symptoms of separation and attachment disorders among young children.

3:00   Conduct psychological assessments at community agency (San Francisco Department of Human Services).

4:00   Intellectual testing of 5-year-old adopted Latino boy who may have been exposed to maternal drug use prior to birth.

5:00   Psychological testing of 7-year-old African-American girl who is anxious and experiences school phobia.

The principles and practices of clinical psychology can be applied to many different areas of research and clinical service. The skills developed by a clinical psychologist can be used to better understand and treat both children and adults as well as a wide variety of special populations such as substance abusers and neglected children. These principles and skills can also be used in a wide range of settings including hospitals, clinics, businesses, government agencies, and even courts. Most clinical psychologists cannot develop and maintain the skills necessary to perform competently with all of these populations and settings. Although many psychologists maintain a general clinical practice, more and more are focusing their skills in an area of specialization. Like many evolving and maturing fields, clinical psychology has developed a number of specialty and subspecialty areas.

Many years ago physicians were trained in general medicine and were often asked to treat all potential medical problems that emerged in the community where they practiced. The era in which almost every physician was a general practitioner is now long gone. As medicine has become increasingly sophisticated, many physicians have focused their training into specialities such as pediatrics, oncology, psychiatry, radiology, internal medicine, neurology, and cardiology. In fact, medical schools have trouble recruiting people to be general practitioners in needy areas. These specialities have further evolved into subspecialties, such as pediatric oncology and geropsychiatry. Specialty residency and fellowship programs were developed to train physicians in these specialty areas and board certification processes were instigated to certify physicians as competent in these specific areas of clinical practice. While many physicians still maintain an essentially general practice (e.g., "family physicians" and "internists"), a large number have chosen to specialize.

Clinical psychology has undergone a very similar developmental process. Psychologists have been historically trained in a general manner and subsequently have applied their skills to all patients and problems they could competently evaluate and treat. As the field has become more sophisticated regarding specific problems of interest to clinical psychology, specialities have emerged. Graduate training programs, internships, and postdoctoral fellowship programs have responded to the era of specialization by training psychologists in these specialty areas. Finally, similar to medical board certification, psychology now offers board certification of psychologists seeking to claim special expertise in one of a number of specialty areas.

Some of the more prominent specialty areas in clinical psychology are health psychology, child psychology, neuropsychology, and forensic psychology. Subspecialty areas have also emerged, such as pediatric neuropsychology and forensic health psychology. Within each specialty area many psychologists focus their research and/or practice on a particular population or problem area. For example, some professionals who specialize in clinical health psychology primarily work in the area of eating disorders, smoking cessation, or alcohol abuse. Some who specialize in neuropsychology focus their attention on elderly stroke victims, patients with epilepsy, or individuals with head and spinal cord injuries. Psychologists who specialize in working with children might focus on children with emotional disorders, traumatic histories, or learning based disorders. Furthermore, many professionals maintain expertise in a technique rather than a problem or patient population. For example, some psychologists have special expertise in group or family therapy approaches. The list of potential specialty and subspecialty areas is remarkably long.

Some of the specialty areas overlap and thus are not mutually exclusive. For example, a pediatric neuropsychologist might specialize in head injuries suffered by children and consequently be called upon to undertake a great deal of forensic work.

Thus, such a psychologist may be said to specialize in forensic pediatric neuropsychology. Another professional may specialize in geriatric health psychology working with Alzheimer's patients. Another psychologist might focus her professional work in the area of chronic pain and workman's compensation litigation and thus specialize in forensic health psychology. In short, there are not only numerous specialty and subspecialty areas but there are many different ways that these areas blend and merge together.

How do we make sense of all these specialty areas? What makes them distinct? Why do so many overlap? Although there are no simple answers to these questions, several principles help to provide some of the answers. First, as clinical psychology evolves, grows, and matures, more and more information has become available through research and practice that can be applied to specific problems and populations. In fact, clinical psychology is no longer limited to issues involving mental illness, and many clinical psychologists do not work with mental illness issues at all. Medical problems such as cancer, head injury, heart disease, and AIDS as well as legal problems such as child custody decisions, competency to stand trial, and product liability are now within the domain of clinical psychology. Thus, as clinical psychology has broadened in scope and focus, specialization has become increasingly necessary. As the field continues to grow and change, new specialties emerge and others diminish. Second, contemporary clinical psychology, as previously discussed, uses an interactive perspective rather than rigid adherence to one particular and limiting orientation. An integrated biopsychosocial model can be used with many problem areas and populations allowing for both growth and overlap of specializations. Third, specific postgraduate training programs as well as board and proficiency certification have become available in a number of specialty areas. The establishment of specific training programs and certification procedures contributes to the official recognition and monitoring of these specialty areas.

This chapter cannot hope to do justice to all of the specialty and subspecialty areas in clinical psychology, but it will discuss the four major contemporary areas of specialization: clinical health psychology, clinical child psychology, neuropsychology, and forensic psychology. The types of clinical and research problems addressed with each of these specialties will be highlighted, along with examples of specific assessment and intervention strategies. Typical subspecialties within each of the specialities will also be described.

Clinical Health Psychology

Clinical health psychology is currently one of the most popular and fastest growing specialties in clinical psychology. The specialty of clinical health psychology formally began around 1980 (Matarazzo, 1980) and has been defined as: ". . . the aggregate of the specific educational, scientific, and professional contributions of the discipline of psychology to the promotion and maintenance of health, the prevention and treatment of illness, the identification of etiologic and diagnostic correlates of health, illness, and related dysfunction, and to the analysis and improvement of the health care system and health policy formation" (Matarazzo, 1982, p. 4). Health psychology is closely related to the field of Behavioral Medicine which is defined as: "The interdisciplinary field concerned with the development and integration of behavioral and biomedical science, knowledge, and techniques relevant to health and illness and the application of this knowledge and these techniques to prevention, diagnosis, treatment, and rehabilitation" (Schwartz & Weiss, 1978, p. 250).

Thus, whereas behavioral medicine is an interdisciplinary field in which M.D.'s, Ph.D.'s, R.N.'s and other professionals practice, **health psychology** involves the contribution of one field (psychology) to problems associated with health and illness. Health psychologists work in numerous and diverse settings including hospitals, clinics, universities, businesses, government agencies, and private practices. They use the principles of psychology and behavior change to study and help people cope better with medical illnesses as well as prevent potential illnesses from developing or worsening. They conduct research on the relationships between behavior and health and consult with organizations to maximize health promoting behavior and policies while minimizing health damaging behavior and policies. Approximately 15 percent of the Gross National Product (GNP), or about 500 billion dollars, is spent each year on health care in the United States, and a national effort has been promoted to reduce these costs through improved health behaviors (Carmody & Matarazzo, 1991; Taylor, 1995). Health psychology offers effective strategies to deal with numerous health related problems and has been at the forefront of improving health in America. The brief clinical health psychology case descriptions, which appear within this section, demonstrate that many of the intervention strategies used in health psychology as well as the problems themselves are complex and multidimensional.

Influenza, measles, tuberculosis, and other infectious diseases were the cause of most deaths in the United States during the first part of the twentieth century and in earlier times. During the past 100 years medical advances have conquered many of these problems. Today, lifestyle factors that reflect health damaging behavior patterns account for most deaths in all developed countries. Smoking, high-fat diets, sedentary lifestyles, unsafe sexual practices, accidents and other "behavioral pathogens" (Matarazzo, 1984) are the culprits in at least 50 percent of the top ten leading causes of death (Centers for Disease Control, 1980; National Center for Health Statistics, 1992, 1993; Taylor, 1995). Heart disease, cancer, stroke and other common killers are also closely associated with lifestyle factors. As a nation, we eat and drink too much, exercise too little, and develop habits that compromise our health. Therefore most health problems of today are intimately tied to problems in behavior. Health psychology hinges on the understanding that by changing unhealthy behavior, a range of significant health problems can be eliminated or minimized (Fig. 11.1).

The principles of clinical psychology have been used to help people live more healthy lifestyles in order to avoid developing illnesses. These principles have also been used to help treat illnesses once they have developed. Diabetes, cancer, heart disease, arthritis, asthma, AIDS, autoimmune diseases such as lupus and multiple sclerosis, chronic pain control, and other serious health problems have all been of interest to health psychologists. Individual and group psychotherapy, education, biofeedback, relaxation training, coping skills training interventions, and other strategies have been effectively used to treat many of these problems. In fact, psychological interventions such as biofeedback and relaxation training have become the primary treatment of choice for a number of health problems such as irritable bowel syndrome and Raynaud's disease. Health psychology presents an excellent example of the contemporary and integrative biopsychosocial approach to both medical and mental health problems. Interventions integrate medical

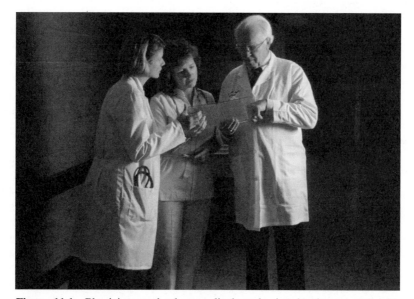

Figure 11.1 Physicians and other medical professionals often consult with health psychologists.

treatment along with education, psychotherapy, social support, social engineering, and other approaches to maximize health and minimize illness. While there are numerous health behaviors and illnesses that are of interest to contemporary clinical health psychology, several stand out as especially compelling current problems that have received tremendous attention from health psychology in recent years. These include smoking, obesity, alcohol consumption, stress management, AIDS, and chronic pain. These issues will be briefly highlighted here. Table 11.1 presents a list of many of the topics of interest to health psychologists.

Smoking

Smoking cigarettes is considered to be the largest preventable cause of premature death in the nation (McGinnis, Richmond, Brandt, Windom, & Mason, 1992; U.S. Department of Health and Human Services, 1983, 1990a; Taylor, 1995). Smoking has been associated with many illnesses including cancer and heart disease (McGinnis et al., 1992; McKim, 1991). Furthermore, smokers are more likely than nonsmokers to engage in other health damaging behaviors such as eating high-fat foods and leading sedentary lifestyles (French, Hennrikus, & Jeffery, 1996). Health psychology has been involved in all aspects of smoking cessation as well as psychoeducational programs to prevent people from beginning the smoking habit. Although almost everyone knows that smoking is damaging to health, approximately 25 percent of the American adult population smokes while as many as 17 percent of high school seniors smoke on a daily basis (U.S. Surgeon Gen-

eral, 1989, 1994). Fortunately, the number of people who smoke has decreased in recent years (McGinnis et al., 1992). Intervention programs and public policies of various sorts have been useful in decreasing the number of smokers.

People generally begin the smoking habit during their teenage years due to peer pressure, cultural norms, modeling of family, friends, and celebrities, as an act of rebellion, an assertion of independence, and a host of other reasons (Chassin, Presson, Rose, & Sherman, 1996; U.S. Surgeon General, 1994). As opposed to many other unhealthy habits such as the consumption of high-fat foods, people generally report that smoking is an acquired taste. In other words, the pleasurable effects of smoking tend to occur after a number of initial attempts at smoking and not during the first few smoking episodes. In fact, initial smoking may result in coughing, headache, nausea or other aversive symptoms. Once accustomed to smoking, however, the addictive qualities of nicotine as well as the psychological dependence associated with smoking result in a very difficult habit for most people to break. Furthermore, anxiety, depression, irritability and anger are associated with nicotine withdrawal (Hall, Munoz, Reus, & Sees, 1993). Therefore, smoking often is used to avoid the negative consequences of nicotine withdrawal.

The majority of people who attempt to quit smoking are unsuccessful (Cepeda-Benito, 1993). While some people are able to quit smoking on their own, many need professional assistance in stopping the habit. Treatments include biological interventions such as the nicotine patch and gum, which supply a constant dose of nicotine without the detrimental effects on lungs or other organs induced by smoking. These treatments provide the drug effect without the psychological and social reinforcement that maintains the psychological dependence on smoking. Other treatment approaches include psychological interventions such as problem solving and coping skills training, hypnotherapy, biofeedback, and behavior modification approaches. Educational and social interventions such as group support are also used (Pomerleau & Pomerleau, 1988; Schwartz, 1987; Zhu, Stretch, Balabanis, Rosbrook, & Bradley, 1996). Finally, social engineering and public policy approaches such as smoking bans in public places also discourage smokers from maintaining their habit. Research in-

Table 11.1 Health Psychology Areas of Focus

Alcohol	Smoking
Irritable Bowel Syndrome	Eating Disorders
Panic Disorders	Hypertension
Raynaud's disease	Asthma
Cardiovascular Disease	Ulcers
Pain	Headache
Diabetes	Cancer
Spinal Injuries	Epilepsy
Sleep Disorders	Cystic Fibrosis
AIDS	Stress
Sexual Disorders	Substance Abuse

dicates that multimodal and integrative biopsychosocial approaches tend to work best in treating smokers (Hall et al., 1993; Hatsukami, Jensen, Allen, & Grillo, 1996; Hughes, 1993; Ockene, 1986; Prochaska, Velicer, DiClemente, & Fava, 1988). Thus fading dependence on nicotine by using a nicotine patch along with cognitive-behavioral coping strategies in the context of a support group may work best. Community-wide interventions such as the Stanford Heart Disease Prevention Project (Meyer, Nash, McAlister, Maccoby, & Farquhar, 1980) among others (Zhu et al., 1996) have also had some success at decreasing smoking behavior in entire communities.

Preventing people from starting to smoke through educational campaigns has also met with some limited success. Peer modeling approaches, role-playing ways to cope with social pressure, self-monitoring of smoking attitudes and behavior, videotaped presentations, and other methods have been used. Although not always effective, research indicates that these programs do prevent many at-risk children and adolescents from beginning to smoke (Carter, Bendell, & Matarazzo, 1985; McGinnis et al., 1992).

Obesity

Obesity, generally defined as weighing 20 percent more than ideal, effects approximately 30 percent of the adult American population (Von Itallie, 1985). While smoking is decreasing in the United States, obesity is on the rise. Especially disturbing is the fact that up to 25 percent of children are obese, with 80 percent of them becoming obese adults (Coates & Thoresen, 1981). Obesity has been associated with coronary heart disease, cancer, gall bladder disease, skeletal-joint problems, diabetes, infections, and many other illnesses (Brownell & Wadden, 1992; Stoll, 1996; Von Itallie, 1985). Morbid obesity (i.e., weighing 100% above ideal weight) is associated with premature death due to a wide spectrum of illnesses. Obesity, like smoking, has become a serious national health problem.

Biopsychosocial factors have been found to contribute to the development of obesity. Research has shown that genetic factors account for up to 60 percent of the variance in body fat (Bouchard & Perusse, 1996; Price, 1987). Lifestyles factors such as sedentary behavior, high-fat food consumption, and television viewing have also been associated with obesity. Psychological and social factors such as stress, depression, access to a variety of highly attractive foods, and culture also play roles in the development of obesity. The complex interaction between biological vulnerability in combination with psychological and social factors clearly demands an integrative biopsychosocial approach to prevention and treatment (Brownell & Wadden, 1992).

Like smoking, the majority of those trying to lose weight are not successful (Agras, Berkowitz, Arnow, & Telch, 1996; National Institute of Health, 1992). While most people try to diet on their own to lose weight, many choose to join community weight loss programs such as Diet Ease, Jenny Craig, Weight Watchers, Overeaters Anonymous, and Take Off Pounds Sensibly (TOPS). These programs also generally use an integrative approach combining medical intervention with social support, education, and counseling. In fact over 400,000 people attend these community programs each year (Taylor, 1995). Others use medically supervised programs offered by medical centers and clinics throughout the country (e.g., Agras et al., 1996). The weight loss industry is a multimillion—perhaps billion—dollar industry. Sadly, the vast majority of those who attempt to lose weight either on their own or in an organized and professionally run program do not maintain their weight loss. In fact about 95 percent of those who lose weight tend to regain all weight loss within 5 years (Brownell, 1993; Wadden, Sternberg, Letizia, Stunkard, & Foster, 1989).

Treatments for obesity reflect the biopsychosocial model. Treatments include surgery, medication, and very low calorie liquid diets for those who are morbidly obese. Behavioral modification, problem-solving coping strategies, hypnotherapy, psychotherapy, group support, nutritional information programs, and exercise programs are also used to treat obesity. Multimodal approaches thus integrate medical intervention along with various forms of education and counseling. In addition to individual treatment, public health and informational approaches have also been used (Jeffrey, 1988; Meyer et al., 1980). Multimodal treatments integrating biopsychosocial factors tend to be most successful (Agras et al., 1996; Brownell, 1993).

Alcohol Consumption

Although **alcohol consumption** in the United States has decreased during the past 20 years, alcohol remains a major threat to the health and well-being of many (U.S. Department of Health and Human Services, 1990b). For example, almost half of all college-age people admitted to an alcohol binge of five or more drinks during the preceding two weeks of the survey (Presley & Meilman, 1992). It has been estimated that 10 percent of the American population has an alcohol problem, whereas about ten million are alcohol dependent (U.S. Department of Health & Human Services, 1990b). Alcohol consumption begins remarkably early in life with over 50 percent of Americans reporting some alcohol use by age 13 (Pandina, 1986). In addition to the numerous physical, psychological, and social problems caused by alcohol-related abuse and dependence, it has been estimated that 50 percent of all traffic accidents are alcohol-related as well as most murders, suicides, rapes, and violent crimes (Taylor, 1995; U.S. Department of Health and Human Services, 1990a; McGuire, 1982). Alcohol appears to disinhibit people's control over their behavior and make them less concerned about the consequences of their actions.

Like smoking and obesity, biopsychosocial factors are associated with both the development of alcohol-related problems and their treatment. Alcohol problems are associated with genetic and biological vulnerability (Finney & Moos, 1991; Goodwin, 1986), and many individuals thus seem to be inherently predisposed to developing an alcohol-related problem. Some people are fortunately unlikely to develop alcohol problems due to inherited inability to drink alcohol. For example, about 25 percent of Asian individuals have a negative physiological reaction to alcohol, which results in little alcohol abuse in that population. While America has an alcohol problem prevalence rate of 10 percent, Taipei has one that is less than 1 percent (Yamamoto, Silva, Sasao, Wang, & Nguyen, 1993). Curiously, the Korean alcoholism rate is 22 percent, which is a rate more than twice that of the United States. Cultural expectations regarding heavy drinking appear to override the physiological tendency towards moderate alcohol consumption in the Korean population (Lee, 1992).

Psychological factors such as anxiety and depression as well as social factors such as peer influence, low income, and stress also play an important role in the development of alcohol problems (Brennan & Moos, 1990; Zucker & Gomberg, 1986). Research suggests that alcohol is often used as a way to buffer stress and thus becomes a maladaptive coping strategy (Seeman, Seeman, & Budros, 1988; Stewart, 1996). Those who experience many negative life events as well as little social support are at risk for developing alcohol problems (Brennan & Moos, 1990; Stewart, 1996). Furthermore, those who feel a sense of powerlessness are at risk (Seeman et al., 1988). Drinking alcohol is temporarily rewarding since it can help people to feel less stressed and distract them from problems in living.

Treatment and prevention programs for alcohol abuse also reflect the biopsychosocial perspective. Alcohol treatment might include the use of Antabuse (a medication that prevents the metabolism of acetaldehyde) which results in severe nausea and vomiting when alcohol is consumed (Nathan, 1993) and medical detoxification in an inpatient hospital facility with individual, family, group, and educational components. Psychotherapy as well as group support through professionally run programs such as Alcoholics Anonymous (AA) are also beneficial. Relapse prevention approaches that focus on specific problem-solving strategies for alcohol abuse have also been used successfully with alcoholics (Marlatt & Gordon, 1985). Once again, multimodal approaches seem to work best. However, relapse is extremely high. For example, only about 50 percent of those treated for alcohol problems remain sober one year following treatment (Nathan, 1996) and 75 percent of those who join AA drop out within a year (Alcoholics Anonymous, 1990).

Stress Management

Stress has been associated with the development and maintenance of numerous physical and mental health problems. Ultimately, the human cost of excess stress is unquantifiable. Psychological and social stress adversely impacts many systems of the body including the immune (Ader & Cohen, 1984; Cohen, Tyrrell, & Smith, 1993) and endocrine systems (Krishman, Doraiswamy, Venkataraman, Reed, & Richie, 1991). Chronic psychosocial stress has been found to damage the brain through hypercortisol activity in the hippocampus and elsewhere

(Sapolsky & Meaney, 1986; Sapolsky, 1990). Thus, chronic stress can actually cause brain damage. People who lack a sense of control and self-efficacy in their lives appear especially vulnerable to stress-related problems (Bandura, 1986; Kobasa, 1982). Finally, environmental stressors such as poverty, violence, and other social ills contribute to poor physical and mental health and similarly need to be addressed at policy, preventative, and intervention levels.

Stress management has been found to help people experiencing many physical and mental health problems including cancer, heart disease, diabetes, AIDS, and chronic pain. Social support has also been found to help in the treatment of stress-related problems (Cohen, 1988) as well as numerous medical problems. For example, social support and stress management strategies provided in group therapy has been found to assist in helping cancer patients live longer (Spiegal, 1989). Stress management techniques such as relaxation training, meditation, biofeedback, diaphragmatic breathing, stress inoculation training, psychotherapy, visual imagery, and other approaches have been found useful in reducing stress.

Acquired Immune Deficiency Syndrome (AIDS)

Tragically, about 2 million Americans are infected with the HIV virus, and close to 200,000 deaths have occurred from **Acquired Immune Deficiency Syndrome (AIDS)** in the United States since 1981 (Brookmeyer, 1996; Centers for Disease Control, 1991; Chesney, 1993). Changing problematic high-risk behavior is the best way to prevent AIDS from spreading since no vaccine is currently available. Engaging in safer-sex as well as avoidance of shared needles among IV drug users are requisites to minimizing the spread of the infection. Multimodal psychoeducational programs that involve informational, motivational, skill-building, sexuality training, and public policy approaches have proved successful in reducing high-risk behaviors in a variety of populations (Ekstrand & Coates, 1990; Kelly & Kalichman, 1995). For example, this type of program reduced unprotected sex in the San Francisco male gay community from 37 percent to 2 percent in one study (Ekstrand & Coates, 1990).

Self-management training and social support have also proved useful in behavior change among high-risk groups (Kelly, St. Lawrence, Hood, & Brasfield, 1989). Finally, enhancing self-efficacy and perceived control over sexual behavior has been found to predict safe sex practices (Gerrard, Gibbons, & Bushman, 1996; O'Leary, 1992). The battle against AIDS provides another classic example of a devastating illness that is completely preventable through behavior change.

Chronic Pain Control

It has been estimated that over 7 million Americans suffer from **chronic pain** with over 65 billion dollars having been spent each year on medications to decrease various types of pain (Bonica, 1992; Taylor, 1995). The severity of pain seems only remotely related to individual reactions to pain. Some people cope remarkably well with severe pain while others do not: some people are incapacitated from somewhat milder forms of pain while others are not. Pain perception is thus largely a subjective experience with biopsychosocial factors interacting to determine the unique pain experience for each person (Banks & Kerns, 1996; Keefe, Dunsmore, & Burnett, 1992). Psychological states such as anxiety and depression as well as pessimism, low self-efficacy, and little sense of control appear closely related to pain experience (Banks & Kerns, 1996; Keefe et al., 1992). Furthermore, those with little social support generally cope less well with pain (Fordyce, 1988; Jamison & Virts, 1990). Relaxation techniques, coping skills training, psychotherapy, group therapy, and cognitive restructuring have all been found to be useful in conjunction with medical interventions in the treatment of chronic pain (Barlow & Rapee, 1991; Keefe et al., 1992).

Conclusion

Health psychologists use the principles and procedures of clinical psychology and apply them to the field of medicine and health. Health psychologists are useful in helping people with a wide variety of health concerns and illnesses. Many health problems are associated with health-damaging behaviors and therefore health psychologists seek to help people develop lifestyles that are health promoting rather than health damaging. Eating healthy low-fat

Case Study: Celeste

Celeste is a 40-year-old Korean-American manager with a Type A personality (e.g., competetive, hard-driving, hostile, time-urgent) and irritable bowel syndrome. She has frequent stomach aches and alternating patterns of constipation and diarrhea. Her father and grandfather both had colon cancer and one of her sisters also struggles with irritable bowel syndrome. She notices that her symptoms are worse when she is under stress. She tends to live life on the edge, always taking on more things than she can comfortably handle and waiting until the last minute to complete work assignments. She always feels that she is in a rush and reports that she frequently eats and even makes phone calls in her car while driving on the highway to work each morning. Certain foods seem to make her symptoms worse as well. Pizza and other high-fat fast foods seem to increase her stomach complaints.

After consulting with her physician, she was referred to a clinical health psychologist for assistance with her symptoms. Reflecting a biopsychosocial intervention approach, in addition to her medical treatment, she participated in efforts to change her lifestyle and increase her social support network. After a careful evaluation, Celeste and the psychologist agreed to work on many of the lifestyle factors that contributed to her symptoms. She agreed to work on developing a comprehensive relaxation program that included regular aerobic exercise, diaphragmatic breathing exercises, relaxation imagery, and cognitive restructuring concerning her need to be in a rush so much of the time. She also worked on changing her eating patterns to avoid problematic fast foods. She worked on getting up earlier to avoid the constant morning rush. She also worked on increasing her social support network of friends and took efforts to develop a satisfying intimate relationship. While it was very difficult for Celeste to alter these patterns, she did achieve reduction in symptoms after several months of consultation.

foods, minimizing alcohol consumption, eliminating smoking and unsafe sexual practices, wearing seat belts, and better managing stress minimize the risk of premature death as well as the risk of developing a long list of health problems. Once health problems occur, health psychologists are involved with helping people cope better with their illnesses and minimize exacerbation or worsening of symptoms. Obtaining social support, learning information about the illness, finding strategies to cope with pain, adhering to the medical treatment regimens, and better understanding underlying causes of noncompliance to medical treatments are all of interest to health psychology.

Child Clinical Psychology

Child clinical psychologists specialize in working with children and their families. Specializing in child

Case Study: Weight Loss Treatment Program

People who are morbidly obese or 100 percent above ideal weight are offered a group treatment program through a university hospital. The program combines a very low-calorie diet along with nutritional information, group support, medical monitoring, and a variety of psychological and social interventions. Patients are interviewed to ensure that they are appropriate for the group. Applicants with severe personality or other mental disorders or medical disorders that contraindicate rapid weight loss are not included in the program. Patients participate in weekly group meetings for 6 months while they use a very low-calorie liquid food product. The weekly group meetings include social support discussion of issues important to individual group members as well as information about diet, exercise, food preparation, and contending with social situations involving food. Patients have a weekly medical appointment to ensure that their medical status is stable and that their weight loss is carefully monitored. Following six months of liquid diet, food is gradually reintroduced beginning with packaged frozen foods and eventually, self-prepared foods. Packaged foods are used to minimize decision making regarding preparation and portion control. After about a year of the weekly program and a significant reduction in weight loss, group members are invited to participate in a twice per month maintenance group where support and information are available to assist in the challenging task of weight loss maintenance.

Case Study: Joe

Joe is a 32-year-old Caucasian man with a severe alcohol problem. He reports that he drinks two bottles of wine per evening as well as a fifth of Scotch over the course of the week. His wife and children are very worried about his alcohol consumption and have insisted that he seek help from a psychologist specializing in alcohol abuse treatment.

Joe admits that he has an alcohol problem and feels that his stressful job contributes to the problem. He works in sales and has trouble reaching his sales quotas each month. Furthermore, he feels that his boss dislikes him a great deal and wants to find a way to fire him. Jack considers himself a wine connoisseur and enjoys collecting, tasting, and reading about fine wines. He says he has

a special fondness for French wines from the St. Emilion region of Southern France.

After several sessions, Joe agrees to participate in an AA program near his home. He also agrees to see his physician to talk about the medical ramifications of his drinking. Psychotherapy focused on his stress at work and his extremely high expectations for himself and for others. Exercise and other more health-promoting behaviors were encouraged. Joe also had several treatment sessions with his wife in attendance to work on marital conflicts both involving and underlying his alcohol consumption. After a drinking binge, Joe was arrested for driving under the influence of alcohol and only then agreed to urine alcohol screening.

---

and family work is enormously popular among clinical psychologists (Mash & Barkley, 1989). In fact, as discussed in Chapter 2, most of the earliest clinical psychologists at the turn of the twentieth century specialized in working with children. Today, these psychologists obtain training in developmental psychology and both child assessment and treatment. They commonly work in community mental health clinics, child guidance clinics, schools, children's hospitals, and private practices. Some of the common problem areas that are the focus of work for child clinical psychologists include physical and/or sexual abuse, attention deficit hyperactivity disorder, conduct disorders, learning disorders, autism, enuresis (bed wetting), depression, and school phobia. These psychologists may provide consultation to school teachers, school counselors, pediatricians, day care workers, parents, and others. They may assist teachers in classroom behavior management or assist parents in developing better parenting skills. Table 11.2 presents a list of topics of interest to child clinical psychologists.

Pediatric psychology is a blend of **child clinical psychology** and health psychology, and is often called child health psychology. Pediatric psychologists are child clinical psychologists who generally work with children and families in hospital settings where significant medical disorders are prominent in the clinical picture. These medical problems might include cancer, epilepsy, diabetes, or cystic fibrosis (Rudolph, Dennig, & Weisz, 1995). The pediatric psychologist might offer pain management

strategies to children or help the family cope more effectively with understanding and assisting a child undergoing significant medical problems. They may help the child and family cope with invasive medical procedures, anxiety and depression, or noncompliance with medical treatment. They may act as a consultant to various medical units and departments to assist physicians, nurses, and other professionals in responding to the emotional and behavioral sequelae of severe medical illnesses in children (Rodrigue, 1994; Rudolph et al., 1995). Pediatric psychologists also may assess neuropsychological functioning, level of cognitive functioning, psychosis, and offer individual, group, and family therapy.

Attention Deficit Hyperactivity Disorder

Attention Deficit Hyperactivity Disorder (ADHD) has received a great deal of national attention in recent years, being featured in the cover stories of major news magazines such as *Time* and *Newsweek* and as the topic of several best-selling books. Child clinical psychologists are frequently asked to conduct evaluations to diagnosis ADHD, provide individual, family, and group treatment for ADHD children, and consult with teachers, pediatricians, and parents about social, behavioral, emotional, medical and educational interventions with ADHD children. Many psychologists are at the forefront of research and public policy campaigns concerning ADHD (e.g., Barkley, 1993; Pelham, 1993). It is currently one of the most frequently encountered

Table 11.2 Examples of Diagnostic Problem Areas of Focus
Among Child Clinical Psychologists

Attention deficit hyperactivity disorder	Conduct disorders
Learning disabilities	Autism
Asperger's disorder	Pervasive developmental disorders
Tourette's disorder	Tics
Encopresis	Enuresis
Separation anxiety	School phobia
Selective mutism	Social anxiety and phobia
Child abuse and neglect	

In Hospital Settings

Cancer	Asthma
Seizures	Diabetes
Headaches	Cystic Fibrosis
Medical problems resulting from child abuse and neglect	
Coping with painful medical procedures	

clinical issues faced by many child clinical psychologists.

ADHD effects approximately 3–5 percent of children, but is primarily found in boys (American Psychiatric Association, 1994a; Barkley, 1993). Symptoms include an inability to sustain attention and concentration as well as problems with impulsivity, overactivity, irritability, and moodiness. Children with ADHD often have trouble getting along with peers and are usually disruptive at home and in the classroom. ADHD children tend to be very active, oppositional, and often get in trouble at both home and school (Barkley, 1989, 1993). Restlessness and impulsivity are generally not tolerated well by parents, peers, and teachers. Attention and organizational problems among ADHD children are usually lifelong problems (Barkley, 1989). Adults who experienced ADHD as children often report that they have similar trouble with attention, impulsivity, and interpersonal relationships as adults.

Biopsychosocial factors play a role in the etiology, manifestation, and treatment of ADHD (Diller, Tanner, & Weil, 1996; Edwards, Schultz, & Long, 1995). Brain functioning in certain regions of the cortex and heredity are believed to play significant roles in the development of ADHD (Beiderman, et al., 1992; Frick, Strauss, Lahey, & Neeper, 1984). People with ADHD tend to have less brain activity in the frontal cortex and basal ganglia area than controls when tested (Zametkin,

et al., 1990). ADHD also appears to be more common in family members with at least one other ADHD member (Barkley, 1993). Psychological and social factors such as child abuse have also been associated with the development of ADHD symptoms (Diller et al., 1996). Children with ADHD usually receive a great deal of negative attention from parents, siblings, teachers, and peers, which results in few friendships, frequent teasing, and other social problems. These children often develop depression and low self-esteem as a result of these social interactions (Barkley, 1989, 1993). They also often experience learning disabilities, and develop conduct and substance abuse disorders later in life.

ADHD is not easy to diagnose. Many biopsychosocial factors might contribute to impulsivity, inattention, and disruptive behavior without constituting ADHD per se. Marital discord, physical and/or sexual abuse, depression, post-traumatic stress disorder, poor child-rearing practices, learning disabilities, conduct disorders and other problems may all result in ADHD-like symptoms (Edwards et al., 1995). Parents, teachers, and pediatricians may also quickly diagnose ADHD without a careful evaluation. Many parents are invested in obtaining an ADHD diagnosis rather than confronting that their child rearing practices are faulty or that there exists other emotional factors to account for the problematic symptoms. A careful diagnosis usually involves a careful history, a close review of the child's behavior at home and at school, as well as psychological, cognitive, and educational testing.

Treatment of ADHD also reflects the bio-psychosocial interplay of factors involved in the development and maintenance of ADHD symptoms. Stimulant medication such as Ritalin is often used and improves ADHD symptoms in approximately 75 percent of all cases (Pelham, 1993; Swanson, et al., 1993). However, stimulant medication has been found to improve attention and concentration even among many non-ADHD children. Cognitive problem-solving strategies to help children learn to think before acting have proved successful with ADHD children (Kendall & Braswell, 1985; Whalen, Henker, & Hinshaw, 1985). Relaxation training and biofeedback has also shown some promise (Raymer & Poppen, 1985). Parent and teacher consultation is also an important adjunct in successful treatment (Barkley, 1993; Fiore, Becker, & Nero 1993; Swanson et al., 1993). Group social skills training is also often used to help ADHD children learn to get along better with other children. A multimodal approach addressing bio-psychosocial factors appears to be most comprehensive and effective (Barkley, 1993; Diller et al., 1996).

Learning Disorders

Learning Disorders (LD) are another common clinical problem faced by child clinical psychologists. A learning disorder is diagnosed when a child experiences a cognitive processing impairment (e.g., visual-motor, auditory), which impedes academic achievement in relation to aptitude measured by intellectual functioning (i.e., IQ). Many children experience problems in reading, writing, mathematics, and other academic areas as a result of one or more learning disorders. While many children perform poorly in various school subjects due to lack of motivation and interest, poor study skills, or psychological, family, or social problems that interfere with school performance, many children have a learning disorder, which hinders their performance. It is estimated that as many as 15 percent of school children have a diagnosable learning disorder with boys being much more vulnerable to this problem than girls (Heaton, 1988). Learning disorders are a risk factor for dropping out of school (Wagner, 1990), adult unemployment (Shapiro & Lentz, 1991), and other psychological and social problems (Russell, 1997;

Spreen, 1988). Children with learning disorders often have negative school experiences and are more likely to experience low self-esteem, depression, anxiety, and disruptive behaviors. Learning disorders often evade detection by parents and teachers who may alternately attribute difficulties in school to laziness, low intellectual ability, oppositionality, or other social or emotional problems.

Like ADHD, learning disorders have received a great deal of clinical, research, and media attention in recent years. Fairly recently, many colleges have begun to offer special admission consideration to learning disabled applicants. Untimed tests are also available at many schools and during national examinations such as the Scholastic Aptitude Test (SAT). Fortunately, learning disorders have received enough attention to alert many parents, teachers, school administrators, and others of this potential basis of children's difficulties in school. However, learning disorders have also become a popular diagnosis, which nonlearning disordered children and their parents seek in order to obtain the advantage of untimed SATs and school exams as well as special consideration for college admission.

Like ADHD, learning disorders are not always easy to diagnose (Russell, 1997). Many different problems can be associated with poor school performance. Psychological and social problems, marital discord, poor motivation, low aptitude, poor nutrition, large class sizes, stress, illness, poor teaching, and a host of other factors may contribute to poor school performance by any given child. Additionally, many children with serious psychiatric or medical problems also appear to have learning disorders (real or supposed). Children with ADHD, Pervasive Developmental Disorders, Asperger's Syndrome, depression, post-traumatic stress disorder, cultural or language differences, and other problems often have trouble with school performance.

The diagnosis of learning disorders is usually made by child clinical psychologists in consultation with educational specialists. Intellectual, educational, and psychological testing along with interviews of teachers, parents, and the child are used to evaluate a potentially learning disordered child. Generally, a learning disorder is defined as a statistically significant difference between aptitude and achievement as well as a diagnosable processing problem, which might include visual or auditory difficulties. However, each state selects a specific criteria for the diagnosis and this criteria varies a great deal from state to state. For example, a 22.5 point difference (one and one-half standard deviation units) between aptitude assessed by a standard IQ test and achievement must be documented to meet the California state criteria for a learning disability.

A classic example is of a learning disability is **dyslexia,** a reading disorder that involves letter reversals such as confusing a "b" with a "d." Dyslexia makes reading and learning difficult, and can involve both visual and/or auditory discrimination problems. Aptitude testing is conducted using the standard IQ tests described in Chapter 8. Achievement testing involves educational testing as also described in Chapter 8. While psychologists frequently conduct both types of testing, they often work in conjunction with educational specialists who provide the achievement testing while the psychologist conducts the aptitude and psychological testing.

In additional to learning disabilities that involve reading, writing, math and other academic skills, learning disabilities that primarily involve social relationships also impact children. Asperger's Syndrome and Nonverbal Learning Disability are two examples in which academic performance may be acceptable but social skills significantly impaired. These children often are unable to adequately interact with peers and teachers and have difficulty interpreting and responding to the subtleties of social interaction.

Prevailing theories concerning the etiology of learning disorders involve genetic and neurological factors. Several studies have suggested that learning disorders are heritable (Cardon, Smith, Fulker, Kimberling, Pennington, & DeFries, 1994; Myers & Hammil, 1990; Pennington & Smith, 1988). Other researchers suggest that early childhood or prenatal brain damage might cause learning disorders (Hynd & Semrud-Clikeman, 1989; Russell, 1997). These biological influences interact with psychological, social, and educational issues to result in the manifestation of learning disorders. Relationships with parents and teachers as well as the child's personality, ability to compensate for deficits, cultural expectations and other factors are all integral to the expression and repercussions of learning disorders. Optimal treatment therefore reflects this biopsychosocial perspective. Special tutoring and computer-assisted techniques that help in compensating for the learning problems have proven useful. Furthermore, psychotherapy, parent education, and teacher consultation are also ideally incorporated into intervention programs. Children often need family and school support as well as psychotherapy to come to terms with a learning disability diagnosis. Feeling different from others, damaged, and contending with the self-esteem, depressive, and anxiety symptoms potentially associated with learning disorders requires individual, family, and/or group psychotherapy.

Child Abuse and Neglect

Many clinical child psychologists and pediatric psychologists are involved in evaluation, treatment, research, and policy development concerning **child abuse and neglect** (Emery & Laumann-Billings, 1998). Sadly, many children are physically, sexually, and/or emotionally abused by parents, stepparents, other family members, family friends, and even strangers. Some high profile cases involving abduction and murder, such as the Polly Klaas case in Petaluma, California, receive national and international attention and highlight the hideous problem of violence towards children. However, unlike such well-known cases, parents rather than strangers are responsible for the vast majority of children being abused, neglected, and even murdered. In fact, it is estimated that about 97 percent of all child abuse cases involve one or both parents as the perpetrator of the abuse (American Humane Association, 1984). Both boys and girls appear to be mistreated at about the same rate.

A number of risk factors are associated with people who are more likely to abuse their children (Faust, Runyon, & Kenny, 1995). The most prominent of these includes a personal history of abuse. Thus, parents who abuse their children generally were abused by their parents when they were children (Faust et al., 1995; Garbarino & Stocking, 1980). Alcohol and drug abuse, socioeconomic stress, occupational and marital stress, poor coping skills, and impulse control problems all contribute to potential abuse (Faust et al., 1995). While child abuse and neglect is found in all segments of society, it generally comes to the attention of child protection services and law enforcement among the poor and disadvantaged.

All psychologists in every state are mandated to report suspected child abuse and neglect to child protective services and/or the police (Deisz, Doueck, & George, 1996; McDevitt, 1996). Therefore all psychologists must be trained in the signs and symptoms of child abuse. Child clinical psychologists are frequently involved in the assessment of possible abuse, in child custody evaluations, and in the treatment of both abused children and their families. Child clinical psychologists also often offer psychoeducational classes to help abusive parents learn better ways of interacting with their children. Child clinical psychologists might also work with legal professionals to determine appropriate home placements for abused children.

Children who are abused often suffer from anxiety, depression, oppositional and conduct disorders, and other problems (Willis, 1995). Troubles with trust, chronic fear, bodily vulnerability, self-esteem, and shame are also common. Abused children are also more likely to develop eating disorders as well (Goldfarb, 1987). Perpetrators of abuse often suffer from alcohol abuse and other problems associated with having been victimized themselves as children. Treatment of both victims and perpetrators of abuse can be very difficult (Kendziora & O'Leary, 1993). Funding of child abuse treatment programs frequently are reduced and eliminated during government budget cutting periods. The embarrassment and humiliation of being abused often prevents children, especially adolescents, from acknowledging victimization and willingly participating in treatment. The same is true of perpetrators, who also may face criminal prosecution. Many abused children find themselves living in various foster homes or with relatives, rendering consistent treatment a challenge. In addition to the victimization of the abuse, usually the child, rather than the victimizing parent, is taken from the home and placed in a new environment. Parents, foster parents, and other guardians are often wary and skeptical of mental health services that may be perceived as being closely connected with law enforcement. Treatment dropout among perpetrators of child abuse is remarkably high and estimated to be about 90 percent in the absence of court involvement and about 40 percent when it is specifically mandated by the courts (Wolfe, Aragona, Kaufman, & Sandler, 1980). Efforts by the courts and policy makers to preserve families by trying to keep abused children

with abusive parents can dangerously backfire with repeated abusive episodes occurring even during treatment.

A unique form of child abuse seen among pediatric psychologists working in hospital settings include Factitious Disorder or Munchausen's by Proxy Disorder (Sanders, 1995). A Factitious Disorder involves the "intentional production or feigning of physical or psychological signs or symptoms" (American Psychiatric Association, 1994a, p. 227). In Munchausen's by Proxy Disorder, a parent (usually the mother) obtains gratification from the attention and support she receives from medical personnel when her child is ill. She therefore intentionally induces illnesses in her child through poisoning or other methods in order to seek treatment in the hospital setting. Frequent and mysterious illnesses among children might suggest that a parent is affected by Munchausen's by Proxy Disorder (Sanders, 1995). Pediatric psychologists might evaluate the mother and child and contact child protective services to investigate allegations of potential abuse.

Anorexia Nervosa

Anorexia nervosa is a self-starvation problem that effects about 1 percent of the adolescent female population. Age of onset is generally around age 17, though it can occur throughout adolescence and even into adulthood (American Psychiatric Association, 1994a; Herzog, 1988). Only about 5 percent of anorexics are males. Anorexia is defined by body weight falling to less than 85 percent of ideal in conjunction with an intense fear of becoming fat and amenorrhea (American Psychiatric Association, 1994a). While all anorexics restrict their food intake, some also engage in episodes of binge eating and purging. Purging might include self-induced vomiting or laxative use. Because anorexia can result in such severe weight loss that health and life are threatened, inpatient hospitalization is needed in severe cases. Pediatric psychologists working in hospital settings are often involved in the diagnosis, treatment, and research of anorexia nervosa.

The etiology, symptoms, and treatment of anorexia reflect the biopsychosocial nature of the disorder and clinical psychology's response to it. Anorexia and other eating disorders may have a genetic component with a 4 to 5 times higher incidence in first degree relatives (Strober & Humphrey, 1987). Anorexia *per se* might not be inherited, yet factors such as personality, impulsivity, body shape, impulse control, anxiety, and other characteristics that might place someone at greater risk for developing an eating disorder may be heritable factors. Once an eating disorder begins, neurochemical factors may perpetuate the problem. Some have suggested that the functioning of the hypothalamus via neurotransmitters such as dopamine, serotonin, and norepinephrine might be involved in anorexia nervosa (Hsu, 1990). Starvation itself also leads to irrational and rigid thinking, which further perpetuates the problem. Psychological factors including a lack of perceived control in life, poor self-esteem, stress, anxiety, and depression also play a role in the development and course of the illness (Striegal-Moore, Silberstein, & Rodin, 1993). Social factors such as cultural ideals of thinness and beauty also play a role in motivating the anorexic's relentless pursuit of thinness (Brownell, 1991; Pike & Rodin, 1991; Striegal-Moore, Silberstein, & Rodin, 1986). Intervention approaches include tube and/or intravenous feeding in medical emergencies, high-calorie liquid diets, and medication to assist with anxiety, depression, and compulsive symptoms. Individual, family,

and group psychotherapy are usually provided in some combination during and following the hospital stay, or in lieu of inpatient treatment where weight loss is less extreme.

Conclusions

Child clinical psychologists and pediatric psychologists work with the unique problems affecting children and adolescents and their families. They also work closely with a wide variety of other professionals involved in the lives of children such as school teachers, pediatricians, and legal authorities. Child clinical psychologists work with the unique problems that face children and families such as attention-deficit hyperactivity disorder, child abuse and neglect, depression, learning disabilities, school phobia, autism, and medical problems that impact children, to name a few (Mash & Barkley, 1989).

Clinical Neuropsychology

The subspecialty of clinical **neuropsychology** focuses on **brain-behavior relationships,** that is, how brain functioning impacts behavior and behavior

---

Case Study: Sam

Sam is a 6-year-old biracial (East Indian and Filipino) boy who experiences difficulties in social relationships at school. His teacher and parents report that he engages in excessive self-stimulation behavior (e.g., rocks, hums) and is rigidly attached to certain objects and routines. They expressed concern that Sam gets upset over little things (e.g., being pushed at school, altered schedules, loud classroom), and shows very little interest in peers or adults.

Sam's parents have a high-conflict relationship and are planning to divorce. They both work many hours each week and frequently travel on business. Sam has a full-time nanny who takes care of him when his parents are working and traveling. Sam's father has an obsessive-compulsive disorder and takes medication to control his behavior. He also participates in an obsessive-compulsive disorder support and information group.

Cognitive testing using the WISC-III revealed that Sam functions in the below average range on overall intellectual functioning, with a lower verbal than perfor-

mance IQ. Sam's performance on the Rey-Osterrieth Complex Figure Test as well as his performance on the Projective Drawing tasks suggest problems in fine motor skills as well as perceptual-motor integration abilities. His language abilities are significantly limited, despite English being his and his parents only language.

Sam's problems in social, behavioral, and intellectual functioning were attributed to childhood autism, which is a severe, pervasive developmental disorder. Autism is a neurologically based psychiatric syndrome that involves problems in social interactions (e.g., lack of spontaneous social behavior and problems in developing appropriate peer relationships and skills), combined with restricted patterns of behavior (e.g., inflexible adherence to specific routines or rituals), and impaired language and communication. The onset of symptoms generally occur prior to the age of 3. The child clinical psychologist recommended a different classroom setting for Sam and a host of behavioral, supportive, and social interventions to assist Sam and his family in addressing his complex needs.

Case Study: Zoe

Zoe is a 13-year-old Caucasian girl who attends the 8th grade. She lives with her adoptive parents and younger adoptive brother and sister. She was adopted when she was 4 months old after Child Protective Services removed her from her home due to physical abuse and neglect. Little is known about the medical, psychological, and social background of Zoe's biological parents.

Zoe is highly disorganized, forgetful, and distracted. Her parents also describe her as "hyper." She can't sit still and is always talking and moving around. She recently was suspended at school when she left a school dance with a few girlfriends to meet up with some older high school boys in a nearby baseball field. The girls drank a large amount of beer and returned to the dance intoxicated. Zoe's parents were especially upset because she was unconcerned about the consequences of her behavior and initially lied about her participation. They also report that when Zoe was 10 she left home late at night and was picked up by the police approximately two miles away at 12:30 A.M. They report

that she left a note about being abducted. Again, the family was concerned about her impulsive behavior, her lying, and inability to understand the consequences of her behavior and exercise better judgment.

A complete psychological evaluation failed to confirm true attentional and other deficits consistent with an ADHD diagnosis. Psychological testing did, however, reveal below average cognitive abilities and poorly modulated feelings of anger and sadness that contributed to Zoe's poor judgment, vulnerability to peer pressure, and impulsive acting out. The psychologist conducting the evaluation suggested that Zoe would benefit from tutorial assistance at school, individual therapy to assist her in contending with painful emotions related to her early history and adolescent autonomy strivings, and family therapy to negotiate rules and limits while addressing adoption issues long buried in the family. Zoe was diagnosed with an adjustment disorder with mixed disturbance of emotions and conduct.

---

problems (Jones & Butters, 1991). Clinical neuropsychologists assess brain and behavior functioning and offer strategies for patients suffering from brain impairment due to problems that result in cognitive and neurological dysfunction. Table 11.3 lists some of the topics of interest to clinical neuropsychologists. Neuropsychologists must be well versed in neuroanatomy, neuropathology as well as clinical

psychology (Report of the International Neuropsychological Society, 1987). They assess a range of cognitive abilities including executive or higher-order cognitive functions, sensory and motor functioning, memory skills and abstract reasoning. Many psychologists who specialize in neuropsychology are often trained as clinical psychologists or they may have received training in cognitive science or neuro-

Case Study: Sally

Sally is a 15-year-old Caucasian girl who was recently hospitalized with anorexia nervosa. She is currently 5'6" tall and weighs only 85 pounds. Her symptoms began when she was 14-years-old following a diet in response to critical comments about her weight made by some girls at school. She first tried to lose weight by exercising and eliminating desserts, enjoying the positive comments about her weight loss made by friends and family members. After she lost several pounds she felt that she was still "too fat" and continued to diet and exercise even more rigorously. She began using laxatives to speed up the weight-loss process and relieve feelings of fullness, guilt, and anxiety after eating even small amounts. She became more withdrawn and depressed. Her school per-

formance decreased and she became more and more obsessed with food and dieting.

Sally's parents brought her to the pediatrician who encouraged her to seek professional help at the Eating Disorders Clinic at a local hospital. Sally denied that she had a problem and refused to get help. After Sally fainted following a run, her mother brought her to the hospital for treatment. She was admitted to the eating disorders unit of the children's hospital. Following an intake interview with Sally and her mother, Sally was provided with intravenous fluids and a regimen to increase weight. Individual, family, and group psychotherapy were provided in conjunction with medical care. Sally was diagnosed with anorexia nervosa.

Table 11.3 Typical Problems Addressed
by Neuropsychologists

Seizures	Tumors
Head traumas	Alzheimer's disease
Stroke	Alcohol
Malingering	Langauge problems
Dementia	Impairment due to injury
Epilepsy	Impairment due to chemotherapy
AIDS	Disease

science. Most neuropsychologists work in hospital, rehabilitation, or clinic settings. Some specialize in working with children, a field referred to as child, or developmental, neuropsychology. Many also work in private or group practice environments.

Assessment is the primary activity of the neuropsychologist who relies upon testing results to provide recommendations for diagnosis, treatment, and rehabilitation. As discussed in Chapter 8, neuropsychologists administer and interpret a wide variety of specialty test batteries such as the Halstead-Reitan Neuropsychological Battery and the Luria-Nebraska Battery as well as individual tests such as the Rey-Osterrieth Complex Figure, the Benton Visual Recognition Test, the Wisconsin Card Sorting Test, and the California Verbal Learning Test, which evaluate language, motor, attention, concentration, and higher order cognitive functioning such as problem solving. Furthermore, more commonly known tests such as the Weschler Adult Intelligence Test-III (WAIS-III) and the Minnesota Multiphasic Personality Inventory-2 (MMPI-2) are often part of a comprehensive neuropsychological evaluation. These tests provide information concerning the cognitive and psychological functioning of people experiencing a wide range of potential problems that impact brain-behavior relationships. Neuropsychologists also provide consultation and rehabilitation services such as psychoeducational support groups, psychotherapy, coping and skill-building strategies, and family support for those experiencing head injuries and diseases impacting brain-behavior relationships. Finally, neuropsychologists conduct research into understanding, assessing, and treating these problems. While neuropsychologists are involved in assessment, treatment, consultation, and research in many problem areas that effect brain functioning,

this section will highlight the problems of epilepsy, degenerative diseases, and head injuries.

Epilepsy

Epilepsy is a seizure disorder defined as excessive discharging of brain cells that are sudden, transient, and recurrent (Goldensohn, Glaser, & Goldberg, 1984; McConnell, & Snyder, 1997; Shuster, 1996). **Seizures** result in intense muscle spasms, a complete or partial loss of consciousness, and sometimes unconscious purposeful behavior. Neurons in the brain become excited due to a variety of reasons that differ from person to person. For example, infections, metabolic abnormalities, and biochemical factors may all contribute to the development of a seizure. In addition to these physiological causes, psychological stress has been found to elicit seizures among those vulnerable to this disorder (Williams, 1982).

Epilepsy effects about 1 percent of the population. Children are more likely to experience epilepsy than adults; children under the age of 5 and at puberty are the most vulnerable (McConnell & Snyder, 1997; Hauser, Annegers, & Anderson, 1983). Curiously, epilepsy is also more likely to occur among lower socioeconomic groups (Hauser et al., 1983). Biopsychosocial factors contribute to the development of epilepsy with genetics, infections, socioeconomics, stress, nutrition, prenatal care, and other factors contributing to the development and maintenance of the disorder (Hanesian, Paez, & Williams, 1988; Stears & Spitz, 1996).

The severity, duration, and age of onset of epilepsy is related to the level of potential impairment in cognitive functioning. Attention-concentration, memory, problem solving, motor, and intellectual abilities all can be significantly impaired due to problems associated with repeated seizures (Ellenberg, Hirtz, & Nelson, 1986; Hanesian, Paez, & Williams 1988). However, anticonvulsant medication causes side effects that adversely impact these skills, thus deficits in cognitive function may be related to medication rather than to the seizures per se (Corbet, Trimble, & Nicol, 1985; McConnell & Snyder, 1997). In addition to neurological functioning, personality and mood are also altered by seizures. Complex partial seizures that are localized in the temporal lobe region of the brain have been associated with changes in mood, sexual activity, and aggressiveness (Trimble, 1985). People with epilepsy are also at higher risk for the development of psychiatric problems such as anxiety, depression, psychosis, and antisocial behavior (Hanesian et al., 1988).

Neuropsychologists are often requested to carefully evaluate the cognitive and personality functioning of patients with epilepsy. Medication and other treatment decisions are often determined partly on the basis of these test results. Neuropsychologists are also frequently asked to differentiate seizures from **pseudoseizure** disorders and **malingering.** Curiously, some people present with seizures that are psychologically based (e.g., "hysterical seizures") or intentionally feigned (Williams & Mostofsky, 1982). Sometimes patients with somatoform disorders, factitious disorders, or motivation to malinger consciously or even unconsciously fake having a seizure disorder for medical attention, financial incentives, or other reasons.

Treatment of epilepsy reflects contemporary, integrative and biopsychosocial perspectives (Shuster, 1996). Anticonvulsant medication such as carbamazepine has proven to be effective in decreasing the frequency and intensity of seizures. Psychotropic medications such as benzodiazepines, antidepressants, and neuroleptics have all been successfully used to minimize the frequency, intensity, or duration (Hanesian et al., 1988; Trimble, 1985; Williams, et al., 1982). When medications prove ineffective and seizures are localized to the temporal lobe, for example, surgery to perform a temporal lobectomy may be performed to prevent onset. Psychotherapy, group therapy, social support, and psychoeducational opportunities are valuable adjuncts to medical treatment (Hanesian et al., 1988; McConnell & Snyder, 1997). These approaches assist patients with the emotional, social, and behavioral challenges of coping with this chronic illness, thereby minimizing any limitations associated with seizures.

Brain Injuries

Brain injuries present another area of focus for neuropsychologists. Accidents causing brain injuries impact over 10 million people each year and may occur from vehicular accidents, falls, war wounds, sport injuries, gun shot wounds, violent assaults and other tragic events. Concussions (jarring the brain) and contusions (shifting of the position of the brain) that occur during accidents can impact brain functions such as memory, attention-concentration, and orientation (Anderson, Bigler, & Blatter, 1995; Newcombe, 1996). Strokes can also impair language, motor skills, personality functioning, and other neurocognitive abilities. Environmental toxins such as poisons, gas fumes, and metals such as mercury and lead can also result in brain injuries. For example, it has been estimated that about 4% of American children have damaging levels of lead in their blood and brains, which can result in impaired intellectual abilities, problems in attention-concentration, confusion, and ADHD-like symptoms (U.S. Department of Health and Human Services, 1985b). Neuropsychologists are asked to evaluate cognitive and psychological functioning as well as develop rehabilitation programs for brain-injured patients. Psychotherapy, group support, education, and medical treatment may all be involved depending upon the nature of the problem and the special needs of the patient and family.

Degenerative Diseases

Degenerative diseases represent an additional spectrum of impairment faced by neuropsychologists. These include Alzheimer's disease, dementia, Parkinson's disease, Huntington's chorea, and infectious diseases such as syphilis and other disorders. Gradual degeneration of neurological functioning results in problems in memory, attention, speech, judgement, movement and other areas of functioning, depending upon the specific disease process in each individual (Tuokko, Kristjansson, & Miller, 1995). Often patients with degenerative diseases develop depression, anxiety, irritability, personality changes, and loss of social support (American Psychiatric Association, 1997; Sultzer, Levin, Mahler, High, & Cummings, 1993). Thus, these individuals also deserve sensitive, comprehensive care.

Dementia associated with Alzheimer's disease is perhaps the most well-known and prevalent degenerative disease. Alzheimer's disease among famous people such as former President Ronald Reagan has greatly increased awareness and interest in this problem. Alzheimer's disease involves memory loss, failure to recognize well known people and objects, difficulty in organizing and planning, suspiciousness, and language problems

(Bogerts, 1993; Edwards, 1994). It is estimated that Alzheimer's disease occurs among more than 4 million people in the United States (Edwards, 1994) and is more common among people with lower educational levels (Korczyn, Kahana, & Galper, 1991).

Alzheimer's disease may be due to genetically and environmentally induced brain atrophy and plaque formation and low levels of the brain neurotransmitters acetylcholine, serotonin, and noradrenalin (La Rue, 1992). Head trauma, malnutrition, drug and toxin exposure, viral infection, personality, and cultural factors all may play a role in the development, progression, and manifestation of Alzheimer's disease (Ikels, 1991; Korczyn et al., 1991).

Neuropsychologists are often requested to evaluate the cognitive and psychological functioning of these patients and assist in making a definitive diagnosis. However, often the diagnosis of Alzheimer's disease is made when no other apparent cause for symptoms can be identified. Often an evaluation helps to rule out other potential explanations for symptoms as well as assists in the rehabilitation efforts. Psychologists also offer services including psychotherapy, group support, psychoeducational instructions, milieu therapy, behavior management, and consultation with physicians, nurses, and other caregivers. Treatment approaches also include careful work with family members who are usually highly stressed by caring for and facing the eventual decline and loss of a loved one. Treatments

also include medication such as Cognex, which prevents the metabolic breakdown of acetylcholine (Winker, 1994).

Conclusions

Neuropsychology is a popular and rapidly developing subspecialty of clinical psychology. It blends psychology and medicine in understanding how problems with the brain impact behavior and psychological functioning. Neuropsychology also highlights the contemporary biopsychosocial model. Brain injuries due to head trauma and disease cause illnesses impacting cognitive and psychological functioning. These disorders impact not only the patient but the patient's family. Genetic vulnerability as well as social and emotional factors interact in many of these problems to result in the development, manifestation and progression of certain diseases. Neuropsychologists can be enormously helpful in assessment, treatment, rehabilitation, and research regarding disorders as diverse as Alzheimer's disease, epilepsy, AIDS, stroke, alcoholism, and gun shot wounds. Neuropsychology also overlaps to some degree with other subspecialty areas in clinical psychology including health psychology, pediatric psychology, and forensic psychology.

Forensic Psychology

Forensic psychology is defined as the "application of psychology to legal issues" (Cooke, 1984, p. 29).

Case Study: Joseph

Joseph is a 71-year-old married Caucasian man who has a doctorate degree and has worked as a highly successful engineer for many years. He was hospitalized on a combined medical/psychiatric unit for depression and a variety of medical problems. He started several companies and had become independently wealthy as a result of his business success. His difficulties involved a number of cognitive and personality changes. He frequently became lost when traveling to familiar places in town, and had difficulty remembering people and places. At times he was overtly hostile to friends and family. His impulsivity resulted in several poor financial decisions that were very costly for his family. The staff of the hospital unit was

interested in determining whether Joseph had a neuropsychological problem associated with dementia. They were unsure if his problems in behavior might be associated with other potential medical or psychiatric problems. An abbreviated version of the Halstead-Reitan Battery was administered. The patient was uncooperative during much of the testing process. He expressed anger and resentment toward the hospital, staff, and examiner. Results indicated that Joseph did in fact experience dementia as well as a concurrent depressive disorder. Results suggested that his level of cognitive functioning (especially abstract reasoning, memory, and new learning) were significantly impaired.

Case Study: Austin

Austin is a 16-year-old Caucasian male who was severely injured in a motorcycle accident associated with his use of the drug *crank* (i.e., methamphetamine). Austin experienced a severe head injury, and was in a coma for one week prior to regaining consciousness. A neuropsychologist administered the Halstead-Reitan Battery and found that Austin evidences impaired judgment, abstract reasoning, and impulse control consistent with his frontal lobe concussion. In addition, Austin has visual deficits associated with his concussion from the impact on his occipital lobe. The neuropsychologist, in conjunction with Austin's physician, provided recommendations, information, and rehabilitation options to Austin and his family. In addition, a drug consultation was recommended for a future date.

Forensic psychologists specialize in utilizing principles of human behavior to inform the judicial and legal systems. They are often trained as clinical psychologists with a specialty in forensic work. Forensic psychologists may conduct psychological evaluations with defendants and present their findings as an expert witness in court. They may also provide evaluations for child custody arrangements, or be asked to predict dangerousness or determine if an individual is competent to stand trial. They may be asked to participate in worker's compensation claims, or serve as a consultant to attorneys who are selecting a jury. Forensic psychologists also assist in documenting mental anguish, pain and suffering, and brain injury in personal injury litigation. Injury may include physical accidents or psychological traumas associated with sexual harassment, rape, discrimination, and others stressful experiences. In addition to being competent psychologists, they must thoroughly understand the law and legal system and be prepared to make court appearances. While forensic psychologists are involved in numerous aspects of the legal system, this chapter will highlight their work in legal cases involving involuntary commitment, the insanity defense, child custody, and jury selection.

Involuntary Commitment

Each state has laws that allow someone to be committed to a psychiatric hospital if they are in serious and immediate danger of hurting themselves or others. While many people may have fleeting suicidal or homicidal thoughts, those who are in danger of acting on these thoughts must be protected from harming themselves or others. However, freedom is a fundamental human right and highly valued in our society. Therefore, depriving a citizen of this important right through forced, **involuntary commitment** to a psychiatric hospital is a serious matter. Throughout the course of history, commitment to a psychiatric facility or prison was exploited as a means of controlling people who maintained unpopular political, religious, or personal beliefs and activities. The ability to commit someone against their will has been clearly abused over the years and continues to occur in many countries. Even with the best intentions, it is often unclear if someone is

Case Study: Margaret

Margaret is a 63-year-old African-American woman who recently suffered a stroke. Since the stroke occurred she has been unable to speak or write. She appears to recognize familiar friends and family members and is frequently upset and frustrated by her inability to communicate. Friends and family were initially very supportive and available to her but have recently appeared more distant. They feel uncomfortable being around her since they cannot communicate effectively. A neuropsychologist was asked to evaluate Margaret and offer treatment recommendations. The neuropsychologist found that Margaret has some ability to communicate via pictures and an adapted keyboard and helped to develop a communication system for Margaret in addition to offering strategies for rehabilitation to the medical team. The neuropsychologist also provided consultation to Margaret and also to her family to help them better understand and cope with Margaret's problems.

indeed in serious danger of hurting themselves or others. Predicting dangerous behavior is very difficult and usually unreliable (Grisso & Appelbaum, 1992). The legal system consults with psychologists to obtain guidance in determining if someone should be involuntarily committed.

In addition to danger to self and others, the criteria for involuntary commitment in most states includes a diagnosable mental illness as well as the inability to adequately care for oneself due to being "gravely disabled." Special efforts are needed to ensure that involuntary commitment laws are not abused. Famous cases such as the *O'Connor* v. *Donaldson* case where a patient without any mental illness and who was not in danger of hurting anyone was hospitalized for many years against his will, highlights this issue. Forensic psychologists are asked to carefully evaluate a patient using assessment techniques such as clinical interviews, cognitive tests, and both objective and projective personality tests to determine if someone is at high risk for harm to self or others as well as to determine whether a mental illness exists that renders them unable to provide adequate self care. Since these criteria are very difficult to evaluate, psychologists make clinical judgements based on the totality of their experience, training, and the data that emerges from their evaluation. They often testify in court as well as consult with both attorneys and judges to make decisions that are ideally in the best interest of both the patient and society.

Insanity Defense

Ever since the **M'Naghten Rule** of 1843, American and British law has struggled with the **insanity defense.** This rule was named after Daniel M'Naghten who attempted to kill the prime minister of England because he felt that the government was persecuting him. Tragically, he mistakenly killed the prime minister's secretary. His symptoms were consistent with what DSM IV would consider paranoid schizophrenia. The M'Naghten Rule suggests that someone is not responsible for their criminal actions if they suffer from a disorder that renders them unaware of what they are doing or that what they are doing is wrong. The M'Naghten Rule has been adapted several times over the years. For example, the **Durham Rule** of 1954 added a "medical disease or defect" to the criteria for insanity. However, since

mental health professionals were unable to reliably demonstrate that a mental illness could cause someone to commit a crime, the Durham Rule was amended by the American Law Institute Rule of 1962, the Diminished Capacity rule of 1979 and the **Insanity Defense Reform Act** of 1984.

Today's version, based on the Insanity Defense Reform Act, states that someone can be found innocent due to reasons of insanity if unable to understand that criminal behavior was wrong at the time of the crime due to a mental disease or mental retardation. Famous cases such as John Hinckley (who attempted to assassinate then President Ronald Reagan), Charles Manson (who participated in multiple murders including the actress Sharon Tate), Jeffrey Dahmer (who committed multiple murders that involved cannibalism), and Dan White (who murdered San Francisco mayor, George Moscone, and claimed that junk food made him unstable) have highlighted the use of the insanity defense. Most people think that the insanity defense is overused and that criminals too often get away with heinous crimes (Hans, 1986). This has led to efforts on the part of several states to abandon the insanity defense altogether (De Angelis, 1994) or develop a "guilty but mentally ill" verdict which would allow both treatment and punishment of criminals who meet this criteria (Callahan, McGreevy, Cirincione, & Stedman, 1992). However, the insanity defense is rarely successful even though it may be used too frequently.

Forensic psychologists are asked to evaluate these accused offenders to determine if they suffer from a mental illness that might meet the legal criteria of insanity and provide expert testimony to the court to assist in determining if the accused should be held responsible for their crime. They complete clinical interviews and conduct psychological evaluations to inform their judgments.

Child Custody

About half of all marriages end in divorce. Many of these marriages involve children, leaving the question of the children's custody a critical and often hotly contested issue (Crosby-Currie, 1996). Many years ago, children from divorced families were routinely given to the father. During the past 30 years, the mother has generally been awarded the children in custody disputes and the father has been allowed visitation rights and ordered to pay child support. In more recent years, these patterns have been challenged, and more and more joint custody arrangements are being worked out in court. **Joint custody** means that both parents retain custody of their children following divorce and that arrangements are made regarding living and financial matters to accommodate the needs and wishes of both parents. While joint custody can often be in the best interest of all of the parties involved, it is not without difficulties and can often be problematic for children. Since many divorces are highly conflictual, cooperation between parents regarding the care of their children is often difficult to establish in joint custody arrangements. Divorced parents must interact frequently in joint custody situations, and children are often placed in the middle of ongoing conflict. When divorced parents remarry and blended families enter the picture, the complexity and challenges often increase.

In addition to **child custody** arrangements due to divorce, custody matters are also decided when parental rights are severed due to child abuse, abandonment, and neglect. Adoption strategies as well as visitation rights are usually worked out through the family court systems. Efforts to keep the best interests of the child in mind while still trying to preserve the rights and freedoms of parents, combined with efforts to keep troubled families together, tend to dominate these decisions.

Forensic psychologists are asked to evaluate parents, children, and other relevant parties (e.g., adoptive parents, foster parents, grandparents who may serve as legal guardians) to assist the court in determining who should have legal custody of children and what arrangements should be outlined for not only custody but visitation and other parental responsibilities. These psychologists may conduct psychotherapy with parents, children, other guardians, and families as well as provide expert testimony concerning their evaluative or intervention work with families.

Jury Selection

Forensic psychologists often work as consultants to attorneys concerning **jury selection.** Famous cases such as the O.J. Simpson double-murder case highlighted the efforts of attorneys to maximize their chances of selecting a jury who would likely be favorable to their client. Jury characteristics such as gender, race, socioeconomic status, occupation, interests, and a host of psychological factors may potentially contribute to the likelihood that a jury will be sympathetic to the defendant or plaintiff. Forensic psychologists also consult with attorneys regarding how to best interact with the selected jury to maximize the chances that the jury will accept their arguments. Presentation styles, attire, mannerisms, and methods of argument are adjusted to enhance the chances that the jury will be favorable to the attorney's point of view. These psychologists might conduct focus groups where research subjects act as juries and are interviewed during and after mock trials to determine which strategies work best.

Conclusions

Forensic psychology is another fast-growing subspecialty in clinical psychology. These psychologists act as consultants and expert witnesses in numerous types of civil and criminal cases. They use their assessment skills as well as their knowledge of the field of psychology to assist courts in determining many legal decisions. They may be hired by the court or by attorneys representing either side of a dispute. While their primary activity is evaluation and expert testimony, many forensic psychologists provide treatment and other services. Forensic psychology, like the other subspecialties reviewed in this chapter, overlap with other subspecialties. For example, forensic and child specialities overlap in child custody work, while neuropsychology and forensic psychology overlap in litigation regarding work-related accidents.

Other Subspecialties

In addition to health, child, neuropsychology, and forensics, there are a number of other subspecialties and areas of expertise in clinical psychology. Furthermore there are specialties within subspecialties. For example, some clinical psychologists specialize in conducting neuropsychological evaluations among elderly persons who experience strokes. Others focus on treatment of children from specific minority populations. Still others specialize in psychopharmacology as it relates to certain illnesses

Case Study: The Lee Family

The Lee family, an affluent Chinese-American family, is in the midst of a child custody dispute. Mr. and Mrs. Lee were granted a divorce several years ago and were awarded joint custody of their 5-year-old son, Mark. Mr. Lee was promoted and transferred to another city about 400 miles away from Mrs. Lee. The Lees decided to have Mark live with Mrs. Lee for two weeks out of the month and live with Mr. Lee for two weeks of the month. Mark would fly between his two homes every other week. After several months of this arrangement, Mark began to show signs of significant stress. He began to develop a bed-wetting problem and was engaging in frequent temper tantrums. Mrs. Lee felt that the joint custody arrangement was unworkable and decided to seek sole legal custody of her son allowing for generous visitation rights with Mark's father. Mr. Lee was outraged at Mrs. Lee's attempt to secure sole custody and fought her attempts. Since Mr. and Mrs. Lee had a bitter divorce and were still very angry with each other, they acted out their conflict regarding the custody arrangements and often did not keep their son's best interests in mind. The court referred the Lee family to a forensic psychologist to conduct a comprehensive family evaluation and make recommendations to the court regarding custody. The psychologist conducted the evaluation using clinical interviews and psychological evaluations of each family member. The psychologist then testified in court regarding these findings and offered recommendations regarding custody.

Case Study: Marie

Marie is a 32-year-old Latino woman who recently made a suicide attempt by cutting her wrists. Luckily, her roommate discovered her and called 911 shortly after she lost consciousness. After receiving medical treatment, she was admitted to a psychiatric unit for evaluation. Marie reported that she felt suicidal after the recent breakup with her boyfriend. She continued to feel suicidal during her hospital stay and admitted that she was angry at her roommate for interrupting her suicide attempt, and demanded to be discharged immediately. The court asked for a psychological evaluation by a forensic psychologist to determine if Marie was still in immediate and serious danger of hurting herself and to determine if she should be hospitalized for an additional 72 hours against her will for evaluation and observation. The psychologist interviewed Marie and asked her to complete a psychological battery including both objective and projective personality measures. The psychologist determined that Marie was still at risk for hurting herself and suggested that Marie continue to be hospitalized.

Case Study: Betty

Betty is a 31-year old Caucasian woman who was denied tenure at a major university. She was furious with the decision and felt that it was an unfair political decision because several members of the department and university tenure review committee did not agree with some of her views about faculty governance and other matters. She also perceived herself to be a victim of gender discrimination since there were no tenured female faculty in her English department. The university reported that her scholarship was not adequate for tenure and that she was only a mediocre teacher. Betty was also suing the university for lost revenue as well as for pain and suffering damages due to the stress she was under as a result of her dismissal. She reported that her stress-related health problems (i.e., lupus and migraine headaches) were primarily due to the university's decision. Her attorney sought to have a psychological evaluation conducted to demonstrate the level of stress she was under. The university also sought an evaluation from another psychologist to demonstrate that the university did not impose undue stress, and in fact, her health problems were a result of Betty's own preexisting emotional instability. The psychologists conducted independent evaluations and presented their results and conclusions to the court.

among certain populations. New subspecialties regularly emerge reflecting psychology's growing and changing evolution. While some specialties have specific professional organizations and standards for training and service, others are so new that these structures are not yet in place.

The Big Picture

Clinical psychology has grown and evolved to the point where subspecialties are necessary and commonplace. Subspecialty areas encompass work in many diverse settings dealing with many diverse problems. Psychology has proved to offer useful services to the legal, medical, psychiatric, and other communities. Paradoxically, the recent proliferation of managed health care has resulted in an emphasis on general and family medical practitioners (primary care providers) rather than specialists. Thus far, this has not been the case of clinical psychology where specialization is the zeitgeist. What had once been viewed as the wave of the future is now very much realized in the current practice. Specialization has proven both viable and valuable, and will likely result in the growth of new specialties as our tools and knowledge base increase regarding specific populations, disorders, and systems. Advances in medical and computer technology as well as new problems may result in psychologists specializing in areas such as infertility, multicultural issues, computer assessment, and other areas yet to emerge in contemporary society. Although the future contemporary clinical psychologist will likely need highly specialized skills in one or several areas of focus, solid basic clinical skills will always be needed regardless of specialization.

Key Points

1. Some of the most popular specialty areas in clinical psychology include health psychology, child psychology, neuropsychology, and forensic psychology. Subspecialty areas have also emerged, such as pediatric neuropsychology. Within each specialty area many psychologists focus their research and/or practice on a particular population or problem area.

2. Health psychologists work in numerous and diverse settings including hospitals, clinics, universities, businesses, government agencies, and private practices. They use the principles of psychology and behavior change to help people cope better with medical illnesses as well as prevent potential illnesses from developing or from getting worse. They conduct research on the relationships between behavior and health and consult with organizations to maximize health-promoting behavior and policies while minimizing health damaging behavior and policies.

3. Common problems of interest to health psychologists include smoking, obesity, alcohol consumption, stress management, AIDS, and chronic pain.

4. Child clinical psychologists commonly work in community mental health clinics, child guidance clinics, schools, children's hospitals, universities, and in private practices. Some of the common problem areas of interest include physical and/or sexual abuse, attention deficit hyperactivity disorder, conduct disorders, autism, enuresis (bed wetting), encopresis (soiling), and school phobia.

5. Pediatric psychology is a blend of child clinical psychology and health psychology. Pediatric psychologists are child clinical psychologists who generally work with children and families in hospital settings where the child has a significant medical disorder. These medical problems might include cancer, epilepsy, diabetes, or cystic fibrosis. The pediatric psychologist might offer pain management strategies to children or help the family cope more effectively with understanding and assisting a child having significant medical problems. They may help the child and family cope with painful medical procedures or assist the family and hospital staff with noncompliance with medical treatment.

6. Clinical neuropsychology focuses on brain-behavior relationships. These are defined as how brain functioning impacts behavior and behavior problems. Clinical neuropsychologists assess brain and behavior functioning and offer strategies for patients suffering from brain impairment due to problems such as dementia, head injuries, tumors, stroke, AIDS, Alzheimer's Disease, epilepsy, and other diseases and traumas that result in cognitive and neurological dysfunction.

7. Forensic psychology involves the application of psychology to legal issues. Forensic psychologists may conduct psychological evaluations with defendants and present their findings as an expert witness in court. They may also provide evaluations for child custody arrangements, or be asked to predict dangerousness or determine if an individual is competent to stand trial. They may be asked to participate in worker's compensation claims, or serve as a consultant to attorneys who are selecting a jury.

8. While forensic psychologists are involved in numerous aspects of the legal system, they may be best known for their work in legal cases involving involuntary commit-ment, the insanity defense, child custody, and jury se-lection.

9. In addition to health, child, neuropsychology, and forensics, there are a number of other subspecialties in clinical psychology. New subspecialties regularly emerge reflecting psychology's growing and changing evolu-tion.

Key Terms

Acquired Immune Deficiency (AIDS)

Alcohol Consumption

Alzheimer's Disease

Anorexia Nervosa

Attention Deficit Hyperactivity Disorder (ADHD)

Brain-Behavior Relationships

Brain Injuries

Child Abuse and Neglect

Child Clinical Psychology

Child Custody

Chronic Pain

Degenerative Diseases

Dementia

Durham Rule

Dyslexia

Epilepsy

Health Psychology

Insanity Defense

Insanity Defense Reform Act

Involuntary Commitment

Joint Custody

Jury Selection

Learning Disorders

M'Naghten Rule

Malingering

Neuropsychology

Obesity

Pseudoseizures

Seizures

Smoking

Stress Management

For Reflection

1. What are some advantages and disadvantages of hav-ing subspecialties in clinical psychology?

2. How might the subspecialties overlap?

3. What types of problems are of interest to those who specialize in clinical health psychology?

4. What types of problems are of interest to those who specialize in child clinical psychology?

5. What types of problems are of interest to those who specialize in neuropsychology?

6. What types of problems are of interest to those who specialize in forensic psychology?

7. Speculate about possible future subspecialties in clini-cal psychology.

CHAPTER 12

Consultative, Teaching, and Administrative Roles in Contemporary Clinical Psychology

Chapter Outline

Highlight of a Contemporary Clinical Psychologist:
   Julie B. (Sincoff) Jampel, Ph.D.

Consultation

Teaching

Administration

HIGHLIGHT OF A CONTEMPORARY CLINICAL PSYCHOLOGIST:

Julie B. (Sincoff) Jampel, Ph.D.

Dr. Jampel uses her skills as a clinical psychologist to counsel students at a university counseling center.

Birth Date: December 1, 1961

College: Harvard University (B.A., Psychology and Social Relations, 1984)

Graduate Program: Yale University (Ph.D., Clinical and Developmental Psychology, 1990)

Clinical Internship: Veterans Administration Medical Center, West Haven, CT, 1989–1990

Postdoctoral Fellowship: Harvard University Health Services, Mental Health Service, 1990–1991

Current Job: Staff Psychologist, Counseling Center, Tufts University, Medford, MA
Lecturer on Psychology, Department of Psychiatry, The Cambridge Hospital, Harvard University School of Medicine

Pros and cons of being a clinical psychologist:

Pros: (1) Being part of the larger field of psychology with its very interesting theories and research.
(2) Performing rewarding work that is challenging and stimulating and that affords an opportunity to get to know a broad range of people.
(3) Having opportunities to observe the whole range of human functioning, including resilience and strength as well as vulnerability.

Cons: (1) At times the work is depressing and demoralizing.
(2) Job opportunities and salaries in some settings may be poor.

Future of clinical psychology: "Although the outlook is dimmer now than previously, clinical psychology will continue to survive and evolve. Clinical psychologists' contributions to health care (e.g., behavioral medicine, pediatric psychology, health psychology, neuropsychology) and to the workplace (organizational consulting, employee assistance programs) may offer the most opportunities in the foreseeable future."

Typical schedule:

9:00   Therapy session with a college student coping with a history of sexual abuse.

10:00   Therapy session with a graduate student from South America who feels alienated.

11:00   Supervise a therapist-in-training regarding the uses and misuses of neutrality and self-disclosure with clients.

12:00   Lunch.

1:00   Intake meeting to discuss Counseling Center clients' disposition.

2:00   Therapy session with a college student

struggling with a learning disability and confusion regarding sexual orientation.

3:00 Supervise a therapist-in-training who is anxious about a suicidal client.

4:00 Therapy session with a graduate student suffering from bipolar disorder.

5:00 Private therapy session with an adult who feels stuck in an unhappy marriage and meaningless job.

Furthermore, participating in case conferences and staff meetings and leading seminars for therapists-in-training are typical weekly activities.

Drs. A, B, and C are all clinical psychologists. Dr. A is a professor at a large university and teaches courses in Abnormal Psychology, Psychological Testing, and Clinical Psychology. Dr. B directs mental health services for a child guidance clinic, overseeing 30 mental health clinicians and managing a multimillion dollar annual budget. Dr. C is a consultant to a law firm and provides advice about stress management, employee relations, ethics, and other matters involving human behavior. Drs. A, B, and C may or may not engage in the traditional clinical psychology activities discussed earlier such as research, psychological testing, or psychotherapy. They may not work with any patients at all. Yet their professional roles and activities are typical of what many clinical psychologists do for a living.

In addition to research, assessment, and psychotherapy, clinical psychologists often spend a significant amount of time involved in other professional activities. Consultation, teaching, and administration are three common professional services offered by clinical psychologists. In a recent survey of over 14,000 practitioner members of the American Psychological Association, psychologists reported spending 11 percent of their time in teaching, 9 percent in administration, and 6 percent in consultation (Phelps, 1996). These activities are not necessarily separate or distinct. Psychologists may both teach and consult in addition to conducting psychotherapy, psychological testing or research. Therefore, a high degree of overlap may exist among these professional activities. The purpose of this chapter is to discuss the consultation, teaching, and administration activities of clinical psychologists.

Consultation

Clinical psychologists are experts in human behavior. They study, research, and treat a wide range of problems and people who are distressed by prob-lematic feelings, thoughts, and behaviors. Psychologists are knowledgeable about theories and principles of human behavior. This expertise can be used to help many individuals, families, groups, and institutions (Fig. 12.1). Clinical psychologists are often asked to consult with others to assist in solving problems in diverse settings. Almost all clinical psychologists participate in some form of professional consultation. Psychologists not only provide consultation but regularly receive consultation from others. Consultation is an integral part of their professional work. Consultation may be provided to other mental health professionals; to organizations, groups, and individuals; and to the general public. Examples of consultation questions in various settings are provided in Table 12.1.

Consultation Defined

Consultation in clinical psychology refers to the application of knowledge and theories of human behavior to specific questions and problems in various community settings such as hospitals, clinics, schools, businesses, and government agencies. Consultation involves offering professional advice to others concerning problems that exist in their setting. Consultation usually involves the participation of a *consultant* with specialized knowledge and skill and a *consultee* or client who benefits from the expertise of the consultant. Unlike one-to-one psychotherapy, a consultant has the opportunity to assist large groups of people and entire organizations through his or her work with a consultee. Wallace and Hall (1996) defined consultation as "a broad helping approach in which qualified psychological consultants help consultees (1) resolve work-related issues pertaining to individuals, clients or programs that they are responsible for, (2) become active agents in achieving solutions to problems, or (3) strengthen consultees' work-related competencies to address similar issues in the future" (p. 10).

Figure 12.1 Psychologists often engage in informal consultation with colleagues.

Consultation might be thought of in terms of the popular phrase, "Two (or more) heads are better than one," especially where one possesses special expertise.

Consultation has become more widely practiced in recent years, with consultation skills more commonly taught to clinical psychology students and professionals (Brown, 1985; Clayton & Bongar, 1994; Conyne & O'Neal, 1992; Wallace & Hall, 1996). In fact, a national survey of psychologists revealed that 71.5 percent agreed that regular consultation is a good or excellent way to obtain information and provide competent professional service (Pope, Tabachnick, & Keith-Spiegel, 1987). Furthermore, the Clayton and Bonger (1994) review of consultation literature reported that consultation activities by psychologists significantly improve quality of care, client satisfaction, and treatment outcome.

Consultation Roles

Consultants may assume many different roles during the course of consultation or between consultation assignments. Lippitt and Lippitt (1986) suggested that the role of consultant is based on a continuum between being directive and being indirective. Consultants in a directive role are generally viewed as offering expert and technical consultation. They help consultees solve problems through their knowledge about issues of interest to the consultees. For example, a consultant may be highly knowledgeable about computer software that keeps track of patients' files. A clinic may hire the consultant to assist in purchasing the software and teaching employees to use it effectively. Nondirective consultants use their skills and expertise to facilitate the consultee's skills. For example, a consultant may be hired to help managers of a company do a better job at interacting with employees who will be "downsized." Managers with the difficult and often painful job of informing employees that their position will be eliminated often need assistance in learning how both to complete this task sensitively and to cope with the employees' distress. The nondirective consultant might conduct role plays and critique the performance to help managers practice this difficult task. Directive consultation generally is task oriented (the consultants provide expert assistance in solving problems), whereas the nondirective approach is process oriented or facilitative (Matthews, 1983). The directive approach generally focuses more on results, while the nondirective approach usually focuses on process or growth (Champion, Kiel, & McLendon, 1990).

Dougherty (1995) defined the following six common consultation roles for clinical psychologists: expert, trainer/educator, advocate, collaborator, fact finder, and process specialist. The

Table 12.1 Examples of Consultation Questions by Setting

Hospital

1. Physicians and nurses on a cardiology unit are wondering how to assist patients in losing weight and exercising after they leave the hospital.
2. Physicians and nurses on a pediatric unit request help in developing a program to minimize adolescents from being sexually involved with other patients on the unit.
3. Physicians and nurses are concerned about how to help dialysis patients cope with feelings of anxiety and depression.

School

1. Teachers in a sixth grade class are concerned about how to best deal with conflicts between the boys and girls in class.
2. Teachers in a third grade class are unsure how to handle the disruptive behavior of a child with an attention deficit disorder.
3. Teachers in a high school are anxious and angry about parents who seem too demanding and entitled. They wonder how to best deal with parents who want too much from them.
4. A school principle seeks guidance about how to best deal with a teacher who openly challenges her during faculty meetings.

Business

1. An employer is concerned about stress associated with numerous layoffs and wonders how he can help his employees best deal with work stress.
2. A small company is unproductive and inefficient due to numerous personality conflicts in the office. The company president hopes that a psychologist can help to figure out ways to help his employees get along better.
3. A company is concerned about a company vice-president who was recently hospitalized with a bipolar illness. The company is unsure how to understand and manage this person once they return to work.
4. A company is interested in hiring employees, especially in selecting employees who are likely to be excellent workers.

Government

1. A police department is interested in helping officers deal with the stress of witnessing and sometimes being the victim of violent crime.
2. A fire department is interested in having a psychologist consult about screening job applicants.
3. A juvenile court system is interested in finding ways to prevent juvenile offenders from repeating their offenses once released.
4. A judge is interested in obtaining consultation regarding child custody evaluations.

expert consultation role is the most common one (Gallessich, 1982). The expert consultant is a technological advisor (Dougherty, 1995) who has the specialized skills, knowledge, or experience that the consultee needs to help solve a problem. For instance, an expert consultant may have special skills in conducting intelligence testing for children applying to a school system's gifted and talented program (GATE). The school hires the consultant to help them understand what the test scores mean and determine how best to screen applicants for the program.

Somewhat similar to the expert role, consultants are often asked to act as trainer/educators. Formal training may occur in workshops, seminars, and classes on a variety of topics. Informal training may occur in one-to-one training sessions with employees or clients. The **trainer/educator** role, like the expert role, assumes that the consultant has specialized information that is useful to the client and can be acquired through education. For example, a consultant may be asked to train employees of a company to manage stress better through the use of relaxation techniques. A trainer/educator consultant may teach day care workers about child illnesses or patterns of physical abuse through several workshop sessions. A consultant who is knowledgeable about domestic violence may also train police officers to recognize the signs and symptoms of this problem.

The **advocate** consultant seeks to convince a consultee to do something that the consultant believes is desirable. Consultants can act as advocates in a wide variety of ways (Kurpius & Lewis, 1988). For example, a consultant to a mental health clinic may advocate for the rights of severely disabled patients who have difficulty advocating for themselves. A consultant hired to participate in a school meeting to discuss an Individual Education Plan (IEP) might advocate for the provision of special education services for a learning disabled child. An advocate consultant may help ensure that a physically disabled child or adult receives access to facilities and maintains optimal independence.

The **collaborator** consultant role suggests that the consultant is an equal partner working with a consultee to achieve a common goal. Both the consultant and consultee stand to benefit from their collaboration. For example, if a researcher is interested in learning more about the effect of exercise in the treatment of depression and knows a great deal about exercise but little about depression, he or she may decide to work with a collaborating consultant who is an expert on depression. As another example, an individual psychotherapist and a group psychotherapist treating the same patient might collaborate in order to coordinate their two psychotherapies and to learn more about the patient's progress in each treatment modality.

The **fact finder** consultation role involves seeking information and relaying the results to consultees who lack the expertise, time, energy, or psychological sensitivities to do the task themselves (Lippitt & Lippitt, 1986; Dougherty, 1995). For instance, a psychologist may be interested in buying a new computer for his research laboratory. He may hire a fact finding consultant who is highly knowledgeable about the use of computers in research to locate an appropriate computer at a reasonable price. Or a company concerned about poor morale might hire an outside fact-finding consultant to investigate the causes of the problem.

Finally, the role of the **process-specialist** consultant is to help the consultee better understand the process of events that might cause problems (Schein, 1988). For example, a clinic manager dissatisfied with how staff meetings are run might hire a process-specialist consultant to observe the meetings and suggest ways to improve communication and staff participation. Consultants thus can assume many different roles or perform several roles during the same consultation experience.

Types of Consultation

Mental Health Consultation   Several types of consultation are typically conducted by clinical psychologists in mental health settings. These include (1) informal peer group consultation, (2) client-centered case consultation, (3) program-centered administrative consultation, (4) consultee-centered case consultation, and (5) consultee-centered administrative consultation (Caplan, 1970; Caplan & Caplan, 1993; Greenblatt, 1985).

Informal peer group consultation is the most widely used and valued method of consultation in psychology (Allen, Nelson, & Sheckley, 1987; Cranston et al., 1988). It involves asking coworkers to consult on a challenging clinical case informally during lunch or other work breaks. For example, a psychologist may struggle with the treatment of a difficult patient where treatment seems stuck. The psychologist may believe that process has stopped and wonders how he or she might best alter the treatment plan to best assist the patient. The psychologist might asked a colleague to discuss the case with him or her in order to develop insight into better treatment strategies.

Client-centered case consultation involves consultation with a fellow professional such as another psychologist who is responsible for the treatment or care of a particular patient. The professional seeks the advice of the consultant in order to meet the specific needs of the patient more adequately. Both consultee and consultant have some responsibility for the care of the patient.

Program-centered administrative consultation focuses on a program or system rather than on an individual case. The consultation may involve an important aspect of the functioning of a clinic, practice, research program, or other more global issue. For example, a psychologist might seek consultation about the curriculum, structure, and advertising strategy of group psychotherapy programs for patients. Or the consultation might concern how best to conduct intake interviews and assign patients to therapists in a large community mental health clinic.

The focus of **consultee-centered case consultation** is on challenges experienced by the consultee rather than on problems concerning an individual case or client. Inexperience, lack of information, and mistakes made by the consultee are often the topic of discussion. For instance, a graduate student in psychology may seek consultation from an experienced supervisor about discomfort and anxiety experienced when conducting psychotherapy with patients who are older than the student.

Finally, **consultee-centered administrative consultation** generally involves working on administrative and personnel issues within an agency. For example, an outpatient clinic board of directors may wish to consult with a psychologist about problems in the leadership performance of their executive director.

Organizational Consultation   Clinical psychologists also frequently provide consultation to an enormous range of nonmental health agencies and organizations. Businesses, nonprofit agencies, and government organizations all employ people who must work cooperatively to achieve a common purpose and keep the organization running effectively and smoothly (Hanna, 1988). As experts in human behavior, psychologists can offer useful advice on dealing with the interpersonal and organizational problems and conflicts that inevitably arise in organizational life.

Organizational consultation generally uses systems theory to understand and intervene in organizations (Hanna, 1988; Kurpius, 1985). As discussed earlier in this book, systems theory proposes that all aspects of a system (whether a family or a professional organization) interact and react to changes and behavior in each element of the system. Each element or subsystem within the large organizational structure is dependent on other elements or subsystems, therefore changes that occur at one level will usually influence changes at other levels (Fuqua & Kurpius, 1993). For example, suppose that one division of a company is losing a great deal of money, has experienced several major failures, and has a leader perceived by most employees as incompetent. The division is unable to maintain employee loyalty and morale, and most of the employees are looking for work elsewhere. Systems theory would predict that the problems within this division are likely to impact the entire company. Losses by the division may need to be compensated for by other more productive and successful divisions within the company. The successful divisions are likely to feel resentful for having to bail out a failing division. As a result, morale will probably decline in the successful divisions. Consultants to organiza-

tions must use systems theory to diagnose organizational problems and provide interventions. They know that tinkering with one aspect of an organization will probably have ripple effects on other parts of the organization, and must be mindful of the entire system when intervening.

Stages of Consultation

Many of the stages that have been used to describe the psychotherapy process apply to consultation as well. These include (1) understanding the question, (2) assessment, (3) intervention, (4) termination, and (5) follow up.

Understanding the Question   First the consultant must size up the situation in order to understand the nature of the referral question and the goals of the consultation. The consultant must determine whether he or she has the training, experience, and expertise to provide a competent and professional consultation. Frequently, the initial question posed by the person(s) seeking consultation changes during the course of the consultation. For example, a personnel director of a company may ask a psychologist to consult on stress management techniques for employees of her company. She tells the psychologist that downsizing and layoffs have resulted in a high degree of stress. She wants the psychologist to offer stress management workshops for small groups of employees as well as individual sessions for those interested in specialized one-on-one help. However, during the initial consultation it becomes clear to the psychologist (and the personnel director) that the management of the company has been ineffective and must be altered to reduce employee stress. Organizational management issues are much more salient than initially thought. The personnel director then decides that dealing with management issues should occur prior to offering the stress management workshops initially requested. Thus, psychologists who act as consultants must fully investigate the nature of the referral questions, knowing that the initial request may not be what is really needed. The consultant must also determine the fit between the needs of the consultee and his or her own expertise.

Sometimes before agreeing to be hired, a consultant must determine whether the organization requesting the consultation is actually ready for the experience. Paradoxically, an organization that initiates contact with a consultant and requests needed help may be resistant to change, to feedback, or to the results of the consultation. An organization's readiness for and openness to consultation are sometimes more important to the success of the consultation project than are the consultant's assessment and intervention. (Beer & Spector, 1993).

Assessment Once the appropriate questions are understood psychologists hired as consultants need to assess the situation fully before offering intervention or advice. The assessment phase usually includes interviews and may also include formal psychological testing and/or review of records or other data. Ideally, the consultant should enter the organizational system "gaining acceptance and approval from consultees and other constituents" (Wallace & Hall, 1996, p. 29). However, the consultees may not trust the consultant if he or she appears to have personality traits, attitudes, or strategies that they view as negative. Even those who are in favor of obtaining help may be resistant and have an agenda concerning the consultant's findings. The consultant must assess the customs, beliefs, rules, and general climate of the organization as well as attempt to develop a trusting relationship with the consultees prior to offering advice (Conoley & Conoley, 1982).

Interviewing is the most common method of conducting a consultation assessment (Molyneaux & Lane, 1982). The consultant may choose to use either structured and standardized interviews or unstructured, conversational, and nonstandardized interviews. The consultant asks questions of relevant people involved with the organization. For example, a researcher may wish to consult with a psychologist on measures to assess depression for a particular study. The consultant interviews the researcher about the goals and design of the study. Once the consultant has a solid understanding of the needs of the researcher, he or she will be able to suggest relevant measures of depression. Or, as another example, suppose the recent reorganization of a small company has proved challenging and stressful for most employees. A psychologist consultant is asked to evaluate the reorganization process and to suggest how best to deal with the associated stress. The psychologist interviews first the company's management team and then each of the key employees. The series of comprehensive interviews enables the

psychologist to assess the problem(s) before offering intervention strategies and advice.

Surveys and questionnaires are a second common method of assessment in consultation. Surveys allow large amounts of information to be collected efficiently and confidentially (Wallace & Hall, 1996). Direct observation is another approach to assessment in consultation (Dougherty, 1990). A consultant may informally observe an organization, sit in on meetings, and/or watch key people work and interact.

Once a comprehensive assessment is complete, the consultant develops a diagnostic impression of the problem(s) and outlines goals for intervention (Wallace & Hall, 1996). The goals should be specific, realistic, measurable, and based on collaboration between consultant and consultees (Wallace & Hall, 1996).

Intervention After the assessment phase, in which the consultant diagnoses a particular problem and sets consultation goals, the consultant can develop an intervention strategy or a response to the consultee's questions and problems. Intervention is the stage when the consultant provides the actual advice or suggestions for change. It is also the stage when implementation occurs. Intervention is what the person(s) seeking consultation hopes to get from the consultant. For instance, a physician may ask a psychologist to consult on a case that he or she is treating: patient with sleep apnea and obesity is not being compliant with the doctor's treatment suggestions. The physician is frustrated and concerned because, without cooperation in her medical treatment, the patient is in jeopardy of dying. The consulting psychologist interviews the physician, the patient, and the patient's spouse and determines that she is highly depressed and wishes to die. The consultant suggests ways for the physician to treat the patient's depression, encourage psychotherapy, and manage the emotional factors affecting her illness.

Consultation intervention may include either individual intervention as in the previous example or group interventions such as training, conflict resolution, or team building (Wallace & Hall, 1996). Implementing the intervention (e.g., team building and training) is usually the responsibility of the consultee, with guidance from the consultant (Caplan, 1970; Dougherty, 1990).

Once an intervention is implemented, an evaluation is typically conducted to determine whether the intervention has been beneficial. Scriven (1967) classifies consultation evaluations as either formative or summative. Formative evaluations examine the process of consultation from start to finish. Each stage of the process is evaluated carefully. Summative evaluations highlight the consultation outcome. They assess whether the goals and objectives of the consultation were adequately reached.

Termination After the goals of the consultation agreements have been met, or if the consultant determines that the goals cannot be achieved, then the termination phase of the consultation occurs (Kurpius, Fuqua, & Rozecki, 1993). Unfortunately, the consultation relationship may be terminated without thoughtful or appropriate consideration. Many authors suggest that careful attention be given to the termination phase to correct this problem (Dustin & Ehly, 1984; Hansen, Himes, & Meier, 1990; Kurpius et al., 1993). For example, Dustin and Ehly (1984) recommend conducting an exit interview at termination. The purpose of the exit interview is to enable the consultant and consultee(s) to discuss the consultation process, share feedback about the experience and intervention, resolve any residual issues, plan for follow-up if appropriate, and obtain closure for all participants.

Follow Up Interventions and advice provided by the consultant may or may not be used. The advice may not be what the consultee wanted to hear, the intervention plans may not be realistic, or they may be too difficult to implement. The consultee may have lost interest in the problems because of new crises that emerged after the initiation or termination of the consultation. Follow-up frequently maximizes the consultee's benefit from the consultation efforts. For example, the previously mentioned patient with sleep apnea may be treated for depression in addition to her sleep apnea, and obesity in accordance with the recommendations of the consultant. However, family conflicts emerge that threaten the progress she has made. Follow-up consultation may prove useful in dealing with these new family concerns so that the therapeutic process can move forward. As another example, a consultant may offer stress management workshops for employees at a company that is undergoing layoffs and organiza-

tional restructuring. Although the workshops may be well received, old patterns of behavior may reemerge and good intentions may fade, causing the intervention to fail several weeks after completion of the workshops. Because behavior and habits are often difficult to change, periodic follow-up sessions or ongoing programs may be needed to maintain new patterns. The sessions may be scheduled during the intervention or termination phase or on an as-needed basis. Many consultants routinely provide follow-up in person, over the telephone, or by letter (Wallace & Hall, 1996).

To Whom Do Clinical Psychologists Offer Consultation?

Consultation to Other Mental Health Professionals Clinical psychologists frequently provide advice and consultation to their peers (Clayton & Bongar, 1994). They may develop a high degree of expertise in a certain area less familiar to other professionals. For instance, a psychologist may be especially skilled in working with children who experience attention deficit hyperactivity disorder (ADHD). Because many different life events and situations may contribute to the impulsive and behavioral overactivity usually associated with ADHD (e.g., physical or sexual abuse, parental neglect, marital discord or divorce, learning disabilities), the diagnosis and treatment of ADHD is complex and should be conducted by specialists. A social worker, psychiatrist, marriage counselor, or fellow psychologist without a high level of expertise in this area may choose to ask another professional with these skills to consult on a given case. The consultant would determine what specific questions or issues need to be addressed (e.g., diagnosis, treatment recommendations) and perhaps meet with the family and child for an assessment. The consultant may offer advice about tests to use or may review testing and interview data to assist in making an appropriate diagnosis.

Psychologists may also consult with a colleague about a patient they treat in psychotherapy when they are unsure how best to handle a particular therapeutic situation. Discussing a case with an objective and unbiased colleague is often very useful. For example, a psychologist may feel frustrated in conducting psychotherapy with a patient who is angry and hostile. The patient experiences a borderline personality disorder, major depression, and chronic low back pain. She frequently expresses anger, resentment, and even rage. During one of her therapy sessions the patient states that she has an urge to strangle the therapist. Furthermore, the patient has access to weapons, and the therapist is concerned that she may show up at a session with a gun. The psychologist tries to be understanding and helpful but feels angry, resentful, and fearful. The psychologist consults with a colleague to discuss the case and obtain advice on how to proceed in the best interest of the patient. The consultant listens carefully to the situation, asking questions of the therapist. They talk about strategies and options for treatment that the therapist can try to incorporate into the treatment sessions as well as discussing the therapist's feelings and reactions. They decide to meet several times to see how the therapy progresses, and the consultant offers follow-up advice.

Psychologists may also seek consultation when conducting psychological evaluations or testing. Some of the data obtained through an evaluation may be difficult to interpret or may conflict with data from other sources (e.g., interview, physician's report, teacher's report). The psychologist conducting the evaluation may seek a second opinion by asking a colleague to consult on the case and review the testing materials. For instance, a psychologist may be asked to conduct an evaluation of a child who does very poorly on school examinations. The child's teachers and parents all feel that the child is very bright and maintains good study skills. They wonder whether the child is overanxious about tests or perhaps has a learning disability that impairs testing performance. The psychologist interviews the parents, several teachers, and the child, and then administered intellectual, educational, and psychological tests to the child. However, the testing data seem somewhat contradictory, and it is unclear what the results actually mean. The psychologist decides to consult with an expert colleague who can review the data, offer an opinion about diagnosis, and suggest treatment plans. The consulting psychologist reviews the testing data and interviews the clinician. The consultant may also decide to interview the family and/or child as well.

Psychologists conducting research also frequently consult with colleagues. A psychologist may seek the consultation of another to assist in interpreting research data, designing appropriate experiments, and determining which specialized equipment to use, or for help in other research questions. For example, a psychologist may be conducting experiments on the psychological benefits of exercise among anxious and depressed patients. She would like to have the patients exercise in a laboratory to determine how much exercise is needed to elevate mood. Unsure of what equipment to use and how intense the exercise sessions should be, she consults with several colleagues who are experts in this field for advice and guidance. The consultants also might provide useful journal articles or other reading materials or invite the psychologist to tour their laboratory to observe their testing and research protocols.

Consultation with Nonmental Health Professionals In addition to consultation with colleagues, many psychologists consult with professionals from other disciplines as well as with individual patients. Clinical psychologists frequently consult with school teachers and administrators, physicians and nurses, attorneys and judges, clergy, the military, and people working in business and industry. The number of potential areas and issues requiring consultation on human behavior is countless. Consultation is so popular that several companies specialize in providing psychological consultation to people in business and industry.

Psychologists also consult with medical personnel (e.g., physicians, nurses, physical therapists, nutritionists) concerning patient care (Miller & Swartz, 1990; McDaniel, 1995; Pillay, 1990). Medical personnel often seek consultation from psychologists and other mental health professionals in order to assist patients experiencing a wide variety of medical problems. Many medical patients need assistance in coping with anxiety or depression associated with their own illness or illness in the family. Others may need assistance in changing their lifestyles to better accommodate their illness or cope more effectively with their medical problems. Still others need help complying with medical instructions to care more appropriately for their needs. In fact, many hospitals offer a consultation-liaison (C&L) service so that psychological consultation can be made available to every medical department at all times. For instance, patients recovering from a heart attack, obtaining dialysis for kidney failure, or receiving radiation/chemotherapy for cancer are

Case Studies: Consultations with Mental Health Colleagues

Dr. A is treating a young Caucasian woman with bulimia. During the course of several months of treatment, the woman inquires about the use of hypnosis as a possible adjunct to treatment. Since Dr. A is unfamiliar with the technique, he suggests that the patient consult with a colleague, Dr. B, who specializes in hypnotic techniques. After discussing the issue with Dr. A, the patient decides to consult with Dr. B. The patient signs a release to allow Dr. A and Dr. B to discuss her case and coordinate treatment. Dr. A continues to provide weekly individual psychotherapy sessions, while Dr. B schedules several hypnotherapy sessions.

Dr. C works in the consultation-liaison service of a large university teaching hospital. The attending psychiatrist on the geropsychiatric unit asks Dr. C for a consultation regarding a 72-year-old African-Amrican female patient who reports feeling severely depressed. The patient has had several trials of antidepressant medication and yet appears disoriented and reports no symptom relief. The psychiatrist

on the unit is considering electroconvulsive therapy (ECT) as a last resort. Prior to administering the ECT treatment, the psychiatrist would like Dr. C to conduct an evaluation and consultation to determine what other personality or neuropsychological factors play a role in her reported symptoms. Dr. C meets with the patient and psychiatrist, conducts an interview, and administers a battery of psychological tests. Dr. C concludes that the patient experiences a senile dementia in addition to depression. Based on Dr. C's findings, the psychiatrist chooses not to administer ECT and further compromise her cognitive functioning.

Dr. D is interested in conducting a research project on the coping responses and strategies of Salvadoran immigrants to the United States. Dr. D decides to consult with his colleague, Dr. E who is a native Salvadoran and psychologist. Dr. E helps Dr. D in securing access to the population of immigrants, translates questionnaires into Spanish, and helps Dr. D better understand the Salvadoran culture to improve his research study.

---

often fearful and depressed. Consultation with a psychologist may assist these patients in coping more effectively with their treatment, diagnosis, feelings, and post-hospital adjustment. Many medical patients engage in health-damaging behavior such as eating too many high fat foods, drinking too much alcohol, smoking cigarettes, and refusing to practice safe sex or wear seat belts. Changing these and other destructive behaviors to improve health and cope more effectively with illness is remarkably difficult. In fact, about 50 percent of all deaths are considered to be caused by lifestyle factors (Center for Disease Control, 1980; Taylor, 1995).

Psychologists frequently consult with teachers and school personnel in day care centers, preschools, elementary schools, secondary schools, and/or special education schools. For instance, a psychologist may consult with a teacher about ways to manage the disruptive classroom behavior of a child. The psychologist might evaluate the child and family, observe the child in the classroom setting, and meet periodically with the teacher to help him or her interact more effectively with the child and class. A school principal may consult with a psychologist about how best to handle requests by parents and students for untimed tests for students with

learning disabilities. Or a psychologist may be requested to consult with a day care center to assist the staff in coping with children who have been victims of sexual abuse.

Many psychologists work regularly with the legal system and consult with attorneys and judges on various cases. For example, psychologists often act as expert witnesses and consultants in child custody cases. Parents who are going through divorce may each seek sole custody of a child or several children. When divorces are bitter and the couple experiences a high degree of conflict, their children may become the battleground for their conflict. The parents may be unable to agree on child placement, child rearing strategies, or anything else pertaining to their children. The psychologist may be asked to evaluate each parent and the child and offer their expert opinion concerning child custody placement. Psychologists are often consultants in criminal cases as well. When a criminal defendant is attempting to use an insanity defense, the psychologist might be asked to conduct an evaluation and consultation, then provide expert opinion to the court about the diagnosis and mental status of the accused.

Psychologists often consult with the clergy as well (Pargament, Falgout, Ensing, Reilly, et al., 1991; Plante, 1996). For example, a clergy member may wish to learn more about how to handle difficult parishioners or best help those suffering from mental illness when they ask for pastoral counseling and advice. Clergy may seek guidance and consultation on the selection process for clergy applicants or for better ways to conduct group sessions during retreats and other group activities.

Psychologists are frequently asked to consult with business personnel from many different industries regarding employee relations, selection, stress management, morale boosting, and so on (Tobias, 1990). For example, many police and fire departments are concerned about helping their employees deal more effectively with the stress associated with their jobs. Psychologists may be asked to consult on individual cases and on developing programs and procedures to help these individuals cope better. They may also be asked to consult on the selection and training of new police and fire recruits.

Effective Consultation

A number of skills are needed to be an effective consultant. Most researchers and practitioners of consultation highlight the primary importance of competent interpersonal and communication skills (Conoley & Conoley, 1992; Dougherty, 1995; Lippitt & Lippitt, 1986). However, excellent group and problem-solving skills (Dougherty, 1995; Schindler-Rainman, 1985), the ability to work with organizations (Schein, 1988), and highly developed professional and ethical behavior (Corey, Corey, & Callanan, 1993) are also imperative. Dougherty (1995) offered consultants a detailed list of skills necessary for effective consultation. Briefly, these include empathy, genuineness, social skills, and ease in working with others. Consultants must be able to create a comfortable, trusting, collaborative environment with consultees. They must be effective

---

Case Studies: Consultation with Nonmental Health Professionals

Dr. F is called by an oncology (cancer specialist) physician treating a 36-year-old Caucasian woman for advanced breast cancer. The physician has been working with the woman for many years regarding her medical problems. Recently she has refused chemotherapy and has failed to undergo scheduled diagnostic tests. Concerned that she might die prematurely, the physician asks Dr. F to consult on the case. Dr. F meets with the patient, her family, and the physician, and determines that the patient is highly depressed and suicidal. Apparently she hopes that she can hasten her death by terminating necessary medical treatment. Dr. F suggests both individual and family psychotherapy, a psychiatric consultation for antidepressant medication, as well as exploration between the patient and her physician of medical alternatives to aversive chemotherapy.

Dr. G is called by a private school headmaster to consult on a difficult situation. The parents of a Caucasian 13-year-old student attending the school insist on special treatment for their child, personalized attention from the teachers, and generally behave in a highly entitled manner. Furthermore, they are often late in paying for tuition and other bills and always have some excuse for the delay. Several teachers have expressed extreme frustration with the parents and have threatened not to include the student in their classes. The headmaster also feels at a loss as to how best deal with the parents' behavior. After interviewing the principal and several teachers, Dr. G helps them develop clear expectations, limits, and consequences for

behavior and coaches them in dealing more firmly and effectively with the parents. A plan is developed prior to each interaction with the parents, and the psychologist reviews the plan and outcome following each interaction. The review helps to fine-tune future interactions, and significantly decreases the tension between the parents and school personnel.

Dr. H is called by an executive director of a nonprofit organization specializing in the diagnosis and treatment of a racially diverse group of learning-disabled children. The executive director is trained in special education and business. She contacted Dr. H to obtain assistance in developing a treatment-outcome and client-satisfaction program for her agency. Various sources of financial support (e.g., health insurance companies; state and county education contracts; federal, state, and private granting agencies) have requested information regarding treatment outcome and client satisfaction prior to considering funding the agency. Dr. H consults with the executive director and reviews the goals of the program, cultural sensitivity of staff, research design strategies, statistical methods, and specific assessment procedures to evaluate treatment outcome and client satisfaction. Dr. H also meets with several other agency administrators and clinical staff members. Together they develop a comprehensive evaluation program with close consultation with Dr. H. The program is implemented and reviewed periodically by Dr. H in order to troubleshoot problems and improve the program.

listeners. They must be able to ask useful questions, provide feedback and criticism in a diplomatic manner, and both give and receive information as necessary. They must be able to define problems and be skilled at gathering, understanding, and interpreting information relevant to the consultation. Consultants must also be able to assess the working atmosphere or climate and culture of an organization. They must understand group dynamics and group process and be able to manage conflict in group settings. Finally, they must be professional and ethical, maintaining the highest level of competence and integrity.

Challenges in Consultation

Although consultants and consultees may readily agree on the need for and goals of a consultation relationship, several challenges often typically emerge. Resistance to the consultant and to his or her suggestions are very common (Wallace & Hall, 1996). Many consultees have mixed feelings about having an outside expert enter their agency, organization, or work environment to tell them what they are doing wrong and how they should solve their problems. Airing dirty laundry before an outsider and admitting that their problems cannot be solved without consultative help is often difficult and threatening. An internal consultant (someone who already works for the organization) may experience resistance as well. Other employees may resent that one of their own peers has been asked to investigate, diagnose and offer suggestions regarding their problems. Although internal consultants are likely to know the organization and its social climate, culture, politics, power issues, and players much better than outside consultants, they may not be taken as seriously by their peers.

Another common problem in consultation is the concern that all the parties involved may not cooperate. Management executives of a company or agency may make the decision to hire a consultant while several employees may feel that consultation is not needed. Therefore not everyone may agree or cooperate. While some may enthusiastically support the consultant's efforts, others may be resentful and even attempt to sabotage the work. Consultees may have hidden agendas as well

(Wallace & Hall, 1996). For example, a school principal may seek consultation from a psychologist about how to handle a very difficult student who does poorly in class and is a discipline problem. The consultant may suggest removing the student from the school. The principal may have wanted to remove the student all along, but sought validation from a professional consultant in order to convince the student's parents and teachers that the decision was justified. Consultants, being human, may also have their hidden agendas. Some may be more interested in promoting their services, seminars, books, training programs, and careers than in helping consultees with a particular problem (Wallace & Hall, 1996).

Additionally, the consultee's expectations may be unreasonably high. By the time many consultees decide to hire a professional consultant, they may want the person to step into the organization and immediately fix the problems(s) (Conyne & O'Neil, 1992). Developing expectations that are reasonable, realistic, and appropriate, as well as intervention plans that are feasible, represent challenging but essential tasks in all consultation relationships.

Finally, consultants themselves may contribute to problems. They may lack adequate knowledge, skill, experience, self-confidence, or professional objectivity and integrity to be effective (Dougherty, 1995).

Clinical psychology consultants are asked to deal with an endless variety of problems, populations, cultures, and questions. As more and more research and practical experience help to develop our understanding of human nature, consultants on human behavior come to be more in demand. A better understanding of behavior and ways to manage or change behavior in various settings is useful in almost all areas of work. Therefore consultation activities provided by clinical psychologists are likely to increase in the future.

Teaching

As discussed in Chapter 3, psychology has its roots in academics, including both research and teaching activities. **Teaching** activities are a part of the professional duties of many psychologists. Although only 30 percent of clinical psychologists work primarily in academic environments such as colleges, universities, and medical schools (Phelps, 1996), most psychologists participate in some teaching activity even if they primarily work in clinical, administrative, consulting, or other professional roles. Nevertheless, teaching and supervision skills are often not a significant part of graduate school training in clinical psychology (Hoffman, 1990; Russell & Petrie, 1994; Watkins, 1992).

Clinical psychologists frequently teach in a wide variety of settings and to a wide variety of audiences. Teaching may involve formal college classroom instruction, individual supervision of a psychologist-in-training, or lecturing on stress-management techniques to business firms or schools. Teaching may also be incorporated into psychotherapy and psychological testing activities. For instance, a psychologist may teach a patient how to use relaxation techniques to counter stress or teach a couple how to communicate better without blaming their partner in an angry and destructive manner. Psychoeducational approaches involve teaching patients to cope with a wide range of medical and psychiatric problems. For example, support and psychoeducational groups helping patients with diabetes, cancer, irritable bowel syndrome, AIDS, and other illnesses use both teaching and psychotherapy methods. Part of the teaching function may be to review specific coping strategies, inform the participants about new treatment medications or procedures, and provide guest speakers on selected topics of interest.

Teaching in Academic Settings

Psychology Departments   Many clinical psychologists teach in psychology departments in colleges and universities across the country. They teach courses such as Abnormal Psychology, Clinical Psychology, Psychological Testing, Introduction to Psychology, Statistics, and Research Methods, among others. In addition to the ordinary duties of teaching such as classroom lectures and discussions; creating, administering, and scoring exams; and counseling students on academic and educational issues, academic psycologists conduct research and offer service to their department and university. They may teach undergraduates, graduates, and postgraduate students.

In addition to offering courses in psychology, many clinical psychology professors provide individual and/or group supervision of clinical cases treated by advanced graduate or postgraduate students (Russell & Petrie, 1994). They review the assessment, treatment, and consultation activities of students working with clinical patients and offer guidance, support, advice, and ensure quality care regarding clinical methods and interventions. Further details regarding clinical supervision are presented in the section on medical schools and hospitals.

Full-time professors in college settings are usually classified as assistant, associate, or full professors. Although their teaching load and research activities may not differ based on academic rank or title, their status within the university as well as salary are determined, at least in part, by their academic rank. Newly hired faculty are generally given the title, assistant professor. An assistant professor has a probationary status and is often provided with a yearly contract for their services until the probationary period is completed. After approximately six years of service, they apply for promotion to associate professor and for tenure. Tenure provides job security by awarding a permanent job to the professor. Their probationary status is terminated with the awarding of tenure. After generally another six years in the rank of associate professor, the person may apply for full professor. Full professor is a rank usually reserved for professors who have made a significant impact on the profession through both research and teaching activities. Associate professors do not need to apply for full professor to maintain their job. Universities also hire part time instructors who are not eligible for tenure or a more permanent full-time position. These part-time teachers are often called lecturers, instructors, or adjunct professors. These positions are also called nontenure track positions. Although tenure has been a part of academic life for many years, it is controversial in that many people feel that the guarantee of a permanent position might result in some professors spending less time and energy on their academic duties following the awarding of tenure.

Other Academic Departments   In colleges and universities clinical psychologists teach in departments other than psychology such as education, counseling, women's studies, business, law, and medicine, among others. They may teach a wide variety of courses full time or part time in these departments.

Medical Schools and Hospitals Clinical psychologists teach in medical schools and hospitals as well. They may teach seminars to various trainees and staff members including medical students, residents, nurses, psychology interns, and postdoctoral psychology fellows, or they may be guest lecturers at courses, seminars, or department grand rounds. Each medical department generally offers weekly or monthly grand rounds presentations where guest speakers provide a lecture on a topic of interest to members of a particular medical speciality such as psychiatry, pediatrics, oncology, cardiology, or neurology. Ongoing seminars (meeting weekly for several months or longer) may focus on numerous topics in psychology. For example, a seminar may be provided for trainees and/or staff on (1) psychosocial factors in the development, maintenance, and treatment of specific or general illnesses, (2) child development, (3) dealing with medical noncompliance, (4) lifestyle management change, and (5) ethics. Clinical psychologists may teach medical school classes on a host of topics such as health psychology, pediatric psychology, and health behavior change.

Clinical psychologists are often asked to provide individual supervision and instruction to staff and trainees at hospital and medical schools. A nurse, a psychiatry or pediatric resident, or a medical student may regularly meet with a psychologist to discuss cases. Psychology interns, postdoctoral psychology fellows, and graduate students also receive individual supervision on their cases by a consulting psychologist. In this way, psychotherapy, psychological testing, and other psychological intervention skills are taught and supervised using a tutorial model (Hoffman, 1990; Romans, Boswell, Carlozzi, & Ferguson, 1995; Russell & Petrie, 1994). Students meet regularly with a supervisor to closely examine their clinical work. They may audio or videotape sessions in order to review them in detail with the supervising psychologist. Videotaping is the most popular method of conducting supervision sessions (Romans, et al., 1995). Frequently supervision is provided in small groups of 3 to 5 trainees (Riva & Cornish, 1995). Supervision training can be general (i.e., emphasis on basic and global skills) or focused (i.e., emphasis on specific skill development) or a combination of both (Schindler & Talen, 1994). Effective clinical supervisors tend

---

Case Studies: Teaching in Academic Settings

Dr. I maintains a full-time private practice in psychotherapy. She also conducts workshops and provides guest lectures on emotional factors associated with chronic physical illnesses. She specializes in the treatment of both children and adults who experience emotional concerns associated with medical illnesses such as cancer, multiple sclerosis, diabetes, lupus, and heart disease. As a clinical faculty member of a local medical school in the department of psychiatry, she supervises two clinical psychology trainees (an intern and a postdoctoral fellow), providing one hour per week of individual supervision of their psychotherapy treatment cases. Her clinical and supervisory skills are useful in training these professionals. She often listens to audiotapes or watches videotapes of the trainees' work and offers suggestions and guidance about treating patients.

Like Dr. I, Dr. J also is a clinical faculty member of a university medical school in the department of psychia-

try. He is a psychologist who teaches an ethics course to psychology trainees and psychiatry residents on a weekly basis. He meets with a group of 10 students for one hour each week to discuss professional ethics. Students describe the ethical dilemmas they experience, and the group discusses ethical principles of behavior with Dr. J's guidance.

Dr. K is a psychologist working full time in a tenure track position at a large university. She teaches two classes each semester (one undergraduate course in Abnormal Psychology and a graduate seminar in Psychological Testing). She also supervises the dissertation projects of several doctoral students in clinical psychology at the university. She conducts research as well and is working on a textbook in Abnormal Psychology. Dr. K also presents guest lectures to local hospitals and other groups on her area of specialization, depression among elderly persons.

to be supportive, interested, and invested in the supervision process, and have solid clinical experience (Russell & Petrie, 1994). Clinical psychologists may be employed as staff members, as full-time or part-time faculty, or as guest lecturers at these medical schools and hospitals.

Teaching in Nonacademic Settings

Clinics Clinical psychologists may teach seminars, provide guest lectures, or give presentations in outpatient community mental health clinics, group private practice clinics, nonprofit institutes, day care centers, and other nonacademic settings. Topics may include how to assess and treat patients experiencing certain disorders (e.g., anxiety, depression, panic, obesity) or how to work more effectively with certain patient populations (e.g., Asian Americans, young children, AIDS patients). Many clinics offer regularly scheduled guest lecture presentations for their staff and trainees so that these professionals can continue to stay up to date on new developments in their field.

Workshops Many clinical psychologists conduct workshops for other psychologists or professionals (e.g., nurses, social workers, physicians). Workshops may last for a single day or for several days, and may offer continuing education credit. Psychologists may provide detailed information and train-

ing on specialized services or on how best to work with certain patient populations. Workshops may also incorporate individual case conferences, individual case supervision, and lectures. Almost all the national and regional psychology professional organizations offer yearly conventions that feature professional workshops.

Business and Industry Clinical psychologists may teach in business and industry environments, focusing on stress management techniques, ways to improve employee morale, and strategies to improve interviewing and communication skills. Their presentations may involve ongoing classroom instruction or a one-time guest lecture.

General Public Clinical psychologists are frequently asked to provide lectures and presentations to the general public at schools, businesses, churches and synagogues, volunteer organizations, bookstores, coffee houses, and other settings. For example, an elementary school may wish to have a psychologist present a lecture on the effects of television violence on children or on how to help children deal with parental divorce. Many organizations ask psychologists to give lectures on stress management, intimate relationships, or how to deal more effectively with specific organizational problems (e.g., layoffs, downsizing, financial restraints) (Fig. 12.2).

Case Studies: Teaching in Nonacademic Locations

Dr. L conducts half-day workshops on stress management for various businesses. He provides information about strategies to maximize effective coping and uses his research on resiliency to help participants examine their lives and determine how they may change aspects that impair their ability to cope with stress. Dr. L also teaches several relaxation techniques, which are practiced during the workshop. He offers a follow-up seminar for those who participate in the workshop to review progress and discuss obstacles.

Dr. M conducts a day-long workshop for mental health professionals on group psychotherapy. She discusses relevant research and offers strategies for both inpatient and outpatient groups on how to deal with problems such as marital discord, eating disorders, panic at-

tacks, and breast cancer. Dr. M uses educational videos to demonstrate effective group therapy techniques and ends her workshop with participants role playing in hypothetical groups. She travels to several cities across the country to present her workshops.

Dr. O is a psychologist who specializes in problems of young children and parents. She offers parenting classes that meet weekly for two hours and are designed for new parents with children aged 0 to 3 months. She hires several students to help with babysitting while the classes meet. Dr. O discusses practical matters such as diapering and feeding babies as well as bonding and psychological development. She invites nurses and pediatricians as occasional guest speakers. Dr. O also offers parenting classes for parents of twins.

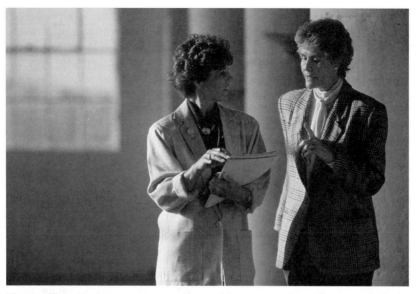

Figure 12.2 Business managers may wish to consult with a psychologist after layoffs

Administration

According to Kilburg (1991), management involves "planning, organizing, leading or directing, decision making, and controlling" (p. 38) such that the manager is ultimately responsible for the "success or failure of (an) enterprise" (p. 38). Effective **administration** involves excellent leadership, decision making, negotiating, and organizational skills. Although these skills may come naturally to some psychologists, they are generally not a specific part of the clinical psychology training process.

Many psychologists provide administrative services (Barton, 1991; Blouke, 1997; Grusky, Thompson, & Tillipman, 1991; Kelly, 1997). Psychologists may work as unit chiefs of hospital psychiatric units, direct mental health services at community mental health clinics, chair psychology departments in colleges or universities, work as deans or provosts in universities, or manage support staff and other clinicians in large group private practices. Psychologists in these roles often have the responsibility of hiring and firing employees, designing and implementing programs and services, managing budgets, and supervising the activities of many other professionals.

Curiously, although many psychologists become administrators, very few have formal training in administration (Barton, 1991; Blouke, 1997; Grusky et al., 1991; Kelly, 1997). For example, it has been estimated that less than 25 percent of mental health administrators representing all mental health disciplines (e.g., psychiatry, psychology, and social work) have had formal training in administration (Barton, 1991). Unlike graduate programs in business administration, graduate programs in psychology rarely offer courses or even guest lectures on administration. Almost no books or professional articles have been published that specifically deal with the issues of clinical psychology administrators. The qualities that make a psychologist a successful clinician, consultant, or researcher are not likely to be the same qualities that make a successful administrator. The ability to conduct high-quality research or to provide effective psychotherapy may involve skills that are very different from managing a budget, negotiating contracts, and dealing with employee conflicts and office politics. Many psychologists do not plan to become administrators but take on the role as their career progresses. Those who have good people skills, pay attention to detail, and manage systems and money well may be encouraged by colleagues and others to assume administrative responsibilities. Effective psychology administrators are organized, effective leaders, and good managers of both people and money (Barton, 1991; Kilburg, 1991; Shore, 1993). Katz (1980) reports that "human skill, the ability to work with others, is essential to effective administration at every level" (p. 82).

Barton (1991) proposed a model curriculum for mental health administration that would include both formal course work and practicum experience. He suggests that a Master's Degree in Mental Health Administration or in Public Health be awarded to those who seek to become administrators in the mental health field. Of course, training would be helpful only for those who are most likely to become administrators. Since a large number of psychologists ultimately provide administrative services, it seems reasonable and prudent for graduate and postgraduate training programs to provide formal training in administration for those who elect this career path.

The following scenario illustrates how psychologists often become administrators. A psychologist may work as a clinician in a community mental health clinic. Over time, the psychologist develops a reputation as being a competent and professional colleague who is organized and effective in his responsibilities. The chief psychologist of the clinic takes another position out of state, and the clinician is invited to act as interim chief until someone else is found for the job. The job search does not result in finding a superior candidate. The psychologist who is acting as chief psychologist takes to the job extremely well, and colleagues working in the agency generally feel that the acting chief of psychology should accept the permanent position. The psychologist agrees to continue in the role, begins to develop management skills, and enjoys the new career direction. Several years later the executive director of the agency retires. The chief psychologist is asked to become the executive director by the agency's board of directors since he knows the agency so well and has done an excellent job in his

---

Case Studies: Administrators in Clinical Psychology

Dr. P is a training director of a clinical internship and postdoctoral fellowship program in clinical psychology. She is responsible for the selection, training, and supervision of 10 trainees in the program and also the management of the budget. She is also responsible for supplying the various service components of the hospital and affiliated agencies with capable trainees. She negotiates problems and conflicts that arise with trainees and secures consulting psychologists who can provide individual and group supervision as well as seminars on topics such as psychotherapy, assessment, and ethics. She organizes site visits from accreditation agencies (e.g., the American Psychological Association), develops advertising strategies, and conducts program evaluations in an effort to improve the training programs.

Dr. Q is chairman of a psychology department at a small liberal arts college. She is responsible for the psychology department budget; hiring new faculty; and managing 10 full-time faculty, 5 part-time adjunct faculty, and a department secretary. She represents the psychology department at university meetings and functions. She

also is currently working with university administrators, fund-development personnel, and an architect concerning plans to build a new sciences building that will house the psychology department. Dr. Q teaches several undergraduates courses per year and conducts research. She conducts department meetings and organizes program/curriculum evaluation projects.

Dr. R is the director of an inpatient psychiatric unit that specializes in the treatment of alcohol abuse and addiction. He manages a staff of 12 clinicians (i.e., several psychologists, social workers, nurses, occupational therapists, and a consulting physician), and a $500,000-per-year budget; negotiates contracts with managed care and other insurance companies; and leads daily rounds to review patient admissions, discharges, and progress. He hires new staff and terminates those who are ineffective, and collaborates with the hospital public relations department to advertise services. Dr. R conducts program and treatment evaluation of the services provided by his unit. He also leads a family support group and follows several patients in treatment.

administrative duties. This scenario occurs frequently among psychologists involved with administration. One thing leads to another, and well-organized and well-liked professionals often move toward administrative and leadership responsibilities.

The Big Picture

Many psychologists thrive in the roles and activities associated with consultation, teaching, and administration. These activities allow the psychologist to positively impact the lives of many more people than generally possible through psychotherapy and psychological testing activities alone. As the mental health and health care fields change, some professionals argue that consultation and teaching activities will be especially important and useful for psychologists to pursue in the future (Kovacs, 1996).

Future contemporary clinical psychologists will likely be asked to consult on problems and issues in human behavior in many different areas both within and outside of the mental health field. Efforts to use our understanding of human behavior will be applied to perhaps all areas of personal and professional life with clinical psychologists at the forefront of these consultative, administrative, and teaching experiences.

Key Points

1. In addition to research, assessment, and psychotherapy, clinical psychologists often spend a significant amount of time involved in other professional activities such as consultation, administration, and teaching.

2. Consultation in clinical psychology generally involves applying knowledge and theories regarding human behavior to specific questions and problems in various community settings such as hospitals, clinics, schools, businesses, and government agencies. Consultation involves offering professional advice to others concerning problems that exist in their setting.

3. Consultants may assume many different roles during the course of a consultation or between consultation assignments. Lippitt and Lippitt (1986) have suggested that the role of consultant is based on a continuum between being directive and indirective.

4. Dougherty (1995) defines the following six common consultation roles for clinical psychologists: expert, trainer/educator, advocate, collaborator, fact finder, and process specialist.

5. Several types of consultation are typically conducted by clinical psychologists in mental health settings. These include (1) client-centered case consultation, (2) program-centered administrative consultation, (3) consultee-centered case consultation, and (4) consultee-centered administrative consultation.

6. Clinical psychologists also frequently provide consultation to an enormous range of nonmental health agencies

and organizations. Businesses, nonprofit agencies, and government organizations all employ people who must work cooperatively to achieve a common purpose and keep the organization running effectively and smoothly.

7. Many of the stages used to describe the psychotherapy process apply to consultation as well. These include (1) understanding the question, (2) assessment, (3) intervention, (4) termination, and (5) follow up.

8. Clinical psychologists frequently provide advice and consultation to their peers. In addition to consultation with colleagues, many psychologists consult with professionals from other disciplines. Clinical psychologists frequently consult with school teachers and administrators, physicians and nurses, attorneys and judges, clergy, the military, and people working in business and industry.

9. A number of skills are needed to be an effective consultant. Most researchers and practitioners of consultation highlight the primary importance of competent interpersonal and communication skills. However, excellent group and problem-solving skills, talents working with organizations, and highly developed professional and ethical behavior are also a must.

10. Although consultants and consultees may readily agree on the need for and goals of a consultation relationship, several problems often typically emerge. Resistance to the consultant and to his or her suggestions are very common. Another common problem in consultation concerns whether or not the involved parties accept the consultation methods and recommendations. Additionally, the consultee's expectations may be unreasonably high. Consultants themselves may contribute to problems. They may lack adequate knowledge, skill, experience, self-confidence, or professional objectivity and integrity to be effective.

11. Teaching activities are at least a part of the professional duties of most psychologists. Although only about 30 percent of clinical psychologists work primarily in academic environments such as colleges, universities, and medical schools, most psychologists participate in some teaching activity even if they primarily work in clinical, administration, consulting or other professional settings.

12. Clinical psychologists frequently teach in a wide variety of settings and to a wide variety of audiences. Teaching may involve formal college classroom instruction, individual supervision of a psychologist-in-training, or lecturing on stress management techniques in business firms or schools. Teaching may also be incorporated into psychotherapy and psychological testing activities.

13. Many psychologists provide administration services. Psychologists may work as unit chiefs of hospital psychiatric units, direct mental health services at community mental health clinics, chair psychology departments in colleges or universities, be on staff at elementary or secondary schools, work as deans or provosts in universities, or manage support staff and other clinicians in large group private practices. Curiously, although many psychologists become administrators, almost none of them have any formal training in administration.

Key Terms

Administration	Consultee-centered case consultation
Advocate	Educator
Client-centered case consultation	Fact Finder
Collaborator	Program-centered administrative consultation
Consultation	Teaching
Consultee-centered administrative consultation	Trainer

For Reflection

1. Who do psychologists consult with in both mental health and nonmental health fields?

2. What are the stages in consultation?

3. What roles are psychologists likely to use in consultation?

4. What are the typical problems associated with consultation?

5. What are the necessary skills needed to be an effective consultant?

6. What type of administrative positions are psychologists likely to hold?

7. In what environments do psychologists teach?

8. What types of lectures might psychologists present to the general public?

9. What is the training like for psychologist administrators?

CHAPTER 13

Ethical Standards in Contemporary Clinical Psychology

Chapter Outline

Highlight of a Contemporary Clinical Psychologist: Thomas G. Plante, Ph.D., ABPP

How Do Professional Ethics Differ from the Law?

The Ethical Principles of Psychologists and Code of Conduct

Why Would a Psychologist Behave in an Unethical Manner?

How Are Ethics Enforced?

What is the Process for Solving Ethical Dilemmas?

Is Behaving in Accordance With the Ethical Principles Always Clear Cut?

HIGHLIGHT OF A CONTEMPORARY CLINICAL PSYCHOLOGIST:

Thomas G. Plante, Ph.D., ABPP

Dr. Plante combines a full-time academic career with a private practice and consultation to religious and other organizations.

Birth Date: January 23, 1960

College: Brown University (Sc.B. in Psychology), 1982

Graduate Program: University of Kansas (M.A. and Ph.D. in Clinical Psychology), 1987

Clinical Internship: Yale University School of Medicine (1986–1987)

Postdoctoral Fellowship: Yale University (1987–1988)

Current Job: Associate Professor of Psychology, Santa Clara University; Clinical Assistant Professor of Psychiatry and Behavioral Sciences, Stanford University School of Medicine; Consulting Associate Professor of Education, Stanford University; Private Practice

Pros and cons of being a clinical psychologist:

Pros: "There is nothing more interesting and compelling than human behavior. Why do people do the things they do or feel the way they feel? Helping people understand their emotional life and find ways to improve the quality of their lives is very rewarding. I can think of numerous times when an assessment, consultation, or treatment resulted in an important change for the better for someone. Furthermore, there are numerous options and opportunities for teaching, research, practice, and consultation in clinical psychology and all of these activities can be very useful to others. Finally, clinical psychology offers a great deal of autonomy and freedom as well."

Cons: "Many economic and political factors threaten the profession. Managed health care, turf battles with other disciplines such as psychiatry, and intraprofession conflicts between science and practice oriented psychologists cause distress. Clinical psychologist often have a great deal of responsibility which can feel overwhelming at times. Salaries also generally tend to be low in comparison to many other professions which require many years of advanced training and advanced degrees."

Future of clinical psychology: Clinical psychology will likely continue to specialize and subspecialize. Internal and external forces will also require the use of empirically validated treatments for most clinical problems. Clinical psychology will also become more and more involved in general health behavior change such as treating lifestyle related health problems and will thus no longer be considered only a mental health profession. Unfortunately, opportunities for independent private practice and other autonomous career options are likely to decrease in the future.

Typical schedule:

9:00   Teach seminar on professional issues and ethics to psychology interns and postdoctoral fellows at Stanford.

10:00   Seminar continues.

11:00   Teach Abnormal Psychology class at Santa Clara University.

12:00   Class continues.

1:00   Meet with research lab group to discuss research projects involving the psychological benefits of exercise.

2:00   Meet individually with students for advising.

3:00   Teach Ethics class at Santa Clara University for undergraduates.

4:00   Class continues.

5:00   Psychological evaluation of 24-year-old Korean man interested in entering religious life as a Catholic priest. Conduct interview and administer several personality tests.

6:00   Psychotherapy session with 50-year-old woman experiencing panic attacks and conflicts with her husband and children.

How should clinical psychologists behave? What are the rules and guidelines for professional behavior among clinical psychologists? Should a psychologist have lunch with his or her patient? Should a psychologist date a current or former patient? Should a psychologist tell his or her friends about a fascinating new patient he or she is treating in psychotherapy?

Whether a psychologist is a researcher, teacher, therapist, or administrator, he or she is expected to maintain the highest professional ethics in all professional activities at all times. In fact, psychology is one of the few fields that have adopted ethical guidelines that hold members to a much higher standard than the law. The most current version of the **Ethics Code** published by the American Psychological Association is provided in the Appendix. Professional ethics form the cornerstone of professionalism in psychology. The American Psychological Association formed an ethics committee in the 1930s, and later developed its first set of ethical principles in 1953. It is especially important for the field of psychology to focus on professional ethics since psychologists generally have a high degree of responsibility that often significantly impacts the lives of others. For example, clinical psychologists who conduct psychotherapy are entrusted with the emotional and often physical vulnerabilities, confidences and well-being of the people who seek their guidance. Clinical psychologists who are teachers or professors are called upon to provide objective, state-of-the-art, and unbiased information to their students. Clinical psychologists conducting research must design and conduct high quality research, pro-

tect the rights of subjects, and carefully interpret and report their results in order to contribute meaningful information and knowledge about human behavior to the professional community. Thus, clinical psychologists must closely and carefully follow ethical principles to ensure that they behave in an appropriate, responsible, and professional manner, protecting the public as well as the profession.

Curiously, the preponderance of media portrayals of clinical psychologists and other mental health professionals in films and on television depict these professionals as engaging in highly unethical, unprofessional, self-serving, and often, illegal behavior. Numerous feature length films such as *The Prince of Tides, Final Analysis, Mr. Jones,* and *Don Juan DeMarco,* as well as television shows such as *Melrose Place,* all depict psychologists and other mental health professionals behaving inappropriately and unethically. Typically, the psychologists or psychiatrists portrayed in the media are involved in unethical dual relationships. In other words, rather than maintaining their professional relationships and boundaries, the psychologists fall in love with or befriend their patients. The development of a personal relationship (usually romantic) outside of the professional relationship is the most common ethical violation illustrated by the media. Using patients for personal gain or gratification, practicing outside of one's area of competence, and breaking confidentiality are also typical depictions. Unfortunately, psychologists are very rarely shown behaving in a professional and ethical manner. In a review of 207 films that included psychiatrists, 35 percent suggested that the mental health professional was more troubled than his or her patients, and 22 percent were involved in manipulative behavior with their patients for the benefit of the themselves (Schneider, 1987). However, some films, such as *Ordinary People* and *Good Will Hunting,* provide fairly realistic portrayals of psychologists behaving in an ethical and professional manner. In real life, many of the mental health professionals depicted in the media would lose their license to practice and perhaps be prosecuted for engaging in the behaviors portrayed.

Unfortunately, psychologists in real life occasionally do commit ethical violations. Psychologists are human and suffer from the same vulnerabilities as the general public. They experience family conflicts, financial hardships, and stress and may behave in unbecoming and even illegal ways. It has been estimated that between 20 percent and 82 percent of psychologists experience relationship problems such as marital conflict, between 13 percent and 57 percent experience depression, and about 11 percent experience substance abuse problems (Deutsch, 1985; Norcross, Strausser-Kirtland, & Missar, 1988). It also has been suggested that between 5 percent and 15 percent of psychologists are impaired (Laliotis & Grayson, 1985). They might, for example, inappropriately break confidentiality, become sexually involved with their patient(s), falsify research data, engage in sexual harassment, encourage their patients to do favors for them such as babysit their child or paint their house, provide ineffective or questionable treatment, or engage in financial mismanagement and fraud. They also make honest mistakes due to ignorance, inattention, or vulnerability. For example, a psychologist who is lonely might be tempted to initiate a friendship or romantic relationship with a highly appealing client. A psychologist with significant financial problems might be tempted to invest in a business deal with a wealthy and successful client.

The American Psychological Association reports that between 1985 and 1994 an average of 337 ethical complaints were received per year (American Psychological Association, 1995d) with over 400 received every year since 1992 (American Psychological Association, 1996). Many other ethical violations may not have been reported to the American Psychological Association or to state ethics and licensing boards. Many of the ethical complaints filed are found to have little or no merit. However, most of the complaints that result in action against the psychologist by the American Psychological Association or local authorities involve breaking confidentiality, sexual misconduct (e.g., sexual relationship with a patient), nonsexual dual relationships (e.g., friendships or business partnerships with patients), and insurance/fee misbehavior (e.g., overbilling insurance, billing for services not rendered). Several authors have reported that the most common ethical violation involves patient confidentiality (Pope & Bajt, 1988; Pope & Vetter, 1992). While many of these violations involve breaking confidentiality without patient permission, a sizable number of cases involve psychologists refusing to break confidentiality when they are ethically and legally required, as in the case of reporting child abuse to the police or state child protective services. Fortunately, however, the vast majority of clinical psychologists do behave in an ethical and professional manner (Koocher & Keith-Spiegal, 1998; Layman & McNamara, 1997). Regardless of what is shown in the media, the unethical psychologist is the exception rather than the rule.

What are the ethical guidelines for psychologists? How exactly should a psychologist behave? How can a psychologist be sure that he or she is behaving appropriately? While certain behaviors seem easy to recognize as unethical such as sexual contact with current patients, falsifying research data or records, breaking patient confidentiality, and overbilling, many other behaviors may not be so clear. The Ethics Code has been updated eight times by the American Psychological Association since the original 1953 document was published; the current version was published in December, 1992 (American Psychological Association, 1992a). The most recent version of the Canadian Code of Ethics for Psychologists was published in 1995 and is more similar than different to the American code (Canadian Psychological Association, 1995). Many of the principles outlined in these various versions were originally highlighted many centuries ago in the Hippocratic Oath. These include competence, respect, confidentiality, informed consent, social justice, and avoiding both harm and exploitation. Thus, many of the fundamental principles outlined several thousand years ago are still in use today. In addition to the Ethics Code, more specific speciality guidelines have also been developed by the American Psychological Association and other organizations to provide further instructions and expectations for professional conduct. For example, the American Psychological Association has published the following speciality guidelines: *Specialty Guidelines for the Delivery of Services by Clinical Psychologists* (American Psychological Association, 1981), *Guidelines for Computer Based Tests and Interpretations* (American Psychological Association, 1987a), *Standards for Educational and Psychological Testing* (American Psychological Association, 1985), and *Guidelines for Providers of Psychological Services to Ethnic, Linguistic, and Culturally Diverse Populations* (American Psychological Association, 1990). Additional guidelines are provided for school psychologists, counseling psychologists, and others.

Koocher and Keith-Speigal (1998) outlined eight general principles for psychologists distilled from the ethics code, specialty guidelines, and additional sources. These include doing no harm, benefiting others, being just and faithful, according dignity, treating others with caring and compassion, pursuing excellence, respecting autonomy, and accepting accountability. These principles are found in the Hippocratic Oath and elsewhere.

In this chapter, the current ethical code for psychologists will be examined and case examples used to illustrate actual ethical violations. Each major division of the Ethics Code will be briefly summarized followed by several illustrative case studies. The case studies are based on actual cases but have been carefully edited and altered to protect the confidentiality of the parties involved. Before the ethical code is outlined, it is important to understand how ethics differ from the law.

How Do Professional Ethics Differ from the Law?

Ethical principles are developed at the national level by the American Psychological Association to protect the public and profession by providing guidelines for professional conduct among psychologists. These principles generally focus on how psychologists should behave. It is important to note that membership in the American Psychological Association is voluntary and adherence to the ethics code developed by the APA is required of APA members only. Most laws involving the delivery of

psychological services and conduct of psychologists are written and enforced at the state level. Because laws differ from state to state, certain unethical behaviors conducted by a psychologist such as having sexual relationships with his or her patients may or may not be illegal, depending upon the jurisdiction. Furthermore, laws and the Ethics Code may not be in agreement regarding a variety of situations. A judge may subpoena a psychologist to release all records concerning a patient, while the Ethics Code prohibits the release of records without patient consent and prohibits releasing material such as psychological testing protocols to be examined and interpreted by unqualified persons such as lawyers and judges. In the case of conflicts between ethics and the law, psychologists are advised to follow the ethical principles and work towards solving the dilemma by making these issues known to relevant parties such as the police, attorneys, and judges. Generally, ethical standards represent a much higher standard than the law.

The Ethical Principles of Psychologists and Code of Conduct

The current version of the ethical principles for psychologists is divided into six general principles and eight ethical standards. The principles serve as aspirational goals while the ethical standards describe a variety of behaviors that define unethical acts. Each of these principles and standards will be highlighted. The complete version of the Ethics Code can be found in Appendix 1.

Other ethical codes generally use similar ethical principles. For example, the Canadian code uses four principles which include (1) respect for the dignity of persons, (2) responsible caring, (3) integrity in relationships, and (4) responsibility to society (Canadian Psychological Association, 1995).

Ethical Principles

Competence   Psychologists must maintain competence in their area(s) of specialization. They must only provide services for which they have the appropriate training and experience and remain up-to-date regarding advances in the field to ensure that they maintain state-of-the-art skills.

It is important for psychologists to be well aware of their strengths and weaknesses, their skills and deficits, and most importantly, their limitations. For example, it has been estimated that about 50 percent of the material that is learned in graduate school becomes obsolete after about 10 to 12 years following graduation (Dubin, 1972). Advances and new discoveries occur so frequently that regular continuing education is necessary and even mandated by law in most states. Psychologists must keep their skills sharp and current and be careful not to offer any service that is less than state-of-the-art. They also must ensure that their personal lives do not interfere with the provision of competent service. However, occasionally a psychologist may work while he or she is ill, tired, or preoccupied. A national survey of psychologists revealed that 59.6 percent acknowledged that they had worked when they were too distressed to be effective (Pope, Tabachnick, & Keith-Spiegel, 1987). It is troubling that the majority of psychologists in the survey have felt that they were unable to be effective due to their personal needs at least at one point during their career.

It is not always obvious what constitutes competence and incompetence. Differences in opinion exist regarding the best ways to teach a class, conduct an assessment, provide psychotherapy for a particular problem, or design a research project to investigate a certain psychological phenomenon. For example, different theoretical orientations or integrative approaches may be employed to treat a particular psychiatric disorder. Some argue that interpersonal psychotherapy should be utilized in treating bulimia. Others purport that cognitive-behavioral psychotherapy is the approach of choice. Still others suggest a combination of the two approaches. Furthermore, because each person who seeks the services of a professional psychologist has unique needs, an individual personality, and a specific constellation of symptoms and biopsychosocial influences, many argue that treatment approaches must be highly individualized and tailored to each person. Competence, therefore, can not usually be assessed in an absolute manner. While some interventions generally can be universally regarded as grossly incompetent (e.g., using leeches to treat depression or ECT to treat anorexia nervosa), most questionable professional behaviors are not so obvious. Often the community standard acts as the criteria for the assessment of professional competence. The community standard is defined by what several reasonable members of the professional psychological community would agree upon as being an appropriate standard of care.

Why would a psychologist provide incompetent service? Why would someone skilled and intelligent enough to earn a doctorate in psychology and a license to practice engage in incompetent professional behavior? A variety of factors may lead a psychologist to provide incompetent service. First, a psychologist, like any human being, may develop a psychiatric disorder or psychological problem that impairs his or her judgement and behavior. For example, a psychologist might develop an alcohol or substance abuse problem that significantly impairs judgment. A psychologist could also develop severe depression and be unable to fully engage in his or her work. A psychologist might have a personality disorder which makes him or her very difficult to train and ultimately precludes competent service. The psychologist might miss patient appointments, fall asleep during sessions, inappropriately become irritable with patients or students, forget to arrive to teach a class, improperly recruit research subjects, or engage in a variety of other problematic behaviors that severely compromise their competence. Psychologists are human and experience the full range of problems humans experience: divorce, illness, financial problems, anxiety, stress, and a host of ills such as greed, dishonesty, and the like. Thus, personal problems and weaknesses in integrity may lead a psychologist to falter.

Second, a psychologist might become so burdened or "burned out" that he or she stops being effective. For example, a psychologist might work in a mental health clinic deluged with a high volume of patients over the course of many years on the job. He or she may begin to feel less and less invested in his or her job and his or her patients. The psychologist might tune out during sessions and try to just get through the therapy hour with a minimum of investment. A psychologist who teaches the same courses year after year at a college or university may become bored and uninspired. The professor may fail to update his or her courses and show no interest in student learning. Thus, burnout may result in incompetent professional activity.

Third, a psychologist could be arrogant and narcissistic, feeling that he or she does not need to stay up-to-date or learn anything else following graduate school. The arrogant psychologist may feel that he or she can handle any problem, teach any class without preparation, publish any data collected, and provide clinical services to whomever seeks treatment. The arrogant psychologist may feel above the professional literature and not alter his or her professional behavior to incorporate the latest research and clinical findings. The arrogant psychologist might enjoy providing a certain type of service and apply it to all of his or her patients whether it is optimal or not. Thus, the arrogant psychologist is not open to new information and consultation from others to ensure professional competence.

Fourth, a psychologist might behave in a selfish manner that contributes to incompetent professional behavior. For example, a psychologist might wish to fill up his or her psychotherapy practice and agree to take any case that comes to his or her attention. The selfish psychologist might agree to treat someone experiencing a certain disorder despite a critical absence of training or experience with the particular disorder. The selfish psychologist might be more interested in earning money or promoting their career than providing quality clinical, teaching, research, or other professional services. The selfish psychologist may put his or her own needs and wishes above those of patients, students, colleagues, and the public. Finally, the uninformed psychologist may provide incompetent services out of ignorance and misinformation. While he or she may be motivated to be competent, inexperience, lack of consultation, and ignorance may prevent competent performance.

Integrity Psychologists must maintain professional and personal integrity and be respectful, fair, and honest in their dealings with others. They must be truthful in describing their services, their areas of expertise, and what can be expected from their services. They must be well aware of their biases, needs, and values and how these may impact their work. Psychologists make all efforts to avoid inappropriate dual relationships.

Unlike many sales and marketing tactics used in business and other areas, psychologists must be careful never to mislead, distort, misrepresent, or deceive. They must be honest and professional in their manner of advertisement and conscientious in their description of their professional services. For example, fees and what can be reasonably expected from a psychotherapy experience must be clearly delineated before services are provided. Importantly, psychologists must be willing to make a referral to another professional if it is in the best interest of the patient.

Psychologists must avoid conflicts of interest and dual relationships with their patients, clients, students, and others. Because psychologists often maintain a position of power in their professional

---

Case Study: Dr. A

Dr. A recently became licensed and opened a private practice. He was very excited about becoming independent and looked forward to developing a satisfying and profitable career. He became disappointed after several months when his practice did not fill up quickly. Furthermore, he was anxious about his financial status, feeling that he would be unable to pay his overhead expenses as well as his home mortgage. Furthermore, his wife was pregnant with their first child, and Dr. A was concerned about a significant increase in family expenses. An uninformed but well meaning colleague referred Dr. A a patient who suffered from panic attacks. The man was wealthy enough to be able to afford treatment and wanted to be seen in psychotherapy several times each week.

Dr. A happily agreed to treat the patient even though he had never treated a patient with panic disorder before and despite his own doubt that three sessions per week were necessary. He thought that he would go to a local bookstore and read a popular press book on panic disorder to learn about it.

Without appropriate training, experience, and consultation in treating panic disorder, Dr. A unethically treated the patient. Dr. A should have referred the patient to a professional with adequate training or experience. He should have obtained appropriate training and supervision prior to treating a panic disorder patient. He also should have declined to see the patient more often than was clinically indicated.

Case Study: Dr. B

Dr. B conducts psychological testing for a mental health clinic. She has been employed by the clinic for about five years and has routinely conducted several evaluations each week. At first, she enjoyed her work and found psychological testing exciting and rewarding. She felt like a detective trying to piece together a puzzle in order to determine exactly which diagnosis was warranted for each of her complex patients. After administering hundreds of evaluations, Dr. B became burned out and resented each additional evaluation she was assigned. She became less and less interested in her job and her patients. She joked with friends and colleagues that she could administer an IQ test in her sleep. Soon she started to take short cuts in her testing administrations. She would give tests too quickly and would skip sections of her evaluation. Finally, her behavior resulted in a significant error that severely impacted her patient. She had been asked to conduct psychological testing to determine if a child was learning disabled. Her testing was done in a sloppy manner and she made several significant calculation errors. She reported that the child was mentally retarded to the parents and the school. The child was placed in a special education class based on Dr. B's evaluation. Six months later, the child was retested and found to function at a much higher level than indicated on Dr. B's evaluation. Her records were requested by the school district and the school psychologist found the errors. Dr. B allowed her boredom and burnout to impact her performance, resulting in significant harm to her patient and the patient's family.

What should Dr. B have done in this situation? What would you do if you were on the ethics board evaluating Dr. B?

---

relationships with patients and students, they must never exploit this power differential and never place their own interests and needs above those they serve. For instance, psychologists should not engage in sexual relationships with patients or students they supervise, no matter how consensual such a relationship may seem. While the issue of sexual relationships between psychologists and their patients and students will be discussed later in this chapter, other nonsexual dual relationships will be briefly discussed here.

Dual relationships are one of the most common ethical violations brought to the attention of ethic boards (American Psychological Association, 1995, 1996). Dual relationships are commonly and casually portrayed in television and films involving psychologists, yet these relationships compromise the effectiveness of the psychologist's work and are often exploitive to the patient, client, or student. While it is common and often expected that business associates and clients have lunch, play golf, or attend social gatherings together, these situations must be avoided by psychologists in order to minimize compromising relationships. Unfortunately, dual relationships are somewhat common among psychologists. For example, a national survey conducted by Pope, Tabachnick, & Keith-Spiegel (1987) revealed that 39.9 percent of psychologists had accepted a patient's invitation to a party, 16 percent had invited patients to a social event, and 28.3 percent had provided psychotherapy services to a friend. Furthermore, Pope et al. (1987) reported that 25 percent of psychology educators (e.g., college professors) had sold products such as cars to their students. No matter how challenging, the maintenance of clear and professional boundaries in all professional relationships is incumbent upon all psychologists.

Some psychologists effectively argue that occasional contact with patients outside of the office can be both ethical and helpful. For example, some psychologists will attend important special events in the life of a patient such as a Bar Mitzvah, confirmation, funeral, graduation, wedding or other once in a lifetime events (Borys & Pope, 1989). Other professionals argue that effective professional service must sometimes occur in the patient's natural environment. For example, a psychologist might meet a patient at an airport to help treat the patient's plane phobia, or at someone's home to conduct clinical services for someone who is physically disabled. These situations can be effectively and ethically conducted if the psychologist is careful to maintain a professional relationship and not develop a potentially exploitive dual relationship.

Teachers and professors also occasionally socialize with their students. In fact, many campuses strongly encourage faculty and students to socialize together at various campus-sponsored events.

"That's enough therapy. From here on out, I think I could do a hell of a lot more for both of us as your agent."

These social contacts between faculty and students can certainly be ethical encounters as long as professional boundaries are maintained and the faculty member does not use their power or status to take advantage of their relationship with their students (e.g., ask students for personal favors, burden students with their personal problems). Of course, sexual intimacies between faculty and their students represent a serious ethical violation.

Some dual relationships are unavoidable (Stockman, 1990). For example, in very small communities a psychologist may be the only mental health professional in town and may need the services of his or her patient because the patient may be the only dentist, car dealer, or grocery store owner in town. A former patient may take a class with a professor who was also his or her therapist because he teaches the only section of a required course. These situations must be handled carefully by the psychologist to minimize any potential harm to others. Psychologists cannot always avoid a dual relationship but they can always be sensitive and thoughtful regarding this issue and proceed with

caution in order to minimize any potential harm to those they serve.

Professional and Scientific Responsibility Psychologists must be willing to consult with other professionals in order to best serve their patients or clients. For example, a psychologist may be treating a person from a different ethnic, cultural, or religious group and he or she may consult with a colleague who is more familiar and experienced with members of the particular group in order to offer the most effective and sensitive service possible. Psychologists may also feel stuck during the course of conducting psychotherapy or while completing an evaluation. They may feel that they are unclear about how to best help one of their patients. Consulting with a colleague often helps to develop a productive direction. Since there are often biological, psychological, and social factors that may influence a particular clinical problem, psychologists also must consult with nonpsychologist professionals, such as physicians, in order to ensure that their

Case Study: Dr. C

Dr. C received a doctorate in physics and was employed by a software company in a middle management position for 15 years. Dr. C became dissatisfied with his career choice and felt that he wanted to make a significant career change. He had been in psychotherapy for several years during and following his divorce and felt that becoming a therapist might be a satisfying career move. He enrolled in a local graduate program in psychology. Dr. C worked in several clinics during his graduate training. He introduced himself as "Dr. C" and had "Dr. C" printed on his business cards. Referring to himself as "Dr." is misleading. His doctorate in physics is not relevant to his new career path, and potential clients are likely to believe that his doctorate is in psychology or a closely related field. Patients have a right to know exactly what service and provider they are paying for.

patients obtain quality service. For example, a psychologist may wish to work closely with a physician while treating a patient that experiences anorexia nervosa to ensure that both medical and psychological services are coordinated. Of course, confidentiality must be maintained or permission of the patient obtained in order to discuss cases with others.

Psychologists conducting research, teaching, or other activities must also consult with others to maintain professional responsibility. For example, a psychologist conducting research may be confused about his or her research findings and the best means of data analysis. The psychologist may feel that consultation with a colleague who is more skilled in research design and statistical analysis would be helpful in order to best investigate the research question. A psychologist who teaches a college course may be unable to answer some questions asked by students, so he or she may wish to consult a colleague in order to better answer the students' questions. In all of these examples, consultation with a colleague can assist the psychologist in providing the most effective and responsible possible service.

In addition to maintaining responsibility for professional behavior, psychologists must also assist in ensuring that colleagues maintain professional ethics. Psychologists must help stop and/or report unethical behavior engaged in by colleagues. Thus, if a psychologist witnesses irresponsible and unethical behavior on the part of a colleague, he or she has an ethical duty to intervene by speaking with the colleague or by reporting the violation to the appropriate authorities. Most cases of irresponsible and unethical behavior committed by colleagues can be rectified through informal and educative consul-

Case Study: Dr. D

Dr. D is treating a patient who experiences obesity. Dr. D is providing a behavioral treatment program to help her patient decrease food consumption, increase exercise, and alter her lifestyle in order to minimize weight problems. Dr. D's patient happens to work in the printing business. Dr. D needs to order more stationary and business cards because she recently moved her office to a new location, so she asks her patient if she would produce the stationary and business cards for her at a discounted price. The patient agrees to produce the materials at a 20 percent discount. Dr. D felt that her patient did only a mediocre printing job and feels angry and resentful. Dr. D should have avoided the dual relationship of having her client also print her stationary and business cards. Dr. D tried to have both a therapeutic professional relationship and a separate business relationship with her patient. This dual relationship may have made it too difficult for the patient to say no to Dr. D, and Dr. D's dissatisfaction with the printing job may interfere with her ability to relate positively to the patient.

What should Dr. D do now?

Case Study: Dr. E

Dr. E is treating a Roman Catholic priest for depression. Dr. E is Jewish and knows very little about the Roman Catholic Church. Some aspects of the Church seem odd to Dr. E and very difficult to understand (e.g., vows of chastity, poverty, and obedience). Dr. E is unfamiliar with church hierarchy and does not understand some of the issues the patient is interested in discussing. Dr. E made it clear to the patient that she was Jewish and that she was unfamiliar with many of the issues involved with being a Roman Catholic priest. The patient decided that he did not want to be treated by a Catholic because he wanted an "unbiased and fresh perspective." Dr. E decided to treat the patient but without consultation from someone who might provide appropriate professional guidance.

---

tation. However, serious violations or conflicts that cannot be resolved through informal means must be reported to the appropriate ethics committee or board.

Respect for People's Rights and Dignity   Psychologists must be respectful of the rights and dignity of others. They must be sensitive to individual and cultural differences, and be aware of gaps in knowledge and areas of bias and prejudice. They must respect the right to freedom, privacy, and confidentiality. Psychologists must not discriminate against others based on sex, religion, ethnicity, sexual orientation, or other factors. Psychologists must be careful to not allow their personal biases and prejudices interfere with their work. Ageism, racism, and sexism have no place in the work of psychologists.

Confidentiality is the cornerstone of psychological services. Everything that is mentioned in the consultation room must be kept confidential. Without the assurance of confidentiality, many patients could not comfortably speak about what is on their minds and would be unable to obtain needed assistance. In fact, many psychologists feel that effective psychotherapy cannot be conducted without the assurance of confidentiality (e.g., Epstein, Steingarten, Weinstein, & Nashel, 1977). However, there are several legal and ethical limits to confidentiality. These generally include serious and immediate danger to self or others, such as suicide and homicide, as well as information concerning the physical, sexual, and emotional abuse or neglect of a child, elderly person, or dependent adult (e.g., disabled adult). Persons seeking services of a psychologist have a right to know about these limits to confidentiality in order to make informed choices about the types of information they choose to disclose.

Patients may choose to waive their right to confidentiality in certain specific circumstances. For example, they may wish to have their psychologist speak with their physician, school teacher, previous

---

Case Study: Dr. F

Dr. F is concerned about one of his colleagues. Dr. F works with Dr. G in a mental health clinic. Dr. G tends to be late for his appointments with his patients, speaks about his patients in derogatory terms, and never has his reports completed in a timely manner. Furthermore, Dr. G supervises several psychology interns and postdoctoral fellows. Several of these students report that Dr. G intimidates them and has them do personal favors for him. Dr. F is very concerned about Dr. G's behavior. Dr. F privately discussed his concerns with Dr. G. Dr. G became enraged and threatened Dr. F. Dr. F felt that although he should report his concerns to Dr. G's supervisor as well as to the ethics board, he didn't want to "make waves." Dr. F had a responsibility to report Dr. G's behavior since the situation could not be resolved informally and both patients and students were at risk due to Dr. G's unethical and unprofessional behavior.

Case Study: Dr. H

Dr. H is working with the children of a famous sports celebrity. She is conducting educational and intellectual testing to determine if one or both of his children have learning disabilities. Dr. H is a big sports fan and is extremely excited about meeting and having the opportunity to work with the family of the sports star. During the course of the evaluation, Dr. H learns a great deal about the family including the fact that the sports celebrity has a learning disability and plans on retiring from sports very soon. Dr. H has difficulty keeping this information to herself. She decides to tell her husband as well as several close friends that she is working with the celebrity. She asks them not to tell anyone about his learning disability and upcoming retirement from sports. Dr. H had a responsibility to keep the identity of her client confidential. Breaking confidentiality was a serious ethical violation and should be reported.

How do you think you would have handled treating the children of this famous patient?

Case Study: Dr. I

Dr. I is conducting an interview with a woman and her two children. The woman is divorced and is concerned that both of her children seem anxious and upset after each visit with their father. The children, aged 7 and 9, report that their father makes them anxious because he drives too fast and erratically after drinking several beers. Furthermore, one of the children reports that their father touches her genitals after drinking. Dr. I informs the mother that he must report the sexual abuse and child endangerment to the county child protection services. The mother angrily states that she does not want Dr. I to break confidentiality and that she is afraid of what her former husband might do when he finds out that the children told someone about the sexual behavior and dangerous driving. They are fearful that it will "just make matters worse, not better." Dr. I capitulates, agreeing not to report the abuse if the father will agree to receive treatment. Dr. I had an obligation to report the abuse and should have informed the family of the limits of confidentiality prior to conducting the interview.

Case Study: Dr. J.

Dr. J is working with a patient who is having an affair. Dr. J feels very strongly that marital affairs are wrong, sinful, and always a bad decision. Dr. J tells his patient that he strongly feels that marital affairs are immoral and destructive and that she would be well advised to stop the affair immediately. The patient, who feels that Dr. J is an excellent psychologist and highly values his opinion, feels upset with Dr. J's strong opinion. She doesn't want to disappoint Dr. J or do something that he feels is so terrible but she is also not willing to terminate the affair. Reluctantly, she decides to see another psychologist and never return to Dr. J for psychotherapy. Dr. J inappropriately imposed his strong views about marital affairs onto his client.

What should Dr. J do if this type of situation occurs with another patient?

Case Study: Dr. K.

Dr. K is Asian-American and is treating a patient who is an African-American male experiencing job dissatisfaction. Dr. K has little experience treating African-American patients. Dr. K feels very uncomfortable with her patient and is hesitant to ask him to elaborate certain cultural issues that emerge (e.g., experience of discrimination at work, strong Christian faith and church ties). She also mistakenly attributes his unfamilar urbane dialect and speech and jargon to his "not being very bright." Dr. K's racism, ignorance, and discomfort prevent her from providing effective service and in fact have detrimental potential for the patient. Furthermore, it is inappropriate for her to fail to obtain consultation regarding a patient from a cultural group with whom she has no experience treating.

therapist, attorney, or other professional in order to obtain helpful background information or consultation. Patients may wish to bring others (e.g., spouse, child, parent, friend) to their sessions, which may potentially compromise their confidentiality. Psychologists must always obtain permission from their patients or clients prior to breaking confidentiality in these circumstances. Normally, written permission is necessary before a psychologist can discuss a patient with someone else.

Psychologists also must respect the rights of others to make their own decisions. They must not impose their wishes and opinions on the student, client, patient, or anyone else they serve even if the psychologist feels that a patient or student is making a poor decision (e.g., to quit school, marry someone who is abusive, use drugs). However, they can certainly provide guidance and discuss the pros and cons of these decisions.

Concern for Other's Welfare Psychologists seek to improve the quality of life of those they serve and avoid harming their clients in any manner. Such concern for other's welfare includes the intention to never exploit their relationships with others. In all professional activities, psychologists work towards enhancing the welfare of clients, patients, and students. Research is conducted to help better understand human behavior as well as to develop methods of improving the human condition. Assessment and treatment are used to improve quality of life and teaching is conducted to enhance knowledge of students. As mentioned earlier in the chapter, psychologists must be highly sensitive to the power differential that exists between them and their clients, patients, and students and avoid misusing or exploiting these relationships (Borys & Pope, 1989; Koocher & Keith-Spiegal, 1998; Stockman, 1990).

Social Responsibility Psychologists work to help others and to advance the science and knowledge of human behavior. They have a social responsibility to speak against causes and policies that contradict or exploit what is known about human behavior and psychological functioning (e.g., policies and causes that support discrimination). Psychologists are expected to contribute some professional time to causes which do not result in financial or other personal gains.

Psychologists are expected to contribute back to society in some professional way. For example, many psychologists agree to treat at least some patients who are unable to pay for services or can only pay a very small amount of money. Some psychologists agree to provide free lectures to schools or civic organizations without financial compensation or the expectation that patient referrals will result from their talk. Some psychologists agree to treat graduate students in psychology for a highly reduced fee. Research psychologists may review manuscripts for publication without payment or other rewards. They also may serve on human subject or granting agency committees in order to contribute to the profession and society.

Case Study: Dr. L

Dr. L is a popular psychology professor on campus. He is an excellent teacher and involves many of his students in his research activities. He is generous with his students, ensuring them co-authorship on research papers and taking a great deal of time to train and mentor them. Dr. L. and his wife just had a baby and needs a nanny as well as general babysitting help. He invites his students to help him care for the baby. Many of the students feel honored that they were asked to care for Dr. L's baby and don't mind that they will not be paid for babysitting. They feel that it is the least they can do for Dr. L because he has been so generous with his time, attention, and effort. Dr. L is not only developing a dual relationship with his students but is also exploiting the power differential between himself and his students by asking them to babysit for him without pay. Dr. L. knows or should know that his young students would feel honored to be asked to babysit and he wrongly uses his allure to obtain free babysitting services.

How should Dr. L meet his babysitting needs?

Case Study: Dr. M

Dr. M has three children and lives in an expensive area of town. She wants to send her children to private school and build an addition to her house. Dr. M is interested in making as much money as possible in her private practice. She charges very high fees and bills by the minute for any telephone contact with her patients even if it is just to change an appointment time. She also bills colleagues whenever they contact her to obtain consultation. Because she is an expert in multiple personality, biofeed-

back, and several other areas, she is often sought after for consultations, lectures, and other professional activities. She refuses to participate in any professional activity without being paid, and never donates any time, money, or consultation at free or reduced prices. Dr. M feels that she owes nothing to society nor to others and feels that her practice is solely a way for her to have the kind of lifestyle she desires. Dr. M is not exercising social responsibility.

Ethical Standards

The ethical standards section of the Ethics Code uses the ethical principles already discussed and applies them to specific and typical professional activities associated with the psychology profession (e.g., teaching, research, psychotherapy, psychological testing). Other psychology ethics codes also generally use a list of ethical standards under the umbrella of ethical principles. The Canadian code, for example, lists a variety of similar ethical standards as they apply to informed consent, therapy, privacy, and care of animals among others (Canadian Psychological Association, 1995). The general standards section of the Ethics Code briefly reviews the ethical principles that must be applied to all professional activities. A review of these standards will be presented here followed by the specific application to a number of professional psychology activities.

General Standards Psychologists must be well aware of the limits and boundaries of their professional competence and never practice outside of their areas of expertise. They must be highly respectful of others and never engage in discrimination, sexual or other forms of harassment, or let their personal problems interfere with their professional work and obligations. They must avoid all potential dual relationships such as business, friendship, or romantic relationships with patients, students, or other types of clients with whom they work in a professional capacity. They must base their judgments on scientific information and avoid any possible harm to others. Psychologists must adequately document their professional work and be careful

with the storage and disposal of professional records. They should ensure that financial arrangements such as fees for service are understood and agreed upon before providing services, and that the fees are not exploitative or misleading. Psychologists must ensure that their employees are properly supervised and that consultations and referrals are made in the best interest of their clients.

Evaluation, Assessment, or Intervention Psychologists must use assessment instruments only for the purposes for which they were developed and validated. They must also only use tests they are qualified to administer and interpret and not encourage unqualified persons to use these tests. It is necessary to provide assessment feedback to clients in an understandable manner and to protect the confidentiality of test results.

Psychologists are entrusted to use psychological testing instruments in an ethical manner at all times. Psychologists must know the strengths and weaknesses of each test they use as well as information regarding the reliability, validity, and standardization. They must ensure that they have adequate training and supervision in each test and are prepared to interpret results thoughtfully and carefully. Since new tests are developed frequently and new versions of tests become available on a regular basis, psychologists must stay up-to-date on the changes that impact their professional work in psychological testing.

Frequently, unqualified persons are interested in administering and/or interpreting psychological tests. For example, school teachers and parents may

Case Study: Dr. N

Dr. N conducts a large number of neuropsychological evaluations at a local rehabilitation hospital. She has been conducting several evaluations each week for the past 10 years. Most of the patients at the hospital experience traumatic brain and/or spinal cord injuries. Dr. N is contacted by an undergraduate student majoring in psychology who is looking for summer work in the field. Following an interview, Dr. N decided to hire the student to conduct neuropsychological evaluations. Dr. N feels that she could use some help and that it would be an excellent training opportunity for the student to learn to administer

neuropsychological tests. Dr. N spends several weeks training the student in testing administration, watches her perform several tests with actual patients, and then has her conduct the testing at the hospital. They meet at the end of each work day to review the testing given on that day, provide supervision, and answer any questions that arise. Dr. N has committed an ethical violation by allowing an unqualified person to administer professional tests. With several weeks of training, an undergraduate psychology student is not adequately trained to competently administer neuropsychological tests.

---

wish to interpret the results of IQ tests given to children without the assistance of a psychologist. Sometimes psychiatrists, social workers, or other mental health professionals wish to administer or interpret psychological tests such as the Rorschach, the Thematic Apperception Test, Projective Drawings, or the Minnesota Multiphasic Personality Inventory-2 (MMPI-2) without appropriate training and supervision. Sometimes these professionals request that psychologists order testing materials for them to use. Most states do not prohibit nonpsychologists such as psychiatrists from using psychological tests. However, psychologists have the ethical obligation to ensure that tests are used appropriately and only by those who have a proper level of training and experience.

Psychologists must protect the security of tests so that there is controlled access to sensitive testing materials. For example, IQ testing will be invalid if

the person being tested has access to the test items prior to being formally administered the test. Just as tests such as the SAT, LSAT, MCAT, GMAT, and other standardized tests must be protected and used carefully so, too, must psychological tests. Therefore, keeping testing supplies in an unlocked or easily accessible location or allowing clients, patients, or students to freely review testing materials would generally constitute an ethical violation. Many psychologists allow clients or patients to take the MMPI-2 home with them to complete since it generally takes about 1.5 hours to finish and it is a pencil-and-paper, self-report test. However, allowing the test to be taken home does not protect the security of the test nor does home-testing constitute standard testing procedure. Furthermore, a patient could have someone else help them with answers or even complete the test for them. If the test is taken home by the client, reliability and

---

Case Study: Dr. O

Dr. O is approached by the board of a computer software company that is interested in hiring a company president. They are hoping that Dr. O would be able to conduct a psychological evaluation to determine which of the three top candidates would make the best company president. The board feels that all three candidates are excellent, and that a better understanding of the psychological functioning, personality, and "character" of each person is needed to make the best decision. Dr. O decides to con-

duct a two-hour interview with each of the three candidates and then ask each to participate in psychological testing. Dr. O decides to use the Rorschach, the MMPI-2, and projective drawings. Based on the testing results, Dr. O recommends one of the candidates as being the most promising company president. Dr. O unethically used testing materials for purposes for which they were not intended. These instruments were neither designed nor validated for personnel selection.

Case Study: Dr. P

Dr. P administered an IQ test to a 7-year-old girl who is applying to attend a school for gifted and talented children. An IQ score of 130 is needed to be admitted into the school. The child obtained a score of 126 on the WISC-III. The child's mother feels that the test was an underestimate of her child's potential and suspects that the psychologist might have made an error in scoring the test. She demands that the psychologist give her a copy of the complete record form of the test so that she can have a school psychologist friend review the scoring. Dr. P feels intimidated by the child's mother and gives her the test. The mother has her child study the test

form provided by the psychologist and then take the test a second time with another psychologist who was unaware of the initial testing. She obtained a score of 139 on the second administration and was admitted to the school. Dr. P had an obligation to protect the security of the test materials and should not have given the mother a copy of the record form. While patients (or parents, if the patient is a minor) do have the legal right to review and copy their medical and other records in most states, they do not have the right to photocopy confidential and copyrighted psychological testing material.

validity as well as the security of the test are threatened.

Advertising and Other Public Statements Psychologists should avoid any false or deceptive public statements misrepresenting themselves, their training, experience, degrees, and activities. Psychologists must make all efforts to correct misleading or deceptive statements made by others on their behalf. Psychologists must not solicit testimonials from current patients or others who are potentially vulnerable.

Psychologists must be very careful in how they represent themselves to the public. They must not mislead or deceive others by overstating or exaggerating their qualifications and abilities. Furthermore, they must ensure that those who represent them not mislead or misrepresent their skills and qualifications. Psychologists who conduct interviews for radio or television programming must be especially

careful to prevent distortion of their statements and qualifications. Because the goal of such programming is often to entertain and sensationalize a topic rather than simply to inform, psychologists must be vigilant in avoiding potential ethical dilemmas (McCall, 1988; McGrath, 1995). Furthermore, interviews may be edited so that careful and thoughtful comments made by a psychologist can be removed while brief but potentially misleading sound bites retained. Psychologists must be careful to avoid having their comments taken out of context or manipulated to make an inappropriate or misleading point.

Therapy Psychologists must structure the therapeutic relationship in a professional manner. This includes clarifying from the outset what can be expected from psychotherapy, fees and confidentiality arrangements, and professional or training status. Psychologists must obtain informed consent prior to providing professional services. As mentioned

Case Study: Dr. Q

Dr. Q successfully treated a wealthy celebrity for depression. Dr. Q feels that if the celebrity would publicly tell others about the treatment, he would become well-known and highly sought out by both new patients and the media. Dr. Q suggests that the celebrity patient and he both

appear on a day-time talk show to discuss her treatment success. The patient reluctantly agrees feeling that she owes Dr. Q a favor for providing such valuable and successful treatment. Dr. Q unethically used his influence to have his famous patient provide a testimonial for his work.

Case Study: Ms. R.

Ms. R is a graduate student in clinical psychology completing her clinical internship at a local hospital. She has completed all of her course work and even her dissertation towards her doctorate. As soon as she completes her internship program, she will be finished with her graduate program and will be awarded her degree. Ms. R's supervisor is a psychiatrist who works at the hospital on a full-time basis. He introduces Ms. R. to patients at the hospital as "Dr. R." Ms. R informs her supervisor that she is not a "Dr." yet. The supervisor says that all students working at the hospital (including medical students) are referred to as "Dr." because it helps the patients have more confidence in their treatment. Because Ms. R feels that her supervisor, a licensed psychiatrist, must know what he is doing she drops the subject and introduces herself to patients as "Dr. R" Ms. R has committed an ethical violation by allowing her status to be misinterpreted by others, misleading patients and staff alike.

How would you have handled this situation?

previously, psychologists must never have sexual relationships with current clients and never begin therapy with someone with whom they have had a sexual relationship in the past. Psychologists must take precautions regarding any potential disruption in the service they provide due to personal problems, illness, relocation, or death. Psychologists should not abandon clients or work towards termination of a professional relationship unless it is in the best interest of the client. Psychologists need to maintain client confidentiality unless a legal or ethical exception emerges such as serious and immediate danger to self and others, or suspected child abuse information which they are mandated to report. Psychologists should maintain professional records in a confidential manner and provide a method in which they remain confidential in the case of the psychologist's death, relocation, or termination at an employment position.

Although it may seem obvious that psychologists should not engage in sexual relationships with their patients, sexual indiscretion is one of the major ethical violations brought to the attention of ethic boards in psychology (American Psychological Association, 1995c). In fact, Pope and Vasquez (1991) report that between 0.9 percent and 3.6 percent of male psychologists and 0.2 percent to 0.5 percent of female psychologists have had sexual relationships with their patients. Other surveys suggest that between 3 percent and 12 percent of psychologists have had sexual contact with their patients (Pope, 1994; Rodolfa, et al., 1994; Stake & Oliver, 1991). Surveys have also supported the finding that male psychologists are much more likely to engage in sexual relationships with their patients than female psychologists (Baur, 1997; Holroyd & Brodsky, 1977; Pope, 1994, Rodolfa et al., 1994)). Furthermore, about 80 percent of psychologists sexually involved with one patient have been sexually involved with other patients (Holroyd & Brofsky, 1977), including sexual involvement with children or adolescents (Bajt & Pope, 1989). One national

Case Study: Dr. S

Dr. S attended a six-week seminar at Harvard University during the summer months. Dr. S, who obtained his degrees at lesser known universities, loved being at such a prestigious university for the six week seminar. Following the seminar, Dr. S adds "Harvard University trained" to his resume, private practice stationary, and private practice brochures. He also mentions having been trained at Harvard University whenever he gives a public lecture. In fact, Dr. S appears to have developed a slight Boston accent! Dr. S behaves unethically in misrepresenting and exaggerating his training and experience at Harvard.

survey found that the vast majority of psychologists have been sexually attracted to some of their clients (87%) with most feeling guilty about these feelings (63%; Pope, Keith- Spiegel, & Tabachnick, 1986).

Psychologists are even more likely to engage in sexual intimacies with their students or supervisees. One survey revealed that 17 percent of female psychologists had sexual relationships with a graduate school professor (Glaser & Thorpe, 1986), while about 12 percent of psychology teachers reported having sexual relationships with students (Pope, Tabachnick, & Keith-Spiegal, 1987). The Ethics Code states that sexual intimacy between psychologist and patient is unethical during ongoing professional services such as psychotherapy as well as for at least two years following the termination of services (American Psychological Association, 1992a). Furthermore, sexual relationships that begin following the two year post-termination rule must demonstrate that they are not exploitive. A number of authors report being uncomfortable with any sexual relationships emerging between psychologist and patient even after two years following the termination of professional services (Gabbard, 1994). Although agreeing with the prohibition on sexual behavior between patients and therapists, some professionals feel that mutual attraction and love can be expected in many psychotherapy relationships and may even assist treatment (Baur, 1997).

Although confidentiality is critical to maintain in any psychotherapeutic relationship and every state has legal limitations on confidentiality (e.g., child abuse reporting laws), a sizeable number of psychologists do not warn their patients that there are limits to confidentiality. One survey revealed that 39 percent of psychologists reported that they did not discuss confidentiality arrangements with their patients and that 19 percent falsely inform their patients that everything that is mentioned in psychotherapy is confidential (Baird & Rupert, 1987).

Professional records must be maintained even following the termination of professional services. Many states have laws that determine how long professional records must be maintained. The American Psychological Association (1981) sug-

gests keeping full patient records for at least 3 years following the termination of professional services for adults and for 3 years past the age of maturity for minors. A summary of the patient record (or the complete record) is suggested to be maintained for an additional 12 years.

In the case of possible death or severe illness, a psychologist should make appropriate arrangements to ensure that client records are kept confidential yet are accessible to clients and their potential future psychologists or other mental health professionals with whom they choose to work. Psychologists should make arrangements for a colleague to handle the transition of records and services if such a crisis or situation unfolds.

Teaching, Training, Supervision, Research, and Publishing Psychologists must be accurate and objective in their teaching activities and teach only in areas that they are qualified. Training or educational programs that they conduct must include accurate descriptions of course information, goals, and evaluation methods. Psychologists must provide timely and appropriate feedback to students they supervise or evaluate. They must obtain informed consent from research subjects and handle animals used in research in a humane manner. They must design and plan their research studies in a responsible manner protecting the rights of others and reporting results in an honest and nonmisleading manner. Psychologists must avoid deception in research and when unavoidable, take necessary precautions to debrief and minimize harm to subjects. Psychologists must never engage in plagiarism and must distribute publication credit based on the legitimate contributions made by each author. Accordingly, psychologists do not duplicate the publication of their own or others' research data. They share data with colleagues when they wish to verify findings.

Forensic Activities Psychologists who provide forensic or legal/court related services are careful to use assessment instruments for the purposes for which they were developed. They are careful to clarify their roles in forensic work and avoid misleading statements.

Psychologists who work in forensic situations often provide expert testimony, consultation, and eval-

Case Study: Dr. T

Dr. T is a single psychologist looking for a mate. Dr. T conducts group psychotherapy and one of the group members mentions after a session that Dr. T should meet her niece. The patient feels that they would make a great couple. Dr. T agrees to go on a blind date with his patient's niece. They hit it off immediately and soon agree to marry. Dr. T continues seeing the patient in group psychotherapy but now also sees the patient at family events with his new wife. Although Dr. T did not have sexual relations with his patient, he developed a dual relationship by involving himself in the patient's family as well as dating and eventually marrying the patient's niece.

Case Study: Dr. U

Dr. U decides to close his practice and move to Hawaii. He provides his patients with one week of notice and closes his practice. Dr. U, in a hurry to begin his new life, makes no arrangements for his patients to continue receiving therapy with colleagues. He reports that they are smart and resourceful enough to find someone else if they need therapy and gives them a list of all the psychologists who are members of the county psychological association. Dr. U has clearly abandoned his patients and has neither ethically nor thoughtfully made appropriate arrangements for their therapy needs.

Case Study: Dr. V

Dr. V is anxious about tenure. She feels that she is not a great researcher but really enjoys teaching and the academic lifestyle. She collected a great deal of data for her doctoral dissertation and decides to see how many professional articles she can publish based on this one study. She decides to write five different papers, each focusing on some small detail of her project. She later decides to publish a review article of her subject area primarily focusing on her five now published articles. Dr. V exploits her data set to give the appearance that she has conducted five separate studies rather than one. Dr. V unethically conducts her research in an irresponsible and misleading manner to increase her chances of obtaining tenure.

Case Study: Dr. W

Dr. W is a professor who supervises several doctoral dissertation projects conducted by graduate students in his department. After working with students for many months and even years in some cases, Dr. W decides without warning to fail several of the students during their final dissertation oral defense. He informs them that their projects are unsatisfactory and not worthy of a dissertation. Dr. W 's actions were irresponsible and unethical because he never provided timely and appropriate feedback to his students during the course of conducting the projects and failed them without warning or feedback.

Case Study: Dr. X

Dr. X is conducting a psychological evaluation in a child custody lawsuit. He conducts an evaluation of the child and both parents who are fighting over custody of the child. He encourages each person to be as honest and open as possible and asserts that he will do whatever is in the best interest of each person. In a vulnerable moment, the father tells Dr. X that he really doesn't want to have custody but that he wants to get back at his wife for her infidelity. The father thinks that this information will be held in confidence. The father is later infuriated that Dr. X included this statement in the evaluation report. Dr. X did not make clear to all of the parties involved what would and would not be communicated in the report and to the court. In fact, Dr. X also tape recorded the evaluation without the knowledge or consent of the parties involved. Dr. X unethically failed to clarify his role in the evaluation, and failed to obtain informed consent and establish the boundaries of confidentiality prior to conducting the evaluations.

uation for legal cases involving, for example, child custody arrangements, workman's compensation, or criminal proceedings to determine sanity. Often there are a number of different and opposing parties involved and invested in the work of the psychologist. These may include the judge, attorneys, defendants, and plaintiffs, among others. Psychologists working in forensic activities must make their role and limits clear to all parties involved to avoid misunderstandings and potential unethical or biased behavior. Furthermore, they must always be vigilant to testify within their areas of expertise and utilize data clearly supported by their evaluation results. The American Psychology-Law Society (Division 41 of the American Psychological Association) has developed specific practice guidelines for psychologists working in legal settings (Committee on Ethical Guidelines for Forensic Psychologists, 1991).

Resolving Ethical Issues   Psychologists must be familiar with the Ethics Code and apply it to their professional work setting. They cooperate with ethics committees and try to resolve ethical dilemmas in an educative rather than punitive manner. If ethical conflicts cannot be resolved informally, psychologists must report ethical violations to the appropriate authority.

Why Would a Psychologist Behave in an Unethical Manner?

Psychologists are, alas, human beings, and they make mistakes in both judgement and behavior. While some psychologists are well aware that they are committing ethical violations, many others are not. Some allow their own needs to supercede those of their patients, students, colleagues, and the greater public. Some psychologists are emotionally disturbed, some are selfish, some are unaware of their missteps, some make errors in judgement, and

Case Study: Dr. Y

Dr. Y is a new assistant professor at a small college. Several of her students tell her about the classroom behavior of Dr. Z. They report that Dr. Z seems to use the same lecture notes from 20 years ago, runs out of things to say in class, and routinely lets class out long before the time period ends. They also state that Dr. Z frequently talks about how much money he makes on a textbook he authored and offers strong opinions about other faculty members and their professional activities. Because Dr. Y does not have tenure, she refuses to get involved in any way. She tells her students that her hands are tied and that some professors are better than others. Dr. Y is not only insensitive to the needs and dilemmas faced by her students, but does nothing to assist in correcting the unethical behavior of Dr. Z.

Case Study: Dr. AA

Dr. AA is conducting an evaluation with an eight-year-old child to determine if the child has an attention deficit hyperactivity disorder (ADHD). The child's parents have few financial resources and hope that their health care insurance will pay for most or all of the costs to complete the evaluation. Dr. AA completes the evaluation and determines that the child does not have ADHD. In fact, Dr. AA failed to find any diagnosable disorder (e.g., depression, oppositional defiant, anxiety). Because no diagnosis can be determined, the insurance provider will not pay for the evaluation. The child's parents feel that they cannot afford the evaluation and ask Dr. AA to list some diagnosis on the insurance forms so that the insurance company will pay for the evaluation. Dr. AA is concerned about his patient's financial problems and agrees to give the child a diagnosis of adjustment disorder with mixed emotional features. While Dr. AA is well meaning in trying to help his patient, he is committing not only an ethical violation but a legal one as well. Committing insurance fraud is a serious legal offense.

---

some innocently fall into behavior that results in an ethical violation.

Many may assume that those who commit ethical violations are incompetent or malicious. However, well meaning psychologists striving to do what they believe is in the best interest of their patients, students, or others commit ethical violations as well. No one is immune from engaging in unethical behavior. Even well-trained, well-meaning, and thoughtful psychologists may commit ethical violations.

Being well informed of the Ethics Code and obtaining consultation when needed can greatly help to minimize the chances of making ethical violations. Furthermore, being attentive to ethical behavior in others can also assist in minimizing the chances that unethical behavior will continue once it has begun.

Sieber (1982) suggested that ethical violations tend to fall into one of six categories. The first category of common error includes inexperience or ignorance on the part of the psychologist leading to an unforeseen ethical dilemma. For example, a psychologist may not realize that photocopying the record form from an intelligence test and giving it to the parents of a child violates the ethical requirement of protecting the security and confidentiality of testing materials.

A second common ethical category involves an underestimate by the psychologist regarding the potential for an ethical problem. For instance, a disorganized psychologist trying to save time may not take appropriate precautions to ensure that research subjects give informed consent prior to participating in a research study and are fully debriefed when the study is completed.

A third category outlined by Sieber includes ethical dilemmas that are unavoidable in the eyes of the psychologist. For example, a psychologist may

---

Case Study: Dr. BB

Dr. BB is treating a graduate student in psychology for anxiety and depressive concerns. The patient is having a very hard time completing his dissertation project. In fact, his graduate program has threatened to terminate his enrollment if he does not complete the project within several months. Dr. BB, wishing to help his patient, offers to give him a project he has been interested in completing and offers to be a member of his dissertation committee. Dr. BB agrees to deceive the graduate program so that they won't find out that Dr. BB is treating the student in psychotherapy. Dr. BB is willing to enter into an unethical dual relationship in an effort to try and help his patient complete his dissertation project.

Both Drs. AA and BB are well meaning in their efforts to go the extra mile for their patients. Their unethical behavior can actually result in advantages to their patients. However, their behavior compromises their therapeutic relationships and the integrity of the profession.

feel it necessary to break confidentiality while working with an adolescent because of concerns about behaviors such as stealing and drug use.

A fourth category subsumes foreseen ethical dilemmas that arise out of a new procedure or approach. For instance, a new treatment may result in unforeseen harm to patients, which the clinician could not have predicted.

A fifth category includes ethical problems that emerge when no clear guidelines exist or guidelines are ambiguous in a particular situation. This can happen as new technology and different approaches develop (e.g., Internet) that impact psychological services and are not addressed directly in the current Ethics Code.

Finally, ethical problems exist when the law contradicts ethical guidelines. For example, a judge may subpoena all of a patient's records from a psychologist. These records may include therapy notes and psychological testing data. Because the Ethics Code states that confidentiality cannot be broken without patient permission (or when someone is in immediate and serious danger) and that testing materials cannot be released to those not qualified to interpret them (e.g., nonpsychologists), then the Ethics Code and legal demands are in conflict.

How Are Ethics Enforced?

All members of the American Psychological Association are instructed to read and agree to follow the Ethics Code (American Psychological Association, 1992a). Members are not only expected to know and follow the Code but are obligated to help correct unethical behavior by colleagues through education or by reporting them to local or national ethics boards. However only about 8 percent of psychologists report that they would be willing to report on a distressed colleague making ethical violations (Wood, Klein, Cross, Lammers, & Elliott, 1985). All authors of articles published in journals published by the American Psychological Association are asked to sign a statement prior to publication indicating that their research was completed in keeping with the ethical guidelines. State licensing examinations and procedures include the Ethics Code in the examination process. Furthermore, a

number of books are published by the American Psychological Association to help psychologists more fully understand professional ethics (e.g., Bersoff, 1995; Canter, Bennett, Jones, & Nagy, 1994). Professional ethics are also generally taught during graduate school and internship/postdoctoral training (Plante, 1995). Therefore, all psychologists are expected to know and follow the ethical standards set forth by the American Psychological Association. Ignorance of the Ethics Code is no excuse for unethical behavior.

Consumers of psychological services also help in enforcing ethical guidelines. Patients, students, clients, supervisors, colleagues, and others who complain about the professional conduct of a psychologist do so by contacting local professional associations or state boards of psychology. These complaints often are directed to local and national ethics boards associated with psychological associations such as the American Psychological Association.

The American Psychological Association maintains a committee to evaluate and monitor ethical violations. Complaints that the committee deem to have merit are investigated and acted upon. Depending upon the results of the investigation, the committee may provide the psychologist with an educative advisory, warnings for minor violations or for ethical but unprofessional conduct, a reprimand or censure for more severe violations, or demand resignation or expulsion from the association for highly serious violations. Furthermore, the American Psychological Association ethics committee works closely with state and local ethics committees and licensing boards to ensure that psychologists who are found to be guilty of ethical violations are appropriately dealt with at the local level (e.g., suspension or revocation of a state license to practice for serious violations).

Each state has independent licensing boards that assist in monitoring the practices of psychologists. The boards process applicants for licensure and assist in monitoring the professional conduct of psychologists once they are licensed. The licensing board can grant, deny, suspend, or revoke, licenses to practice. For example, a license can be denied if the applicant does not meet minimum standards for training or has failed to pass the licensing examinations. Licenses can be suspended or revoked when a psychologist has been found to be engaging in unethical or illegal activity. The most common reasons that malpractice claims are filed result from inappropriate sexual behavior on the part of the psychologist, suicide of a patient, and inappropriate treatment conducted with a patient. Sexual dual relationships account for the majority of claims paid to plaintiffs by the American Psychological Association's liability insurance carrier (Pope, 1991).

What Is the Process for Solving Ethical Dilemmas?

When ethical dilemmas arise, it is important to consult the Ethics Code to determine precisely what the written guidelines instruct. Second, consultation with colleagues concerning the conduct or issue in question can be extremely useful (Fig. 13.1). If it has been determined that an ethical violation has or may have occurred, the psychologist discovering the violation has a duty to bring it to the attention of the offending psychologist. For minor violations committed by error or oversight, educating the person about the ethical principles involved is generally an adequate means of correcting the problematic conduct. If the collegial educative process does not

result in ethical behavior, or if the violation is serious, the psychologist has the ethical responsibility to inform the ethics board at the state or national level. The ethics board then collects information and determines whether the infraction is worthy of investigation and either action or dismissal.

Is Behaving in Accordance With the Ethical Principles Always Clear Cut?

While it seems obvious that psychologists should maintain professional competence, never have sexual relationships with current or recent patients or students, and maintain patient confidentiality, numerous ethical dilemmas emerge that are more ambiguous and highly challenging to resolve. Pope and Vetter (1992) report several cases that surfaced from a national survey of 1319 members of the American Psychological Association. While easy answers to many cases cannot be found, careful analysis and professional consultation usually results in the soundest decision and professional judgement.

For example, Pope and Vetter (1992) describe the following case scenarios for consideration.

Case 1: A psychologist who has been treating

Figure 13.1 When an ethical dilemma arises, a psychologist may consult with colleagues

a women for three years in psychotherapy coincidentally begins to date her best and closest friend.

Case 2: A psychologist in a rural community is active in his church group. Members of the church group wish to consult with him on a professional basis because they know and trust him and he is the only professional in the area that offers particular speciality services.

Case 3: A psychologist conducts psychotherapy with a child. Soon after the beginning of therapy, the child's mother and the therapist develop a strong mutual attraction. The psychologist considers referring the patient elsewhere but feels that therapeutic gains will be lost.

Case 4: A psychologist is providing psychotherapy to another psychologist. The patient reveals that he has committed a serious ethical violation. The patient states that due to patient confidentiality, the therapist cannot report the violation.

Case 5: The rules of a university medical center dictate that a psychologist must give Principal Investigator (P.I.) status on research grants to a physician even if the physician is not actually the P.I. on the project.

How should these actual cases be handled? Each of the cases mentioned do not have simple and clear cut answers. Careful review and consideration of the Ethics Code as well as appropriate consultation is generally required in order to make reasonable professional and ethical judgements.

The Big Picture

The Ethics Code provides useful guidelines for psychologists as well as the public concerning the standards of professional conduct. The American Psychological Association has carefully revised the Code eight times since the first edition was published in 1953. They have worked to ensure that a great deal of input from members of the organization occurs with each revision. The Code is "living" in that it is frequently discussed in professional journals and circles and is updated often. Many professionals have suggested that the current Ethics Code is a significant improvement over earlier versions, including greater detail and clarification regarding many of the principles (Koocher, 1994; Vasquez, 1994). Furthermore, the American Psychological Association spends more money on issues of professional ethics than any other professional organization (Chalk, Frankel, & Chafer, 1980).

However, not everyone is satisfied with the Ethics Code (Gabbard, 1994; Keith-Spiegel, 1994; Koocher & Keith-Spiegel, 1998; Lakin, 1994; Payton, 1994; Sonne, 1994). Some have argued that the Code does not go far enough in its emphasis on the declaration of respect for the worth and dignity of individuals. Payton (1994) reports that the Code should go further in addressing issues of relevance to ethnic minority group members as well as women, gay men and lesbians. Others are concerned that the code does not go far enough in protecting patients and students from sexual exploitation by psychologists (Gabbard, 1994; Koocher & Keith-Spiegel, 1998; Layman & McNamara, 1997). In fact, unlike previous versions of the Ethics Code, the current version allows for sexual relationships between psychologists and patients under special circumstances two years following the termination of services. Some argue that issues pertaining to multipatient therapies such as family therapy, couples therapy, and group therapy are not adequately addressed in the Ethics Code (Lakin, 1994). Some cynically state that the Code is designed to protect psychologists more than the public (Payton, 1994). Finally, some argue that much of the Code is too vague and does not provide specific guidelines in a number of important areas (Koocher & Keith-Spiegel, 1998).

However imperfect, the Ethics Code provides a working standard of conduct by which persons who receive psychological services can judge professional behavior. All psychologists are expected to both know and follow the Ethics Code. Professional ethical guidelines in psychology are not simply strict laws to follow or violate. Infractions are not generally met with a punitive response (unless the violation is very serious with potential significant harm to the public.) Rather, professional ethics in psychology are meant to be educative and ethical dilemmas are generally resolved informally among colleagues. Diligent attention to ethical behavior upholds the stature, helpfulness, and humanitarian goals of the clinical psychology profession.

Although many future revisions of the ethics code is assured, the basic principles of ethical behavior outlined many years ago by Hippocrates are likely to be applicable indefinitely. Future clinical psychologists will always be expected to behave in a competent, professional, ethical manner and maintain integrity and responsibility in their professional roles and responsibilities. It is unlikely that these basic tenets will ever change.

Key Points

1. Whether a psychologist is a researcher, teacher, therapist, or administrator, he or she is expected to maintain the highest professional ethics in all professional activities at all times.

2. Most complaints that result in action against psychologists by the American Psychological Association involve breaking confidentiality, sexual misconduct (e.g., sexual relationship with a patient), nonsexual dual relationships (e.g., friendships or business partnerships with patients), and insurance/fee misbehavior (e.g., over billing insurance, billing for services not rendered).

3. Since 1953, the American Psychological Association has had an Ethics Code that specifically outlined the behavior expected of all psychologists. The Ethics Code has been updated eight times since 1953 and the current version was published in December, 1992 (American Psychological Association, 1992).

4. The current version of the ethical principles for psychologists is divided into six general principles and eight ethical standards. The general principles include (1) competence, (2) integrity, (3) professional and scientific responsibility, (4) respect for people's rights and dignity, (5) concern for others' welfare, and (6) social responsibility. The ethical standards include (1) general standards, (2) advertising and other public statements, (3) therapy privacy and confidentiality, (4) teaching, training, supervision, research, and publishing, (5) forensic activities, and (6) resolving ethical issues.

5. Psychologists must maintain competence in their area(s) of specialization and work. They must only provide services that they have the appropriate training and experience to legitimately offer to the public. They must also stay up-to-date on changes and advances in the field in order to ensure that they maintain state-of-the-art skills.

6. Psychologists must maintain professional and personal integrity and be respectful, fair, and honest in their dealings with others. They must be truthful in describing their services, their areas of expertise, and what can be expected from participation in their services. They must be well aware of their biases, needs, and values and how each of these impact their work.

7. Psychologists should make all efforts to avoid inappropriate dual relationships.

8. Psychologists must be willing to consult with others as indicated in order to best serve their patients or clients. They must also help to avoid unethical behavior engaged in by colleagues. Psychologists must be responsible for their own conduct and accept their obligations to the larger profession and public welfare.

9. Psychologists must be respectful of the rights and dignity of others. They must be sensitive to individual and cultural differences as well as vigilant in providing nondiscriminatory services. They must respect the rights to freedom, privacy, and confidentiality of their patients and clients.

10. Psychologists work to improve the quality of life and never incur harm through their work with others. Psychologists must never exploit their relationships with others.

11. Psychologists work to help others and advance the science and knowledge of human behavior. Psychologists are expected to contribute some professional time to causes that do not result in financial or other personal gains.

12. Many may assume that those who commit ethical violations are usually incompetent or malicious. However, well meaning psychologists seeking to best serve the interests of their patients, students, or others commit ethical violations. No one is immune from engaging in unethical behavior. Even well-trained, well-meaning, and thoughtful psychologists are capable of committing an ethical violation.

13. Ethical principles are developed at the national level by the American Psychological Association to protect the public and profession as well as to provide guidelines for conduct among psychologists. All psychologists are expected to know and follow the ethical standards set forth by the American Psychological Association. Ignorance of the Ethics Code is no excuse for unethical behavior.

Key Terms

Confidentiality   Dual Relationships   Ethics Code

For Reflection

1. What are the general principles and ethical standards of the American Psychological Association Ethics Code?

2. Why bother having an Ethics Code?

3. What are the most common ethical violations?

4. Why would a psychologist make an ethical violation?

5. What is a dual relationship and why should it be avoided?

6. Why shouldn't psychologists have sexual relationships with patients or students following the termination of their professional relationship?

7. What are some of the pros and cons to the Ethics Code?

8. How are ethical dilemmas resolved?

9. How might the Ethics Code be changed in the future?

10. How do ethics and the law relate?

PART 3

Where Is Clinical Psychology Going and Should I Go with It?

CHAPTER 14

Current and Future Trends and Challenges in Contemporary Clinical Psychology

Chapter Outline

Highlight of a Contemporary Clinical Psychologist: Nicholas A. Cummings, Ph.D., Sc.D.

Trends in Society

Research Issues

Practice Issues

Reaching Beyond Mental Health in Contemporary Clinical Psychology

Training Issues

HIGHLIGHT OF A CONTEMPORARY CLINICAL PSYCHOLOGIST:

Nicholas A. Cummings, Ph.D., Sc.D.

Dr. Cummings is past-president of the American Psychological Association and founder of the first psychology preferred provider organization, American Biodyne.

Birth Date: July 25, 1924

College: University of California, Berkeley (A.B. Psychology), 1948

Graduate Program: Claremont College (M.A. Psychology), 1952; Adelphi University (Ph.D. Clinical Psychology), 1958

Clinical Internship: New Hope Guild Center, Brooklyn, NY; Creedmoor State Hospital, Queens, NY; Patton State Hospital, Patton, CA

Postdoctoral Fellowship: William Alanson White, New York

Current Job: President, Foundation for Behavioral Health; President, U.K. Behavioural Health, Ltd.; Chairman, The Nicholas & Dorothy Cummings Foundation, Inc.

Job Locations: Reno, NV; Scottsdale, AZ, London, U.K.

Pros and cons of being a clinical psychologist:

Pros: "Clinical psychology has an array of exciting challenges as the healthcare system in America is continuing to industrialize. Psychologists can be entrepreneurs, executives, supervisors, program planners, outcomes researchers, and perform many other exciting roles, including that of master therapist/supervisor."

Cons: "Those who cannot make the appropriate paradigm shifts should not go into clinical psychology, as they will be shutout."

Future of clinical psychology: "Fifty percent of those practicing today will not make it into the next century. Those who prosper will have the roles described above. Masters level clinicians will do most of the psychotherapy and most treatment will have empirically derived protocols. The future of clinical psychology is in behavioral health as medicine, surgery and mental health/chemical dependency integrate as primary care. Clinical psychologists should join physicians in regional group practices as practitioner/owners."

Typical schedule:

6:00   Telephone calls to east coast consulting with managed care companies regarding strategies to provide comprehensive mental health services at affordable costs

7:00	Telephone calls continue.	1:00	Writing on current book about the integration of behavioral and primary health care.
8:00	Running or biking.		
9:00	Teleconference to London concerning integration of behavioral and primary care health provision.	2:00	Writing continues.
		3:00	Writing continues.
10:00	Consult with attorneys regarding malpractice case acting as an expert witness.	4:00	Consult with several psychologists concerning methods to provide quality substance abuse treatment in a new large group practice.
11:00	Consultation continues.		
12:00	Return calls & lunch	5:00	Consultation continues.
		6:00	Return calls. Prepare for next day.

Clinical psychology has evolved and changed rapidly during its 100-year history. The influence of leaders in the field such as Sigmund Freud, B. F. Skinner, and Carl Rogers, and events such as the two world wars, the availability of National Institute of Mental Health (NIMH) training grants, and the advent of managed health care have expedited change and development. However, it is difficult to imagine a more rapidly changing period in clinical psychology than the present. Today, clinical psychology looks very different than it did, not only 20 or 30 years ago, but even 5 years ago. Of course, changes in society as well as in many other professions have paralleled this evolution. For example, recent advances in science, technology, and information systems, as well as the innovation of managed health care and a growing sensitivity to multicultural and diversity issues, have all contributed to the evolution and advancement of contemporary clinical psychology. Where is clinical psychology going? What is its future? What are some of the current hot topics in clinical psychology? What are its current and future challenges? These are some of the questions addressed in this chapter.

One of the best examples of a current hot topic in clinical psychology is the advent of managed health care. Some have suggested that managed health care may alter clinical psychology in a permanent and profound way (Anders, 1996; Benedict & Phelps, 1998; Cummings, 1984, 1995; Fox, 1994; Kovacs, 1996). Although managed health care will be addressed in more detail later, a brief introduction to this important issue is warranted to demonstrate how quickly fundamental aspects of clinical psychology can change. Since the 1970s (and much earlier for physicians), someone who wanted to see a clinical psychologist for psychotherapy or other psychological service could choose to be treated by any licensed psychologist in his or her geographical area. The psychologist would conduct as many sessions as necessary to best treat the patient, using whatever theoretical orientation(s) and techniques he or she deemed appropriate in order to provide competent and professional service. Insurance carriers such as Blue Cross/Blue Shield would rarely question the treatment plan, and would typically reimburse between 50 percent and 80 percent of the fees regardless of whether the treatment lasted for 3 sessions or for 300. A similar scenario existed for physicians of all specialities.

Over the past several years (primarily during the late 1980s and 1990s), this scenario has changed radically. Today, the patient typically contacts his or her insurance carrier to determine which therapists in the patient's area are part of the insurance company's preferred provider list. The patient then contacts the professional and is allowed a specific number of sessions authorized by the insurance carrier. The authorized number of sessions is usually just a few (e.g., three to six). The patient pays nothing or a nominal fee (i.e., co-payment) for the sessions. However, the provider accepts a discount or a reduction (usually about 30%) in his or her usual fee in order to be on the provider panel. Additional sessions or other treatment modalities (e.g., inpatient care, group psychotherapy, family psychotherapy) must be authorized by the insurance company before these services can be provided. The insurance company representatives carefully examine the treatment plan offered by the provider and encourage very brief, problem-focused services. In many ways, the changes in managed health care are permanently changing the science and practice of clinical psychology (e.g., emphasis on low-cost, brief crisis intervention) as well as the entire health care system. These changes significantly impact all major areas of clinical psychology including research, training, and practice, as well as the larger cultural climate for public demand for psychological services. For example, since most managed care companies will not authorize treatment conducted by trainees, many hospitals and clinics cannot continue to train psychology trainees and expect to get insurance reimbursement for their services.

Trends in Society

Clinical psychology must change and adapt to a changing world just like any other field of study or practice. It would be foolish for clinical psychology to keep its "head in the sand" and try to resist societal changes (Benedict & Phelps, 1998; Cummings, 1995; Klein, 1996; Plante, 1996b). Rather, clinical psychology must grow and develop based on the issues and concerns of the world at large as well as to changes within the field as new research discoveries and clinical practice strategies emerge. In the words of Rachel Klein, "psychology has to move with the times and should welcome the opportunity" (Klein, 1996, p. 216). Issues such as family changes, multicultural sensitivity, scientific advances, financial challenges, and gender shifts in professions will be highlighted here.

Contemporary Changes in the American Family

The American family has changed a great deal in recent years. The traditional image of a married couple living with two or more of their own children is no longer the norm (U.S. Bureau of the Census, 1990). Today, 50 percent of marriages end in divorce, about 20 percent of adults over the age of 18 live alone, and approximately 55 percent of people report cohabitating together prior to marriage (U.S. Bureau of the Census, 1990). Many households include single or remarried parents with blended families. It has been estimated that about 33 percent of children born in the 1980s will live with a stepparent before they reach 18 years of age (Kantrowitz & Wingert, 1990). Families today may include adopted or "test tube" children, children and parents of mixed ethnicity, race, and religious backgrounds, gay and lesbian parents, single parents, and unmarried parents.

The changing face of the American family has implications for clinical psychology and related fields. Families who experience stress associated with, for example, being a single parent, integrating children in blended families under one roof, or dealing with discrimination associated with sexual orientation or interracial issues, have unique needs and concerns. Clinical psychologists must be sensitive to the issues associated with the changing American family and must be able to provide competent assessment, treatment, and consultation to these families.

Multicultural and Diversity Issues

The United States has quickly become an ethnically and culturally diverse nation. It has been estimated that approximately 25 percent of the American population consists of ethnic minorities, with 43 percent in California (Sue, Zane, & Young, 1994; U.S. Bureau of the Census, 1990). Of the approximately 250 million Americans in the United States, about 30 million are African Americans; 25 million Latino Americans; and 10 million Asian Americans (Sue et al., 1994). The increase in numbers of ethnic minorities and immigrants has been dramatic. During the 1980s, the number of Asian Americans rose by over 100 percent, and by 2000 the majority of people living in California will be ethnic minority group members. About 33 percent of the American population will be comprised of ethnic minorities in 2000 with 50 percent by the year 2050 (U.S. Bureau of the Census, 1995). Increasing attention and interest have been focused in recent years on the role of **multicultural** and **diversity** issues in all aspects of society (Hall, 1997; Trickett, Watts, & Birman, 1994). Psychologists, as well as professionals from other fields, have acquired greater insight into the role of culture and diversity in the development of behavior and behavioral problems (Bernal & Castro, 1994; Fowers & Richardson, 1996; Hall, 1997).

The role of social context and culture are powerful influences on behavior. The understanding of culture is critical to the understanding of psychological and physical symptoms as well as in developing treatment interventions. For example, conversion disorders, which were rather common during Freud's time, are less common today in Western culture. The cultural context of the emotional and sexually repressive Victorian era along with the oppression of women have been associated with the frequency of conversion disorders 100 years ago (Shorter, 1994). Certain hypochondriacal and conversion disorders are found in some cultures but not others. For example, "koro" involves the belief that genitals are retracting into the stomach region and primarily occurs among Asian men (Rubin, 1982). Other culture specific illnesses include "dhat," anxiety about semen loss among men in India, hot sensations in the head among African individuals, and burning sensations in the hands and feet among Pakistanis (Ebigno, 1986). These symptoms tend to be culture bound and all involve anxiety and depressive affect associated with bodily complaints that have no known physiological cause.

Even disorders that appear to be universally found among all cultures manifest differently depending on the specific culture. For example, schizophrenia seems to be found in all cultures. However, whereas schizophrenics from American and other industrialized Western countries generally experience auditory hallucinations, those from Latin American and African countries typically experience visual hallucinations (Ndetei & Singh, 1983). Although it is unclear what might contribute to these cultural differences in the manifestation of symptoms, psychologists and other mental health professionals must be sensitive to cultural issues with all they treat (Garb, 1997).

The American Psychological Association (APA, 1990) has urged psychologists to "become familiar with indigenous beliefs and practices and respect them" (p. 3). Guidelines developed by the APA assert that both researchers and clinicians must develop and maintain a "sociocultural framework" (p. 45) and "consider diversity of values, interactional styles, and cultural expectations in a systematic fashion" (p.45) in their efforts to provide professional psychological service (American Psychological Association, 1993a). Eighty-percent of graduate training programs now require coursework on multicultural issues (Bernal & Castro, 1994) with most of the remaining programs soon to follow (Hall, 1997). Moreover, psychologists must "recognize ethnicity and culture as significant parameters in understanding psychological processes" (p. 46). Thus, social factors such as ethnicity and culture are now highlighted as critical factors to consider and integrate in clinical psychology. Symp-

toms occur in the context of culture and thus culture must be understood to understand and treat problems.

Increasing attention and sensitivity toward various ethnic and cultural groups (e.g., African Americans, Mexican Americans, Asian Americans) have also generalized to other nonethnic minority groups (e.g., gays and lesbians, women, persons with physical disabilities, various religious groups). This development has led to new strategies and methods for helping those with emotional and behavioral concerns among these groups. The traditional 50-minute hour of individual insight oriented psychotherapy in the psychologist's office may be of limited value for many. Customary methods of conducting research as well as practice must be carefully examined and potentially altered to accommodate people from diverse backgrounds (American Psychological Association, 1993a; Brown, 1990; Garb, 1997; Greene, 1993; Hall, 1997; Lopez et al., 1989; Tharp, 1991). The vast majority of studies on psychotherapy outcome have used Americans or British subjects who tend to be fairly homogeneous in terms of race, income, and background. Since most therapies were developed from research and practice with middle- or upper-economic level Caucasians, their generalizability to minority groups has been seriously and legitimately questioned (Hall, 1997; Landrine, 1992; Lopez et al., 1989; Trickett et al., 1994). For example, psychological treatment integrating traditional ethnic healing methods (e.g., the use of sweat lodges, talking circles) is now advised for many Native Americans (LaFromboise, 1988), and sensitivity to the role of family hierarchy and the "loss of face" (i.e., shamed among others) dynamic is important for many Asian-American clients (Murase, 1977; Sue et al., 1994). Furthermore, researchers and clinicians are more sensitive to the notion that tremendous diversity in perspectives, needs, and issues exists within each ethnic or minority group (Bernal & Castro, 1994; Fowers & Richardson, 1996; Landrine, 1992; Sue et al., 1994). Therefore, generalizing assessment, treatment, or research strategies to all ethnic or minority groups is inappropriate. Acculturation and assimilation factors as well as unique individual differences must be taken into consideration when working with members of diverse groups (Lopez et al., 1989).

More minority representation is needed within the field of psychology to provide better service to minority group members (Bernal & Castro, 1994; Hall, 1997; Landrine, 1992; Lopez et al., 1989). Although the United States has become a highly diverse nation, the vast majority of clinical psychologists are Caucasian. For example, fewer than 5 percent of the clinical psychology division of the American Psychological Association (Division 12) is Asian, Hispanic, or African American (American Psychological Association, 1993a). Of all the psychology doctorates awarded in 1993, fewer than 10 percent were awarded to ethnic minority group members (American Psychological Association, 1995b). The American Psychological Association has thus encouraged graduate training programs to increase minority group representation in graduate and postgraduate (e.g., internship and postdoctoral fellowship) admissions. As a result of these efforts, 17 percent of incoming doctoral students in psychology are now ethnic minority group members (Norcross, Hanych, & Terranova, 1996).

Advances in Science, Technology, and Medicine

Recent advances and significant discoveries in science, technology, and medicine have greatly impacted clinical psychology as well as many other fields. Every day newspapers across the country report the latest developments in these areas. The enthusiasm generated by these reports typically reinforces the old medical model notion that the mind and body are separate and that biology is at the root of most human behavior. Thus the biopsychosocial model is challenged by the seventeeth-century medical model even as current scientific advances unfold. The development of Prozac to treat depression, efforts to find the "fat gene" and develop fat substitutes, and medication treatments (e.g., Ritalin) to treat attention deficit disorders are excellent examples demonstrating how scientific advances influence attitudes about mind-body relationships.

Research conducted by pharmaceutical companies as well as by other investigators have resulted in the development of Prozac to treat depression. Prozac was introduced in 1987 and quickly became enormously popular. In fact, it has been estimated that over 20 million people take Prozac worldwide (Horgan, 1996) and it is the topic of several best-sellers as well (Kramer, 1993; Wurtzel, 1995). Im-

proved medications to treat depression (such as Prozac) and other psychiatric symptoms (e.g., anxiety, bulimia) have fueled support for the biological foundation of many psychological problems. Advocates argue that if medication greatly reduces symptoms of depression or other psychiatric concerns, then biological factors such as chemical imbalances in the brain may be at the root of symptoms. This is faulty thinking. As discussed earlier, medications impacting behavior do not provide a causal link between biological causes of behavior. Contrary to research findings, many maintain the attitude that psychosocial interventions (such as psychotherapy) are of marginal value in comparison with these powerful new medications. The *remedicalization* of psychiatry with increasing emphasis on biological interventions (e.g., medication) and less emphasis on psychosocial treatments (e.g., psychotherapy) further diminishes adherence to a more comprehensive biopsychosocial framework (Fleck, 1995).

The same trend is illustrated by the treatment of obesity. Scientific efforts to discover the fat gene as well as the development of fat substitutes reinforce a strictly biological view of obesity and overeating, ignoring the role of psychosocial factors (Bouchard, 1995; Gibbs, 1996; Zhang, Proenca, Barone, Leopold, & Friedman, 1994). However, research continues to support the biopsychosocial perspective in obesity treatment (e.g., Brownell, 1991).

Medication treatment for attention deficit hyperactivity disorder (ADHD) provides yet another example of the impact of scientific advances on clinical psychology. Many parents and teachers show more interest in using medication to control the symptoms of ADHD (e.g., impulsivity, distractibility) than in using psychosocial interventions (e.g., parenting skill development, stimulus control procedures). As in the previous examples, medication treatment for ADHD perpetuates the notion that these symptoms are due solely to biological issues and thus need biological solutions, whereas research supports the biopsychosocial perspective (e.g., Barkley, 1989).

Technological advances (e.g., computer technology, fax machines, cellular phones, video, electronic mail, and virtual reality) also have an impact on clinical psychology. For instance, maintaining confidentiality when using computers to keep track of patient information is an important and controversial issue. Potential access to computer files and discs containing sensitive and confidential patient information and the breaking of security codes are of great concern to many. The use of the Internet (e.g., e-mail) as well as the telephone to conduct psychotherapy or psychological consultation is also controversial (Bloom, 1992; Haas, Benedict, & Kobos, 1996; Roan , 1992; Sleek, 1997). Some argue that the telephone and the Internet may be acceptable avenues for conducting psychological services, while others feel it would be unethical to use these unsecured methods. Some say that telephone or Internet access to psychotherapy might have important advantages such as immediate access to services, privacy, and availability of services for more people (Haas et al., 1996; Mermelstein & Holland, 1991; Tausig & Freeman, 1988; Tolmach, 1985). However, others have cautioned that these services may be counterproductive in crisis situations and therefore may be abused (Haas et al., 1996; Nagy, 1987).

Virtual reality has also been used to treat anxiety and other psychological disorders (Binik, Cantor, Ochs, & Meana, 1997; Glantz, Durlach, Barnett, & Aviles, 1996). Patients and therapists can use virtual reality technology in exposure-style treatments. For example, a person with a phobic reaction can visualize the feared object in a realistic yet safe manner using this approach.

Many technological advances have also increased the ability of clinical psychologists to obtain important information about issues of interest. For example, countless World Wide Web (WWW) locations provide information on topics such as mental health resources, self-help newsletters, mental health legal issues, and family issues; there is even a WWW page dedicated to Freud (Zuckerman, 1996). The ease of accessing so much information can help psychologists maintain state-of-the-art services.

Money

During the economic boom of the 1960s and 1970s, federal money from the NIMH and other government agencies was available to fund clinical psychology research, supplement the expense of training psychologists in graduate and postgraduate programs, and provide services for those in need (e.g., the community mental health movement). During the "lean and mean 90s" efforts to reduce costs, to become more efficient, and to decrease services

have affected many different segments of society and many different industries. Topics such as downsizing, layoffs, restructuring, and reduction in services have been highlighted on a daily basis in newspapers across the country. Attempts to balance the federal deficit have also resulted in cuts in programs affecting clinical psychology.

Money (or more specifically, the lack of money) is currently an important issue concerning research, practice, and training in clinical psychology. For example, for over 30 years after World War II, the NIMH awarded generous research and training grants to clinical psychology graduate students, interns, and postdoctoral fellows in order to increase the number of qualified psychologists as well as to advance the science of psychology. In fact, most psychology graduate students in accredited training programs between the end of World War II and 1980 received a NIMH training grant to help pay for their education. Furthermore, generous research grants were awarded to psychologists in university and hospital settings to support research efforts. During the early years of the Reagan administration, when the government tried to cut federal spending, these grants were quickly decreased and ultimately eliminated. Federal grants to support behavioral science research have also dwindled significantly in recent years. Today, only about 15 percent of federal grant applications are funded (National Advisory Mental Health Council, 1995). The number of NIMH-supported postdoctoral training positions in 1994 is 20 percent lower than those funded between 1976 and 1980, although the number of psychology postdoctoral fellows and psychologists in general has risen dramatically (National Advisory Mental Health Council, 1995). In fact, in 1995 the National Science Foundation (NSF) proposed that all behavioral science funding be eliminated. Reductions in financial support mean that the ability to conduct quality psychological research is much more challenging. Furthermore, reductions in federal money mean fewer jobs for psychologists and fewer clinical services in many settings such as VA hospitals, community mental health clinics, and state and county hospitals.

Financial constraints have also resulted in more debt among clinical psychology students. The median level of debt among new professionals with doctorates in clinical psychology is $23,000, and the mean is $28,288 (American Psychological Association, 1995a). Federal grant support is available for fewer than 20 percent of these new professionals; thus, they must use their own (or their family's) financial resources as well as student loans to pay for graduate training. The median starting salary for doctorates in clinical psychology is only about $41,500 (American Psychological Association, 1995a). Modest starting salaries in combination with large educational debts lead to a high degree of stress for many new psychologists.

Gender Shifts in Professions

Over the past several decades, more and more women have entered traditionally male professions such as law, psychology, business, and medicine (Denmark, 1994; Pion, Mednick, Astin, Hall, Kenkel, Keita, Kohout, & Kelleher, 1996). This trend has been especially true in applied areas of psychology such as clinical psychology (Pion et al., 1996; Snyder, McDermott, Leibowitz, & Kutter, under review). Whereas about 60 percent of APA members are men, the majority of new doctorates in clinical psychology are now awarded to women (American Psychological Association, 1995e; Dey, Astin, & Korn, 1991; Norcross et al., 1996). Between 1973 and 1991, the number of men who entered the field of psychology rose by 130 percent, whereas the number of women choosing psychology as a career increased by 530 percent (American Psychological Association, 1995d; National Science Foundation, 1994). Although most of the doctorates in clinical psychology were awarded to men in 1971 (74%) and 1981 (55%), the proportion dropped to only 36 percent by 1991 (Pion et al., 1996). Specifically, the number of doctorates awarded to men in clinical psychology during 1991 was 676 (36%) compared with 1203 (64%) awarded to women (Pion et al., 1996). These trends are also evident at the bachelor's degree level. In 1970, 43 percent of bachelor degrees in psychology were awarded to women; by 1991, about 75 percent of these degrees were awarded to women (National Science Foundation, 1994). Overall, it is estimated that within a few years women in clinical psychology will outnumber men by a 2-to-1 ratio (Snyder et al., under review).

Many have suggested that the gender shift in psychology is a positive trend resulting in, for example, more professional sensitivity to women's issues (Denmark, 1994; Pion et al., 1996; Plante &

Anderson, under review). An increase in diversity adds new perspectives, awarenesses, and approaches to any field. Professions and services are enriched when people of different gender, ethnicity, religious persuasion, and other differences enter the discipline. Furthermore, an increase in diversity allows more choice for those seeking psychological services as well as role models for students interested in the field (Denmark, 1994). However, many people of both genders are concerned that the shift from a male-dominated to a female-dominated profession might mean that clinical psychology could be devalued in status and perceived importance, resulting in lower salaries (Goodheart & Markham, 1992; Snyder et al., under review).

Research Issues

Research in clinical psychology has evolved beyond attempts to answer fairly simple and straightforward questions examining main effects. For example, research questions such as "does psychotherapy work better than no treatment?" have been duly addressed. We know that psychotherapy does indeed work and that psychological interventions from a biopsychosocial perspective appear to be superior to no intervention or more limited interventions (e.g., medication alone). Therefore more complicated and sophisticated research designs and questions are being implemented today. These research questions tend to look for interactions rather than main effects, for example, under which conditions, with which patients, treated by which therapists, and using which techniques will interventions work best.

As clinical psychology has evolved and matured, the need for newer research designs and methodologies has led to a move toward greater methodological pluralism. In addition to traditional research and statistical methods, qualitative, descriptive, and narrative approaches have been used in an attempt to better answer important research questions (Bergin & Garfield, 1994). Investigating clinical rather than simply statistical significance has also been advanced as a more useful way to make sense of research data (Kazdin, 1994). The use of effect size and meta-analysis techniques as well as more sophisticated statistical analysis aided by computer technology has increased the utility as well as the complexity of research methodologies and data analysis approaches (Kazdin, 1994).

Cost containment concerns have also led many new research investigations to incorporate cost-effectiveness or cost-benefit analysis into their designs (Newman & Taylor, 1996; Yates, 1994). Thus, it is important not only to determine what works and what doesn't work in clinical psychology but also to investigate the cost versus the benefits of assessment, treatment, consultation, and other clinical psychology activities. Recent research has focused on cost-effective, brief, and empirically validated treatment approaches (Barlow, 1996, Rehm, 1997; VandenBos, 1996).

Some authors criticize the historically narrow focus of psychological research, stating that "too many psychologists hug the intellectual shoreline and are content to paddle quietly in their own small ponds" (Beven, 1991, p. 481) and that psychology is "a collection of studies rather than a coherent discipline" (Schneider, 1996, p. 715). Many authors have argued that psychology research of the future must work harder to answer the "big questions about [the world]" (Bevan, 1991, p. 481). Significant contemporary problems of society such as homelessness, violence, racism, terrorism, and the role of psychology and behavior in diseases such as AIDS must be better addressed with research. Calls for more creative, risky, and multidisciplinary research has been made by many as well. In the words of Stanley Schneider (1996) "There is almost universal agreement that multidisciplinary approaches are necessary to study contemporary scientific problems" (p. 718) and that "we should think about application, clinical relevance, and policy implications even if we are engaged in the most basic research" (p. 716).

Practice Issues

Managed Health Care

Traditionally, physicians treated patients simply as they saw fit, and medical insurance paid for whatever procedures the doctors ordered. The physician decided what diagnostic and treatment approaches were in the best interest of the patient, and insurance companies supported and funded the physician's discretion in making professional judgments.

Lacking medical degrees, clinical psychologists could not be reimbursed by medical insurance companies. In the 1970s, however, psychologists lobbied state legislatures to pass "freedom-of-choice" laws that would allow anyone who held a license to practice in the mental health field (e.g., psychologists, social workers) to be eligible for medical insurance reimbursement. While physicians vigorously argued that only physicians (such as psychiatrists) should be allowed to treat patients in psychotherapy (and therefore be reimbursed by medical insurance), psychologists successfully argued that a mental health professional did not need to be a physician in order to conduct psychotherapy and other psychological services (e.g., psychological testing, consultation). By 1983, 40 of the 50 states had passed legislation allowing people to obtain psychological services from any licensed mental health profession and be eligible to receive some insurance reimbursement (Nietzel, Bernstein, & Milich, 1991).

Psychology enjoyed the advantages of freedom-of-choice legislation for about 10 to 20 years (although this time frame varies significantly from state to state). Psychologists, like physicians, quickly became accustomed to treating patients as they saw fit and having insurance companies reimburse them and their patients for their professional services. Thus, psychologists could offer various types of psychotherapy (e.g., psychodynamic, cognitive-behavioral, humanistic, family systems, eclectic) and various types of modalities (e.g., individual, couple, family, group) for any diagnosable problem. Typically, insurance would reimburse 50 percent to 80 percent of the fees charged by the psychologist, and patients paid the remaining portion. With these arrangements, psychologists and patients decided on a treatment plan without input from or parameters from other parties such as insurance companies.

These private, fee-for-service insurance arrangements began to change radically during the latter part of the 1980s. Health care costs rose steadily and dramatically during the 1970s and 1980s. Significant improvements in medical technology, newer and more expensive diagnostic tools such as CAT, PET, and MRI scans, as well as newer and more expensive treatments resulted in enormous amounts of costly medical insurance claims. Furthermore, very ill patients could live longer using these newer technologies, so costs continued to escalate for the treatment of chronic and terminal conditions. Medical education and physician salaries continued to rise as well. In fact, health care costs have increased about 2.7 times the rate of inflation in recent years (Cummings, 1995; Resnick & DeLeon, 1995). By 1995, health care costs have increased to over one thousand billion dollars per year, accounting for about 15 percent of the gross national product (GNP) (Cummings, 1995). By 2000 health care costs will account for over 20 percent of the GNP (Resnick & DeLeon, 1995).

These escalating costs have clearly become unacceptable to insurance companies and other organizations (such as government agencies) who pay for medical services. Furthermore, it has been estimated that about 30 percent of all health care costs are for procedures that are unnecessary, ineffective, inappropriate, or fraudulent (Resnick & DeLeon, 1995). In 1983 Congress passed legislation that initiated a new method of paying hospitals with a fixed and predetermined fee for treating Medicare patients. Under this plan, payment was determined by the patient diagnosis rather than by the actual total cost of treatment. Patients were categorized into diagnosis-related groups (DRGs), and the costs were calculated based on the average cost per patient for a given diagnosis. Thus, a hospital would receive a fixed fee for treating a patient with a particular diagnosis. If the hospital needed more time or money to treat the patient, monies would not be available for the additional services; or if the patient could be treated using less than the designated amount, hospitals would keep the difference to pay for other costs. Following the advent of DRGs in the early and mid 1980s, managed health care plans such as **health maintenance organizations (HMOs)** and preferred provider organizations (PPOs) exploded onto the health care scene during the late 1980s and the 1990s. The aim of these programs was to provide a more cost-effective way to pay for health services including those services offered by mental health professionals such as clinical psychologists. While 96 percent of people who had health care insurance still had fee-for-service plans in 1984, only 37 percent still had these plans by 1990 (Weiner & de Lissovoy, 1993). The number of Americans with fee-for-service plans continues to diminish rapidly (Cummings, 1995; Broskowski, 1995). In fact, over 35 million Americans now belong to a health maintenance organization, and

about 130 million Americans are covered by some form of **managed health care** (Cummings, 1995).

Contrary to the traditional fee-for-service plan outlined above, an HMO provides comprehensive health (and usually mental health services) within one organization. An employer (or employee) pays a monthly fee to belong to the HMO. Whenever health care is needed, members obtain all their care from the HMO for no additional cost above the monthly membership fee or a small co-payment fee (e.g., $5 per office visit). Patients have little or no choice regarding which doctor or other health care provider can treat them. Furthermore, they must obtain all their services (from flu shots to brain surgery) from health care professionals working at the HMO. Unlike private practitioners, these providers are paid a yearly salary rather than a certain fee for each patient they treat. In order to be profitable, the HMO must control costs and minimize any unnecessary and expensive services. For example, Cummings (1995) reported that only 38 large HMOs "the size and efficiency of Kaiser-Permanente can treat 250 million Americans with only 290,000 physicians, half the present number, and with only 5% of the gross national product" (p. 13). Thus, it is theoretically possible for physicians and organizations to provide medical services at a fraction of the cost associated with traditional fee-for-service arrangements. The important concern is if these more efficient services are of high quality and in the best interest of patient care.

A **Preferred Provider Organization (PPO)** is a compromise between the traditional fee-for-service and the HMO style of health care. A PPO is a network of providers who agree to treat patients affiliated with the PPO network for discounted rates. Therefore, traditional private practice professionals in all medical specialities as well as clinical psychologists and other mental health professionals can choose to apply to be on the PPO network. A patient who is on a PPO plan must be treated by professionals in the community who have agreed to serve on the PPO panel of providers. Furthermore, large health organizations such as clinics and hospitals also may apply to be on the PPO network panel. The PPO network and the providers of professional services (including hospitals) agree to set fees for various types of professional services such as surgery, office visits, and psychotherapy. A patient who needs services may contact one of a number of hospitals, clinics, or private practice providers. Some of the services, however, still need to be authorized by the PPO network organization before they can be guaranteed payment. Thus permission is needed by the insurance company before many major diagnostic or treatment services can be offered by any provider on the panel.

With the advent of HMOs and PPOs, spiraling health care costs and some unnecessary procedures have been better contained. The HMO and PPO companies determine, along with the professional treating a patient, the most cost-effective and reasonable diagnostic or treatment plan to follow. Therefore the insurance companies paying for physical and mental health care services now have an important vote in the types of services that can be rendered. Some arguments have been made that ultimately these changes in managed health care do not save money (Fraser, 1996). In fact, some argue that the monies going to health care have shifted from hospitals and providers to the managed care insurance industry (Matthews, 1995). Evidence that the managed-care insurance industry is one of the most profitable industries in the United States, with CEOs and other top executives enjoying salaries of over 6 million dollars per year, supports this claim (Matthews, 1995).

Generally, providers and patients are not as satisfied with these managed care programs as are those who still use the traditional fee-for-service professionals. While costs are theoretically contained in managed-care models, freedom of choice for both patient and provider is strictly controlled. A recent survey of over 17,000 HMO patients revealed general dissatisfaction with their health plans, while patients still on the fee-for service plans expressed the most satisfaction (Rubin et al., 1993). These survey results have raised concerns about the quality of service provided by managed health care. Managed care companies now routinely survey their members concerning client satisfaction (Broskowski, 1995). The need for accountability has also resulted in the requirement that managed-care organizations routinely report information on "9 quality of care indicators, over 60 usage indicators, measures of access to care and member satisfaction, and over 12 indicators of financial performance" (Broskowski, 1995 p. 160). This information is part of what is called the HEDIS Report (Corrigan & Nielson, 1993).

Psychologists and other mental health professionals tend to be unhappy with managed health care (Anders, 1996; Davenport & Woolley, 1997; Fox, 1994; Fraser, 1996; Karon, 1995; Murphy, DeBernardo, & Shoemaker, 1998; Newman & Taylor, 1996; Phelps, 1996; Phelps, Eisman, & Kohout, 1998; Saeman, 1996) and have even formed special interest groups to curtail its impact and abuses (e.g., the National Coalition of Mental Health Professionals and Consumers). A recent survey of over 14,000 members of the American Psychological Association revealed that 78 percent of the group felt that managed care had a negative impact on their professional work, with only 10.4 percent reporting a positive impact (Phelps, 1996). A survey of over 200 Diplomats in clinical psychology from the American Board of Professional Psychology revealed that over 90 percent felt that managed health care was a negative and problematic trend (Plante, Boccaccini, & Andersen, in press). In another national survey, 49 percent of 718 psychologists surveyed reported that their patients were negatively impacted by managed care that delayed or denied services while 90 percent reported that managed care reviewers interfered with appropriate treatment (Tucker & Lubin, 1994). Other surveys have demonstrated that psychologists generally feel that managed health care has requested that practitioners compromise professional ethics to contain costs (Murphy et al., 1998). The president of the American Psychiatric Association, Harold Eist, has stated, "We are under attack by a rapacious, dishonest, disruptive, greed-driven insurance-managed care big business combine that is in the process of decimating all health care in America, but most egregiously, the care of the mentally ill" (Saeman, 1996).

The mental health professional's deep discontent with managed-care stems from several concerns. First, all professional decisions (such as type and frequency of therapy services) must be authorized by the managed care insurance company. The cases must go through utilization review, which means that a representative of the insurance company reviews the services and plans of the professional before authorization for services can occur. Often the insurance agent with whom the psychologist works in this regard is not a licensed mental health professional. Therefore, many psychologists resent that they must "sell" their treatment plans to someone who is not as well trained in providing professional services. Furthermore, many feel that these reviewers are primarily interested in minimizing costs for the insurance company rather than being concerned about what is in the best interest of the patient (Anders, 1996).

Second, concerns about patient confidentiality have arisen. Details about the patient must be disclosed in order to obtain authorization for services. Many mental health professionals (as well as patients) feel that their confidentiality is compromised by informing the insurance company about intimate details of the patient's life and problems. Many patients fear that this information might be misused or provided to their employer.

Third, many psychologists feel overwhelmed by the paper work that is required of managed-care providers. In addition to lengthy application forms for each separate panel to which the professional belongs (copies of malpractice insurance, license, transcripts from all professional training, updated curriculum vitae, documentation of medical staff affiliations), other lengthy forms often need to be completed after each session with a patient.

Fourth, many psychologists resent having to accept significant reductions in their typical fees for managed care patients. For example, a psychologist might charge $100 per hour for services, but in order to be admitted to a PPO panel, he or she might have to accept a $65 per hour rate. Furthermore, the additional paper work and time on the telephone for authorization and utilization review is not reimbursed.

Fifth, psychologists (and patients) often feel that too few sessions are authorized by the managed-care company (Murphy et al., 1998). For example, only 3 or 5 sessions might be authorized for services. Many psychologists feel that patients that truly need more services are being denied access to treatment (Phelps et al., 1998). And finally, many psychologists resent having someone tell them how they should treat their patients. For example, a managed-care company might urge the psychologist to have the patient enter group rather than individual therapy in order to save costs, given the typically lower fee for group as opposed to individual treatment.

Furthermore, many psychologists are concerned about the growing use of capitation methods by managed care companies. The capitation program is similar to the DRG program already out-lined. In a capitation program, the insurance company will pay a set fee for the treatment of a given patient no matter what treatment or how many sessions are required. For example, when a managed care insurance company refers a patient to a practitioner, the company may pay $250 for whatever services are needed. If services can be provided within 1 to 3 sessions, the practitioner covers his or her costs. If many more services are needed (e.g., 20 sessions), the professional loses a good deal of time and income. Many managed-care companies have thus transferred the risks of expensive services from the insurance company to the practitioner. In the words of Bertram Karon, "What started reasonably is becoming a national nightmare" (Karon, 1995, p. 5).

Some psychologists, however, have noted that managed care offers a variety of hidden benefits (Anonymous, 1995; Clement, 1996, Hayes, 1996). For example, justifying treatment plans to managed care companies encourages professionals to think clearly about how best to treat their patients in a cost-effective manner, keeping their clinical skills sharp and motivation for success high. Furthermore, managed care promotes interdisciplinary collaboration by forcing professionals to work with other professionals (such as physicians) also treating a given patient as well as with professionals representing the managed-care company. Finally, managed health care demands that professionals be held more accountable for everything they do and for the price of their services. These changes have encouraged psychologists and other professionals to use empirically validated treatment approaches as well as brief, problem-focused treatments (Barlow, 1996; Bickman, 1996; Clement, 1996; Hayes, 1996; Rehm, 1997; Speer & Newman, 1996).

What is the future of managed health care and what will the role of clinical psychology be in the future marketplace? These are difficult questions to answer. However, it appears clear that clinical psychology must adjust to these rapid changes in the health care delivery and reimbursement system or be excluded from them. Kiesler and Morton (1988) predicted "declining provider autonomy, increasing integration of services, increasing emphasis on treatment outcomes, increasing management purview and control . . . and more consumer control via government and administrative decree" (Kiesler & Morton, 1988, p. 997). Many experts

(Cummings, 1984, 1995; Kiesler & Morton, 1987, 1988) predict that multidisciplinary group practices that focus on brief, problem-focused and family-centered treatments with an emphasis on demonstrating effective treatment outcome and client satisfaction will be the future of clinical psychology practice. Some, however, have suggested that psychologists should no longer participate in the health care and managed health care systems and return to fee-for-service approaches such as those used by attorneys and accountants (Kovacs, 1996; Murphy et al., 1998). Kovacs (1996), for example, states that, "the best hope we confront as a group of professionals is for us to remain in traditional independent practice and to leave the health care delivery system entirely" (p. 14). Clinical psychologists can likely expect an era of increased accountability along with many restrictions and limits on the types and length of services they provide.

Prescription Privileges

Historically, psychiatrists have been the only mental health professionals legally allowed to prescribe medication for their patients. Curiously, however, any physician from any speciality area (e.g., cardiology, urology, internal medicine) may legally prescribe psychotropic medications even if the physician lacks mental health training or experience. In fact, the majority (approximately 80%) of psychotropic medications prescribed to alleviate anxiety and depression are prescribed by general family practice or internal medicine physicians and not by psychiatrists (DeLeon & Wiggins, 1996). Although a number of psychologists actively conduct research on the neurobiology and psychopharmacology of behavior, and approximately two-thirds of graduate training programs in psychology offer psychopharmacology courses to their students (Popanz, 1991), psychologists have not obtained legal permission to prescribe medications to the public.

A highly controversial issue facing clinical psychology is the possibility of obtaining the legal and professional ability to prescribe psychotropic medications. The American Psychological Association, after careful study, has supported efforts to develop a curriculum to adequately train psychologists in psychopharmacology and to lobby state legislative groups to pass laws allowing psychologists to prescribe medications (American Psychological Asso-

ciation, 1992b; Cullen, 1998; Martin, 1995; Smyer et al., 1993).

During the past several decades, there has been an explosion of research on the effects of various medications on psychiatric problems such as anxiety, depression, impulsivity, and thought disturbance. New and effective medications have become available to assist those experiencing a wide range of emotional and behavioral problems. For example, the development and popularity of Prozac has led numerous people to become interested in using the drug to combat depression and other problematic symptoms such as bulimia. Additionally, the influence of alcohol, cocaine, nicotine, and other substances on behavior (such as substance abuse, domestic violence, and crime) continues to be a major issue for all health care and mental health professionals. These substance abuse problems are often treated with medications such as antabuse for alcohol addiction and methadone for heroine addiction. Advances in the development and availability of psychotropic medication as well as the influence of substance use and abuse on behavior have set the stage for the controversial issue of the development of prescription privileges for psychologists. Furthermore, as more integrative and biopsychosocial perspectives replace traditional one-dimensional theoretical models (e.g., psychodynamic, behavioral) of diagnosis and treatment, biological and medication issues become increasingly relevant for practicing psychologists.

Prescription privileges for psychologists is a hotly debated topic both within and outside the profession. For example, both the American Medical Association and as the American Psychiatric Association are adamantly opposed to allowing psychologists the privilege of prescribing medication (American Medical Association, 1984). A recent survey of approximately 400 family practice physicians revealed strong opposition to psychologists obtaining prescription privileges (Bell, Digman, & McKenna, 1995). They claim that a medical degree is necessary to competently administer medications that deal with the complexities of mind-body interactions. Even within psychology, many are opposed to having psychologists prescribe medication for their patients (DeNelsky, 1991, 1996; Hayes & Heiby, 1996). Some psychologists are adamantly opposed to prescription privileges (DeNelsky, 1996). Some are concerned that allowing psychologists to prescribe medication would distract them from their traditional focus on non-biological emotional and behavioral interventions (e.g., psychotherapy, education; Hayes & Hieby, 1996; DeNelsky, 1996). Some have argued that by obtaining prescription privileges psychology would lose its unique identity and psychologists would become "junior psychiatrists" (DeNelsky, 1996, p. 208; Lorion, 1996). Finally, many are concerned about the practical problems associated with prescription privileges such as sizable increases in the costs of malpractice insurance or the increased influence of pharmaceutical companies on the field of psychology (Hayes & Hieby, 1996).

On the other hand, many have argued for the development of prescription privileges for psychologists (Brentar, & McNamara, 1991; Cullen, 1998; Cullen & Newman, 1997; DeLeon, 1993; DeLeon, Fox, & Graham, 1991; DeLeon & Wiggins, 1996; Fox, Schwelitz, & Barclay, 1992; Klein, 1996). The majority of clinical psychologists support prescription privileges (Frederick/Schneiders, 1990; Pimental, Stout, Hoover, & Kamen, 1997). Furthermore, about half of all graduate students in clinical psychology wish to be able to prescribe medication with the majority wanting the option available for the profession (Smith, 1992). Proponents argue that with appropriate and intensive training for those who wish to prescribe medications, psychologists would be excellent candidates to provide psychotropic medications for patients (Cullen & Newman, 1997; Lorion, 1996; Smyer et al., 1993) including the underserved populations (e.g., the elderly, the military, people with low socioeconomic status, and people who live in rural areas) who have little opportunity to be treated by a psychiatrist (Brentar & McNamara, 1991; DeLeon & Wiggins, 1996; Smith, 1992). Many point out that other nonphysicians (e.g., nurse practitioners, optometrists, podiatrists, dentists) already have the appropriate training and legal authority to prescribe a limited array of medications. In fact, nurse practitioners have prescription privileges in 49 states, physician assistants can legally prescribe medication in 40 states, and optometrists can prescribe medication in all 50 states (DeLeon & Wiggins, 1996). Because medical schools in the United States typically spend only an average of 104 hours of classroom instruction on pharmacology (Association for Medical School Pharmacology, 1990), psychologists have argued

that obtaining a medical degree is not necessarily needed to prescribe medications if sufficient and specific training is available. Despite the advantage of no longer having to send patients to other professionals for medication, psychologists generally tend to have mixed feelings about obtaining prescription privileges and thus are not uniformly in favor of it (Boswell & Litwin, 1992; DeNelsky, 1996; Evans & Murphy, 1997; Hayes & Heiby, 1996; Plante et al., 1997).

The Task Force on Psychopharmacology of the American Psychological Association (Smyer et al., 1993) has outlined a curriculum for psychologists who are interested in being trained to prescribe medication. The program includes basic psychopharmacology education, collaborative practice, and, finally, prescription privilege. The basic psychopharmacology education would offer 26 graduate credits (390 lecture hours) of biochemistry, physiology, pharmacology, biological bases of behavior, and other relevant topics. Collaborative practice would follow a consultation-liaison model in which the psychologist would work closely with a skilled licensed professional in managing the integration of medications and psychosocial interventions for patients with a range of psychiatric problems. The prescription privilege endorsed by the Task Force would involve a limited-practitioner approach similar to that of dentists. Thus psychologists would be able to prescribe medications for problems in which they specialitize such as anxiety, depression, and thought disorders. The Task Force also recommended mandatory postdoctoral supervised experience and training and continuing education training.

In 1991 the United States Department of Defense under the CHAMPUS (Civilian Health and Medical Program of the Uniformed Service) program developed a psychopharmacology training program for several psychologists at the postdoctoral level (Sammons & Brown, 1997). After several years of study, these psychologists have been allowed to prescribe medications for patients in the military. The success of this program has led to further enthusiasm for the development of prescription privileges for psychologists outside the military environment. In fact, by 1998 legislation for psychology prescription privileges was introduced in six states including California, Florida, Hawaii, Louisiana, Missouri, and Tennessee (Cullen, 1998).

Medical Staff Privileges

Historically, only physicians were allowed to treat patients independently in a hospital setting and serve on the medical staff of a hospital. **Medical staff privileges** allowed a physician to admit and discharge patients as needed as well as organize or manage the treatment plan of patients while hospitalized. Therefore, if a psychologist was treating a patient in an outpatient environment (such as a community mental health clinic or in private practice) who then later required hospitalization, the psychologist would have to turn the hospital portion of the care over to a physician (such as a psychiatrist), who would admit, discharge, and direct treatment. The psychologist would be allowed to see the hospitalized patient only as a visitor (just like family members) and not as a professional. The psychologist also could not offer treatment services (such as psychotherapy) while the patient was in the hospital setting.

Psychologists have been interested in obtaining medical staff privileges to provide independent inpatient care for their patients. Many psychologists feel that physicians (such as psychiatrists) do not need to supervise their work in hospital settings. Physicians, however, have generally opposed medical staff privileges for psychologists (American Medical Association, 1984). After about 10 years of legislative advocacy and activity, approximately 16 percent of clinical psychologists have obtained full medical staff privileges in the United States (Litwin, Boswell, & Kraft, 1991). Yet, many hospital-affiliated psychologists continue to struggle to maintain autonomous status within hospital settings (Enright, Resnick, DeLeon, Sciara, & Tanney, 1990; Litwin, Boswell, & Kraft, 1991). In 1978, legislation was passed allowing psychologists to be able to obtain medical staff privileges independently in California. However, many hospitals and physician groups fought the legislation. A past president of the American Psychiatric Association (ApA) stated that it was a "dangerous trend" for psychologists to obtain hospital staff appointments (Fink, 1986, p. 816). The American Medical Association also passed a resolution stating that they must "fight incursions of nurse midwives, podiatrists, nurse practitioners, physician's assistants, psychologists. . . into medical practice via prescribing privileges, independent practice, mandated third-party reim-

bursement or other expansion of their scope of practice" (American Medical Association, 1984, p.79). In 1990 the *CAPP* v *Rank* lawsuit in California upheld the hospital privilege statute for psychologists. Since that time approximately 15 states have enacted similar legislation.

Private Practice

The number of clinical psychologists choosing to work in full-time or part-time **private practice** has grown steadily in the past several decades. Currently, about 35 percent to 40 percent of clinical psychologists primarily work in solo or group private practices (Newman & Taylor, 1996; Norcross, Prochaska, & Gallagher, 1989; Norcross, Karg, & Prochaska, 1997; Phelps, 1996). Over two-thirds of clinical psychologists maintain at least some part-time private practice activities (Kohout, Wicherski, Popanz, & Pion, 1990; Norcross et al., 1989; Norcross et al., 1997). This proportion represents a 47 percent increase since 1973 (Garfield & Kurtz, 1974; Norcross et al., 1989, 1997). While survey results have revealed a larger and larger percentage of clinical psychologists conducting at least part-time private practice activities, experts generally now predict that this trend will quickly reverse itself owing to the rapid changes in the health care delivery and insurance reimbursement systems (Broskowski, 1995; Cummings, 1995; Fox, 1994). For example, a recent survey of over 15,000 members of the American Psychological Association revealed that over 40 percent of practitioners who obtained their license prior to 1980 were working in solo independent practice, compared with only about 30 percent of those who obtained their license after 1990 (Newman & Taylor, 1996). Managed health care has made it increasingly difficult to develop and maintain an independent practice in clinical psychology. In the words of Russ Newman, director of the Practice Directorate of the American Psychological Association, "It is going to be very difficult to continue as a solo practitioner in the integrated marketplace of the future" (Nickelson, 1995, p. 367).

Managed-care companies, in their efforts to provide cost-effective services, have looked to master's-degree trained counselors as a lower cost alternative to clinical psychologists. Furthermore, the companies are less likely to pay for services that have been traditionally an integral part of a psychologist's independent practice (e.g., long-term insight-oriented psychotherapy). Managed care companies often find it more convenient and cost effective to work with large multidisciplinary health care facilities rather than a host of independent practitioners. In fact, some authors have suggested that solo private practice (as commonly provided by clinicians in the 1980s and 1990s) will no longer exist within the next several years and that by 2000, 50 percent of all psychotherapists' practices existing in 1995 will be out of business (Cummings, 1995). Thus, in the words of Nicholas Cummings, "the golden era of clinical psychology is over" (Cummings, 1984, p. 19). The future of independent practice of clinical psychology is likely to look very different than it does now. Large multidisciplinary group practices offering a range of services that are solution-focused and based on solid treatment-outcome research are most likely to develop (Cummings, 1995), perhaps ushering in a different type of golden age that more efficiently addresses patient problems.

Specialization

With advances in research and practice, the need for **specialization** in clinical psychology has become apparent. A general clinical psychologist, like a general practice physician, is likely to have significant limitations in terms of the depth the professional can provide in certain areas of practice and research. As clinical psychology has evolved and more and more information on human behavior has become available, practitioners have endeavored to specialize in areas such as neuropsychology, geropsychology, brief treatments, health psychology, infant psychology, and forensic psychology. Furthermore, efforts to subspecialize (e.g., pediatric neuropsychology versus geriatric neuropsychology) have begun. In fact the American Board of Professional Psychology (ABPP) has increased the number of specialization diplomate categories from four to nine within several years, reflecting the increased number of psychologists specializing in various areas. Some have expressed concern about overspecialization and loss of valuable general skills (Matarazzo, 1987; Plante, 1996b), arguing that it is important for psychologists to realize that there is

only one psychology, with many different applications.

Specialization has also resulted in further certification requirements for psychologists. For example, Division 40 (Neuropsychology) and Division 38 (Health Psychology) have developed guidelines regarding the appropriate training and experience necessary to specialize in these areas. The potential access to prescription privileges in the future will create yet another new specialty area for psychologists. The American Psychological Association has developed a "college" that educates and certifies psychologists in subspecialty areas such as alcohol and substance abuse. Thus, a generic psychologist license no longer allows someone to practice in all areas of professional practice.

Empirically Validated Treatments

Historically psychologists and other providers of professional psychological services could evaluate and treat each patient as they saw fit. They could choose to use any treatment strategies, theoretical orientations, and methods that they felt were clinically indicated. Treatment could be short or long, insight oriented or behavior-change oriented, and conducted with or without research support. But the drastic changes in health care have forced mental health professionals to examine more closely effective treatment outcome and client satisfaction, and have resulted in efforts to use only **empirically validated treatments,** that is, structured treatment approaches that have substantial research support. Empirically validated treatments have received a great deal of attention and support from the American Psychological Association and other professional organizations such as the American Psychiatric Association (American Psychological Association, 1995g; Chambless et al., 1996; Crits-Christoph, Chambless, Frank, Brody, et al., 1995; Hayes, Follette, Dawes, & Grady, 1995; Rehm, 1997; Sanderson, 1994; Sanderson & Woody, 1995; Wilson, 1997). The clinical psychology division of the American Psychological Association (Division 12) has been at the forefront in developing guidelines for both researchers and clinicians regarding research-supported empirically validated treatments (Chambless et al., 1996; Task Force on Promotion and Dissemination of Psychological Procedures, 1995). The APA clinical division was

"Wow! You need professional help."

the first to establish a task force, develop criteria, and conduct an exhaustive review of the treatment outcome literature to develop these guidelines. Empirically validated treatment approaches have been developed for a variety of clinical problems such as depression (Cornes & Frank, 1994), anxiety (Newman & Borkovec, 1995), obsessive-compulsive disorder (Foa, 1996), bulimia nervosa (Wilson, 1997), and conduct disordered children (Feldman & Kazdin, 1995). Table 14.1 provides examples of empirically validated treatments for several disorders.

Some professionals feel that because individuals are unique and have different personalities, symptoms, and coping resources, it is impossible to fit the same treatment approach to every patient based on empirical research support (Fensterheim & Raw, 1996; Garfield, 1996; Ingram, Kendall, & Chen, 1991; Nezu, 1996; Plante et al., in press; Silverman, 1996). Therefore, many clinicians resist being instructed to provide treatments that they feel may not be useful to particular patients. Others, however, applaud the attempt to give treatment a more empiri-

Table 14.1 Examples of Empirically Validated Treatments

Anxiety and Stress	Cognitive behavior therapy for panic disorder
	Exposure and response prevention for obsessive-compulsive disorder
	Exposure treatment for simple phobia
Depression	Interpersonal psychotherapy
	Cognitive therapy
	Brief dynamic therapy
Bulimia	Interpersonal psychotherapy
	Cognitive therapy
Oppositional Defiant Disorder	Parent training
Substance Abuse	Brief dynamic therapy and cognitive therapy for opiate dependence
	Behavior therapy for cocaine abuse

Source: From Chambless et al., 1996.

cal and research supported basis (Barlow, 1996; Clement, 1996; Hayes, 1996; Meehl, 1997; Nathan, 1996; Rehm, 1997; Wilson, 1996, 1997).

Reaching Beyond Mental Health in Contemporary Clinical Psychology

Clinical psychology has been closely associated with the mental health field for many years. However, many psychologists feel that psychology is an important health care discipline in itself, offering potentially useful services beyond mental health issues (Belar, 1995; Fox, 1994; Kovacs, 1996; McDaniel, 1995; Resnick & DeLeon, 1995; VandenBos, 1993). Because so many health problems are associated with behavior (e.g., alcohol, smoking, drug use, violence, sedentary lifestyles, risky sexual behavior), many psychologists have suggested that psychology can be helpful in altering high-risk behaviors in a wide variety of areas (Belar, 1995; McDaniel, 1995; Resnick & DeLeon, 1995). For example, unsafe sexual practices may lead to sexually transmitted diseases such as AIDS. Obesity, smoking, and sedentary lifestyles have been associated with cardiovascular diseases and cancer. Although approximately half of all traffic accidents are associated with alcohol consumption (McGuire, 1982), an additional problem is that large numbers of Americans choose not to use seat belts (McGinnis, 1984). Overall, it has been estimated that about half of all deaths are caused by lifestyle factors under behavioral control (Center for Disease Control, 1980; Taylor, 1995). In fact, a number of psychosocial factors (e.g., lack of trust, impulsivity, immature ego defenses) reliably predict premature death (Friedman, et al., 1995). Psychologists, it is argued, are excellent candidates to assist in research, teaching, public policy, and clinical practice to improve health promoting behaviors in the population and minimize health damaging behaviors. Therefore many have suggested that psychology be considered not only an independent mental health discipline but also an independent general health care discipline (Belar, 1995; Fox, 1994; McDaniel, 1995; Resnick & DeLeon, 1995; VandenBos, 1993). Clinical psychology may be useful for a variety of health care behaviors including those not generally associated with mental illness.

Training Issues

As outlined earlier, training models in clinical psychology include the scientist-practitioner, or Boulder, model; the scholar-practitioner, or Vail, model; the Ph.D. or the Psy.D. degree programs; and the university or the free standing professional school models. Today, within 20 years of the professional school movement, more than 50 percent of all doctorates awarded in clinical psychology are awarded from free standing professional schools of psychology rather than through more traditional university psychology training programs. Therefore, the types of training models and contexts have changed tremendously during the past several decades. Which training models will survive and thrive and which will not has important implications for the future of clinical psychology. For instance, a recent APA president has suggested that the Psy.D. degree rather than the traditional Ph.D. be awarded to all those who plan on being practitioners in clinical psychology (Shapiro & Wiggins, 1994). Although this suggestion is not likely to be embraced by both research and practice-oriented psychologists who value the Ph.D. degree, it does highlight the chasm between the science and practice of clinical psychology.

The proliferation of free standing professional schools of psychology has been controversial. Since admission standards (i.e., GPA, GRE scores, acceptance rates) at professional schools tend to be lower than those of university programs (Mayne et al., 1994a), some surveys have found that many psychologists are concerned that professional standards have decreased with the advent of professional schools. For example, a recent survey of over 200 diplomates in clinical psychology found that over 70 percent believed that the advent of free standing schools of psychology has been a negative influence on the profession (Plante et al., in press). Many free standing professional schools are unaccredited by the American Psychological Association and several enroll any interested student without screening their academic or psychological readiness for graduate study.

With the explosion of graduate students attending free standing professional schools of psychology and the emphasis on practitioner training (Shapiro & Wiggins, 1994), the proportion of psychologists conducting research and seeking academic careers relative to the total number of new psychologists has declined. Therefore, a smaller proportion of current and future psychologists will dedicate their careers to academic and research pursuits. Some have expressed concern that these shifts will result in a much more practice-oriented than science-oriented profession, thereby eroding the scientific base of clinical psychology (Rice, 1997). Such concerns have contributed to significant conflicts within the American Psychological Association and the development of the more research-oriented American Psychological Society in 1988.

New discoveries, specializations, and the demands of society influence training as well. For example, efforts to obtain prescription privileges for psychologists mean that graduate and postgraduate training programs may need to provide comprehensive training in psychopharmacology and related areas (e.g., biochemistry) not typically or historically offered in clinical psychology training programs (American Psychological Association, 1992b; DeLeon & Wiggins, 1996; Smyer et al., 1993). Society's focus on violence, ethnic diversity, technological advances, and cost-effective treatment all influence the training emphasis in clinical psychology. For instance, efforts to provide more training in brief and empirically validated treatments (Clement, 1996; Critis-Chistoph et al., 1995; Garfield, 1996; Hayes et al., 1995; Hayes, 1996; Nathan, 1996; Wilson, 1996) reflect managed care's emphasis on cost-effective treatment outcome.

Many psychologists have suggested that shifts in training models and focus must occur in order for clinical psychology to survive and thrive (Rice, 1997). Broskowski (1995) stated: "The dominant ideologies for training psychologists have not kept pace with contemporary realities. Training for clinical psychology is dominated either by a clinical practice model that stresses solo practice and traditional long-term therapy methods or a scientist-professional paradigm geared to forms of basic research but not health services research." (p. 161). Former American Psychological Association president Ronald Fox has called for more uniform standards in professional education as well as an expansion of training away from the traditional mental

health model to a more general health and well-being model (Fox, 1994). Many authors (Fox , 1994; McDaniel, 1995; Resnick & DeLeon, 1995; Vanden-Bos, 1993) suggest that psychology educators, for example, should train students to offer preventive care, short-term acute care, rehabilitation services, and long-term care for those dealing with chronic illnesses. Thus, the shift to primary care in the health field as opposed to narrowly defined mental health roles has been advocated by many (Belar, 1995; Fox, 1994; McDaniel, 1995; Resnick & DeLeon, 1995; VandenBos, 1993). This emphasis has important implications for training programs and career options for psychologists. Furthermore, as clinical psychology has developed more integrative and biopsychosocial perspectives and is evolving toward more involvement in general health care, training professionals in a one-dimensional theoretical orientation has become outdated. In the words of past APA presidents Robert Resnick and Patrick De-Leon, "professional psychology must expand its traditional training boundaries or face being relegated to an unneeded and perhaps unnecessary discipline" (Resnick & DeLeon, 1995, p. 4). Finally, Kovacs (1996) states, "There are many ways that young professionals can find and create careers for themselves . . . but they require shattering an identity that has constrained us" (p. 14).

Other trends in training include mandatory postdoctoral training and new joint degree programs. Almost all states now require postdoctoral supervisory experiences and training prior to obtaining a state license as a psychologist. These requirements, as well as the need for postdoctorate education, have resulted in efforts to develop accredited mandatory postdoctoral residency programs in psychology (Larsen, Belar, Bieliauskas, Klepac, Stigall, & Zimet, 1993). In recent years, there has developed a number of joint degree programs that combine psychology training with other fields, such as business and law. For example, Widener University has recently developed a Psy.D./MBA degree program, and the University of Nebraska has developed a Ph.D./J.D. program. As clinical psychology matures, more and more emphasis in research and practice will be placed on continuing education, specialization, and interdisciplinary training.

The Big Picture

Clinical psychology is changing and growing at a rapid pace. Some of these changes are very positive; some clearly negative. On the positive side, psychology has greatly contributed to a better understanding of human behavior and ways to improve the quality of life for many. Assessment, treatment, research, teaching, and consultation are all much more effective today than in the past. Psychology has also attained increasing independence as a discipline. Licensing laws, medical staff privileges, prescription privileges, and freedom of choice legislation have all contributed to the development of psychology as a respected independent profession. As the profession and field has matured, a more in-depth and sophisticated understanding of human behavior has unfolded. Unfortunately, however, the trend toward managed health care and further constraints in funding for research and prac-

tice potentially threaten the growth and types of services psychology can provide. In addition, sizable increases in the number of students being trained as psychologists, especially at large free standing professional schools of psychology, may intensify competition for available job positions.

Despite the challenges confronting this as well as all related fields, clinical psychology as a profession remains a fascinating and exciting endeavor with a tremendous potential to help individuals, groups, and society in the course of a truly fulfilling professional career. Although the future of clinical psychology is uncertain, it is likely to continue to be a rewarding career for many. Future clinical psychologists must be flexible to adapt to changing needs and requirements as society and the discipline evolves and changes.

Key Points

1. Clinical psychology has evolved and changed rapidly during its 100-year history. It is difficult to imagine a more rapidly changing period in clinical psychology than the present time. However, change was certainly rapid for clinical psychology both before World War I and between World Wars I and II. Today clinical psychology looks very different than it did, not only 20 or 30 years ago, but even 5 years ago.

2. The United States has quickly become an ethnically and culturally diverse nation. Increasing attention and interest have been focused in recent years on the role of multicultural and diversity issues in all aspects of society. Psychologists, as well as other professions, have acquired greater insight into the role of culture and diversity in the development of behavior and behavioral problems.

3. Recent advances and significant discoveries in science, technology, and medicine have greatly impacted clinical psychology as well as many other fields.

4. During the "lean and mean 90s," efforts to reduce costs, to become more efficient, and to decrease services have affected many different industries and segments of society. Topics such as downsizing, layoffs, and reduction in services all have been highlighted on a daily basis in newspapers across the country. Attempts to balance the federal deficit have also resulted in cuts in programs effecting clinical psychology.

5. Research in clinical psychology has evolved beyond attempts to answer fairly simple and straightforward

questions examining main effects. As clinical psychology has evolved and matured, the need for newer research designs and methodologies has led to a move toward greater methodological pluralism.

6. One of the best examples of a current "hot topic" in clinical psychology involves the advent of managed health care. Some have suggested that managed health care may alter the field of clinical psychology in a permanent way. With the advent of HMOs and PPOs, much of the spiraling health care costs and unnecessary procedures are contained. The HMO and PPO companies determine, along with the professional treating a patient, the most cost-effective and reasonable diagnostic or treatment plan should be followed. Therefore the insurance companies paying for professional health and mental health care services now have an important say in the types of services that can be rendered.

7. A highly controversial issue facing clinical psychology is the possibility of obtaining the legal and professional ability to prescribe psychotropic medications. The American Psychological Association, after careful study, has supported efforts to develop a curriculum to adequately train psychologists in psychopharmacology and to lobby state legislative groups to pass laws allowing psychologists to prescribe medications.

8. Psychologists in many states have obtained medical staff privileges in order to provide independent inpatient care for their patients. After about 10 years of legislative advocacy and activity, approximately 16 percent of clinical psychologists have obtained full medical staff privileges in the United States. Yet many hospital-affiliated psychologists continue to struggle to maintain autonomous status within hospital settings.

9. Whereas survey results have revealed a larger and larger percentage of clinical psychologists conducting at least part-time private practice activities, experts generally now predict that the private practice trend will quickly reverse itself owing to the rapid changes in the health care delivery and insurance reimbursement systems.

10. With advances in research and practice, the need for specialization in clinical psychology has become apparent. As clinical psychology has evolved and more information on human behavior has become available, practitioners have endeavored to specialize in areas such as neuropsy-

chology, geropsychology, brief treatments, health psychology, infant psychology, and forensic psychology.

11. Psychologists, it is argued, are excellent candidates to assist in research, teaching, public policy, and clinical practice to improve health promoting behaviors in the population and minimize health-damaging behaviors. Therefore many have suggested that psychology be considered not only an independent mental health discipline but also an independent general health care discipline.

12. The types of training models have changed tremendously during the past several decades. Which training models will survive and thrive and which will not has important implications for the future of clinical psychology.

Key Terms

Diversity	Medical Staff Privileges	Prescription Privileges
Empirically Validated Treatments	Multicultural	Private Practice
Health Maintenance Organization (HMO)	Preferred Provider Organization (PPO)	Specialization
Managed Health Care		

For Reflection

1. How do changes in society impact clinical psychology?

2. What is managed health care and how does it impact clinical psychology?

3. How are financial issues associated with the future of clinical psychology?

4. How do diversity issues effect clinical psychology?

5. What are medical staff privileges and why are they important to clinical psychologists?

6. What are prescription privileges and why are they important to clinical psychology?

7. What training issues effect the future of clinical psychology?

8. How might an interested student learn more about the field of clinical psychology?

9. What is likely to happen to private practice in clinical psychology in the future?

10. How is clinical psychology more than a mental health discipline?

11. What are empirically validated treatments?

12. What are some pros and cons to using empirically validated treatments?

CHAPTER 15

Becoming a Clinical Psychologist: A Road Map

Chapter Outline

Highlight of a Contemporary Clinical Psychologist: Dianne L. Chambless, Ph.D.

College

Applying to Graduate Programs in Clinical Psychology

Graduate School in Clinical Psychology

Clinical Internship

Postdoctoral Fellowship

Specialization

Certification and/or Licensure

Employment

The American Board of Professional Psychology (ABPP) Diploma

Is Clinical Psychology Right for Me?

How to Get More Information About Current Issues in Clinical Psychology

HIGHLIGHT OF A CONTEMPORARY CLINICAL PSYCHOLOGIST:

Dianne L. Chambless, Ph.D.

Dr. Chambless is a full-time academic who has spear-headed the development of an APA list of empirically validated treatments.

Birth date: February 26, 1948

College: Newcomb College of Tulane University, Political Science, 1969

Graduate Program: Temple University, 1979 (Ph.D., Clinical Psychology)

Clinical Internship: Philadelphia Veterans

Administration Hospital and Behavior Therapy Unit of Temple University Medical School

Current Job: Professor of Psychology, University of North Carolina at Chapel Hill

Pros and cons of being a clinical psychologist:

Pros: "First, clinical psychology's unusual scientist-practitioner blend of activities and values allows me to fulfill two strong needs of mine—to be of use to others and to search for new knowledge and understanding. I love the intellectual challenge of research and scholarship, but I also need to know that my research will, at least potentially, help solve important human problems. Second, the breadth of activities in which clinical psychologists are trained and engaged means I'll never be bored with my work, as so many people are. I've been a full-time clinician, a full-time academician, and have done a mix of both types of work at different points in my career."

Cons: "For me there are no cons. I can only mention minor annoyances. First, the position of clinical psychology vs. psychiatry, especially biological psychiatry. Our profession is under-valued and under-funded. It is far harder to find research funding for psychotherapy research and psychosocial approaches to psychopathology than for biological research and pharmacotherapy, despite the large body of research demonstrating the importance of psychological variables and approaches. Second, when I worked in medical schools and hospital environments, I chaffed at the restrictions on the activities and responsibilities of psychologists imposed not because medical training was required for some responsibility, but because the tradition was that physicians should be in charge. My own solution to that was simple: I moved to a psychology department. However, for psychologists whose work can only be done in medical settings (e.g.,

311

clinical health psychologists) I see this as a continuing problem. Finally, although it does not affect me personally, I do worry about my students' future. Too many people are graduating with degrees in clinical psychology for the job market in the foreseeable future."

Future of Clinical Psychology: I suspect that the changes wrought by the crisis in health care funding will lead clinical psychologists to return to their roots as scientist-practitioners. Emphasis on cost efficiency will probably mean that much direct clinical service in agencies will be provided by masters level clinicians, with the doctoral level providers serving as diagnosticians, trainers, supervisors, and program evaluators, in addition to providing a smaller degree of direct services. I expect clinical health psychology will continue to grow, and that more clinical psychologists will turn their attention to the problems of ethnic minority group members and the elderly. A smaller number of clinical psychologists will be able to be successful in private practice. Although the academically oriented will continue to find work in university settings, I expect the expansion in the number of clinical psychology programs to cease.

Typical Schedule:

7:00 Review student's research proposal on social phobia or conduct peer review of an article submitted for publication concerning obsessive-compulsive disorder.

8:00 Review work continues.

9:00 Break (exercise)

10:00 Screening with potential patient (35-year-old Caucasian women with obsessive-compulsive disorder) for psychotherapy research project

11:00 Screening continues.

12:00 Meet with graduate student for research supervision.

1:00 University or department committee meeting concerning rank and tenure

2:00 Break (talk to husband).

3:00 Graduate class on research methods in clinical psychology or practicum team meeting

4:00 Class continues.

5:00 Class continues.

6:00 Correspondence and paperwork

7:00 Break (dinner)

8:00 Prepare for next day's undergraduate class, grade papers, or watch videotapes for psychotherapy supervision.

Students wishing to become clinical psychologists do so for a variety of reasons. Many are interested in being helpful to others, whereas others are fascinated by human behavior. Some are interested in the interface between psychology and biology as manifested in health issues. Others are sensitive to human suffering and the nuances of human relationships, feeling naturally drawn to clinical psychology as a field of study. Still others are primarily interested in contributing to improvements in society at large. Many are interested in all of these aspects of clinical psychology. Many people cynically believe that those who wish to become clinical psychologists are primarily interested in solving their own personal or family problems. Although some studies have indeed suggested that psychologists enter the field in order to help resolve personal or family conflicts or problems (Elliott & Guy, 1993; Guy, 1987; Sussman, 1992), other studies have found little or no association with personal and family problems and choice of psychology as a profession (Murphy & Halgin, 1995; Norcross & Guy, 1989).

Although numerous terminal master's degree programs are available in clinical psychology, the American Psychological Association "recognizes the doctorate as the minimum educational requirement for entry into professional practice as a psychologist" (American Psychological Association, 1987b, p. 3). Therefore, in this chapter, the stages towards the doctorate in clinical psychology and subsequent postdoctoral training and licensing will be discussed.

A career as a clinical psychologist is rife with both tremendous challenges and unanticipated rewards. The road to becoming a clinical psychologist is a long one divided by several distinct stages that include college, graduate school, clinical internship, postdoctoral fellowship, licensure, and finally employment and advanced certification. In this chapter, each of these progressive stages will be reviewed. Although college students may not need details on postdoctoral training, licensing, employment, and board certification this early in their careers, this information is included in this chapter to provide a complete "road map" of the training process.

College

Most college students who plan on becoming clinical psychologists will decide to major in psychology. However, while a psychology major is obviously advantageous, english, biology, math, sociology, or any other major will not preclude a student from being accepted into graduate school in psychology. Prerequisite courses such as General Psychology, Statistics, Research Methods, Personality, Biopsychology, Learning/Cognition, and Abnormal Psychology are generally required or highly recommended to students who choose not to major in psychology as undergraduates (Lawson, 1995; Mayne, Norcross, & Sayette, 1994b; Smith, 1985). Additional courses in math and science are also recommended.

Overall, students interested in becoming clinical psychologists and gaining admission into high-quality graduate programs must take their college experience very seriously (Table 15.1). Solid grades and high quality research and clinical experiences during the college years are important to acquire. Specifically, students must obtain a solid GPA, high scores on the Graduate Record Examination, obtain some clinical (e.g., work with patients or clients located at various social services agencies such as a homeless or battered women's shelter, suicide prevention hotline, school for developmentally disabled children, psychiatric unit of a local hospital) and research experience (e.g., working with a pro-

Table 15.1   Ten Important Goals During the College Experience

---

High Grade Point Average
High Graduate Record Examination Scores
Quality Research Experience
Quality Clinical Experience
Excellent Verbal Skills
Excellent Interpersonal Skills
Reliability and Dependability
Excellent Productivity
Excellent Letters of Recommendation
High Motivation

---

fessor or other researchers on psychology-related experiments), and receive excellent letters of recommendation. Each of these elements as well as other important aspects of the college experience will be highlighted in this chapter.

Grade Point Average (GPA)

Whereas there are no absolute cutoffs, except for some set by the occasional graduate program, a 3.0 GPA should be generally viewed as a minimum while a 3.5 or higher is generally expected by graduate training programs. A recent study (Mayne, Norcross, & Sayette, 1994a) revealed that the mean GPA score for all clinical psychology graduate programs is 3.3 ($SD = 0.2$). However, Lawson (1995), reported a mean GPA of 3.46 for incoming graduate students in psychology doctoral programs. While grade point average does not necessarily correlate strongly with graduate school performance in clinical psychology (Dollinger, 1989) or necessarily with intelligence, success as a psychologist, or with therapeutic skill, it does serve at least as an index of motivation and discipline. A high degree of motivation and determination are qualities found in successful graduate students. Ironically, once enrolled in a graduate program or employed as a psychologist, grades per se take on a relatively inconsequential role in later success (barring impressively poor grades). However, as an undergraduate, GPA is one way to be distinguished among the large number of graduate school applicants.

Graduate Record Exam (GRE)

Students interested in applying to graduate school in psychology generally take the GRE during the fall term of their senior year. In fact, about 90 percent of all doctoral graduate programs in clinical psychology require that the GRE be taken in order to be considered for admission (Steinpreis, Queen, & Tennen, 1992). The Graduate Record Examination is administered by the Educational Testing Service (Princeton, New Jersey) and yields four scores: Verbal, Quantitative, Analytic, and Psychology, the latter being administered in a separate testing session. The Verbal, Quantitative, and Analytical sections make up the GRE General Test while the Psychology portion is one of many GRE

Subject Tests. The GRE General Test and Subject Tests are administered at different times. A total of 800 points is possible in each area. Each score has a mean of 500 and a standard deviation of 100.

Generally, graduate programs will focus on the combined Verbal/Quantitative total, looking for approximately 1200 (e.g., 600 Verbal, 600 Quantitative) as a common cutoff. Higher scores on the Psychology section of the GRE are often expected by high quality graduate programs (i.e., above 600). However, a recent study (Mayne, Norcross, & Sayette, 1994a) revealed that the mean GRE scores for graduate programs in clinical psychology is 581 (*SD* = 46) for the Quantitative measure, 580 (*SD* = 48) for the Verbal scale, 579 (*SD* = 46) for the Analytic scale, and 587 (*SD* = 47) for the Psychology subject test. According to this study, GRE scores tended to be higher among research-oriented Ph.D. programs compared to, for example, practice-oriented Ph.D. or Psy.D. graduate programs. Lawson (1995) reports mean GRE scores for incoming psychology doctoral students of 598 (Verbal), 612 (Quantitative), 633 (Analytic), and 616 (Psychology). Many students obtain self-study GRE materials or enroll in GRE preparatory classes offered by several companies such as Stanley Kaplan in order to help maximize their performance. Students unable to afford the costs of these preparatory programs are well advised to discipline themselves to study and prepare on their own or with friends in order to maximize performance. There are many self-study preparation books available. Although the GRE is required by most doctoral programs in psychology, the test's ability to predict performance in graduate school is modest at best (Sternberg & Williams, 1997).

Research Experience

Most high-quality graduate programs in clinical psychology expect applicants to have some research experience prior to admission to graduate school. In fact, survey research has indicated that quality research experience was the top-rated variable listed by graduate program directors as being important in graduate school admissions (Eddy, Lloyd, & Lubin, 1987). However, Lawson (1995) reported that work and clinical experience tend to be rated higher than research experience for clinical or counseling psychology programs. In general, any involve-

ment in a quality research project or projects with college psychology professors or with other psychology professionals working in settings such as hospitals, clinics, and industry is valued. Quality research is not always easy to define. Professionals often disagree concerning the quality and value of various research projects. Generally, research that is conducted by well-trained professionals, is methodologically rigorous, and contributes to the professional community of scholars—evidenced by being presented at regional or national professional conferences and/or published in refereed professional journals—would be considered quality research.

Research experience at the undergraduate level typically occurs by working with a psychology faculty member who has undergraduate students help him or her as research assistants. It is not imperative that the research be clinically oriented. Rather, obtaining solid research experience with a professor who is productive and enjoyable to work with is important. Furthermore, having the opportunity to present research findings at professional or student research conferences and co-author manuscripts for publication in professional journals is also highly beneficial. Most areas of the country, for example, offer undergraduate psychology research conferences each spring (e.g., Greater Boston Undergraduate Psychology Research Conference, Western Undergraduate Psychology Research Conference), allowing undergraduates to present their research in paper or poster presentation form to peers and faculty from a variety of schools. Often, college students working as research assistants may score questionnaires, run subjects through laboratory procedures, and conduct literature reviews as part of their work with the professor or other psychology professional.

Closely associated with research experience, computer, data analysis, and statistical skills are also important to obtain during the college years. In addition to standard word processing skills, developing competence with statistical packages such as SYSTAT, Statistical Analysis System (SAS), Statistical Package for the Social Sciences (SPSS), or Bio-Medical Data Package (BMDP) is extremely valuable. Although many students interested in clinical psychology careers may be uninterested in computer, mathematical, and statistical concepts and activities, these skills are generally extremely important to develop among all clinical psychologists.

"You're kidding! You count S.A.T.s?"

Even those who hope to conduct primarily psychotherapy in their professional career must use these skills to manage their finances, examine treatment outcome and client satisfaction, complete necessary paperwork, and be good consumers of research in order to maintain state-of-the-art service.

Clinical Experience

Most undergraduate psychology departments and colleges offer externships or field placements in clinical settings where students can gain exposure to the signs, symptoms, and language of clinical problems. In fact, over two-thirds of colleges and universities offer practicum experiences in psychology (VandeCreek & Fleisher, 1984). Typical examples of volunteer placements include local hospitals, community mental health centers, drug and alcohol rehabilitation half-way houses, schools or summer camps for disabled children, homeless or battered women's shelters, and crisis or suicide hotlines. These experiences help students obtain experience with clinical populations as well as provide some important beginning skills and knowledge about clinical problems and interventions.

Students might ask their professors or fellow students about opportunities that are worthwhile. If a college does not have an organized internship or service-learning program, a student could still find appropriate and useful volunteer or even paid experiences by calling local social service agencies. Hospitals, crisis hotlines, schools for developmentally disabled children or adults, shelters for battered women, homeless persons, or abused children are excellent starting points. Local United Way agencies and church groups also may be helpful in finding appropriate positions for students.

Determining what is a quality clinical experience is sometimes difficult. Generally, a clinical experience that allows the student to observe a wide range of activities with a number of patients and allows the student to talk about their experiences with a professional in the clinical setting is more likely to be a quality experience. The best type of location is one that encourages and values student learning and is not merely interested in obtaining free labor. For example, observing and/or working directly with patients would be preferred relative to spending too much time doing clerical work such as filing and typing. Often the experiences of previous students who have worked in the particular clinical setting can assist in determining if the experience would be worthwhile.

Verbal Skills

Beyond the confines of the GRE, the field of clinical psychology is highly dependent upon a range of verbal skills. These include writing ability, public speaking ability, and the ongoing ability to verbally communicate with colleagues and clients in a direct, clear, and sensitive fashion. Often, professors will infer the intelligence and social skills of a student largely on the basis of their ability to express themselves through written and oral communication. Thus, honing writing and speaking skills is an important element of the college experience.

Interpersonal Skills

Challenging to measure or quantify, this realm of social transaction is perhaps the most important quality to possess as a psychology student and eventual professional. Good interpersonal and social skills, empathy for others, and effective communication are critical to becoming an effective psychotherapist, consultant, teacher, and overall professional clinical psychologist. In clinical psychology, the ability to deal directly, sensitively, and in a reassuring manner is critical to success with both colleagues and clients. It is perhaps a well-kept secret that in addition to valuing competence, experience, and intellectual potential, graduate, intern, postdoctoral, and employment sites often give the edge to those whom they simply like and expect to be agreeable and engaging. Good interpersonal skills are important contributors to therapeutic alliance and effectiveness as well as appreciated among co-workers and supervisors.

Reliability and Dependability

The field of clinical psychology, like most professional careers, requires consistency and almost unerring reliability. Unreliability as manifested in lateness, tardy reports, inefficiency, sloppiness, and general "flakiness" is highly problematic at all stages in training and in employment as a clinical psychologist. Clinical, teaching, and research duties require an unselfish focus and conscientious levels

of effort and dedication. Clinical psychologists as well as students in psychology must be able to be depended upon, for example, to finish what they say they will finish or arrive when agreed. A psychologist must earn the trust of others as someone capable of fulfilling a responsible, professional role.

Productivity

In any competitive field, the ability to work efficiently and produce high quality, thoughtful, accurate, and important work, and to do so fairly quickly, is a great advantage. For instance, research productivity is most apparent in one's list of publications and presentations; clinical and teaching experience are expressed in both variety and hours logged. However, even more than quantity, the quality of one's work is ultimately most compelling. A lot of quality work is even more impressive!

Letters of Recommendation

Much like interpersonal skills, a strong vote of support from a professor or supervisor can go a long and indefinable way towards enhancing one's appeal as a prospective graduate student. Not only does this necessitate quality work and positive relationships, but involves establishing a mentor relationship with one or more professors or supervisors. The better an advisor knows, respects, and likes the person they are writing about, the better able he or she will be to strike both an informed professional and personal tone in a letter of recommendation. Letters of recommendation can figure in prominently, as they are the only part of an application (beyond a personal statement) which speaks of the applicant as a real live person in relation to others.

Motivation

Motivation is perhaps the key ingredient to a successful undergraduate record. Motivation helps to pull a student through aversive tasks such as studying for the GREs and adds enthusiasm and dedication to more enjoyable tasks. In other words, motivation helps to overcome the many obstacles posed by exams, papers, applications and the like, and is often apparent in graduate school applications through the depth and breadth of psychology experience pursued during college. Many highly motivated students have become successful psychologists despite significant weaknesses in academic or even interpersonal realms, utilizing their energy and drive to compensate for other relative shortcomings.

Applying to Graduate Programs in Clinical Psychology

Because quality graduate programs can be highly competitive, it is usually helpful to cast a wide net by applying to a fairly large number of programs in various parts of the country. Even schools that are not necessarily prestigious can be highly competitive. There are approximately 2000 clinical psychology graduate school openings available each year and the acceptance rate for all APA-accredited doctoral graduate programs in clinical psychology is about 10 percent (Mayne, Norcross, & Sayette, 1994a; Norcross, Sayette, & Mayne, 1996). However, some programs are extremely competitive, accepting fewer than 2 percent of their applicants, whereas other programs are much less competitive, accepting greater than 60 percent of their applicants (Mayne, Norcross, & Sayette, 1994a; Norcross, Sayette, & Mayne, 1996). Generally, university-based programs are more competitive than free standing professional schools. University programs also tend to be significantly less expensive than most free standing professional schools.

In order to determine which schools to apply to, it is important to consider the type and quality of the programs as well as which geographic locations would be acceptable. Several resources such the *Insider's Guide to Graduate Programs in Clinical and Counseling Psychology* by Norcross, Sayette, & Mayne (1996) and *Graduate Study in Psychology* published by the American Psychological Association (1995c) may be helpful in creating a list of the programs most likely to be of interest. Psychology faculty are also likely to be good sources of information. Once a list of 20–35 programs is developed, obtaining catalogs and application packets from these program will help to further narrow the list. A final list of perhaps 13–16 schools should be developed and reviewed by professors or other professionals for final advice. A combination of competitive and less competitive "safety" schools should be considered. Although each applicant must decide to which programs he or she will apply, the national application average is about 13 (Mayne, Norcross, & Sayette, 1994b; Norcross, Sayette, & Mayne, 1996).

The application forms must be completed thoughtfully and correctly, avoiding typographical or grammatical errors. Because most programs request applicants to write a personal statement as well as submit a curriculum vita (C.V.), applicants must take these tasks very seriously. While there is generally no right or wrong way to complete the personal statement, revealing family secrets and personal problems is usually not advised. The focus of the statement should be more professional than personal, highlighting career, intellectual, and service interests and goals. The statement requires the applicant to discuss the reasons why he or she is interested in graduate school in clinical psychology as well as the particular factors leading them to apply to each specific graduate program. Furthermore, the personal statement generally requests that applicants outline their career and educational goals and specify how the specific program can help meet these goals.

The curriculum vita (C.V.) is an academic resume. The C.V. outlines the applicant's addresses and phone numbers, educational experiences (e.g., schools attended and degrees obtained), relevant work experiences, and professional presentations and publications (if any). Unlike a resume, a C.V. is not confined to one page. While the C.V. of a college student, graduate student, or working professional differ a great deal, several general principles should be followed for all C.V.s. Preparation of a C.V. should include concise and honest descriptions of relevant work, educational, and other professional experiences (e.g., volunteer positions). Headings such as "Education, Honors and Awards, and Professional Activities" should be used (see Table 15.2). Asking a professor, career counselor, and several friends to review the completed personal statement and C.V. for feedback is generally beneficial. Making a photocopy of all application materials is wise in case any application materials get lost or destroyed. Using overnight delivery services or certified mail will help ensure that the application materials have indeed reached the intended destinations. Also, requests for transcripts and GRE scores are usually needed well in advance of the

Table 15.2 General Headings and Subheadings for a Curriculum Vita

General information (i.e., name, address, telephone number, e-mail address)
Education (i.e., university, degree, year of graduation, major field(s) of study)
Honors and Awards
Professional Memberships (e.g., American Psychological Association, Student Affiliate)
Professional Activities (e.g., relevant work and volunteer positions with dates, location, supervisors' names, and brief description of activities)
Research (i.e., presentations at regional or national conferences, publications)
References (i.e., names, addresses, phone numbers, e-mail addresses of three or four professional references)

application deadlines. Excellent guidelines for preparing graduate school applications can be found in the guidebook by Norcross, Sayette, & Mayne (1996).

Once applications have been mailed and received, the applicant must wait for responses. A telephone or in-person interview may be requested by interested schools. It is important to always be professional with all representatives of the graduate program. This includes faculty, secretaries, and current graduate students. Even during informal chats with students and secretarial staff, an applicant may be judged and evaluated by each and every interaction. Students are advised to avoid silly or "flip" messages on their home answering machines.

If one is fortunate enough to be invited for an on-site or telephone interview, he or she has passed the first critical cut of applicants. Graduate programs often interview only a small proportion of their applicants and thus the odds of getting an acceptance to the program increases substantially once an applicant reaches this stage of the process. In preparation for the interview, it is critical that the applicant be very familiar with the training program, interests of the faculty, and educational requirements and thus should read the brochures and course catalog carefully. Once on-site for an interview, applicants should be sure to dress in a professional manner as well as maintain a high level of interest, energy, and enthusiasm for the program throughout the day and with all interactions with faculty, graduate students, and staff. Thoughtful questions for each interviewer should be prepared in advance. Additional guidelines for how to best prepare and participate in the interview process can be found in the guidebook by Norcross, Sayette, and Mayne (1996).

Graduate School in Clinical Psychology

Graduate training in psychology involves course work, clinical training, research experience, and often teaching experience. There are approximately 180 accredited doctoral graduate programs in clinical psychology in the United States and Canada and many nonaccredited programs as well. About 1300 doctorates in clinical psychology are awarded each year (American Psychological Association, 1995a). Graduate school in clinical psychology is designed to take five years to complete including the required one year clinical internship. However, the national average is closer to about six to eight years. This additional length of time is generally due to students taking longer than expected to complete their doctoral dissertations. In most graduate programs, the doctoral dissertation is a comprehensive and high-quality original research study that is supervised by a faculty committee of three to five professors with one professor acting as chairperson.

Students interested in graduate school in clinical psychology can choose between several different training models and types of programs to best suit their needs and interests. Each of the following choices and issues merit informed and careful consideration.

Ph.D. or Psy.D.

A student interested in obtaining a doctorate in clinical psychology can choose between two types of doctorates: the traditional **Ph.D. (or Doctor of Philosophy)** or the newer **Psy.D. (Doctor of Psychology)**. Historically, the Ph.D. was awarded to graduate students training in psychology at the doctoral level. The most common model of training was and still is the scientist-practitioner model (Raimy, 1950), which encourages equal and integrated training emphases on both research and clinical practice. The model seeks to train graduate students in becoming both competent practitioners of clinical psychology providing skilled psychotherapy, psychological assessment, and consultation services as well as competent researchers being able to conduct rigorous scientific studies. Most universities with graduate training programs in clinical psychology award the Ph.D. degree.

Several universities such as the University of Denver and Rutgers University offer separate programs for Ph.D. students and Psy.D. students. The Psy.D. degree was proposed as a viable alternative to the traditional Ph.D. Rather than a scientist-practitioner model that equally blends research and clinical practice into training graduate students, the new Psy.D. model sought to train students in the scholar-practitioner model with much more emphasis on clinical practice and minimal emphasis on research skills. Thus, the goal of the Psy.D. training model is to spend most of the graduate training years preparing students to become practitioners of clinical psychology services (e.g., psychotherapy, psychological assessment, clinical consultation) with minimal focus on training professionals to become researchers. While research is generally valued in Psy.D. programs, the training model assumes that graduates will become practitioners and consumers of research rather than actually conduct research studies during their careers. The majority of graduate training programs currently award students the traditional Ph.D. degree, yet more and more programs (especially free standing professional schools that exist outside of the university environment) are offering the Psy.D. degree. Of the approximately 4000 psychology doctorates earned in 1994, 82 percent were Ph.D.s while 16 percent were Psy.D. degrees [with the remaining 2 percent Ed.D.s (doctorates in education with a psychology emphasis) (Sheridan, Matarazzo, & Nelson, 1995)].

Currently, Psy.D. graduate programs tend to be larger than Ph.D. programs and tend to be less competitive regarding admission. Ph.D. program acceptance rates average between 6 percent and 10 percent, while Psy.D. programs accept about 23 percent of their applicants (Mayne, Norcross, & Sayette, 1994b). However, research has indicated that Ph.D. and Psy.D. students perform equally well on graduate school qualifying examinations, grades (Peterson & Baron, 1975) and on clinical internships (Shemberg & Leventhal, 1981; Snepp & Peterson, 1988). However, concerns about the quality of Psy.D. training programs remain (Strickland, 1985). These concerns generally highlight the very large number of students being admitted to these programs.

University Versus Free Standing Professional Schools

Historically, graduate training in clinical psychology has been the domain of university programs throughout the United States and Canada. However, during the early 1970s, a number of free standing professional schools opened to train graduate students in psychology. **Free standing professional schools** are not university based or affiliated. These programs originally emerged and proliferated in California with the opening of the California School of Professional Psychology (CSPP). CSPP now operates four campuses in California (Alameda, San Diego, Los Angeles, and Fresno), enrolling approximately 5000 students. These free standing schools of psychology are not affiliated with any universities and maintain independent faculty, staff, and students. Today, free standing professional schools can be found throughout the United States with the majority still located in California. Approximately 50 percent of all doctorates in clinical psychology are now awarded by these schools (Stricker & Cummings, 1992). The free standing schools tend to have extremely large entry classes relative to university-based programs, older students, and tend to be less competitive regarding admission. Whereas many of these schools offer the Psy.D. degree, many offer a Ph.D. degree or both. Furthermore, many of the free standing schools admit older students who may look at psychology as being a second career. Financial aid also tends to be less available in free standing schools relative to university programs, and the expense is prohibitive for many students (Norcross, Sayette, & Mayne, 1996). Finally, students attending free standing schools generally do not have the opportunity to be exposed to the entire field of psychology since nonclinical areas of psychology such as cognitive, developmental, social, learning, physiological, and others are not represented at these schools.

Accreditation

Since 1948, the American Psychological Association has accredited graduate training programs in clinical psychology. They also accredit programs in other areas of applied psychology such as counseling, school, and industrial/organizational psychology. The American Psychological Association lists specific criteria for **accreditation** and regularly (usually every three to five years) conducts on site visitations to graduate training programs to ensure that all criteria for accreditation are met. It is assumed that any APA accredited program would offer a high quality graduate training experience.

However, not all graduate programs in psychology are accredited by the American Psychological Association or even by local accreditation agencies such as the Western Association of Colleges and Schools (WASC). Accreditation by the American Psychological Association as well as regional accreditation agencies is important to maximize the chances of obtaining quality graduate education, clinical internship, and postdoctoral training. APA accreditation increases the chance of obtaining a license to practice in any state as well as the ability to be employed in any appropriate setting. In fact, obtaining training from an APA accredited program is often a requirement for employment for many positions including all Veteran Administration (VA) Hospitals. Furthermore, APA-accredited training is a requirement for obtaining board certification or the diploma from the American Board of Professional Psychology (ABPP) and for inclusion in the *National Register of Health Service Providers in Psychology*. The *National Register* is frequently used by insurance companies and others to determine which psychologists will be eligible to receive insurance reimbursement for professional services (Sheridan et al., 1995). Finally, the American Psychological Association has advised state licensing boards that only students from accredited programs should be allowed to obtain a license to practice psychology stating that "by 1995 applicants for licensure shall have completed a doctoral program in psychology that is accredited by the Ameri-

can Psychological Association" (American Psychological Association, 1987b, p. 3).

Training Curriculum and Emphasis

Although the American Psychological Association outlines a core curriculum for all accredited clinical psychology training programs, all accredited graduate training programs are not exactly alike. Each program maintains its own unique perspective and curriculum based on the faculty and traditions of the program. Not everyone is content with the way in which clinical psychologists are trained (Fox, 1994; Shapiro & Wiggins, 1994), because there is disagreement concerning how best to organize and structure graduate training in clinical psychology. These differences of opinion are thus reflected in the diversity of training programs available. While some programs heavily emphasize research skills and productivity (about 35% of programs), others may emphasize clinical training (about 25% of programs). Still other programs pride themselves on providing an equal balance between research and clinical training. Some programs focus their clinical training towards certain theoretical orientations such as cognitive-behavioral models, psychodynamic models, humanistic models, family systems models, or others, while many programs emphasize eclectic training in utilizing a variety of theoretical models and perspectives. For example, a recent survey of graduate school training directors found that 55 percent of training programs emphasize a cognitive-behavioral approach, 23 percent emphasize a psychodynamic approach, and 10 percent focused on an humanistic-existential orientation (Wisocki, Grebstein, & Hunt, 1994). Another survey revealed that 49 percent emphasize a cognitive-behavioral approach, 28 percent emphasize a psychodynamic approach, and 19 percent emphasize a family systems approach (Norcross, Sayette, & Mayne, 1996). Some programs demand highly rigorous research dissertation projects while others allow theoretical papers or case studies to be written for dissertation projects. Some programs are primarily interested in training researchers, other are interested in training practitioners, while others maintain no specific agenda in the future employment of their students. Individual programs may offer specialty emphasis in areas such as health psychology, child clinical psychology, or minority psychology.

It is not always possible to determine the training emphasis of each program by reviewing the course catalog or application materials. Often one must have these questions answered by current graduate students, recent graduates of the training program, or by current faculty.

Graduate training programs generally offer the same core curriculum suggested by the American Psychological Association (Table 15.3). This core curriculum has not changed significantly since it was proposed about 50 years ago (Shakow, 1947). This includes courses on the biological bases on behavior, the social bases of behavior, individual differ-

ences, cognition and learning, as well as courses in professional ethics. Graduate courses in statistics, research methods, assessment, and psychopathology are also required. In addition to course work, graduate training also usually includes practicum or field placements. These placements allow graduate students to work with clinical populations providing individual, couple, family, and group psychotherapy with a variety of patient populations (e.g., adults, children, inpatient, outpatient) as well as providing opportunities to acquire experience with psychological testing (e.g., intelligence, neuropsychological, personality). Graduate training also provides research training. Typically a master's thesis as well as a doctoral dissertation are conducted, allowing

Table 15.3 Typical Graduate School Program and Schedule

First Year

Fall Term	**Spring Term**
Statistics	Biological Basis of Abnormal Behavior
Psychopathology	Personality Testing
Research Methods	Interviewing Techniques
Intelligence Testing	History and Systems of Psychology
Multicultural Issues	Individual Differences
Master's Thesis Research	Master's Thesis Research

Second Year

Fall Term	**Spring Term**
Psychological Testing	Development Psychology
Advanced Personality	Multivariate Statistics II
Multivariate Statistics	Social Psychology
Clinical Psychotherapy	Clinical neuropsychology
Practicum	Practicum
Master's Thesis Research	Master's Thesis Research

Third Year

Fall Term	**Spring Term**
Advanced Human Learning and Memory	Professional Ethics
Human Sexuality	Elective
Dissertation	Dissertation
Practicum	Practicum

Fourth Year

Fall Term	**Spring Term**
Electives	Electives
Dissertation Research	Dissertation Research

Fifth Year

Full Time Clinical Internship

Note: Although graduate programs may be completed in five years, a high degree of variability exists such that many students take longer than five years to complete their requirements.

the student to conduct quality research project under the supervision and guidance of several graduate school faculty members. The master's thesis is typically completed by the end of the second year of graduate study while the dissertation is completed by the end of the fourth or fifth year. The dissertation project acts as a final capstone research experience where a student completes a comprehesive study under faculty supervision. The dissertation is often seen as the defining accomplishment of the doctoral degree. The student then defends the project in an oral examination among a group of faculty members. Finally, most graduate training programs require comprehensive qualifying examinations to determine the competence of their students in academic psychology, research, and clinical work prior to being allowed to complete their internships and doctoral degree. A typical graduate program in clinical psychology includes the courses and schedule as listed in Table 15.3.

Clinical Internship

Almost all graduate training programs in clinical psychology require that students complete a one year full-time (or two years part-time) clinical **internship** prior to being awarded the doctorate. As of 1994, there were 435 American Psychological Association accredited internship programs in the United States and Canada (Sheridan et al., 1995). This training almost always occurs outside of the graduate training program in hospitals, clinics, and various clinical settings throughout the United States. Students apply for internships following the successful completion of all graduate course work, practicum training (i.e., small, part-time local internship experiences), and research requirements of the graduate program. Therefore, the clinical internship generally serves as a capstone or final integrating experience prior to obtaining the doctorate.

Many students are unable to complete their dissertation projects prior to attending their internship. These students often must return to their graduate training programs following the completion of internship in order to complete (and defend before a committee of faculty) their doctoral dissertations.

Many of the strategies and principles for applying to graduate school are applicable to clinical internship programs. Many training sites are very selective and seek graduate students who have outstanding academic credentials as well as excellent clinical training and experiences. The American Psychological Association accredits about 400 internship programs as they do the approximately 180 graduate training programs. A complete list of accredited internship programs can be found in a yearly updated directory of internships published and provided by the Association of Psychology Postdoctoral and Internship Centers (APPIC). The directory is available through APPIC and all graduate programs and internship sites have a copy of the directory. Applications are obtained by contacting each internship site. Most applications must be completed on or around December 1st of each year for those interested in the programs that begin the following July 1st or September 1st. For example, application materials are due around December 1, 1997 for internship training beginning on July 1, 1998 or September 1, 1998. All internship programs maintain their own selection and interviewing process. However, internship programs are not allowed to make offers of admission until the second Monday in February of each year at 10:00 AM Eastern Standard Time. Therefore, applicants wait by their telephones on that day to find out which internship sites have offered to admit them. Applicants then have four hours to make their final decision to accept or reject an internship offer. The applicant, however, is not allowed to accept or "hold" more than one offer at a time. Therefore, they must inform programs that accept them if they plan on not accepting their offer of admission (Association of Psychology Postdoctoral and Internship Centers, 1996).

Activities during the clinical internship usually focus specifically on clinical training. Psychotherapy, psychological testing, and consultation with a variety of patient populations is expected. Interns typically work in collaboration with a variety of professionals (e.g., physicians, nurses, social workers, counselors) in most settings. Interns also typically participate in seminars on topics such as psychotherapy, psychological testing, professional ethics, among others. Some internship training sites specialize in certain patient populations (e.g., children, adolescents, college students, adults, the elderly) while certain sites specialize in particular types of professional services (e.g., testing, psychotherapy, consultation, acute hospital care). Research experience and training may also be a part of the internship experience. Following the successful completion of the clinical internship and all of the requirements of the graduate training program (including the doctoral dissertation), the doctorate is awarded.

Postdoctoral Fellowship

Contrary to what many assume, being awarded the doctorate is not the end of the organized training line for those wishing to become clinical psychologists. Almost all states now require one to two years of postdoctoral training before one is eligible to take the licensing examination. Anyone wishing to practice clinical psychology must obtain a license to practice from their state licensing board. Some psychologists who choose not to practice (e.g., full-time academics) do not necessarily need a license or a **postdoctoral fellowship** in order to teach and conduct their research in college or university settings. The criteria for postdoctoral training vary from state to state. The American Psychological Association does not currently provide accreditation for postdoctoral training sites despite doing so for both graduate and internship training facilities. However, an organization affiliated with the American Psychological Association (the Association of Psychology Postdoctoral and Internship Centers, APPIC) does provide a list of member organizations that offer postdoctoral training meeting APPIC guidelines for quality training.

Postdoctoral training occurs in a wide variety of settings including hospitals, clinics, counseling centers, universities, and even private practices. Postdoctoral training can include clinical work such as psychotherapy, psychological testing, and consultation as well as research, teaching, and many other professional activities. Some postdoctoral fellowships (especially research fellowships) last three or four years. The American Psychological Association as well as interested affiliated organizations such as APPIC are working towards more structured criteria, expectations, and accreditation procedures for postdoctoral training.

Finally, once postdoctoral training is successfully completed, one is now eligible to take the licensing examination in order to be fully licensed as a psychologist and eligible to practice and func-

tion as an independent professional. Four years of college followed by at least four years of graduate school, a year of clinical internship and finally one or more years of postdoctoral training have been completed before licensing is possible.

Specialization

Clinical psychology offers many specialties. Various specialities and subspecialties (e.g., pediatric neuropsychology) have developed and become popular while others are popular for awhile and fade in interest over time (Sayette & Mayne, 1990; Plante, 1996b). For example, neuropsychology and health psychology have become very popular specialities in recent years (American Psychological Association, 1995b). Postdoctoral training is generally the time when most of the intensive specialization training occurs. Some authors have warned that clinical psychology students often try to specialize too early in their careers and do not adequately obtain basic clinical psychology skills prior to specialization (Matarazzo, 1987; Plante, 1996b). Matarazzo (1987) warned that it is important to keep in mind that psychology is one field that has many applications rather than a set of numerous and distinct specialties. Each specialization, through their representative professional organization(s), typically offers guidelines for the specific training and educational requirement that are suggested to become competent in a speciality area. For instance, Division 38 (Health Psychology) and Division 40 (Neuropsychology) of the American Psychological Association offer guidelines on training in these speciality areas. Furthermore, the board certification or ABPP diploma process (discussed later in this chapter) offers certification in a variety of speciality areas.

Certification and/or Licensure

Certification and licensure procedures are legally defined and regulated at the state level by state boards of psychology. The role of the psychology board is to set minimum standards for admission to the profession, conduct licensing examinations, and regulate the practice of psychology in order to protect the public from professional misconduct.

Certification laws control the use of the word *psychologist* such that only those who meet legal state standards are allowed to call themselves or represent themselves to the public as psychologists. While certification laws protect the title psychologist from being misused, certification laws do not impact the practice of psychological services.

Licensing laws are more restrictive than certification laws. In addition to protection of the title psychologist, licensing laws provide guidelines and restrictions in defining what constitutes the practice of psychological services. Almost all licensing laws provide a generic license for psychologists without acknowledgment or restrictions on speciality or sub-specialty (e.g., child clinical psychology, neuropsychology, clinical health psychology, counseling psychology). Therefore, contrary to what many believe, states do not generally recognize or have a specific license available for clinical psychologists separate from other practicing psychologists (e.g., counseling psychologists). In fact, in many states, such as California, it is not permissible to advertise to the public as a "clinical psychologist" or a "licensed clinical psychologist" because the state does not issue specialty licenses.

Since the certification and licensing processes are conducted at the state level, each state develops its own laws and procedures. However, since 1955, the American Psychological Association has offered states a set of guidelines now called the "Model Act for State Licensure of Psychologists" (American Psychological Association, 1955; 1967; 1987b) which outlines suggested rules and regulations for state licensing. The Model Act includes minimum educational requirements as well as guidelines concerning the suspension and revocation of licenses. While state licensing boards are not required to use the Model Act, the vast majority of states do in fact use the APA document in drafting state licensing laws and regulations.

Because most states maintain licensing laws rather than certification laws, licensing laws will be highlighted here. First, an application must be submitted to the state board of psychology in order to be allowed to take the licensing examination. While this procedure differs from state to state, all boards review applications to ensure that the state criteria for exam eligibility have been met. This includes ensuring that the applicant has an appropriate doctorate in psychology with the required amount of both predoctoral and postdoctoral supervisory experiences and training. Once the state licensing board reviews the application and determines that it meets all of the necessary criteria, the applicant is allowed to take the written portion of the examination.

The Written Examination

All states administer the same biannual national written examination for licensing [i.e., the **Examination for Professional Practice in Psychology (EPPP)**]. This exam consists of 200 multiple choice items covering a variety of relevant areas within the field of psychology. The exam does not focus solely on the clinical practice of psychology as many people often assume. Questions about test construction, statistics, social psychology, experimental psychology, industrial/organizational psychology, developmental psychology, etc. are all included in the written licensing examination. Many applicants choose to take structured preparatory courses provided by a few independent businesses such as the Association for Advanced Training in the Behavioral Sciences. These programs sell study materials including audiotape lectures, practice examinations, and detailed outlines of various domains likely to be addressed on the examination. For an additional charge, these companies also offer face-to-face classroom instruction to assist in concentrated preparation. Because these preparatory courses can be expensive, costing $500 or more, some applicants for licensure prefer to share the materials and thus the expense with a colleague who is also taking the examination at the same time. Others choose to borrow materials from a colleague who recently took the examination. While the biannual national examination is renewed and updated each time it is given, certain areas of psychology such as statistics do not change radically between administrations. Some choose not to use any of these testing materials at all. With adequate preparation, many successfully pass the written examination.

States do vary in designating what constitutes a passing score. Some states consider a fixed number of correct items such as 150 out of 200 as the criterion for passing, while others use the national median, which changes with each testing administration. Approximately 2200 people take the examination across the United States each time it is given. An applicant may take the exam again if not passed on the first (or subsequent) attempt(s).

The Oral Examination

After successful completion of the written examination, many states then require an oral (or sometimes an essay) examination before obtaining the license. The oral examination differs from state to state. Typically, questions about legal issues pertaining to the practice of psychology (such as limits on confidentiality, treatment of minors, child abuse reporting laws, involuntary commitment) are discussed along with ethical issues and clinical questions regarding diagnosis and treatment of hypothetical patients. The examiners, typically licensed psychologists who volunteer to conduct the examinations, assess the applicant's understanding of the laws and ethics of professional practice as well as probing clinical skills, sensitivity to multicultural issues, and clinical judgment to determine if the applicant is competent to act as an independent and thus unsupervised professional.

Once an applicant successfully passes the state licensing requirements, he or she is issued a license number by the state and can finally represent themselves to the public as a psychologist capable of independent practice. In most states, the license must be renewed every year or two. In order to do so, the psychologist will typically need to document that they have not been convicted of any felony offenses, are not in trouble due to ethical violations, demonstrate successful completion of a certain number of continuing education credits (usually about 20 hours per year), and pay a licensing fee. The number of hours and the types of courses acceptable for continuing education vary from state to state. Topics for continuing education include the current understanding of the assessment and treatment of various psychiatric diagnoses, learning new assessment or treatment techniques, understanding specific concerns of diverse populations, how to avoid legal and ethical dilemmas, and other topics.

Employment

The transition from student/trainee to an independent professional can be both exciting and challeng-ing. Most professional training programs do surprisingly little to prepare students for this transition. Because graduate training programs tend to emphasize the academic, clinical, and research training of graduate students, they usually offer little if any attention to career development and professional issues (Plante, 1995, 1996b). Furthermore, many of the academic faculty at most graduate programs are often not involved with many of the professional issues that many of their students will typically experience during their nonacademic careers (e.g., developing a private or group practice, licensure and continuing education requirements, dealing with managed health care and hospital politics, working with a wide variety of clinicians from different disciplines). Therefore, many new clinical psychologists are unprepared for the transition to employment.

Numerous myths about employment must be dealt with in order to successfully cope with the transition. For example, Olson, Downing, Heppner, and Pinkney (1986) reported a number of myths that afflict many early career psychologists:

1. As soon as I unpack my bags, I'll be settled.
2. My new associates will welcome me enthusiastically and accept me as one of them.
3. I will never be an apprentice again.
4. I will easily master the varied demands of my job.
5. I must perform perfectly, lest someone discover that I am a fraud.
6. Because I have worked so hard to get here, I will love my job.

One of the great advantages of being a clinical psychologist is that there are a wide variety of employment settings in which to work. Many psychologists wish to enter the academic world. Some look towards large research universities while others look towards small liberal arts colleges that emphasize teaching. Others wish for an academic career in a medical center environment while still other psychologists are interested in clinical practice. Some prefer medical centers, outpatient clinics, or solo or group private practice. Still others are interested in careers in administration and program development. Many new professionals wish to combine academic work with clinical practice. Median starting salaries vary depending upon speciality area and job location. For example, starting salaries in community mental health centers are about $37,000, while hospital salaries yield about $42,000 and business and industry about $50,000 initially (American

Psychological Association, 1995a, 1997b). Private practitioners can earn much more. Strategies for finding a suitable first job vary significantly depending on which career direction the psychologist chooses (American Psychological Association, 1997b, Kilburg, 1991; Sternberg, 1997). Strategies for academic and clinical positions will be highlighted here.

Academic Positions

Full-time tenure-track academic positions are a popular choice for many new psychologists. After being in school for so many years and being influenced by college and graduate school professors, academic careers are appealing to many. Although doctorates in clinical psychology can include the Ph.D. or Psy.D. degrees, tenure track academic positions in university settings generally prefer the Ph.D. rather than the Psy.D. degree. Tenure-track academic positions are also very competitive and can be hard to find (Brems, Lampman, & Johnson, 1995). The *American Psychological Association Monitor, The Chronicle of Higher Education,* and the *American Psychological Society Observer* are the most likely places to find these jobs advertised. Current professors may also provide an insider's view of good jobs that are available or at least imminent. After completing the application procedure (typically mailing a Curriculum Vitae, reprints of published professional articles, a cover letter outlining teaching and research interests, and having three letters of recommendation), the applicant must wait to be selected for a job interview. Typically, academic departments invite a very small number of top applicants (typically about three) for job interviews. The interview usually lasts a full day or two and includes individual meetings with the department chair, faculty members on the search committee, and sometimes the dean and student representatives. Additionally, most applicants are asked to present their research to a group of faculty and students during a one hour "job talk." Applicants may also be asked to give a guest lecture in a psychology course as well. Finally, lunch and dinner with faculty also can be expected during the interview.

Clinical Positions

If a psychologist is primarily seeking a clinical position in an outpatient clinic, hospital, or group pri-

vate practice, the application and interview strategy will be very different from those for an academic position. Typically, these jobs will be advertised in the *APA Monitor* only for organizations who wish to pursue a national search for a job candidate. Not all clinical settings are interested in interviewing people from all over the United States and therefore will not advertise in the *APA Monitor* or other national publications. The costs for advertising in these national publications can be high, and many organizations may not be interested in the expense of having job candidates fly in from all over the country to interview for their job opening. Therefore, finding out about job openings can be challenging. Often, word of mouth is the best and most opportune way to find out about job openings (American Psychological Association, 1997b). Also, contacting various hospitals, clinics, group practices, state and county psychological associations, postgraduate training institutes, and colleagues may help to determine if positions are available. Positions are also often listed at local professional conferences (e.g., state psychological associations). Networking is the key to ultimately securing clinical jobs.

Clinical job applications usually require a Curriculum Vitae, cover letter outlining clinical interests and experiences, and three letters of recommendation. Often, a sample assessment or other clinical report (removed of all identifying patient information) is requested. All materials are reviewed and a small number of applicants are selected for interviews. The interview often includes individual (and sometimes) group interviews with staff and administrators. In some institutions, the applicant will be asked to present a clinical case in front of staff in a clinical case conference or treatment rounds format.

The American Board of Professional Psychology (ABPP) Diploma

Five years after being awarded the doctorate, a clinical psychologist is eligible to become a **diplomate,** an advanced level of certification. The American Board of Professional Psychology (ABPP) diploma is a post-licensing certification that reflects advanced competency in a subspecialty of psychology. The American Board of Professional Psychology acts as the credentialing agency for psychology diplomas in a variety of speciality areas including clinical psychology, neuropsychology, counseling psychology, health psychology, family psychology, behavior therapy, school psychology, industrial/organizational psychology, and forensic psychology. The ABPP is an independent organization closely associated with the American Psychological Association. It is modeled after medical boards in that following medical school and residency training, a physician may apply to be board certified in a speciality area (e.g., Child Psychiatry, Neurology). These board exams are very common in medicine and are becoming increasingly common for psychologists.

The ABPP diploma application and examination process is a challenging, time-consuming, and expensive endeavor. So, why do it? First, board certification, modeled after medical boards, recognizes an advanced level of professional competence in a speciality area of practice. This certification process and demonstration of advanced competence is often helpful to the public and other consumers of psychological services such as hospitals, clinics, training programs, insurance companies, and courts by suggesting that very high quality skills and services can be expected from a diplomate. The ABPP diploma is becoming more strongly suggested and even required in some employment settings such as university medical centers. For example, at Stanford University Medical School, clinical and medical staff faculty are required to be board certified in order to be promoted in the academic ranks. Therefore, in order for a Clinical Assistant Professor to be promoted to a Clinical Associate Professor or Clinical Professor position, the ABPP diploma is required. Higher salaries are offered for psychologists who are diplomates in some settings such as in the military and VA Hospitals. Thus, several thousand dollars each year might be added to the salary of psychologists in these settings.

The ABPP diploma is also expected in a variety of professional circles in order to be considered an expert. For example, the diploma is almost a requisite in many neuropsychology and forensic psychology environments. Thus, credibility and effectiveness in court testimony, for example, is enhanced by having the ABPP diploma. The ABPP also allows for licensing reciprocity in many states. Therefore, psychologists who are diplomates often do not need to go through the licensing process of examinations if they move from state to state. Finally, distinguishing oneself professionally and attaining the satisfaction of such an accomplishment often serve as sufficient motivators for pursuing diplomate status. Approximately 3 percent of all members of the American Psychological Association become diplomates, and about 10 percent of all eligible psychologists become diplomates (American Psychological Association, 1997a). Therefore, diplomates are a select group of psychologists. Although the numbers are growing, the majority of clinical psychologists choose not to become diplomates.

Professionals are eligible to apply for an ABPP diploma in one of nine areas (Clinical, Counseling, School, Family, Health, Behavior Therapy, Neuropsychology, Forensic, Group) five years after completing their doctoral degree. The application process includes completing an application outlining training and employment background as well as providing the committee with letters of recommendation from three or more professionals who are either diplomates themselves or fellows of the American Psychological Association. Once these materials are reviewed and deemed acceptable by the screening committee, the applicant is asked to provide work samples to submit to the committee.

The work samples typically include complete written transcripts and videotapes of a one-hour psychotherapy session and a one-hour diagnostic interview or testing session. Additionally, a written description of the patient background, diagnosis, treatment plan, and the role of the session example in the context of the overall assessment or treatment plan is required. The work samples are then reviewed by the committee.

The final step in the process is the oral examination. In 1997 the oral examination was changed from a full day to a half day. A committee of three diplomate examiners including a nonvoting chairperson conducts the examination. The examination includes: (1) a discussion of the applicant's theoretical orientation and professional activities, (2) a discussion and defense of the applicant's work samples, and (3) a discussion of ethical vignettes presented by the committee.

Is Clinical Psychology Right for Me?

What does it take to become a clinical psychologist? Is it right for me? Certainly drive and dedication are needed to complete the lengthy training process in order to become a psychologist. A natural curiosity and interest in human behavior and a desire to improve the quality of life for others are also important factors. Anyone interested in the field of clinical psychology as a career option must, of course, decide for himself or herself whether clinical psychology is a good career path to follow (Table 15.4). Decisions about types of training programs, specializations, and career emphasis (e.g., research, teaching, administration, practice) must be made as well. Generally, psychologists express a high degree of satisfaction with their career choice. This book was written in the hope of providing enough background about the field for a student to make an informed decision.

How to Get More Information About Current Issues in Clinical Psychology

Where does a student obtain the most up-to-date information about clinical psychology? Useful sources of information include books about the field (including this one), some focusing on admission to graduate school and other training experiences (e.g., Keith-Spiegal, 1991; Mayne, Norcross, & Sayette, 1994b; Megargee, 1990), and others on the role and activities of clinical and other psychologists (e.g., Kilburg, 1991; Sternberg, 1997). A number of excellent professional journals, newsletters, and other periodicals also provide compelling and timely information. These include *Professional Psychology: Research and Practice,* the *Journal of Consulting and Clinical Psychology,* the *National Psy-*

Table 15.4 Some Pros and Cons of Becoming a Clinical Psychologist

Pros
Exciting range of employment settings
Exciting range of employment activities
Opportunity to play significant role in helping others
Opportunities for both personal and professional growth

Cons
Long training process
Moderate salaries
Increased competition for jobs
Reduced research and training funding

chologist, the *American Psychological Association Monitor,* the *American Psychologist,* the *Clinical Psychologist,* and *Clinical Psychology: Science and Practice,* among others. The American Psychological Association and appropriate divisions (e.g., Division 12-Clinical Psychology), and state and county psychological associations are additional resources. Students may also join the American Psychological Association as student affiliated members at a very low cost. Interested students can contact APA at 202-336-5500 or via the internet at WWW.APA.ORG. Students from Canada may wish to contact the Canadian Psychological Association via the internet at WWW.CPA.CA. Finally, individual clinical psychologists themselves may offer help to interested persons. Obtaining information from several different sources (e.g., professional organizations, books, journals, professionals in the field, students in various stages of training) is highly advised.

Big Picture

Such a detailed description of the step-by-step process towards becoming a clinical psychologist may seem long and daunting as delineated here. After completing college, it takes at least six years of full-time training to become a licensed psychologist. Such is the preparation required to ensure competency, if not excellence, in psychologists' contributions to patient care, diagnosis, teaching, and research. Becoming a clinical psychologist allows one to teach at the university level and elsewhere, conduct research, provide consultation to a wide variety of profes-

sionals and organizations, conduct psychotherapy, and psychological testing with one's own patients, and work in numerous professional settings. While the process is lengthy, it is important not to lose sight of the fact that each step is ripe with new experiences, rewards, exciting skill development, and the ongoing satisfaction of moving toward a personal and professional goal in a field designed ultimately to contribute to the quality of human life.

How will the road to becoming a clinical psychologist change in the future? The application and training process will likely change. For example, the graduate curriculum must accommodate important changes in society such as multiculturalism. Postdoctoral training is likely to become mandatory while continuing education will become more rigorous in the future. The training process must adapt to the changing needs of both students and society for clinical psychology to remain both relevant and vibrant.

Key Points

1. The road to becoming a clinical psychologist is a long one divided by several distinct stages that include college, graduate school, clinical internship, postdoctoral fellowship, licensure, and finally employment and advanced certification (e.g., the diplomate).

2. Overall, students interested in becoming clinical psychologists and gaining admission into high-quality graduate programs must take their college experience very seriously. Solid grades and high-quality research and clinical experiences during the college years are important to acquire. Specifically, students must obtain a solid GPA, high scores on the Graduate Record Examination, obtain some clinical and research experience, and receive excellent letters of recommendation.

3. Graduate training in psychology involves course work, clinical training, and research experiences. There are approximately 180 accredited doctoral graduate programs in clinical psychology in the United States and Canada and many nonaccredited programs as well. Graduate school in clinical psychology generally takes five years to complete including the required one year clinical internship.

4. A student interested in obtaining a doctorate in clinical psychology can choose between two types of doctorates: the traditional Ph.D. (or Doctor of Philosophy) or the newer Psy.D. (Doctor of Psychology). The most common model of training is the scientist-practioner, or Boulder, model, which encourages equal training emphases on both research and clinical practice.

5. The Psy.D. degree seeks to train students in the scholar-practitioner, or Vail, model with much more emphasis on clinical practice and minimal emphasis on research skills. While the majority of graduate training programs currently award students the traditional Ph.D. degree, more and more programs (especially free standing professional schools) are offering the Psy.D. degree.

6. Historically, graduate training in clinical psychology has been the domain of university programs throughout the United States and Canada. However, during the early 1970s, a number of free standing professional schools opened to train graduate students in psychology. Approximately 50 percent of all doctorates in clinical psychology are now awarded by these schools. The free standing schools tend to have large entry classes, older students, and tend to be less competitive regarding admission than university based programs.

7. Since 1948, the American Psychological Association has accredited graduate training programs in clinical psychology. Accreditation by the American Psychological Association as well as regional accreditation agencies are important to maximize the chances of obtaining quality graduate education, clinical internship, and postdoctoral training. APA accreditation also improves the odds of being able to obtain a license to practice in any state and the ability to be employed in any appropriate setting.

8. All accredited graduate training programs are not alike. Each program maintains its own personality based on the faculty and traditions of the program.

9. Almost all graduate training programs in clinical psychology require that students complete a one year, full-time (or two years, part-time) clinical internship prior to being awarded the doctorate. As of 1994, there were 435 American Psychological Association accredited internship programs in the United States and Canada. This training almost always occurs outside of the graduate training program in hospitals, clinics, and various clinical settings throughout the United States. The activities during the clinical internship focus specifically on clinical training such as psychotherapy, psychological testing, and consultation with a variety of patient populations.

10. Almost all states now require one to two years of postdoctoral training before one is eligible to take the licensing examination. Postdoctoral training occurs in a wide variety of settings including hospitals, clinics, counseling centers, universities, and even private practices. Postdoctoral training can include clinical work such as psychotherapy, psychological testing, and consultation as well as research, teaching, and many other professional activities. The American Psychological Association, as well as interested affiliated organizations such as APPIC, are working towards more structured criteria, expectations, and accreditation for postdoctoral training.

11. Since the certification and licensing processes are conducted at the state level, each state develops its own laws and procedures. However, since 1955 the American Psychological Association has offered states a set of guidelines called the Model Act, which outlines suggested rules and regulations for state licensing.

12. All states use the same national written examination for licensing (the EPPP). This exam consists of 200 multiple choice items covering a variety of relevant areas within the field of psychology. After successful completion of the written examination, many states then require an oral (or sometimes an essay) examination before obtaining the license.

13. One of the great advantages of being a clinical psychologist is that there are a wide variety of employment settings in which to work. Becoming a clinical psychologist allows one to teach at the university level, conduct research, provide consultation to a wide variety of professionals and organization, conduct psychotherapy, psychological testing, and work in a many different environments.

14. Five years after being awarded the doctorate, a clinical psychologist is eligible to become a diplomate, an advanced level of certification. The ABPP diploma is a post-licensing certification that reflects advanced competency in a specialty area of psychology. The American Board of Professional Psychology (ABPP) acts as the credentialing agency for psychology diplomates in a variety of speciality areas such as clinical psychology.

Key Terms

Accreditation

Certification

Diplomate

Doctor of Philosophy (Ph.D.)

Doctor of Psychology (Psy.D.)

Examination for Professional Practice in Psychology (EPPP)

Free Standing Professional School

Graduate Record Examination (GRE)

Internship

Licensure

Postdoctoral Fellowhip

For Reflection

1. What should a college student do during college to increase their chance of being admitted to a high quality graduate program in clinical psychology?

2. What is the difference between a Ph.D. and a Psy.D. degree?

3. What is the difference between university and free standing professional schools for graduate training?

4. How long does it take from graduate school to licensure to become a clinical psychologist?

5. Why is accreditation important in selecting a graduate training program?

6. Which is the least regulated part of training for clinical psychology?

7. What is the ABPP diploma?

8. Why is licensure important?

9. What are the major training models in clinical psychology?

10. In general, how does the application process differ between academic and clinical positions?

GLOSSARY

Accreditation organizational review of curriculum to ensure training programs meet minimal standards of quality

Acquired Immune Deficiency Syndrome (AIDS) persons infected with one of several HIV viruses that may result in a serious and life-threatening disorder impacting the immune system

Active Listening interviewing technique using a variety of methods to maximize understanding of what is being said

Administration clinical psychology activity involving management of people and organizations

Advocate consultation approach that seeks to convince a consultee to do something that the consultant believes is desirable

Alzheimer's Disease degenerative disease involving memory loss, failure to recognize well known people and objects, difficulty in organizing and planning, suspiciousness, and language problems

American Board of Professional Psychology acts as the credentialling agency for postlicensing psychology diplomas in a variety of speciality areas, including clinical psychology

American Psychological Association founded in 1892 and is currently the largest organization of psychologists anywhere in the world representing all specialities within psychology

American Psychological Society founded in 1988 and includes members primarily interested in the research and scientific aspects of psychology

Analogue studies that use procedures, subjects, and measures that approximate a real life clinical situation and are usually conducted in a laboratory where experimental conditions can be best controlled

Anorexia Nervosa a self-starvation problem that effects about 1 percent of the adolescent female population

Assessment clinical psychology activity involving various techniques, such as interviews and tests, to evaluate and answer clinical questions

Attention Deficit Hyperactivity Disorder (ADHD) a disorder that includes an inability to sustain attention and concentration as well as problems with impulsivity, overactivity, irritability, and moodiness

Beck Scales a series of inventories to assess depression, anxiety, hopelessness, and suicidal ideation developed by psychiatrist Aaron Beck

Behavioral applies theories of learning and conditioning to the understanding of human behavior and the treatment of behavioral and psychological problems

Behavioral Rehearsal behavioral technique where someone practices how he or she might handle a given problem situation

Between Group research designs that use two or more separate groups of subjects, each of which receives a different type of intervention or, in the case of a control condition, no intervention

Bias attempt to minimize potential error in research by controlling potentially influencing variables—also involves a point of view that is imposed on the patient or client

Binet Scales revised versions of the first standardized intelligence test, developed by Alfred Binet in 1905. The current version, called the Stanford-Binet, was published in 1986.

Biofeedback behavioral technique that provides physiological information such as heart rate and blood pressure to patient in an attempt to learn to control these reactions to stress

Biological Vulnerability genetic or other biological factors that put someone more at risk for the development of problems later

Biopsychosocial an integrative perspective that suggests that biological, psychological, and social influences interact to contribute to both physical and mental health and illness

Boston Process Approach neuropsychological assessment approach developed by Edith Kaplan that uses a variety of tests to understand the process of brain-behavior functioning

Boulder Model clinical psychology training model developed at a conference in Boulder Colorado that places equal weight in both science and practice—also called the scientist-practitioner model

Brain-Behavior Relationships the focus of the neuropsychology subspeciality that highlights the examination of how the brain impacts behavior and how behavior impacts the brain

Brain Injuries trauma to the brain from vehicular accidents, falls, war wounds, sport injuries, gun shot wounds, violent assaults, and other tragic events that impact cognitive functioning

Case Studies research approach that conducts an in-depth analysis of one person

Certification legal process that controls the word *psychologist* from being misused

Child Abuse and Neglect physical, sexual, or emotional misuse of children which puts them in danger or risk of physical or emotional injury

Child Behavior Checklist (CBCL) popular testing instrument used with children, parents, and teachers to assess behavioral problems among children aged 4 to 18

Child Clinical Psychology subspeciality areas that focuses on the problems and concerns of children and their families

Child Custody the legal determination of who is the legal guardian of a minor following divorce, death, or mental disability

Chronic Pain consistent discomfort or pain associated with a large range of medical and psychiatric conditions

Clarification interviewing technique where questions are asked to ensure that the message is being fully understood

Classical conditioning behavioral technique that maintains learning occurs and subsequently, behavior, through the association of conditioned and unconditioned stimuli

331

Client-centered humanistic theoretical orientation that highlights nondirective techniques such as active listening, empathy, congruence, and unconditional positive regard to understand and help others

Client-centered Case Consultation involves consultation with a fellow professional such as another psychologist who is responsible for the treatment or care of a particular patient

Client-Therapist Variation Strategy treatment outcome research approach that alters the types of therapists or patients to determine which combinations optimize treatment outcome

Clinical Psychology discipline that uses what is known about the principles of human behavior to help people with the numerous troubles and concerns they experience during the course of life in their relationships, emotions, and physical selves

Cognitive-Behavioral approach that uses the principles of learning, conditioning, and information processing to understand, assess, and treat emotional and behavioral problems

Collaborative multisite research projects common and popular research strategy that uses researchers and subjects from a variety of locations

Collaborator consultant role that suggests that the consultant is an equal partner working with a consultee to achieve a common goal

Common Factors elements of treatment that are curative and common in many different types of treatment approaches

Community Mental Health Movement attempt during the late 1950s and 1960s to develop outpatient community mental health services outside of the inpatient mental hospital setting

Community-wide Intervention common and popular research approach that attempts to get large segments of entire communities to change behavior

Comparative Treatment Strategy treatment outcome research approach that generally compares different strategies (e.g., psychodynamic versus behavioral techniques) for producing change in a clinical problem

Competence ethical principle requiring that psychologists perform only the duties that they have appropriate levels of training and experience to perform

Computerized Axial Tomography (CAT) neuroimaging technique that provides computer-enhanced multiple X-ray like pictures of the brain from multiple angles

Confidentiality ethical and legal issue restraining a psychologist from disclosing information about a patient or research subject to a third party

Congruence or genuineness, refers to harmony between ones feelings and actions

Constructive Treatment Strategies attempt to answer the question, "What might be added to an effective treatment to make it even more effective?" The constructive treatment approach adds various components to the treatment to determine whether the additions will improve treatment outcome.

Consultation clinical psychology activity that uses knowledge about human behavior to help individuals, groups, and organizations function better

Consultee-centered Administrative Consultation consultation model that involves working on administrative and personnel issues within an agency

Consultee-centered Case Consultation consultation model such that challenges experienced by the consultee rather than problems concerning an individual case or client are the focus

Contingency Management behavioral technique that focuses on changing behavior by altering the consequences that follow behavior

Controlled Observation behavioral technique that attempts to observe behavior in a prescribed manner by forcing the behavior of interest to occur in a simulated manner

Correlational research design that examines the degree of association between two or more variables

Counseling Psychologists specialty of psychology similar to clinical psychology but generally with a historical focus on vocational and college counseling of people mostly free of major psychiatric disturbance

Counterconditioning behavioral technique that attempts to develop a more adaptive response to environmental stimuli

Countertransference psychodynamic concept where therapist responds to the transference of the patient through projecting their needs, wishes, and dynamics onto the patient

Cross-sectional research design that provides a "snapshot" view of behavior at a given moment in time

Curative Factors elements of the psychotherapy experience that contribute to the cure or the significant reduction in symptoms

Defense Mechanisms psychodynamic term refers to strategies used to cope with anxiety and other uncomfortable emotions and impulses

Dementia a particular neurological and psychiatric condition that results in a significant decrease in intellectual, memory, learning, and problem-solving functioning

Dementia Praecox historical term referring to today's notion of schizophrenia

Denial defense mechanism such that person believes that problematic feelings, thoughts, or behaviors do not exist

Diathesis-stress a causal perspective for illness or problems in that it suggests that a biological or other type of vulnerability in combination with psychosocial or environmental stress creates the necessary conditions for illness to occur

Differentiation family systems term to describe the need for family members to develop more adaptive separation and independence from other family members

Diplomate advanced level of certification awarded to eligible psychologists several years following training

Disengagement family systems term for a family member being uninterested or uninvolved with family members

Dismantling treatment outcome research approach that seeks to identify the active ingredient of a particular treatment strategy after the treatment has been determined effective

Diversity refers to differences in age, gender, ethnicity, sexual preference, socioeconomic, and religious orientations

Doctor of Philosophy (Ph.D.) traditional doctorate that balances research and practice or focuses on research only

Doctor of Psychology (Psy.D.) newer doctoral degree that focuses on clinical practice

Dualism seventeenth-century notion that the mind and body are separate and do not significantly interact or influence each other

Dual Relationships ethical term referring to psychologists maintaining outside relationships as friends, lovers, or business partners with their clients or patients

Durham Rule 1954 law that added a "medical disease or defect" to the criteria for insanity

Dyslexia type of learning disability that involves difficulty reading

Educator type of consultation role such that the consultant has specialized information that is useful to the client and can be acquired through education

Ego psychodynamic term that refers to the rational and reasonable aspects of our personality helping us to adapt to a challenging world

Electroencephalography (EEG) technique that assesses electrical brain wave activity

Empathy humanistic term conveying a sense of being heard and understood

Empirically Validated Treatments treatment approaches that have been found to be effective according to research studies and that use treatment manuals

Enmeshment family systems term that refers to maladaptive and over involvement in the lives of family members

Epilepsy type of seizure disorder

Ethics Code ethical principles and standards published by the American Psychological Association (and other psychological associations) to provide ethical guidelines for their members

Evoked Potentials electrical brain wave readings

Examination for Professional Practice in Psychology (EPPP) national 200-item examination used to license psychologists

Experimental Designs methods used to construct experiments to minimize error or bias in the results. Each design has unique advantages and disadvantages.

Experimental Mortality subject drops out from an experiment

Exposure behavioral term that refers to gradual or all at once approach to the feared situation or stimuli

Fact Finder consultation role involves seeking information and relaying the results to consultees who lack the expertise, time, energy, or psychological sensitivities to do the task themselves

Family Systems theoretical orientation that places a deemphasis on the problems of any one member of a family in favor of attention to the family system as a whole

Forensic Psychology clinical psychology subspeciality utilizing principles of human behavior to inform the judicial and legal systems

Free Association psychodynamic term that refers to saying whatever is on one's mind without censoring

Free Standing Professional School graduate training in clinical psychology not affiliated with a college or university

Functional Analysis behavioral term for investigating the specific factors that precede and result from a behavior of interest

Geropsychology clinical psychology subspeciality utilizing principles of human behavior to assist elderly persons

Gestalt humanistic approach that focuses on being keenly aware of one's "here and now" or present experience

Graduate Record Examination (GRE) standardized examination for those interested in applying for graduate school

Health Maintenance Organization (HMO) provides comprehensive health, and usually mental health services, within one organization

Health Psychology clinical psychology subspeciality utilizing principles of human behavior to prevent health problems from occurring or helping those with health problems cope better

History threat to validity of a research study and refers to events outside the experimental situation that could have a significant impact on the results of the study

Humanistic a theoretical approach that emphasizes each individual's perception and experience of his or her world and tends to view people as being active, thinking, creative, and growth oriented

Id psychodynamic term that refers to all primitive impulses

Insanity Defense legal term that suggests that someone is not responsible for their criminal actions if they suffer from a disorder that renders them unaware of what they are doing or that what they are doing is wrong

Insanity Defense Reform Act states that someone can be found innocent due to reasons of insanity if unable to understand that criminal behavior was wrong at the time of the crime due to a mental disease or mental retardation.

Insight understanding of factors that contribute to problems or concerns

Instrumentation threat to validity of research that refers to the influences of the tests and measurement devices used to measure constructs in the study

Integrative combining two or more approaches to assessment, treatment, consultation, and other professional activities

Integrity ethical term and principle that focuses on honesty

Intellectual Testing assessment approaches used to measure cognitive abilities

Intelligence Quotient (IQ) term used to refer to score obtained on tests of intellectual functioning

Internship required one year of full-time clinical training prior to being awarded a doctorate in clinical psychology

Involuntary Commitment being held in a hospital setting without agreeing to the hospitalization

Joining family systems term referring to the therapist's attempt to connect with the family and become part of the family unit rather than act in an detached observer manner in the sessions

Joint Custody legal term for both parents who are divorced, maintaining legal custody of their children

Jury Selection the use of principles of psychology to choose jury members that might maximize an advantage to one side of the legal case

Kaufman Scales cognitive tests that measure intellectual and achievement functioning

Learning Disorders cognitive processing problems in reading, writing, math, and other skills important to success in school

Licensure state document and registration that allows a psychologist to practice and offer services to the public

Longitudinal   research method that follows the responses of subjects over time

Magnetic Resonance Imaging (MRI)   neuroimaging technique that analyzes the nuclear magnetic movements of hydrogen in the water and fat of the body

Malingering   faking an illness to obtain some desired gain

Managed Health Care   organizational and insurance attempts to control the high cost of health care

Marriage, Family, and Child Counseling   master's-level discipline and license that focuses on counseling

Maturation   threat to validity of study and refers to changes within subjects over the passage of time that may influence the experimental results

Medical Staff Privileges   ability to admit, treat, and discharge patients in a hospital setting

Mental Status Interview   series of screening questions to quickly assess a patient's cognitive functioning

Meta-analysis   statistical technique that uses data from a variety of studies to determine overall effects

Milan approach   family systems approach that highly values neutrality as well as acceptance and respect for the family system

Millon Clinical Multiaxial Inventories (MCMI)   popular personality tests based on DSM IV organization of personality disorders

Minnesota Multiphasic Personality Inventory (MMPI)   popular personality test

Mixed Group   research design where experiments are constructed in such a way that different groups of subjects receive different treatment or experimental experiences (between group) while subject responses are assessed over time at different phases of the experiment (within group)

M'Naghten Rule   legal term that suggests that someone is not responsible for their criminal actions if they suffer from a disorder that renders them unaware of what they are doing or that what they are doing is wrong

Moral Therapy   historical therapy sought to treat patients as humanely as possible and encouraged the nurturance of interpersonal relationships

Multicultural   attention and sensitivity to issues related to a variety of ethnic, racial, gender, sexual orientation, and religious issues and values

Multiple-Treatment Interference   threat to validity of study and refers to exposing a subject to several treatment conditions or factors such that the experimenter cannot isolate any specific condition or factors

Narrative   family systems approach that suggests that family members conceptualize their problems and concerns through a series of stories about their lives and various members of the family system

Naturalistic Observation   involves entering into the world of the patient in order to observe the person interacting with the environment in which problems occur

Neuroimaging   techniques that involve obtaining a picture of internal brain and other bodily organs and structures

Neuropsychological Testing   assessment that measures brain-behavior relationship such as cognitive functioning, memory, visual motor skills, and language functioning

Neuropsychology   the subspecialty of clinical psychology that focuses on brain-behavior relationships

Obesity   generally defined as being over 20% above expected weight

Object Relations   a psychodynamic approach that views infants as being relationship seeking rather than pleasure seeking and believes that the early relationship with the mother provides the framework for the development of the sense of self and later psychological functioning

Objective Testing   highly-structured tests that compare scores to national norms

Oedipal Complex   psychodynamic term referring to child's admiration and love of their parent of the opposite sex and disdain for parent of the same sex

Operant Perspective   behavioral approach that maintains that all behavior can be understood through a functional analysis of antecedents (the conditions present just before a target behavior occurs) and consequences (what occurs following the target behavior) of behavior

Paradoxical   family systems techniques that involve prescribing the symptom of concern in an exaggerated form, thus seeming to contradict the goals of intervention

Parametric   treatment outcome research approach that changes a specific aspect of the treatment to determine whether the change can enhance treatment effectiveness

Paraphrasing   interviewing technique that involves rephrasing the content of what is being said

Peak Experience   humanistic concept that refers to moments in life when self-actualization is actually reached

Personality Testing   assessment that assesses personality styles and psychological functioning

Polygraph   machine that measures physiological activity such as heart rate and blood pressure

Positron Emission Tomography (PET)   a type of neuroimaging technique that uses radioactive isotopes injected into the bloodstream of a patient to create gamma rays in the body allowing for views of internal structures

Postdoctoral Fellowship   training after the completion of the doctoral degree that is required prior to licensing in most states

Preferred Provider Organization (PPO)   managed care organization that maintains a list of practitioners who will see patients on an insurance plan for reduced costs

Prescription Privileges   ability to prescribe psychotropic medication

Private Practice   providing professional services on one's own without being employed by an agency

Process Research Strategy   attempts to answer the question, "How does the actual process of therapy impact treatment outcome?" This research approach seeks to determine which aspects of the psychotherapeutic process are associated with positive treatment outcome

Program-centered Administrative Consultation   consultation model that focuses on a program or system rather than on an individual case

Projective Drawings   technique that requires the subject or patient to draw pictures of objects or persons such as a tree, house, person, or family and is interpreted

Projective Testing testing that provides unstructured or ambiguous stimuli such as inkblots or drawings

Pseudo Seizures factitious seizures

Psychiatric Nurses nursing that specializes in the care of psychiatric patients in both outpatient and inpatient settings

Psychiatry medical speciality that focuses on abnormal behavior

Psychodynamic theoretical approach that focuses on unconscious conflicts, defenses, early childhood experiences, dreams, impulses, and fantasies

Psychological Testing assessment that examines personality, cognitive, mood, learning, and other skills

Psychosexual stages psychodynamic approach to development that examines where energy is directed during early childhood and adolescence

Psychotherapy the informed and intentional application of clinical methods and interpersonal stances derived from established psychological principles for the purpose of assisting people to modify their behaviors, cognitions, emotions, and/or other personal characteristics in directions that the participants deem desirable (Norcross, 1990, p. 218)

Psychotherapy Treatment Outcome results of psychological intervention to determine if person(s) is (are) improved following treatment

Psychotropic Medication medications used to alter psychological functioning and mood

Quasi-Experimental research designs used when random assignment to experimental and control conditions is not possible because of ethical or other limitations

Rapport term used to describe the comfortable working relationship that develops between the professional and the client

Reactivity threat to validity of study regarding the subject's potential response to participating in an experiment

Reflection rephrasing the feelings of what is being said in order to encourage the person to express and better understand his or her feelings

Reframing family systems term involves reinterpretation of a behavior or issue in a new and different light

Repression psychodynamic term referring to the defense mechanism that keeps uncomfortable thoughts and feelings out of consciousness

Research clinical psychology activity involving the use of the scientific method to answer questions of interest to researchers and society

Research Program a series of experiments or research studies that attempt to answer questions one step at a time

Revisionists psychodynamic theorists who altered or expanded upon Freud's theory

Rorschach projective inkblot test used to assess psychological functioning

Scholar-Practitioner Model graduate training model that focuses on training practitioners who are consumers of research but are likely not to conduct research—also know as the Vail model

School Psychologists professionals who use knowledge about human behavior and apply that knowledge in a school setting

Scientist-Practitioner Model graduate training model that focuses on a balance between research and practice—also known as the Boulder model

Seizures intense muscle spasms, a complete or partial loss of consciousness, and sometimes unconscious purposeful behavior

Selection Bias threat to validity of a study and refers to a differential and problematic selection procedure for choosing research subjects

Self Actualization humanistic term that refers to the forward movement in life towards greater growth, peace, and acceptance of self and others

Self-efficacy cognitive term that refers to the belief that one can accomplish a goal

Self-monitoring behavioral technique that includes maintaining a diary or log where one can record problematic behaviors as well as other important information such as feelings and thoughts associated with each behavioral occurrence

Sentence Completion projective assessment where subjects are asked to complete an incomplete sentence with the first thing that comes to their mind

Sixteen Personality Factors Questionnaire (16PF) popular personality assessment questionnaire that assumes that the person does not experience significant psychiatric disturbance

Social Learning cognitive-behavioral approach that suggests that behavior is learned by modeling others

Social Work generally a master's-level discipline that has historically focused on patient case management, patient advocacy, and a liaison to optimal social service agencies and benefits

Specialization a specific area of expertise

Statistical Regression threat to validity of study and concerns the tendency of extreme scores on a measure to move toward the mean over time

Stress Management a variety of techniques and strategies to cope more effectively with stress

Strategic family systems approach that utilizes direct involvement by the clinician to combat resistance by directing and altering the behavior of others

Structural family systems approach that focuses on appropriate and adaptive levels of differentiation among family members

Structured Interview interview techniques that involve highly specific questions and often scoring procedures

Summarization interviewing technique that involves both paraphrasing and reflection in attempting to pull together several points into a coherent brief review of the message

Superego represents the internalization of familial, cultural, and societal norms and mores

Symptom Checklist-90-Revised (SCL-90-R) a brief and multidimensional self-report measure to screen persons for major psychiatric symptoms

Teaching clinical psychology activity involving dispensing information to others and engaging them in learning

Testing a potential threat to both internal and external validity of a research study. As a threat to internal validity, testing concerns the influence of the testing or evaluation process itself on research results, such as in the use of repeated measures obtained on the same subjects over time. As a threat to external validity, testing refers to the use of a questionnaire or other assessment device that may sensitize and alter the subject's response and, therefore, influence the dependent measure

Thematic Apperception Test (TAT) projective assessment that asks persons to examine pictures and tell a story about each one

Theoretical Orientation philosophical perspectives used to approach assessment, treatment, consultation, and research

Thought Stopping cognitive technique to eliminate problematic and maladaptive thoughts

Threats to External Validity factors that decrease the generalizability of a research study

Threats to Internal Validity factors that decrease the experimental control and precision of a research study

Trainer consultation role that assumes that the consultant has specialized information that is useful to the client and can be acquired through education

Transference psychodynamic term that involves the projection of early relationship dynamics onto the therapist who represents an authority figure similar to the patient's parents, for example

Treatment clinical psychology activity involving intervention strategies to help others improve their lives

Treatment Outcome Research Strategy various research methods to determine if and how treatment works

Treatment Package Strategy approach attempts to answer the basic question, "Does treatment work?" This approach seeks to determine whether a specific treatment is effective for a specific clinical problem or disorder

Unconditional positive regard humanistic term for allowing a client to discuss his or her concerns without judgement

Vail Model graduate training model that suggests that clinical psychologists are generally practitioners and consumers of research—also referred to as the scholar-practitioner model

Veterans Administration government agency that manages numerous hospitals and clinics throughout the United States to assess and treat veterans

Wechsler Scales a series of intellectual assessments for children and adults that are individually administered

Within Group research approach that examines research effects within the same group of subjects

Working Through psychodynamic term that refers to assimilating and incorporating new insights into daily life

APPENDIX

Ethical Principles of Psychologists and Code of Conduct

CONTENTS

Introduction

The American Psychological Association's (APA's) Ethical Principles of Psychologists and Code of Conduct (hereinafter referred to as the Ethics Code) consists of an Introduction, a Preamble, six General Principles (A-Fl), and specific Ethical Standards. The Introduction discusses the intent, organization, procedural considerations, and scope of application of the Ethics Code. The Preamble and General Principles are aspirational goals to guide psychologists toward the highest ideals of psychology. Although the Preamble and General Principles are not themselves enforceable rules, they should be considered by psychologists in arriving at an ethical course of action and may be considered by ethics bodies in interpreting the Ethical Standards. The Ethical Standards set forth enforceable rules for conduct as psychologists. Most of the Ethical Standards are written broadly, in order to apply to psychologists in varied roles, although the application of an Ethical Standard may vary depending on the context. The Ethical Standards are not exhaustive. The fact that a given conduct is not specifically addressed by the Ethics Code does not mean that it is necessarily either ethical or unethical.

Membership in the APA commits members to adhere to the APA Ethics Code and to the rules and procedures used to implement it. Psychologists and students, whether or not they are APA members, should be aware that the Ethics Code may be applied to them by state psychology boards, courts, or other public bodies.

This Ethics Code applies only to psychologists' work-related activities, that is, activities that are part of the psychologists' scientific and professional functions or that are psychological in nature. It includes the clinical or counseling practice of psychology, research, teaching, supervision of trainees, development of assessment instruments, conducting assessments, educational counseling, organizational consulting, social intervention, administration, and other activities as well. These work-related activities can be distinguished from the purely private conduct of a psychologist, which ordinarily is not within the purview of the Ethics Code.

The Ethics Code is intended to provide standards of professional conduct that can be applied by the APA and other bodies that choose to adopt them. Whether or not a psychologist has violated the Ethics Code does not by itself determine whether he or she is legally liable in a court action, whether a contract is enforceable, or whether other legal consequences occur. These results are based on legal rather than ethical rules. However, compliance with or violation of the Ethics Code may be admissible as evidence in some legal proceedings, depending on the circumstances.

In the process of making decisions regarding their professional behavior, psychologists must consider the Ethics Code, in addition to applicable laws and psychology board regulations. If the Ethics Code establishes a higher standard of conduct than is required by law, psychologists must meet the higher ethical standard. If the Ethics Code standard appears to conflict with the requirements of law, then psychologists make known their commitment to the Ethics Code and take steps to resolve the conflict in a responsible manner. If neither law nor the Ethics Code resolves an issue, psychologists should consider other professional materials[1] and the dictates of their own conscience, as well as seek consultation with others within the field when this is practical.

The procedures for filing, investigating, and resolving complaints of unethical conduct are described in the current Rules and Procedures of the APA Ethics Committee. The actions that APA may take for violations of the Ethics Code include actions such as reprimand, censure, termination of APA membership, and referral of the matter to other bodies. Complainants who seek remedies such as monetary damages in alleging ethical violations by a psychologist must resort to private negotiation, administrative bodies, or the courts. Actions that violate the Ethics Code may lead to the imposition of sanctions on a psychologist by bodies other than APA, including state psychological associations, other professional groups, psychology boards, other state or federal agencies, and payers for health services. In addition to actions for violation of the Ethics Code, the APA Bylaws provide that APA may take action against a member after his or her conviction of a felony, expulsion or suspension from

---

[1]Professional materials that are most helpful in this regard are guidelines and standards that have been adopted or endorsed by professional psychological organizations. Such guidelines and standards, whether adopted by the American Psychological Association (APA) or its Divisions, are not enforceable as such by this Ethics Code, but are of educative value to psychologists, courts, and professional bodies. Such materials include, but are not limited to, the APA's *General Guidelines for Providers of Psychological Services* (1987), *Specialty Guidelines for the Delivery of Services by Clinical Psychologists, Counseling Psychologists, Industrial/Organizational Psychologists, and School Psychologists* (1981), *Guidelines for Computer Based Tests and Interpretations* (1987), *Standards for Educational and Psychological Testing* (1985), *Ethical Principles in the Conduct of Research With Human Participants* (1982), *Guidelines for Ethical Conduct in the Care and Use of Animals* (1986), *Guidelines for Providers of Psychological Services to Ethnic, Linguistic, and Culturally Diverse Populations* (1990), and *Publication Manual of the American Psychological Association* (3rd ed., 1983). Materials not adopted by APA as a whole include the APA Division 41 *(Forensic Psychology)/American Psychology-Law Society's Specialty Guidelines for Forensic Psychologists* (1991).

an affiliated state psychological association, or suspension or loss of licensure.[2]

Preamble

Psychologists work to develop a valid and reliable body of scientific knowledge based on research. They may apply that knowledge to human behavior in a variety of contexts. In doing so, they perform many roles, such as researcher, educator, diagnostician, therapist, supervisor, consultant, administrator, social interventionist, and expert witness. Their goal is to broaden knowledge of behavior and, where appropriate, to apply it pragmatically to improve the condition of both the individual and society. Psychologists respect the central importance of freedom of inquiry and expression in research, teaching, and publication. They also strive to help the public in developing

[2]This version of the APA Ethics Code was adopted by the American Psychological Association's Council of Representatives during its meeting, August 13 and 16, 1992, and is effective beginning December 1, 1992. Inquiries concerning the substance or interpretation of the APA Ethics Code should be addressed to the Director, Office of Ethics, American Psychological Association, 750 First Street, NE, Washington, DC 20002-4242.

This Code will be used to adjudicate complaints brought concerning alleged conduct occurring on or after the effective date. Complaints regarding conduct occurring prior to the effective date will be adjudicated on the basis of the version of the Code that was in effect at the time the conduct occurred, except that no provisions repealed in June 1989, will be enforced even if an earlier version contains the provision. The Ethics Code will undergo continuing review and study for future revisions; comments on the Code may be sent to the above address.

The APA has previously published its Ethical Standards as follows:
American Psychological Association. (1953). *Ethical standards of psychologists.* Washington, DC: Author.
American Psychological Association. (1958). *Standards of ethical behavior for psychologists.* American Psychologist, 13, 268–271.
American Psychological Association. (1963). *Ethical standards of psychologists.* American Psychologist, 18, 56–60.
American Psychological Association. (1968). *Ethical standards of psychologists.* American Psychologist, 23, 357–361.
American Psychological Association. (1977, March). *Ethical standards of psychologists.* APA Monitor, pp. 22–23.
American Psychological Association. (1979). *Ethical standards of psychologists.* Washington, DC: Author.
American Psychological Association. (1981). *Ethical principles of psychologists.* American Psychologist, 36. 633–638.
American Psychological Association. (1990). *Ethical principles of psychologists* (Amended June 2, 1989). American Psychologist, 45, 390–395

Request copies of the APA's Ethical Principles of Psychologists and Code of Conduct from the APA Order Department, 750 First Street, NE, Washington, DC 20002-4242, or phone (202) 336-5510.

informed judgments and choices concerning human behavior. This Ethics Code provides a common set of values upon which psychologists build their professional and scientific work.

This Code is intended to provide both the general principles and the decision rules to cover most situations encountered by psychologists. It has as its primary goal the welfare and protection of the individuals and groups with whom psychologists work. It is the individual responsibility of each psychologist to aspire to the highest possible standards of conduct. Psychologists respect and protect human and civil rights, and do not knowingly participate in or condone unfair discriminatory practices.

The development of a dynamic set of ethical standards for a psychologist's work-related conduct requires a personal commitment to a lifelong effort to act ethically; to encourage ethical behavior by students, supervisees, employees, and colleagues, as appropriate; and to consult with others, as needed, concerning ethical problems. Each psychologist supplements, but does not violate, the Ethics Code's values and rules on the basis of guidance drawn from personal values, culture, and experience.

General Principles

Principle A: Competence

Psychologists strive to maintain high standards of competence in their work. They recognize the boundaries of their particular competencies and the limitations of their expertise. They provide only those services and use only those techniques for which they are qualified by education, training, or experience. Psychologists are cognizant of the fact that the competencies required in serving, teaching, and/or studying groups of people vary with the distinctive characteristics of those groups. In those areas in which recognized professional standards do not yet exist, psychologists exercise careful judgment and take appropriate precautions to protect the welfare of those with whom they work. They maintain knowledge of relevant scientific and professional information related to the services they render, and they recognize the need for ongoing education. Psychologists make appropriate use of scientific, professional, technical, and administrative resources.

Principle B: Integrity

Psychologists seek to promote integrity in the science, teaching, and practice of psychology. In these activities psychologists are honest, fair, and respectful of others. In describing or reporting their qualifications, services, products, fees, research, or teaching, they do not make statements that are false, misleading, or deceptive. Psychologists strive to be aware of their own belief systems, values, needs, and limitations and the effect of these on their work. To the extent feasible, they attempt to clarify for relevant parties the roles they are performing and to function appropriately in accordance with those roles. Psychologists avoid improper and potentially harmful dual relationships.

Principle C: Professional and Scientific Responsibility

Psychologists uphold professional standards of conduct, clarify their professional roles and obligations, accept appropriate responsibility for their behavior, and adapt their methods to the needs of different populations. Psychologists consult with, refer to, or cooperate with other professionals and institutions to the extent needed to serve the best interests of their patients, clients, or other recipients of their services. Psychologists' moral standards and conduct are personal matters to the same degree as is true for any other person, except as psychologists' conduct may compromise their professional responsibilities or reduce the public's trust in psychology and psychologists. Psychologists are concerned about the ethical compliance of their colleagues' scientific and professional conduct. When appropriate, they consult with colleagues in order to prevent or avoid unethical conduct.

Principle D: Respect for People's Rights and Dignity

Psychologists accord appropriate respect to the fundamental rights, dignity, and worth of all people. They respect the rights of individuals to privacy, confidentiality, self-determination, and autonomy, mindful that legal and other obligations may lead to inconsistency and conflict with the exercise of these rights. Psychologists are aware of cultural, individual, and role differences, including those due to age, gender, race, ethnicity, national origin, religion, sexual orientation, disability, language, and socioeconomic status.

Principle E: Concern for Others' Welfare

Psychologists seek to contribute to the welfare of those with whom they interact professionally. In their professional actions, psychologists weigh the welfare and rights of their patients or clients, students, supervisees, human research participants, and other affected persons, and the welfare of animal subjects of research. When conflicts occur among psychologists' obligations or concerns, they attempt to resolve these conflicts and to perform their roles in a responsible fashion that avoids or minimizes harm. Psychologists are sensitive to real and ascribed differences in power between themselves and others, and they do not exploit or mislead other people during or after professional relationships.

Principle F: Social Responsibility

Psychologists are aware of their professional and scientific responsibilities to the community and the society in which they work and live. They apply and make public their knowledge of psychology in order to contribute to human welfare. Psychologists are concerned about, and work to mitigate, the causes of human suffering. When undertaking research, they strive to advance human welfare and the science of psychology. Psychologists try to avoid misuse of their work. Psychologists comply with the law and encourage the development of law and social policy that serve the interests of their patients and clients and the public. They are encouraged to contribute a portion of their professional time for little or no personal advantage.

Ethical Standards

1. General Standards

These General Standards are potentially applicable to the professional and scientific activities of all psychologists.

1.01 Applicability of the Ethics Code

The activity of a psychologist subject to the Ethics Code may be reviewed under these Ethical Standards of the Ethics Code may be reviewed under these Ethical Standards only if the activity is part of his or her work-related functions or the activity is psychological in nature. Personal activities having no connection to or effect on psychological roles are not subject to the Ethics Code.

1.02 Relationship of Ethics and Law

If psychologists' ethical responsibilities conflict with law, psychologists make known their commitment to the Ethics Code and take steps to resolve the conflict in a responsible manner.

1.03 Professional and Scientific Relationship

Psychologists provide diagnostic, therapeutic, teaching, research, supervisory, consultative, or other psychological services only in the context of a defined professional or scientific relationship or role. (See also Standards 2.01,

Evaluation, Diagnosis, and Interventions in Professional Context, and 7.02, Forensic Assessments.)

1.04 Boundaries of Competence

A. Psychologists provide services, teach, and conduct research only within the boundaries of their competence, based on their education, training, supervised experience, or appropriate professional experience.

B. Psychologists provide services, teach, or conduct research in new areas or involving new techniques only after first undertaking appropriate study, training, supervision, and/or consultation from persons who are competent in those areas or techniques.

C. In those emerging areas in which generally recognized standards for preparatory training do not yet exist, psychologists nevertheless take reasonable steps to ensure the competence of their work and to protect patients, clients, student, research participants, and others from harm.

1.05 Maintaining Expertise

Psychologists who engage in assessment, therapy, teaching, research, organizational consulting, or other professional activities maintain a reasonable level of awareness of current scientific and professional information in their fields of activity, and undertake ongoing efforts to maintain competence in the skills they use.

1.06 Basis for Scientific and Professional Judgments

Psychologists rely on scientifically and professionally derived knowledge when making scientific or professional judgments or when engaging in scholarly or professional endeavors.

1.07 Describing the Nature and Results of Psychological Services

A. When psychologists provide assessment, evaluation, treatment, counseling, supervision, teaching, consultation, research, or other psychological services to an individual, a group, or an organization, they provide, using language that is reasonably understandable to the recipient of those services, appropriate information beforehand about the nature of such services and appropriate information later about result sand conclusions. (See also Standard 2.09, Explaining Assessment Results).

B. If psychologists will be precluded by law or by organizational roles from providing such information to par-

ticular individuals or groups, they so inform those individuals or groups at the outset of the service.

1.08 Human Differences

Where differences of age, gender, race, ethnicity, national origin, religion, sexual orientation, disability, language, or socioeconomic status significantly affect psychologists' work concerning particular individuals or groups, psychologists obtain the training, experience, consultation, or supervision necessary to ensure the competence of their services, or they make appropriate referrals.

1.09 Respecting Others

In their work-related activities, psychologists respect the rights of others to hold values, attitudes, and opinions that differ from their own.

1.10 Nondiscrimination

In their work-related activities, psychologists do not engage in unfair discrimination based on age, gender, race ethnicity, national origin, religion, sexual orientation, disability, socioeconomic status, or any basis proscribed by law.

1.11 Sexual Harassment

A. Psychologists do not engage in sexual harassment. Sexual harassment is sexual solicitation, physical advances, or verbal or nonverbal conduct that is sexual in nature, that occurs in connection with the psychologist's activities or roles as a psychologist, and that either: (1) is unwelcome, offensive, or creates a hostile workplace environment, and the psychologist knows or is told this; or (2) is sufficiently severe or intense to be abusive to a reasonable person in the context. Sexual harassment can consist of a single intense or severe act or of multiple persistent or pervasive acts.

B. Psychologists accord sexual-harassment complaints with dignity and respect. Psychologists do not participate in denying a person academic admittance or advancement, employment, tenure, or promotion, based solely upon their having made, or their being the subject of, sexual-harassment charges. This does not preclude taking action based upon the outcome of such proceedings or consideration of other appropriate information.

1.12 Other Harassment

Psychologists do not knowingly engage in behavior that is harassing or demeaning to persons with whom they interact in their work based on factors such as those persons' age, gender, race, ethnicity, national origin, religion, sexual orientation, disability, language, or socioeconomic status.

1.13 Personal Problems and Conflicts

A. Psychologists recognize that their personal problems and conflicts may interfere with their effectiveness. Accordingly, they refrain from undertaking an activity when they know or should know that their personal problems are likely to lead to harm to a patient, client, colleague, student research participant, or other person to whom they may owe a professional or scientific obligation.

B. In addition, psychologist have an obligation to be alert to signs, and to obtain assistance for, their personal problems at an early state, in order to prevent significantly impaired performance.

C. When psychologist become aware of personal problems that may interfere with their performing work-related duties adequately, they take appropriate measures, such as obtaining professional consultation or assistance, and determine whether they should limit, suspend, or terminate their work-related duties.

1.14 Avoiding Harm

Psychologists take reasonable steps to avoid harming their patients or clients, research participants, students, and others with whom they work, and to minimize harm where it is foreseeable and unavoidable.

1.15 Misuse of Psychologists' Influence

Because psychologists' scientific and professional judgments and actions may affect the lives of others, they are alert to and guard against personal, financial, social, organizational, or political factors that might lead to misuse of their influence.

1.16 Misuse of Psychologists' Work

A. Psychologists do not participate in activities in which it appears likely that their skills or data will be misused by others, unless corrective mechanisms are available. (See also Standard 7.04, Truthfulness and Candor.)

B. If psychologist learn of misuse or misrepresentation of their work, they take reasonable steps to correct or minimize the misuse or misrepresentation.

1.17 Multiple Relationships

A. In many communities and situations, it may not be feasible or reasonable for psychologist to avoid social or other nonprofessional contact with persons such as patients, clients, students, supervisees, or research participants. Psychologists must always be sensitive to the potential harmful effects of other contacts on their work and on those persons with whom they deal. A psychologist refrains from entering into or promising another personal, scientific, professional, financial, or other relationship with such persons if it appears likely that such a relationship reasonably might impair the psychologist's objectivity or otherwise interfere with the psychologist's effectively performing his or her functions as a psychologist, or might harm or exploit the other party.

B. Likewise, whenever feasible, a psychologist refrains from taking on professional or scientific obligations when preexisting relationships would create a risk of such harm.

C. If a psychologist finds that, due to unforeseen factors, a potentially harmful multiple relationship has arisen, the psychologist attempts to resolve it with due regard for the best interests of the affected person and maximal compliance with the Ethics Code.

1.18 Barter (With Patients or Clients)

Psychologists ordinarily refrain from accepting goods, services, or other nonmonetary remuneration from patients or clients in return for psychological services because such arrangements create inherent potential for conflicts, exploitation, and distortion of the professional relationship. A psychologist may participate in bartering *only* if (1) it is not clinically contraindicated, *and* (2) the relationship is not exploitative. (See also Standards 1.17, Multiple Relationships, and 1.25, Fees and Financial Arrangements.)

1.19 Exploitative Relationships

A. Psychologists do not exploit persons over whom they have supervisory, evaluative, or other authority such as students, supervisees, employees, research participants, and clients or patients. (See also Standards 4.05–4.07 regarding sexual involvement with clients or patients.)

B. Psychologists do not engage in sexual relationships with students or supervisees in training over whom the psychologist has evaluative or direct authority, because such relationships are so likely to impair judgment or be exploitative

1.20 Consultations and Referrals

A. Psychologists arrange for appropriate consultations and referrals based principally on the best interests of their patients or clients, with appropriate consent, and subject to other relevant considerations, including applicable law and contractual obligations. (See also Standards 5.01, Discussing the Limits of Confidentiality, and 5.06, Consultations.)

B. When indicated and professionally appropriate, psychologists cooperate with other professionals in order to serve their patients or clients effectively and appropriately.

C. Psychologists' referral practices are consistent with law.

1.21 Third-Party Requests for Services

A. When a psychologist agrees to provide services to a person or entity at the request of a third party, the psychologist clarifies to the extent feasible, at the outset of the service, the nature of the relationship with each party. This clarification includes the role of the psychologist (such as therapist, organizational consultant, diagnostician, or expert witness), the probable uses of the services provided or the information obtained, and the fact that there may be limits to confidentiality.

B. If there is a foreseeable risk of the psychologist's being called upon to perform conflicting roles because of the involvement of a third party, the psychologist clarifies the nature and direction of his or her responsibilities, keeps all parties appropriately informed as matters develop, and resolves the situation in accordance with this Ethics Code.

1.22 Delegation to and Supervision of Subordinates

A. Psychologists delegate to their employees, supervisees, and research assistants only those responsibilities that such persons can reasonably be expected to perform competently, on the basis of their education, training, or experience, either independently or with the level of supervision being provided.

B. Psychologists provide proper training and supervision to their employees or supervisees and take reasonable steps to see that such persons perform services responsibly, competently, and ethically.

C. If institutional policies, procedures, or practices prevent fulfillment of these obligations, psychologists attempt to modify their role or to correct the situation to the extent feasible.

1.23 Documentation of Professional and Scientific Work

A. Psychologists appropriately document their professional and scientific work in order to facilitate provision of services later by them or by other professionals, to ensure accountability, and to meet other requirements of institutions or the law.

B. When psychologists have reason to believe that records of their professional services will be used in legal proceedings involving recipients of or participants in their work, they have a responsibility to create and maintain documentation in the kind of detail and quality that would be consistent with reasonable scrutiny in an adjudicative forum. (See also Standard 7.01, Professionalism.)

1.24 Records and Data

Psychologists create, maintain, disseminate, store, retain, and dispose of records and data relating to their research, practice, and other work in accordance with law and in a manner that permits compliance with the requirement of this Ethics Code. (See also Standard 5.04, Maintenance of Records.)

1.25 Fees and Financial Arrangements

A. As early as is feasible in a professional or scientific relationship, the psychologist and the patient, client, or other appropriate recipient of psychological services reach an agreement specifying the compensation and the billing arrangements.

B. Psychologists do not exploit recipients of services or payors with respect to fees.

C. Psychologists' fee practices are consistent with law.

D. Psychologists do not misrepresent their fees.

E. If limitations to services can be anticipated because of limitations in financing, this is discussed with the patient, client, or other appropriate recipient of services as early as feasible. (See also Standard 4.08, Interruption of Services.)

F. If the patient, client, or other recipient of services does not pay for services as agreed, and if the psychologist wishes to use collection agencies or legal measures to collect the fees, the psychologist first informs the person that such measures will be taken and provides that person an opportunity to make prompt payment. (See also Standard 5.11, Withholding Records for Nonpayment.)

1.26 Accuracy in Reports to Payors and Funding Sources

In their reports to payors for services or sources of research funding, psychologists accurately state the nature of the research or service provided, the fees or charges, and where applicable, the identity of the provider, the findings, and the diagnosis. (See also Standard 5.05, Disclosures.)

1.27 Referrals and Fees

When a psychologist pays, receives payment from, or divides fees with another professional other than in an employer-employee relationship, the payment to each is based on the services (clinical, consultative, administrative, or other) provided and is not based on the referral itself.

2. Evaluation, Assessment, or Intervention

2.01 Evaluation, Diagnosis, and Interventions in Professional Context

A. Psychologists perform evaluations, diagnostic services, or interventions only within the context of a defined professional relationship. (See also Standard 1.03, Professional and Scientific Relationship.)

B. Psychologists' assessments, recommendations, reports, and psychological diagnostic or evaluative statements are based on information and techniques (including personal interviews of the individual when appropriate) sufficient to provide appropriate substantiation for their findings. (See also Standard 7.02, Forensic Assessments.)

2.02 Competence and Appropriate Use of Assessments and Interventions

A. Psychologists who develop, administer, score, interpret, or use psychological assessments techniques, interviews, tests, or instruments do so in manner and for purposes that are appropriate in light of the research on or evidence of usefulness and proper application of the techniques.

B. Psychologists refrain from misuse of assessment techniques, interventions, results, and interpretations and take reasonable steps to prevent others from misusing the information these techniques provide. This includes reframing from releasing raw test results or raw data to persons, other than to patients or clients as appropriate, who are not qualified to use such information. (See also Standards 1.02, Relationship of Ethics and Law, and 1.04, Boundaries of Competence.)

2.03 Test Construction

Psychologist who develop and conduct research with tests and other assessments techniques use scientific procedures and current professional knowledge for test design, standardization, validation, reduction or elimination of bias, and recommendations for use.

2.04 Use of Assessment in General With Special Populations

A. Psychologists who perform interventions or administer, score, interpret, or use assessment techniques are familiar with the reliability, validation, and related standardization or outcome studies of, and proper applications and uses of, the techniques they use.

B. Psychologists recognize limits to the certainty with which diagnoses, judgments, or predictions can be made about individuals.

C. Psychologists attempt to identify situations in which particular interventions or assessment techniques or norms may not be applicable or may require adjustment in administration or interpretation because of factors such as individuals' gender, age, race, ethnicity, national origin, religion, sexual orientation, disability, language, or socioeconomic status.

2.05 Interpreting Assessment Results

When Interpreting assessment results, including automated interpretations, psychologists take into account the various test factors and characteristics of the person being assessed that might affect psychologists' judgements or reduce the accuracy of their interpretations. They indicate any significant reservations they have about the accuracy or limitations of their interpretations.

2.06 Unqualified Persons

Psychologists do not promote the use of psychological assessment techniques by unqualified persons. (See also Standard 1.22, Delegation to and Supervision of Subordinates.)

2.07 Obsolete Tests and Outdated Test Results

A. Psychologists do not base their assessment or intervention decisions or recommendations on data or test results that are outdated for the current purpose.

B. Similarly, psychologists do not base such decisions or recommendations on tests and measures that are obsolete and not useful for the current purpose.

2.08 Test Scoring and Interpretation Services

A. Psychologists who offer assessment or scoring procedures to other professionals accurately describe the purpose, norms, validity, reliability, and applications of the procedures and any special qualifications applicable to their use.

B. Psychologists select scoring and interpretation services (including automated services) on the basis of evidence of the validity of the program and procedures as well as on other appropriate considerations.

C. Psychologists retain appropriate responsibility for the appropriate application, interpretation, and use of assessment instruments, whether they score and interpret such tests themselves or use automated or other services.

2.09   Explaining Assessment Results

Unless the nature of the relationship is clearly explained to the person being assessed in advance and precludes provision of an explanation of results (such as in some organizational consulting, preemployment or security screenings, and forensic evaluations), psychologists ensure that an explanation of the results is provided using language that is reasonably understandable to the person on behalf of the client. Regardless of whether the scoring and interpretation are done by the psychologist, by assistants, or by automated or other outside services, psychologists take reasonable steps to ensure that appropriate explanations of results are given.

2.10   Maintaining Test Security

Psychologists make reasonable efforts to maintain the integrity and security of tests and other assessment techniques consistent with law, contractual obligations, and in a manner that permits compliance with the requirements of this Ethics Code. (See also Standard 1.02, Relationship of Ethics and Law.)

3.   Advertising and Other Public Statements

3.01   Definition of Public Statements

Psychologists comply with this Ethics Code in public statements relating to their professional services, products, or publications or the field of psychology. Public statements include but are not limited to paid or unpaid advertising, brochures, printed matter, directory listings, personal resumes or curricula vitae, interviews or comments for use in media, statements in legal proceedings, lectures and public oral presentations, and published materials.

3.02   Statements by Others

A. Psychologists who engage others to create or place public statements that promote their professional practice, products, or activities retain professional responsibility for such statements.

B. In addition, psychologists make reasonable efforts to prevent others whom they do not control (such as employees, publishers, sponsors, organizational clients, and representatives of the print or broadcast media) from making deceptive statements concerning psychologists' practice or professional or scientific activities.

C. If psychologists learn of deceptive statements about their work made by others, psychologists make reasonable efforts to correct such statements.

D. Psychologists do not compensate employees of press, radio, television, or other communication media in return for publicity in a news item.

E. A paid advertisement relating to the psychologist's activities must be identified as such, unless it is already apparent from the context.

3.03   Avoidance of False or Deceptive Statements

A. Psychologists do not make public statements that are false, deceptive, misleading, or fraudulent, either because of what they state, convey, or suggest or because of what they omit, concerning their research, practice, or other work activities or those of persons or organizations with which they are affiliated. As examples (and not in limitation) of this standard, psychologist do not make false or deceptive statements concerning (1) their training, experience, or competence; (2) their academic degrees; (3) their credentials; (4) their institutional or association affiliations; (5) their services; (6) the scientific or clinical basis for, or results or degree of success of, their services; (7) their fees; or (8) their publications or research findings. (See also Standards 6.15, Deception in Research, and 6.18 Providing Participants With Information About the Study.)

B. Psychologists claim as credentials for their psychological work, only degrees that (1) were earned from a regionally accredited educational institution or (2) were the basis for psychology licensure by the state in which they practice.

3.04   Media Presentations

When psychologists provide advice or comment by means of public lectures, demonstrations, radio or television programs, prerecorded tapes, printed articles, mailed material, or other media, they take reasonable precautions to ensure that (1) the statements are based on appropriate psychological literature and practice, (2) the statements are otherwise consistent with this Ethics Code, and (3) the recipients of the information are not encouraged to infer that a relationship has been established with them personally.

3.05 Testimonials

Psychologists do not solicit testimonials from current psychotherapy clients or patients or other persons who because of their particular circumstances are vulnerable to undue influence.

3.06 In-Person Solicitation

Psychologists do not engage directly or through agents, in uninvited in-person solicitation of business from actual or potential psychotherapy patients or clients or other persons who because of their particular circumstance are vulnerable to undue influence. However, this does not preclude attempting to implement appropriate collateral contacts with significant others for the purpose of benefiting an already engaged therapy patient.

4. Therapy

4.01 Structuring the Relationship

A. Psychologists discuss with clients or patients as early as is feasible in the therapeutic relationship appropriate issues, such as the nature and anticipated course of therapy, fees, and confidentiality. (See also Standards 1.25, Fees and Financial Arrangements, and 5.01, Discussing the Limits of Confidentiality.)

B. When the psychologist's work with clients or patients will be supervised, the above discussion includes that fact, and the name of the supervisor, when the supervisor has legal responsibility for the case.

C. When the therapist is a student intern, the client or patient is informed of that fact.

D. Psychologists make reasonable efforts to answer patients' questions and to avoid apparent misunderstandings about therapy. Whenever possible, psychologists provide oral and/or written information, using language that is reasonably understandable to patient or client.

4.02 Informed Consent to Therapy

A. Psychologists obtain appropriate informed consent to therapy or related procedures, using language that is reasonably understandable to participants. The content of informed consent will be on many circumstances; however, informed consent generally implies that the person (1) has the capacity to consent, (2) has been informed of significant information concerning the procedure, (3) has freely and without undue influence expressed consent, and (4) consent has been appropriately documented.

B. When persons are legally incapable of giving informed consent, psychologists obtain informed permission from a legally authorized person, if such substitute consent is permitted by law.

C. In addition, psychologists (1) inform those persons who are legally incapable of giving informed consent about the proposed interventions in a manner commensurate with the persons' psychological capacities, (2) seek their assent to those interventions, and (3) consider such persons' preferences and best interests.

4.03 Couple and Family Relationships

A. When a psychologist agrees to provide services to several persons who have a relationship (such as husband and wife or parents and children), the psychologist attempts to clarify at the outset (1) which of the individuals are patients or clients and (2) the relationship the psychologist will have with each person. This clarification includes the role of the psychologist and the probable uses of the services provided or the information obtained. (See also Standard 5.01, Discussing the Limits of Confidentiality.)

B. As soon as it becomes apparent that the psychologist may be called on to perform potentially conflicting roles (such as martial counselor to husband or wife, and then witness for one party in a divorce proceeding), the psychologist attempts to clarify and adjust, or withdraw from, roles appropriately. (See also Standard 7.03, Clarification of Role.)

4.04 Providing Mental Health Services to Those Served by Others

In deciding whether to offer or provide services to those already receiving mental health services elsewhere, psychologists carefully consider the treatment issues and the potential patient's or client's welfare. The psychologist discusses these issues with the patient or client, or another legally authorized person on behalf of the client, in order to minimize the risk of confusion and conflict, consults with the other service providers when appropriate, and proceeds with caution and sensitivity to the therapeutic issues.

4.05 Sexual Intimacies With Current Patients or Clients

Psychologists do not engage in sexual intimacies with current patients or clients.

4.06 Therapy With Former Sexual Partners

Psychologist do not accept as therapy patients or clients persons with whom they have engaged in sexual intimacies.

4.07 Sexual Intimacies With Former Therapy Patients

A. Psychologists do not engage in sexual intimacies with a former therapy patient or client for at least two years after cessation or termination of professional services.

B. Because sexual intimacies with a former therapy patient or client are so frequently harmful to the patient or client, and because such intimacies undermine public confidence in the psychology profession and thereby deter the public's use of needed services, psychologists do not engage in sexual intimacies with former therapy patients and clients even after a two-year interval except in the most unusual circumstances. The psychologist who engages in such activity after the two years following cessation or termination of treatment bears the burden of demonstrating that there has been no exploitation, in light of all relevant factors, including (1) the amount of time that has passed since therapy terminated, (2) the nature and duration of therapy, (3) the circumstances of termination, (4) the patient's or client's personal history, (5) the patient's or client's current mental status, (6) the likelihood of adverse impact on the patient or client and others, and (7) any statements or actions made by the therapist during the course of therapy suggesting or inviting the possibility of a posttermination sexual romantic relationship with the patient or client. (See also Standard 1.17, Multiple Relationships.)

4.08 Interruption of Services

A. Psychologists make reasonable efforts to plan for facilitating care in the event that psychological services are interrupted by factors such as the psychologist's illness, death, unavailability, or relocation or by the client's relocation or financial limitations. (See also Standard 5.09, Preserving Records and Data.)

B. When entering into employment or contractual relationships, psychologists provide for orderly and appropriate resolution of responsibility for patient or client care in the event that the employment or contractual relationship ends, with paramount consideration given to the welfare of the patient or client.

4.09 Terminating the Professional Relationship

A. Psychologists do not abandon patients or clients. (See also Standard 1.25, under Fees and Financial Arrangements.)

B. Psychologists terminate a professional relationship when it becomes reasonably clear that the patient or client no longer needs the service, is not benefiting, or is being harmed by continued service.

C. Prior to termination for whatever reason, except where precluded by the patient's or client's conduct, the psychologist discusses the patient's or client's views and needs, provides appropriate pretermination counseling, suggests alternative service providers as appropriate, and takes other reasonable steps to facilitate transfer of responsibility to another provider if the patient or client needs one immediately.

5.00 Privacy and Confidentiality

These Standards are potentially applicable to the professional and scientific activities of all psychologists.

5.01 Discussing the Limits of Confidentiality

A. Psychologists discuss with persons and organizations with whom they establish a scientific or professional relationship (including, to the extent feasible, miners and their legal representatives) (1) the relevant limitations on confidentiality, including limitations where applicable in group, marital, and family therapy or in organizational consulting, and (2) the foreseeable uses of the information generated through their services.

B. Unless it is not feasible or is contraindicated, the discussion of confidentiality occurs at the outset of the relationship and thereafter as new circumstances may warrant.

C. Permission for electronic recording of interviews is secured from clients and patients.

5.02 Maintaining Confidentiality

Psychologists have a primary obligation and take reasonable precautions to respect the confidentiality rights of those with whom they work or consult, recognizing that confidentiality may be established by law, institutional rules, or professional or scientific relationships. (See also Standard 6.26, Professional Reviewers.)

5.03 Minimizing Intrusions on Privacy

A. In order to minimize intrusions on privacy, psychologists include in written and oral reports, consultations, and the like, only information germane to the purpose for which the communication is made.

B. Psychologists discuss confidential information obtained in clinical or consulting relationships, or evaluative data concerning patients, individual or organizational clients, students, research participants, supervisees, and employees, only for appropriate scientific or professional purposes and only with persons clearly concerned with such matters.

5.04 Maintenance of Records

Psychologists maintain appropriate confidentiality in creating, storing, accessing, transferring, and disposing of records under their control, whether these are written, automated, or in any other medium. Psychologists maintain and dispose of records in accordance with law and in a manner that permits compliance with the requirements of this Ethics Code.

5.05 Disclosures

A. Psychologists disclose confidential information without the consent of the individual only as mandated by law, or where permitted by law for a valid purpose, such as (1) to provide needed professional services to the patient or the individual or organizational client, (2) to obtain appropriate professional consultations, (3) to protect the patient or client or others from harm, or (4) to obtain payment for services, in which instance disclosure is limited to the minimum that is necessary to achieve the purpose.

B. Psychologists also may disclose confidential information with the appropriate consent of the patient or the individual or organizational client (or of another legally authorized person on behalf of the patient or client), unless prohibited by law.

5.06 Consultations

When consulting with colleagues, (1) psychologists do not share confidential information that reasonably could lead to the identification of a patient, client, research participant, or other person or organization with whom they have a confidential relationship unless they have obtained the prior consent of the person or organization or the disclosure cannot be avoided, and (2) they share information only to the extent necessary to achieve the purposes of the consultation. (See also Standard 5.02, Maintaining Confidentiality.)

5.07 Confidential Information in Databases

A. If confidential information concerning recipients of psychological services is to be entered into databases or systems of records available to persons whose access has not been consented to by the recipient, then psychologists use coding or other techniques to avoid the inclusion of personal identifiers.

B. If a research protocol approved by an institutional review board or similar body requires the inclusion of personal identifiers, such identifiers are deleted before the information is made accessible to persons other than those of whom the subject was advised.

C. If such deletion is not feasible, then before psychologists transfer such data to others or review such data collected by others, they take reasonable steps to determine that appropriate consent of personally identifiable individuals has been obtained.

5.08 Use of Confidential Information for Didactic or Other Purposes

A. Psychologists do not disclose in their writings, lectures, or other public media, confidential, personally identifiable information concerning their patients, individual or organizational clients, students, research participants, or other recipients of their services that they obtained during the course of their work, unless the person or organization has consented in writing or unless there is other ethical or legal authorization for doing so.

B. Ordinarily, in such scientific and professional presentations, psychologists disguise confidential information concerning such persons or organizations so that they are not individually identifiable to others and so that discussions do not cause harm to subjects who might identify themselves.

5.09 Preserving Records and Data

A psychologist makes plans in advance so that confidentiality of records and data is protected in the event of the psychologist's death, incapacity, or withdrawal from the position or practice.

5.10 Ownership of Records and Data

Recognizing that ownership of records and data is governed by legal principles, psychologists take reasonable and lawful steps so that records and data remain available to the extent needed to serve the best interests of patients, individual or organizational clients, research participants, or appropriate others.

5.11 Withholding Records for Nonpayment

Psychologists may not withhold records under their control that are requested and imminently needed for a patient's or client's treatment solely because payment has not been received, except as otherwise provided by law.

6.00 Research and Publishing

6.01 Design of Education and Training Programs

Psychologists who are responsible for education and training programs seek to ensure that the programs are competently designed, provide the proper experiences, and meet the requirements for licensure, certification, or other goals for which claims are made by the program.

6.02 Descriptions of Education and Training Programs

A. Psychologists responsible for education and training programs seek to ensure that there is a current and accurate description of the program content, training goals and objectives, and requirements that must be met for satisfactory completion of the program. This information must be made readily available to all interested parties.

B. Psychologists seek to ensure that statements concerning their course outlines are accurate and not misleading, particularly regarding the subject matter to be covered, bases for evaluating progress, and the nature of course experiences. (See also Standard 3.03, Avoidance of False or Deceptive Statements.)

C. To the degree to which they exercise control, psychologists responsible for announcements, catalogs, brochures, or advertisements describing workshops, seminars, or other nondegree-granting educational programs ensure that they accurately describe the audience for which the program is intended, the educational objectives, the presenters, and the fees involved.

6.03 Accuracy and Objectivity in Teaching

A. When engaged in teaching or training, psychologists present psychological information accurately and with a reasonable degree of objectivity.

B. When engaged in teaching or training, psychologists recognize the power they hold over students or supervisees and therefore make reasonable efforts to avoid engaging in conduct that is personally demeaning to students or supervisees. (See also Standards 1.09, Respecting Others, and 1.12, Other Harassment.)

6.04 Limitation on Teaching

Psychologists do not teach the use of techniques or procedures that require specialized training, licensure, or expertise, including but not limited to hypnosis, biofeedback, and projective techniques, to individuals who lack the prerequisite training, legal scope of practice, or expertise.

6.05 Assessing Student and Supervisee Performance

A. In academic and supervisory relationships, psychologists establish an appropriate process for providing feedback to students and supervisees.

B. Psychologists evaluate students and supervisees on the basis of their actual performance on relevant and established program requirements.

6.06 Planning Research

A. Psychologists design, conduct, and report research in accordance with recognized standards of scientific competence and ethical research.

B. Psychologists plan their research so as to minimize the possibility that results will be misleading.

C. In planning research, psychologists consider its ethical acceptability under the Ethics Code. If an ethical issue is unclear, psychologists seek to resolve the issue through consultation with institutional review boards, animal care and use committees, peer consultations, or other proper mechanisms.

D. Psychologists take reasonable steps to implement appropriate protections for the rights and welfare of human participants, other persons affected by the research, and the welfare of animal subjects.

6.07 Responsibility

A. Psychologists conduct research competently and with due concern for the dignity and welfare of the participants.

B. Psychologists are responsible for the ethical conduct of research conducted by them or by others under their supervision or control.

C. Researchers and assistants are permitted to perform only those tasks for which they are appropriately trained and prepared.

D. As part of the process of development and implementation of research projects, psychologists consult those with expertise concerning any special population under investigation or most likely to be affected.

6.08 Compliance With Law and Standards

Psychologists plan and conduct research in a manner consistent with federal and state law and regulations, as well as professional standards governing the conduct of research, and particularly those standards governing research with human participants and animal subjects.

6.09 Institutional Approval

Psychologists obtain from host institutions or organizations appropriate approval prior to conducting research, and they provide accurate information about their research proposals. They conduct the research in accordance with the approved research protocol.

6.10 Research Responsibilities

Prior to conducting research (except research involving only anonymous surveys, naturalistic observations, or similar research), psychologists enter into an agreement with participants that clarifies the nature of the research and the responsibilities of each party.

6.11 Informed Consent to Research

A. Psychologists use language that is reasonably understandable to research participants in obtaining their appropriate informed consent (except as provided in Standard 6.12, Dispensing With Informed Consent). Such informed consent is appropriately documented.

B. Using language that is reasonably understandable to participants, psychologists inform participants of the nature of the research; they inform participants that they are free to participate or to decline to participate or to withdraw from the research; they explain the foreseeable consequences of declining or withdrawing; they inform participants of significant factors that may be expected to influence their willingness to participate (such as risks, discomfort, adverse effects, or limitations on confidentiality, except as provided in Standard 6.15, Deception in Research); and they explain other aspects about which the prospective participants inquire.

C. When psychologists conduct research with individuals such as students or subordinates, psychologists take special care to protect the prospective participants from adverse consequences of declining or withdrawing from participation.

D. When research participation is a course requirement or opportunity for extra credit, the prospective participant is given the choice of equitable alternative activities.

E. For persons who are legally incapable of giving informed consent, psychologists nevertheless (1) provide an appropriate explanation, (2) obtain the participant's assent, and (3) obtain appropriate permission from a legally authorized person, if such substitute consent is permitted by law.

6.12 Dispensing With Informed Consent

Before determining that planned research (such as research involving only anonymous questionnaires, naturalistic observations, or certain kinds of archival research) does not require the informed consent of research partici-

pants, psychologists consider applicable regulations and institutional review board requirements, and they consult with colleagues as appropriate.

6.13 Informed Consent in Research Filming or Recording

Psychologists obtain informed consent from research participants prior to filming or recording them in any form, unless the research involves simply naturalistic observations in public places and it is not anticipated that the recording will be used in a manner that could cause personal identification or harm.

6.14 Offering Inducements for Research Participants

A. In offering professional services as an inducement to obtain research participants, psychologists make clear the nature of the services, as well as the risks, obligations, and limitations. (See also Standard 1.18, Barter [With Patients or Clients].)

B. Psychologists do not offer excessive or inappropriate financial or other inducements to obtain research participants, particularly when it might tend to coerce participation.

6.15 Deception in Research

A. Psychologists do not conduct a study involving deception unless they have determined that the use of deceptive techniques is justified by the study's prospective scientific, educational, or applied value and that equally effective alternative procedures that do not use deception are not feasible.

B. Psychologists never deceive research participants about significant aspects that would affect their willingness to participate, such as physical risks, discomfort, or unpleasant emotional experiences.

C. Any other deception that is an integral feature of the design and conduct of an experiment must be explained to participants as early as is feasible, preferably at the conclusion of their participation, but no later than at the conclusion of the research. (See also Standard 6.18, Providing Participants With Information About the Study.)

6.16 Sharing and Utilizing Data

Psychologists inform research participants of their anticipated sharing or further use of personally identifiable research data and of the possibility of unanticipated future uses.

6.17 Minimizing Invasiveness

In conducting research, psychologists interfere with the participants or milieu from which data are collected only in a manner that is warranted by an appropriate research design and that is consistent with psychologists' roles as scientific investigators.

6.18 Providing Participants With Information About the Study

A. Psychologists provide a prompt opportunity for participants to obtain appropriate information about the nature, results, and conclusions of the research, and psychologists attempt to correct any misconceptions that participants may have.

B. If scientific or humane values justify delaying or withholding this information, psychologists take reasonable measures to reduce the risk of harm.

6.19 Honoring Commitments

Psychologists take reasonable measures to honor all commitments they have made to research participants.

6.20 Care and Use of Animals in Research

A. Psychologists who conduct research involving animals treat them humanely.

B. Psychologists acquire, care for, use, and dispose of animals in compliance with current federal, state, and local laws and regulations, and with professional standards.

C. Psychologists trained in research methods and experienced in the care of laboratory animals supervise all procedures involving animals and are responsible for ensuring appropriate consideration of their comfort, health, and humane treatment.

D. Psychologists ensure that all individuals using animals under their supervision have received instruction in research methods and in the care, maintenance, and handling of the species being used, to the extent appropriate to their role.

E. Responsibilities and activities of individuals assisting in a research project are consistent with their respective competencies.

F. Psychologists make reasonable efforts to minimize the discomfort, infection, illness, and pain of animal subjects.

G. A procedure subjecting animals to pain, stress, or privation is used only when an alternative procedure is unavailable and the goal is justified by its prospective scientific, educational, or applied value.

H. Surgical procedures are performed under appropriate anesthesia; techniques to avoid infection and minimize pain are followed during and after surgery.

I. When it is appropriate that the animal's life be terminated, it is done rapidly, with an effort to minimize pain, and in accordance with accepted procedures.

6.21 Reporting of Results

A. Psychologists do not fabricate data or falsify results in their publications.

B. If psychologists discover significant errors in their published data, they take reasonable steps to correct such errors in a correction, retraction, erratum, or other appropriate publication means.

6.22 Plagiarism

Psychologists do not present substantial portions or elements of another's work or data as their own, even if the other work or data source is cited occasionally.

6.23 Publication Credit

A. Psychologists take responsibility and credit, including authorship credit, only for work they have actually performed or to which they have contributed.

B. Principal authorship and other publication credits accurately reflect the relative scientific or professional contributions of the individuals involved, regardless of their relative status. Mere possession of an institutional position, such as Department Chair, does not justify authorship credit. Minor contributions to the research or to the writing for publications are appropriately acknowledged, such as in footnotes or in an introductory statement.

C. A student is usually listed as principal author on any multiple-authored article that is substantially based on the student's dissertation or thesis.

6.24 Duplicate Publication of Data

Psychologists do not publish, as original data, data that have been previously published. This does not preclude republishing data when they are accompanied by proper acknowledgment.

6.25 Sharing Data

After research results are published, psychologists do not withhold the data on which their conclusions are based from other competent professionals who seek to verify the substantive claims through reanalysis and who intend to use such data only for that purpose, provided that the confidentiality of the participants can be protected and unless legal rights concerning proprietary data preclude their release.

6.26 *Professional Reviewers*

Psychologists who review material submitted for publication, grant, or other research proposal review respect the confidentiality of and the proprietary rights in such information of those who submitted it.

7. *Forensic Activities*

7.01 *Professionalism*

Psychologists who perform forensic functions, such as assessments, interviews, consultations, reports, or expert testimony, must comply with all other provisions of this Ethics Code to the extent that they apply to such activities. In addition, psychologists base their forensic work on appropriate knowledge of and competence in the areas underlying such work, including specialized knowledge concerning special populations. (See also Standards 1.06, Basis for Scientific and Professional Judgments; 1.08, Human Differences; 1.15, Misuse of Psychologists' Influence; and 1.23, Documentation of Professional and Scientific Work.)

7.02 *Forensic Assessments*

A. Psychologists' forensic assessments, recommendations, and reports are based on information and techniques (including personal interviews of the individual, when appropriate) sufficient to provide appropriate substantiation for their findings. (See also Standards 1.03, Professional and Scientific Relationship; 1.23, Documentation of Professional and Scientific Work; 2.01, Evaluation, Diagnosis, and Interventions in Professional Context; and 2.05, Interpreting Assessment Results.)
B. Except as noted in (C), psychologists provide written or oral forensic reports or testimony of the psychological characteristics of an individual only after they have conducted an examination of the individual adequate to support their statements or conclusions.
C. When, despite reasonable efforts, such an examination is not feasible, psychologists clarify the impact of their limited information on the reliability and validity of their reports and testimony, and they appropriately limit the nature and extent of their conclusions or recommendations.

7.03 *Clarification of Role*

In most circumstances, psychologists avoid performing multiple and potentially conflicting roles in forensic mat-

ters. When psychologists may be called on to serve in more than one role in a legal proceeding—for example, as consultant or expert for one party or for the court and as a fact witness—they clarify role expectations and the extent of confidentiality in advance to the extent feasible, and thereafter as changes occur, in order to avoid compromising their professional judgment and objectivity and in order to avoid misleading others regarding their role.

7.04 *Truthfulness and Candor*

A. In forensic testimony and reports, psychologists testify truthfully, honestly, and candidly and, consistent with applicable legal procedures, describe fairly the bases for their testimony and conclusions.
B. Whenever necessary to avoid misleading, psychologists acknowledge the limits of their data or conclusions.

7.05 *Prior Relationships*

A prior professional relationship with a party does not preclude psychologists from testifying as fact witnesses or from testifying to their services to the extent permitted by applicable law. Psychologists appropriately take into account ways in which the prior relationship might affect their professional objectivity or opinions and disclose the potential conflict to the relevant parties.

7.06 *Compliance With Law and Rules*

In performing forensic roles, psychologists are reasonably familiar with the rules governing their roles. Psychologists are aware of the occasionally competing demands placed upon them by these principles and the requirements of the court system, and attempt to resolve these conflicts by making known their commitment to this Ethics Code and taking steps to resolve the conflict in a responsible manner. (See also Standard 1.02, Relationship of Ethics and Law.)

8. *Resolving Ethical Issues*

8.01 *Familiarity With Ethics Code*

Psychologists have an obligation to be familiar with this Ethics Code, other applicable ethics codes, and their application to psychologists' work. Lack of awareness or misunderstanding of an ethical standard is not itself a defense to a charge of unethical conduct.

8.02 *Confronting Ethical Issues*

When a psychologist is uncertain whether a particular situation or course of action would violate this Ethics

Code, the psychologist ordinarily consults with other psychologists knowledgeable about ethical issues, with state or national psychology ethics committees, or with other appropriate authorities in order to choose a proper response.

8.03 Conflicts Between Ethics and Organizational Demands

If the demands of an organization with which psychologists are affiliated conflict with this Ethics Code, psychologists clarify the nature of the conflict, make known their commitment to the Ethics Code, and to the extent feasible, seek to resolve the conflict in a way that permits the fullest adherence to the Ethics Code.

8.04 Informal Resolution of Ethical Violations

When psychologists believe that there may have been an ethical violation by another psychologist, they attempt to resolve the issue by bringing it to the attention of that individual if an informal resolution appears appropriate and the intervention does not violate any confidentiality rights that may be involved.

8.05 Reporting Ethical Violations

If an apparent ethical violation is not appropriate for informal resolution under Standard 8.04 or is not resolved properly in that fashion, psychologists take further action appropriate to the situation, unless such action conflicts with confidentiality rights in ways that cannot be resolved. Such action might include referral to state or national committees on professional ethics or to state licensing boards.

8.06 Cooperating With Ethics Committees

Psychologists cooperate in ethics investigations, proceedings, and resulting requirements of the APA or any affiliated state psychological association to which they belong. In doing so, they make reasonable efforts to resolve any issues as to confidentiality. Failure to cooperate is itself an ethics violation.

8.07 Improper Complaints

Psychologists do not file or encourage the filing of ethics complaints that are frivolous and are intended to harm the respondent rather than to protect the public.

REFERENCES

Achenbach, T. V. (1991). *Manual for the Child Behavior Checklist/4-18 and 1991 Profile.* Burlington, VT: University of Vermont, Department of Psychiatry.

Ader, R., & Cohen, N. (1984). Behavior and the immune system. In W. D. Gentry (Ed.), *Handbook of behavioral medicine* (pp. 117–173). New York: Guilford.

Aglioni, G. (1982). *History and systems.* Berkeley, CA: Association for Advanced Training in the Behavioral Sciences.

Agras, W. S., & Berkowitz, R. (1980). Clinical research in behavior therapy: Halfway there? *Behavior Therapy, 11,* 472–488.

Agras, W. S., Berkowitz, R. I., Arnow, B. A., Telch, C. F. (1996). Maintenance following a very-low calorie diet. *Journal of Consulting and Clinical Psychology, 64,* 610–613.

Agras, W. S., Telch, C. F., Arnow, B., Eldredge, K., Detzer, M. J., Henderson, J., & Marnell, M. (1995). Does interpersonal therapy help patients with binge eating disorder who fail to respond to cognitive-behavioral therapy? *Journal of Consulting and Clinical Psychology, 63,* 356–360.

Albee, G. W., & Gullotta, T. P. (Eds.). (1997). *Primary prevention works.* Thousands Oaks, CA: Sage.

Albee, G. W. & Perry, M. (1996). Are we preventing diseases or promoting competencies? *Journal of Mental Health, 5,* 421–422.

Alcoholics Anonymous (1990). *Comments on A.A.'s triennial surveys.* New York: Alcoholics Anonymous World Services.

Allen, G. J., Nelson, W. J., & Sheckley, B. G. (1987). Continuing education activities of Connecticut psychologists. *Professional Psychology: Research and Practice, 18,* 78–80.

Allison, J., Blatt, S. J., & Zimet, C. N. (1968). *The interpretation of psychological tests.* New York: Harper & Row.

American Association of Retired Persons (1989). *A profile of older Americans.* Washington, DC: Author.

American Cancer Society (1989). *Cancer facts and figures–1989.* Atlanta, GA: Author.

American Cancer Society (1996). *Cancer facts and figures–1996.* Atlanta, GA: Author.

American Heart Association. (1993). *Heart and stroke facts.* Dallas, TX: Author.

American Humane Association (1984). *Highlights of official child abuse and neglect reporting–1982.* Denver, CO: Author.

American Medical Association (1984). *Proceedings of the house of delegates of the American Medical Association.* Chicago: Author.

American Psychiatric Association (1994a). *Diagnostic and Statistical Manual, Fourth Edition (DSM-IV).* Washington, DC: Author.

American Psychiatric Association (1994b). *Quick Reference to the Diagnostic Criteria from DSM-IV.* Washington, DC: Author

American Psychiatric Association (1995). *1993 APA directory survey, with new member updates for 1994 and 1995. APA research office.* Unpublished manuscript, Washington, DC: Author.

American Psychiatric Association (1997). *American Psychiatric Association practice guideline for the treatment of patients with Alzheimer's disease.* Washington, DC: American Psychiatric Association Press.

American Psychological Association (1955). Joint report of the APA and CSPA (Conference of State Psychological Associations). *American Psychologist, 10,* 727–756.

American Psychological Association (1967). A model for state legislation affecting the practice of psychology 1967: Report of the APA Committee on Legislation. *American Psychologist, 22,* 1095–1103.

American Psychological Association (1981). Specialty guidelines for the delivery of services by clinical psychologists. *American Psychologist, 36,* 640–651.

American Psychological Association (1985). *Standards for educational and psychological testing.* Washington, DC: Author.

American Psychological Association (1987a). *Guidelines for computer based tests and interpretations.* Washington, DC: Author.

American Psychological Association (1987b). Model act for state licensure of psychologists. *American Psychologist, 42,* 696–703.

American Psychological Association (1988). *State of the states and provinces: A survey of state and provincial psychological associations.* Washington, DC: Author.

American Psychological Association (1990). *Guidelines for providers of psychological services to ethnic, linguistic, and culturally diverse populations.* Washington, DC: Author.

American Psychological Association (1992a). Ethical principles of psychologists and code of conduct. *American Psychologist, 47,* 1597–1611.

American Psychological Association (1992b). *Report of the Ad Hoc Task Force on Psychopharmacology.* Washington, DC: Author.

American Psychological Association (1993a). *Directory of the American Psychological Association, 1993 edition.* Washington, DC: Author.

American Psychological Association (1993b). Guidelines for providers of psychological services to ethnic, linguistic, and culturally diverse populations. *American Psychologist, 48,* 45–48.

American Psychological Association (1995a). *1993 Doctorate Employment Survey.* Washington, DC: Author.

American Psychological Association (1995b). *Current major field of APA members by employment status: 1995.* Unpublished manuscript. Washington, DC: Author.

American Psychological Association (1995c). Report of the ethics committee, 1994. *American Psychologist, 50,* 706–713.

American Psychological Association (1995d). *Report of the task force on the changing gender composition of psychology.* Washington, DC: Author.

American Psychological Association (1995e). Training in and dissemination of empirically-validated psychological treatments: Reports and recommendations. *The Clinical Psychologist, 48,* 3–23.

American Psychological Association (1996). Report of the ethics committee, 1995. *American Psychologist, 51,* 1279–1286.

American Psychological Association (1997a). *Directory of the American Psychological Association, 1993 edition.* Washington, DC: Author.

American Psychological Association (1997b). *1995 Doctorate Employment Survey.* Washington, DC: Author.

Anastasi, A. (1988). *Psychological testing (6th ed.).* New York: Macmillan.

Anders, G. (1996). *Health against wealth: HMOs and the breakdown of medical trust.* Boston: Houghton Mifflin.

Andersen, B. L. (1992). Psychological interventions for cancer patients to enhance the quality of life. *Journal of Consulting and Clinical Psychology, 60,* 552–568.

Andersen, B. L. (1996). Introduction to the featured section: Psychological and behavioral studies in cancer prevention and control. *Health Psychology, 15,* 411–412.

Anderson, C. V., Bigler, E. D., & Blatter, D. D. (1995). Frontal lobe lesions, diffuse damage, and neuropsychological functioning in traumatic brain-injured patients. *Journal of Clinical and Experimental Neuropsychology, 17,* 900–908.

Anderson, E. M., & Lambert, M. J. (1995). Short-term dynamically oriented psychotherapy: A review and meta-analysis. *Clinical Psychology Review, 15,* 503–514.

Anderson, N. B., & Jackson, J. S. (1987). Race, ethnicity, and health psychology: The example of essential hypertension. In C. M. Stone, S. M. Weiss, J. D. Matarazzo, N. E. Miller, J. Rodin, C. D. Belar, M. J. Follick, & J. E. Singer (Eds.), *Health psychology: A discipline and a profession.* Chicago: University of Chicago Press.

Andreasen, N. C. (Ed.) (1989). *Brain imaging: Applications in psychiatry.* Washington, DC: American Psychiatric Association.

Andreasen, N. C., & Black, D .W. (1995). *Introductory textbook of psychiatry* (2nd ed.). Washington, DC: American Psychiatric Association.

Andrews, G., & Harvey, R. (1981). Does psychotherapy benefit neurotic patients? A reanalysis of the Smith, Glass, and Miller data. *Archives of General Psychiatry, 38,* 1203–1208.

Andrews, J. (1991). *The active self in psychotherapy: An integration of therapeutic styles.* Boston: Allyn & Bacon.

Anisman, H. (1984). Vulnerability to depression: Contribution of stress. In R. Post & J. Ballenger (Eds.), *Neurobiology of mood disorders.* Baltimore: Williams & Wilkins.

Annis, H. M. (1990). Relapse to substance abuse: Empirical findings within a cognitive-social learning approach? *Journal of Psychoactive Drugs, 22,* 117–124.

Anonymous (1995). Hidden benefits of managed care. *Professional Psychology: Research and Practice, 26,* 235–237.

Ansbacher, H. L. (1951). The history of the leaderless group discussion technique. *Psychological Bulletin, 48,* 383–391.

Apfel, R. J., & Simon, B. (1985). Patient-therapist sexual contact: I. Psychodynamic perspectives on the causes and results. *Psychotherapy and Psychosomatics, 43,* 57–62.

Arkowitz, H. (1989). The role of theory in psychotherapy integration. *Journal of Integrative and Eclectic Psychotherapy, 8,* 8–16.

Arkowitz, H. (1992). Integrative theories of therapy. In D. K. Freedheim (Ed.), *History of psychotherapy: A century of change* (pp. 261–303). Washington, DC: American Psychological Association.

Arling, G. (1976). The elderly widow and her family, neighbors, and friends. *Journal of Marriage and the Family, 38,* 757–768.

Arnkoff, D. B., & Glass, C. R. (1992). Cognitive therapy and psychotherapy integration. In D. K. Freedheim (Ed.), *History of psychotherapy: A century of change* (pp. 657–694). Washington, DC: American Psychological Association.

Association for Medical School Pharmacology (1990). *Knowledge objectives in medical pharmacology* (2nd ed.). Washington, DC: Author.

Association of Psychology Postdoctoral and Internship Centers (APPIC) (1996). *APPIC directory* (25th ed.). Washington, DC: Author.

Baekeland, F., & Lundwall, L. (1975). Dropping out of treatment: A critical review. *Psychological Bulletin, 82,* 738–783.

Baird, K. A., & Rupert, P. A. (1987). Clinical management of confidentiality: A survey of psychologists in seven states. *Professional Psychology: Research and Practice, 18,* 347–352.

Bajt, T. R., & Pope, K. S. (1989). Therapist-patient sexual intimacy involving children and adolescents. *American Psychologist, 44,* 555.

Baldessarini, R. J. (1990). Drugs and the treatment of psychiatric disorders. In A. Goodman Gilman, T. W. Rall, A. S. Nies, & P. Taylor (Eds.), *The pharmacological basis of therapeutics* (8th ed., pp. 383–435). Elmsford, NY: Pergamon Press.

Baldessarini, R. J., & Cole, J. O. (1988). Chemotherapy. In A. M. Nicholi, Jr. (Ed.), *The new Harvard guide to psychiatry.* Cambridge, MA: Harvard University Press.

Bandura, A. (1969). *Principles of behavior modification.* New York: Holt, Reinehart, & Winston.

Bandura, A. (1982). Self-efficacy mechanisms in human agency. *American Psychologist, 37,* 122–147.

Bandura, A. (1986). *Social foundations of thought and action: A social cognitive theory.* Englewood Cliffs, NJ: Prentice–Hall.

Bandura, A. (1989). Human agency in social cognitive theory. *American Psychologist, 33,* 344–358.

Banks, S. M., & Kerns, R. D. (1996). Explaining high rates of depression in chronic pain: A diathesis-stress framework. *Psychological Bulletin, 119,* 95–110.

Barker, S. L., Funk, S. C., & Houston, B. K. (1988). Psychological treatment versus nonspecific factors: A meta-analysis of conditions that engender comparable expectations of improvement. *Clinical Psychology Review, 8,* 579–594.

Barkley, R. A. (1989). Attention deficit-hyperactivity disorder. In E. J. Mash & R. A. Barkley (Eds.), *Treatment of childhood disorders* (pp. 39–72). New York: Guilford.

Barkley, R. A. (1993). *Hyperactive children: A handbook for diagnosis and treatment.* New York: Guilford.

Barlow, D. H. (1988). *Anxiety and its disorders.* New York: Guilford Press.

Barlow, D. H. (1996). Health care policy, psychotherapy research, and the future of psychotherapy. *American Psychologist, 51,* 1050–1058.

Barlow, D. H., & Craske, M. G. (1989). *Mastery of your anxiety and panic.* Albany, NY: Graywind.

Barlow, D. H., Hayes, S. C., & Nelson, R. O. (1984). *The scientist practitioner: Research and accountability in clinical and educational settings.* New York: Pergamon.

Barlow, D. H., & Repee, R. M. (1991). *Mastering stress: A lifestyle approach.* Dallas, TX: American Health Publishing.

Barton, W. E. (1991). Toward a model curriculum in mental health administration. *Administration and Policy in Mental Health, 18,* 237–246.

Barton, W. E., & Barton, G. M. (1983). *Mental health administration.* New York: International Universities Press.

Bateson, G., Jackson, D., Haley, J., & Weakland, J. (1956). Toward a theory of schizophrenia. *Behavioral Science, 1,* 251–264.

Baur, S. (1997). *The intimate hour: Love and sex in psychotherapy.* New York: NY: Houghton Mifflin.

Baxter, L. R., Schwartz, J. M., Bergman, K. S., Szuba, M. P., Guze, B. H., Mazziotta, J. C., Alazraki, A., Selin, C. E., Ferng, H. K., Munford, P., & Phelps, M. E. (1992). Caudate glucose metabolic rate changes with both drug and behavior therapy for obsessive-compulsive disorder. *Archives of General Psychiatry, 49,* 681–689.

Bay-Hinitz, A. K., Peterson, R. F., & Quilitch, H. R. (1994). Cooperative games: A way to modify aggressive and cooperative behavior in young children. *Journal of Applied Behavior Analysis, 27,* 435–446.

Bayley, N. (1993). *Bayley Scale of Infant Development (2nd ed).* San Antonio, TX: Psychological Corporation.

Beck, A. (1987). *Manual for the Beck Depression Inventory.* San Antonio, TX: Psychological Corporation.

Beck, A. (1988). *Manual for the Beck Hopelessness Scale.* San Antonio, TX: Psychological Corporation.

Beck, A. (1990). *Manual for the Beck Anxiety Inventory.* San Antonio, TX: Psychological Corporation.

Beck, A. (1991). *Manual for the Beck Scale for Suicide Ideation.* San Antonio, TX: Psychological Corporation.

Beck, A. (1993). *Manual for the Beck Anxiety Inventory.* San Antonio, TX: Psychological Corporation.

Beck, A. T. (1963). Thinking and depression. *Archives of General Psychiatry, 9,* 324–333.

Beck, A. T. (1976). *Cognitive therapy and emotional disorders.* New York: International Universities Press.

Beck, A. T., Steer, R. A., & Brown, G. K. (1996). *Manual for the Beck Depression Inventory - II.* San Antonio, TX: Psychological Corporation.

Beckham, E.E. (1990). Psychotherapy of depression at the crossroads: Directions for the 1990s. *Clinical Psychology Review, 10,* 207–228.

Beer, M., & Spector, B. (1993). Organizational diagnosis: Its role in organizational learning. *Journal of Counseling and Development, 71,* 642–650.

Beiderman, J., Faraone, S. V., Keenan, K., Benjamin, J., Krifcher, B., Moore, C., Sprich-Buckminster, S., Ugaglia, K., Jellinek, M. S., Steingard, R., Spencer, T., Norman, D., Kolodny, R., Kraus, I., Perrin, J., Keller, M., & Tsuang, M. T. (1992). Further evidence for family-genetic risk factors in attention deficit hyperactivity disorder: Patterns of comorbidity in probands and relative in psychiatrically and pediatrically referred samples. *Archives of General Psychiatry, 49,* 728–738.

Belar, C. D. (1995). Collaboration in capitated care: Challenges for psychology. *Professional Psychology: Research and Practice, 26,* 139–146.

Belar, C. D., Bieliauskas, L. A., Larsen, K. G., Mensh, I. N., Poey, K., & Roehike, H.J. (1989). The National Conference on Internship Training in Psychology. *American Psychologist, 44,* 60–65.

Bell, J. E. (1961). Family group therapy. *Public Health Monograph No. 64.* Washington, DC: US Government Printing Office.

Bell, P. F., Digman, R. H., & McKenna, J. P. (1995). Should psychologists obtain prescription privileges? A survey of family physicians. *Professional Psychology: Research and Practice, 26,* 371–376.

Bellak, L. (1986). *The Thematic Apperception Test, the Children's Apperception Test, and the Senior Apperception Technique in Clinical Use* (4th ed.). New York: Grune & Stratton.

Bellock, A. S., & Herson, M. (Eds.) (1990). *Handbook of comparative treatments for adult disorders.* New York: Wiley.

Bem, D. J., & Funder, D. C. (1978). Predicting more of the people more of the time: Assessing the personality of situations. *Psychological Review, 85,* 485–501.

Benedict, J. G., & Phelps, R. (1998). Introduction: Psychology's view of managed care. *Professional Psychology: Research and Practice, 29,* 29–30.

Benton, A. (1963). *Benton Visual Retention Test.* San Antonio, TX: Psychological Corporation.

Bentz, V. J. (1985). Research findings from personality assessment of executives. In H. J. Bernardin & D. A. Bownas (Eds.), *Personality assessment in organizations.* New York: Praeger.

Bergin, A. E. (1971). The evaluation of therapeutic outcomes. In A. E. Bergin & S. L. Garfield (Eds.), *Handbook of psychotherapy and behavior change: An empirical analysis* (pp. 217–270). New York: Wiley.

Bergin, A. E., & Garfield, S. L. (1994). Overview, trends, and future issues. In A. E. Bergin & S. L. Garfield (Eds.), *Handbook of psychotherapy and behavior change* (4th ed.). New York: Wiley.

Bergin, A. E., & Lambert, M. J. (1978). The evaluation of therapeutic outcomes. In A. E. Bergin & S. L. Garfield (Eds.), *Handbook of psychotherapy and behavior change: An empirical analysis* (2nd ed.). New York: Wiley.

Berkman, L. F., & Syme, S. L. (1979). Social networks, host resistance, and mortality: A nine-year followup study of Alameda

County residents. *American Journal of Epidemiology, 109,* 186–204.

Berman, J. S., & Norton, N. C. (1985). Does professional training make a therapist more effective? *Psychological Bulletin, 98,* 401–406.

Bernal, M. E., & Castro, F. G. (1994). Are clinical psychologists prepared for service and research with ethnic minorities: Report of a decade of progress. *American Psychologist, 49,* 797–805.

Berrigan, L. P., & Garfield, S. L. (1981). Relationship of missed psychotherapy appointments to premature termination and social class. *The British Journal of Clinical Psychology, 20,* 239–242.

Bersoff, D. N. (1995). *Ethical conflicts in psychology.* Washington, DC: American Psychological Association.

Bertelsen, B., Harvald, B., & Hauge, M. (1977). A Danish twin study of manic-depressive disorders. *British Journal of Psychiatry, 130,* 330–351.

Betz, N., & Shullman, S. (1979). Factors related to client return following intake. *Journal of Counseling Psychology, 26,* 542–545.

Beutler, L. E. (1986). Systematic eclectic psychotherapy. In J. C. Norcross (Ed.), *Handbook of eclectic psychotherapy* (pp. 94–131). New York: Brunner/Mazel.

Beutler, L. E., & Fisher, D. (1994). Combined specialty training in counseling, clinical, and school psychology: An idea whose time has returned. *Professional Psychology: Research and Practice, 25,* 62–69.

Beutler, L. E., Mohr, D. C., Grawe, K., Engle, D., & MacDonald, R. (1991). Looking for differential treatment effects: Cross-cultural predictions of differential therapeutic efficacy. *Journal of Psychotherapy Integration, 1,* 121–141.

Beutler, L. E., Williams, R. E., Wakefield, P. J., & Entwistle, S. R. (1995). Bridging scientist and practitioner perspectives in clinical psychology. *American Psychologist, 50,* 984–994.

Bevan, W. (1991). Contemporary psychology: A tour inside the onion. *American Psychologist, 46,* 475–483.

Bickman, L. (1987). Graduate education in psychology. *American Psychologist, 42,* 1041–1047.

Bickman, L. (1996). A continuum of care: More is not always better. *American Psychologist, 49,* 689–701.

Binik, Y. M., Cantor, J., Ochs, E., & Meana, M. (1997). From the couch to the keyboard: Psychotherapy in cyberspace. In S. Kiesler (Ed.), *Culture of the internet.* Mahwah, NJ: Erlbaum.

Blanchard, E. B. (1987). Long-term effects of behavioral treatment of chronic headaches. *Behavior Therapy, 18,* 375–385.

Blascovich, J., & Katkin, E. S. (1993). *Cardiovascular reactivity to psychological stress and disease.* Washington, DC: American Psychological Association.

Blatt, S. J. (1975). The validity of projective techniques and their research and clinical contribution. *Journal of Personality Assessment, 39,* 327–343.

Bloom, B. (1992). Computer-assisted intervention: A review and commentary. *Clinical Psychology Review, 128,* 169–198.

Bloom, B. L. (1981). Focused single-session therapy: Initial development and evaluation. In S. H. Budman (Ed.), *Forms of brief therapy* (pp. 167–216). New York: Guilford Press.

Blouke, P. S. (1997). Musings of a bureaucratic psychologist. *Professional Psychology: Research and Practice, 28,* 326–328.

Bogerts, B. (1993). Images in psychiatry: Alois Alzheimer. *American Journal of Psychiatry, 160,* 1868.

Bohart, A. C. (1982). Similarities between cognitive and humanistic approaches in psychotherapy. *Cognitive Therapy and Research, 6,* 245–250.

Boice, R., & Myers, P. E. (1987). Which setting is healthier and happier, academe or private practice? *Professional Psychology: Research and Practice, 18,* 526–529.

Boll, T. (1981). The Halstead-Reitan Neuropsychological Battery. In S. B. Fisher & T. J. Boll (Eds.), *Handbook of clinical neuropsychology* (Vol. 1, pp. 577–607). New York: Wiley-Interscience.

Bonica, J. J. (1992). Pain research and therapy: Past and current status and future goals. In C. E. Short & A. van Posnik (Eds.), *Animal pain: Proceedings of the symposium on animal pain and its control* (Ithaca, NY, June 25–28, 1990).

Boring, E. G. (1923 June 6). Intelligence as the tests test it. *The New Republic,* 35–37.

Borys, D. S., & Pope, K. S. (1989). Dual relationships between therapist and client: A national study of psychologists, psychiatrists, and social workers. *Professional Psychology: Research and Practice, 20,* 283–293.

Boscolo, L., Cecchin, G., Hoffman, L., & Penn, P. (1987). *Milan systemic family therapy: Conversations in theory and practice.* New York: Basic Books.

Boswell, D. L., & Litwin, W. J. (1992). Limited prescription privileges for psychologists: A 1 year follow-up. *Professional Psychology: Research and Practice, 23,* 108–113.

Bouchard, C. (1995). Genetics of obesity: An update on molecular markers. *International Journal of Obesity, 19,* S10–S13.

Bouchard, C., & Perusse, L. (1996). Current status of the human obesity gene map. *Obesity Research, 4,* 81–90.

Bouchard, T. J., Jr., & McGue, M. (1990). Genetic and environmental influences on adult personality: An analysis of adopted twins reared apart. *Journal of Personality, 58,* 263–295.

Bowen, M. (1978). *Family therapy in clinical practice.* New York: Aronson.

Breggin, P. R. (1991). *Toxic psychiatry.* New York: St. Martin's Press.

Brehm, S. S., & Brehm, J. W. (1981). *Psychological reactance: A theory of freedom and control.* New York: Academic Press.

Breiter, H. C., Rauch, S. L., Kwong, K. K., & Baker, J. R. (1996). Functional magnetic resonance imaging of symptom provocation in obsessive-compulsive disorder. *Archives of General Psychiatry, 53,* 595–606.

Brems, C., Johnson, M. E., & Gallucci, P. (1996). Publication productivity of clinical and counseling psychologists. *Journal of Clinical Psychology, 52,* 711–722.

Brems, C., Lampman, C., & Johnson, M. E. (1995). Preparation of applications for academic positions in psychology. *American Psychologist, 50,* 533–537.

Brennan, P. L., & Moos, R. H. (1990). Life stressor, social resources, and late-life problem drinking. *Psychology and Aging, 5,* 491–501.

Brentar, J., & McNamara, J. R. (1991). The right to prescribe medication: Considerations for professional psychology. *Professional Psychology: Research and Practice, 22,* 179–187.

Breuer, J., & Freud, S. (1957). *Studies in hysteria.* New York: Basic Books. (Original work published in 1895)

Brody, N. (1983). Where are the emperor's clothes? *Behavioral and Brain Sciences, 6,* 303–308.

Brody, N. (1997). Intelligence, schooling and society. *American Psychologist, 52,* 1046–1050.

Brookmeyer, R. (1996). AIDS, epidemics, and statistics. *Biometrics, 52,* 781–796.

Broskowski, A. T. (1995). The evolution of health care: Implications for the training and careers of psychologists. *Professional Psychology: Research and Practice, 26,* 156–162.

Brotemarkle, B. A. (1947). Fifty years of clinical psychology: Clinical psychology 1896–1946. *Journal of Consulting Psychology, 11,* 1–4.

Brous, J. F. & Olendzki, M. C. (1985). The "offset effect" of mental health treatment on ambulatory medical care utilization and charges: Month-by-month and grouped-month analyses of a five-year study. *Archives of General Psychiatry, 42,* 573–580.

Brown, D. (1985). The preservice training and supervision of consultants. *Counseling Psychologist, 13,* 410–425.

Brown, L. S. (1990). Taking account of gender in the clinical assessment interview. *Professional Psychology: Research and Practice, 21,* 12–17.

Brownell, K. D. (1993). Whether obesity should be treated. *Health Psychology, 12,* 339–341.

Brownell, K. D. (1991a). Dieting and the search for the perfect body: Where physiology and culture collide. *Behavior Therapy, 22,* 1–12.

Brownell, K. D. (1991b). Personal responsibility and control over our bodies: When expectations exceeds reality. *Health Psychology, 10,* 303–310.

Brownell, K. D., & Jeffery, R. W. (1987). Improving long-term weight loss: Pushing the limits of treatment. *Behavior Therapy, 18,* 353–374.

Brownell, K. D., & Wadden, T. A. (1992). Etiology and treatment of obesity: Understanding a serious, prevalent, and refractory disorder. *Journal of Consulting and Clinical Psychology, 55,* 139–144.

Bruce, M. L., & Kim, K. M. (1992). Differences in the effects of divorce on major depression in men and women. *American Journal of Psychiatry, 149,* 914–917.

Buck, J. N. (1948). The H-T-P technique: A qualitative and quantitative scoring manual. *Journal of Clinical Psychology, 4,* 319–396.

Bugental, J. T. F. (1978). *Psychotherapy and process: The fundamentals of an existential humanistic approach.* Reading, MA: Addison-Wesley.

Burish, T. G., & Trope, D. M. (1992). Psychological techniques for controlling the adverse side effects of cancer chemotherapy: Findings from a decade of research. *Journal of Pain and Symptom Management, 7,* 287–301.

Burton, R. (1977). *Anatomy of melancholy.* New York: Random House.(Reprint of 1621 edition).

Buss, D. (1994). *The evolution of desire. Strategies of human mating.* New York: Basic Books.

Butcher, J. N., Dahlstrom, W. G., Graham, J. R., Tellegen, A., & Kraemmer, B. (1989). *Minnesota Multiphasic Personality Inventory (MMPI-2). Manual for administration and scoring.* Minneapolis: University of Minnesota Press.

Butcher, J. N., Williams, C. L., Graham, J. R., Archer, R. P., Tellegen, A., Ben-Porath, Y. S., & Kraemmer, B. (1992). *Minnesota Multiphasic Personality Inventory-Adolescent (MMPI-A). Manual for administration and scoring.* Minneapolis: University of Minnesota Press.

Callahan, R. J., McGreevy, M. A., Cirincione, C., & Stedman, H. J. (1992). Measuring the effects of the guilty but mentally ill (GBMI)verdict: Georgia's 1982 GBMI reform. *Law and Human Behavior, 16,* 447–462.

Campbell, D. T., & Stanley, J. C. (1963). *Experimental and quasi-experimental designs for research.* Chicago: Dorsey Press.

Canadian Psychological Association (1995). *Canadian code of ethics for psychologists.* Ottowa, Canada: Author.

Canter, M. B., Bennett, B. E., Jones, S. E., & Nagy, T. F. (1995). *Ethics for psychologists: A commentary on the APA Ethics Code.* Washington, DC: American Psychological Association.

Caplan, G. (1970). *The theory and practice of mental health consultation.* New York: Basic Books.

Caplan, G., & Caplan, R. B. (1993). *Mental health consultation and collaboration.* San Francisco: Jossey-Bass.

Cardon, L. R., Smith, S. D., Fulker, D. W., Kimberling, W. J., Pennington, B. F., & DeFries, J. C. (1994). Quantitative trait locus for reading disability on chromosome 6. *Science, 266,* 276–279.

Carmody, T. P., & Matarazzo, J. D. (1991). Health psychology. In M. Hersen, A. E. Kazdin, & A. S. Bellack (Eds.). *The clinical psychology handbook* (2nd ed.). New York: Pergamon.

Carpenter, P. J., & Range, L. M. (1982). Predicting psychotherapy duration from therapists' sex, professional affiliation, democratic values, and community mental health ideology. *Journal of Clinical Psychology, 38,* 90–91.

Carter, B. D., Bendell, D., & Matarazzo, J. D. (1985). Behavioral health: Focus on preventive child health behavior. In A. R. Zeiner, D. Bendell, & C. E. Walker (Eds.), *Health psychology: Treatment and research issues* (pp. 1–61). New York: Plenum.

Casey, R. J., & Berman, J. S. (1985). The outcome of psychotherapy with children. *Psychological Bulletin, 98,* 388–400.

Cattell, R. B. (1963). Theory of fluid and crystallized intelligence: A critical experiment. *Journal of Educational Psychology, 54,* 1–22.

Cattell, R. B. (1971). *Abilities: Their structure, growth, and action.* Boston: Houghton Mifflin.

Cattell, R. B. (1979). Are culture-fair intelligence tests possible and necessary. *Journal of Research and Development in Education, 12,* 3–13.

Cattell, R. B., Cattell, A. K., & Cattell, H. E. P. (1993). *Sixteen Personality Factors Questionnaire, Fifth Edition.* Champaign, IL: Institute for Personality and Ability Testing.

Center for Disease Control (1980). *Risk factor update.* Atlanta, GA: US Department of Health and Human Services.

Center for Disease Control (1991, October). *HIV/AIDS surveillance report.* Atlanta, GA: US Department of Health and Human Services.

Cepeda-Benito, A. (1993). Meta-analytical review of the efficacy of nicotine chewing gum in smoking treatment programs. *Journal of Consulting and Clinical Psychology, 61,* 822–830.

Chalk, R., Frankel, M. S., & Chafer, S. B. (1980). *AAAS Professional Ethics Project.* Washington, DC: American Association for the Advancement of Science.

Chambless, D. L. (1996). In defense of dissemination of empirically supported psychological interventions. *Clinical Psychology: Science and Practice, 3,* 230–235.

Chambless, D. L., Sanderson, W. C., Shoham, V., Johnson, S. B., Pope, K. S., Crits-Chistoph, P., Baker, M., Johnson, B., Woody, S. R., Sue, S., Beutler, L., Williams, D., & McCurry, S. (1996). An update on empirically validated therapies. *The Clinical Psychologist, 49,* 5–18.

Champion, D. P., Kiel, D. H., & McLendon, J. A. (1990). Choosing a consulting role. *Training and Development Journal,* (February), 66–69.

Chassin, L., Presson, C. C., Rose, J. S., & Sherman, S. J. (1996). The natural history of cigarette smoking from adolescence to adulthood: Demographic predictors of continuity and change. *Health Psychology, 15,* 478–484.

Chesney, M. A. (1993). Health psychology in the 21st century: Acquired immunodeficiency syndrome as a harbinger of things to come. *Health Psychology, 12,* 259–268.

Clark, D. M. (1988). A cognitive model of panic attacks. In S. Rachman & J. D. Maser (Eds.), *Panic: Psychological perspectives* (pp. 71–89). Hillsdale, NJ: Erlbaum.

Clarke, W. V. (1956). The construction of an industrial selection personality test. *Journal of Psychology, 41,* 379–394.

Clarkin, J. F., & Hull, J. W. (1991). The brief psychotherapies. In M. Hersen, A.E. Kazdin, & A.S. Bellack (Eds.), *The clinical psychology handbook* (2nd ed.). New York: Pergamon.

Classen, C., Koopman, C., Angell, K., & Spiegel, D. (1996). Coping styles associated with psychological adjustment to advanced breast cancer. *Health Psychology, 15,* 434–437.

Clayton, S., & Bonger, B. (1994). The use of consultation in psychological practice: Ethical, legal, and clinical consideration. *Ethics and Behavior, 4,* 43–57.

Clement, P. W. (1996). Evaluation in private practice. *Clinical Psychology: Science and Practice, 3,* 146–159.

Coates, T. J., & Thoresen, C. E. (1981). Treating obesity in children and adolescents: Is there any hope? In J. M. Ferguson & C. B. Taylor (Eds.), *The comprehensive handbook of behavioral medicine* (Vol. 2, pp 204–231). New York: Spectrum.

Cohen, R. Y., Stunkard, A., & Felix, M. R. J. (1986). Measuring community change in disease prevention and health promotion. *Preventive Medicine, 15,* 411–421.

Cohen, S. (1988). Psychosocial models of the role of social support in the etiology of physical disease. *Health Psychology, 7,* 269–297.

Cohen, S., Tyrrell, D. A. J., & Smith, A. P. (1993). Negative life events, perceived stress, negative affect, and susceptibility to the common cold. *Journal of Personality and Social Psychology, 64,* 131–140.

Cole, N. S. (1981). Bias in testing. *American Psychologist, 36,* 1067–1077.

Colson, D., Lewis, L., & Horowitz, L. (1985). Negative outcome in psychotherapy and psychoanalysis. In D. T. Mays & C. M. Franks (Eds.), *Negative outcome in psychotherapy and what to do about it* (pp. 59–75). New York: Springer.

Committee on Ethical Guidelines for Forensic Psychologists (1991). Specialty guidelines for forensic psychologists. *Law and Human Behavior, 15,* 655–665.

Conners, C. K. (1989). *Conners' Rating Scales: Administration Manual.* North Tonawanda, NY: Multi-Health Systems.

Conoley, J. C., & Conoley, C. W. (1992). *School consultation: Practice and training* (2nd ed.). Boston: Allyn & Bacon.

Consumer Reports (1995, November) *Mental health: Does therapy help?* pp. 734–739.

Contrada, R. J., & Krantz, D. S. (1988). Stress, reactivity, and Type A behavior: Current status and future directions. *Annals of Behavioral Medicine, 10,* 64–70.

Conyne, R., & O'Neal, J. (1992). Closing the gap between consultation training and practice. In R. Conyne & J. O. O'Neal (Eds.), *Organizational consultation: A casebook* (pp. 1–16). Newbury Park, CA: Sage.

Cooke, G. (1984). Forensic psychology. In R. G. Corsini (Ed.), *Encyclopedia of psychology (Vol. 2).* New York: Wiley.

Cooper, N. A., & Clum, G. A. (1989). Imaginal flooding as a supplementary treatment for PTSD in combat veterans: A controlled study. *Behavior Therapy, 20,* 381–392.

Corbet, J., Trimble, M., & Nicol, T. (1985). Behavioral and cognitive impairment in children with epilepsy: The long-term effects of anticonvulsant therapy. *Journal of the American Academy of Child Psychiatry, 24,* 17–23.

Corey, G., Corey, M. S., & Callanan, P. (1993). *Issues and ethics in the helping professions* (4th ed.). Pacific Grove, CA: Brooks Cole.

Cormier, W. H., & Cormier, L. S. (1979). *Interviewing strategies for helpers: A guide to assessment, treatment, and evaluation.* Monterey, CA: Brooks/Cole.

Cornes, C. L., & Frank, E. (1994). Interpersonal psychotherapy for depression. *The Clinical Psychologist, 47,* 9–10.

Corrigan, N., & Nielsen, D. (1993). Toward the development of uniform reporting standards for managed care organizations: The Health Plan Employer Data and Information Set (Version 2.0). *Journal of Quality Improvement, 19,* 566–575.

Costa, P., & McCrae, R. (1985). *NEO-Personality Inventory manual.* Odessa, FL: Psychological Assessment Resources.

Costa, P., & McCrae, R. (1989). *NEO-PI/NEO-FFI manual supplement.* Odessa, FL: Psychological Assessment Resources.

Costa, P., & McCrae, R. (1992). *Revised NEO-Personality Inventory (NEO-PI-R) and NEO Five Factor Inventory (NEO-FFI): Professional manual.* Odessa, FL: Psychological Assessment Resources.

Craighead, W. E. (1990). There's a place for us: All of us. *Behavior Therapy, 21,* 3–23.

Cranston, C., Ulrey, G., Hansen, R., Hudler, M., Marshall, R., & Wuori, D. (1988). Interprofessional collaboration: Who is doing it? Who isn't? *Journal of Developmental and Behavioral Pediatrics. 9,* 134–139.

Craske, M. G., Brown, T. A., & Barlow, D. H. (1991). Behavioral treatment of panic disorder: A two year follow-up. *Behavior Therapy, 19,* 577–592.

Crits-Christoph, P. (1996). The dissemination of efficacious psychological treatments. *Clinical Psychology: Science and Practice, 3,* 260–263.

Critis-Christoph, P., Chambless, D., Frank, E., Brody, C., et al. (1995). Training in empirically validated treatments: What are clinical psychology students learning? *Professional Psychology: Research and Practice, 26,* 514–522.

Crits-Christoph, P., & Mintz, J. (1991). Implications of therapist effects for the design and analysis of comparative studies of psychotherapies. *Journal of Consulting and Clinical Psychology, 59,* 20–26.

Cronbach, L. J. (1956). Assessment of individual differences. *Annual Review of Psychology, 7,* 173–196.

Crosby-Currie, C. A. (1996). Children's involvement in contested custody cases: Practices and experiences of legal and mental health professionals. *Law and Human Behavior, 20,* 289–311.

Cullen, E. A. (1998). Legislative wrap-up: 1997 state prescription privilege activities. *The California Psychologist, 31,* 8–9.

Cullen, E. A., & Newman, R. (1997). In pursuit of prescription privileges. *Professional Psychology: Research and Practice, 28,* 101–106.

Cummings, C., Gordon, J., & Marlatt, G. A. (1980). Relapse: Prevention and prediction. In W. Miller (Ed.), *The addictive behaviors.* Oxford: Pergamon Press.

Cummings, N. A. (1977). The anatomy of psychotherapy under national health insurance. *American Psychologist, 32,* 71–78.

Cummings, N. A. (1984). The future of clinical psychology in the United States. *The Clinical Psychologist, 37,* 19–20.

Cummings, N. A. (1995). Impact of managed care on employment and training: A primer for survival. *Professional Psychology: Research and Practice, 26,* 10–15.

Dahlstrom, W. G., Welsh, G. S., & Dahlstrom, L. E. (1975). *An MMPI handbook: Vol. 2. Research developments and applications.* Minneapolis: University of Minnesota Press.

Davenport, D. S., & Woolley, K. K. (1997). Innovative brief pithy psychotherapy: A contribution from corporate managed mental health care. *Professional Psychology: Research and Practice, 28,* 197–200.

Davison, G. C., & Lazarus, A. A. (1994). Clinical innovation and evaluation: Integrating practice with inquiry. *Clinical Psychology: Science and Practice, 1,* 157–168.

Dawes, R. M. (1979). The robust beauty of improper linear models in decision making. *American Psychologist, 34,* 571–582.

Dawes, R. M. (1994). *House of cards: Psychology and psychotherapy built on myth.* New York: Free Press.

DeAngelis, T. (1989). Suit opens doors to analysis training. *The APA Monitor, 20,* 16.

Deakin, J. F. W., & Graeff, F. G. (1991). Critique: 5-HT and mechanisms of defense. *Journal of Psychopharmacology, 5,* 305–315.

Deisz, R., Doueck, H. J., & George, N. (1996). Reasonable cause: A qualitative study of mandated reporting. *Child Abuse and Neglect, 20,* 275–287.

DeLeon, P. H. (1993). Legislative issues. *The Independent Practitioner, 13,* 170–172.

DeLeon, P. H., Fox, R. E., & Graham, S. R. (1991). Prescription privileges: Psychology's next frontier? *American Psychologist, 46,* 384–393.

DeLeon, P. H., & Wiggins, J. G. (1996). Prescription privileges for psychologists. *American Psychologist, 51,* 225–229.

Delis, D. C., Kramer, J., Kaplan, E., & Ober, B. A. (1987). *California Verbal Learning Test.* San Antonio, TX: Psychological Corporation.

Delis, D. C., Kramer, J., Kaplan, E., & Ober, B. A. (1994). *California Verbal Learning Test–Children's Version.* San Antonio, TX: Psychological Corporation.

DeNelsky, G. Y. (1991). Prescription privileges for psychologists: The case against. *Professional Psychology: Research and Practice, 22,* 188–193.

DeNelsky, G. Y. (1996). The case against presccription privleges for psychologists. *American Psychologist, 51,* 207–212.

Denmark, F. L. (1994). Engendering psychology. 101st annual conference of the American Psychological Association distinguished contribution to psychology in the public interest award address. *American Psychologist, 49,* 329–334.

Derogatis, L. R. (1982). *Manual for the Brief Symptom Inventory.* Riderwood, MD: Clinical Psychometric Research.

Derogatis L. R. (1983). *SCL-90-R administration, scoring & procedures manual-II for the revised version and other instruments of the psychopathology rating scale series.* Riderwood, MD: Clinical Psychometric Research.

Deutsch, C. J. (1985). A survey of therapists' personal problems and treatment. *Professional Psychology: Research and Practice, 16,* 305–315.

Devanand, D. P., Dwork, A. J., Hutchinson, E. R., Bolwig, T. G., & Sackheim, H. A. (1994). Does ECT alter brain structure? *American Journal of Psychiatry, 151,* 957–970.

Devanand, D. P., & Sackheim, H. A. (1995). "Does ECT alter brain structure?": Reply. *American Journal of Psychiatry, 152,* 1403.

Dey, E. L., Astin, A. W., & Korn, W. S. (1991). *The American freshman: Twenty-five year trends, 1966–1990.* Los Angeles: Higher Education Research Institute, University of California, Los Angeles.

Dial, T. H., Tebbutt, R., Pion, G. M., Kohout, J., VandenBos, G. R., Johnson, M., Schervish, P. H., Whiting, L., Fox, J. C., & Merwin, E. I. (1990). Human resources in mental health. In R. W. Manderscheid & M. A. Sonnenschein (Eds.), *Mental health, United States, 1990* (pp. 33–58). San Francisco: Jossey-Bass.

Digman, J. M. (1990). Personality structure: Emergence of the five-factor model. *Annual Review of Psychology, 41,* 417–470.

Diller, L. H., Tanner, J. L., & Weil, J. (1996). Etiology of ADHD: Nature or nurture? *American Jounal of Psychiatry, 153,* 451–452.

Dishman, R. K. (1982). Compliance/adherence in health-related exercise? *Psychosomatic Medicine, 49,* 375–382.

Dobson, K. S., & Block, L. (1988). Historical and philosophical bases of cognitive-behavioral therapies. In K. S. Dobson (Ed.), *Handbook of cognitive-behavioral therapies* (pp. 3–38). New York: Guilford Press.

Dodd, J. A. (1970). A retrospective analysis of variables related to duration of treatment in a university psychiatric clinic. *Journal of Nervous and Mental Disease, 151,* 75–85.

Dollard, J., & Miller, N. (1950). *Personality and psychotherapy: An analysis in terms of learning, thinking, and culture.* New York: McGraw-Hill.

Dollinger, S. J. (1989). Predictive validity of the Graduate Record Examination in a clinical psychology program. *Professional Psychology: Research and Practice, 20,* 56–58.

Dorwart, R. A., Chartock, L. R., Dial, T., Fenton, W., Knesper, D., Koran, L., Leaf, P. J., Pinus, H., Smith, R., Weissman, S., Winkelmeyer, R. (1992). A national study of psychiatrists' professional activities. *American Journal of Psychiatry, 149,* 1499–1505.

Dougherty, A. M. (1990). *Consultation: Practice and perspectives.* Pacific Grove, CA: Brooks/Cole.

Dougherty, A. M. (1995). *Consultation: Practice and perspectives in school and community settings* (2nd ed.). Pacific Grove, CA: Brooks/Cole.

Dubin, S. S. (1972). Obsolescence or lifelong education: A choice for the professional. *American Psychologist, 27,* 486–496.

Dunn, L. M., & Dunn, L. M. (1981). *Peabody Picture Vocabulary Test-Revised: Manual.* Circles Pines, MN: American Guidance Service.

Dush, D. M., Hirt, M. L., & Schroeder, H. E. (1989). Self-statement modification in the treatment of child behavior disorders: A meta-analysis. *Psychological Bulletin, 106,* 97–106.

Dustin, D., & Ehly, S. (1984). Skills for effective consultation. *School Counselor, 32,* 23–29.

Dykens, E. M., & Hodapp, R. M. (1997). Treatment issues in genetic mental retardation syndromes. *Professional Psychology: Research and Practice, 28,* 263–270.

Eaker, E. D., Pinsky, J., & Castelli, W. P. (1992). Myocardial infarction and coronary death among women: Psychosocial predictors from a 20-year follow-up of women in the Framingham study. *American Journal of Epidemiology, 135,* 854–864.

Eaton, W. W., Holzer, C. E., Von Korff, M., Anthony, J. C., Helzer, J. E., George, L., Burnam, A., Boyd, J. H., Kessler, L. G., & Locke, B. Z. (1984). The design of the epidemiologic catchment area surveys. *Archives of General Psychiatry, 41,* 942–948.

Ebigno, P. O. (1986). A cross sectional study of somatic complaints of Nigerian females using the Enugu Somatization Scale. *Culture, Medicine, and Psychiatry, 10,* 167–186.

Eddy, B., Lloyd, P. J., & Lubin, B. (1987). Enhancing the application to doctoral professional programs: Suggestions from a national survey. *Teaching of Psychology, 14,* 160–163.

Edelbrock, H. P., & Costello, A. J. (1984). Structured psychiatric interviews for children and adolescents. In G. Goldstein & M. Herson (Eds.), *Handbook of psychological assessment* (pp. 276–290). Elmsford, NY: Pergamon Press.

Edelson, M. (1994). Can psychotherapy research answer this psychotherapist's questions? In P. F. Tally, H. H. Strupp, & S. F. Butler (Eds.), *Psychotherapy research and practice: Bridging the gap* (pp. 124–142). New York: Basic Books.

Edwards, A. L. (1959). *Edwards Personal Preference Schedule.* New York: Psychological Corporation.

Edwards, A. J. (1994). *When memory fails: Helping the Alzheimer's and dementia patient.* New York: Plenum.

Edwards, M. C., Schultz, E. G., & Long, N. (1995). The role of the family in the assessment of attention deficit hyperactivity disorder. *Clinical Psychology Review, 15,* 375–394.

Ekstrand, M. L., & Coates, T. J. (1990). Maintenance of safer sexual behaviors and predictors of risky sex. The San Francisco men's health study. *American Journal of Public Health, 80,* 973–977.

Elkin, I. (1994). The NIMH Treatment of depression collaborative research program: Where we began and where we are. In A. E. Bergin & S. L. Garfield (Eds.), *Handbook of psychotherapy and behavior change* (4th ed., pp. 114–139). New York, Wiley.

Elkin, I., Parloff, M. B., Hadley, S. W., & Autry, J. H. (1985). NIMH Treatment of Depression Collaborative Research Program: Background and research plan. *Archives of General Psychiatry, 42,* 305–316.

Elkin, I., Shea, M. T., Watkins, J. T., Imber, S. D., Sotsky, S. M., Collins, J. F., Glass, D. R., Pilkonis, P. A., Leber, W. R., Docherty, J. P., Fiester, S. J., & Parloff, M. B. (1989). National Institute of Mental Health Treatment of Depression Collaborative Research Program: General effectiveness of treatments. *Archives of General Psychiatry, 46,* 971–982.

Ellenberg, J., Hirtz, D., & Nelson, K. (1986). Do seizures in children cause intellectual deterioration? *New England Journal of Medicine, 314,* 1085–1088.

Elliott, D. M., & Guy, J. D. (1993). Mental health professionals versus non-mental-health professionals: Childhood trauma and adult functioning. *Professional Psychology: Research and Practice, 24,* 83–90.

Ellis, A. (1962). *Reason and emotion in psychotherapy.* New York: Stuart.

Ellis, A. (1977). *Sex without guilt.* Hollywood, CA: Wilshire.

Ellis, A. (1980). Rational-emotive therapy and cognitive behavior therapy: Similarities and differences. *Cognitive Therapy & Research, 4,* 325–340.

Ellis, A. & Grieger, R. (Eds.) (1977). *Handbook of rational-emotive therapy.* New York: Springer.

Ellsworth, R. B. (1981). *CAAP Scale: The Measurement of Child and Adolescent Adjustment.* Palo Alto, CA: Consulting Psychologists Press, Inc.

Emery, R. E., & Laumann-Billings, L. (1998). An overview of the nature, causes, and consequences of abusive family relationships: Towards differentiating maltreatment and violence. *American Psychologist, 53,* 121–135.

Engel, G. L. (1977). The need for a new medical model: A challenge for biomedicine. *Science, 196,* 129–136.

Engel, G. L. (1980). The clinical application of the biopsychosocial model. *American Journal of Psychiatry, 137,* 535–544.

Enright, M. F., Resnick, R., DeLeon, P. H., Sciara, A. D., & Tanney, M. F. (1990). The practice of psychology in hospital settings. *American Psychologist, 45,* 1059–1065.

Epstein, S. (1979). The stability of behavior: I. On predicting most of the people much of the time. *Journal of Personality and Social Psychology, 37,* 1097–1126.

Erickson, M. H. (1980). *The collected papers of Milton H. Erickson on hypnosis.* New York: Irvington.

Evans, G. D., & Murphy, M. J. (1997). The practicality of predoctoral prescription training for psychologists: A survey of directors of clinical training. *Professional Psychology: Research and Practice, 28,* 113–117.

Exner, J. E. (1974). *The Rorschach: A comprehensive system.* New York: Wiley.

Exner, J. E. (1976). Projective techniques. In I. B. Weiner (Ed.), *Clinical methods in psychology* (pp. 61–121). New York: John Wiley & Sons.

Exner, J. E. (1986). *The Rorschach: A comprehensive system (Vol. 1: Basic foundations, 2nd ed.).* New York: Wiley.

Exner, J. E., & Weiner, I. (1995). *The Rorschach: A comprehensive system (Vol. 3: Assessment of children and adolescents, 2nd ed.).* New York: Wiley.

Eysenck, H. J. (1952). The effects of psychotherapy: An evaluation. *Journal of Consulting Psychology, 16,* 319–324.

Eysenck, H. J. (1958). Personality tests: 1950–1955. In G. W. T. H. Fleming and A. Walk (Ed.), *Recent progress in psychiatry* (Vol. 3, pp. 118–159). New York: Grove Press.

Eysenck, H. J. (1960). *Handbook of abnormal psychology: An experimental approach.* London: Pitman.

Eysenck, H. J. (1970). A mish-mash of theories. *International Journal of Psychiatry, 9,* 140–146.

Eysenck, H. J. (1978). An exercise in meta-silliness. *American Psychologist, 33,* 517.

Eysenck, H. J. (1983). [Review of *The benefits of psychotherapy*]. *Behaviour Research and Therapy, 21,* 315–320.

Eysenck, H. J., & Eysenck, S. B. G. (1975). *Manual for the Eysenck Personality Questionnaire.* San Diego: Educational and Individual Testing Service.

Fairbairn, W. R. D. (1954). *An object relations theory of the personality.* New York: Basic Books.

Farrell, A. D., Complair, P. S., & McCullough, L. (1987). Identification of target complaints by computer interview: Evaluation of the computerized assessment system for psychotherapy evaluation and research. *Journal of Consulting and Clinical Psychology, 55,* 691–700.

Faust, D. (1986). Research on human judgment and its application to clinical practice. *Professional Psychology: Research and Practice, 17,* 420–430.

Faust, J., Runyon, M. K., & Kenny, M. C. (1995). Family variables associated with the onset and impact of intrafamilial childhood sexual abuse. *Clinical Psychology Review, 15,* 443–456.

Feather, B. W., & Rhoads, J. M. (1972). Psychodynamic behavior therapy: I. Theory and rationale. *Archives of General Psychiatry, 26,* 496–502.

Feighner, J. P., Brown, S. L., & Oliver, J. E. (1973). Electrosleep therapy. *Journal of Nervous and Mental Disease, 157,* 121–128.

Feldman, J. M., & Kazdin, A. E. (1995). Parent management training for oppositional and conduct problem children. *The Clinical Psychologist, 48,* 3–5.

Fensterheim, H., & Raw, S. D. (1996). Psychotherapy research is not psychotherapy practice. *Clinical Psychology: Science and Practice, 3,* 168–171.

Fiester, A. R., & Rudestam, K. E. (1975). A multivariate analysis of the early dropout process. *Journal of Consulting and Clinical Psychology, 43,* 528–535.

Fink, P. J. (1986). Dealing with psychiatry's stigma. *Hospital and Community Psychiatry, 37,* 814–818.

Finney, J. W., & Moos, R. H. (1991). The long-term course of treated alcoholism, I: Mortality, relapse, and remission rates and comparisons with community controls. *Journal of Studies on Alcoholism, 52,* 44–54.

Fiore, T. A., Becker, E. A., & Nero, R. C. (1993). Educational interventions for students with attention deficit disorder. *Exceptional Children, 60,* 163–173.

First, M. B., Spitzer, R. L., & Williams, J. B. W. (1996). *Structured Clinical Interview for DSM-IV Axis I Disorder.* Washington, DC: Biometrics Research.

First, M. B., Gibbon, M., Spitzer, R. L., Williams, J. B., & Benjamin, L. (1997). *Structured clinical interview for DSM-IV axis II personality disorders (SCID-II).* Washington, DC: American Psychiatric Press.

First, M. B., Spitzer, R. L., Gibbon, M., & Williams, J. B. (1997). *Structured clinical interview for DSM-IV axis I disorders (SCID-I), clinical version.* Washington, DC: American Psychiatric Press.

Fischbach, G. D. (1992). Mind and brain. *Scientific American, 267,* 48–57.

Fischer, H. (1992). *Anatomy of Love: The Mysteries of Mating, Marriage, and Why We Stray.* New York, NY: Ballantine Books.

Fischer, J., & Corcoran, K. (1994). *Measures for clinical practice: A sourcebook* (Vol. 2, Adults). New York: Free Press.

Fitzgibbon, M. L., Stolley, M. R., Avellone, M. E., Sugerman, S., & Chavez, N. (1996). Involving parents in cancer risk reduction: A program for Hispanic American families. *Health Psychology, 15,* 413–422.

Fleck, S. (1995). Dehumanizing developments in American psychiatry in recent decades. *Journal of Nervous and Mental Disease, 183,* 195–203.

Foa, E. B. (1996). The efficacy of behavioral therapy with obsessive-compulsives. *The Clinical Psychologist, 49,* 19–22.

Foa, E. B., & Stekete, G. (1977). Emergent fears during treatment of three obsessive compulsives: Symptom substitution or deconditioning? *Journal of Behaviour Therapy and Experimental Psychiatry, 8,* 353–358.

Fordyce, W. E. (1988). Pain and suffering: A reappraisal. *American Psychologist, 43,* 276–283.

Forer, B. R. (1957). *The Forer Structured Sentence Completion Test.* Los Angeles, CA: Western Psychological Service.

Fowers, B. J., & Richardson, F. C. (1996). Why is multiculturalism good? *American Psychologist, 51,* 609–621.

Fowler, R. D. (1995). 1994 report of the chief executive officer: The winds of change. *American Psychologist, 50,* 600–611.

Fox, B. H. (1988). Psychogenic factors in cancer, especially its incidence. In S. Maes, D. Spielberger, P. B. Defares, & I. G. Sarason (Eds.), *Topics in health psychology* (pp. 37–55). New York: Wiley.

Fox, R. E. (1994). Training professional psychologists for the twenty-first century. *American Psychologist, 49,* 200–206.

Fox, R. E., Schwelitz, F. D., & Barclay, A. G. (1992). A proposed curriculum for psychopharmacology training for professional psychologists. *Professional Psychology: Research and Practice, 23,* 216–219.

Frank, G. (1984). The Boulder model: History, rationale, and critique. *Professional Psychology: Research and Practice, 15,* 417–435.

Frank, J. D. (1961). *Persuasion and healing.* Baltimore: Johns Hopkins Press.

Frank, J. D. (1973). *Persuasion and healing.* Baltimore, MD: Johns Hopkins University Press.

Frank, J. D. (1982). Therapeutic components shared by all psychotherapies. In J. H. Harvey & M. M. Parks (Eds.), *The Master Lecture Series: Vol 1. Psychotherapy research and behavior change* (pp. 73–122). Washington, DC: American Psychological Association.

Frank, L. K. (1948). *Projective methods.* Springfield, IL: Charles C. Thomas.

Frankl, V. (1963). *Man's search for meaning.* New York: Washington Square Press.

Frankl, V. (1965). *The doctor and the soul.* New York: Knopf.

Fraser, J. S. (1996). All that glitters is not always gold: Medical offset effects and managed behavioral health care. *Professional Psychology: Research and Practice, 27,* 335–344.

Frederick/Schneiders, Inc. (1990, December). *Survey of American Psychological Association Members.*

Fredrickson, M., & Matthew, K. A. (1990). Cardiovascular responses to behavioral stress and hypertension: A meta-analytic review. *Annals of Behavioral Medicine, 12,* 30–39.

Freedman, R. R. (1993). Raynaud's disease and phenomenon. In R. J. Gatchel & E. B. Blanchard (Eds.). *Psychophysiological Disorders.* Washington, DC: American Psychological Association.

French, S. A., Hennrikus, D. J., & Jeffery, R. W. (1996). Smoking status, dietary intake, and physical activity in a sample of working adults. *Health Psychology, 15,* 448–454.

Freud, S. (1959). The question of lay analysis. In *Standard edition* (Vol. 20). London: Hogarth Press. (Originally published, 1926).

Freud, S. (1963). Introductory lectures in psychoanalysis. In J. Strachey (Ed. and Trans.), *The standard edition of the complete psychological works of Sigmund Freud* (Vol. 16, pp. 241–489). London: Hogarth Press. (Original work published in 1917).

Freud, S. (1964). New introductory lectures on psychoanalysis. In J. Strachey (Ed. and Trans.), *The standard edition of the complete psychological works of Sigmund Freud* (Vol. 22, pp. 1–182). London: Hogarth Press. (Original work published in 1933).

Friedman, H. S., Tucker, J. S., Schwartz, J. E., Tomlinson-Keasey, C., Martin, L. R., Wingard, D. L., & Criqui, M. H. (1995). Psychosocial and behavioral predictors of longevity: The aging and death of the "Termites." *American Psychologist, 50,* 69–78.

Fuqua, D., & Kurpius, D. (1993). Conceptual models in organizational consultation. *Journal of Counseling and Development, 71,* 607–618.

Gabbard, G. O. (1994). Reconsidering the American Psychological Association's policy on sex with former patients: Is it justifi-able? *Professional Psychology: Research and Practice, 25,* 329–335.

Gallagher-Thompson, D., Hanley-Peterson, P., & Thompson, L. W. (1990). Maintenance of gains versus relapse following brief psychotherapy for depression. *Journal of Consulting and Clinical Psychology, 58,* 371–374.

Gallessich, J. (1982). *The profession and practice of consultation.* San Francisco: Jossey-Bass.

Garb, H. N. (1988). Comment on "The Study of Clinical Judgment: An Ecological Approach." *Clinical Psychology Review, 8,* 441–444.

Garb, H. N. (1989). Clinical judgment, clinical training, and professional experience. *Psychological Bulletin, 105,* 387–396.

Garb, H. N. (1997). Race bias, social class bias, and gender bias in clinical judgement. *Clinical Psychology: Science and Practice, 4,* 99–120.

Garbarino, J., & Stocking, S. H. (1980). *Protecting children from abuse and neglect.* San Francisco: Jossey-Bass.

Gardner, H. (1983). *Frames of mind: The theory of multiple intelligences.* New York: Basic Books.

Gardner, H. (1986). The waning of intelligence tests. In R. J. Sternberg & D. K. Detterman (Eds.), *What is intelligence?* Norwood, NJ: Ablex.

Gardner, H. (1994). *Creating minds.* New York: Basic.

Garfield, S. L. (1986). Research on client variables in psychotherapy. In S. L. Garfield & A. E. Bergin (Eds.), *Handbook of psychotherapy and behavior change* (3rd ed., pp. 213–256). New York: Wiley.

Garfield, S. L. (1993). Methodological problems in clinical diagnosis. In P. B. Sutker & H. E. Adams (Eds.), *Comprehensive handbook of psychopathology* (2nd ed., pp. 27–46). New York: Plenum.

Garfield, S. L. (1994). Eclecticism and integration in psychotherapy: Developments and issues. *Clinical Psychology: Science and Practice, 1,* 123–137.

Garfield, S. L. (1996). Some problems associated with "validated" forms of psychotherapy. *Clinical Psychology: Science and Practice, 3,* 218–229.

Garfield, S. L., & Bergin, A. E. (Eds.). (1986). *Handbook of psychotherapy and behavior change* (3rd ed.). New York: Wiley.

Garfield, S. L., & Kurtz, R. (1974). A survey of clinical psychologists: Characteristics, activities, and orientations. *The Clinical Psychologist, 28,* 7–10.

Garfield, S. L., & Kurtz, R. (1976). Clinical psychologists in the 70s. *American Psychologist, 31,* 1–9.

Gatchel, R. J., & Blanchard, E. B. (Eds.) (1993). *Psychophysiological Disorders.* Washington, DC: American Psychological Association.

Gerrard, M., Gibbons, F. X., & Bushman, B. J. (1996). Relation between perceived vulnerability to HIV and precautionary sexual behavior. *Psychological Bulletin, 119,* 390–409.

Gershon, E. S. (1990). Genetics. In F. K. Goodwin & K. R. Jamison (Eds.), *Manic-depressive illness* (pp. 373–401). New York: Oxford University Press.

Gibbs, W. W. (1996). Gaining on fat. *Scientific America, 275,* 88–94.

Gill, M. M. (1984). Psychoanalytic, psychodynamic, cognitive behavior, and behavior therapies compared. In H. Arkowitz and S. B. Messer (Ed.), *Psychoanalytic therapy and behavior therapy: Is integration possible?* (pp. 179–188). New York: Plenum.

Glantz, K., Durlach, N. I., Barnett, R. C., Aviles, W. A. (1996). Virtual reality (VR) for psychotherapy: From the physical to the social environment. *Psychotherapy, 33,* 464–473.

Glaser, R., & Thorpe, J. (1986). Unethical intimacy: A survey of sexual contact and advances between psychology educators and female graduate students. *American Psychologist, 41,* 43–51.

Goldberg, I. D., Krantz, G., & Locke, B. Z. (1970). Effect of a short-term outpatient psychiatric therapy benefit on the utilization of medical services in a prepaid group practice medical program. *Medical Care, 8,* 419–428.

Goldberg, P. A. (1965). A review of sentence completion methods in personality assessment. *Journal of Projective Techniques and Personality Assessment, 29,* 12–45.

Golden, C. J., Hammeke, T. A., & Purisch, A. D. (1980). *The Luria-Nebraska Neuropsychological Battery.* Los Angeles: Western Psychological Services.

Goldensohn, E., Glaser, G., & Goldberg, M. (1984). Epilepsy. In L. Rowland (Ed.). *Meritt's Textbook of Neurology* (pp. 629–649). Philadelphia: Lea & Febiger.

Goldfarb, L. A. (1987). Sexual abuse antecedent to anorexia nervosa, bulimia, and compulsive overeating: Three case reports. *International Journal of Eating Disorders, 6,* 675–680.

Goldfarb, L. A., Dykens, E., Gerrard, M. (1985). The Goldfarb Fear of Fat Scale. *Journal of Personality Assessment, 49,* 329–332.

Goldfried, M. R. (1991). Research issues in psychotherapy integration. *Journal of Psychotherapy Integration, 1,* 5–25.

Goldfried, M. R., Greenberg, L. S., & Marmar, C. (1990). Individual psychotherapy: Process and outcome. In M. R. Rosenzweig & L. W. Porter (Eds.), *Annual review of psychology.* Palo Alto, CA: Annual Reviews.

Goldfried, M. R., & Wolfe, B. E. (1996). Psychotherapy practice and research: Repairing a strained alliance. *American Psychologist, 51,* 1007–1016.

Goleman, D. (1995). *Emotional intelligence: Why it can matter more than IQ.* New York: Bantam.

Goodglass, H. (1986). The flexible battery in neuropsychological assessment. In T. Incagnoli, G. Goldstein, & C. J. Golden (Eds), *Clinical applications of neuropsychological test batteries* (pp. 121–134). New York: Plenum Press.

Goodheart, C. D., & Markham, B. (1992). The feminization of psychology: Implications for psychotherapy. *Psychotherapy, 29,* 130–138.

Goodwin, D. W. (1986). Heredity and alcoholism. *Annals of Behavioral Medicine, 8,* 3–6.

Gottesman, I. I. (1991). *Schizophrenia genesis: The origins of madness.* New York: W. H. Freeman.

Gottesman, I. I., & Prescott, C. A. (1989). Abuses of the MacAndrew MMPI Alcoholism Scale: A critical review. *Clinical Psychology Review, 9,* 223–242.

Gough, H. G. (1962). Clinical versus statistical prediction in psychology. In L. Postman (Ed.), *Psychology in the making: Histories of selected research problems.* New York: Knopf.

Gough, H. G. (1984). A managerial potential scale for the California Psychological Inventory, *Journal of Applied Psychology, 69,* 233–240.

Graham, J. R. (1990). *MMPI-2: Assessing personality and psychopathology.* New York: Oxford University Press.

Grant, D. A., & Berg, E. A. (1948). A behavioral analysis of degree of reinforcement and ease of shifting to new responses in Weigl-type card-sorting program. *Journal of Experimental Psychology, 38,* 404–411.

Grant, D. A., & Berg, E. A. (1993). *Wisconsin Card Sorting Test.* Odessa, FL: Psychological Assessment Resources.

Grantham, R. J. (1973). Effects of counselor sex, race, and language style on black students in initial interviews. *Journal of Counseling Psychology, 20,* 553–559.

Gray, J. A. (1991). Fear, panic, and anxiety: What's in a name? *Psychological Inquiry, 2,* 72–96.

Greenblatt, M. (1985). Mental health consultation. In H. I. Kaplan & B. J. Sadock (Eds.), *Comprehensive textbook of psychiatry* (4th ed.). Baltimore: Williams & Wilkins.

Greene, B. (1993). Human diversity in clinical psychology: Lesbian and gay sexual orientations. *The Clinical Psychologist, 46,* 74–82.

Greenfield, P. M. (1997). You can't take it with you: Why ability assessments don't cross cultures. *American Psychologist, 52,* 1115–1124.

Greenough, W. T., Withers, G. S., & Wallace, C. S. (1990). Morphological changes in the nervous system arising from behavioral experience: What is the evidence that they are involved in learning and memory? In L. R. Squire & E. Lindenlaub (Eds.), *The biology of memory, Symposia Medica Hoescht 23* (pp. 159–183). Stuttgart/New York: Schattauer Verlag.

Greist, J. H. (1990). Treatment of obsessive-compulsive disorder: Psychotherapies, drugs, and other somatic treatments. *Journal of Clinical Psychiatry, 51,* 44–50.

Grencavage, L. M., & Norcross, J. C. (1990). Where are the commonalities among the therapeutic common factors? *Professional Psychology: Research and Practice, 21,* 372–378.

Grisso, T., & Appelbaum, P. S. (1992). Is it unethical to offer predictions of future violence? *Law and Human Behavior, 16,* 621–633.

Grusky, O., Thompson, W. A., & Tillipman, H. (1991). Clinical versus administrative backgrounds for mental health administrators. *Administration and Policy in Mental Health, 18,* 271–278.

Guilford, J. P. (1967). *The nature of human intelligence.* New York: McGraw-Hill.

Guilford, J. P. (1979). Intelligence isn't what it used to be: What to do about it. *Journal of Research and Development in Education, 12,* 33–46.

Guilford, J. P. (1985). The structure-of-intellect model. In B. B. Wolman (Ed.), *Handbook of intelligence* (pp. 225–266). New York: Wiley.

Guion, R. M., & Gottier, R. F. (1965). Validity of personality measures in personnel selection. *Personnel Psychology, 18,* 135–164.

Gutkin, T. B., Reynolds, C. R., & Galvin, G. A. (1984). Factor analysis of the Wechsler Adult Intelligence Scale-Revised

(WAIS-R): An examination of the standardization sample. *Journal of School Psychology, 22,* 83–93.

Guy, J. D. (1987). *The personal life of the psychotherapist.* New York: Wiley.

Haas, L. J., Benedict, J. G., & Kobos, J. C. (1996). Psychotherapy by telephone: Risks and benefits for psychologists and consummers. *Professional Psychology: Research and Practice, 27,* 154–160.

Hale, R. L. (1991). Intellectual assessment. In M. Hersen, A. E. Kazdin, & A. S. Bellack (Eds.), *The clinical psychology handbook (2nd ed.).* New York: Pergamon.

Haley, J. (1973). *Uncommon therapy.* New York: W. W. Norton.

Haley, J. (1976). *Problem solving therapy: New strategies for effective family therapy.* San Francisco: Jossey-Bass.

Haley, J. (1987). *Problem-solving therapy* (2nd ed.). San Francisco: Jossey-Bass.

Hall, C. C. I. (1997). Cultural malpractice: The growing obsolescence of psychology with the changing U.S. population. *American Psychologist, 52,* 642–651.

Hall, S. M., Munoz, R. F., Reus, V. I., & Sees, K. L. (1993). Nicotine, negative affect, and depression. *Journal of Consulting and Clinical Psychology, 61,* 761–767.

Halstead, W. C. (1947). *Brain and intelligence: A quantitative study of the frontal lobes.* Chicago: University of Chicago Press.

Hanesian, H., Paez, P., & Williams, D. T. (1988). The neurologically impaired child and adolescent. In C. J. Kestenbaum & D. T. Williams (Eds.), *Handbook of clinical assessment of children and adolescents* (Vol. 1, pp. 415–445). New York: New York University Press.

Hanna, D. (1988). *Designing organizations for high performance.* Reading, MA: Addison-Wesley.

Hans, V. P. (1986). An analysis of public attitudes toward the insanity defense. *Criminology, 4,* 393–415.

Hansen, J., Himes, B., & Meier, S. (1990). *Consultation: Concepts and practices.* Englewood Cliffs, NJ: Prentice-Hall.

Harris, D. B. (1972). Review of the DAP. In O. K. Buros (Ed.), *The seventh mental measurement yearbook* (pp. 401–405). Highland Park, NJ: Gryphon Press.

Hathaway, S. R. (1943). *The Minnesota Multiphasic Personality Inventory.* Minneapolis: University of Minnesota Press.

Hatsukami, D., Jensen, J., Allen, S., & Grillo, M. (1996). Effects of behavioral and pharmacological treatment on smokeless tobacco users. *Journal of Consulting and Clinical Psychology, 64,* 153–161.

Hattie, J. A., Sharpley, C. F., & Rogers, H. F. (1984). Comparative effectiveness of professional and paraprofessional helpers. *Psychological Bulletin, 95,* 534–541.

Hauser, W., Annegers, J., & Anderson, V. (1983). Epidemiology and genetics of epilepsy. *Research in Nervous and Mental Disorders, 61,* 267–294.

Havens, L. (1994). Some suggestions for making research more applicable to clinical practice. In P. F. Tally, H. H. Strupp, & S. F. Butler (Eds.), *Psychotherapy research and practice: Bridging the gap* (pp. 88–98). New York: Basic Books.

Havik, O. E., & VandenBos, G. R. (1996). Limitations of manualized psychotherapy for everyday clinical practice. *Clinical Psychology: Science and Practice, 3,* 264–267.

Hawkins, R. P. (1987). Selection of target behaviors. In R. O. Nelson & S. C. Hayes (Eds.), *Conceptual foundations of behavioral assessment* (pp. 311–385). New York: Guilford.

Hayes, S. (1996). Creating the empirical clinician. *Clinical Psychology: Science and Practice, 3,* 179–181.

Hayes, S. C., & Heiby, E. (1996). Psychology's drug problem: Do we need a fix or should we just say no? *American Psychologist, 51,* 198–206.

Hayes, S. C., Follette, W. C., Dawes, R. D., & Grady, K. (Eds.). (1995). *Scientific standards of psychological practice: Issues and recommendations.* Reno, NV: Context Press.

Haynes, S. G., Feinleib, M., Kannel, W. B. (1980). The relationship of psychosocial factors to coronary heart disease in the Framingham study III. Eight-year incidence of coronary heart disease. *American Journal of Epidemiology, 111,* 37–58.

Hayward, P., Wardle, J., & Higgitt, A. (1989). Benzodiazepine research: Current findings and practical consequences. *British Journal of Psychiatry, 28,* 307–327.

Heaton, R. K. (1988). Introduction to special series. *Journal of Consulting and Clinical Psychology, 56,* 787–788.

Helms, J. E. (1992). Why is there no study of cultural equivalence in standardized cognitive ability testing? *American Psychologist, 47,* 1083–1101.

Herbert, D. L., Nelson, R. O., & Herbert, J. D. (1988). Effects of psychodiagnostic labels, depression, severity, and instructions on assessment. *Professional Psychology: Research and Practice, 19,* 496–502.

Herrnstein, R. J. & Murray, C. (1994). *The bell curve: Intelligence and class structure in American life.* New York: Free Press.

Herzog, D. B. (1988). Eating disorders. In A. M. Nicoli, Jr. (Ed.), *The new Harvard guide to psychiatry* (pp. 434–445). Boston: Harvard University Press.

Hoffman, L. W. (1990). *Old scapes, new maps: A training program for psychotherapy supervisors.* Cambridge, MA: Milusik Press.

Hogan, R., Hogan, J., & Roberts, B. W. (1996). Personality measurement and employment decisions: Questions and answers. *American Psychologist, 51,* 469–477.

Hollon, S. D. (1996). The efficacy and effectiveness of psychotherapy relative to medications. *American Psychologist, 51,* 1025–1030.

Hollon, S. D., & Beck, A. T. (1994). Cognitive and cognitive-behavioral therapies. In A. E. Bergin and S. L. Garfield (Eds.), *Handbook of psychotherapy and behavior change* (4th ed., pp. 428–466). NY: John Wiley & Sons.

Hollon, S. D., & Garber, J. (1988). Cognitive therapy. In L. Y. Abramson (Ed.), *Social cognition and clinical psychology* (pp. 204–253). New York: Guilford.

Holroyd, J., & Brodsky, A. (1977). Psychologists' attitudes and practices regarding erotic and nonerotic physical contact with clients. *American Psychologist, 32,* 843–849.

Holtzman, W. H. (1975). New developments in Holtzman Inkblot Technique. In P. McReynolds (Ed.), *Advances in psychological assessment* (Vol. 3). San Francisco: Jossey-Bass.

Holtzman, W. H., Thorpe, J. W., Swartz, J. D., & Herron, E. W. (1961). *Inkblot perception and personality: Holzman Inkblot Technique.* Austin, TX: University of Texas Press.

Horgan, J. (1996). Why Freud isn't dead. *Scientific American, 275,* 106–111.

Horowitz, M. J. (1974). Microanalysis of working through in psychotherapy. *American Journal of Psychiatry, 131,* 1208–1212.

Horowitz, M. J. (1988). *Introduction to psychodynamics: A new synthesis.* New York: Basic Books.

Horowitz, M., Marmar, C., Krupnick, J., Wilner, N., Kaltreider, N., Wallerstein, R. (1984). *Personality styles and brief psychotherapy.* New York: Basic Books.

Horvath, A. O., & Symonds, B. D. (1991). Relationship between working alliance and outcome in psychotherapy: A meta-analysis. *Journal of Counseling Psychology, 38,* 139–149.

Horvath, P. (1988). Placebos and common factors in two decades of psychotherapy research. *Psychological Bulletin, 104,* 214–225.

House, J. A., Robbins, C., & Metzner, H. L. (1982). The association of social relationships and activities with mortality: Prospective evidence from the Tecumseh Community Health Study. *American Journal of Epidemiology, 116,* 123–140.

House, J. S., Landis, K. R., & Umberson, D. (1988). Social relationships and health. *Science, 241,* 540–545.

Howard, K. I., Kopta, S. M., Krause, M. S., & Orlinsky, D. E. (1986). The dose-effect relationship in psychotherapy. *American Psychologist, 41,* 159–164.

Hsu, L. K. G. (1990). *Eating disorders.* New York: Guilford.

Hubert, N., Wachs, T. D., Peters-Martin, P., & Gandour, M. (1982). The study of early temperament: Measurement and conceptual issues. *Child Development, 53,* 571–600.

Hughes, J. R. (1993). Pharmacotherapy for smoking cessation: Unvalidated assumptions, anomalies, and suggestions for future research. *Journal of Consulting and Clinical Psychology, 61,* 751–760.

Hynd, G. W., & Semrud-Clikeman, M. (1989). Dyslexia and brain morphology. *Psychological Bulletin, 106,* 447–482.

Ikels, C. (1991). Aging and disability in China: Cultural issues in measurement and interpretation. *Social Science Medicine, 32,* 649–665.

Ingram, R. E., Kendall, P. C., & Chen, A. H. (1991). Cognitive-behavioral interventions. In C. R. Snyder, D. R. Forsyth (Eds.), *Handbook of social and clinical psychology: The health perspective,* pp. 509–522. NY: Pergamon.

Ingram, R. E., & Scott, W. D. (1990). Cognitive behavior therapy. In A. S. Bellack, M. Hersen, & A. E. Kazdin (Eds.), *International handbook of behavior modification and therapy* (2nd ed., pp. 53–65). NY: Plenum.

Insel, T. R. (Ed.). (1984). *New findings in obsessive-compulsive disorder.* Washington, DC: American Psychiatric Press.

Insel, T. R. (1992). Toward a neuroanatomy of obsessive-compulsive disorder. *Archives of General Psychiatry, 49,* 739–744.

Insel, T. R., Champoux, M., Scanlan, J. M., & Suomi, S. J. (1986, May). *Rearing condition and response to anxiogenic drug.* Paper presented at the annual meeting of the American Psychiatric Association, Washington, DC.

International Neuropsychological Society. (1987). Report of the INS–Division 40 Task Force on Education, Accreditation, and Credentialing. (1987). *The Clinical Neuropsychologist, 1,* 29–34.

Jacobson, N. S. (1985). Family therapy outcome research: Potential pitfalls and prospects. *Journal of Marital and Family Therapy, 11,* 149–158.

Jacobson, N. S., & Margolin, G. (1979). *Marital therapy: Strategies based on social learning and behavior exchange principles.* New York: Brunner/Mazel.

Jacobson, N. S., & Revenstorf, D. (1988). Statistics for assessing the clinical significance of psychotherapy techniques: Issues, problems, and new developments. *Behavioral Assessment, 10,* 133–145.

Jamison, R. N., & Virts, K. L. (1990). The influence of family support on chronic pain. *Behaviour Research and Therapy, 28,* 283–287.

Jastak, S., & Wilkinson, G. S. (1993). *Wide Range Achievement Test-3.* Wilmington, DE: Jastak Associates.

Jeffrey, R. W. (1988). Dietary risk and their modification in cardiovascular disease. *Journal of Consulting and Clinical Psychology, 56,* 350–357.

Jenkins, C. D. (1988). Epidemiology of cardiovascular diseases. *Journal of Consulting and Clinical Psychology, 56,* 324–332.

Jones, B. P., & Butters, N. (1991). Neuropsychological assessment. In M. Hersen, A. E. Kazdin, & A. S. Bellack (Eds.). *The clinical psychology handbook* (2nd ed.). New York: Pergamon.

Jones, M. C. (1924). The elimination of children's fears. *Journal of Experimental Psychology, 7,* 383–390.

Jones, M. L., Ulicny, G. R., Czyzewski, M. J., & Plante, T. G. (1987). Employment in caregiving jobs for mentally disabled young adults: A feasibility study. *Journal of Employment Counseling, 24* (9), 122–129.

Jones, S. L. (1994). A constructive relationship for religion with the science and profession of psychology: Perhaps the boldest model yet. *American Psychologist, 49,* 184–199.

Jorgensen, R. S., Johnson, B. T., Kolodziej, M. E., Schreer, G. E. (1996). Elevated blood pressure and personality: A meta-analytic review. *Psychological Bulletin, 120,* 293–320.

Jorm, A. F. (1989). Modifiability of trait anxiety and neuroticism: A meta-analysis of the literature. *Australian and New Zealand Journal of Psychiatry, 23,* 21–29.

Julien, R. M. (1995). *A primer of drug action* (7th ed.). New York: W. H. Freeman.

Kagan, J., Reznick, J. S., & Snidman, N, (1988). Biological bases of childhood shyness. *Science, 240,* 167–171.

Kahn, M. W., & Heiman, E. (1978). Factors associated with length of treatment in a barrio-neighborhood mental health service. *International Journal of Social Psychiatry, 24,* 259–262.

Kantrowitz, B., & Wingert, P. (1990, Winter/Spring). Step by Step. *Newsweek Special Edition,* pp. 24–34.

Kaplan, E., Fein, D., Morris, R., Delis, D. C. (1991). *WAIS-R as a Neuropsychological Instrument.* San Antonio, TX: Psychological Corporation.

Kaplan, G. A., & Reynolds, P. (1988). Depression and cancer mortality and morbidity: Prospective evidence from the Alameda County study. *Journal of Behavioral Medicine, 11,* 1–13.

Kaplan, H. I., & Sadock, B. J. (1993). *Pocket handbook of psychiatric drug treatment.* Baltimore, MD: Williams & Wilkins.

Karasu, T. B. (1986). Specificity versus nonspecificity. *American Journal of Psychiatry, 143,* 687–695.

Karon, B. P. (1995a). Becoming a first-rate professional psychologist despite graduate education. *Professional Psychology: Research and Practice, 26,* 211–217.

Karon, B. P. (1995b). Provision of psychotherapy under managed health care: A growing crisis and national nightmare. *Professional Psychology: Research and Practice, 26,* 5–9.

Katz, R. L. (1980). Human relations skills can be sharpened. In Paths towards personal progress: Leaders are made not born. *Harvard Business Review,* 82–93.

Kaufman, A. S., & Kaufman, N. L. (1983). *Kaufman Assessment Battery for Children (K-ABC): Administrative and Scoring Manual.* Circles Pines, MN: American Guidance Service.

Kaufman, A. S., & Kaufman, N. L. (1990). *Kaufman Brief Intelligence Test (K-BIT): Administrative and Scoring Manual.* Circles Pines, MN: American Guidance Service.

Kaufman, A. S., & Kaufman, N. L. (1993). *Kaufman Adolescent and Adult Intelligence Test (KAIT): Administrative and Scoring Manual.* Circles Pines, MN: American Guidance Service.

Kaufman, A. S., & Kaufman, N. L. (1994). *Kaufman Short Neuropsychological Assessment Procedure (K-SNAP): Administrative and Scoring Manual.* Circles Pines, MN: American Guidance Service.

Kazdin, A. E. (1991). Treatment research: The investigation and evaluation of psychotherapy. In M. Hersen, A. E. Kazdin, & A. S. Bellack (Eds.), *The clinical psychology handbook (2nd ed.).* New York: Pergamon.

Kazdin, A. E. (1994). Methodology, design, and evaluation in psychotherapy research. In A. E. Bergin & S. L. Garfield (Eds.), *Handbook of psychotherapy and behavior change* (4th ed.). New York: Wiley.

Kazdin, A. E., & Bass, D. (1989). Power to detect differences between alternative treatments in comparative psychotherapy outcome research. *Journal of Consulting and Clinical Psychology, 57,* 138–147.

Kazdin, A. E., & Wilson, G. T. (1978). *Evaluation of behavior therapy: Issues, evidence, and research strategies.* Cambridge, MA: Ballinger.

Keefe, F. J., Dunsmore, J., & Burnett, R. (1992). Behavioral and cognitive-behavioral approaches to chronic pain: Recent advances and future directions. Special issue: Behavioral medicine: An update for the 1990s. *Journal of Consulting and Clinical Psychology, 60,* 528–536.

Keith-Spiegal, P. (1991). *The complete guide to graduate school admission: Psychology and related fields.* Hillsdale, NJ: Erlbaum.

Keith-Spiegal, P. (1994). The 1992 ethics: Boon or bane? *Professional Psychology: Research and Practice, 25,* 315–316.

Kelly, J. A., & Kalichman, S. C. (1995). Increased attention to human sexuality can improve HIV–AIDS prevention efforts: Key research issues and directions. *Journal of Consulting and Clinical Psychology, 63,* 907–918.

Kelly, J. A., St. Lawrence, J. S., Hood, H. V., & Brasfield, T. L. (1989). Behavioral intervention to reduce AIDS risk activities. *Journal of Consulting and Clinical Psychology, 57,* 60–67.

Kelly, T. A. (1997). A wake-up call: The experience of a mental health commissioner in times of change. *Professional Psychology: Research and Practice, 28,* 317–322.

Kemp, S. (1990). *Medieval psychology.* New York: Greenwood Press.

Kendall, P. C., & Bemis, K. M. (1983). Thought and action in psychotherapy: The cognitive behavioral approaches. In M. Hersen, A. E. Kazdin, & A. S. Bellak (Eds.), *The clinical psychology handbook* (pp. 565–592). Elmsford, NY: Pergamon Press.

Kendall, P. C., & Braswell, L. (1985). *Cognitive behavioral therapy with impulsive children.* New York: Guilford.

Kendall, P. C., & Norton-Ford, J. D. (1982). Therapy outcome research methods. In P. C. Kendall & J. N. Butcher (Eds.), *Handbook of research methods in clinical psychology* (pp. 429–460). New York: Wiley.

Kendziora, K., & O'Leary, S. G. (1993). Dysfunctional parenting as a focus for prevention and treatment of child behavior problems. In H. Ollendick & R. J. Prinz (Eds.), *Advances in child clinical psychology* (Vol. 15, pp. 175–206). New York: Plenum.

Kenrick, D. T., & Funder, D. C. (1988). Profiting from controversy: Lessons from the person-situation debate. *American Psychologist, 43,* 23–34.

Kernberg, O. (1973). Summary & conclusion of "Psychotherapy and psychoanalysis: Final report of the Menninger Foundation's psychotherapy research project." *International Journal of Psychiatry, 11,* 62–77.

Kernberg, O. (1975). *Borderline conditions and pathological narcissism.* New York: Jason Aronson.

Kernberg, O. (1976). *Object relations theory and clinical psychoanalysis.* New York: Jason Aronson.

Kernberg, O. (1984). *Severe personality disorders: Psychotherapeutic strategies.* New Haven, CT: Yale University Press.

Kiesler, C. A., & Morton, T. L. (1987). Responsible public policy in a rapidly changing world. *The Clinical Psychologist, 40,* 28–31.

Kiesler, C. A., & Morton, T. L. (1988). Psychology and public policy in the "Health Care Revolution." *American Psychologist, 43,* 993–1003.

Kiesler, C. A., & Zaro, J. (1981). The development of psychology as a profession in the United States. *International Review of Applied Psychology, 30,* 341–353.

Kilburg, R. R. (1991). *How to manage your career in psychology.* Washington, DC: American Psychological Association.

Kirsch, I. (1990). *Changing expectations: A key to effective psychotherapy.* Pacific Grove, CA: Brooks/Cole.

Kirschner, D. A., & Kirschner, S. (1986). *Comprehensive family therapy: An integration of systemic and psychodynamic treatment models.* New York: Brunner/Mazel.

Klein, M. (1952). Some theoretical conclusions regarding the emotional life of the infant. In M. Klein (Ed.). *Envy and gratitude and other works, 1946–1963* (pp. 61–93). New York, Delta.

Klein, R. G. (1995). The role of methylphenidate in psychiatry. *Archives of General Psychiatry, 52,* 429–433.

Klein, R. G. (1996). Comments on expanding the clinical role of psychologists. *American Psychologist, 51,* 216–218.

Kleinke, C. L. (1994). *Common principles of psychotherapy.* Pacific Grove, CA: Brooks/Cole.

Klosko, J. S., Barlow, D. H., Tassinari, R., & Cerny, J. A. (1990). A comparison of alprazolam and behavior therapy in treatment of panic disorder. *Journal of Consulting and Clinical Psychology,* *58,* 77–84.

Kobasa, S. C. (1982). The hardy personality: Toward a social psychology of stress and health. In G. S. Sanders & J. Suls (Eds.), *Social psychology of health and illness* (pp. 3–32). Hillsdale, NJ: Erlbaum.

Kohout, J. L., Wicherski, M. M., Popanz, T. J., & Pion, G. M. (1990). *1989 salaries in psychology. Report of the 1989 APA Salary Survey.* Washington, DC: American Psychological Association.

Kohut, H. (1971). *The analysis of the self.* New York: International Universities Press.

Kohut, H. (1977). *The restoration of the self.* New York: International Universities Press.

Kohut, H. (1984). *How does analysis cure?* Chicago: University of Chicago Press.

Kolko, D. J., Kazdin, A. E., & Meyer, E. C. (1985). Aggression and psychopathology in childhood firesetters: Parent and child report. *Journal of Consulting and Clinical Psychology, 53,* 377–385.

Koocher, G. P. (1994). The commerce of professional psychology and the new ethics code. *Professional Psychology: Research and Practice, 25,* 355–361.

Koocher, G. P., & Keith-Spiegal, P. (1998). *Ethics in Psychology.* New York: Oxford.

Koran, L. M., Thienemann, M. L., & Davenport, R. (1996). Quality of life for patients with obsessive-compulsive disorder. *American Journal of Psychiatry, 153,* 783–788.

Korczyn, A. D., Kahana, E., & Galper, Y. (1991). Epidemiology of dementia in Ashkelon, Israel. *Neuroepidemiology, 10,* 100.

Korman, M. (Ed.) (1976). *Levels and patterns of professional training in psychology.* Washington, DC: American Psychological Association.

Kovacs, A. (1996, March/April). Advice to the new professional. *The National Psychologist, 5,* 14.

Kovacs, M. (1985). The Children's Depression Inventory (CDI). *Psychopharmacology Bulletin, 21,* 995–998.

Kramer, P. D. (1993). *Listening to Prozac.* New York: Viking Press.

Krantz, D. S., Constrada, R. J., Hill, D. R., & Friedler, E. (1988). Environmental stress and biobehavioral antecedents of coronary heart disease. *Journal of Consulting and Clinical Psychology, 56,* 333–341.

Krasner, L., & Ullmann, L. P. (Eds.) (1965). *Research in behavior modification: New developments and implications.* New York: Holt, Rinehart, & Winston.

Krishnan, K. R., Doraiswamy, P. M., Ventkataraman, S., Reed, D., & Richie, J. C. (1991). Current concepts in hypothalamopituitaryadnrenal axis regulation. In J. A. McCubbin, P. G. Kaufmann, & C. B. Nemeroff (Eds.), *Stress, neuropeptidues, and sytemic disease* (pp. 19–35). San Diego: Academic Press.

Kurpius, D. (1985). Consultation interventions: Successes, failures, and proposals. *Conseling Psychologist, 13,* 368–389.

Kurpius, D., Fuqua, D., & Rozecki, T. (1993). The consulting process: A multidimensional approach. *Journal of Counseling and Development, 71,* 601–606.

Kurpius, D. J., & Lewis, J. E. (1988). Introduction to consultation: An intervention for advocacy and outreach. In D. J. Kurpius & D. Brown (Eds.), *Handbook of consultation: An intervention for advocacy and outreach* (pp. 1–4). Alexandria, VA: American Association for Counseling and Development.

Lafferty, P., Beutler, L. E., & Crago, M. (1991). Differences between more and less effective psychotherapists: A study of select therapist variables. *Journal of Consulting and Clinical Psychology, 57,* 76–80.

LaFromboise, T. D. (1988). American Indian mental health policy. *American Psychologist, 43,* 388–397.

Lakin, M. (1994). Morality in group and family therapies: Multiperson therapies and the 1992 Ethics Code. *Professional Psychology: Research and Practice, 25,* 344–348.

Laliotis, D. A., & Grayson, J. H. (1985). Psychologist heal thyself: What is available for the impaired psychologist? *American Psychologist, 40,* 84–96.

Lam, D. J. (1991). The Tao of clinical psychology: Shifting from a medical to a biopsychosocial paradigm. *Bulletin of the Hong Kong Psychological Society, 26,* 107–113.

Lambert, L. E., & Wertheimer, M. (1988). Is diagnostic ability related to relevant training and experience? *Professional Psychology: Reearch and Practice, 19,* 50–52.

Lambert, M. J. (1986). Implications of psychotherapy outcome research for eclectic psychotherapy. In J. C. Norcross (ed.), *Handbook of eclectic psychotherapy* (pp. 436–462). New York: Brunner/Mazel.

Lambert, M. J. (1992). Psychotherapy outcome reserch: Implications for integrative and eclectic therapists. In J. C. Norcross & M. R. Goldfried (Eds.), *Handbook of psychotherapy integration.* New York: Basic.

Lambert, M. J., & Bergin, A. E. (1994). The effectiveness of psychotherapy. In A. E. Bergin & S. L. Garfield (Eds.), *Handbook of psychotherapy and behavior change* (4th ed., pp. 143–189). New York: Wiley.

Lambert, M. J., Shapiro, D. A., & Bergin, A. E. (1986). The effectiveness of psychotherapy. In S. L. Garfield and A. E. Bergin (Eds.), *Handbook of psychotherapy and behavior change* (3rd ed., pp 157–211). New York: Wiley.

Lambert, N., Eland, H., & Nihira, K. (1992). *AAMR Adaptive Behavior Scales-School (2nd ed.).* Monterey, CA: Publishers Test Service.

Landman, J. T., & Dawes, R. (1982). Psychotherapy outcome: Smith Glass's conclusions stand up under scrutiny. *American Psychologist, 37,* 504–516.

Landrine, H. (1992). Clinical implications of cultural differences: The referential versus indexical self. *Clinical Psychology Review, 12,* 401–415.

Lanyon, B. P., & Lanyon, R. I. (1980). *Incomplete Sentence Task: Manual.* Chicago: Stoelting.

Larsen, K. G., Belar, C. D., Bieliauskas, L. A., Klepac, R. K., Stigall, T. T., & Zimet, C. N. (1993). *Proceedings from the National Conference on Postdoctoral Training in Professional Psychology.* Washington, DC: Association of Psychology Postdoctoral and Internship Centers.

La Rue, A. (1992). *Aging and neuropsycological assessment.* New York: Plenum.

Lawson, T. J. (1995). Gaining admission into graduate programs in psychology: An update. *Teaching of Psychology, 22,* 225–227.

Layman, M. J., & McNamara, J. R. (1997). Remediation for ethics violations: Focus on psychotherapists' sexual contact with clients. *Professional Psychology: Research and Practice, 28,* 281–292.

Lazarus, A. A. (1971). *Behavior therapy and beyond.* New York: McGraw-Hill.

Lazarus, A. A. (1981). *The practice of multimodal therapy.* New York: McGraw-Hill.

Lazarus, A. A. (Ed.) (1985). *Casebook of multimodal therapy.* New York: Guilford.

Lazarus, A. A. (1986). Multimodal therapy. In J.C. Norcross (Ed.), *Handbook of eclectic psychotherapy* (pp. 286–326). New York: Guilford.

Lazarus, A. A. (1989). *The practice of multimodal therapy.* Baltimore: Johns Hopkins University Press.

Lazarus, A. A. (1995). Integration and clinical verisimilitude. *Clinical Psychology: Science and Practice, 2,* 399–402.

Lazarus, A. A. (1996). The utility and futility of combining treatments in psychotherapy. *Clinical Psychology: Science and Practice, 3,* 59–68.

Lebow, J. L. (1984). On the value of integrating approaches to family therapy. *Journal of Marital and Family Therapy, 10,* 127–138.

Lechnyr, R. (1992). Cost savings and effectiveness of mental health services. *Journal of the Oregon Psychological Association, 38,* 8–12.

Lechnyr, R. (1993). The cost savings of mental health services. *EAP Digest, 22,* 1–3.

Lee, C. K. (1992). Alcoholism in Korea. In J. Helzer & G. Canino (Eds.), *Alcoholism-North America, Europe and Asia: A coordinated analysis of population data from ten regions* (pp. 247–262). London: Oxford University Press.

Levy, L. (1962). The skew in clinical psychology. *American Psychologist, 29,* 441–449.

Levy, L. H. (1984). The metamorphosis of clinical psychology: Towards a new charter as human services psychology. *American Psychologist, 39,* 486–494.

Levy, S. M. (1983). Host differences in neoplastic risk: Behavioral and social contributions to disease. *Health Psychology, 2,* 21–44.

Lewinsohn, P. M., & Shaffer, M. (1977). Use of home observations as an integral part of the treatment of depression: Preliminary report and case studies. *Journal of Consulting and Clinical Psychology, 37,* 87–94.

Lewis, G., David, A., Andreasson, S., & Allsbeck, P. (1992). Schizophrenia and city life. *Lancet, 340,* 137–140.

Lewis, J. F., & Mercer, J. R. (1978). The System of Multicultural Pluralistic Assessment (SOMPA). In W. A. Coulter & H. W. Morrow (Eds.), *Adaptive behavior: Concepts and measurement* (pp. 185–212). Orlando, FL: Grune & Stratton.

Lewis, O. (1969). A Puerto Rican boy. In J. C. Finney (Ed.), *Culture, change, mental health, and poverty.* New York: Simon and Schuster.

Lex, B. W. (1985). Alcohol problems in special populations. In J. H. Mendelson & N. K. Mello (Eds.), *The diagnosis and treatment of alcoholism* (2nd ed., pp. 89–187). New York: McGraw-Hill.

Liberman, B. L. (1978). The role of mastery in psychotherapy: Maintenance of improvement and prescriptive change. In J. D. Frank, R. Hoehn-Saric, S. D. Imber, B. L. Liberman, & A. A. Stone (Eds.), *Effective ingredients of successful psychotherapy* (pp. 1–34). New York: Brunner/Mazel.

Linehan, M. M. (1993). *Cognitive-behavioral treatment of borderline personality disorder.* New York: Guilford Press.

Linkins, R. W., & Comstock, G. W. (1988). Depressed mood and development of cancer. *American Journal of Epidemiology, 128,* 894–901.

Lippitt, G., & Lippitt, R. (1986). *The consulting process in action* (2nd ed.). La Jolla, CA: University Associates.

Lipsey, M. & Wilson, D. (1993). The efficacy of psychological, educational, and behavioral treatment: Confirmation from meta-analysis. *American Psychologist, 48,* 1181–1209.

Litwin, W. J., Boswell, D. L., & Kraft, W. A. (1991). Medical staff membership and clinical privileges: A survey of hospital-affiliated psychologists. *Professional Psychology: Research and Practice, 22,* 322–327.

Loehlin, J. C. (1992). *Genes and environment in personality development.* Newbury Park, CA: Sage.

London, P. (1988). Metamorphosis in psychotherapy: Slouching toward integration. *Journal of Integrative and eclectic Psychotherapy, 7,* 3–12.

Lopez, S. R., Grover, K. P., Holland, D., Johnson, M. J., Kain, C. D., Kanel, K., Mellins, C. A., & Rhyne, M. C. (1989). Development of culturally sensitive psychotherapists. *Professional Psychology: Research and Practice, 20,* 369–376.

Lorion, R. P. (1996). Applying our medicine to the psychopharmacology debate. *American Psychologist, 51,* 219–224.

Lubin, B., Larsen, R. M., Matarazzo, J. D., & Seever, M. (1985). Psychological test usage patterns in five professional settings. *American Psychologist, 40,* 857–861.

Luborsky, L., & DeRubeis, R. J. (1984). The use of psychotherapy treatment manuals—a small revolution in psychotherapy research style. *Clinical Psychology Review, 4,* 5–14.

Luborsky, L., Singer, B., & Luborsky, L. (1975). Comparative studies of psychotherapy. *Archives of General Psychiatry, 32,* 995–1008.

Lykken, D. T. (1991). *Science, lies and controversy: An epitaph for the polygraph.* Invited address upon receipt of the Senior Career award for Distinquished Contribution to Psychology in the Public Interest, American Psychological Association.

Lyons, L. C., & Woods, P. J. (1991). The efficacy of rational-emotive therapy: A quantitative review of the outcome research. *Clinical Psychology Review, 11,* 357–369.

MacDonald, G. (1996). Inferences in therapy: Processes and hazards. *Professional Psychology: Research and Practice, 27,* 600–603.

Machover, K. (1949). *Personality projection in the drawing of the human figure.* Springfield, IL: Charles C. Thomas.

MacKinnon, D. W. (1944). The structure of personality. In J. McVicker Hunt (Ed.), *Personality and the behavior disorders* (Vol. 1, pp. 3–48). New York: Ronald Press.

Magnusson, D. (1981). *Toward a psychology of situations: An interactional perspective.* Hillsdale, NJ: Erlbaum.

Maher, B. A. & Maher, W. B. (1985a). Psychopathology: I. From ancient times to the eighteenth century. In G. A. Kimble & K. Schlesinger (Eds.), *Topics in the history of psychology* (pp. 251–294). Hillsdale, NJ: Erlbaum.

Maher, B. A. & Maher, W. B. (1985b). Psychopathology: II. From the eighteenth century to modern times. In G. A. Kimble & K. Schlesinger (Eds.), *Topics in the history of psychology* (pp. 295–329). Hillsdale, NJ: Erlbaum.

Mahler, M. (1952). On child psychosis and schizophrenia: Autistic and symbiotic infantile psychoses. *Psychoanalytic Study of the Child, 7,* 206–305.

Mahoney, M. J. (1974). *Cognition and behavior modification.* Cambridge, MA: Ballinger.

Mahoney, M. J. (1988). The cognitive sciences and psychotherapy: Patterns in developing relationships. In K. S. Dobson (Ed.), *Handbook of cognitive-behavioral therapies* (pp. 357–386). New York: Guilford Press.

Mariotto, M. J., & Paul, G. L. (1974), A multimethod validation of the Inpatient Multidimensional Psychiatric Scale with chronically institutionalized patients. *Journal of Consulting and Clinical Psychology, 42,* 497–508.

Marlatt, G. A., & Gordon, J. R. (Eds.) (1985). *Relapse prevention: Maintenance strategies in the treatment of addictive behaviors.* New York: Guilford Press.

Martin, S. (1995, September). APA to pursue prescription privileges. *APA Monitor,* p.6.

Mash, E. J. & Barkley, R. A. (Eds.) (1989). *Treatment of childhood disorders.* New York: Guilford.

Maslow, A. H. (1954). *Motivation and personality.* New York: Harper.

Maslow, A. H. (1971). *The farther reaches of human nature.* New York: Viking Press.

Masterson, J. L. (1981). *The narcissistic and borderline disorders: An integrated developmental approach.* New York: Brunner/Mazel.

Matarazzo, J. D. (1980). Behavioral health and behavioral medicine: Frontiers for a new health psychology. *American Psychologist, 35,* 807–817.

Matarazzo, J. D. (1982). Behavioral health's challenge to academic, scientific, and professional psychology. *American Psychologist, 37,* 1–14.

Matarazzo, J. D. (1984). Behavioral immunogens and pathogens in health and illness. In B. L. Hammonds & C. J. Scheirer (Eds.), *Psychology and health: The master lecture series* (Vol. 3, pp. 9–43). Washington, DC: American Psychological Association.

Matarazzo, J. D. (1987). There is only one psychology, no specialties, but many applications. *American Psychologist, 42,* 893–903.

Matarazzo, J. D. (1992). Psychological testing and assessment in the 21st century. *American Psychologist, 47,* 1007–1018.

Matt, G. E. (1989). Decision rules for selecting effect sizes in meta-analysis: A review and reanalysis of psychotherapy outcome studies. *Psychological Bulletin, 105,* 106–115.

Matthews, J. (1983). *The effective use of management consultants in higher education.* Boulder, CO: National Center for Higher Education Management Services.

Matthews, J. (1995, December 28). CEOs feeling flush: HMO execs cut costs and salaries by not their own. *Washington Post.*

Matthews, K. A., Woodall, K. L., & Allen, M. T. (1993). Cardiovascular reactivity to stress predicts future blood pressure status. *Hypertension, 22* (4), 479–485.

May, R. (1977). *The meaning of anxiety.* New York: Norton.

May, R., Angel, E., & Ellenberger, H. (Eds.) (1958). *Existence: A new dimension in psychiatry and psychology.* New York: Basic Books.

Mayne, T. J, Norcross, J. C., & Sayette, M. A. (1994a). Admission requirements, acceptance rates, and financial assistance in clinical psychology programs: Diversity across the practice-research continuum. *American Psychologist, 49,* 806–811.

Mayne, T. J., Norcross, J. C., & Sayette, M. A. (1994b). *Insider's guide to graduate programs in clinical psychology.* New York, Guilford.

Mays, D. T., & Frank, C. M. (1980). Getting worse: Psychotherapy or no treatment. The jury should still be out. *Professional Psychology, 11,* 78–92.

Mays, D. T., & Frank, C. M. (1985). *Negative outcome in psychotherapy and what to do about it.* New York: Springer.

Mazziotta, J. C. (1996). Mapping mental illness: A new era. *Archives of General Psychiatry, 53,* 574–576.

McArthur, D. S., & Roberts, G. E. (1982). *Roberts Apperception Test for Children: Manual.* Los Angeles: Western Psychological Services.

McCall, R. B. (1988). Science and the press: Like oil and water? *American Psychologist, 43,* 87–94.

McCall, R. B., & Garriger, M. S. (1993). A meta–analysis of infant habituation and recognition memory performance as predictors of later IQ. *Child Development, 64,* 57–79.

McCaul, K. D., Branstetter, A. D., Schroeder, D. M., & Glasgow, R. E. (1996). What is the relationship between breast cancer risk and mammography screening? A meta-analytic review. *Health Psychology, 15,* 423–429.

McConnell, H. W., & Snyder, P. J. (Eds.) (1997). *Psychiatric comorbidity in epilepsy: Basic mechanisms, diagnosis, and treatment.* Washington, DC: American Psychiatric Association Press.

McDaniel, S. H. (1995). Collaboration between psychologists and family physicians: Implementing the biopsychosocial model. *Professional Psychology: Research and Practice, 26,* 117–122.

McDevitt, S. (1996). The impact of news media on child abuse reporting. *Child Abuse and Neglect, 20,* 261–274.

McGinnis, J. M. (1984). Occupant protection as a priority in national efforts to promote health. *Health Education Quarterly, 11,* 127–131.

McGinnis, M., Richmond, J. B., Brandt, E. N., Windom, R. E., & Mason, J. O. (1992). Health progress in the United States: Results of the 1990 objectives for the nation. *Journal of the American Medical Association, 268,* 2545–2552.

McGlashan, T. H. (1986). The chestnut lodge follow-up study. *Archives of General Psychiatry, 43,* 20–30.

McGrath, E. (1995). Are we trading our souls for a sound bite? *APA Monitor, 24,* 5.

McGue, M., & Lykken, D. T. (1992). Genetic influence on risk of divorce. *Psychological Science, 3,* 368–373.

McGuffin, P., Katz, R., & Bebbington, P. (1988). The Camberwell Collaborative Depression Study. III. Depression and adversity in the relatives of depressed probands. *British Journal of Psychiatry, 152,* 775–782.

McGuire, F. L. (1982). Treatment of the drinking driver. *Health Psychology, 1,* 137–152.

McKim, W. A. (1991). *Drugs and behavior: An introduction to behavioral pharmacology* (2nd ed.). Englewood Cliffs, NJ: Prentice-Hall.

McLeod, J. D., Kessler, R. C., & Landis, K. R. (1992). Speed of recovery from major depressive episodes in a community sample of married men and women. *Journal of Abnormal Psychology, 101,* 277–286.

McNeill, B. W., May, R. J., & Lee, V. E. (1987). Perceptions of counselor source characteristics by premature and successful terminators. *Journal of Counseling Psychology, 34,* 86–89.

McReynolds, P. (1987). Lightner Witmer: Little-known founder of clinical psychology. *American Psychologist, 42,* 849–858.

Mechanic, D., & Rochefort, D. A. (1992). A policy for inclusion for the mentally ill. *Health Affairs, 11,* 128–150.

Meehl, P. E. (1954). *Clinical versus statistical prediction.* Minneapolis: University of Minnesota Press.

Meehl, P. (1962). Schizotaxia, schizotypy, schizophrenia. *American Psychologist, 17,* 827–838.

Meehl, P. (1965). Seer over sign: The first good example. *Journal of Experimental Research in Personality, 1,* 27–32.

Meehl, P. (1997). Credentialed persons, credentialed knowledge. *Clinical Psychology: Science and Practice, 4,* 91–98.

Megargee, E. J. (1990). *A guide to obtaining a psychology internship.* Muncie, IN: Accelerated Development.

Meichenbaum, D. H. (1977). *Cognitive-behavior modification.* New York: Plenum.

Mercer, J.R., & Lewis, J. F. (1979). *System of Multicultural Pluralistic Assessment.* Cleveland, OH: Psychological Corporation.

Mermelstein, H. T., & Holland, J. C. (1991). Psychotherapy by telephone: A therapeutic tool for cancer patients. *Psychosomatics, 32,* 407–412.

Messer, S. B. (1983). Integrating psychoanalytic and behaviour therapy: Limitations, possibilities, and trade-offs. *British Journal of Clinical Psychology, 22,* 131–132.

Meyer, A. J., Nash, J. D., McAlister, A. L., Maccoby, M., & Farquhar, J. W. (1980). Skills training in a cardiovascular health education campaign. *Journal of Consulting and Clinical Psychology, 2,* 129–142.

Meyer, A. J., Maccoby, M., Farquhar, J. W. (1980). Reply to Kasl and Levethal et al. *Journal of Consulting and Clinical Psychology, 48,* 159–163.

Michels, R. (1995). Dehumanizing developments in American psychiatry. *Journal of Nervous and Mental Disease, 183,* 204–205.

Milberg, W., Hebben, N., & Kaplan, E. (1986). The Boston Process Approach to neuropsychological assessment. In I. Grant & K. M. Adams (Eds.), *Neuropsychological assessment of neuropsychiatric disorders* (pp. 65–86). New York: Oxford University Press.

Miller, J. G. (1946). Clinical psychology in the Veterans Administration. *American Psychologist, 1,* 181–189.

Miller, J. G. (1978). *Living systems.* New York: McGraw Hill.

Miller, N. E. (1987). Education for a lifetime of learning. In G. C. Stone, S. M. Weiss, J. D. Matarazzo, N. E. Miller, J. Rodin, C. D. Belar, M. J. Follick, & J. E. Singer (Eds.). *Health psychology: A discipline and a profession* (pp. 3–14). Chicago: University of Chicago Press.

Miller, T. Q., Smith, T. W., Turner, C. W., Guijarro, M. L., & Hallet, A. J. (1996). A meta-analytic review of research on hostility and physical health. *Psychological Bulletin, 119,* 322–348.

Miller, T., & Swartz, L. (1990). Clinical psychology in general hospital settings: Issues in interprofessional relationships. *Professional Psychology: Research and Practice, 21,* 48–53.

Miller, W. R., & DiPilato, M. (1983). Treatment of nightmares via relaxation and desensitization: A controlled evaluation. *Journal of Consulting and Clinical Psychology, 51,* 870–877.

Millon, T. (1981). *Disorders of personality: DSM-III, Axis II.* New York: John Wiley.

Millon, T. (1987). *Manual for the Millon Clinical Multiaxial Inventory-II.* Minneapolis, MN: NCS Assessments.

Millon, T., Green, C., & Meagher, R. B. (1982). *Manual for the Millon Behavioral Health Inventory.* Minneapolis, MN: NCS Assessments.

Millon, T., Millon, C., & Davis, R. (1982). *Manual for the Millon Adolescent Personality Inventory.* Minneapolis, MN: NCS Assessments.

Millon, T., Millon, C., & Davis, R. (1994). *Manual for the Millon Adolescent Clinical Inventory.* Minneapolis, MN: NCS Assessments.

Millon, T., Millon, C., & Davis, R. (1997). *Manual for the Millon Clinical Multiaxial Inventory-III.* Minneapolis, MN: NCS Assessments.

Minuchin, S. (1974). *Families and family therapy.* Cambridge, MA: Harvard University Press.

Minuchin, S., & Fishman, H. C. (1981). *Family therapy techniques.* Cambridge, MA: Harvard University Press.

Mischel, W. (1968). *Personality and assessment.* New York: Wiley.

Mischel, W. (1973). Toward a cognitive social learning reconceptualization of personality. *Psychological Review, 80,* 252–283.

Mischel, W. (1986). *Introduction to personality* (4th ed.). New York: Holt, Rinehart, & Winston.

Mjoseth, J. (February, 1998). New diagnostic system could benefit psychologists. *APA Monitor, 29.*

Mogul, K. M. (1982). Overview: The sex of the therapist. *American Journal of Psychiatry, 139,* 1–11.

Mohr, D. C. (1995). Negative outcome in psychotherapy: A critical review. *Clinical Psychology: Science and Practice, 2,* 1–27.

Mohr, D. C., Beutler, L. E., Engle, D., Shoham-Salomon, V., Bergan, J., Kaszniak, A. W., & Yost, E. (1990). Identification of patients at risk for nonresponse and negative outcome in psychotherapy. *Journal of Consulting and Clinical Psychology, 58,* 622–628.

Molyneaux, D., & Lane, V. (1982). *Effective interviewing: Techniques and analysis.* Boston: Allyn & Bacon.

Mora, G. (1985). History of psychiatry. In H. Kaplan & B. J. Sadock (Eds.), *Comprehensive textbook of psychiatry* (Vol. 4, pp. 1034–2054). Baltimore, MD: Williams & Wilkins.

Murase, K. (1977). Minorities: Asian-American. *Encyclopedia of Social Work, 2,* 953–960.

Murphy, M. J., DeBernardo, C. R., & Shoemaker, W. E. (1998). Impact of managed care on independent practice and professional ethics: A survey of independent practitioners. *Professional Psychology: Research and Practice, 29,* 43–51.

Murphy, P. M., Cramer, D., & Lillie, F. J. (1984). The relationship between curative factors perceived by patients in their psychotherapy and treatment outcome: An exploratory study. *British Journal of Medical Psychology, 57,* 187–192.

Murphy, R. A., & Halgin, R. P. (1995). Influences on the career choice of psychotherapists. *Professional Psychology: Research and Practice, 26,* 422–426.

Murray, H. A. (1938). *Explorations in personality.* New York: Oxford.

Murray, H. A., & Bellak, L. (1942). *Thematic Apperception Test.* Cambridge, MA: Harvard University Press.

Murray, H. A. (1943). *Thematic Apperception Test.* Cambridge, MA: Harvard University Press.

Myers, P. I., & Hammil, D. D. (1990). *Learning disabilities: Basic concepts, assessment practices, and instructional strategies* (4th ed.). Austin, TX: Pro-Ed.

Naglieri, J. A., & Bardos, A. N. (1997). *Manual for the General Ability Measure for Adults.* Minnetonka, MN: NCS Assessments.

Nagy, T. (1997, November). Electronic ethics. *APA Monitor, 26,* 3.

Nathan, P. E. (1993). Alcoholism: Psychopathology, etiology, and treatment. In P. B. Sutker & H. E. Adams (Eds.), *Comprehensive handbook of psychopathology* (pp. 451–476). New York: Plenum.

Nathan, P. E. (1996). Validated forms of psychotherapy may lead to better-validated psychotherapy. *Clinical Psychology: Science and Practice, 3,* 251–255.

National Advisory Mental Health Council (1995). Basic behavioral science research for mental health: A national investment. *American Psychologist, 50,* 485–495.

National Association of Social Workers (1995). *NASW Membership Demographics.* Washington, DC: National Association of Social Workers.

National Center for Health Statistics (1992). *Vital statistics of the United States, 1992.* Washington, DC: Government Printing Office.

National Center for Health Statistics (1993). *Health, U.S., 1992.* Hyattsville, MD: Public Health Service.

National Institutes of Health (1992). Methods for voluntary weight loss and control. *Technology Assessment Conference Statement, March 30–April 1, 1992.* Bethesda, MD: National Institutes of Health.

National Mental Health Association (1986). *The prevention of mental-emotional disabilities. Report of the Commission on Prevention.* Alexandria, VA: Author.

National Science Foundation (1994). *Women, minorities, and persons with disabilities in science and engineering: 1994* (NSF 94–333). Arlington, VA: Author.

Ndetei, D. M., & Singh, A. (1983). Hallucinations in Kenyan schizophrenic patients. *Acta Psychiatrica Scandinavica, 67,* 144–147.

Neisser, U., Boodoo, G., Bouchard, T. J., Boykin, A. W., Ceci, S. J., Halpern, D. F., Loehlin, J. C., Perloff, R., Sternberg, R. J., & Urbina, S. (1996). Intelligence: knowns and unknowns. *American Psychologist, 51,* 77–101.

Newcombe, F. (1996). Very late outcome after focal wartime brain wounds. *Journal of Clinical and Experimental Neuropsychology, 18,* 1–23.

Newman, M. G., & Borkovec, T. D. (1995). Cognitive-behavioral treatment for generalized anxiety disorder. *The Clinical Psychologist, 48,* 5–7.

Newman, R., & Taylor, G. (1996, June). Practitioner survey results offer comprehensive view of psychology practice. *Practioner Update, 4,* 1–4.

Nezu, A. M. (1996). What are we doing to our patients and should we care if anyone else knows? *Clinical Psychology: Science and Practice, 3,* 160–163.

Nguyen, T. D., Attkisson, C. C., & Stegner, B. L. (1983). Assessment of patient satisfaction: Development and refinement of a Service Evaluation Questionnaire. *Evaluation and Program Planning, 6,* 299–313.

Nicholson, R. A., & Berman, J. S. (1983). Is follow-up necessary in evaluating psychotherapy? *Psychological Bulletin, 93,* 261–278.

Nickelson, D. W. (1995). The future of professional psychology in a changing health care marketplace: A conversation with Russ Newman. *Professional Psychology: Research and Practice, 26,* 366–370.

Nietzel, M. T., Bernstein, D. A., & Milich, R. (1991). *Introduction to clinical psychology* (3rd ed.). Englewood Cliffs, NJ: Prentice-Hall.

Nietzel, M. T., Russell, R. L., Hemmings, K. A., & Gretter, M. L. (1987). Clinical significance of psychotherapy for unipolar depression: A meta-analytic approach to social comparison. *Journal of Consulting and Clinical Psychology, 55,* 156–161.

Norcross, J. C. (1990). An eclectic definition of psychotherapy. In J. K. Zeig & W. M. Munion (Eds.), *What is psychotherapy, 28,* 439–472.

Norcross, J. C. (1995). Dispelling the DoDo bird verdict and exclusivity myth in psychotherapy. *Psychotherapy, 32,* 500–504.

Norcross, J. C., Alford, B. A., & DeMichele, J. T. (1992). The future of psychotherapy: Delphi data and concluding observations. *Psychotherapy, 29,* 150–158.

Norcross, J. C. & Goldfried, M. R. (Eds.) (1992). *Handbook of psychotherapy integration.* New York: Basic Books.

Norcross, J. C. & Guy, J. D. (1989) Ten therapists: The process of becoming and being. In W. Dryden & L. Spurling (Eds.), *On becoming a psychotherapist* (pp. 215–239). London: Tavistock/Routledge.

Norcross, J. C., Hanych, J. M., & Terranova, R. D. (1996). Graduate study in psychology: 1992–1993. *American Psychologist, 51,* 631–643.

Norcross, J. C., Karg, R. S., & Prochaska, J. O. (1997a). Clinical psychologists in the 1990's. Part I. *The Clinical Psychologist, 50,* 4–9.

Norcross, J. C., Karg, R. & Prochaska, J. O. (1997b). Clinical psychologists in the 1990's: Part II. *The Clinical Psychologist, 50,* 4–11.

Norcross, J. C. & Prochaska, J. O. (1983a). Clinicians' theoretical orientations: Selections, utilization, and efficacy. *Professional Psychology: Research and Practice, 14,* 197–208.

Norcross, J. C. & Prochaska, J. O. (1983b). Psychotherapists in independent practice: Some findings and issues. *Professional Psychology: Research and Practice, 14,* 869–881.

Norcross, J. C. & Prochaska, J. O. (1988). A study of eclectic (and integrative) views revisited. *Professional Psychology: Research and Practice, 19,* 170–174.

Norcross, J. C., Prochaska, J. O., & Gallagher, K. M. (1989). Clinical psychologists in the 1980s: I. Demographics, affiliations, and satisfactions. *The Clinical Psychologist, 42,* 29–39.

Norcross, J. C., Sayette, M. A., & Mayne, T. J. (1996). *Insider's guide to graduate programs in clinical and counseling psychology.* New York: Guilford.

Norcross, J. C., Strausser-Kirtland, D., & Missar, C. D. (1988). The processes and outcomes of psychotherapists' personal treatment experiences. *Psychotherapy, 25,* 36–43.

Nurnberger, J. I., & Gershon, E. S. (1992). Genetics. In E. S. Paykel (Ed.), *Handbook of affective disorders* (pp. 126–145). New York: Guilford.

O'Leary, A. (1992). Self-efficacy and health: Behavioral and stress-physiological mediation. *Cognitive Therapy and Research, 16,* 229–245.

O'Leary, K. D., & Becker, W. C. (1967). Behavior modification of an adjustment class: A token reinforcement program. *Exceptional Children, 33,* 637–642.

O'Leary, K. D., & Wilson, G. T. (1987). *Behavior therapy: Application and outcome.* Englewood Cliffs, NJ: Prentice-Hall.

Ockene, J. K. (Ed.). (1986). *The pharmacologic treatment of tobacco dependence: Proceedings of the World Congress, November 4–5, 1985.* Cambridge, MA: Institute for the Study of Smoking Behavior and Policy, Harvard University.

Olson, S. K., Downing, N. E., Heppner, P. P., & Pinkney, J. (1986). Is there life after graduate school? Coping with the transition to postdoctoral employment. *Professional Psychology: Research and Practice, 17,* 415–419.

Ornberg, B., & Zalewski, C. (1994). Assessment of adolescents with the Rorschach: A critical review. *Assessment, 1,* 209–217.

OSS Assessment Staff (1948). *Assessment of men: Selection of personnel for the Office of Strategic Services.* New York: Rinehart.

Overall, J. E., & Pfefferbaum, B. (1962). The Brief Psychiatric Rating Scale for Children. *Psychopharmacology Bulletin, 18,* 10–16.

Pandina, R. J. (1986). Methods, problems, and trends in studies of adolescent drinking practices. *Annals of Behavioral Medicine, 8,* 20–26.

Pargament, K. I., Falgout, K., Ensing, D. S., Reilly, B., et al. (1991). The Congregation Development Program: Data–based consultation with churches and synagogues. *Professional Psychology: Research and Practice, 22,* 393–404.

Parker, K. C. H. (1983). A meta-analysis of the reliability and validity of the Rorschach. *Journal of Personality Assessment, 47,* 227–231.

Parker, K. C. H., Hanson, R. K., & Hunsley, J. (1988). MMPI, Rorschach, and WAIS: A meta-analytic comparison of reliability, stability, and validity. *Psychological Bulletin, 103,* 367–373.

Patterson, G. R. (1977). Naturalistic observation in clinical assessment. *Journal of Abnormal Child Psychology, 5,* 307–322.

Payton, C. R. (1994). Implications of the 1992 Ethics Code for diverse groups. *Professional Psychology: Research and Practice, 25,* 317–320.

Peck, C. P., & Ash, E. (1964). Training in the Veterans Administration. In L. Blank & H. P. David (Eds.), *Sourcebook for training in clinical psychology* (pp. 61–81). New York: Springer.

Pelham, W. E. (1993). Pharmacotherapy for children with attention-deficit hyperactivity disorder. *School Psychology Review, 22,* 199–227.

Pennebaker, J. W. (1990). *Opening up: The healing power of confidence in others.* New York: William Morrow.

Pennington, B. F., & Smith, S. D. (1988). Genetic influences on learning disabilities: An update. *Journal of Consulting and Clinical Psychology, 56,* 817–823.

Perls, F. S. (1947). *Ego, hunger and aggression: A revision of Freud's theory and method.* New York: Random House.

Perls, F. S. (1969). *Gestalt therapy verbatim.* Lafayette, CA: Real People Press.

Peterson, D. R. (1968). The doctor of psychology program at the University of Illinois. *American Psychologist, 23,* 511–516.

Peterson, D. R., & Baron, A. (1975). Status of the University of Illinois doctor of psychology program, 1974. *Professional Psychology, 6,* 88–95.

Phelps, R. (1996, February). Preliminary practitioner survey results enhance APA's understanding of health care environment. *Practitioner Focus, 9,* 5.

Phelps, R., Eisman, E. J., & Kohout, J. (1998). Psychological practice and managed care: Results of the CAPP practitioner survey. *Professional Psychology: Research and Practice, 29,* 31–36.

Phillips, E. L., & Fagan, P. J. (1982, August). *Attrition: Focus on the intake and first therapy interviews.* Paper presented at the 90th annual convention of the American Psychological Association, Washington, DC.

Piaget, J. (1952). *The origins of intelligence in children.* New York: International Universities Press.

Piaget, J. (1970). *Science of education and the psychology of the child.* New York: Orion.

Piaget, J. (1972). Intellectual evolution from adolescence to adulthood. *Human Development, 15,* 1–12.

Pike, K. M., & Rodin, J. (1991). Mothers, daughters, and disordered eating. *Journal of Abnormal Psychology, 100,* 1–7.

Pilkonis, P. A., Imber, S. D., Lewis, P., & Rubinsky, P. (1984). A comparative outcome study of individual, group, and cojoint psychotherapy. *Archives of General Psychiatry, 41,* 431–437.

Pillay, A. L. (1990). The increasing demand for clinical psychological consultations in the smaller general hospital. *South African Journal of Psychology, 20,* 163–169.

Pimental, P. A., Stout, C. E., Hoover, M. C., & Kamen, G. B. (1997). *Professional Psychology: Research and Practice, 28,* 123–127.

Pion, G. M., Mednick, M. T., Astin, H. S., Hall, C. C. I., Kenkel, M. B., Keita, G. P., Kohout, J. L., Kelleher, J. C. (1996). The shifting gender composition of psychology: Trends and implications for the discipline. *American Psychologist, 51,* 509–528.

Piotrowski, C., & Keller, J. W. (1989). Psychological testing in outpatient mental health facilities: A national study. *Professional Psychology: Research and Practice, 20,* 423–425.

Plante, T. G. (1988). Postdoctoral training in clinical psychology: As amorphous as an inkblot. *Professional Psychology: Research and Practice, 19,* 251–253.

Plante, T. G. (1995). Training child clinical predoctoral interns and postdoctoral fellows in ethics and professional issues: An experiential model. *Professional Psychology: Research and Practice, 26,* 616–619.

Plante, T. G. (1996a). Catholic priests who sexually abuse minors: Why do we hear so much yet know so little? *Pastoral Psychology, 44,* 305–310.

Plante, T. G. (1996b). Ten principles of success for psychology trainees embarking on their careers. *Professional Psychology: Research and Practice, 27,* 304–307.

Plante, T. G., Andersen, E., & Boccaccini, M. Empirically validated treatments and related contemporary changes in professional psychology practice: what do clinical ABPs think? Under review.

Plante, T. G., Boccaccini, M., & Andersen, E. (1998). Attitudes concerning professional issues impacting psychotherapy among members of the American Board of Professional Psychology. *Psychotherapy, 35,* 34–42.

Plante, T. G., Couchman, C., & Diaz, A. (1995). Measuring mental health treatment outcome and client satisfaction among children and families. *Journal of Mental Health Administration, 22,* 261–269.

Plante, T. G., Couchman, C., & Hoffman, C. (1998). Measuring treatment outcome and client satisfaction among children and families: A case report. *Professional Psychology: Research and Practice, 29,* 52–55.

Plante, T. G., Goldfarb, L. P., & Wadley, V. (1993). Are stress and coping associated with aptitude and achievement testing performance among children? A preliminary investigation. *Journal of School Psychology, 31,* 259–266.

Plante, T. G., Manual, G. M., & Bryant, C. (1996). Defensiveness and cognitive functioning among sexual offending Roman Catholic priests, *Pastoral Psychology, 45,* 129–139.

Plante, T. G., Lantis, A., & Checa, G. (1997). The influence of gender, hypertension risk, and aerobic fitness on cardiovascular responses to laboratory-induced stress. *International Journal of Stress Management, 4,* 89–99.

Plante, T. G., Pinder, S. L., & Howe, D. (1988). Introducing the Living with Illness Group: A specialized treatment for patients with chronic schizophrenic conditions. *Group, 12,* 198–204.

Plante, T. G. & Sykora, C. (1994). Are stress and coping associated with WISC–III performance among children? *Journal of Clinical Psychology, 50,* 759–762.

Plaud, J. J., & Gaither, G. A. (1996). Behavioral momentum: Implications and development from reinforcement theories. *Behavior Modification, 20,* 183–201.

Plomin, R. (1990). The role of inheritance in behavior. *Science, 248,* 183–188.

Pomerleau, O. F., & Pomerleau, C. S. (1977). *Break the smoking habit.* Champaign, IL: Research Press.

Pomerleau, O. F., & Pomerleau, C. S. (Eds.). (1988). *Nicotine replacement: A critical evaluation.* New York: Alan R. Liss.

Popanz, T. (1990). *Graduate training in psychopharmacology, substance abuse, and basic science: 1980–1990.* Washington, DC: American Psychological Association.

Pope, K. S. (1991). Ethical and legal issues in clinical practice. In M. Hersen, A. E. Kazdin, & A. S. Bellack (Eds.), *The Clinical Psychology Handbook* (2nd ed.). New York: Pergamon.

Pope, K. S. (1994). *Sexual involvement with therapists: Patient assessment, subsequent therapy, forensics.* Washington, DC: American Psychological Association.

Pope, K. S. & Bajt, T. R. (1988). When laws and values conflict: A dilemma for psychologists. *American Psychologist, 43,* 828–829.

Pope, K. S., Keith-Spiegal, P., & Tabachnick, B. G. (1986). Sexual attraction to clients: The human therapist and the (sometimes) inhuman training system. *American Psychologist, 41,* 147–158.

Pope, K. S., Tabachnick, B. G., & Keith-Spiegal, P. (1987). Ethics of practice: The beliefs and behaviors of psychologists as therapists. *American Psychologist, 42,* 993–1006.

Pope, K. S. & Vetter, V. A. (1992). Ethical dilemmas encountered by members of the APA: A national survey. *American Psychologist, 47,* 397–411.

Presley, C. A. & Meilman, P. W. (1992). *Alcohol and drugs on American college campuses: A report to college presidents.* Carbondale: Southern Illinois University Press.

Price, R. A. (1987). Genetics of human obesity. *Annals of Behavioral Medicine, 9,* 9–14.

Prochaska, J. O. (1984). *Systems of psychotherapy: A transtheoretical analysis* (2nd ed.). Homewood, IL: Dorsey.

Prochaska, J. O. (1995). Common problems: Common solutions. *Clinical Psychology: Science and Practice, 2,* 101–105.

Prochaska, J. O., & Norcross, J. C. (1994). *Systems of psychotherapy: A transtheoretical analysis* (3rd. ed.). Pacific Grove, CA: Brooks/Cole.

Prochaska, J. O., Velicer, W. F., DiClemente, C. C., & Fava, J. (1988). Measuring processes of change: Applications to the cessation of smoking. *Journal of Consulting and Clinical Psychology, 56,* 520–528.

Rabin, A. S., Kaslow, N. J., & Rehm, L. P. (1985). Factors influencing continuation in a behavioral therapy. *Behaviour Research and Therapy, 23,* 695–698.

Rachman, S. J., & Wilson, G. T. (1980). *The effects of psychological therapy* (2nd ed.). New York: Pergamon.

Raimy, V. C. (Ed.) (1950). *Training in clinical psychology.* New York: Prentice-Hall.

Raven, J. C. (1993). *Raven's Progressive Matrices.* Enberg, England: Author.

Raymer, R., & Poppen, R. (1985). Behavioral relaxation training with hyperactive children. *Journal of Behavior Therapy and Experimental Psychiatry, 16,* 309–316.

Reed, T. E., & Jensen, A. R. (1991). Arm nerve conduction velocity (NCV), brain NCV, reaction time, and intelligence. *Intelligence, 15,* 33–47.

Regier, D. A., Myers, J. K., Kramer, M., Robins, L. N., Blazer, D. G., Hough, R. L., Eaton, W. W., & Locke, B. Z. (1984).

The NIMH epidemiologic catchment area program. *Archives of General Psychiatry, 41,* 934–941.

Rehm, L. P. (1997). Continuing education for empirically supported treatments. *The Clinical Psychologist, 50,* 2–3.

Reisman, J. M. (1976). A history of clinical psychology. New York: Irvington.

Reitan, R. M. & Davison, L. A. (1974). *Clinical neuropsychology: Current status and applications.* Washington, DC: V. H. Winston & Sons.

Rende, R., & Plomin, R. (1992). Diathesis-stress models of psychopathology: A quantitative genetic perspective. *Applied & Preventive Psychology, 1,* 177–182.

Resnick, R. J., & DeLeon, P. H. (1995). The future of health care reform: Implications of 1994 elections. *Professional Psychology: Research and Practice, 26,* 3–4.

Rice, C. E. (1997). Scenarios: The scientist-practitioner split and the future of psychology. *American Psychologist, 52,* 1173–1181.

Riggs, D. S., & Foa, E. B. (1993). Obsessive-compulsive disorder. In D. H. Barlow (Ed.), *Clinical handbook of psychological disorders* (2nd ed.). New York, Guilford.

Riva, M. T., & Cornish, J. A. E. (1995). Group supervision practices at psychology predoctoral internship programs: A national survey. *Professional Psychology: Research and Practice, 26,* 523–525.

Roan, S. (1992, November 24). Calling for help. *Los Angeles Times,* pp. E1, E6.

Robins, L. N., Helzer, J. E., Croughan, J., & Ratcliff, K. S. (1994). The National Institute of Mental Health Diagnostic Interview Schedule. In J. E. Mezzich, M. R. Jorge, & I. M. Salloum (Eds.), *Psychiatric epidemiology: Assessment concepts and methods* (pp. 227–248). Baltimore: Johns Hopkins University Press.

Rodnick, E. H. (1985). Clinical psychology. In H. I. Kaplan & B. J. Sadock, *Comprehensive textbook of psychiatry* (4th ed.). Baltimore: Williams & Wilkins.

Rodolfa, E., Hall, T., Holms, V., Davena, A., Komatz, D., Antunez, M., & Hall, A. (1994). The management of sexual feelings in therapy. *Professional Psychology: Research and Practice, 25,* 168–172.

Rodrigue, J. R. (1994). Beyond the individual child: Innovative systems approaches to service delivery in pediatric psychology. *Journal of Child Clinical Psychology, 23,* 32–39.

Roe, A., Gustad, J. W., Moore, B. V., Ross, S., & Skodar, M. (Eds.) (1959). *Graduate education in psychology.* Washington, DC: American Psychological Association.

Roger, C. R. (1951). *Client-centered therapy.* Boston: Houghton Mifflin.

Rogers, C. R. (1957). *Psychotherapy and personality change.* Chicago: University of Chicago Press.

Rogers, C. R. (1961). *On becoming a person.* Boston: Houghton Mifflin.

Romans, J. S. C., Boswll, D. L., Carlozzi, A. F., & Ferguson, D. B. (1995). Training and supervision practices in clinical, counseling, and school psychology programs. *Professional Psychology: Research and Practice, 26,* 407–412.

Rorschach, H. (1921/1942). *Psychodiagnostics: A diagnostic test based on perception.* New York: Grune and Stratton.

Rorschach, H. (1951). *Rorschach Technique.* New York: Grune and Stratton.

Rosenhan, D. L., & Seligman, M. E. (1989). *Abnormal psychology* (2nd ed.). New York: W. W. Norton.

Rosenthal, R. (1987). Pygmalion effects: Existence, magnitude, and social importance. *Educational Researcher, 16,* 37–41.

Roth, M. (1996). The panic-agoraphobic syndrome: A paradigm of the activity group of disorders and its implications for psychiatric practice and theory. *American Journal of Psychiatry, 153,* 111–124.

Rotter, J. B. (1954). *Social learning and clinical psychology.* Englewood Cliffs, NJ: Prentice-Hall.

Rotter, J. B., & Rafferty, J. E. (1950). *The Rotter Incomplete Sentences Test.* New York: Psychological Corporation.

Rounsaville, B. J., O'Malley, S., Foley, S., & Weissman, M. W. (1988). Role of manual-guided training in the conduct and efficacy of interpersonal psychotherapy for depression. *Journal of Consulting and Clinical Psychology, 56,* 681–688.

Rubin, H. R., Gandek, B., Rogers, W. H., Kosinski, M., McHorney, C. A., & Ware, J. E. (1993). Patients' rating of outpatient visits in different practice settings: Results from the Medical Outcomes Study. *Journal of the American Medical Association, 270,* 835–840.

Rubin, R. T. (1982). Koro (Shook Yang): A culture-bound psychogenic syndrome. In C. T. H. Friedmann & R. A. Fauger (Ed.), *Extraordinary disorders of human behavior* (pp. 155–172). New York: Plenum.

Rudolph, K. D., Dennig, M. D., & Weisz, J. R. (1995). Determinants and consequences of children's coping in medical setting: Conceptualization, review, and critique. *Psychological Bulletin, 118,* 328–357.

Russell, O. (Ed.). (1997). *Seminars in the psychiatry of learning disabilities.* Washington, DC: American Psychiatric Association Press.

Russell, R. K., Petrie, T. A. (1994). Issues in training effective supervisors. *Applied and Preventive Psychology, 3,* 27–42.

Sachs, J. S. (1983). Negative factors in brief psychotherapy: An empirical assessment. *Journal of Consulting and Clinical Psychology, 51,* 557–564.

Saeman, H. (1996a). Psychologists cheer as top psychiatrist jeers managed care. *The National Psychologist, 5(3),* 1–4.

Saeman, H. (1996b). Psychologists frustrated with managed care, economic issues, but plan to 'hang tough,' survey reveals. *The National Psychologist, 5(2),* 1–2.

Salvio, M., Beutler, L. E., Wood, J. M., & Engle, D. (1992). The strength of the therapeutic alliance in three treatments for depression. *Psychotherapy Research, 2,* 31–36.

Sammons, M. T., & Brown, A. B. (1997). The Department of Defense Psychopharmacology Demonstration Project: An evolving program for postdoctoral education in psychology. *Professional Psychology: Research and Practice, 28,* 107–112.

Sanchez, P. N., & Kahn, M. W. (1991). Differentiating medical from psychosocial disorders: How do medically and nonmedically trained clinicians differ? *Professional Psychology: Research and Practice, 22,* 124–126.

Sanders, M. J. (1995). Symptom coaching: Factitious disorder by proxy with older children. *Clinical Psychology Review, 15,* 423–442.

Sanderson, W. C. (1994). Introduction to series on empirically validated psychological treatments. *The Clinical Psychologist, 47,* 9.

Sanderson, W.C., & Woody, S. (1995). Manuals for empirically validated treatments. *The Clinical Psychologist, 48,* 7–12.

Sandoval, J. (1989). The WISC-R and internal evidence of test bias with minority groups. *Journal of Counseling and Clinical Psychology, 47,* 919–927.

Sanford, N. (1953). Clinical method: Psychotherapy. *Annual Review of Psychology, 4,* 317–342.

Sapolsky, R. M. (1990, January). Stress in the wild. *Scientific American,* 116–123.

Sapolsky, R. M., & Meaney, M. J. (1986). Maturation of the adrenal stress response: Neuroendocrine control mechanisms and the stress hyporesponsive period. *Brain Research Review, 11,* 65–76.

Satir, V. (1967). *Conjoint family therapy.* Palo Alto, CA: Science and Behavior Books.

Satir, V. (1972). *Peoplemaking.* Palo Alto: Science and Behavior Books.

Sattler, J. M. (1988). *Assessment of children* (3rd ed.). San Diego: Author.

Sattler, J. M. (1992). Assessment of children's intelligence. In C. E. Walker, M. C. Roberts (Eds.), *Handbook of clinical child psychology,* pp. 85–100. NY: John Wiley & Sons.

Sayette, M. A. & Mayne, T. J. (1990). Survey of current clinical and research trends in clinical psychology. *American Psychologist, 45,* 1263–1266.

Schein, E. H. (1988). *Process consultation: Lessons for managers and consultants* (Vol. 2). Reading, MA: Addison-Wesley.

Scherg, H. (1987). Psychosocial factors and disease bias in breast cancer patients. *Psychosomatic Medicine, 49,* 302–312.

Schiele, J. H. (1991). An epistemological perspective on intelligence assessment of African-American children. *Journal of Black Psychology, 17,* 23–36.

Schindler, N. J., & Talen, M. R. (1994). Focus supervision: Management format for supervision practices. *Professional Psychology: Research and Practice, 25,* 304–306.

Schindler-Rainman, E. (1985). Invited commentary: The modern consultant—a renaissance person. *Consultation, 4,* 264–267.

Schneider, I. (1987). The theory and practice of movie psychiatry. *American Journal of Psychiatry, 144,* 996–1002.

Schneider, S. F. (1996). Random thoughts on leaving the fray. *American Psychologist, 51,* 715–721.

Schofield, W. (1952). Research in clinical psychology: 1951. *Journal of Clinical Psychology, 8,* 255–261.

Schofield, W. (1964). *Psychotherapy: The purchase of friendship.* Englewood Cliffs, NJ: Prentice-Hall.

Schwartz, G. E. (1982). Testing the biopsychosocial model: The ultimate challenge facing behavioral medicine? *Journal of Consulting and Clinical Psychology, 50,* 1040–1053.

Schwartz, G. E. (1984). Psychobiology of health: A new synthesis. In B. L. Hammonds & C. J. Scheirer (Eds.), *Psychology and health: The master lecture series* (Vol. 3, pp. 149–193). Washington, DC: American Psychological Association.

Schwartz, G. E. (1991). The data are always friendly: A systems approach to psychotherapy integration. *Journal of Psychotherapy Integration, 1,* 55–69.

Schwartz, G. E., & Beatty, J. (1977). *Biofeedback: Theory and research.* New York: Academic Press.

Schwartz, G. E., & Weiss, S. M. (1978a). Behavioral medicine revisted: An amended definition. *Journal of Behavioral Medicine, 1,* 249–251.

Schwartz, G. E., & Weiss, S. M. (1978b). Yale Conference on Behavioral Medicine: A proposed definition and statement of goals. *Journal of Behavioral Medicine, 1,* 3–12.

Schwartz, J. L. (1987). *Review and evaluation of smoking cessation methods: The United States and Canada, 1978–1985.* Washington, DC: Division of Cancer Prevention and Control, National Cancer Institute.

Scott, A. I. F. (1995). Does ECT alter brain structure? *American Journal of Psychiatry, 152,* 1403–1408.

Scriven, M. (1967). The methodology of evaluation. In R. Tyler, R. Gagne, & M. Scriven (Eds.), *Perspectives of curriculum evaluation* (American Educational Research Association Monograph Series on Curriculum Evaluation) (pp. 39–83). Chicago: Rand McNally.

Searles, J. S. (1985). A methodological and empirical critique of psychotherapy outcome meta-analysis. *Behaviour Research and Therapy, 23,* 453–463.

Seeman, M., Seeman, A. Z., & Budros, A. (1988). Powerlessness, work, and community: A longitudinal study of alienation and alcohol use. *Journal of Health and Social Behavior, 29,* 185–198.

Seligman, M. E. P. (1975). *Helplessness: On depression, development and death.* San Francisco: Freeman.

Seligman, M. E. P. (1994). *What you can change and what you can't.* New York: Knopf.

Seligman, M. E. P. (1995). The effectiveness of psychotherapy: The Consumer Reports Study. *American Psychologist, 50,* 965–974.

Seligman, M. E. P. (1996). Science as an ally of practice. *American Psychologist, 51,* 1072–1079.

Seligman, M. E. P., Peterson, C., Kaslow, N. J., Tanenbaum, R. L., Alloy, L. B., & Abramson, L. Y. (1984). Explanatory style and depressive symptoms among school children. *Journal of Abnormal Psychology, 93,* 235–238.

Selvini Palazzoli, M., Boscolo, L., Cecchin, G., & Prata, G. (1980). Hypothesizing-circularity-neutrality: Three guidelines for the conductor of the session. *Family Process, 19,* 73–85.

Shakow, D. (1947). Recommended graduate training program in clinical psychology. *American Psychologist, 2,* 539–558.

Shakow, D. (1976). What is clinical psychology? *American Psychologist, 31,* 553–560.

Shakow, D. (1978). Clinical psychology seen some 50 years later. *American Psychologist, 33,* 148–158.

Shapiro, A. E., & Wiggins, J. G. (1994). A PsyD degree for every practitioner: Truth in labeling. *American Psychologist, 49,* 207–210.

Shapiro, D. & Shapiro, D. (1982). Meta-analysis of comparative therapy outcome studies: A replication and refinement. *Psychological Bulletin, 92,* 581–604.

Shapiro, D. L. (1984). *Psychological evaluation and expert testimony: A practical guide to forensic work.* New York: Van Nostrand Reinhold.

Shapiro, E. S., & Lentz, F. E. (1991). Vocational-technical programs: Follow-up of students with learning disabilities. *Exceptional Children, 58,* 47–59.

Sharow, D. (1947). Recommended graduate training program in clinical psychology. *American Psychologist, 2,* 539–558.

Shemberg, K. M., & Leventhal, D. B. (1981). Attitudes of internship directors toward preinternship training and clinical training models. *Professional Psychology, 12,* 639–646.

Sheridan, E. P., Matarazzo, J. D., & Nelson, P. D. (1995). Accreditation of psychology's graduate professional education and training programs: An historical perspective. *Professional Psychology: Research and Practice, 26,* 386–392.

Shneidman, E. S. (1951). *Thematic test analysis.* New York: Grune and Stratton.

Sholomskas, D. E., Barlow, D. H., Cohen, J., Gorman, J., Moras, K., Papp, L., Shear, M. K., & Woods, S. W. (1990). *Drug/behavior treatment of panic: Study design.* Paper presented at the annual meeting of the American Psychiatric Association, New York.

Shore, M. F. (1993). Thoughts on twenty years of mental health administration. *Administration and Policy in Mental Health, 21,* 117–121.

Shorter, E. (1994). *From the mind into the body: The cultural origins of psychosomatic symptoms.* New York, NY: Free Press.

Shuster, E. A. (1996). Epilepsy in women. *Mayo Clinic Proceedings, 71,* 991–999.

Sieber, J. E. (1982). Ethical dilemmas in social research. In J. E. Sieber (Ed.), *The ethics of social research: Survey and experiments.* New York: Springer-Verlag.

Silverman, W. H. (1996). Cookbooks, manuals, and paint-by-numbers: Psychotherapy in the 90's. *Psychotherapy, 33,* 207–215.

Silverman, W. K., & Nelles, W. B. (1988). The Anxiety Disorders Interview Schedule for Children. *Journal of the American Academy of Child and Adolescent Psychiatry, 27,* 772–778.

Singer, M. T., & Lalich, J. (1996). *Crazy therapies: What are they? Do they work?* San Francisco: Jossey-Bass.

Skinner, B. F. (1948). *Walden Two.* New York: Macmillan.

Skinner, B. F. (1953). *Science and human behavior.* New York: Macmillan.

Sklar, L. S., & Anisman, H. (1981). Stress and cancer. *Psychological Bulletin, 89,* 369–406.

Sleek, S. (1997, August). Providing therapy from a distance. *APA Monitor, 28,* 1, 38

Sloane, R. B., Staples, F. R., Cristol, A. H., Yorkston, N. J., & Whipple, K. (1975). *Psychotherapy versus behavior therapy.* Cambridge, MA: Harvard University Press.

Smith, B. S. (1992). *Attitudes toward prescribing privileges among clinical graduate students.* Unpublished doctoral research project. Indiana State University.

Smith, M. L. (1982). What research says about the effectiveness of psychotherapy. *Hospital and Community Psychiatry, 33,* 457–461.

Smith, M. L., & Glass, G. V. (1977). Meta-analysis of psychotherapy outcome studies. *American Psychologist, 32,* 752–760.

Smith, M. L., Glass, G. V., & Miller, T. (1980). *The benefits of psychotherapy.* Baltimore: Johns Hopkins University Press.

Smith, R. A. (1985). Advising beginning psychology majors for graduate school. *Teaching of Psychology, 12,* 194–198.

Smith, T. W., Turner, C. W., Ford, M. H., Hunt, S. C., Barlow, G. K., Stults, B. M., & Williams, R. R. (1987). Blood pressure reactivity in adult male twins. *Health Psychology, 6,* 209–220.

Smyer, M. A., Balster, R. L., Egli, D., Johnson, D. L., Kilbey, M. M., Leith, N. J., & Puente, A. E. (1993). Summary of the report of the ad hoc task force on psychopharmacology of the American Psychological Association. *Professional Psychology: Research and Practice, 24,* 394–403.

Snepp, F. P., & Peterson, D. R. (1988). Evaluative comparison of PsyD and PhD students by clinical internship supervisors. *Professional Psychology: Research and Practice, 19,* 180–193.

Snyder, C. R., McDermott, D. S., Leibowitz, R. Q., & Kutter, C. A female clinical psychology? Through a looking glass gently into the 21st century. Under review.

Sonne, J. L. (1994). Multiple relationships: Does the new ethics code answer the right questions? *Professional Psychology: Research and Practice, 25,* 336–343.

Sopchak, A. L., Sopchak, A. M., & Kohlbrenner, R. J. (1993). *Interpersonal relatedness from projective drawings: Applicability in diagnostic and therapeutic practice.* Charles C. Thomas: Springfield, IL.

Sparrow, S. S., Balla, D. A., & Cicchetti, D. V. (1987). *Vineland Adaptive Behavior Scales: Manual.* Circles Pines, MN: American Guidance Service.

Spearman, C. (1927). *The abilities of man.* New York: Macmillan.

Speer, D. C., & Newman, F. L. (1996). Mental health services outcome evaluation. *Clinical Psychology: Science and Practice, 3,* 105–129.

Spiegal, D. (1990). Can psychotherapy prolong cancer survival? *Psychosomatics, 31,* 361–366.

Spiegal, D. (1992). Effects of psychosocial support on patients with metastatic breast cancer. *Journal of Psychosocial Oncology, 10,* 113–120.

Spiegal, D., Bloom, J. R., Kramer, H. C., & Gottheil, E. (1989). Effect of psychosocial treatment on survival of patients with metastatic breast cancer. *Lancet, 14,* 888–891.

Spitzer, R. L., Williams, J. B. W., Gibbon, M., & First, M. B. (1990). *Structured clinical interview for DSM-III-R (SCID).* Washington, DC: American Psychiatric Press.

Spoont, M. R. (1992). Modulatory role of serotonin in neural information processing: Implications for human psychopathology. *Psychological Bulletin, 112,* 330–350.

Spreen, O. (1988). Prognosis of learning disability. *Journal of Consulting and Clinical Psychology, 56,* 836–842.

Strupp, H. H. (1980). Success and failure in time-limited psychotherapy: Furthr evidence (Comparison 4). Archives of General Psychiatry, 37, 947–954.

Strupp, H. H., & Binder, J. L. (1984). *Psychotherapy in a new key: A guide to time-limited dynamic therapy.* New York: Basic Books.

Stake, J. E., & Oliver, J. (1991). Sexual contact and touching between therapist and client: A survey of psychologists' attitudes and behavior. *Professional Psychology: Research and Practice, 22,* 297–307.

Stears, J. C., & Spitz, M. C. (1996). The imaging of epilepsy. *Seminars in Ultrasound, 17,* 221–250.

Stein, D. M., & Lambert, M. J. (1984). On the relationship between therapist experience and psychotherapy outcome. *Clinical Psychology Review, 4,* 1–16.

Steinpreis, R., Queen, L., & Tennen, H. (1992). The education of clinical psychologists: A survey of training directors. *The Clinical Psychologist, 45,* 87–94.

Sternberg, R. J. (1996). *Successful intelligence: How practical and creative intelligence determines success in life.* New York: Simon & Schuster.

Sternberg, R. J. (1997a). The concept of intelligence and its role in lifelong learning and success. *American Psychologist, 52,* 1030–1037.

Sternberg, R. J. (Ed.) (1997b). *Career paths in psychology: Where your degree can take you.* Washington, DC: American Psychological Association.

Sternberg, R. J., & Detterman, D. K. (Eds.). (1986). *What is intelligence?* Norwood, NJ: Ablex.

Sternberg, R. J., & Kaye, D. B. (1982). Intelligence. In H. E. Mitzel, J. H. Best, & H. E. Rabinowitz (Eds.), *Encyclopedia of educational research* (5th ed., pp. 924–933). New York: Free Press.

Sternberg, R. J., & Williams, W. M. (1997). Does the Graduate Record Examination predict meaningful success in the graduate training of psychologists? A case study. *American Psychologist, 52,* 630–641.

Stewart, S. H. (1996). Alcohol abuse in individuals exposed to trauma: A critical review. *Psychological Bulletin, 120,* 83–112.

Stiles, W. B., Shapiro, D. A., & Elliot, R. (1986). Are all psychotherapies equivalent? *American Psychologist, 41,* 165–180.

Stockman, A. F. (1990). Dual relationships in rural mental health practice: An ethical dilemma. *Journal of Rural Community Psychology, 11,* 31–45.

Stoll, B. A. (1996). Obesity, social class and Western diet: A link to breast cancer prognosis. *European Journal of Cancer, 32A,* 1293–1295.

Stone, M. H. (1985). Negative outcome in borderline states. In D. T. Mays & C. M. Franks (Eds.), *Negative outcome in psychotherapy and what to do about it.* (pp. 145–170). New York: Springer.

Stone, M. H. (1990). Treatment of borderline patients: A pragmatic approach. *Psychiatric Clinics of North America, 13,* 265–285.

Stricker, G., & Trierweiler, S. J. (1995). The local clinical scientist: A bridge between science and practice. *American Psychologist, 50,* 995–1002.

Strickland, B. R. (1985). Over the Boulder(s) and through the Vail. *The Clinical Psychologist, 38,* 52–56.

Striegal-Moore, R. H., Silberstein, L. R., & Rodin, J. (1986). Toward an understanding of risk factors for bulimia. *American Psychologist, 3,* 246–263.

Striegal-Moore, R. H., Silberstein, L. R., & Rodin, J. (1993). The social self in bulimia nervosa: Public self-consciousness, social anxiety, and perceived fraudulence. *Journal of Abnormal Psychology, 102,* 297–303.

Strober, M., & Humphrey, L. L. (1987). Familial contributions to the etiology and course of anorexia nervosa and bulimia. Special Issue: Eating disorders. *Journal of Consulting and Clinical Psychology, 55,* 654–659.

Strother, C. R. (1956). *Psychology and mental health.* Washington, DC: American Psychological Association.

Strupp, H. H. (1963). The outcome problem in psychotherapy revisited. *Psychotherapy: Theory, Research, and Practice, 1,* 1–13.

Strupp, H. H. (1980). Success and failure in time-limited psychotherapy: A systematic comparison of two cases (comparison 1). *Archives of General Psychiatry, 37,* 595–603.

Strupp, H. H. (1995). The psychotherapist's skill revisited. *Clinical Psychology: Science and Practice, 2,* 70–74.

Strupp, H. H., & Binder, J. L. (1984). *Psychotherapy in a new key: A guide to time-limited dynamic psychotherapy.* New York: Basic Books.

Sue, S. (1983). Ethnic minority issues in psychology: A reexamination. *American Psychologist, 38,* 583–592.

Sue, S. (1988). Psychotherapeutic services for ethnic minorities. *American Psychologist, 43,* 301–308.

Sue, S., McKinney, H. L., & Allen, D. B. (1976). Predictors of the duration of therapy for clients in the community mental health system. *Community Mental Health Journal, 12,* 365–375.

Sue, S., Zane, N., & Young, K. (1994). Research on psychotherapy with culturally diverse populations. In A. E. Bergin & S. L. Garfield (Eds.), *Handbook of psychotherapy and behavior change* (4th ed.). New York: Wiley.

Suinn, R. M., & Oskamp, S. (1969). *The predictive validity of projective measures: A fifteen-year evaluative review of the research.* Springfield, IL: Charles C. Thomas.

Sultzer, D. L., Levin, H. S., Mahler, M. E., High, W. M., & Cummings, J. L. (1983). A comparison of psychiatric symptoms in vascular dementia and Alzheimer's disease. *American Journal of Psychiatry, 150,* 1806–1812.

Sussman, M. B. (1992). *A curious calling: Unconscious motivations for practicing psychotherapy.* Northvale, NJ: Aronson.

Suzuki, L. A., & Valencia, R. R. (1997). Race-ethnicity and measured intelligence: Educational implications. *American Psychologist, 52,* 1103–1114.

Svartberg, M., & Stiles, T. C. (1991). Comparative effects of short-term psychodynamic psychotherapy: A meta-analysis. *Journal of Consulting and Clinical Psychology, 59,* 704–714.

Swanson, J. M., McBurnett, K., Wigal, T., Pfiffner, L. J., Lerner, M. A., Williams, L., Christian, D. L., Tamm, L., Willcut, E., Crowley, K., Clevenger, W., Khouzam, N., Woo, C., Crinella, F. M., & Fisher, T. D. (1993). Effect of stimulant medication on children with attention deficit disorder: A "review of reviews." *Exceptional Children, 60,* 154–162.

Swartz, J. D. (1978). Review of the TAT. In O.K. Buros (Ed.), *The eighth mental measurements handbook* (pp. 1127–1130). Highland Park, NJ: Gryphon Press.

Sweet, J. J., Rozensky, R. H., & Tovian, S. M. (Eds.). (1991). *Handbook of clinical psychology in medical settings.* New York: Plenum.

Tageson, W. C. (1982). *Humanistic psychology: A synthesis.* Homewood, IL: Dorsey Press.

Tally, P. F., Strupp, H. H., & Butler, S. F. (Eds.). (1994). *Psychotherapy research and practice: Bridging the gap.* New York: Basic Books.

Task Force on Promotion and Dissemination of Psychological Procedures (1995). Training in and dissemination of empirically validated psychological treatments: Report and recommendations. *The Clinical Psychologist, 48,* 3–23.

Taube, C. A., Burns, B. J., & Kessler, L. (1984). Patients of psychiatrists and psychologists in office-based practice: 1980. *American Psychologist, 39,* 1435–1447.

Tausig, J. E., & Freeman, E. W. (1988). The next best thing to being there. Conducting the clinical research interview by telephone. *American Journal of Orthopsychiatry, 58,* 418–427.

Taylor, C. B., Agras, W. S., Losch, M., Plante, T. G., & Burnett, K. (1991). Improving the effectiveness of computer-assisted weight loss. *Behavior Therapy, 22,* 229–236.

Taylor, S. E. (1995). *Health Psychology* (3rd ed.). New York, NY: McGraw-Hill, Inc.

Temoshok, L. (1987). Personality, coping style, emotion and cancer: Towards an integrative model. *Cancer Surveys, 6,* 545–567.

Tharp, R. G. (1991). Cultural diversity and treatment of children. *Journal of Consulting and Clinical Psychology, 59,* 799–812.

Thoresen, C. E., & Powell, L. H. (1992). Type A behavior pattern: New perspectives on theory, assessment and intervention. Special Issues: Behavioral medicine: An update for the 1990s. *Journal of Consulting and Clinical Psychology, 60,* 595–604.

Thorndike, R. L., Hagen, E. P., & Sattler, J. M. (1986). *The Stanford-Binet Intelligence Scale: Fourth Edition, Technical manual.* Chicago: Riverside.

Thurstone, L. L. (1931). Multiple factor analysis. *Psychological Review, 38,* 406–427.

Thurstone, L. L. (1938). *Primary mental abilities.* Chicago, IL: University of Chicago Press.

Tobias, L. L. (1990). *Psychological consultation to management: A clinician's perspective.* New York: Brunner/Mazel.

Tolmach, J. (1985). "There ain't nobody on my side": A new day treatment program for Black urban youth. *Journal of Clinical Child Psychology, 14,* 214–219.

Tomkins, S. S. (1947). *The thematic apperception test.* New York: Grune & Stratton.

Trevisaw, M. S. (1996). Review of the Draw-a-Person: Screening procedures for emotional disturbance. *Measurement and Evaluation in Counseling and Development, 28,* 225–228.

Trickett, E. J., Watts, R. J., & Birman, D. (Eds.) (1994). *Human diversity: Perspectives on people in context.* San Francisco, CA: Jossey-Boss.

Trimble, M. (1985). Psychosomatic aspects of epilepsy. *Advances in Psychosomatic Medicine, 13,* 133–150.

Truax, C. B., & Mitchell, K. M. (1971). Research on certain therapist interpersonal skills in relation to process and outcome.

In A. E. Bergin and S. L. Garfield (Eds.), *Handbook of psychotherapy and behavior change* (pp. 299–344). New York: Wiley.

Trull, T. J., & Widiger, T. A. (1997). *Manual for the Structured Interview for the Five-Factor Model of Personality* (*SIFFM*). Odessa, FL: Psychological Assessment Resources.

Tucker, L. & Lubin, W. (1994). *National survey of psychologists. Report from Division 39, American psychological Association.* Washington, DC: American Psychological Association.

Tuokko, H., Kristjansson, E., & Miller, J. (1995). Neuropsychological detection of dementia: An overview of the neuropsychological component of the Canadian Study of Health and Aging. *Journal of Clinical and Experimental Neuropsychology, 17,* 352–373.

Turk, D. C., & Fernandez, E. (1990). On the putative uniqueness of cancer pain: Do psychological principles apply? *Behavioural Research and Therapy, 28,* 1–13.

Turnbull, W. W. (1979). Intelligence testing in the year 2000. *Intelligence, 3,* 275–282.

U.S. Bureau of the Census (1990). *Census of population and housing summary* (Tape File 1C, CD-ROM). Washington, DC: Government Printing Office.

U.S. Bureau of the Census (1995). *Statistical abstract of the U.S.* (115th ed.). Washington, DC: Author.

U.S. Department of Health and Human Services. (1983). *The health consequences of smoking: Cardiovascular disease. A report to the Surgeon General* (DHHS Publication No. PHS 84-50204). Washington, DC: Public Health Service, Office on Smoking and Health.

U.S. Department of Health and Human Services (1985a). *Health: United States 1985* (DHHS Publication No. PHS 86-1232). Washington, DC. Author.

U.S. Department of Health and Human Services. (1985b). *Preventing lead poisoning in young children. Second revision of the statement by the Centers for Disease Control.* Washington, DC: U.S. Government Printing Office.

U.S. Department of Health and Human Services (1990a). *Healthy people 2000.* Washington, DC: Author.

U.S. Department of Health and Human Services. (1990b). *Seventh annual report to the U.S. Congress on alcohol and health from the Secretary of Health and Human Services.* Rockville, MD: National Institute on Alcohol Abuse and Alcoholism.

U.S. Surgeon General (1989). *Reducing the health consequences of smoking: 25 years of progress.* Washington, DC: U.S. Government Printing Office.

U.S. Surgeon General (1994). *Preventing tobacco use among young people.* Washington, DC: U.S. Government Printing Office.

VandeCreek, L., & Fleisher, M. (1984). The role of practicum in undergraduate psychology curriculum. *Teaching of Psychology, 11,* 9–14.

VandenBos, G. (1993). The U.S. mental health policy: Proactive evolution in the midst of health care reform. *American Psychologist, 48,* 283–290.

VandenBoss, G. R. (1996). Outcome assessment of psychotherapy. *American Psychologist, 51,* 1005–1006.

VandenBos, G. R., & DeLeon, P. H. (1988). The use of psychotherapy to improve physical health. *Psychotherapy, 25,* 335–343.

Vasquez, M. J. (1991). Sexual intimacies with clients after termination: Should a prohibition be explicit? *Ethics & Behavior, 1,* 45–61.

Vasquez, M. J. T. (1994). Implications of the 1992 ethics code for the practice of individual psychotherapy. *Professional Psychology: Research and Practice, 25,* 321–328.

Vaugh, M., & Beech, H. R. (1985). Which obsessionals fail to change? In D. T. Mays & C. M. Franks (Eds.), *Negative outcome in psychotherapy and what to do about it.* (pp. 192–209). New York: Springer.

Vernon, P.E. (1950). The validation of civil service selection board procedures. *Occupational Psychology, 24,* 75–95.

Von Itallie, T.B. (1985). Health implications of overweight and obesity in the United States. *Annals of Internal medicine, 103,* 983–988.

Voth, H. M., & Orth, M. H. (1973). *Psychotherapy and the role of the environment.* New York: Behavioral Press.

Wachtel, P. L. (1975). Behavior therapy and the facilitation of psychoanalytic exploration. *Psychotherapy: Theory, Research, and Practice, 12,* 68–72.

Wachtel, P. L. (1977). *Psychoanalysis and behavior therapy: Toward an integration.* New York: Basic Books.

Wachtel, P. L. (1982). What can dynamic therapies contribute to behavior therapy? *Behavior Therapy, 13,* 594–609.

Wachtel, P. L. (1984). On theory, practice, and the nature of integration. In H. Arkowitz and S.R. Messer (Eds.), *Psychoanalytic therapy and behavior therapy: Is integration possible?* (pp. 31–52). New York: Plenum.

Wachtel, P. L. (1987). *Action and insight.* New York: Guilford.

Wadden, T. A., Sternberg, J. A., Letizia, K. A., Stunkard, A. J., & Foster, G. D. (1989). Treatment of obesity by very low calorie diet, behavior therapy, and their combination: A five-year perspective. *International Journal of Obesity, 13,* 39–46.

Wagner, M. (1990, April). *The school programs and school performance of secondary students classified as learning disabled: Findings from the National Longitudinal Transition study of special education students.* Paper presented at Division G, American Educational Research Association Annual Metting, Boston.

Wallace, W. A., & Hall, D. L. (1996). *Psychological consultation: Perspectives and applications.* Pacific Grove, CA: Brooks/Cole.

Wandersman, A., Poppen, P. J., & Ricks, D. F. (Eds.). (1976). *Humanism and behaviorism: Dialogue and growth.* Elmsford, NY: Pergamon.

Watkins, C. E. (1992). Reflections on the preparation of psychotherapy supervisors. *Journal of Clinical Psychology, 48,* 145–147.

Watson, J. B., & Rayner, R. (1920). Conditioned emotional reactions. *Journal of Experimental Psychology, 3,* 1–14.

Watzlawick, P., Weakland, J., & Fisch, R. (1974). *Change: Principles of problem formation and problem resolution.* New York: Norton.

Wechsler, D. (1981). *Wechsler Adult Intelligence Scale-Revised.* San Antonio, TX: Psychological Corporation.

Wechsler, D. (1989). *Wechsler Preschool and Primary Scale of Intelligence-Revised.* San Antonio, TX: Psychological Corporation.

Wechsler, D. (1991). *Wechsler Intelligence Scale for Children-Third Edition.* San Antonio, TX: Psychological Corporation.

Wechsler, D. (1997a). *Wechsler Adult Intelligence Scale-Third Edition.* San Antonio, TX: Psychological Corporation.

Wechsler, D. (1997b). *Wechsler Memory Scale-Third Edition.* San Antonio, TX: Psychological Corporation.

Weinberger, J. (1995). Common factors aren't so common: The common factors dilemma. *Clinical Psychology: Science and Practice, 2,* 45–69.

Weiner, I. B. (1975). *Principles of psychotherapy.* New York: John Wiley & Sons.

Weiner, I. B. (1996). Some observations on the validity of the Rorschach Inkblot method. *Psychological Assessment, 8,* 206–213.

Weiner, J. P. & de Lissovoy, G. (1993). Razing a Tower of Babel: A taxonomy for managed care and health insurance plans. *Journal of Health, Politics, Policy, and Law, 18,* 75–103.

Weisz, J. R., Weiss, B., Alicke, M. D., & Klotz, M. L. (1987). Effectiveness of psychotherapy with children and adolescents: A meta-analysis for clinicians. *Journal of Consulting and Clinical Psychology, 55,* 542–549.

Weller, E. B., & Weller, R. A. (1988). Neuroendrocrine changes in affectively ill children and adolescents. *Endocrinology and metabolism clinics of North America, 17,* 41–53.

West, S. G., & Graziano, W. G. (1989). Long-term stability and change in personality: An introduction. *Journal of Personality, 57,* 175–193.

Whalen, C. K., Henker, B., & Hinshaw, S. P. (1985). Cognitive-behavioral therapies for hyperactive children: Premises, problems, and prospects. *Journal of Abnormal Child Psychology, 13,* 391–410.

Whitaker, C., & Keith, D. (1981). Symbolic experiential family therapy. In A. Gurman and D. Kniskern (Eds.), *Handbook of family therapy* (pp. 187–225). New York: Brunner/Mazel.

White, M. (1986). Negative explanation, restraint, and double description: A template for family therapy. *Family Process, 25,* 169–184.

White, M., & Epston, D. (1990). *Narrative means to therapeutic ends.* New York: Brunner/Mazel.

Wiens, A. N. (1989). Structured clinical interviews for adults. In G. Goldstein & M. Herson (Eds.), *Handbook of psychological assessment* (pp. 309–328). Elmsford, NY: Pergamon Press.

Wiggins, J. S., & Pincus, A. L. (1989). Conceptions of personality disorders and dimensions of personality. *Psychological Assessment, 1,* 305–316.

Wilfley, D. E., Agras, W. S., Telch, C. F., Rossiter, E. M., Schneider, J. A., Cole, A. G., Sifford, L., & Raeburn, S. D. (1993). Group cognitive-behavioral therapy and group interpersonal therapy for the nonpurging bulimic: A controlled comparison. *Journal of Consulting and Clinical Psychology, 61,* 296–305.

Williams, D. (1982). The treatment of seizures: Special psychotherapeutic and psychobiological techniques. In H. Sands (Ed.), *Epilepsy: A handbook for the mental health professional* (pp. 58–74). New York: Brunner/Mazel.

Williams, D., & Mostofsky, D. (1982). Psychogenic seizures in childhood and adolescence. In T. Riley & A. Roy (Eds.), *Pseudoseizures* (pp. 169–184). Baltimore: Williams and Wilkins.

Willis, D. (1995). Psychological impact of child abuse and neglect. *Journal of Clinical Child Psychology, 24,* 2–4.

Wilson, E. O. (1978). *On human nature.* Cambridge, MA: Harvard University Press.

Wilson, E. O. (1983). Sociobiology and human beings. *Psychohistory Review, 11,* 5–14.

Wilson, E. O. (1991). Animal communication. In W.S.Y. Wang (Ed.), *The emergence of language: Development and evolution: Readings from "Scientific American" magazine,* pp. 3–15. NY: W.H. Freeman.

Wilson, G. T. (1981). Some comments on clinical research. *Behavioral Assessment, 3,* 217–226.

Wilson, G. T. (1996). Empirically validated treatments: Reality and resistance. *Clinical Psychology: Science and Practice, 3,* 241–244.

Wilson, G. T. (1997). Cognitive behavioral treatment of bulimia nervosa. *The Clinical Psychologist, 50,* 10–12.

Wilson, G. T., & Frank, C. M. (Eds.) (1982). *Contemporary behavior therapy: Conceptual and empirical foundations.* New York: Guilford Press.

Wilson, G. T., & Rachman, S. (1983). Meta-analysis and the evaluations of psychotherapy outcome: Limitations and liabilities. *Journal of Consulting and Clinical Psychology, 51,* 54–64.

Windle, C. (1952). Psychological tests in psychopathological prognosis. *Psychological Bulletin, 49,* 451–482.

Winker, M. A. (1994). Tacrine for Alzheimer's disease: Which patient, what dose? *Journal of the American Medical Association, 271,* 1023–1024.

Wisocki, P. A., Grebstein, L. C., & Hunt, J. B. (1994). Directors of clinical training: An insider's perspective. *Professional Psychology: Research and Practice, 25,* 482–488.

Wolfe, D. A., Aragona, J., Kaufman, K., & Sandler, J. (1980). The importance of adjudication in the treatment of child abuse: Some preliminary findings. *Child Abuse and Neglect, 4,* 127–135.

Wolpe, J. (1958). *Psychotherapy by reciprocal inhibition.* Stanford, CA: Stanford University Press.

Wolpe, J., & Lazarus, A. A. (1966). *Behavior therapy techniques: A guide to treatment of neuroses.* New York: Pergamon Press.

Wood, B. J., Klein, S., Cross, H. J., Lammers, C. J., & Elliott, J. K. (1985). Impaired practitioners: Psychologists' opinions about prevalence, and proposals for intervention. *Professional Psychology: Research and Practice, 16,* 843–850.

Wurtzel, E. (1995). *Prozac nation.* New York: Riverhead.

Yalom, I. D. (1980). *Existential psychotherapy.* New York: Basic Books.

Yalom. I. D. (1985). The theory and practice of group psychotherapy (3rd ed.). New York: Basic Books.

Yalom, I. D., & Lieberman, M. A. (1971). *A study of encounter group casualties.* Archives of General Psychiatry, 25, 16–30.

Yamamoto, J., Silva, A., Sasao, T., Wang, C., & Nguyen, L. (1993). Alcoholism in Peru. *American Journal of Psychiatry, 150,* 1059–1062.

Yates, A. J. (1986). Behaviour therapy and psychodynamic psychotherapy: Basic conflict or reconciliation and integration? *British Journal of Clinical Psychology, 212,* 107–125.

Yates, B. T. (1994). Toward the incorporation of costs, cost-effectiveness analysis, and cost-benefit analysis into clinical research. *Journal of Consulting and Clinical Psychology, 62,* 729–736.

Zametkin, A. J., Nordahl, T., Gross, M., King, A. C., Semple, W. E., Rumsey, J., Hamburger, S., & Cohen, R. M. (1990). Cerebral glucose metabolism in adults with hyperactivity of childhood onset. *New England Journal of Medicine, 323,* 1361–1366.

Zhang, X. R., Proenca, M., Barone, M., Leopold, L., & Friedman, J. M. (1994). Positional cloning of the mouse obese gene and its human homologue. *Nature, 372,* 425–432.

Zhu, S. H., Stretch, V., Balabanis, M., & Rosbrook, B. (1996). Telephone counseling for smoking cessation: Effects of single-session and multiple-session interventions. *Journal of Consulting and Clinical Psychology, 64,* 202–211.

Zimet, C. N., & Throne, F. M. (1965). *Preconference materials.* Conference on the Professional Preparation of Clinical Psychologists. Washington, DC: American Psychological Association.

Ziskin, J., & Faust, D. (1988). *Coping with psychiatric and psychological testimony* (Vols. 1–3, 4th ed.). Marina Del Rey, CA: Law and Psychology Press.

Zubin, J. (1954). Failures of the Rorschach technique. *Journal of Projective Techniques, 18,* 303–315.

Zubin, J., & Spring, B. (1977). Vulnerability: A new view of schizophrenia. *Journal of Abnormal Psychology, 86,* 103–126.

Zucker, R. A., & Gomberg, E. S. L. (1986). Etiology of alcoholism reconsidered: The case for a biopsychosocial process. *American Psychologist, 41,* 783–793.

Zuckerman, E. (1996, March/April). Surfing the Internet for psychology. *The National Psychologist, 5,* 8.

PHOTO CREDITS

Chapter 1
Page 3: Courtesy Patrick H. Deleon.

Chapter 2
Page 23: Courtesy Gerdenio "Sonny" Manuel.
Page 24: © 1998 by Sidney Harris. *Page 30:*
Courtesy Archives of the History of American
Psychology, University of Akron. *Page 32:* Courtesy
Clark University Archives.

Chapter 3
Page 37: Courtesy Amy Basell Crowe.

Chapter 4
Page 53: Courtesy Marcia Johnston Wood.
Page 64: © 1998 by Mark Litzler.

Chapter 5
Page 72: Courtesy Paul L. Watchel. *Page 73:* Robert
Mankoff © 1995 from The New Yorker Collection.
All Rights Reserved.

Chapter 6
Page 97: Courtesy Alan E. Kazdin.

Chapter 7
Page 125: Courtesy Stanley Sue. *Page 133:* Zigy
Kaluzny/Tony Stone Images/New York, Inc.
Page 145 (left): S. Grant/Monkmeyer/Grantpix.
Page 145 (right): Grant Le Duc/Monkmeyer/LeDuc.

Chapter 8
Page 151: Courtesy Lori Goldfarb Plante. *Page 158:*
Courtesy The Psychological Corporation, San
Antonio, Texas. *Page 171:* Hermann Rorschach,
Rorschach ®Test. ©Verlag Hans Huber AG, Bern,
Switzerland, 1921, 1948, 1994. *Page 174:* Chast
© 1989 from The New Yorker Collection. All
Rights Reserved. *Page 175:* Reprinted by
permission of the publisher from Henry A. Murray,
THEMATIC APPERCEPTION TEST, Cambridge,
Mass.: Harvard University Press; © 1943 by the
President and Fellows of Harvard College; © 1971
by Henry A. Murray.

Chapter 9
Page 185: Courtesy of John C. Norcross. *Page 189:*
Zigy Kaluzny/Tony Stone Images/New York, Inc.
Page 195: Robert E. Daemmrich/Tony Stone
Images/New York, Inc. *Page 198:* Judy S. Gelles/
Stock, Boston.

Chapter 10
Page 206: Courtesy Allen Sherman. *Page 208:* Bruce
Eric Kaplan © 1994 from The New Yorker
Collection. All Rights Reserved. *Page 215:*
PEANUTS reprinted by permission of United
Features Syndicate, Inc.

Chapter 11
Page 220: Courtesy Micheline Beam. *Page 223:*
Will & Demi McIntyre/Photo Researchers.

Chapter 12
Page 245: Courtesy Julie B. Jampel. *Page 247:*
Rhoda Sidney/Stock, Boston. *Page 260:* Bruce
Ayres/Tony Stone Images/New York, Inc.

Chapter 13
Page 264: Courtesy Thomas G. Plante. *Page 271:*
William Hamilton © 1997 from The New Yorker
Collection. All Rights Reserved. *Page 285:* Bruce
Ayres/Tony Stone Images/New York, Inc.

Chapter 14

Page 291: Courtesy Nicholas A. Cummings. *Page 306:* Robert Mankoff © 1996 from The New Yorker Collection. All Rights Reserved.

Chapter 15

Page 311: Courtesy Dianne L. Chambless. *Page 315:* Mike Twohy © 1991 from The New Yorker Collection. All Rights Reserved.

NAME INDEX

SUBJECT INDEX